Genetic diversity of European livestock breeds

The EAAP series is published under the direction of Jean Boyazoglu, Jean Renaud and Siem Korver.

EAAP – European Association for Animal Production

The European Association for Animal Production wishes to express its appreciation to the
Ministero delle Risorse Agricole, Alimentari e Forestali
Associazione Italiana Allevatori
Associazione Nazionale Allevatori Bovini Razza Frisona Italiana
and
Raisio Group - Feed Industry (Finland)
for their valuable support of its activities
and to the
FAO Animal Production and Health Division for its contribution to the development of
the EAAP Animal Genetic Databank

Genetic diversity of European livestock breeds

Results of monitoring by the EAAP Working Group on Animal Genetic Resources
EAAP Animal Genetic Data Bank, Institute of Animal Breeding and Genetics, School of Veterinary Medicine, Hannover, Germany

(EAAP Publication No. 66, 1993)

Detlef L. Simon and Doris Buchenauer

Wageningen Pers
Wageningen, September,1993

CIP-DATA KONINKLIJKE BIBLIOTHEEK,
DEN HAAG

ISSN 0071-2477
ISBN 90-74134-10-6 bound
NUGI 835

Subject headings:
European breeds
Endangered breeds
Genetic diversity
Effective population size

© Wageningen Pers, Wageningen,
The Netherlands, 1993

Printed in The Netherlands

Preface

Genetic variation in animals has developed during millions of years. In the course of time the usefulness of different genes and gene combinations has undergone severe tests, especially concerning adaptability of different conditions and resistance to diseases and parasites. During the last ten millenia man has partly influenced this evolution: many breeds adapted to local needs and environments have been developed. Only a few species are used by man, but there are many breeds within each species, the total number being ca. 4 000. Only recently the importance of breed diversity has generally been recognized besides species variety. The breed differences have been estimated to comprise half of the total biodiversity in farm animal species.

The possibilities of making changes in the genetic make-up of farm animals and of concentrating on the utilization of the breeds considered to be the best, have increased in recent decades, thanks to the availability of modern reproduction, computer and communication techniques, and of advanced theories. The increasing rate of changes, increased uniformity of breeding objectives and disappearance of many breeds have awakened concerns about losses of genetic variation both within and between breeds. Activities for preventing gene and breed losses have been started in many parts of the world, in order to maintain the possibility of adjusting animals to future, unpredictable needs. The Food and Agriculture Organization (FAO) of United Nations has, since the 1940's, played a central role in stimulating activities for conservation of genetic variation, especially of breeds in the world, including Europe. An important step was the FAO/UNEP Technical Consultation on AGR Conservation and Management, in 1980.

The book in hand is a result of many years of work by the Working Party on Animal Genetic Resources (AGR), set up by the Commission on Animal Genetics of the European Association for Animal Production (EAAP), in 1980, on recommendation of the FAO/-UNEP consultation. In order to document and evaluate European livestock resources the party has organized three surveys on breeds concerning the five species on which EAAP has study commissions.

The 1st survey aimed at describing the situation in 1982. The 2nd survey was made in 1985, and the data from this survey were transferred to the EAAP Data Bank on AGR, established at the Institute of Animal Breeding and Genetics, School of Veterinary Medicine Hannover, in 1988. The 3rd survey was initiated in 1988 and concerned data of all breeds, not only of endangered ones.

The need of publishing the information collected in the 1985- and 1988-surveys was long realized. Because of the incompleteness of the data from many countries and on many breeds, hundreds of enquiries were sent to selected experts for supplementing it, and so the numbers of breeds of which information was obtained increased decisively. It was decided to put the main emphasis on the facts about breeds at the cost of the history of the data bank and the description of collecting the information. It was hoped that in this way the book would best serve those involved with conservation and management of different breeds, and the possible combining of related/similar breeds, and those looking for suitable candidates for given purposes and environments.

Many kinds of new and useful information have been obtained on breeds of the five species kept in Europe. It will hopefully be useful in planning conservation activities and future utilization of many populations. Much of the information is difficult or even impossible to find elsewhere. Valuable experience of developing questionnaires, collecting channels and time schedules, evaluation and summarization of data, and criteria of choosing breeds for conservation has also been obtained.

The book is an invaluable source of information on European breeds. Special thanks for getting the book done belong to Prof. Dr. D. Simon and Dr. Doris Buchenauer, who have devoted much of their time and energy to this work and solved many scientific and practical problems of handling the mixed collection of incomplete questionnaires. There are good reasons to believe that it will help to get still more complete and precise data of both European and other breeds, and will be used for planning activities for sustainable use of animal genetic resources in the whole world.

Sincere thanks are also given to the other members of the working party, Prof. I. Bodò, Mr. L. Ollivier and Mr. D. Steane, for their irreplaceable contributions to the surveys and the planning of this book. The country coordinators providing the data deserve warm thanks. They are encouraged to make an additional effort to check and, if necessary, to correct the information printed on each population in the book.

Kalle Maijala
Prof. Emer.
Chairman of the EAAP Working Party
on AGR in 1981-93

Foreword

This is the first detailed report of the Animal Genetic Data Bank of the European Association of Animal Production EAAP which was established in 1987 at the Institute of Animal Breeding and Genetics of the Hannover School of Veterinary Medicine. Preliminary reports were given by SIMON (1990, 1992a) and BUCHENAUER and SIMON (1993).

This report has four main objectives which are related to the growing awareness of people and present concepts for conservation of animal genetic diversity:

Firstly, to present a register of breeds of the major farm animal species in Europe, i.e. cattle, sheep, goats, pigs and of horses; this can facilitate a wider use of minor breeds which may have a specific potential for a particular environment.

Secondly, to define the status of endangeredness of breeds and draw attention to it.

Thirdly, to form groups of similar breeds where this information can be used to decide on conservation of an individual breed in the context of others.

Fourthly, to present in a condensed form most of the information needed in order to decide whether a particular breed, which is endangered, should be conserved and whether this could be done in cooperation with other breeds.

The presentation and evaluation of breeds within this book are mainly performed on the basis of information which we received on questionnaires from informants. Numerous additional inquiries were made, and additional sources were used to some extent. However, some information is still missing and information available may not be the latest one or it may not be correct in any case. We are aware of these limitations; on the other hand we feel it necessary to make known the information on livestock breeds in Europe which could be accumulated by now. If the reader discovers inadequacies and if corrections are possible, we kindly ask him to let us know. This will help to improve the usefulness of the EAAP-Animal Genetic Data Bank and to give more precise answers on inquiries in future.

The basis for this report was laid by the EAAP Working Group on Animal Genetic Resources with its chairman Prof. Maijala, Finland, and its members (since 1985) Prof. Bodo, Hungary, Dr. Ollivier, France, Mr. David Steane, United Kingdom (and Prof. D. Simon, Germany). In part this is also their work and we are grateful for their activities and for the numerous discussions within this group.

This publication would not have been possible without the motivation and time consuming support of numerous informants, colleagues and institutions in European countries. They deserve our most sincere recognition and thanks; they are so numerous that they cannot be listed here.

We are also indebted to the Animal Production and Health Division of the Food and Agriculture Organisation FAO in Rome with its former representatives Prof. Jasiorowski, Prof. Cunningham, Dr. Hodges and Dr. Madalena, and with its senior officer for Animal Genetic Resources, Dr. Hammond, for many discussions, for supplying information on breeds from the former USSR, for providing some of the operating costs of the Data Bank and for providing the necessary funds for this publication.

We thank the Deutsche Forschungsgemeinschaft DFG for the funds provided for the initiation of the Animal Genetic Data Bank at the Hannover School of Veterinary Medicine, Hannover.

Our sincere thanks go to the personnel of the Institute of Animal Breeding and Genetics, Hannover, for the great care, interest and motivation shown in all stages of preparing this publication and in operating the data bank. The work and commitment of our programmer Mr. Wrede deserves special acknowledgement.

It is our hope that this publication will be useful both to make known the specific potential and risk status of livestock breeds in Europe and to provide most of the necessary information if decisions on conservation of a particular breed become necessary.

Hannover, 1993   Detlef L. Simon
                                                                    Doris Buchenauer

Contents

1   Introduction

1.1   Formation of concept

This publication has four main objectives: To decide on and to present

- a register of breeds of the major livestock species in Europe,
- the status of endangeredness of individual breeds,
- groups of similar breeds,
- structured information on individual breeds.

In pursuit of these objectives several decisions had to be made:

The local breed name in the original language is generally used for the identification of a breed. If more than one local breed name is in use, the breed is listed by each of these names, however with the same entry number and the same international breed name.

The entry number EN is a serial number in this book allocated to each breed for a clear identification; entry numbers are ordered within species.

The international breed name should enable a better recognition of breeds on an international level. A clear international naming is also necessary to define relationships among breeds in different countries, which resulted from splitting of populations, transfer of breeding animals, incrossings and outcrossings. Obviously no agreement exists among countries how to name a particular breed. We therefore newly decided on an international breed name for each breed. For this we mainly used an English translation of the local breed name, considering also tradition, origin and appearance of the breed and the naming by MASON (1969,1988).

Status of endangeredness. A new system has been developed, mainly based on the effective population size Ne (FALCONER, 1989) in relation to the expected increase of inbreeding during the next 50 years, including other factors such as population trend, absence of herdbook, number of herds, percentage of purebreeding and percentage of incrossing.

Similar breeds. Groups of similar breeds were formed on the basis of information on origin and development, on incrossing, phenotypic appearance and on transfer of genetic material between breeds, as far as we could obtain these pieces of information from our informants. Although still incomplete this section required considerable efforts.

Country name: As a consequence of political changes in Europe during recent years new countries were formed, some were divided, some were integrated into others. This development was taken into account as explained in chapter 3 on page 22. In order to save space the international car registration symbol was used as an abbreviation of the country name in most of the tables and presentations, an explanation is given in table 4, page 23.

1.2 Structure of presentation

Chapter 2, 'Monitoring of Animal Genetic Diversity', deals in short with the importance of monitoring animal genetic diversity, with the basic work and achievements of the EAAP Working Group for Animal Genetic Resources, and with the operation of the EAAP-Animal Genetic Data Bank in Hannover.

The information on animal genetic diversity in Europe is presented in five different ways:

-   Alphabetic register of livestock breeds by local breed name within species and country, additionally giving an Entry Number, international breed name and the page number where the "full" information on the breed is presented. This should enable a quick overview on which breeds are where available (Chapter 3: Listing of livestock breeds in countries of Europe).

-   List of endangered breeds in the four categories: potentially endangered, minimally endangered, endangered and critically endangered; by local breed name and species, additionally giving the effective population size Ne, page number of 'full' information and page number of group of similar breeds (Chapter 4.2: Listing of endangered breeds).

-   Groups of similar breeds with local breed name and additional information on country, status of endangeredness, page number of "full" information and international breed name. The information on similar breeds can be useful for the decision whether a particular breed should be conserved as a unique genetic resource or whether breeds with similar genetic potential should be included in a programme of concerted actions (Chapter 4.3: Groups of similar breeds).

-   Chapter 4.4, 'Grouping of breeds according to specific factors', gives an impression of the diversity of livestock breeds in Europe. Breeds are ordered by specific criteria, such as population size, cryoconservation, number of herds, withers height, live weight of adults, coat colour, specific abilities, management conditions, etc. The results are presented in 27 tables usually presenting the number of breeds which fall into a particular category. This may help to find breeds with a specific genetic potential.

-   Presentation of "full" information on individual breeds, in alphabetic order by local breed name within species and country; some 60 items are presented in a structured form on half a page per breed, which characterize the breed and should be important for decisions on conservation and use (Chapter 5: Presentation of individual breeds).

1.3 Guide for users

Depending on the question of interest the information in the book may be looked up as follows:

Question	Look up information in Chapter number ...
Sheep breeds in Ireland (local breed names)	3 Listing of livestock breeds in countries of Europe a) Country: Ireland b) Species: Sheep; page 33
How many sheep breeds are mainly used for milk production	4.4 Grouping of breeds according to specific factors a) Survey of tables: page 112/113 b) Look up table 40; result: 48 breeds
Status of endangered- ness of sheep breeds in Ireland	4.2 Listing of endangered breeds a) Species: Sheep; page 60-63 b) Status: Search in 4 classes c) Country: Ireland
Breeds similar to German Pinzgauer cattle in other countries with status of endangered- ness	5 Presentation of individual breeds a) Country: Germany b) Species: Cattle c) Breed: Pinzgauer; page 263 d) Line 21-24: 4 similar breeds Line 20: Page no. of group of similar breeds: "77" e) Look up page no.77, group/subgroup 3/4
Reasons for endangered- ness of German Pinz- gauer Cattle	5 Presentation of individual breeds a) Country: Germany b) Species: Cattle c) Breed: Pinzgauer; page 263 d) Line no. 19: Watch: .....
How many sheep breeds with 4 horns of females are registered; additional information on these breeds	4.4 Grouping of breeds according to specific factors a) Survey of tables: page 112/113 b) Look up table 39, result: '4' 5 Presentation of individual breeds c) Search in species sheep for four breeds with information "4 horns" in line No. 10
Number of sires repre- sented in cryostorage of semen of French Salers cattle	5 Presentation of individual breeds a) Country: France b) Species: Cattle c) Breed: Salers; page 196 d) Line 18: Semen: "35" sires

3

2   Monitoring of Animal Genetic Diversity

A breed is usually regarded as a group of interbreeding animals which have more in common with each other than with other animals. Similarity of breed members may result from the same genes of only one locus or from similarity in many traits, i.e. from numerous genes. Similarity of breed members therefore is a relative quantity, as is uniqueness in comparison with other breeds.

Breeds have to be reproduced in order to survive for a longer time. If reproduction is performed with a high number of male and female breeding animals of the same breed, and in absence of severe selection and of other disturbing factors, the uniqueness of the breed can be maintained over many generations. However, if the parents of the next generation are very limited in number or are highly selected or originated in part from another breed, the chance is reduced that all genes which make up the breed today will be transferred into the following generations. As a consequence the original uniqueness of the breed is in danger of getting lost. If the uniqueness of breeds should be maintained over time, this requires monitoring of animal genetic diversity and appropriate actions.

2.1   Monitoring, prerequisite for conservation

Monitoring of animal genetic diversity means obtaining, registering, evaluating and making known information which is important to avoid further losses of animal genetic diversity.
Since conservation normally requires reproduction and mating, a minimum number of breeding animals is required. These should be unrelated in order to avoid inbreeding and random loss of genes by genetic drift. This is also true of cryogenic storage of semen, embryos and other genetic material since after reactivation mating of unrelated animals should be again possible. Therefore the unit of observation in monitoring should not be individual animals, but the interbreeding group of animals, which may be called a population, breed, line or variety. In this publication we use the term breed for each group of interbreeding animals which was reported to us neglecting situations where two "breeds" in two countries may represent the same genetic material.

Monitoring should involve information which is essential to concepts for avoiding further losses of genetic diversity. The knowledge of the following aspects is of special interest:

- which breeds exist and where
- the number of male and female breeding animals of the breed
- the time trend of these numbers
- the number of breeding herds
- the specific potential of a breed in a given habitat
- similarities with other breeds
- the degree of incrossing from other breeds

- the importance of a breed for people in a given area
- chances of concerted actions across countries
- conservation programmes which are under way
- persons with special knowledge of the breed
- economic and other factors working against the breed

This information should be continously updated in order to register changes in the risk status of a breed.

Additional aspects of monitoring animal genetic diversity, such as how to obtain information on breeds, which information for which objective, criteria for conservation, coordination of several monitoring institutions, were discussed by SIMON (1992a,b).

2.2 The EAAP Working Group on Animal Genetic Resources*)

Following recommendations of the FAO/UNEP Technical Consultation on Animal Genetic Resources (AGR), Conservation and Management (FAO, 1981), the Commission on Animal Genetics of the European Association for Animal Production (EAAP) established a Working Group on Animal Genetic Resources in 1980. The objectives were to (1) consider the conclusions of the FAO/UNEP consultation, (2) make proposals under the auspices of the EAAP Genetics Commission and implement activities for AGR conservation and development in Europe, (3) liaise with FAO/UNEP about AGR in Europe.

The working group has organized three surveys on European livestock breeds in the five species for which EAAP has study commissions (cattle, goats, horses, pigs and sheep) (MAIJALA et al., 1984).

2.2.1 First EAAP survey (1982)

Since there was no up-to-date, comprehensive survey of Animal Genetic Resources available in Europe, the Working Group decided to organize one describing the situation in 1982.

Three different questionnaires were worked out and used: (1) Breeds within country, (2) attitudes towards conservation within country, and (3) details of endangered breeds within country. Replies were received from 22 countries on the five EAAP species and also on poultry and fur-animals from some countries. The replies were supplemented from the literature, especially from MASON (1969).

------

*) The text of chapter 2.2 is mainly based on the report of K. Maijala (1992)

Numbers of breeds in total and endangered

A list of breeds existing in the countries was prepared on the basis of replies from 22 countries and on literature from additional 8 countries (MAIJALA et al., 1984). Each breed within a country was counted as a "country population". There were 350, 103, 280, 146 and 384 country populations of cattle, goats, horses, pigs and sheep, respectively, making a total of 1263.

130 "breeds" existed in at least two countries, and hence the number of breeds was much smaller than that of country populations. For example, there were 24 "Friesian" cattle-populations, 14 "Saanen" goat-, 16 "Thoroughbred" horse-, 22 "Large White" pig-, and 19 "Merino" sheep-populations. Thus, the numbers of different breeds decreased to 181, 77, 149, 66 and 264, i.e. to a total of 737.

The criteria for endangerment were based on numbers of males and females. In all, 81 cattle-, 12 goat-, 51 horse-, 30 pig- and 67 sheep-breeds, i.e. a total of 241 "breeds" were considered endangered. These were listed with present numbers of females and trends during the last 10 and 3 years.

Motives for conservation and activities

The EAAP Working Group considered that there are many motives for conserving AGR, the most important being to avoid (1) loss of genetic material which could be valuable for future production requirements, and (2) loss of genetic material, e.g. breeds, before adequate evaluation has been carried out; it was considered well-founded also for cultural-historical reasons. With the aid of the questionnaires and literature, an idea was obtained of the organization and forms of and attitudes to conservation in different countries. Some governments had started activities already in the 1960's, and in some countries private organizations had been established in the 1970's.

Planning of data bank and other aspects

It was found important to develop a data bank, where information of breeds needing conservation would be collected and stored. A preliminary plan for it was prepared. In addition, following aspects were discussed: genetic losses within breeds, criteria in choosing breeds for conservation, available conservation techniques, recommendations for conservation, and encouraging private organizations interested in conserving indigenous breeds for cultural-historical reasons. Conservation costs could be lowered by using animals as pasture and/or working animals in nature protection and similar areas. Recommendations were given to FAO and UNEP as well as suggestions for the European organization (MAIJALA et al., 1984). A preliminary report of the survey was given in the annual meeting of EAAP in 1982 and the final one in 1983.

2.2.2 Second EAAP survey (1985)

In its report, the working group suggested to the EAAP genetics commission that the work should be continued for (1) organizing 3-yearly surveys, (2) reporting annually to the genetics commission, (3) recommending any action considered desirable. For the survey a new questionnaire was developed which could be used equally for the five species cattle, goats, horses, pigs and sheep. The questionnaire had the following five sections:

A) General information: 1. Country, 2. Species, 3. Breed/population, 4. Main location, 5. Main organization concerned with the breed, 6. Preparation of replies.
B) Origin and development of breed: 1. Origin, 2. Immigration to the breed, 3. Similarities with other breeds, 4. Breeding population numbers, 5. Average ages of mature males/females used for breeding.
C) Breed description: 1. Colour, 2. Horns, 3. Hair and wool, 4. Appearance, 5. Genetic peculiarities.
D) Qualification of breed: 1. Present main use, 2. Other important uses, 3. Present management levels, 4. Special qualifications.
E) Performance records: 1. Name of standard breed, 2. Absolute production level in comparison with standard, 3. Validity of comparisons (production conditions).

The forms were distributed to the country delegates of the EAAP Genetics Commission with necessary advice. Replies were received from 17 countries, concerning 148 cattle-, 45 goat-, 73 horse-, 64 pig- and 183 sheep-breeds, a total of 513 "breeds". The frequency of answers to different questions varied greatly both within and between species. The results were reported to the EAAP-meeting in 1985, and later published (MAIJALA, 1987).

In 1987 the EAAP Genetics Commission approved the following recommendations of the working group for future surveys:

- to cover all breeds, not only the endangered ones, of the five species cattle, goats, horses, pigs and sheep,
- to use the English language in the answers,
- to repeat surveys in three year intervals,
- to ask for the relative performance of the breed in comparison to a so called "standard breed" living in the same country and preferably under the same conditions,
- to set up a data bank.

The Institute of Animal Breeding and Genetics decided to set up the data bank and was enabled to do so by a grant of the Deutsche Forschungsgemeinschaft DFG.

2.2.3 Third EAAP survey (1988)

The forms of the 85-survey were used as basis for planning the third survey. Some changes were made on the basis of discussions with the Nordic Working Party on AGR, and with the Animal Production and Health Division of FAO. Developments in biotechnology were taken into account, place was reserved for the absolute production level of standard breeds, the scale for relative production level was widened, and questions on genetic distance, DNA-storage and live animal conservation programmes were added. Thus, a questionnaire with seven sections was used.

The forms were again distributed to country delegates of the Genetics Commission and to experts with special knowledge of the breeds. For breeds already recorded in the Data Bank a printout of available information was prepared which only had to be re-examined and supplemented by informants.

Replies were received from 12 countries (SIMON, 1989). These concerned 68 cattle-, 9 goat-, 30 horse-, 35 pig-, and 83 sheep-"breeds", making a total of 225 country populations or breeds.

2.2.4 Division of labour between EAAP and FAO, additional efforts

During the meeting of the joint EAAP/FAO Working Group, Berlin, 1991, it was agreed that in future the EAAP Data Bank Hannover will concentrate on collecting data from Europe, while data from outside Europe will be collected by FAO. Preliminary plans were made for a global network of interactive regional data banks, co-ordinated by FAO.
In view of the planned publication on breed resources in Europe it became clear that additional efforts would be needed to improve the completeness of the data.

2.3   The EAAP Animal Genetic Data Bank Hannover

2.3.1 Development of data bank

It was one of the recommendations of the FAO/UNEP Technical Consultation on Animal Genetic Resources Conservation and Management, Rome, 1980, to set up data banks for animal genetic resources (FAO, 1981). Actions were initiated both by FAO and other organizations in different regions.

In Europe the EAAP Working Group on Animal Genetic Resources was set up, whose two surveys of 1982 and 1985 laid the ground for an Animal Genetic Data Bank for Europe. Founding of the data bank became possible in 1987 by a grant of the Deutsche Forschungsgemeinschaft DFG to the Institute of Animal Breeding and Genetics at the School of Veterinary Science, Hannover, Germany.

As hardware an IBM compatible workstation is in use with 5 1/4" and 3 1/2" drives for floppy disks and a streamer to safegard the data. The databank system dBASE III$^+$ is in operation until now; we are screening the market for possible improvements. Additional programmes had to be developed for data entry, for data bank operations, for evaluations and for various printouts. Although hard- and software is important the crucial factor for the usefulness of the databank is the success in collecting breed information which is complete, correct and relevant to the present situation. This area requires most of the efforts and costs of operating the data bank.

In November 1987 FAO and EAAP made an agreement that identical questionnaire forms should be used in Europe and in other regions, and that all information on breed resources should be combined in the data bank Hannover, which in future should serve as the Global Animal Genetic Data Bank. In addition a combined EAAP/FAO working group was set up.

Following this agreement the activity of the data bank in collecting breed information was extended to regions outside Europe, i.e. to Africa, Canada and the USA. In Bolivia, Chile and Peru a survey of South American Camelides was organized (with support of FAO) and breed information from regional data banks in China and India were transferred to Hannover.

2.3.2 The EAAP-/FAO-Questionnaire

This was developed in 1987 and 1988 in the combined EAAP-FAO working group. It is the result of a compromise in the pursuit of two objectives: to get complete information on breeds and to keep the addressed people motivated to supply it. The information asked in the questionnaire can be regarded as a core information which is necessary for the characterization of a breed and which should be made available as a minimum for each breed in each country. This should not interfere with possibilities of national data banks of asking for additional information on a national level.

The same questionnaire is in use for the five major livestock species cattle, sheep, goats, pigs, horses and for buffaloes. It covers seven main sections as outlined in tables 1 and 2. The questionnaire is available in the four languages English, French, German and Spanish. It has been in use since 1988 with the additional question on the number of herds in which a breed is kept.

The information which was obtained in the surveys of 1982 and 1985 had to be transformed into the structure of the 1987 questionnaire and was entered into the data bank. New information is normally sent to the data bank in the form of filled-in questionnaires by informants. However, if national or regional institutions prefer to run their own data bank they can be supplied with software from Hannover for the data input on a PC and the transfer to Hannover can be performed by floppy disk. Up to now software from the EAAP data bank is used in 9 national or regional centers, ranging from China to the USA and Brazil.

Table 1: Main items asked in the EAAP-/FAO-questionnaire

A. General information (page 1)
  - Country and species (buffalos, cattle, goats, sheep, horses, or pigs)
  - Breed or population (local and international name)
  - Main organization concerned with the breed
  - Preparation of replies (name, organization, time)

B. Origin and development of breed (page 2)
  - Origin (from which breeds, from which country, herdbook since when), immigration into the breed (breed, country, time, percentage of matings)
  - Breeding population numbers 1986 (males, females; males in A.I., herd size, changes in numbers)
  - Average age of mature animals used for breeding (δ, $\female$))

C. Breed description (page 3)
  - Colour (unicoloured, colour combinations, special signs)
  - Horns (number, shape)
  - Appearance (adult weight, withers height)
  - Genetic peculiarities (chromosome abberrations, marker genes)

D. Qualification of breed (page 4)
  - Present main use (ranking of eight alternatives)
  - Other important uses
  - Special qualifications (with references)

E. Management conditions (page 5)
  - Type, housing period, feeding
  - Specific natural environment

F. Performance records (page 5 and 6)
  - Name of standard breed for comparisons within country
  - Approximate production level of standard breed in main traits
  - relative comparisons with standard breed in specific traits
  - Validity of comparisons (production conditions)

G. Additional information (page 7)
  - Estimate of genetic distance to other breeds
  - Storage of DNA in a gene-library
  - Programmes to conserve live animals of the breed
  - Additional information can be obtained where

Table 2: Questionnaire of EAAP Animal Genetic Data Bank

A. General information

1 Country   *Germany*

2 Species: 11=Buffalo, 12=Cattle, 13=Goats, 14=Sheep |1¦2|
           21=Horses, 31=Pigs

3 Breed or population

3.1 local name   *Hinterwälder*

3.2 international name   *Hinterwälder*
    (see Mason's Dictionary)

4 Main location of breed

4.1 region with country   *Hochschwarzwald*

5.1 Main organisation concerned with the breed;
    normally Breed Society; (name, address):

    Zuchtverband für Fleckvieh und Wäldervieh,
    31535 Titisee-Neustadt

    If not 5.1 (Breed Society), please complete:

5.2 University/state institution/others _____

6 Preparation of replies
    Information for this questionnaire was given

6.1 on **page 1 to 3** by

    Name: *Arbeitsgemeinschaft Deutscher*

    Organisation   *Tierzüchter, Bonn*

6.2 on **page 4 to 7** by

    Name: *see above*

    Institution:

6.3 Date of preparation: *March* (month) *1989* (year)

EAAP Animal Genetic Data Bank
Institute for Animal Breeding and Genetics
Hannover School of Veterinary Medicine
Bünteweg 17p
D-30559 Hannover, Germany

B. Origin and development of breed

1   Origin   Year

1.1 Breed was mainly established out of the following
    local breeds
    Autochthon breed   around | 1 , 8 , 0 , 0 |

1.2 Breed was mainly imported

    from   country   -
                breed   -   in | ⌊ , , , ⌋ |
    and from   country   -
                breed   -   in | ⌊ , , , ⌋ |

1.3 Breed is known by its local name since | 1 , 8 , 6 , 5 |

1.4 Herdbook established (please mark "x") | X | | 1 , 8 , 8 , 9 |

2   Immigration has taken place in the last years:
    for cattle, buffalo, and horses since 1950, for
    sheep and goats since 1960, and for pigs since 1970.
    (code: 1=5%, 2=5-20%, 3=>20%, estimated % of matings)

    | 1 | from breed *Vorderwälder* country *Germany*   in | 1 , 9 , 7 , 2 |
    | 1 | from breed *Vorderwälder* country *Germany*   in | 1 , 9 , 7 , 2 |
    | | from breed   country   in | ⌊ , , , ⌋ |
          from breed   country   in | ⌊ , , , ⌋ |

3   **Breeding population numbers in 1986**

3.1 Females (numbers being bred)   3.1.1 total   *2300*
                                     3.1.2 registered in herdbook   *259*

3.2 Per cent females being bred pure (mated to males of own breed)   *95*

3.3 Number of males total in service   *45*

3.4 Out of the above males, the number in AI-service   *5*

3.5 Changes in numbers of females:
    (1=increasing, 2=stable, 3=decreasing)
    until 1986 | *3* | since 1986 | *2* |

3.6 Average herd size (females) 1986   total   *8*
    in private herds   *8*   in other herds   -

4   **Average age** of animals used for breeding (months)
    females   *104*   males   *30*

5   **Storage of semen and embryos**   Number of males, sires and
                                                  dams represented
5.1 semen | X | in case of storage   males   *12*
5.2 embryos | | please mark "X"   sires   dams
5.3 Additional information on storage can be obtained by
    Zuchtverband für Fleckvieh und Wäldervieh, 31535 Titisee-Neustadt

C Breed description (please mark with "x")

1 Coat colour	black	grey	blue	red	brown	yellow	white	blond
1.1 predominantly uncoloured								
1.2 colour combinations as follows				X		X	X	

1.3 special colour characteristics
(e.g. spotted, saddle, white head, etc)
White head, spotted around the eyes

2 Skin colour _____

3 Horns

		4	2	0
male			X	
female			X	

3.1 typical number of horns (please mark with "x")

3.2 knobs only (spurs) (please mark with "x")

3.3 remarkable horn shape (or size)
which ? _lyra-formed horns_

4 Hair and/or wool? (only sheep and goats)

4.1 hair (please mark with "x") [X]

4.2 wool (1=fine, 2=medium/crossbred, 3=coarse/carpet, 4=mixed) (code) [ ]

5 Adult size and weight (metric measurements)

5.1 wither height (cm) males _130_ females _118_

5.2 live weight (kg) males _700_ females _420_

6 Other specific visible traits, i.e. fat tail, hump, etc
please describe _____

7 Genetic peculiarities
7.1 chromosome aberrations _____

7.2 typical marker and/or major genes   gene _____ gene-frequency

7.3 other _____

7.4 additional information on genetic peculiarities can be obtained by the following institution or person:

_____

13

D   Qualification of breed

1   Present main use

1.1	milk
1.2	tractive power
1.3	meat
1.4	wool
1.5	fur
1.6	vegetation management
1.7	sport, hobby
1.8	other (state below)

1

2

3

please indicate 1st, 2nd and
3rd rankings according to
present importance

2   Are there other uses which are of importance - please specify

_____

3   Breed has <u>special</u> qualification (other than stated above) in the following
       fields (please mark with "x")

3.1   quality of product for human consumption |__|
       specify _____

3.2   resistance against specific pathogenic agent | X |
       specify **no IBR/IPV-infections** _____

3.3   adaptability to climate |__|
       specify _____

3.4   fertility (e.g. twinning, long breeding season) |__|
       specify _____

3.5   adaptability to marginal land (e.g. mountain, marsh, wetland, semi desert) | X |
       specify **very good legs to graze on steep mountains**

3.6   other |__|
       specify _____

3.7   experimental results in the above fields have been published

3.7.1 by   **none** _____ for field |3,2| *

       in (reference) _____

3.7.2 by   _____ for field |3,5| *

       in (reference) **none** _____

3.8   Additional information on the above qualifications can be obtained from
       the following institution or persons:
       Zuchtverband für Fleckvieh und Wäldervieh, 31535 Titisee-Neustadt

       _____ for field |3,2| |3,5| *

       and from _____

       _____ for field |_,_| |_,_| *

_____

*please fill in the field number (3.1 to 3.6) for which additional information can be obtained

E   Management conditions

1   Type | 2 | 2 Housing period | 3 | 3 Feeding of adults | 2 |

1 = stationary	1 = no housing	1 = total grazing
2 = transhumant	2 = up to 2 months	2 = grazing+fodder
3 = nomadic	3 = 2 to 6 months	3 = mixed
	4 = over 6 months	4 = concentrate
	5 = total housing	5 = total concentrate

4   Special conditions, i.e. lack of water supply,
     specify _____

_____

F   Summary performance record

1   Standard breed for comparisons with country

The performance of breed (B) in specific traits is to be compared with the performance of a
standard breed (SB), same trait, same measurement; *preferably one of the following most
frequent breeds should be used as standard breed:*

Buffalo	
Cattle	H. Friesians, Simmental, Jersey, Hereford, Charolais
Goats	Malta, Saanen, Toggenburg, Alpine
Sheep	Border-Leicester, Merino, Suffolk, Texel, Scottish Blackface, East Friesian, Finnsheep
Horses	Arab, Thoroughbred, Halbred, Fjord, Percheron, Quarter Horse
Pigs	Landrace, Large White, Pietrain, Duroc

If none of the above breeds is present in the country, the most popular breed should be used
as standard breed.

1.1   Name of standard breed chosen   ***Simmental***

1.2   Approximate production of standard breed within country

trait		buffalo/cattle	goat/sheep	pigs
1.2.1	milk yield per year kg	*5000*		
1.2.2	fat per cent %	*4.01*		
1.2.3	daily gain (males g	*1200*		
1.2.4	litter size n			
1.2.5	lean meat %			

15

Summary performance record (continued)

2   Relative comparisons

The absolute production level of breed B in comparison to the standard breed_____
is

(code) 1 = very much lower   (- 51 to -100%)
            2 = much lower   (- 16 to - 50%)
            3 = lower   (- 6 to - 15%)
            4 = <u>about equal</u>   (- 5 to + 5%)
            5 = higher   (+ 6 to + 15%)
            6 = much hgher   (+ 16 to + 50%)
            7 = very much higher   (+ 51 to +100%)
            8 = more than 100 per cent higher (+101 to +200%)
            9 = more than 200 per cent higher   (>200%)

in the following traits (please enter codes in table):

trait	buffalo + cattle		sheep + goats		pigs		horses	
2.01	milk yield	2	milk yield		daily gain		pulling power	
2.02	% fat	4	% fat		feed conversion ratio		fertility	
2.03	% protein	4	% protein		muscularity		handling ease	
2.04	pulling power		daily gain		% lean		daily gain	
2.05	milkability	4	muscularity		meat quality		age at sexual maturity	
2.06	daily gain	2	carcass leanness		litter size		speed in gallop	
2.07	muscularity	3	litter size		mortality		speed in trotters	
2.08	calving rate	4	length of mating season		handling ease		adaptability: (in dressage)	
2.09	calving ease	5	lambing interval		farrowing interval		(in jumping)	
2.10	calf mortality	2	age at sexual maturity		age at sexual maturity		(in military)	
2.11	calving interval	3	wool or fiber yield		liveweight at slaughter			
2.12	handling ease	4	wool or fiber thickness					
2.13	age at sexual maturity	5						
2.14		6						

16

3   Validity of comparisons

The production conditions for Breed B (the one in question)

3.1   are about equal with the conditions for standard breed SB in above trait number(s) (please enter trait numbers)

2.02	2.03	2.05	2.08	2.11	2.14				

3.2   are probably not as good as for the standard breed SB in above trait number(s) (please enter trait numbers)

2.01	2.06	2.07	2.12						

3.3   are probably better than for the standard breed SB in above trait number(s) (please enter trait numbers)

2.09	2.10	2.13							

G   **Additional information on the breed**

1   Genetic distance

Estimates of genetic distance to the following other breeds are available:

1.1   (Breed)   1.2   (in country)

1.1.1   _____   1.2.1   _____

1.1.2   _____   1.2.2   _____

1.1.3   _____   1.2.3   _____

1.1.4   _____   1.2.4   _____

Additional information on genetic distance can be obtained by

1.3.1   _____

_____ and by

1.3.2   _____

_____

2   Storage of genetic material in a "gene-library"

[ ] please mark "x" if genetic material of the breed such as DNA-sequences was entered in a gene library

Additional information on this kind of storage can be obtained by:

2.1   _____

_____ and by

2.2   _____

_____

3   Activities to conserve live animals of the breed

3.1   The following specific programs exist to live animal conservation (please indicate number of males and females, location, sponsor, etc), excluding individual breeders who are part of an overall program:

Förderverein Hinterwäldervieh e.V. Schonau. Premium for matings

3.2   Additional information on conservation of live animals of the breed can be obtained from:

3.2.1   *Zuchtverb. für Fleckvieh u. Wäldervieh, D-31535 Titisee-Neustadt*

and from

3.2.2   _____

Before the data are entered into the data bank every breed record is checked for completeness and for possible errors by a person with experience in animal breeding. Correct interpretation of incoming information sometimes requires flexibility and imagination, for example if the origin of a breed of fighting bulls is explained in Spanish or if the height and weight of a Scottish draught horse is defined in "hands" and "stones".

2.3.3 Use of the EAAP Animal Genetic Data Bank

The purpose of the data bank can be seen in collecting, examining and storing the available information on livestock breeds in Europe and to give correct answers to questions in the context of proper use and - if necessary - of conservation of a breed.

Examples for utilization of a particular breed:
- Based on the information on the specific potential of a breed, the breed may be used in a new location with similar environmental conditions.
- Based on the information on breed history, immigration, and genetic distance, the chance of utilization of heterosis in crosses with other breeds can be estimated.
- Knowledge of the specific genetic potential in quantitative traits can be used to develop a synthetic breed which combines the advantages of several breeds.
- Knowledge of the presence of major genes in a breed can be used to study their effects in more details, to identify and isolate them by recombinant DNA-techniques, and use them for later gene transfers if this seems feasible (SMITH et al., 1987).
- Knowledge of the genetic potential of a breed in relation to others can be used in experiments to detect linkage of quantitative trait loci with genetic markers as a basis to improve estimation of breeding values (PATERSON et al., 1988).

Examples of use of information in the context of conservation:
- The knowledge of the number of male and female breeding animals is the main factor to define the status of endangeredness of a breed.
- The information 'decline of the number of males' can be used to prepare a list of breeds which probably will become endangered. This list can draw the attention of people without prior knowledge of the breed, to its genetic potential and to the danger of losing it.
- The information on semen and embryos stored for conservation, and the number of males represented by them, is necessary to decide whether something should be done in this respect. The same holds for the information 'programmes for conservation of live animals'.
- The information 'same breed exists in different countries' can be used to combine the resources from different locations in order to increase the effective population size and to use limited funds for conservation in a more efficient way.
- The information 'similarity among breeds, breed history, genetic distance to other breeds' can help to decide whether a given breed is a unique genetic group and deserves to be conserved or whether it would be justified to combine the resources of similar genetic background into one population (SIMON and SCHULTE-COERNE, 1979).

Examples of inquiries of the data bank.
Inquiries vary extremely in objectives. Some examples are given in the following:
- Scientific aspects: Scientists make inquiries on population size, special qualification of a breed, genetic pecularities, similarities to other breeds, conservation activities in general and in certain breeds. They use this information for books, papers, theses as well as for lectures. They also require the address of specialists who know more details to specific questions.
- Breeding aspects: Breeders of rare breeds ask for addresses of breeders of the same breed to exchange breeding animals, they ask for immigration of breeds into a specific breed, for qualification and suitability of related breeds to use for breeding in small populations. Breeders want to know about conservation programmes for live animals. People wanting to build up a herd ask which breed would be suited best for a given environment. Breeding journals are demanding reports on qualifications of "old" breeds. Breed societies compare data on population size from different countries.
- Public aspects: Magazine, journals, newspapers, television ask for the importance of genetic diversity and conservation of live animals, use of traditional breeds for ecological purposes, use of old breeds in extensified agricultural conditions. Private people want information on old breeds in general.
- The Commission of the European Communities CEC - in the process of developing support programmes for an extensive agriculture and for conservation of biological diversity - asks for compilations of breeds of specific farm animal species which meet certain requirements. Lists of ruminant breeds were compiled in 1992, lists of horse breeds in 1993 and sent to the EC-Commission in Brussels.

2.3.4 How to obtain information on breeds

This is a matter of an appropriate questionnaire and of good informants.

It has already been pointed out that the questionnaire should cover only main items and should not be too complicated. If additional information is needed this can be obtained after specific questions from the informant.

The amount of required information can be seen in relation to the specific objectives which one has in mind. For example, if it is essential to evaluate the risk status of a breed in a short time, different information is needed than for arguments to conserve a breed as a human heritage. Table 3 gives an impression which of 34 questions from the EAAP/FAO-questionnaire are relevant to five different objectives (SIMON, 1992a).

Table 3: Information required for different objectives

Information (from EAAP/FAO-questionnaire)	Risk status	Unique-ness	Human heritage	Better use	Concerted actions
A) General information					
country, species		+	+	+	+
local breed name	+	+	+	+	+
internat. breed name	+	+	+	+	+
breed organization				+	+
expert person	+	+	+	+	+
B) Origin, Development					
autochthone breed		+	+		
mixture, of which breeds		+			+
herdbook established	+	+	+		+
% of pure matings	+	+	+		+
number breeding males	+		+		+
number breeding females	+		+		+
change in numbers	+				+
number of herds	+		+		+
age of breeding animals	+				
C) Breed description					
coatcolour		+	+		
horns: number, shape		+	+		
adult withers height		+	+	+	
adult live weight		+	+	+	
D) Qualification					
present main use	+	+	+	+	+
other important uses	+	+		+	+
specific qualification	+	+		+	+
E) Management condition					
type			+	+	
housing period			+	+	
feeding			+	+	
special environment		+	+	+	
F) Performance					
standardbreed (SB)		+		+	
production level of SB		+		+	
rel.deviations from SB		+		+	
G) Addit. information					
estim. genetic distance		+			+
semen in cryo-store	+				+
embryos in cryo-store	+				+
number parents involved	+				+
live animal programmes	+				+
genetic markers		+			+

The informant preferably should be a motivated animal breeding scientist. The EAAP Working Group on Animal Genetic Resources contacted the delegates of EAAP member countries in the EAAP Genetics Commission. However, the relatively poor result of the third survey of 1988 (information on 225 breeds from 12 countries) draws attention to the main problem of an Animal Genetic Data Bank: to obtain complete, correct and up-to-date information. The data bank reacted to the poor result by writing hundreds of individual letters to individual people whom we expected to have good knowledge of a given breed. This approach was repeated several times, if necessary. As a result of these efforts the quality of information per breed could be improved and the number of breeds could be increased from 225 to 877 for this report. This, of course, was only possible because of the good cooperation of hundreds of colleagues in European countries.

3   Listing of livestock breeds in countries of Europe

The presentations of breeds in this and the following chapters cover 877 breeds on which a reasonable amount of information could be obtained until August 1st, 1993. 78 additional breeds are registered in the data bank but not yet included in this publication. The information either arrived after the fixed date or needs further completion. These breeds are listed in table number 50 in chapter 6.

Due to political changes in Europe during recent years the assignment of breeds to a specific country is sometimes not straightforward or the local breed name may have changed. We proceeded as follows:

-    CSFR: Breeds which could not be assigned to the newly formed countries CZECH REPUBLIC or SLOVAKIAN REPUBLIC were listed under CSFR.

-    USSR: Breeds which could not be assigned to the newly formed countries ARMENIA, BELORUSSE, GEORGIA, KAZAKH, UKRAINE, UZBEKIA or other were listed under USSR. Russian local breed names were used.

-    YUGOSLAVIA: Breeds which could not be assigned to the newly formed countries CROATIA, SLOVENIA or other were listed under YUGOSLAVIA. Serbo-croatian local breed names were used.

-    GERMAN DEMOCRATIC REPUBLIC, GDR: Breeds which were reported for the region of the former GDR are marked with * and assigned to GERMANY.

Table 4 informs on the number of breeds per country and species of which information is available in the data bank; in table 5 these breeds are listed by local breed name with additional information on entry number EN, international breed name and the number of the page where the "full" information on the breed is presented in chapter 5.

Table 4: Number of breeds in EAAP Animal Genetic Data Bank

Country Name	Country Code	Number of breeds Cattle	Sheep	Goats	Pigs	Horses	Total
Armenia	ARM	0	0	0	1	0	1
Austria	A	8	1	0	0	2	11
Belgium	B	5	1	3	3	3	15
Belorusse	BEL	1	0	0	1	0	2
Bulgaria	BG	2	0	0	0	0	2
Croatia	HR	3	3	1	1	2	10
CSFR	CS	1	2	2	5	1	11
Czech Republic	CZ	1	2	0	1	1	5
Denmark	DK	4	3	1	2	2	12
Estonia	EW	3	0	0	1	0	4
Faeroe Islands	FR	1	1	0	0	0	2
Finland	SF	4	2	1	2	11	20
France	F	39	55	5	17	31	147
Georgia	GO	3	0	0	1	0	4
Germany	D	25	25	5	16	11	82
Greece	GR	3	12	2	0	2	19
Hungary	H	1	3	0	1	6	11
Iceland	IS	2	1	0	0	1	4
Ireland	IRL	12	5	1	2	5	25
Italy	I	31	51	22	9	12	125
Kazakh	KAZ	3	0	0	2	0	5
Latvia	LV	1	0	0	1	0	2
Lithuania	LT	2	0	0	1	0	3
Luxembourg	L	4	1	0	1	3	9
Netherlands	NL	4	7	2	3	3	19
Norway	N	3	6	1	2	4	16
Poland	PL	4	8	0	6	2	20
Portugal	P	8	9	3	1	3	24
Romania	RO	5	5	1	7	0	18
Slovakia	SK	2	0	0	1	0	3
Slovenia	SLO	1	2	0	3	1	7
Spain	E	25	17	6	3	1	52
Sweden	S	2	3	1	0	2	8
Switzerland	CH	6	9	9	3	3	30
Ukraine	UR	6	0	0	3	0	9
United Kingdom	GB	30	47	2	12	10	101
USSR	USSR	17	0	0	11	0	28
Uzbekia	UZB	1	0	0	0	0	1
Yugoslavia	YU	4	2	0	3	1	10
Total		277	283	68	126	123	877

Table 5: Listing of Livestock Breeds in Countries of Europe

Country Species Entry Number	Local Breed Name	International Breed Name	Breed presentation page no.
Armenia (ARM)			
Pigs			
966	Lesogornaya porodnaya gruppa	Forest Mountain	131
Austria (A)			
Cattle			
88	Fleckvieh	Simmental	131
139	Kärntner Blondvieh	Austrian Blond	132
178	Murbodner	Murboden	132
190	Österreichisches Braunvieh	Austrian Brown	133
202	Pinzgauer	Pinzgau	133
256	Tiroler Grauvieh	Tyrol Grey	134
259	Tuxer	Tux	134
268	Waldviertler Vieh	Waldviertel	135
Sheep			
521	Kärntner Brillenschaf	Carinthian	135
521	Seeländer Schaf	Carinthian	135
Horses			
788	Norisches Kaltblut	Noric	136
815	Vollblutaraber	Arab	136
Belgium (B)			
Cattle			
33	Blanc Bleu Belge	Belgian Blue	137
273	Blanc-Rouge de Belgique	Belgian White-and-Red	139
198	Pie-Noire-Holstein	Holstein	137
199	Pie-Rouge	Belgian Red Pied	138
224	Rood Ras van Belgie	Belgian Red	138
199	Roodbont	Belgian Red Pied	138
273	Witrood Ras Van Belgie	Belgian White-and-Red	139
Sheep			
561	Mouton Laitier Belge	Belgian Milk Sheep	139
Goats			
308	Blanche	Campine	140
317	Chamoisee	Belgian Fawn	140
361	Toggenburger	Toggenburg	141
Pigs			
906	Belgisch Landvarken	Belgian Landrace	141
937	Grand Yorkshire Belge	Large White	142
988	Pietrain	Pietrain	142
Horses			
728	Cheval de Sport Belge	Belgian Sport Horse	143
729	Cheval de Trait Ardennais	Ardennes	143
731	Cheval de Trait Belge	Flemish	144

29

Goats
  309 Bonte geit (extinct)   Dutch Pied Original   402
  341 Nederlandse Landgeit   Dutch Landrace   402
Pigs
  938 Groot Yorkshire-S   Large White / sire line   403
  939 Groot Yorkshire-Z   Large White / dam line   403
  980 Nederlands Landras   Dutch Landrace   404
Horses
  750 Gelders Paard   Gelderland   404
  752 Groninger Paard   Groningen   405
  816 Warmbloed Paard Nederlands   Netherlands Riding Horse   405

Norway (N)
Cattle
  187 Norsk rodtfe   Norwegian Red   406
  235 Sidet tronderfe og nordland   Blacksided Trondheim   406
  254 Telemark   Telemark   407
Sheep
  476 Dala   Dala   407
  496 Gammelnorsk   Old Norwegian   408
  566 Norsk Pels-Sau   Norwegian Fur Sheep   408
  614 Rygja sau   Rygja Sheep   409
  569 Spaelsau   Old Norwegian Short Tailed   409
  638 Steigar sau   Steigar Sheep   410
  496 Utegangarsau   Old Norwegian   408
Goats
  342 Norsk Geit   Norwegian Landrace   410
Pigs
  983 Norsk Landrace   Norwegian Landrace   411
  984 Norsk Yorkshire   Large White   411
Horses
  746 Fjordhest   Fjord   412
  786 Lyngshest   Nordland   412
  786 Nordlandshest   Nordland   412
  789 Norsk Kaldblods Traver   Norwegian Heavy Trotter   413
  814 Tyngre Doelehest   Doele Draught Horse   413

Poland (PL)
Cattle
   72 Czerwona Polska   Polish Red   414
  183 Nizinna Czerwono-Biala   Polish Red-and-White   414
  185 Nizinna-Czarno-Biala   Polish Black-and-White   415
  237 Simentalska   Polish Simmental   415
Sheep
  582 Corriedale   Polish Corriedale   416
  517 Kamieniecka   Kamieniec   416
  571 Olkuska   Olkusz   417
  583 Polish Merino   Polish Merino   417
  584 Polska owca gorska   Polish Mountain   418
  586 Pomorska   Pomeranian Coarsewool   418
  678 Wielkopolska Sheep   Wielkopolska   419
  680 Wrzosowka   Wrzosowka   419

Pigs
  930 Duroc   Duroc   420
  992 Polska biala zwisloucha   Polish Landrace   420
  995 Pulawska   Pulawy   421
 1019 Wielka biala polska   Large White   421
 1024 Zlotnicka biala   Zlotniki White   422
 1025 Zlotnicka pstra   Zlotniki Black and White   422
Horses
  763 Hucul   Hutsul   423
  771 Koniki Polskie   Polish Konik   423

Portugal (P)
Cattle
    5 Alentejana   Alentejana   424
   11 Arouquesa   Arouquesa   424
   21 Barrosa   Barrosa   425
  167 Marinhoa   Marinhoa   425
  168 Maronesa   Maronesa   426
  170 Mertolenga   Mertolenga   426
  172 Mirandesa   Mirandesa   427
  212 Raca Brava   Fighting Bull   427
Sheep
  406 Badana   Badana   428
  443 Campanica   Campanica   428
  454 Churra Algarvia   Algarve Churra   429
  455 Churra da Terra Quente   Churra da Terra Quente   429
  494 Galega Bragancana   Braganca+Miranda Galician   430
  494 Galega Mirandesa   Braganca+Miranda Galician   430
  547 Merino Portugues   Portuguese Merino   430
  557 Mondegueira   Mondegueira   431
  615 Saloia   Saloia   431
  626 Serra da Estrela   Serra da Estrela   432
Goats
  318 Charnequeira   Charnequeira   432
  354 Serpentina   Serpentina   433
  355 Serrana   Serrana   433
Pigs
  902 Alentejana   Alentejana   434
Horses
  749 Garrano   Garrano   434
  780 Lusitano   Lusitanian   435
  807 Sorraia   Sorraia   435

Romania (RO)
Cattle
   19 Baltata cu negru romanesca   Romanian Holstein-Friesian   436
   20 Baltata Romanesca   Romanian Simmental   436
   47 Bruna de Maramures   Romanian Brown   437
  201 Pinzgau de Transilvania   Romanian Pinzgau   437
  248 Sura de Stepa   Romanian Steppe   438

Pigs
934 Colorada	Extremadura Red	474
934 Extremena retinta	Extremadura Red	474
971 Manchada de Jabugo	Andalusian Spotted	474
981 Negra Iberica	Iberian Black	475
934 Olivenza	Extremadura Red	474

Horses
742 Espanol-Andaluz	Andalusian	475

Sweden (S)
Cattle
86 Fjällras	Swedish Mountain	476
225 Röd Kullig Lantras	Swedish Red Polled	476

Sheep
505 Gutefar	Gotland Sheep	477
580 Pälsfar	Swedish Fur Sheep	477
612 Ryafar	Rya Sheep	478

Goats
359 Svensk Lantras	Swedish Landrace	478

Horses
787 Nordsvensk häst	North Swedish Horse	479
805 Skogsruss	Gotland Pony	479

Switzerland (CH)
Cattle
40 Braunvieh	Brown Swiss	480
83 Eringer Rind	Herens	480
116 Hinterwälder	Hinterwald	481
214 Rätisches Grauvieh	Raetian Grey Cattle	481
230 Schwarzfleckvieh	Holstein-Friesian	482
240 Simmentaler Fleckvieh	Simmental	482

Sheep
485 Besch da pader	Engadine Red	484
432 Braunköpfiges Fleischschaf	Oxford Down	483
441 Bündner Oberländerschaf	Buendner Oberland	483
451 Charollais Suisse	Charollais	484
485 Engadiner Schaf	Engadine Red	484
609 Roux du Valais	Valais Red	485
621 Schwarzbraunes Bergschaf	Swiss Black-Brown Mountain	485
637 Spiegelschaf	Spiegel	486
609 Walliser Landschaf	Valais Red	485
666 Walliser Schwarznasenschaf	Valais Blacknose	486
669 Weißes Alpenschaf	Swiss White Alpine	487

Goats
303 Appenzellerziege	Appenzell	487
312 Bündner Strahlenziege	Grisons Striped	488
332 Gemsfarbige Gebirgsziege	Chamois Coloured	488
352 Nera Verzasca	Verzasca	490
344 Pfauenziege	Peacock Goat	489
349 Saanen	Saanen	489
357 Sardonaziege	St. Gallen Booted Goat	490
352 Schwarzer Tessiner	Verzasca	490

357	St Galler Stiefelgeiss	St. Gallen Booted Goat	490
362	Toggenburger	Toggenburg	491
366	Walliser Schwarzhalsziege	Valais Blackneck	491

Pigs

1020	Schwalbenbauch Mangalitza	Swallow-Bellied Mangalitsa	492
1007	Schweizerisches Edelschwein	Large White	492
1008	Schweiz. Veredeltes Landschwein	Swiss Landrace	493
1020	Wollschwein	Swallow-Bellied Mangalitsa	492

Horses

740	Demi Sang Suisse	Halfbred	493
747	Franches-Montagnes	Freiberg	494
756	Haflinger	Haflinger	494

Ukraine (UR)

Cattle

27	Belogolovaya ukrainskaya	Ukrainian Whiteheaded	495
49	Buraya karpatskaya	Carpathian Brown	495
146	Krasnaya polskaya	Polish Red	496
147	Krasnaya stepnaya	Red Steppe	496
154	Lebedinskaya	Lebedin	497
231	Seraya ukrainskaya	Ukrainian Grey	497

Pigs

976	Mirgorodskaya	Mirgorod	498
1014	Ukrainskaya stepnaya belaya	Ukrainian White Steppe	498
1015	Ukrainskaya stepnaya ryabaya	Ukrainian Spotted Steppe	499

United Kingdom (GB)

Cattle

1	Aberdeen-Angus	Aberdeen-Angus	499
18	Ayrshire	Ayrshire	500
24	Beef Shorthorn Cattle	Beef Shorthorn	500
26	Belgian Blue	Belgian Blue	501
28	Belted Galloway	Belted Galloway	501
38	Blonde d'Aquitaine	Blonde d'Aquitaine	502
43	British Charolais	Charolais	502
44	British Limousin	Limousin	503
45	British White	British White	503
81	Dexter	Dexter	504
82	English Longhorn	Longhorn	504
96	Galloway	Galloway	505
103	Gloucester	Gloucester	505
108	Guernsey	Guernsey	506
112	Hereford	Hereford	506
114	Highland	Highland	507
117	Holstein-Friesian	Holstein-Friesian	507
123	Irish Moiled	Irish Moiled	508
133	Jersey	Jersey	508
159	Lincoln Red	Lincoln Red	509
181	Murray Grey	Murray Grey	509
188	North Devon	Devon	510
204	Pinzgauer	Pinzgau	510
216	Red Poll	Red Poll	511
188	Red Ruby	Devon	510

EN	Local Breed Name	International Breed Name	Page

Pigs
910 Breitovskaya	Breitov	558
949 Kemerovskaya	Kemerovo	559
951 Krupnaya belaya	Large White	559
969 Livenskaya	Livny	560
979 Muromskaya	Murom	560
1000 Severokavkazskaya	North Caucasus	561
1001 Sibirskaya chernopestraya	Siberian Black Pied	561
1002 Sibirskaya severnaya	North Siberian	562
1010 Tarskaya (extinct)	Siberian	562
1012 Tsivilskaya	Tsivilsk	563
1016 Urzhumskaya	Urzhum	563

Uzbekia (UZB)
Cattle
53 Bushuevskaya	Bushuev	564

Yugoslavia (YU)
Cattle
52 Busha	Busa	564
71 Crno-belo	Holstein-Friesian	565
127 Istarsko govece	Istrian	565
238 Simentalska rasa	Simmental	566

Sheep
461 Cigaja	Tsigai	566
588 Pramenka	Yugoslavian Zackel	567
588 Sjenicka	Yugoslavian Zackel	567
588 Svrljiska	Yugoslavian Zackel	567

Pigs
925 Dom. mesnata svinja	Large White	567
978 Moravka	Morava	568
1003 Slavenske ciernostrakate	Slovakian Black Pied	568

Horses
712 Bosanski brdski konj	Bosnian Pony	569

4   Characterization of breeds

4.1   Criteria for the status of endangeredness of a breed

4.1.1 Risk definition in the literature

The risk that the genetic potential of a breed is getting lost depends on several factors. Several proposals have been made to define the status of endangeredness of a breed, four of them will be presented here.

The EAAP Working Group procedure

In its first report (MAIJALA et.al., 1984) the EAAP Working Group on Animal Genetic Resources in Europe used the following criteria for considering breeds to be endangered (table 6):

```
Table 6: Criteria for considering a breed to be endangered,
         EAAP Working Group procedure (1984)

Species      Criteria and conditions
───────────────────────────────────────────────────────────────
Cattle       <1000♀♀ or (1000-5000♀♀ and (decreasing or <20♂♂))
Sheep,Goats  < 500♀♀ or ( 500-1000♀♀ and (decreasing or <20♂♂))
Pigs         < 200♀♀ or ( 200- 500♀♀ and (decreasing or <20♂♂))
───────────────────────────────────────────────────────────────
♀♀ = number of female, ♂♂ = number of male breeding animals
```

The FAO proposal

An FAO expert consultation, Rome, 1992, defined the risk status of a breed mainly as a function of the number of female breeding animals. Four grades are used:

```
Table 7: Risk status of a breed, FAO proposal

Number of female breeding animals        Risk status
───────────────────────────────────────────────────────────
      <   100                            critical
100   - 1000                             endangered
1000  - 5000                             vulnerable
50000 - 10000                            rare
───────────────────────────────────────────────────────────
```

In addition "other factors such as reproductive rates, agronomic systems and patterns of use should be considered" (FAO, 1992).

The CEC proposal

A working group set up by the Commission of the European Communities CEC for endangered ruminant breeds suggested threshold numbers of reproducing females, below which a breed should or can be regarded as endangered; the thresholds differ for cattle, sheep and goats and depend on changes of the number of breeding animals during the last five years:

Table 8: Risk status of ruminant breeds, CEC proposal

Threshold numbers of reproducing animals below which a breed should be regarded as endangered

Species	Change in number during last 5 years		
	decreasing	stable	increasing
cattle	7500	5000	4000
sheep	9000	7500	6000
goat	9000	7500	6000

In order to become a candidate for conservation, it is additionally required that a herdbook exists and that the breed be regarded as autochthonous (AVON, 1992).

The DGfZ proposal

A working group of the Deutsche Gesellschaft für Züchtungskunde, DGfZ, the German branch of EAAP, suggested that a population should be regarded as endangered if one of the following five conditions is true (DGfZ, 1991):

1) The Effective Population size Ne decreases below Ne = 50, where Ne is a criterion which corresponds to the probability of the increase of inbreeding and genetic drift in a reproducing population with unequal numbers of male and female breeding animals.
   Ne = 50 is equivalent to an increase of inbreeding in the order of 1 % per generation; Ne = 50 is also equivalent to a ratio of the number of male and female breeding animals of 25/25, 20/35, 15/80 or 13/325, etc.
2) The population size (number of females) decreases more than 10% per year.
3) The number of breeding herds decreases below 10.
4) The proportion of matings with animals from different population(s) is higher than 10%.
5) The economic conditions for the population rapidly get worse relative to other populations.

48

The four proposals share the notion that the status of endangeredness of a breed should be based not only on the absolute number of breeding animals but also on additional criteria, such as a change in these numbers during recent years. The DGfZ proposal also asks for the number of breeding herds in which the breed is kept and for the percentage of pure breeding.

A major difference among the four proposals is the number of breeding females below which a breed is regarded as endangered. The threshold numbers of reproducing females are highest in the CEC-, intermediate in the EAAP - or FAO -, and lowest in the DGfZ-proposal.

The DGfZ proposal concentrates on ensuring a minimal Effective Population size Ne, and - since Ne is related to the amount of inbreeding and genetic drift - on maintaining inbreeding and genetic drift in the population below a defined level.

The formula for $Ne = 4 \cdot m \cdot f/(m+f)$ (FALCONER, 1989) with m and f the number of male and female breeding animals attributes more weight to the number of breeding males m, or to the sex, which is normally represented with the lower numbers. The formula assumes random relationship among mates and random variation in the number of off-spring per mating.

These assumptions are generally not true, particularly in small populations, and they can hardly be evaluated when no herdbook is established or complete pedigree information is missing. This means that under real life conditions, the threshold numbers of male and female breeding animals should be higher than expressed by Effective Population size estimated by the above cited formula.

4.1.2 New approach to define the status of endangeredness

Our main criterion to define the status of endangeredness is the minimum effective population size which is necessary to limit the accumulated inbreeding to a given value in 50 years of conservation. Additional factors are change in the number of breeding animals, absence of herdbook, number of herds, percentage of purebreeding and percentage of incrossing.

4.1.2.1 Accumulated inbreeding in 50 years

This is a function of ΔF, the expected increase of inbreeding per generation and of the number of generations within 50 years. ΔF is a function of the effective population size Ne, $\Delta F = 1/2 \, Ne$, where $Ne = 4 \cdot m \cdot f/(m+f)$; as mentioned above the formula assumes random mating, no selection among offspring groups and no increased genetic relationship among parents.

These assumptions should be true of Ne = 100, which corresponds to m = 26 males (if we assume p = 20 females mated to each male), but are not realistic for a low value of Ne, such as Ne = 15, which corresponds to only m = 4 males (with p = 20). For low values a correction of Ne appears necessary in order to take account of the probability of an increased genetic relationship among mates.

Example:
For a small population with m = 4 males and f = 80 females the above cited formulae estimate Ne = 15 and ΔF = 3,3 %. However, in a real life situation, if the population size of a breed went down to only 4 males and 80 females, we can expect a higher than average relationship among mates. If we assume that in this decreased population 50 % of mates have one parent in common and the other 50 % one grandparent, this corresponds to an average coefficient of inbreeding of ΔF 7,8 % in the offspring, if WRIGHT's (1923) formula $\Delta F = 1/2^{1+n_1+n_2}$ is used for a specific mating situation (n_1, n_2 = number of generation from sire and dam respectively to common ancestor).

For the correction of small values of Ne we suggest a pragmatic solution as follows:

a) The condition of ΔF = 0,5 % per generation corresponding to Ne = 100 and m=26 males (p=20 females) is regarded as acceptable and normal for a long term conservation.
b) For a small population of Ne = 15 with m=4 males and f=4x20 = 80 females we assume an increased genetic relationship among parents resulting in an increased coefficient of inbreeding ΔF = 7,8 % instead of ΔF = 3,3 %. This is an increase in the order of factor 7,8/3,3 = 2,6.
c) If we assume a linear increase in average genetic relationship among mates from Ne = 100 to Ne = 15 or Ne = 4 a linear correction of the expected increase of inbreeding by the formula ΔF = (2,6-0,016 Ne/2Ne) and backtransformation to a corrected effective population size Ne_c = 1/(2 ΔF_c) can be performed (table 9). For example Ne = 50 with normally ΔF = 1% is reduced to a corrected value of Ne_c = 27,8 with ΔF_c = 1,8% and Ne = 15 to Ne_c = 6,4 with ΔF_c = 7,8%. For values of Ne < 100, the corrected values Ne_c form the basis for the definition of the status of endangeredness of a breed.

Table 9: Correction of expected increase of inbreeding ΔF
         and of effective population size Ne for assumed
         increased average genetic relationship among mates,
         4 ≤ Ne ≤ 100

Effective Population size Ne	Increase of inbreeding per generation (%)		Effective Population size corrected
	ΔF	ΔF-corrected	
100	0,5	0,5	100
90	0,56	0,64	77,6
80	0,62	0,82	60,6
70	0,71	1,05	47,3
60	0,83	1,36	36,6
50	1,0	1,8	27,8
40	1,25	2,45	20,4
30	1,67	3,53	14,1
20	2,5	5,7	8,8
15	3,3	7,8	6,4
10	5,0	12,0	4,1
4	12,5	31,8	1,6

Sometimes no information on the number of male and female breeding animals is available, only the total number T of both sexes. In this case we assume for all species a mating ratio of p = 20 females per male and Ne can be derived from T as $Ne_2 = 0,181$ T. Values of $Ne_2 < 100$ were again corrected to Ne_c as outlined above.

The number of generations within the time interval of 50 years depends on the length of the generation interval and this again on the species.
The length of the generation interval was estimated on the assumption of the average age of male and female breeding animals at the time of birth of their offspring during conservation. There are two conflicting objectives, on the one hand lengthening the generation interval during conservation, on the other hand limiting the number of offspring from the individual parent. In this situation we assumed the length of the generation interval as listed in table 10 as a realistic compromise:

Table 9: Assumed generation interval GI and number
of generations in 50 years of conservation

Species	GI (years)	Number of generations
Pigs	1,5	33
Sheep/Goats	2,5	20
Cattle	3,5	14
Horses	4,5	11

The maximum value of inbreeding which is acceptable per generation depends on the number of generations in 50 years and on the maximum accumulated value of inbreeding F_x after 50 years, which appears acceptable. For the definition of classes of endangeredness we assumed the following five levels of accumulated inbreeding in 50 years:
Fx < 5%, 5-15%, 16-25%, 26-40% and > 40%. The resulting values of maximum inbreeding per generation ΔF and the minimal effective population size Ne or Ne_c is presented in table 11.

Table 11: Maximum increase of inbreeding per generation ΔF (%)
and minimal effective population size Ne

Species	number of generations	Fx= 5 %		Fx= 15 %		Fx= 25 %		Fx= 40%	
		ΔF	Ne	ΔF	Ne	ΔF	Ne	ΔF	Ne
Pigs	33	0,16	303	0,45	111	0,76	66	1,21	41
Sheep Goats	20	0,25	200	0,75	67	1,25	40	2,00	25
Cattle	14	0,36	139	1,07	47	1,79	28	2,86	17
Horses	11	0,45	111	1,36	37	2,27	22	3,64	14

It can be seen that the minimal effective population size necessary to limit the accumulated inbreeding to a given value after 50 years of conservation depends on the species.

Table 12 presents the defined classes of endangeredness with the range of effective population size for the five species, which correspond to the assumed maximal accumulated inbreeding Fx after 50 years of conservation as reproducing population.

Table 12: Minimal values of effective population size
(or corrected values Ne_c as explained above)
for 5 classes of endangeredness

Species	Normal	Potentially endangered	Minimally endangered	endangered	critically endangered
	Fx < 5%	Fx 5-15 %	Fx 16-25%	Fx 26-40 %	Fx > 40 %
Pigs	$\geq$ 304	111 - 303	66 -110	41 - 65	< 41
Sheep Goats	$\geq$ 201	67 - 200	40 - 66	25 - 39	< 25
Cattle	$\geq$ 140	47 - 139	28 - 46	17 - 27	< 17
Horses	$\geq$ 112	37 - 111	22 - 36	14 - 21	< 14

4.1.2.2 Additional factors for risk definition

a)   Number of animals registered in herdbook is unknown
We assume that for planned matings during conservation pedigree information of breeding animals is required. Since according to table 12 approximately Ne = 200 is required for accumulated inbreeding Fx < 5 % and Ne = 200 corresponds to approximately f = 1000 females (with p = 20) this would mean a minimal number of 1000 females in herdbook. If these are 25 % of the total number of females, a total number of at least 4000 females are required for a meaningful reproduction.
As a consequence, if only the total number of females is known and this is less than f = 4000, the breed is classified downward by one class.

b) Percentage of purebreeding of females is less than 100 %
Again a minimal number of 1000 purebreeding females in herdbook is assumed to be necessary. The breed is classified downward from 'normal' to 'potentially endangered' if the number of females is less than the given value in table 13 for a given percentage of purebreeding.

Table 13: Classification of a breed as potentially
endangered if purebreeding is less than 100 %
and the number of females is below a given value

Percentage of Purebreeding	Minimal number of females total	in herdbook
90	4400	1100
80	5000	1250
75	5300	1330
70	5700	1420
60	6800	1700
50	8000	2000
40	10000	2500

c) Number of females is decreasing

In this case it is assumed that twice the number of purebreeding females in herdbook is required than if the number of females is stable or increasing. The breed is classified downward by one class if the absolute number of females is less or equal to the given numbers:

Condition	Pure breeding	
	100 %	<100 %
female total	8000	10.000
female in herdbook	2000	2.500

d) Number of herds

If the number of herds in which a breed is kept is small, the risk of losing a breed by accident, disease or lack of interest is increased. As a consequence the breed is classified downward by one class
- if the number of herds is known to be less than 10
- or if the number of females is less or equal to the given numbers:

Species	Number of females	
	total	in herdbook
Cattle, sheep Goats, pigs	< 800	< 200
Horses	< 200	< 50

e) Immigration or incrossing

This situation results in a loss of genes which were originally present in the breed. As a consequence, the breed is classified downward by one class if immigration or incrossing is greater or equal to 10 percent of the matings.

Based on the criteria explained above a breed is assigned to one of the five classes of endangeredness: "critically endangered", "endangered", "minimally endangered", "potentially endangered" and "normal".

In chapter 5, where the "full" information on each breed is presented, the criteria which are critical for the breed are listed under the heading "watch" in the following order: number of males, number of females, number of females in herdbook, trend of females, number of herds, percentage of purebreeding and percentage of incrossing.

4.2 Listing of endangered breeds

The status of endangeredness of a breed is defined on the basis of a combination of the effective population size Ne, change in number of breeding animals, absence of herdbook, number of herds, percentage of purebreeding and percentage of incrossing (see chapter 4.1.2).

Table 14 presents the number of breeds which, according to these criteria, fall into a particular group of endangeredness. It can be seen that out of a total of 877 breeds 158 breeds are critically endangered and less than half of the breeds (412) can be regarded as normal or not endangered.

Table 14: Status of endangeredness of breeds

Status of endangeredness	Cattle	Sheep	Goats	Pigs	Horses	Total
Normal	128	149	31	55	49	412
Potentially endangered	53	47	12	23	27	162
Minimally endangered	26	34	4	11	14	89
Endangered	12	12	4	5	10	43
Critically endangered	57	37	16	27	21	158
No information	1	4	1	5	2	13
Total	277	283	68	126	123	877

In table 15 breeds are listed in alphabetic order within species and within the four classes of endangeredness "potentially endangered", "minimally endangered", "endangered" and "critically endangered". Breeds which are not endangered are not listed here. The following information is presented on each breed:

Entry number EN, local breed name, country, effective population size, BP and SB, where

BP =   the corresponding page number of section 5:
"Presentation of individual breeds", where the "full" information on the breed can be found.

SB =   the corresponding page number of section 4.3:
"Groups of similar breeds", where information on similar breeds can be found with which cooperation in conservation could be considered.

For countries and local breed names see also explanation on page 22.

Table 15: Listing of endangered breeds

Entry Number	Local Breed Name	Country	Effective Pop. Size	Page No. BP	SB
POTENTIALLY ENDANGERED:	**CATTLE**				
3	Alatauskaya	Kazakh	18568	387	78
5	Alentejana	Portugal	1749	424	79
8	Angler	Germany	891	254	78
25	Belgian Blue	Ireland	76	313	81
173	Bianca val padana	Italy	126	330	82
273	Blanc-Rouge de Belgique	Belgium	2277	139	76
39	Brachyceros	Greece	1810	295	80
41	Brava	France	154	183	76
48	Brune des Alpes	France	3385	184	79
49	Buraya karpatskaya	Ukraine	1779	495	79
53	Bushuevskaya	Uzbekia	394	564	
58	Camargue	France	381	185	76
68	Cinisara	Italy	1514	327	80
74	Deutsche Rotbunte	Germany	9089	255	76
77	Deutsches Braunvieh	Germany	11799	256	79
79	Deutsches Schwarzbuntes Rind	Germany*	60	257	75
82	English Longhorn	United Kingdom	114	504	78
85	Ferrandais	France	61	187	76
87	Flamande	France	220	187	78
103	Gloucester	United Kingdom	98	505	80
110	Hereford	France	82	189	77
116	Hinterwälder	Switzerland	173	481	77
119	Inra 95	France	133	190	82
120	Irish Blonde d'Aquitaine	Ireland	107	314	81
127	Istarsko govece	Yugoslavia	57	565	80
128	Istobenskaya	USSR	993	551	75
132	Jersey	Ireland	60	317	82
144	Krasnaya gorbatovskaya	USSR	176	553	79
149	Krasnyi belorusskii skot	Belorusse	2498	144	78
154	Lebedinskaya	Ukraine	1939	497	79
161	Maas-Rijn-Yssel	Netherlands	200	397	76
173	Modenese	Italy	126	330	82
174	Modicana	Italy	6340	331	80
181	Murray Grey	United Kingdom	194	509	76
183	Nizinna Czerwono-Biala	Poland	442	414	76
185	Nizinna-Czarno-Biala	Poland	5176	415	75
188	North Devon	United Kingdom	941	510	78
194	Pezzata rossa d'Oropa	Italy	243	331	77
195	Pezzata Rossa Italiana	Italy	1517	332	77
89	Pie Rouge de l'Est	France	2708	194	77
202	Pinzgauer	Austria	1332	133	77
203	Pinzgauer	Germany	63	263	77
212	Raca Brava	Portugal	732	427	76
41	Race Espagnole	France	154	183	76

Entry No. EN	Local Breed Name	Country	Effect. Pop. Size	Page No. BP	SB
214	Rätisches Grauvieh	Switzerland	114	481	81
216	Red Poll	United Kingdom	152	511	78
188	Red Ruby	United Kingdom	941	510	78
217	Reggiana	Italy	178	335	82
161	Roodbont	Netherlands	200	397	76
242	Sivo govedo Dalmacije	Croatia	100	147	80
245	Sortbroget Dansk Malkekvaeg	Denmark	9143	161	75
256	Tiroler Grauvieh	Austria	158	134	81
261	Valdostana Pezzata Nera	Italy	66	339	75
264	Villard de Lans	France	69	197	81
267	Vosgienne	France	312	197	78
271	White Park	United Kingdom	73	513	82
272	Whitebred Shorthorn	United Kingdom	222	514	82
273	Witrood Ras Van Belgie	Belgium	2277	139	76

MINIMALLY ENDANGERED: CATTLE

Entry No. EN	Local Breed Name	Country	Effect. Pop. Size	Page No. BP	SB
13	Asturiano Montana	Spain	138	451	79
16	Aure et Saint-Girons	France	41	180	80
29	Berrenda negra andaluza	Spain	125	451	76
34	Blanca Cacerena	Spain	45	452	79
52	Busha	Yugoslavia	14480	564	80
55	Cachena	Spain	42	453	80
56	Caldelana	Spain	37	453	76
13	Casina	Spain	138	451	79
84	Faeroesk	Faeroe Islands	155	167	82
113	Hessisches Rotvieh	Germany	64	260	78
115	Hinterwälder	Germany	186	261	77
140	Kerry Cattle	Ireland	120	317	76
143	Krasnaya estonskaya	Estonia	3014	166	78
146	Krasnaya polskaya	Ukraine	82	496	78
148	Krasnaya tambovskaya	USSR	426	553	79
152	Lakenvelder	Netherlands	113	397	75
162	Magyar szürke	Hungary	210	304	80
170	Mertolenga	Portugal	1143	426	79
182	Negra de las Campinas andaluzas	Spain	52	458	76
218	Rendena	Italy	143	336	79
225	Röd Kullig Lantras	Sweden	73	476	78
227	Sarda	Italy	759	337	79
237	Simentalska	Poland	57	415	77
246	Suksunskii skot	USSR	60	555	79
266	Vorderwälder	Germany	1337	265	77
270	Westfälisches Rotvieh	Germany	58	266	78
274	Yakutskii skot	USSR	60	557	75

Entry No.	Local EN Breed Name	Country	Effect. Pop. Size	Page No. BP	SB

ENDANGERED: CATTLE

17	Ayrshire	Ireland	36	312	78
42	Breton Pie Noire	France	47	184	75
76	Deutsche Schwarzbunte (Original)	Germany	25	256	75
86	Fjällras	Sweden	159	476	76
93	Froment du Leon	France	15	188	82
106	Groninger Blaarkop	Netherlands	36	396	76
150	Krasnyi megrelskii skot	Georgia	157	253	79
153	Länsisuomenkarja	Finland	55	169	78
177	Mostrenca	Spain	54	457	82
180	Murnau-Werdenfelser	Germany	25	262	81
192	Palmera	Spain	23	459	82
177	Palurda	Spain	54	457	82
248	Sura de Stepa	Romania	32	438	80

CRITICALLY ENDANGERED: CATTLE

2	Agerolese	Italy	15	324	79
4	Albera	Spain	11	450	82
6	Alpha 16 (terminated)	France	miss	178	81
7	Alpine Herens	France	5	179	80
10	Armoricaine	France	8	179	78
22	Basco-Bearnaise	France	19	181	81
27	Belogolovaya ukrainskaya	Ukraine	20	495	76
51	Burlina	Italy	11	325	75
54	Cabannina	Italy	19	326	80
57	Calvana	Italy	8	326	82
60	Cardena Andaluza	Spain	4	454	76
61	Ceske strakate	Czech Republic	686	157	77
69	Coopelso 93	France	miss	186	81
101	Donnersberger Rotvieh	Germany	20	258	78
90	Frieiresa	Spain	24	455	80
95	Galloway	Iceland	4	310	76
97	Garfagnina	Italy	14	328	81
99	Gascon Areole	France	17	189	81
102	Glanrind	Germany	19	259	81
109	Harzer Rotvieh	Germany	13	260	78
123	Irish Moiled	United Kingdom	13	508	78
104	Iskursko govedo	Bulgaria	11	145	80
126	Istarsko govedo	Croatia	25	146	80
129	Itäsuomenkarja	Finland	7	168	78
136	Katerini	Greece	20	295	80
139	Kärntner Blondvieh	Austria	8	132	81
151	Kurganskaya	USSR	20	554	78
155	Limiana	Spain	17	455	80
158	Limpurger	Germany	40	262	81
160	Lourdaise	France	16	191	
164	Mallorquina	Spain	5	456	79
169	Menorqina	Spain	21	456	79

Entry No.	Local EN Breed Name	Country	Effect. Pop. Size	Page No. BP	SB
171	Mestnaya estonskaya	Estonia	9	166	78
178	Murbodner	Austria	19	132	81
179	Murciana	Spain	6	458	79
189	Original Allgäuer Braunvieh	Germany	24	263	79
258	Ottonese	Italy	5	338	82
191	Pajuna	Spain	13	459	79
201	Pinzgau de Transilvania	Romania	18	437	77
200	Pinzgauer	Italy	7	333	77
205	Pisana	Italy	7	333	79
207	Pohjoissuomenkarja	Finland	25	169	76
208	Pontremolese	Italy	10	334	82
210	Pustertaler Schecken	Germany	8	264	77
211	Pustertaler Sprinzen	Italy	5	335	77
220	Rodopska kusoroga	Bulgaria	7	146	80
231	Seraya ukrainskaya	Ukraine	29	497	80
191	Serrana	Spain	13	459	79
232	Serrana Negra	Spain	7	460	76
235	Sidet tronderfe og nordland	Norway	20	406	76
251	Sykia	Greece	8	296	80
254	Telemark	Norway	11	407	78
255	Terrena	Spain	13	461	80
258	Tortonese	Italy	5	338	82
259	Tuxer	Austria	18	134	76
258	Varzese	Italy	5	338	82
263	Vianesa	Spain	26	462	80
265	Vogelsberger Rind	Germany	17	265	78
268	Waldviertler Vieh	Austria	12	135	81
276	Yurinskaya	USSR	7	558	79

DEFINITION OF STATUS NOT POSSIBLE BECAUSE OF MISSING INFORMATION: CATTLE

| 204 | Pinzgauer | United Kingdom | miss | 510 | 77 |

Entry Local	Country	Effect.	Page No.
No. EN Breed Name		Pop. Size	BP SB

POTENTIALLY ENDANGERED: SHEEP

Entry No. EN	Breed Name	Country	Effect. Pop. Size	BP	SB
404	Aure et de Campan	France	2339	198	93
404	Aurois	France	2339	198	93
405	Avranchin	France	1448	199	88
408	Bagnolese	Italy	6335	341	94
420	Bizet	France	474	201	93
443	Campanica	Portugal	2864	428	95
446	Castlemilk Moorit Sheep	United Kingdom	70	518	91
451	Charollais Suisse	Switzerland	107	484	88
453	Chios	Greece	362	297	89
464	Clun Forest	France	741	206	89
474	Cotswold Sheep	United Kingdom	360	520	88
481	Dorset Down	France	1750	208	89
484	Drentse Heideschaap	Netherlands	462	398	90
489	Finnois	France	192	208	90
630	Glossa	Greece	270	300	92
500	Granadina	Spain	13784	465	93
503	Grivette	France	511	209	93
515	Inra 401	France	190	210	87
522	Kempische Heideschaap	Netherlands	132	399	90
654	Kivircik	Greece	3620	301	93
529	Leineschaf	Germany	277	269	88
530	Licka Ovca	Croatia	181	148	92
532	Lincoln Longwool	United Kingdom	375	526	88
534	Locale	Italy	272	354	92
536	Maellana	Spain	267	466	94
543	Menorquina	Spain	268	466	89
555	Merinos Precoce	France	546	215	87
500	Montesina	Spain	13784	465	93
668	Moorschnucke	Germany	231	277	90
624	Moscia Calabrese	Italy	2715	361	89
568	North Ronaldsay	United Kingdom	117	528	91
500	Ojalada	Spain	13784	465	93
500	Ojinegra	Spain	13784	465	93
574	Ouessant	France	491	218	94
579	Paska Ovca	Croatia	724	148	92
584	Polska owca gorska	Poland	905	418	92
591	Race de l'est a Laine Merinos	France	2362	219	87
592	Race de Thones et de Marthod	France	390	219	94
593	Racka	Hungary	377	306	92
601	Romanov	France	1846	221	90
605	Rouge de l'ouest	United Kingdom	381	530	87
610	Rubia de El Molar	Spain	179	470	95
614	Rygja sau	Norway	6335	409	90
624	Sciara	Italy	2715	361	89
629	Shropshire	United Kingdom	285	531	89
630	Skopelos	Greece	270	300	92
633	Solognot	France	309	223	87
643	Sumavska	Czech Republic	938	158	92

Entry No.	Local EN Breed Name	Country	Effect. Pop. Size	Page No. BP	SB
648	Texel	Finland	100	171	88
654	Thraki	Greece	3620	301	93
668	Weiße hornlose Heidschnucke	Germany	231	277	90
674	Wensleydale Longwool	United Kingdom	221	536	88
676	Whitefaced Woodland	United Kingdom	128	537	94
680	Wrzosowka	Poland	145	419	90
658	Zuslachtena valasska	CSFR	12218	152	92

MINIMALLY ENDANGERED: SHEEP

Entry No.	Local EN Breed Name	Country	Effect. Pop. Size	Page No. BP	SB
411	Baregeois	France	387	199	93
417	Berrichon de l'Indre	France	135	200	87
485	Besch da pader	Switzerland	138	484	92
430	Bovska Ovca	Slovenia	200	447	89
433	Brentegana	Italy	543	344	91
441	Bündner Oberländerschaf	Switzerland	69	483	92
458	Ciavenasca	Italy	543	346	94
599	Coete	Spain	61	469	95
617	Demontina	Italy	362	360	91
480	Di Corteno	Italy	362	349	91
485	Engadiner Schaf	Switzerland	138	484	92
488	Finarda	Italy	905	350	91
496	Gammelnorsk	Norway	147	408	90
510	Hvidhovedet Marsk	Denmark	735	162	88
523	Kymi	Greece	182	298	92
526	Landais	France	51	211	93
533	Livo	Italy	79	354	91
535	Lourdais	France	274	212	93
539	Manx Loaghtan	United Kingdom	160	526	91
545	Merina	Spain	185	467	87
546	Merino de Grazalema	Spain	155	467	87
558	Mourerous	France	125	215	91
561	Mouton Laitier Belge	Belgium	42	139	89
565	Norfolk Horn	United Kingdom	140	527	89
558	Peone	France	125	215	91
599	Roja Mallorquina	Spain	61	469	95
609	Roux du Valais	Switzerland	59	485	91
616	Saltasassi	Italy	453	359	91
617	Sambucana	Italy	362	360	91
620	Schoonebeker Heideschaap	Netherlands	109	400	90
632	Solcavsko-Jezerska	Slovenia	267	447	91
657	Trimeticcia di Segezia	Italy	109	363	87
496	Utegangarsau	Norway	147	408	90
659	Varesina	Italy	163	364	91
660	Veluwse Heideschaap	Netherlands	94	401	90
663	Vissana	Italy	181	364	92
609	Walliser Landschaf	Switzerland	59	485	91
667	Weiße gehörnte Heidschnucke	Germany	61	277	90
675	Whiteface Dartmoor	United Kingdom	335	536	88
681	Zakynthos	Greece	87	302	91

Entry Local No. EN Breed Name	Country	Effect. Page No. Pop. Size BP SB

ENDANGERED: SHEEP

456 Churra Lebrijana	Spain	86	463	95
460 Cigaja	Hungary	84	305	93
462 Cikta	Hungary	65	305	92
490 Florina	Greece	55	297	92
495 Galway	Ireland	177	318	88
521 Kärntner Brillenschaf	Austria	45	135	91
520 Kärntner Brillenschaf	Germany	29	269	91
570 Nostrana	Italy	272	356	95
490 Pellagonia	Greece	55	297	92
594 Raiole	France	59	220	89
611 Ruda Dubrovacka Sheep	Croatia	191	149	92
623 Schwarzköpfiges Fleischschaf	Germany*	561	274	89
521 Seeländer Schaf	Austria	45	135	91
637 Spiegelschaf	Switzerland	63	486	91

CRITICALLY ENDANGERED: SHEEP

400 Alpagota	Italy	109	340	91
470 Alpine	France	362	206	91
401 Altamurana	Italy	14	340	89
665 Bayernwaldschaf	Germany	24	276	92
413 Bellunese	Italy	2	343	91
421 Blackface	France	181	202	94
431 Braunes Bergschaf	Germany	25	267	91
434 Brianzola	Italy	4	345	91
435 Brigasca	Italy	18	345	92
436 Brigasque	France	181	203	92
440 Brogne	Italy	109	346	91
445 Castillonnais	France	56	204	93
447 Caussenard des Garrigues	France	181	204	89
466 Coburger Fuchsschaf	Germany	23	268	90
470 Commun des Alpes	France	362	206	91
471 Cornella bianca	Italy	3	348	92
477 Dansk Landfar	Denmark	51	161	90
492 Frabosana	Italy	199	350	92
497 Garessina	Italy	8	351	91
498 Garfagnina bianca	Italy	16	351	92
511 Ibicenca	Spain	9	465	94
516 Istriana	Italy	19	352	91
525 Lamon	Italy	5	353	91
540 Marrane	Italy	13	355	94
542 Matesina	Italy	31	356	87
553 Merinos de Rambouillet	France	29	214	87
559 Mouton Boulonnais	France	181	216	88
571 Olkuska	Poland	47	417	88
578 Palmera	Spain	12	468	94
585 Pomarancina	Italy	145	358	92
590 Pusterese	Italy	4	358	92

Entry	Local	Country	Effect.	Page No.	
No. EN	Breed Name		Pop. Size	BP	SB

595	Rauhwolliges Pommer. Landschaf	Germany*	27	273	88
603	Rosset	Italy	24	359	94
606	Rouge du Roussillon	France	2	222	95
619	Savoiarda	Italy	8	361	94
645	Tacola	Italy	8	362	91
662	Vierhornschaf	Germany	7	276	91
665	Waldschaf	Germany	24	276	92
682	Zucca Modenese	Italy	13	365	92

DEFINITION OF STATUS NOT POSSIBLE BECAUSE OF MISSING INFORMATION: SHEEP

403	Ardes	France	miss	198	93
463	Ciuta	Italy	miss	347	94
467	Colbred	United Kingdom	miss	520	88
607	Rough Fell	United Kingdom	miss	530	94

| Entry | Local | Country | Effect. | Page No. | |
No. EN	Breed Name		Pop. Size	BP	SB

POTENTIALLY ENDANGERED: GOATS

300	Alpina	Italy	1086	365	97
304	Balkanska Koza	Croatia	18	149	98
307	Blanca Serrana Andaluza	Spain	317	471	98
308	Blanche	Belgium	151	140	97
317	Chamoisee	Belgium	117	140	97
319	Chevre du Rove	France	373	226	98
325	Di Cosenza	Italy	7240	368	97
326	Di L' Aquila	Italy	543	368	97
341	Nederlandse Landgeit	Netherlands	150	402	98
357	Sardonaziege	Switzerland	67	490	97
356	Skopelos	Greece	1448	303	98
357	St Galler Stiefelgeiss	Switzerland	67	490	97
364	Valgerola	Italy	127	375	98

MINIMALLY ENDANGERED: GOATS

313	Cabra Mallorquina	Spain	347	471	98
334	Hneda kratkosrsta	CSFR	149	153	97
336	Irish Goat	Ireland	494	320	97
345	Poitevin	France	381	227	97

ENDANGERED: GOATS

312	Bündner Strahlenziege	Switzerland	47	488	97
327	Di Potenza	Italy	79	369	97
358	Suomenvuohi	Finland	41	171	98
361	Toggenburger	Belgium	34	141	97

CRITICALLY ENDANGERED: GOATS

302	Angora Goat	United Kingdom	37	538	
305	Bastarda	Italy	4	366	97
328	Cilentana Grigia	Italy	2	369	97
323	Derivata di Siria	Italy	22	367	98
305	Di Benevento	Italy	4	366	97
324	Di Campobasso	Italy	8	367	97
328	Di Salerno	Italy	2	369	97
329	Di Teramo	Italy	50	370	97
330	Erzgebirgsziege	Germany	18	280	97
331	Garganica	Italy	25	370	97
333	Girgentana	Italy	30	371	98
337	Istriana	Italy	4	372	98
344	Pfauenziege	Switzerland	25	489	97
347	Roccaverano	Italy	18	373	98
353	Sempione	Italy	6	374	98
360	Thüringer Waldziege	Germany	18	280	97
363	Val di Livo	Italy	13	375	98
365	Vallesana	Italy	3	376	98

DEFINITION OF STATUS NOT POSSIBLE BECAUSE OF MISSING INFORMATION: GOATS

309	Bonte geit (extinct)	Netherlands	miss	402	97

Entry No. EN	Local Breed Name	Country	Effect. Pop. Size	Page No. BP	SB
POTENTIALLY ENDANGERED: PIGS					
905	Belgicka Landrase	CSFR	194	154	101
912	British Saddleback	United Kingdom	257	540	102
934	Colorada	Spain	1810	474	103
919	Deutsche Landrasse B	Germany	257	283	101
928	Duroc	Germany*	226	286	103
930	Duroc	Poland	218	420	103
934	Extremena retinta	Spain	1810	474	103
936	Gloucestershire Old Spot	United Kingdom	202	541	104
944	Hampshire	Romania	569	442	102
949	Kemerovskaya	USSR	5322	559	103
953	Landrace	France	2147	231	101
969	Livenskaya	USSR	3167	560	101
979	Muromskaya	USSR	835	560	101
934	Olivenza	Spain	1810	474	103
993	Porcul de Banat	Romania	562	444	102
994	Presticke	Czech Republic	705	158	102
1020	Schwalbenbauch Mangalitza	Switzerland	115	492	102
997	Schwäbisch-Hällisches Schwein	Germany	128	288	102
998	Schwerfurter Fleischrasse	Germany*	800	289	104
999	Semirechenskaya	Kazakh	1720	389	101
1000	Severokavkazskaya	USSR	12755	561	103
1001	Sibirskaya chernopestraya	USSR	593	561	104
1010	Tarskaya	USSR	5035	562	101
1015	Ukrainskaya stepnaya ryabaya	Ukraine	624	499	103
1020	Wollschwein	Switzerland	115	492	102
1022	Yorkshire	Romania	255	444	101
MINIMALLY ENDANGERED: PIGS					
909	Berkshire	United Kingdom	218	539	103
924	Deutsches Sattelschwein	Germany*	66	285	102
948	Kakhetinskaya	Georgia	140	253	104
959	Large Black	United Kingdom	135	542	103
972	Mangalica	Hungary	178	306	102
973	Mangalita	Romania	246	443	102
975	Middle White	United Kingdom	128	543	101
995	Pulawska	Poland	109	421	104
1009	Tamworth	United Kingdom	159	543	103
1018	Welsh	United Kingdom	308	544	102
1025	Zlotnicka pstra	Poland	95	422	104
ENDANGERED: PIGS					
915	Corse	France	566	228	104
941	Hampshire	France	27	230	102
956	Landrace Belga	Italy	99	378	101
984	Norsk Yorkshire	Norway	82	411	101
985	Pen Ar Lan P 77	France	44	234	104

CRITICALLY ENDANGERED: PIGS

Entry No.	Breed Name	Country	Pop. Size	BP	SB
900	Acadie P22	France	13	228	104
903	Angler Sattelschwein	Germany	26	281	102
904	Bela Zlahtna	Slovenia	34	448	101
907	Belgische Landrasse	Germany*	53	282	101
996	Buntes Schwein	Germany	17	288	104
913	Chester White	United Kingdom	17	540	102
974	Chinois	France	41	233	104
914	Cinta Senese	Italy	13	376	102
927	Duroc	France	10	229	103
932	Duroc	United Kingdom	59	541	103
935	Gascon	France	28	229	103
942	Hampshire	Germany*	6	286	102
943	Hampshire	Italy	13	377	102
945	Hampshire	United Kingdom	15	542	102
947	Jia-Xing	France	6	230	104
950	Krskopoljski crnopasasti prasic	Slovenia	28	449	102
966	Lesogornaya porodnaya gruppa	Armenia	33	131	104
967	Limousin	France	13	232	102
971	Manchada de Jabugo	Spain	4	474	104
974	Mei-Shan	France	41	233	104
977	Mora Romagnola	Italy	2	379	103
982	Normand	France	33	233	102
986	Penshire P66	France	32	234	104
987	Pie noir du Pays Basque	France	13	235	102
996	Schwarz-Weißes Bentheimer	Germany	17	288	104
1005	Sortbroget	Denmark	44	164	104
1011	Tia Meslan P44	France	8	236	104
1013	Turopolljac	Croatia	19	150	104
1024	Zlotnicka biala	Poland	14	422	101

DEFINITION OF STATUS NOT POSSIBLE BECAUSE OF MISSING INFORMATION: PIGS

Entry No.	Breed Name	Country	Pop. Size	BP	SB
916	Crna Slavonska	Slovenia	miss	448	103
978	Moravka	Yugoslavia	miss	568	103
990	Pietrain	Italy	miss	380	103
1003	Slavenske ciernostrakate	Yugoslavia	miss	568	104
1006	Spotted	Italy	miss	380	104

Entry Local No. EN Breed Name	Country	Effect. Pop. Size	Page No. BP	SB
POTENTIALLY ENDANGERED: HORSES				
707 Ardennais	France	789	237	109
708 Ardennais du nord	France	143	238	109
713 Boulonnais	France	137	239	109
714 Breton	France	1794	240	109
716 Cavallo Agricolo Italiano	Italy	1200	381	109
719 Cavallo della Giara	Italy	144	383	111
720 Cavallo Maremmano	Italy	519	383	109
725 Cavallo Siciliano	Italy	141	386	109
735 Comtois	France	1328	242	109
743 Exmoor Pony	United Kingdom	138	547	110
746 Fjordhest	Norway	233	412	110
747 Franches-Montagnes	Switzerland	370	494	109
756 Haflinger	Switzerland	58	494	111
763 Hucul	Poland	155	423	111
764 Irish Draught Horse	Ireland	336	323	109
769 Kisberi felver	Hungary	296	307	109
780 Lusitano	Portugal	488	435	108
782 Mezöhegyesi felver	Hungary	109	308	109
784 New Forest	France	190	247	110
785 Noniusz	Hungary	319	309	108
790 Percheron	France	633	248	109
794 Pottok	France	89	249	111
795 Puoliverinen	Finland	44	176	108
822 Shetland Pony	Finland	87	176	111
808 Suffolk Punch	United Kingdom	61	549	110
708 Trait du nord	France	143	238	109
814 Tyngre Doelehest	Norway	106	413	110
818 Zweibrücker	Germany	505	294	108
MINIMALLY ENDANGERED: HORSES				
711 Barbe	France	59	239	108
726 Cheval de selle	Luxembourg	34	395	108
730 Cheval de Trait Ardennais	Luxembourg	33	395	109
738 Dartmoor	France	59	243	110
741 Den Jydske Hest	Denmark	61	164	110
748 Frederiksborgheste	Denmark	59	165	110
749 Garrano	Portugal	727	434	111
761 Hrvatski Hladnokrvnjak	Croatia	97	150	109
766 Islandais	France	36	245	110
786 Lyngshest	Norway	66	412	110
821 New Forest Pony	Finland	26	175	110
786 Nordlandshest	Norway	66	412	110
798 Sächsisches Warmblut	Germany	55	292	109
800 Schwarzwälder Füchse	Germany	31	293	110
800 St. Märgener Füchse	Germany	31	293	110
817 Welsh	France	260	251	110

ENDANGERED: HORSES

705	Arab Horse	Ireland	23	322	108
723	Cavallo Sanfratellano	Italy	28	385	109
724	Cavallo Sardo	Italy	272	385	109
757	Haflinger	United Kingdom	27	548	111
772	Landais	France	43	245	111
774	Lipicai	Hungary	90	308	108
783	Morgan Horse	United Kingdom	37	548	108
791	Mulassier	France	61	248	109
791	Poitevin	France	61	248	109
799	Schleswiger Kaltblut	Germany	19	292	110
806	Skyos Pony	Greece	47	304	111

CRITICALLY ENDANGERED: HORSES

701	Altwürttemberger	Germany	6	289	108
706	Arabialainen	Finland	7	173	108
709	Auxois	France	31	238	109
722	Cavallo Norico	Italy	5	384	110
819	Connemara Pony	Finland	5	173	111
750	Gelders Paard	Netherlands	17	404	108
751	Gidran	Hungary	37	307	108
820	Gotland Russ	Finland	7	174	110
752	Groninger Paard	Netherlands	19	405	108
759	Highland	France	21	244	110
762	Hucul	CSFR	14	156	111
767	Islannin hevonen	Finland	7	174	110
770	Kladrubsky	Czech Republic	21	159	108
776	Lipizzan	France	6	246	108
777	Lipizzano	Italy	10	386	108
797	Rottaler	Germany	3	291	108
801	Senner	Germany	0	293	108
802	Shagya arab	Hungary	17	309	108
807	Sorraia	Portugal	9	435	111
811	Täysverinen	Finland	3	177	108
823	Welsh Pony (A, B & D)	Finland	11	178	110

DEFINITION OF STATUS NOT POSSIBLE BECAUSE OF MISSING INFORMATION: HORSES

712	Bosanski brdski konj	Yugoslavia	miss	569	111
778	Ljutomerski kasac	Slovenia	miss	449	108

4.3   Similar breeds

Breeds are developed by selection of certain types of animals of a species which are bred for specific phenotypic appearance and/or specific performances. The breed is defined as a group of domesticated animals resembling each other in appearance and in physiological characteristics and sharing the same breed history. Based on these descriptions animals can be recognized as members of a particular breed. This distinguishes them from other animals in the same species.

The beginning of systematic breeding differs among species. In sheep early attempts are known to breed for fine wool. In the 18th century the breeding results of Thouroughbred and different breeds of riding and coach horses induced English breeders to apply these breeding methods to other species. Several sheep and cattle breeds were developed at this time. In the 19th century the time of systematic breeding began. The number of breeds increased. Breeding associations were founded. Trading of breeding stocks became of economic value. For this reason many breeds were transferred to geographical areas they had not originally been bred for. Large White became popular in continental Europe and influenced many populations, and, based on imports from Switzerland, large Simmental populations were developed in South Germany and Austria from 1830 onwards. In the middle of the 20th century breeds were consolidated, performance tests were introduced. Purebreeding and inbreeding as well as breeding for special types and phenotypic appearances were important strategies. After World War II the main breeding aim was breeding for high performances, so a few highly selected breeds superseded traditional local breeds.

Similarity among breeds is an important issue if one deals with endangered breeds. If additional breeding stock is needed for an endangered breed, breeders look for similar breeds to enlarge their own population without losing the breed characteristics. In order to help in such situations, an attempt was made to form groups of similar breeds. This was done using the information we received from our informants and of the relevant literature. However, it has to be pointed out, that this can only be regarded as a first attempt which needs further improvement.

4.3.1 Criteria of similarities

In order to find similarities among breeds, they can be categorized according to different aspects:

-    geographical origin,
-    breed history and development of breeds,
-    influence of specific ancestors, such as Merino, Shorthorn, Gidran, Nonius,
-    phenotypic characteristics, such as colour, horned or polled, lop or erect ears,
-    demand for food quality and housing, resulting in intensive or extensive breeds,
-    breeds of special performance, e.g. dairy or meat breeds, fine wool breeds,
-    genetic polymorphisms, such as blood groups and protein polymorphisms,
-    DNA polymorphism, such as RFLPs and microsatellites.

We used a combination of these criteria. In general information on genetic or DNA polymorphisms was not available, so this kind of information could not be used to define similarities or genetic distances among breeds.

We proceeded as follows:
Each species was classified into several main groups. Most main groups were divided into subgroups to clarify relationships in more detail. Cattle and pigs were categorized according to their coat colour, goats according to famous breeds and their descendants as well as coat colours, sheep according to the wool characteristics and their genetic background or geographical origin, horses according to their so called temperament. The species are too different and, besides, the information varied, so the same procedure could not be followed for all species.

The grouping of similar breeds is presented in tables 16, 17, 18 , 19 and 20. For each species the specific procedure for the formation of groups is explained at the beginning of each section. In the tables the following information is presented:

-   Group number
-   Subgroup number
-   Country (international car registration symbol)
-   Local breed name
-   Entry number
-   Status of endangeredness, N = normal, PE = potentially endangered, ME = minimally endangered, E = endangered, CE = critically endangered
-   Page number of breed presentation (BP), where the "full" information on this breed can be found
-   International breed name

For this chapter the following literature was used: Alderson (1992), Behrens, Doehner, Schelje und Waßmuth (1969), Dimitriev and Ernst (1989), Evans et al. (1977), Frahm (1990), Gall (1982), Goodall (1980), Hammond et al. (1961), Haring (1976), Hinrichsen (1993), Kober (1992), Künzi and Stranzinger (1993), Mason (1988), Mathes (in prep.), Mendel (1993), Porter (1991), Reddick (1976), Sambraus (1986).

4.3.2 Groups of similar breeds - CATTLE

The categorization of cattle was performed according to the coat colour: ten main groups were formed. Large main groups were classified into subgroups due to a more precise characterization of the colour patterns, geographical origin or genetic relationship.

Black and White Pattern group
Holstein-Friesian: All breeds of this group were incrossed by U.S. or Canadian HF-bulls to reach the high level of milk yield of the today's production. A detailed investigation would probably show that the same bulls are preferred in different countries, and so relationships exist among these Holstein-Friesian populations.
Original Black Pied group: The breeds of this group are local Black Pieds without the influence of modern Holstein-Friesian from overseas.
Russian Black Pied: This group includes various populations of cattle, originating from different maternal stocks under different climatic and feeding conditions. The crossings of the local low-grade cattle with imported sires started at different times. Dutch Black Pied, East Friesian, Swiss Brown, Simmental and Tyrolian bulls were used as well as Russian breeding stocks were exchanged among these breeds.
Other Black Pied: This group contains one new synthetic breed, German Black Pied Dairy, which is composed of the old East German Black Pied, Holstein-Friesian and Jersey. Furthermore there are three other Black Pied breeds which could neither be identfied as original Black and White breed nor as Holstein-Friesian breed exactly.
White Belted group: The Belted Galloway and the Lakenvelder are old breeds. Since the 1960s Belted Galloway and U.S. Lakenvelder have been incrossed into the Dutch Lakenvelder.
Colour Sided: Tux descended apparently from Herens. Among other breeds it has developed Gorbatov, Red Tambov and Yurino. Blacksided Trondheim is related to Swedish Mountain and North Finncattle. Black Berrendo descended probably from Black Iberian, but it has been selected for long times for its coat pattern, which is similar to that of the Pinzgauer. Dagestan Mountain is a subvariety of Greater Caucasus.
Whiteheaded: Ukrainian Whiteheaded derived from Groningen Whiteheaded. Groningen was formed by incrossing of Shorthorn into the old local Black and White population.

Black group
Iberian Black: Serrana Black (Avilena-Black Iberian) was formed in 1980 by uniting the Avilena and Serrana/Black Iberian. Friesian, Brown and Charolais bulls are used to increase the production. Andalusian Black is very similar to Serrana. Andalusian Grey is a colour variety of Andalusian Black. Caldelana strongly resembles the Black Iberian of Central Spain and probably it comes originally from there. Fighting bulls have developed into a type of Black Iberian but with Retinta and Northwestern Chestnut breeds. Other colours are possible. Camargue is also used for bull fights.
English Black: The indigenous Scottish breed Aberdeen Angus was exported to many countries. Murray Grey derived from crossing Aberdeen Angus and White Shorthorn, the offspring was selected for the special colour. Aberdeen Angus was crossed with German dual purpose breeds to create German Angus. Galloway is thought to have links with Aberdeen Angus and Highland in previous times. Kerry is the origin of Dexter.

Red Pattern group

Red Pied group: Red Pied populations derived from the original Black Pied breeds because those own the gene for red factor as well. The red populations separated from the Black Pied groups and established independent breeds. In the development and improvement of red breeds, Meuse-Rhine-Yssel (MRY) and German Red Pied played a major role. Belgian Red Pied was formed by MRY, local cattle and some Shorthorn, Polish Red-and-White by German Red Pied and MRY as well as Pie Rouge de Plaines. In Danish Red are German Red Pied, MRY and some Shorthorn included; Belgian White and Red consists of Shorthorn, MRY and local cattle. In Normande and Main-Anjou Shorthorn was introduced. Red Holstein from the U.S.A. were used to improve all the European Red Pied to a different extent.

Simmental group: The ancestor of Simmental is Berner Cattle which was exported to different countries, e.g. in France it became well-known as Montbeliard. Since 1830 large Simmental populations have been developed in South Germany and Austria. All the other breeds of this group have been influenced or improved by Simmental.

Black Forest: The Black Forest breeds Hinterwald and Vorderwald resemble Simmental in colour patterns and in the white head but they are aboriginal independent breeds.

Pinzgauer group: Pinzgau has been exported to different countries. Pustertaler Sprinzen are a variety of Pinzgau.

Hereford group: The old native breed of West England with the dominant white head is distributed world-wide.

Ayrshire group: Ayrshire originated in the late 18th and early 19th century in South West Scotland from Teeswater, local cattle and some Highland. It is the origin of Finnish Ayrshire and Swedish Ayrshire, and partly also ancestor of Red Trondheim and Norwegian Red and White.

White lineback: The breeds of this group resemble oneanother in some colour patterns only; there were no relationships found among them.

Red groups

English Red: Devon exists in two breeds, North Devon and South Devon. It is supposed that between the two Devon breeds there was a certain amount of incrossing and also between them and the Hereford and with the Guernsey. But closer links are between the North Devon and the Sussex. Red Poll was developed in the early 19th century in East England from Suffolk Polled and Norfolk Horned.

Shorthorn group: Shorthorn originated in North East England in the late 18th century from Holderness and Teeswater. The three colours red, roan and white are possible as well as occasionally red-and-white or roan-and-white. The breed developed Beef Shorthorn (in the U.S.A. Polled Shorthorn) and Dairy Shorthorn (in the U.S.A. Milking Shorthorn). White Bred Shorthorn is a selected strain of the Dairy Shorthorn. Shorthorn genes including breeds are Armorican, Belgian breeds, Danish Red Pied, German Shorthorn, Kurgan, Lincoln Red and Main-Anjou.

Central European Red: This group can be subdivided into: **Northern Central type:** Angeln, Danish Red, Flemish (Danish Red x Flemish), Belgian Red (similar to Flemish x Shorthorn) and Polish Red (Angeln x local Red). **German Red Hill group:** Westphalian Red, Hessian Red, Harz, Donnersberg and Vogelsberg. **Baltic type:** The breeds in this group combine Angeln and Danish with local cattle. All German Red breeds are severly improved by Angeln; Flemish is improved by Danish Red. There are close links between Angeln and Danish Red. In Danish Red incrossing of Red Holstein started some years ago.

Scandinavian Red: Icelandic derives from Norwegian, this moreover is similar to Swedish Red Polled, which is a variety of Swedish Polled. Between Swedish Polled and West Finncattle are links and Estonian Native was improved by West Finncattle, besides jersey.

Russian Red: Russian red breeds result from crossing various North/Central European breeds into local cattle at different times. Bestuzhev: Friesian, Simmental, Shorthorn, Kholmogory, local cattle. Gorbatov Red: Tux and local Oka. Kalmyk derives probably from Indian or other Asian cattle. Mingrelian Red: native cattle from the Caucasus. Red Steppe were developed from Red East Friesian, Angeln and Ukrainian Grey by Mennonites in the late 18th century. They were later improved by East Friesian and Swiss Brown. Suksun originated in the second half of the 19th century from crossing Danish Red and local cattle. In the beginning of the 20th century they were improved by Danish Red and Angeln and in the 1930s influenced by Red Steppe, Latvian Brown and Estonian Red. Tambov Red: local cattle, Tyrolean Cattle, some Devon and Simmental. Yurino: local Chuvash-Mari, Tyrolean Cattle, Swiss Brown, Simmental, Kholmogory and Gorbatov Red.

Iberian Red: Alentejana is the origin of Mertolenga and similar to Retinta. White Caceres is a colour variety of Retinta. Links are supposed between the Retinta and Pajuna as well as Murcian. The Balearic Island breeds Majorcan and Minorcan derive from Marinera, which belongs to the "Red Convexo" types of Southern Spain. Red Berrendo has the same ancestors like Retinta; for a long time it was selected from them because of the colour distribution. The mountain breed Monchina is probably a mixture of native Cantabriaus with Tudanca and Pyrenean. Carrena is the lowland strain of Asturian being improved with Brown Swiss and Friesian, whereas Casina is the smaller sized mountain strain. Limousin is used to improve the Murcian, Pajuna and Retinta.

Brown group

Brown Swiss group: Brown Swiss was included to form and improve the other breeds of this group. Additional incrossings of Brown Swiss from the U.S.A. are known in the following breeds: Brown Swiss, German Brown, Austrian Brown, Brown Mountain, French Brown, Romanian Brown and Carpathian Brown.

Alpine Brown: Herens is distributed in Switzerland and in France. Aosta Chestnut resulted from crossing Herens with Aosta Black Pied. Tarentaise belongs only locally in this group.

Brown Mountain: This is a heterogenous group; there exist no relations among them except the colour.

Iberian Brown: Marinhoa is a variety of Mirandesa. Mirandesa and Barrosa are included in Arouquesa and Maronesa. Barrosa and Cachena are similar. Limiana and Vianesa belong to the group "Morenas del Noreste".

Balkan Brown: Rodopi, Greek Shorthorn and Busa are similar, the colours vary from brown shades to red and black. All three breeds are improved by Brown Swiss (CH) and Bulgarian Brown.

British Brown: These breeds have only in common that they belong to the same colour group and region.

Grey Cattle group

Grey Steppe/Podolian: Grey Steppe originated in the Steppe of Ukrainia from where it moved west and immigrated into Italy in ancient times, where it formed the Podolian cattle. Dalmatian Grey is improved by Tyrol Grey. Istrian (YU) is crossed with Brown Swiss (CH, U.S.A.), Romagnola and Maremmana. Istrian (HR) is improved by Romagnola. Sykia is a smaller variety of the Grey Steppe type. Hungarian Steppe is crossed with Maremmana and Yugoslavian Podolian. Maremmana is incrossed with Chianina and Charolais. Romagnola is improved with Chianina, Reggiana and Maremmana. Sardo-Modicana derived from Modicana and Sardinian. Cinisara is similar to Modicana.

Grey Mountian: Grey Alpine and Tyrol Grey are identical breeds, they are incrossed with Raetian Grey Cattle. Garfagnina, an Alpine Grey cattle, is improved by Italian Brown. Gascon and its variety Gascon Areole, the grey cattle breeds of the Gascony, are improved by Piedmont.

Blue Cattle group: This group consists of Belgian Blue which is imported from many other countries.

Blond Cattle

Blonde d'Aquitaine group: Blonde d'Aquitaine exists in three countries. The artificial line Coopelso 93 contains Blonde d'Aquitaine and Charolais. Villar de Lans is a variety of the main breed. Basco Bearnais is another Pyrenean breed, but not absorbed by Blonde d'Aquitaine so far.

Gelbvieh group: German Yellow combined several local cattle varieties which were crossed with uni-coloured Simmental and some Shorthorn. Later on it was improved by Danish Red and Flemish. German Yellow is included in the other listed breeds.

Limousin group: Limousin exists in four countries. Parthenais belongs to the same colour group but is not related.

Channel Island Cattle group: This group consists of Jersey, living in five different countries, the related other Channel Island breed Guernsey and its relative, the Froment du Leon. The latter is considered to be the basic breed for Guernsey.

Italian Blond: Montana is incrossed with Reggiana and Italian Brown. Pontremolese is upgraded by Italian Brown. The Italian Blonds are displaced by the Browns.

Iberian Blond: The northern breeds of the Iberian Penisula are mostly blond. Unfortunately the Data Bank does not have information on these breeds. Canary Island originated from Galician Blond.

White Cattle

British White: White Park is an ancient breed. British White was formed by White Park and White Shorthorn. White Bred Shorthorn is a colour-selected line of Dairy Shorthorn.

Charolais group: The group contains Charolais in four countries.

Italian White: Calvana is a smaller variety of Chianina, which derived by crossing Podolian with local cattle; and it is the origin of Marchigiana and was improved by Romagnola. Modenese is a result from crossing Reggiana and Romagnola. This group is related to the Podolian group and of lighter colour.

Multicoloured group: In this group are unimproved cattle breeds which vary in coat colour. Relationships among these breeds are not documented.

Table 16: Groups of similar breeds - CATTLE -

Group
  Subgroup

Coun- try	Local Breedname	Entry Number	ST. END.	BP page	International Breedname
1 Black and White Pattern group					
1 1 Holstein-Friesian group					
NL	Zwartbont	277	N	398	Holstein-Friesian
GB	Holstein-Friesian	117	N	507	Holstein-Friesian
DK	Sortbroget Dansk Malkekvaeg	245	PE	161	Holstein-Friesian
D	Deutsche Schwarzbunte	75	N	255	Holstein-Friesian
F	Prim' Holstein	209	N	195	Holstein-Friesian
B	Pie-Noire-Holstein	198	N	137	Holstein
IRL	Friesian	91	N	313	Holstein-Friesian
L	Black and White	32	N	392	Holstein-Friesian
I	Frisona	92	N	328	Holstein-Friesian
CH	Schwarzfleckvieh	230	N	482	Holstein-Friesian
PL	Nizinna-Czarno-Biala	185	PE	415	Polish Black-and-White
1 2 Original Black Pied group					
I	Valdostana Pezzata Nera	261	PE	339	Aosta Black Pied
I	Burlina	51	CE	325	Burlina
F	Breton Pie Noire	42	E	184	Breton Black Pied
D*	Deutsches Schwarzbuntes Rind	79	PE	257	German Black Pied
D	Deutsche Schwarzbunte (Original)	76	E	256	Ger. Original Black Pied
EW	Cherno-pestraya estonskaya	65	N	165	Estonian Black Pied
LT	Cherno-pestraya litovskaya	66	N	390	Lithuanian Black Pied
1 3 Russian Black Pied group					
USSR	Cherno-pestraya	64	N	550	Russian Black Pied
USSR	Yaroslavskaya	275	N	557	Yaroslavl
USSR	Kholmogorskaya	141	N	552	Kholmogory
USSR	Tagilskaya	252	N	556	Tagil
USSR	Istobenskaya	128	PE	551	Istoben
USSR	Yakutskii skot	274	ME	557	Yakut
KAZ	Aulieatinskaya	15	N	387	Aulie-Ata
1 4 Other Black Pied					
D*	Schwarzbuntes Milchrind	229	N	264	German Black Pied Dairy
CS	Nizinne cernostrakate	184	N	151	Czech Black Pied
YU	Crno-belo	71	N	565	Holstein-Friesian
RO	Baltata cu negru romanesca	19	N	436	Rom. Holstein-Friesian
1 5 White Belted group					
GB	Belted Galloway	28	N	501	Belted Galloway
NL	Lakenvelder	152	ME	397	Dutch Belted

Table 16: Groups of similar breeds - CATTLE -, continued

Coun- try	Local Breedname	Entry Number	ST. END.	BP page	International Breedname

1 6 Colour Sided

A	Tuxer	259	CE	134	Tux
N	Sidet tronderfe og nordland	235	CE	406	Blacksided Trondheim
E	Berrenda negra andaluza	29	ME	451	Black Berrendo
GO	Dagestanskii gornyi skot	107	N	252	Dagestan/Georg. Mountain
GO	Gruzinskii gornyi skot	107	N	252	Dagestan/Georg. Mountain
SF	Pohjoissuomenkarja	207	CE	169	North Finncattle
S	Fjällras	86	E	476	Swedish Mountain

1 7 Whiteheaded

NL	Groninger Blaarkop	106	E	396	Groningen Whiteheaded
UR	Belogolovaya ukrainskaya	27	CE	495	Ukrainian Whiteheaded

2 Black group
2 1 Iberian Black

E	Serrana Negra	232	CE	460	Serrana Black
E	Negra de las Campinas andaluzas	182	ME	458	Andalusian Black
E	Cardena Andaluza	60	CE	454	Andalusian Grey
E	Caldelana	56	ME	453	Caldelana
E	Toro de Lidia	257	N	461	Fighting bull
P	Raca Brava	212	PE	427	Fighting Bull
F	Brava	41	PE	183	Fighting Bull
F	Race Espagnole	41	PE	183	Fighting Bull
F	Camargue	58	PE	185	Camargue

2 2 English Black

GB	Aberdeen-Angus	1	N	499	Aberdeen-Angus
IRL	Angus	9	N	312	Angus
GB	Murray Grey	181	PE	509	Murray Grey
D	Deutsche Angus	80	N	254	German Angus
GB	Galloway	96	N	505	Galloway
D	Galloway	94	N	258	Galloway
IS	Galloway	95	CE	310	Galloway
GB	Dexter	81	N	504	Dexter
IRL	Kerry Cattle	140	ME	317	Kerry
GB	Welsh Black	269	N	513	Welsh Black

3 Red Pattern group
3 1 Red Pied group

NL	Maas-Rijn-Yssel	161	PE	397	Meuse-Rhine-Yssel
NL	Roodbont	161	PE	397	Meuse-Rhine-Yssel
L	Meuse-Rhine-Yssel	215	N	393	Red and White
D	Deutsche Rotbunte	74	PE	255	German Red Pied
B	Pie-Rouge	199	N	138	Belgian Red Pied
B	Roodbont	199	N	138	Belgian Red Pied
PL	Nizinna Czerwono-Biala	183	PE	414	Polish Red-and-White
F	Pie Rouge des Plaines	196	N	194	Pie Rouge des Plaines

Coun- try	Local Breedname	Entry Number	ST. END.	BP page	International Breedname
DK	Dansk Rodbroget Kvaeg	73	N	159	Danish Red Pied
B	Blanc-Rouge de Belgique	273	PE	139	Belgian White-and-Red
B	Witrood Ras Van Belgie	273	PE	139	Belgian White-and-Red
F	Normande	186	N	193	Normande
F	Maine-Anjou	163	N	192	Maine-Anjou
F	Ferrandais	85	PE	187	Ferrandais

3 2 Simmental group

CH	Simmentaler Fleckvieh	240	N	482	Simmental
A	Fleckvieh	88	N	131	Simmental
D	Deutsches Fleckvieh	78	N	257	German Simmental
F	Pie Rouge de l'Est	89	PE	194	French Simmental
F	Montbeliard	176	N	192	Montbeliard
F	Race d'Abondance	213	N	195	Abondance
I	Valdostana Pezzata Rossa	262	N	339	Aosta Red Pied
I	Pezzata rossa d'Oropa	194	PE	331	Oropa
I	Pezzata Rossa Italiana	195	PE	332	Italian Red Pied
CZ	Ceske strakate	61	CE	157	Bohemian Red Pied
SK	Slovenske strakate	244	N	445	Slovakian Simmental
PL	Simentalska	237	ME	415	Polish Simmental
GB	Simmental	239	N	512	Simmental
IRL	Irish Simmental	125	N	316	Simmental
YU	Simentalska rasa	238	N	566	Simmental
HR	Simentalac	236	N	147	Simmental
RO	Baltata Romanesca	20	N	436	Romanian Simmental
USSR	Simmentalskaya	241	N	555	Russian Simmental
USSR	Sychevskaya	250	N	556	Sychevka

3 3 Black Forest

D	Hinterwälder	115	ME	261	Hinterwald
CH	Hinterwälder	116	PE	481	Hinterwald
D	Vorderwälder	266	ME	265	Vorderwald

3 4 Pinzgauer group

A	Pinzgauer	202	PE	133	Pinzgau
D	Pinzgauer	203	PE	263	Pinzgau
I	Pinzgauer	200	CE	333	Pinzgau
SK	Slovenske pinzgavske	243	N	445	Slovakian Pinzgau
RO	Pinzgau de Transilvania	201	CE	437	Romanian Pinzgau
GB	Pinzgauer	204		510	Pinzgau
I	Pustertaler Sprinzen	211	CE	335	Pustertaler Sprinzen
D	Pustertaler Schecken	210	CE	264	Pustertaler Sprinzen

3 5 Hereford group

GB	Hereford	112	N	506	Hereford
IRL	Hereford	111	N	314	Hereford
F	Hereford	110	PE	189	Hereford
KAZ	Kazakhskaya belogolovaya	138	N	388	Kazakh Whiteheaded

Coun- try	Local Breedname	Entry Number	ST. END.	BP page	International Breedname

3 6 Ayrshire group

GB	Ayrshire	18	N	500	Ayrshire
IRL	Ayrshire	17	E	312	Ayrshire
SF	Suomen Ayrshire	247	N	170	Ayrshire

3 7 White lineback

SF	Itäsuomenkarja	129	CE	168	East Finncattle
GB	Irish Moiled	123	CE	508	Irish Moiled
GB	English Longhorn	82	PE	504	Longhorn
N	Telemark	254	CE	407	Telemark
F	Vosgienne	267	PE	197	Vosges

4 Red group
4 1 English Red

GB	North Devon	188	PE	510	Devon
GB	Red Ruby	188	PE	510	Devon
GB	Sussex	249	N	512	Sussex
GB	Red Poll	216	PE	511	Red Poll

4 2 Shorthorn group

GB	Beef Shorthorn Cattle	24	N	500	Beef Shorthorn
GB	Lincoln Red	159	N	509	Lincoln Red
IRL	Irish Shorthorn	124	N	316	Shorthorn
GB	Shorthorn	233	N	511	Shorthorn
USSR	Kurganskaya	151	CE	554	Kurgan
F	Armoricaine	10	CE	179	Armorican

4 3 Central European Red

D	Angler	8	PE	254	Angeln
DK	Rod Dansk Malkerace	222	N	160	Danish Red
F	Flamande	87	PE	187	Flemish
B	Rood Ras van Belgie	224	N	138	Belgian Red
D	Westfälisches Rotvieh	270	ME	266	Westphalian Red
D	Hessisches Rotvieh	113	ME	260	Hessian Red
D	Harzer Rotvieh	109	CE	260	Harz
D	Donnersberger Rotvieh	101	CE	258	Donnersberg
D	Vogelsberger Rind	265	CE	265	Vogelsberg
PL	Czerwona Polska	72	N	414	Polish Red
UR	Krasnaya polskaya	146	ME	496	Polish Red
BEL	Krasnyi belorusskii skot	149	PE	144	Byelorussian Red
EW	Krasnaya estonskaya	143	ME	166	Estonian Red
LT	Krasnaya litovskaya	145	N	391	Lithuanian Red
LV	Buraya latviiskaya	50	N	389	Latvian Brown

4 4 Scandinavian Red

IS	Icelandic Dairy Cattle	118	N	310	Icelandic Cattle
N	Norsk rodtfe	187	N	406	Norwegian Red
S	Röd Kullig Lantras	225	ME	476	Swedish Red Polled

Coun- try	Local Breedname	Entry Number	ST. END.	BP page	International Breedname
SF	Länsisuomenkarja	153	E	169	West Finncattle
EW	Mestnaya estonskaya	171	CE	166	Estonian Native

4 5 Russian Red
USSR	Bestuzhevskaya	31	N	550	Bestuzhev
USSR	Krasnaya gorbatovskaya	144	PE	553	Gorbatov Red
USSR	Kalmytskaya	135	N	551	Kalmyk
GO	Krasnyi megrelskii skot	150	E	253	Mingrelian Red
UR	Krasnaya stepnaya	147	N	496	Red Steppe
USSR	Suksunskii skot	246	ME	555	Suksun
USSR	Krasnaya tambovskaya	148	ME	553	Tambov Red
USSR	Yurinskaya	276	CE	558	Yurino

4 6 Iberian Red
P	Alentejana	5	PE	424	Alentejana
P	Mertolenga	170	ME	426	Mertolenga
E	Retinta	219	N	460	Retinta
E	Blanca Cacerena	34	ME	452	White Caceres
E	Mallorquina	164	CE	456	Majorcan
E	Menorqina	169	CE	456	Minorcan
E	Pajuna	191	CE	459	Pajuna
E	Serrana	191	CE	459	Pajuna
E	Berrenda roja andaluza	30	N	452	Red Berrendo
E	Monchina	175	N	457	Monchina
E	Murciana	179	CE	458	Murcian
E	Asturiano Montana	13	ME	451	Asturian Mountain
E	Casina	13	ME	451	Asturian Mountain
E	Asturiana de Valles	12	N	450	Asturian Valley
E	Carrenana	12	N	450	Asturian Valley

5 Brown group
5 1 Brown Swiss group
CH	Braunvieh	40	N	480	Brown Swiss
D	Original Allgäuer Braunvieh	189	CE	263	Original German Brown
D	Deutsches Braunvieh	77	PE	256	German Brown
A	Österreichisches Braunvieh	190	N	133	Austrian Brown
SLO	Rjavo govedo	221	N	446	Slovenian Brown
F	Brune des Alpes	48	PE	184	French Brown
I	Bruna	46	N	325	Brown Mountain
I	Rendena	218	ME	336	Rendena
I	Sarda	227	ME	337	Sardinian
I	Agerolese	2	CE	324	Agerose
F	Aubrac	14	N	180	Aubrac
I	Pisana	205	CE	333	Pisana
USSR	Shvitskaya	234	N	554	Russian Brown
USSR	Kostromskaya	142	N	552	Kostroma
GO	Kavkazskaya buraya	137	N	252	Caucasian Brown
KAZ	Alatauskaya	3	PE	387	Ala-Tau

Table 16: Groups of similar breeds - CATTLE -, continued

Coun-try	Local Breedname	Entry Number	ST. END.	BP page	International Breedname
UR	Lebedinskaya	154	PE	497	Lebedin
RO	Bruna de Maramures	47	N	437	Romanian Brown
UR	Buraya karpatskaya	49	PE	495	Carpathian Brown

5 2 Alpine Brown

CH	Eringer Rind	83	N	480	Herens
F	Alpine Herens	7	CE	179	Herens
I	Valdostana Castana	260	N	338	Aosta Chestnut
F	Tarentaise	253	N	196	Tarentaise

5 3 Brown Mountain

I	Cabannina	54	CE	326	Cabannina
F	Salers	226	N	196	Salers
F	Bazadais	23	N	181	Bazadais
F	Aure et Saint-Girons	16	ME	180	Aure et Saint-Girons

5 4 Iberian Brown

P	Mirandesa	172	N	427	Mirandesa
P	Marinhoa	167	N	425	Marinhoa
P	Barrosa	21	N	425	Barrosa
E	Cachena	55	ME	453	Cachena
P	Arouquesa	11	N	424	Arouquesa
P	Maronesa	168	N	426	Maronesa
E	Limiana	155	CE	455	Limiana
E	Vianesa	263	CE	462	Vianesa
E	Frieiresa	90	CE	455	Frieiresa
E	Terrena	255	CE	461	Terrena

5 5 Balkan Brown

BG	Rodopska kusoroga	220	CE	146	Rodopi
GR	Brachyceros	39	PE	295	Greek Shorthorn
YU	Busha	52	ME	564	Busa

5 6 British Brown

GB	Highland	114	N	507	Highland
GB	Gloucester	103	PE	505	Gloucester

6 Grey Cattle group

6 1 Grey Steppe / Podolian

UR	Seraya ukrainskaya	231	CE	497	Ukrainian Grey
RO	Sura de Stepa	248	E	438	Romanian Steppe
HR	Sivo govedo Dalmacije	242	PE	147	Dalmatian Grey
YU	Istarsko govece	127	PE	565	Istrian
HR	Istarsko govedo	126	CE	146	Istrian
GR	Sykia	251	CE	296	Sykia
GR	Katerini	136	CE	295	Katerini
I	Piemontese	197	N	332	Piedmont
BG	Iskursko govedo	104	CE	145	Iskar Grey

Coun- try	Local Breedname	Entry Number	ST. END.	BP page	International Breedname
H	Magyar szürke	162	ME	304	Hungarian Grey
I	Maremmana	166	N	330	Maremmana
I	Podolica	206	N	334	Podolian
I	Romagnola	223	N	336	Romagnola
I	Modicana	174	PE	331	Modicana
I	Sardo-Modicana	228	N	337	Sardo-Modicana
I	Cinisara	68	PE	327	Cinisara

6 2 Grey Mountain

I	Grigia Alpina	105	N	329	Grey Alpine
CH	Rätisches Grauvieh	214	PE	481	Raetian Grey Cattle
A	Tiroler Grauvieh	256	PE	134	Tyrol Grey
I	Garfagnina	97	CE	328	Garfagnina
F	Gascon	98	N	188	Gascon
F	Gascon Areole	99	CE	189	Gascon Areole

7 Blue Cattle group

B	Blanc Bleu Belge	33	N	137	Belgian Blue
F	Blanc-Bleu-Belge	35	N	182	Belgian Blue
IRL	Belgian Blue	25	PE	313	Belgian Blue
GB	Belgian Blue	26	N	501	Belgian Blue
F	Bleue du Nord	36	N	182	Bleue du Nord

8 Blond Cattle
8 1 Blonde d'Aquitaine group

F	Blonde d'Aquitaine	37	N	183	Blonde d'Aquitaine
GB	Blonde d'Aquitaine	38	N	502	Blonde d'Aquitaine
IRL	Irish Blonde d'Aquitaine	120	PE	314	Blonde d'Aquitaine
F	Coopelso 93 (terminated)	69	CE	186	Coopelso 93
F	Villard de Lans	264	PE	197	Villard de Lans
F	Basco-Bearnaise	22	CE	181	Basco-Bearnais

8 2 Gelbvieh group

D	Gelbes Frankenvieh	100	N	259	German Yellow
D	Glanrind	102	CE	259	Glan
D	Limpurger	158	CE	262	Limpurger
D	Murnau-Werdenfelser	180	E	262	Murnau-Werdenfels
A	Kärntner Blondvieh	139	CE	132	Austrian Blond
A	Murbodner	178	CE	132	Murboden
A	Waldviertler Vieh	268	CE	135	Waldviertel

8 3 Limousin group

F	Limousin	156	N	191	Limousin
L	Limousin	157	N	393	Limousin
GB	British Limousin	44	N	503	Limousin
IRL	Irish Limousin	122	N	315	Limousin
F	Alpha 16 (terminated)	6	CE	178	Alpha 16
F	Parthenaise	193	N	193	Parthenais

Coun- try	Local Breedname	Entry Number	ST. END.	BP page	International Breedname

8 4 Channel Island Cattle group

GB	Jersey	133	N	508	Jersey
IRL	Jersey	132	PE	317	Jersey
F	Jersiais	134	N	190	Jersey
DK	Jersey	130	N	160	Jersey
D	Jersey	131	N	261	Jersey
GB	Guernsey	108	N	506	Guernsey
F	Froment du Leon	93	E	188	Froment du Leon

8 5 Italian Blond

I	Ottonese	258	CE	338	Montana
I	Tortonese	258	CE	338	Montana
I	Varzese	258	CE	338	Montana
I	Pontremolese	208	CE	334	Pontremolese
I	Reggiana	217	PE	335	Reggiana

8 6 Iberian Blond

E	Canaria	59	N	454	Canary Island
E	Palmera	192	E	459	Palmera

9 White Cattle
9 1 British White

GB	White Park	271	PE	513	White Park
GB	Whitebred Shorthorn	272	PE	514	Whitebred Shorthorn
GB	British White	45	N	503	British White

9 2 Charolais group

F	Charolais	62	N	185	Charolais
L	Charolais	63	N	392	Charolais
GB	British Charolais	43	N	502	Charolais
IRL	Irish Charolais	121	N	315	Charolais

9 3 Italian White

I	Calvana	57	CE	326	Calvana
I	Chianina	67	N	327	Chianina
I	Marchigiana	165	N	329	Marchigiana
I	Bianca val padana	173	PE	330	Modenese
I	Modenese	173	PE	330	Modenese

10 Multicoloured group

E	Albera	4	CE	450	Alberes
F	Corse	70	N	186	Corsican
E	Mostrenca	177	E	457	Donana Cattle
E	Palurda	177	E	457	Donana Cattle
FR	Faeroesk	84	ME	167	Faeroes Cattle
F	Inra 95	119	PE	190	Inra 95

4.3.3 Groups of similar breeds - SHEEP -

The categorization of sheep breeds is usually performed by the fleece characteristics. These are classified in Merino and sheep in Merino type, longwool breeds and longwool crosses, shortwool breeds and shortwool crosses, coarse wool breeds and coarse hair sheep. Another classification is related to the landscape where the breeds exist. Such a scheme distinguishes between marsh-, heath-, mountain sheep and breeds for maritime and continental climates. In this presentation breeds were categorized according to the wool characteristics, geographical origins, types of use and genetic backgrounds. For the later purposes certain breeds which were very important for other populations, e.g. by incrossing, were classified as a subgroup of a larger group to which they belong. It was difficult to apply this scheme to the British breeds but it was attempted. British crossbreds are included even if it is doubtful to do so.

Merinos are grouped, according to their geographical presence, into Iberian-, French-, Italian-, German-, and East-European Merino. These groups have the same ancestory. During the breed's history, breeding stock was exchanged among the different countries, therefore relationship within the groups and among the different groups can be presumed.

The breeds of the Merino descendant group were developed from Merino and other breeds. Berrichon du Cher e.g. is composed of Merino, South Down, Leicester Longwool, Dishley Merino and Boischaut. A sub-breed is Berrichon de l'Indre. Berrichon is included in Solognot and Charmoise. Ile-de-France, a product of crossing Merino and Leicester Longwool, was used in forming Weißes Alpenschaf. Inra 401, an artificial line, was developed from Romanow and Berrichon du Cher.

In the Continental longwool group one finds Bleu du Maine and Texel as two of the subgroups. Bleu du Maine was developed from Leicester Longwool, Wensleydale, Kent and Choletais, a local marsh sheep. Rouge de l'Ouest is similar to Bleu du Maine and has the same genetic background. Texel descended from an unpretending marsh sheep, to which British meat breeds, mainly Lincoln and Leicester, were introduced. The third subgroup contains other marsh sheep like the native Danish Marsh sheep and the Leinesheep. In the breed history of the Leinesheep Leicester Longwool, Cotswold and Berrichon played an important role. The breed of today is improved by Texel. The geographical origin of the Pomeranian Coarsewool are the coasts of the Baltic Sea. It is included in the Olkusz and Kaminiec.

The British longwool group contains many breeds which were very important for the development or improvement of other breeds. Leicester Longwool originated from Old Leicester and formed together with Cheviot the Border Leicester. From this Border Leicester, one has developed the Bluefaced Leicester. Leicester Longwool is included in Cotentin and in the similar Avranchin, Boulonnais, Charolais, Roussin de la Hague, Cotswold and also in its derivatives German Whiteheaded Mutton and Valais Blacknose, Wensleydale, Whiteface Dartmoor and Lincoln Longwool. Lincoln together with Merino and Leicester

Longwool has formed Corriedale, which moreover is included in the Wielkopolka. Border Leicester is included in Colbred, Welsh Half, Greyface Dartmoor, and together with Bluefaced Leicester in Cambridge. Bluefaced Leicester is part of Welsh Mule.

The Shortwool and Down group consists of a common group and a group containing breeds which are important to other countries as well.
A main breed of the common group is the Southdown of the U.K. Together with Wiltshire it is included in Hampshire Down, which, as well, formed Cotswold and Oxford Down. From Southdown Vendeen and Shropshire were developed, the latter of which is included in Clun Forest. Along with Hampshire, Southdown is included in Dorset Down. Clun Forest and Poll Dorset are closely related. They stemmed from Portland and Merino.
Suffolk, which exists in several countries and influences local populations by crossbreeding systems, was derived from Norfolk Horn and Southdown.
Oxford Down is included in the Swiss Oxford Down as well as in the German Blackheaded Mutton.

The subgroup Friesian of the Milksheep group could also belong to landraces of marsh types with coarse wool. The East Friesian Milksheep is known for its high fertility as far back as the 16th century. The Belgian Milksheep is based on a similar marsh-type sheep as the East Friesian Milksheep, from which the British Milksheep has been developed.
The South European Milksheep group contains breeds from different geographical origins. Several other breeds which are used for milking could be placed into this group. But from these breeds, the milk yield was quite low or the genetic background or other similarities fitted better into another group.

Heath sheep, small and short-tailed sheep, descending from the European Mufflon, still show an unpretending landrace character. They are distributed over areas of poor vegetation from the Shetlands, Scotland, Britany, Northern Germany, Scandinavia to Siberia. They are arranged according to their geographical distribution into four groups:
Schnucken group: The German Grey Heath is the origin of the White Horned and the White Polled Heath.
Dutch Heath: The small Drenthe Heath Sheep is the origin of the Bentheimer and, together with a local sheep, of the Schoonebeker. Kempen and Mergelland are similar to Drenthe. The Velouve Heath has the wool characteristics of Drenthe (long cover-hair and fine under-wool).
Nordic group: Gotland, Swedish Fur and Rya are varieties of the Swedish Landrace; Swedish Fur Sheep descended from Gotland. The origin of the Danish Landrace is the Danish Heath. Therefore the breed is placed into this group, even if it is improved by Leicester Longwool and Oxford Down. Old Norwegian is the basic breed of Icelandic, Norwegian Fur Sheep and together with Icelandic the origin of the Faeroes. Finnsheep, an old native, very prolific breed, became popular in crossbreeding systems in many countries. Greenland is believed to belong to this group, but there was no information available to document this. Romanov descended from the Russian Short-tailed sheep, and it improved the Polish heath breed Wrzosowka. Coburg and Rhoen are landraces suited for

poor vegetation habitats and rough climates and because of these traits, they are placed into this group.

North-West group: Soay is similar to the domesticated sheep of the neolithic period and Bronze Age in regard to the comparison of bones. It is included in Castlemilk Moorit together with Shetland and Manx Loaghtan. The latter is similar to Hebridean; Jacobs-sheep is a variety of Hebridean. North Ronaldsey is another short-tailed island breed.

Mountain group:

Mountain breeds also belong to the category of landraces bearing coarsewool; they are divided into four Alpine subgroups (Lop-eared Alpine group, Bergamasca, Semi-lop-eared group and Zaupel descendant group), an Apennine group, Zackel group, Tsigai group, Massif Central group, Pyrenean group, Iberian Mountain group and British Hill group. This classification was carried out according to geographical origins and according to the importance and influence of certain breeds which influenced other breeds significantly. In some cases these groups are subgroups of geographical groups. Many of the mountain breeds are used for milking and cheese production. But due to the breed history and other similarities, they are kept in the mountain group.

All Alpine mountain breeds are traced back to the Zaupel sheep, which is extinct. Zaupel and the similar Steinschaf were small sheep having a straight nose and small ears. Berga-masca from the Pre-Alpine region of Bergamo is a tall sheep with a Roman nose and very large lopped ears. This breed has influenced a large variety of Alpine populations, which can be categorized as Lop-eared Alpine group. Bellunese derived from Alpagota and Lamon, an obsolete naming of Biellese was Biellese-Bergamasca reflecting the importance of Bergamasca. Bretegana originated from Lamon. This is true also of Brogne, but Berga-masca is included as well.

Bergamasca group is a subgroup with the same characteristics, however the relations to the Bergamasca are better documented, which may be shown by a few examples.

Carinthian is a result of Bergamasca, Padua sheep and local Steinschaf. A variety of Carinthian is Spiegel, which is the origin of Tyrol Mountain and Pusterese. Zakynthos is formed by Bergamasca.

Semi-lop eared group: Breeds of this group indicate that their ancestors are Bergamasca as well as Zaupel/Steinschaf or the influence of Bergamasca is not so pronounced as in the other groups. Brigasca/Brigasque lives on both sides of the Italian-French border and it is similar to Frabasona, which is moreover similar to Langhe. Engadine Red and Pusterese resulted from Bergamasca and Steinschaf whereas in Pusterese also Lamon is included.

Zaupel/Steinschaf group: The breeds in this group mostly resemble the Zaupel and Steinschaf from all mountain breeds. The Steinschaf is the origin of the Buender Oberland, Tiroler Steinschaf and together with Bergamasca the origin of Carinthian, Tyrol Mountain, Pusterese and German Mountain.

To the Apennine group belong breeds which are local in the region from Tuscany/Emilia to Abruzzo. The breeds derived from Merino, local sheep, Bergamasca and Sopravissana.

The geographical distribution of the Zackel group is East- and Southeast-Europe. Sheep of the Zackel group are small, unimproved and undemanding animals, bearing a coarse wool of usually white, also black, brown or pied colours, long spiral horns in males (females are horned or polled) and a long thin tail. Sumava is similar to the Valachian, but heavier. Pramenca is the basis of many local varieties. Ruda is more improved than common Zackel.

Tsigai group is also localized in Southeast Europe. Zackel influenced Tsigai to a certain extent. Many Tsigai populations are improved by Merino with the result of a finer wool.

Massif Central group: Lacaune, a dairy breed, is the origin of Blanc du Massif Central and Ardes. The latter has been absorbed by Lacaune and is extinct. Grivette is similar to Rava.

Pyrenean group: The mentioned breeds resulted from local populations of the central Pyrenees which have been incrossed by Merino, except Landais which derived from Pyrenaen.

Iberian Mountain group: The breeds of this group are white with coloured marks on face and legs, males are occasionally horned, females are polled.

British Hill group: North country Cheviot, a variation of Cheviot, is the origin of Wicklow Cheviot, and Cheviot has improved Dala and Steigar. In North-England Blackfaced Mountain originated; Scotland includes Derbyshire Gritstone and Rough Fell.

Local Coarsewool group includes mainly unimproved landraces of South-European origin.

Italian/French Coarsewool: Comisana was formed from Maltese and Sicilian sheep and is similar to Bagnolese. Ciavenasca and Ciuta were similar, but Ciuta is extinct. Rosset resembles Savoiarda; these breeds as well as Thones-Marthod exist in Prealpine regions and could be placed into Mountain group.

The common Iberian Coarsewool is a heterogenous group, any relationsships were not obvious.

Barbary descendants: The breeds of this group derived from local populations into which the North African Barbary has been incrossed.

Churra type: Churra is a Spanish breed of mixed wool with several local subbreeds.

Bordaleiro Type is a Portugese breed which resulted from crossing Merino with Churro. From this breed subbreeds have been developed.

Table 17: Groups of similar breeds - SHEEP -
Group
   Subgroup

Coun-try	Local Breedname	Entry Number	ST. END.	BP page	International Breedname

1 Merino

<u>1 1 Iberian Merino</u>

E	Merina	545	ME	467	Spanish Merino
E	Merino de Grazalema	546	ME	467	Merino Grazalema
P	Merino Portugues	547	N	430	Portuguese Merino

<u>1 2 French Merino</u>

F	Merinos d'Arles	554	N	214	Arles Merino
F	Race de l'est a Laine Merinos	591	PE	219	Merino de l'Est
F	Merinos Precoce	555	PE	215	Precoce
F	Merinos de Rambouillet	553	CE	214	Rambouillet

<u>1 3 Italian Merino</u>

I	Gentile di Puglia	499	N	352	Gentile di Puglia
I	Matesina	542	CE	356	Matesina
I	Sopravissana	634	N	362	Sopravissana
I	Trimeticcia di Segezia	657	ME	363	Segezia Triple Cross

<u>1 4 German Merino</u>

D	Merinolandschaf	550	N	271	German Merino
D*	Merinofleischschaf	548	N	270	German Mutton Merino
D	Merinofleischschaf	549	N	270	German Mutton Merino
D*	Merinolangwollschaf	551	N	271	Merino Longwool

<u>1 5 East European Merino</u>

CZ	Czech Merino	475	N	157	Merino
PL	Polish Merino	583	N	417	Polish Merino
RO	Merinos de Palas	552	N	439	Palas Merino
RO	Merinos Transilvanean	556	N	439	Transylvanian Merino

<u>1 6 Merino descendants</u>

F	Berrichon du Cher	418	N	201	Berrichon du Cher
F	Berrichon de l'Indre	417	ME	200	Berrichon de l'Indre
F	Solognot	633	PE	223	Solognot
F	Charmoise	450	N	205	Charmoise
F	Ile-de-France	513	N	210	Ile-de-France
CH	Weißes Alpenschaf	669	N	487	Swiss White Alpine
GB	Ile-de-France	514	N	525	Ile-de-France
F	Inra 401	515	PE	210	Inra 401

2 Continental longwool group

<u>2 1 Bleu du Maine group</u>

F	Bleu du Maine	425	N	203	Bleu du Maine
D	Blauköpfiges Fleischschaf	424	N	267	Bleu du Maine
GB	Bleu du Maine	426	N	515	Bleu du Maine
F	Rouge de l'ouest	604	N	221	Rouge de l'Ouest
GB	Rouge de l'ouest	605	PE	530	Rouge de l'Ouest

Table 17: Groups of similar breeds - SHEEP -, continued

Coun-try	Local Breedname	Entry Number	ST. END.	BP page	International Breedname

2 2 Texel group

NL	Texelaar	653	N	401	Texel
L	Texel	652	N	394	Texel
D	Texel	650	N	275	Texel
F	Texel	649	N	225	Texel
GB	British Texel	439	N	517	Texel
IRL	Texel	651	N	319	Texel
SF	Texel	648	PE	171	Texel

2 3 Marsh sheep

DK	Hvidhovedet Marsk	510	ME	162	Marsh Sheep
D	Leineschaf	529	PE	269	Leine
D*	Rauhwolliges Pommer. Landschaf	595	CE	273	Pomeranian Coarsewool
PL	Pomorska	586	N	418	Pomeranian Coarsewool
PL	Olkuska	571	CE	417	Olkusz
PL	Kamieniecka	517	N	416	Kamieniec

3 British longwool group

GB	Border Leicester	428	N	516	Border Leicester
GB	Bluefaced Leicester	427	N	515	Bluefaced Leicester
GB	Leicester Longwool	528	N	525	Leicester Longwool
F	Mouton Boulonnais	559	CE	216	Boulonnais
F	Mouton Charollais	560	N	216	Charollais
CH	Charollais Suisse	451	PE	484	Charollais
GB	British Charollais	437	N	516	Charollais
F	Cotentin	473	N	207	Cotentin
F	Avranchin	405	PE	199	Avranchin
GB	Romney Sheep	602	N	529	Romney
GB	Cotswold Sheep	474	PE	520	Cotswold Sheep
CH	Walliser Schwarznasenschaf	666	N	486	Valais Blacknose
D	Weißköpfiges Fleischschaf	670	N	278	Ger. Whiteheaded Mutton
GB	Cambridge	442	N	518	Cambridge
GB	Colbred	467		520	Colbred
IRL	Galway	495	E	318	Galway
GB	Welsh Half-bred	671	N	534	Welsh Half-bred
GB	Welsh Mule	673	N	535	Welsh Mule
GB	Wensleydale Longwool	674	PE	536	Wensleydale
GB	Whiteface Dartmoor	675	ME	536	Whiteface Dartmoor
F	Rouge de Hague	608	N	222	Roussin de la Hague
F	Roussin	608	N	222	Roussin de la Hague
PL	Wielkopolska Sheep	678	N	419	Wielkopolska
GB	Lincoln Longwool	532	PE	526	Lincoln Longwool
PL	Corriedale	582	N	416	Polish Corriedale
GB	Teeswater	647	N	533	Teeswater
GB	Greyface Dartmoor	502	N	523	Greyface Dartmoor

Coun- try	Local Breedname	Entry Number	ST. END.	BP page	International Breedname

4 Shortwool and Down
4 1 Common group

GB	Hampshire Down	507	N	523	Hampshire Down
F	Hampshire	506	N	209	Hampshire Down
GB	Southdown	636	N	532	Southdown
F	Southdown	635	N	223	Southdown
F	Mouton Vendeen	562	N	217	Vendeen
GB	Vendeen	661	N	534	Vendeen
GB	Dorset Down	482	N	521	Dorset Down
F	Dorset Down	481	PE	208	Dorset Down
GB	Clun Forest	465	N	519	Clun Forest
F	Clun Forest	464	PE	206	Clun Forest
GB	Poll Dorset	483	N	522	Dorset Horn/Poll
GB	Dorset Horn	483	N	522	Dorset Horn/Poll
GB	Wiltshire Horn	679	N	537	Wiltshire Horn
GB	Portland	587	N	529	Portland
GB	Ryeland	613	N	531	Ryeland
GB	Shropshire	629	PE	531	Shropshire

4 2 Suffolk group

GB	Norfolk Horn	565	ME	527	Norfolk Horn
GB	Suffolk sheep	642	N	533	Suffolk
IRL	Suffolk	641	N	319	Suffolk
F	Suffolk	639	N	224	Suffolk
D	Suffolk	640	N	275	Suffolk

4 3 Oxford group

GB	Oxford Down	575	N	528	Oxford Down
CH	Braunköpfiges Fleischschaf	432	N	483	Oxford Down
D	Schwarzköpfiges Fleischschaf	622	N	274	Ger. Blackheaded Mutton
D*	Schwarzköpfiges Fleischschaf	623	E	274	Ger. Blackheaded Mutton

5 Milksheep
5 1 Friesian group

NL	Friese Melkschaap	493	N	399	Friesian Milksheep
D	Ostfriesisches Milchschaf	573	N	272	East Friesian
D*	Ostfriesisches Milchschaf	572	N	272	East Friesian
B	Mouton Laitier Belge	561	ME	139	Belgian Milk Sheep
GB	British Milksheep	438	N	517	British Milksheep

5 2 South European Milksheep group

I	Altamurana	401	CE	340	Altamurana
I	Leccese	527	N	353	Leccese
I	Moscia Calabrese	624	PE	361	Sciara
I	Sciara	624	PE	361	Sciara
F	Caussenard des Garrigues	447	CE	204	Caussenard des Garrigues
F	Caussenard du Lot	448	N	205	Caussenard du Lot

Table 17: Groups of similar breeds - SHEEP -, continued

Coun-try	Local Breedname	Entry Number	ST. END.	BP page	International Breedname
F	Raiole	594	E	220	Raiole
F	Manech (Tete Noire)	537	N	213	Black-Face Manech
F	Manech (Tete Rousse)	538	N	213	Red-Face Manech
F	Basco-Bearnaise	412	N	200	Basco-Bearnais
E	Menorquina	543	PE	466	Minorcan
SLO	Bovska Ovca	430	ME	447	Bovec
GR	Chios	453	PE	297	Chios

6 Heath group
6 1 Schnucken group

D	Graue gehörnte Heidschnucke	501	N	268	German Grey Heath
D	Weiße gehörnte Heidschnucke	667	ME	277	White Horned Heath
D	Moorschnucke	668	PE	277	White Polled Heath
D	Weiße hornlose Heidschnucke	668	PE	277	White Polled Heath

6 2 Dutch Heath

NL	Drentse Heideschaap	484	PE	398	Drenthe Heath Sheep
D	Bentheimer Landschaf	414	N	266	Bentheim
NL	Kempische Heideschaap	522	PE	399	Kempen Heath Sheep
NL	Mergelland Schaap	544	N	400	Mergelland
NL	Schoonebeker Heideschaap	620	ME	400	Schoonebeker
NL	Veluwse Heideschaap	660	ME	401	Veluwe Heath

6 3 Nordic group

DK	Dansk Landfar	477	CE	161	Danish Landrace
S	Gutefar	505	N	477	Gotland Sheep
S	Pälsfar	580	N	477	Swedish Fur Sheep
S	Ryafar	612	N	478	Rya Sheep
F	Romanov	601	PE	221	Romanov
PL	Wrzosowka	680	PE	419	Wrzosowka
N	Gammelnorsk	496	ME	408	Old Norwegian
N	Utegangarsau	496	ME	408	Old Norwegian
N	Spaelsau	569	N	409	Old Norw. Short Tailed
N	Rygja sau	614	PE	409	Rygja Sheep
N	Norsk Pels-Sau	566	N	408	Norwegian Fur Sheep
FR	Foroyskur Seydur	491	N	168	Faeroes Sheep
IS	Icelandic Sheep	512	N	311	Icelandic Sheep
SF	Suomenlammas	644	N	170	Finnsheep
F	Finnois	489	PE	208	Finnsheep
DK	Gronlandsk Fär	504	N	162	Greenland Sheep
D	Coburger Fuchsschaf	466	CE	268	Coburg
D	Rhönschaf	597	N	273	Rhoen

Coun- try	Local Breedname	Entry Number	ST. END.	BP page	International Breedname

6 4 North-West group

GB	Castlemilk Moorit Sheep 446		PE	518	Castlemilk Moorit
GB	Manx Loaghtan 539		ME	526	Manx Loaghtan
GB	Hebridean 508		N	524	Hebridean
D	Vierhornschaf 662		CE	276	Jacob Sheep
GB	North Ronaldsay 568		PE	528	North Ronaldsay
GB	Soay 631		N	532	Soay

7 Mountain group
7 1 Lop Eared Alpine group

I	Alpagota 400		CE	340	Alpagota
I	Bellunese 413		CE	343	Bellunese
I	Biellese 419		N	344	Biellese
I	Brentegana 433		ME	344	Brentegana
I	Brianzola 434		CE	345	Brianzola
I	Brogne 440		CE	346	Brogne
I	Garessina 497		CE	351	Garessina
I	Livo 533		ME	354	Livo
I	Saltasassi 616		ME	359	Saltasassi
I	Demontina 617		ME	360	Sambucana
I	Sambucana 617		ME	360	Sambucana
I	Tacola 645		CE	362	Tacola
F	Alpine 470		CE	206	French Alpine
F	Commun des Alpes 470		CE	206	French Alpine
F	Mourerous 558		ME	215	Mourerous
F	Peone 558		ME	215	Mourerous
F	Prealpes du Sud 589		N	218	Prealpes du Sud

7 2 Bergamasca group

I	Bergamasca 415		N	343	Bergamasca
I	Di Corteno 480		ME	349	Corteno
I	Fabrianese 487		N	349	Fabrianese
I	Finarda 488		ME	350	Finarda
I	Istriana 516		CE	352	Istrian
I	Lamon 525		CE	353	Lamon
I	Varesina 659		ME	364	Varesina
A	Kärntner Brillenschaf 521		E	135	Carinthian
A	Seeländer Schaf 521		E	135	Carinthian
D	Kärntner Brillenschaf 520		E	269	Carinthian
CH	Spiegelschaf 637		E	486	Spiegel
D	Braunes Bergschaf 431		CE	267	Brown Mountain
I	Tiroler Bergschaf 656		N	363	Tyrol Mountain
CH	Roux du Valais 609		ME	485	Valais Red
CH	Walliser Landschaf 609		ME	485	Valais Red
D	Weißes Bergschaf 416		N	278	White Mountain
SLO	Solcavsko-Jezerska 632		ME	447	Solca
GR	Zakynthos 681		ME	302	Zakynthos

Coun-try	Local Breedname	Entry Number	ST. END.	BP page	International Breedname
7 3 Semi Lop Eared group					
I	Brigasca	435	CE	345	Brigasca
F	Brigasque	436	CE	203	Brigasca
I	Frabosana	492	CE	350	Frabosana
I	Delle Langhe	478	N	348	Langhe
I	Pusterese	590	CE	358	Pusterese
CH	Besch da pader	485	ME	484	Engadine Red
CH	Engadiner Schaf	485	ME	484	Engadine Red
7 4 Zaupel / Steinschaf group					
D	Bayernwaldschaf	665	CE	276	Bavarian Forest
D	Waldschaf	665	CE	276	Bavarian Forest
CH	Bündner Oberländerschaf	441	ME	483	Buendner Oberland
CH	Schwarzbraunes Bergschaf	621	N	485	Swiss Black-Brown Mount.
H	Cikta	462	E	305	Cikta
7 5 Apennine group					
I	Appenninica	402	N	341	Apennine
I	Cornella bianca	471	CE	348	Cornella White
I	Garfagnina bianca	498	CE	351	Garfagnina White
I	Locale	534	PE	354	Locale
I	Massese	541	N	355	Massese
I	Pagliarola	576	N	357	Pagliarola
I	Pomarancina	585	CE	358	Pomarancina
I	Vissana	663	ME	364	Vissana
I	Zucca Modenese	682	CE	365	Zucca Modenese
7 6 Zackel group					
GR	Vlahiko	664	N	301	Greek Zackel
GR	Sarakatsaniko	664	N	301	Greek Zackel
GR	Sazakatsaniko	429	N	296	Mountain breeds
GR	Boutsiko	429	N	296	Mountain breeds
GR	Vlahiko	429	N	296	Mountain breeds
GR	Siteia	429	N	296	Mountain breeds
GR	Karagouniko	518	N	298	Karagouniko
GR	Kymi	523	ME	298	Kymi
GR	Mytilini	563	N	299	Mytilene
GR	Lesvos	563	N	299	Mytilene
GR	Florina	490	E	297	Pellagonia
GR	Pellagonia	490	E	297	Pellagonia
CZ	Sumavska	643	PE	158	Sumava
GR	Serres	627	N	299	Serrai
GR	Sfakia	628	N	300	Sfakia
GR	Glossa	630	PE	300	Skopelos
GR	Skopelos	630	PE	300	Skopelos
RO	Turcana	600	N	440	Romanian Zackel
YU	Pramenka	588	N	567	Yugoslavian Zackel

Coun-try	Local Breedname	Entry Number	ST. END.	BP page	International Breedname
YU	Sjenicka	588	N	567	Yugoslavian Zackel
YU	Svrljiska	588	N	567	Yugoslavian Zackel
HR	Ruda Dubrovacka Sheep	611	E	149	Dubrovnik
HR	Licka Ovca	530	PE	148	Lika
HR	Paska Ovca	579	PE	148	Pag Island
H	Racka	593	PE	306	Racka
CS	Zuslachtena valasska	658	PE	152	Valachian
PL	Polska owca gorska	584	PE	418	Polish Mountain

7 7 Tsigai group

YU	Cigaja	461	N	566	Tsigai
GR	Kivircik	654	PE	301	Kivircik
GR	Thraki	654	PE	301	Kivircik
RO	Tigaie	655	N	440	Tsigai
H	Cigaja	460	E	305	Tsigai
CS	Cigaja	459	N	152	Tsigai

7 8 Massif Central group

F	Lacaune	524	N	211	Lacaune
F	Blanc du Massif Central	423	N	202	Blanc du Massif Central
F	Ardes (extinct)	403		198	Ardes
F	Limousin	531	N	212	Limousin
F	Bizet	420	PE	201	Bizet
F	Rava	596	N	220	Rava
F	Grivette	503	PE	209	Grivette
F	Noir du Velay	564	N	217	Velay Black

7 9 Pyrenean group

F	Aure et de Campan	404	PE	198	Aure-Campan
F	Aurois	404	PE	198	Aure-Campan
F	Castillonnais	445	CE	204	Castillonnais
F	Tarasconnais	646	N	224	Tarasconnais
F	Landais	526	ME	211	Landais
F	Lourdais	535	ME	212	Lourdais
F	Baregeois	411	ME	199	Baregeois

7 10 Iberian Mountain group

E	Granadina	500	PE	465	Montesina
E	Montesina	500	PE	465	Montesina
E	Ojalada	500	PE	465	Montesina
E	Ojinegra	500	PE	465	Montesina
E	Pallaresa	577	N	468	Pallaresa
E	Xisqueta	577	N	468	Pallaresa

Table 17: Groups of similar breeds - SHEEP -, continued

Country	Local Breedname	Entry Number	ST. END.	BP page	International Breedname

7 11 British Hill group

Country	Local Breedname	Entry Number	ST. END.	BP page	International Breedname
GB	Badger faced Welsh Mountain	407	N	514	Badger Faced Welsh Moun.
GB	Cheviot	452	N	519	Cheviot
GB	Exmoor Horn	486	N	522	Exmoor Horn
GB	North Country Cheviot	567	N	527	North Country Cheviot
N	Dala	476	N	407	Dala
N	Steigar sau	638	N	410	Steigar Sheep
IRL	Wicklow Cheviot	677	N	320	Wicklow Cheviot
GB	Rough Fell	607		530	Rough Fell
GB	Welsh Hill Speckled Face	672	N	535	Welsh Hill Speckled Face
GB	Derbyshire Gritstone	479	N	521	Derbyshire Gritstone
GB	Herdwick	509	N	524	Herdwick
IRL	Blackface Mountain	422	N	318	Blackfaced Mountain
F	Blackface	421	CE	202	Blackface
GB	Whitefaced Woodland	676	PE	537	Whitefaced Woodland

8 Local Coarsewool group

8 1 Italian / French Coarsewool

Country	Local Breedname	Entry Number	ST. END.	BP page	International Breedname
I	Bagnolese	408	PE	341	Bagnolese
I	Ciavenasca	458	ME	346	Ciavenasca
I	Ciuta (extinct)	463		347	Ciuta
I	Comisana	469	N	347	Comisana
I	Marrane	540	CE	355	Marrane
I	Rosset	603	CE	359	Rosset
I	Savoiarda	619	CE	361	Savoiarda
F	Corse	472	N	207	Corsican
F	Ouessant	574	PE	218	Ushant
F	Race de Thones et de Marthod	592	PE	219	Thones-Marthod

8 2 Common Iberian Coarsewool

Country	Local Breedname	Entry Number	ST. END.	BP page	International Breedname
P	Badana	406	N	428	Badana
E	Chamarita	449	N	463	Chamarita
E	Ibicenca	511	CE	465	Ibiza
E	Maellana	536	PE	466	Maellana
E	Palmera	578	CE	468	Palmera
E	Segurena	625	N	470	Segurena

Table 17: Groups of similar breeds - SHEEP -, continued

Coun-try	Local Breedname	Entry Number	ST. END.	BP page	International Breedname

8 3 Barbary descendants

I	Barbaresca della Campania	409	N	342	Campanian Barbary
I	Barbaresca Siciliana	410	N	342	Sicilian Barbary
I	Nostrana	570	E	356	Nostrana
I	Pinzirita	581	N	357	Pinzirita
I	Sarda	618	N	360	Sardinian
F	Rouge du Roussillon	606	CE	222	Roussillon Red
E	Cartera	444	N	462	Cartera
E	Coete	599	ME	469	Red Majorcan
E	Roja Mallorquina	599	ME	469	Red Majorcan
E	Guirra	598	N	469	Levantina Red
E	Roja Levantina	598	N	469	Levantina Red
E	Sudat	598	N	469	Levantina Red

8 4 Churra Type

E	Churra Lebrijana	456	E	463	Andalusian Churra
P	Churra Algarvia	454	N	429	Algarve Churra
P	Churra da Terra Quente	455	N	429	Churra da Terra Quente
E	Churra Tensina	457	N	464	Tensina Churra
E	Colmenarena	468	N	464	Colmenar
P	Galega Bragancana	494	N	430	Bragan.+Miranda Galician
P	Galega Mirandesa	494	N	430	Bragan.+Miranda Galician
P	Mondegueira	557	N	431	Mondegueira
E	Rubia de El Molar	610	PE	470	Somosierra Blond

8 5 Bordaleiro-type

P	Campanica	443	PE	428	Campanica
P	Saloia	615	N	431	Saloia
P	Serra da Estrela	626	N	432	Serra da Estrela

4.3.4 Groups of similar breeds - GOATS -

The situation of the goat populations is characterized by the fact that in north and central Europe distinct breeds are found, whereas in southern Europe there are mainly little defined, mixed populations. These are often named after the area where they live. In this presentation the goat breeds are arranged in 10 groups, according to famous breeds with great influences, coat colours or geographical origin.

The groups Saanen, Chamois and Toggenburg are based on the actual Swiss breed of the same name, which genetically influenced the other populations of the group.

The Swiss Mountain group contains the other Swiss goats, the relationship of which is not clear, although Sardonaziege and St. Gallener Stiefelgeiss show similarities.

The breeds of the Maltese/Alpine/Garganica group are composed by local goat and Maltese - like Ionica and Malaga; or, like in the other breeds, they include Alpine (Cosenza) and/or Alpine, besides Malaga.

In the Southern white group local populations are included which are predominantly white, but the relationships are not known.

In the White and black group Vallesano originated from Valais Blacknose. Serpentina is not related to these breeds and shows a different black marking.

The Black or red group includes also the pied of these colours; all three colours can occur in the same population.

The Southern multicoloured group includes populations without a predominant colour. Many colours are possible.

In the Nordic landrace group Dutch Landrace is incrossed into Danish, into which also Saanen, Harz and also Norwegian are incrossed. Norwegian is incrossed into Swedish and Finnish.

Table 18: Groups of similar breeds - GOATS -
Group
    Subgroup

Coun-try	Local Breedname	Entry Number	ST. END.	BP page	International Breedname

1 Saanen group

CH	Saanen	349	N	489	Saanen
F	Gessenay	350	N	227	Saanen
F	Saanen	350	N	227	Saanen
I	Saanen	348	N	373	Saanen
D	Saanenziege	367	N	281	German Improved White
D	Weiße Deutsche Edelziege	367	N	281	German Improved White
B	Blanche	308	PE	140	Campine
CS	Bila kratkosrsta	306	N	153	White Shorteared Goat
RO	Carpatina Cashgora	315	N	441	Carpathian Goat
CH	Appenzellerziege	303	N	487	Appenzell
IRL	Irish Goat	336	ME	320	Irish Goat

2 Chamois group

CH	Gemsfarbige Gebirgsziege	332	N	488	Chamois Coloured
D	Alpenziege	310	N	279	German Improved Fawn
D	Bunte Deutsche Edelziege	310	N	279	German Improved Fawn
D	Erzgebirgsziege	330	CE	280	Erzgebirg Goat
F	Alpine	301	N	225	Alpine
I	Alpina	300	PE	365	Alpine
I	Camosciata delle Alpi	314	N	366	Camosciata Alpine
B	Chamoisee	317	PE	140	Belgian Fawn
CS	Hneda kratkosrsta	334	ME	153	Brown Shorteared Goat

3 Toggenburg

CH	Toggenburger	362	N	491	Toggenburg
B	Toggenburger	361	E	141	Toggenburg
GB	Pure Toggenburg	346	N	538	Toggenburg
D	Thüringer Waldziege	360	CE	280	Thuringian Forest
F	Poitevin	345	ME	227	Poitou
NL	Bonte geit (extinct)	309		402	Dutch Pied Original

4 Swiss Mountain group

CH	Sardonaziege	357	PE	490	St. Gallen Booted Goat
CH	St Galler Stiefelgeiss	357	PE	490	St. Gallen Booted Goat
CH	Bündner Strahlenziege	312	E	488	Grisons Striped
CH	Nera Verzasca	352	N	490	Verzasca
CH	Schwarzer Tessiner	352	N	490	Verzasca
CH	Pfauenziege	344	CE	489	Peacock Goat

5 Maltese / Alpine / Garganica group

I	Maltese	339	N	372	Maltese
I	Di L' Aquila	326	PE	368	Aquila
I	Di Cosenza	325	PE	368	Cosenza
I	Di Campobasso	324	CE	367	Campobasso
I	Ionica	335	N	371	Ionica
I	Garganica	331	CE	370	Garganica

Table 18: Groups of similar breeds - GOATS -, continued

Coun-try	Local Breedname	Entry Number	ST. END.	BP page	International Breedname
I	Cilentana Grigia	328	CE	369	Salerno
I	Di Salerno	328	CE	369	Salerno
I	Di Teramo	329	CE	370	Teramo
I	Di Potenza	327	E	369	Potenza
I	Bastarda	305	CE	366	Benevento
I	Di Benevento	305	CE	366	Benevento
E	Costena	321	N	472	Malaga
E	Malaguena	321	N	472	Malaga

6 Southern white group

I	Girgentana	333	CE	371	Girgentana
I	Istriana	337	CE	372	Istrian Goat
I	Sempione	353	CE	374	Sempione
E	Blanca Serrana Andaluza	307	PE	471	Andalusian White

7 White with Black group

CH	Walliser Schwarzhalsziege	366	N	491	Valais Blackneck
I	Vallesana	365	CE	376	Vallesana
P	Serpentina	354	N	433	Serpentina

8 Black or red group

F	Chevre du Rove	319	PE	226	Rove
I	Derivata di Siria	323	CE	367	Syrian Derivative
E	Castiza	316	N	472	Andalusian Black
E	Negra Serrana	316	N	472	Andalusian Black
E	Murciana-Granadina	340	N	473	Murcia-Granada
E	Cabra Mallorquina	313	ME	471	Majorcan Goat
P	Charnequeira	318	N	432	Charnequeira

9 Southern multicoloured group

I	Valgerola	364	PE	375	Valgerola
I	Val di Livo (extinct)	363	CE	375	Val di Livo
I	Roccaverano	347	CE	373	Roccaverano
I	Sarda	351	N	374	Sardinian
F	Corse	320	N	226	Corsican
HR	Balkanska Koza	304	PE	149	Balkan Goat
GR	Skopelos	356	PE	303	Skopelos
GR	Local breeds	338	N	302	Local breeds
P	Serrana	355	N	433	Serrana
E	Montejaquena	343	N	473	Montejaquena
E	Payoya	343	N	473	Montejaquena

10 Nordic Landrace group

NL	Nederlandse Landgeit	341	PE	402	Dutch Landrace
DK	Dansk Landrace	322	N	163	Danish Landrace
N	Norsk Geit	342	N	410	Norwegian Landrace
S	Svensk Lantras	359	N	478	Swedish Landrace
SF	Suomenvuohi	358	E	171	Finnish Landrace

4.3.5 Groups of similar breeds - PIGS -

Pigs are divided into eight groups. The groups were formed according to the phenotypic appearance, as colours and ear position. Large groups were divided into subgroups if a closer similarity was found in the exterior or genetic relationship.

The group "White pigs with erect ears" is subdivided into the groups Large White/Yorkshire and descendants of these breeds. Large White/Yorkshire from the United Kingdom was introduced to other countries, whereby the animals were bred pure or were incrossed with local breeds to improve the performance of these local breeds.

The same procedure was applied in the group "White breeds with lop ears". The subgroup, "Improved landraces" is based on the West European lean and meaty landraces and the breeds they have influenced significantly. The subgroup "Local landraces" shows more of the original character of a landrace. To a certain extent these breeds have also been improved by the modern white breeds, e.g. the French breed Normand has some influence of Large White.

Saddleback breeds were also distinguished by the ear position. Between the lop-eared Saddlebacks from Germany and the Prestice exchanges of breeding animals have taken place and these continental breeds were influenced by British Saddleback; particularly Prestice was improved by Wessex. Basque black pied is similar to Limousin and both resemble the Schwäbisch-Hällisches Schwein. The group Saddleback with erect ears describes a heterogenous group. Bazna is white belted with semi-lop ears, but it originated from Berkshire and Mangalitza about 1872. But because of its exterior and long time of breed existence it is grouped into the Saddlebacks. The outstanding breed of this group, which should be treated as a subgroup, is Hampshire, whose white belt is usually smaller than in the other Saddlebacks, more like a ring, and the white colour includes the front legs.

The Black Group was differentiated between solid black breeds and blacks with white markings (the Berkshire and their descendants). Large Black/Cornwall from the U.K. from the group of solid blacks, has influenced other breeds. Allentejana is similar to Extremadura Red. Black Slavonian originated from Berkshire, Poland China, Mangalitza and Cornwall at about 1860. Also, Moravska was composed of Berkshire and Mangalitza and improved by Large Black. Because of the age of these breeds and their solid colour, they are grouped into the solid black group and not into the Berkshire group. Berkshire, an old British breed, formed a remarkable great number of other breeds, particularly in East Europe.

The Red breed group is subdivided into two subgroups. One is the originally American Duroc, which is now found in many countries. The second subgroup Other red breeds includes Tamworth and two South European breeds. All of these 3 breeds show original characteristics of old local breeds.

From the spotted pigs Pietrain was imported by many countries to be used as a pure breed and for crossbreeding systems. Pietrain was composed of Bayeux, Tamworth and a local breed in the first quarter of this century. It can be assumed that Pietrain was used to improve other local spotted breeds, but, except for Slovakian Black Pied, there is not much reported about it. In Sortbroget, Turopolje and Slovakian Black Pied, there is an incrossing of Berkshire and other breeds.

Native unimproved breeds are found in different places. There are no relationships found among these or other breeds.

Artifical and exotic breeds were used for experimental purposes as well as to fulfil special needs.

Table 19: Groups of similar breeds - PIGS -
Group
   Subgroup

Coun-try	Local Breedname	Entry Number	ST. END.	BP page	International Breedname

1 White breeds with erect ears
1 1 Large White / Yorkshire
GB	Yorkshire	1023	N	544	Large White
SF	Yorkshire	1021	N	172	Large White
B	Grand Yorkshire Belge	937	N	142	Large White
N	Norsk Yorkshire	984	E	411	Large White
IRL	Large White Pigs	963	N	321	Large White
F	Large White	960	N	232	Large White
I	Large White	961	N	379	Large White

1 2 Large White / Yorkshire descendants
D	Deutsches Edelschwein	923	N	285	Large White
D*	Deutsches Edelschwein	922	N	284	Large White
CH	Schweizerisches Edelschwein	1007	N	492	Large White
NL	Groot Yorkshire-S	938	N	403	Large White / sire line
NL	Groot Yorkshire-Z	939	N	403	Large White / dam line
GB	Middle White	975	ME	543	Middle White
CS	Vile uslechtile	1017	N	156	Large White
PL	Wielka biala polska	1019	N	421	Large White
SLO	Bela Zlahtna	904	CE	448	Slovenian White
YU	Dom. mesnata svinja	925	N	567	Large White
RO	Large White	962	N	443	Large White
RO	Yorkshire	1022	PE	444	Yorkshire
LT	Litovskaya belaya	968	N	391	Lithuanian White
LV	Latviiskaya belaya	964	N	390	Latvian White
UR	Ukrainskaya stepnaya belaya	1014	N	498	Ukrainian White Steppe
KAZ	Semirechenskaya	999	PE	389	Semirechensk
USSR	Krupnaya belaya	951	N	559	Large White
USSR	Livenskaya	969	PE	560	Livny
USSR	Muromskaya	979	PE	560	Murom
USSR	Sibirskaya severnaya	1002	N	562	North Siberian
USSR	Tarskaya (extinct)	1010	PE	562	Siberian
USSR	Tsivilskaya	1012	N	563	Tsivilsk
USSR	Urzhumskaya	1016	N	563	Urzhum

2 White breeds with lop ears
2 1 Improved landraces
DK	Dansk Landrace	917	N	163	Danish Landrace
N	Norsk Landrace	983	N	411	Norwegian Landrace
SF	Maatiaissika	970	N	172	Finnish Landrace
NL	Nederlands Landras	980	N	404	Dutch Landrace
B	Belgisch Landvarken	906	N	141	Belgian Landrace
D	Deutsche Landrasse B	919	PE	283	Belgian Landrace
D*	Belgische Landrasse	907	CE	282	Belgian Landrace
D	Deutsche Landrasse/Sauenlinie	921	N	283	German Landrace/dam line

Table 19: Groups of similar breeds - PIGS -, continued

Coun-try	Local Breedname	Entry Number	ST. END.	BP page	International Breedname
D	Deutsche Landrasse/Universal	920	N	284	German Landrace/univ.
D*	Deutsche Landrasse	918	N	282	German Landrace
CH	Schweiz. Veredeltes Landschwein	1008	N	493	Swiss Landrace
CS	Belgicka Landrase	905	PE	154	Belgian Landrace
CS	Landrace	952	N	155	Czech Landrace
GB	British Landrace	911	N	539	British Landrace
IRL	Irish Landrace	946	N	321	Irish Landrace
L	Landrace belge	958	N	394	Belgian Landrace
F	Landrace Belge	957	N	231	Belgian Landrace
F	Landrace	953	PE	231	French Landrace
I	Landrace Belga	956	E	378	Belgian Landrace
I	Landrace	954	N	378	Italian Landrace
EW	Estonskaya bekonnaya	933	N	167	Estonian Bacon
PL	Zlotnicka biala	1024	CE	422	Zlotniki White
PL	Polska biala zwisloucha	992	N	420	Polish Landrace
USSR	Breitovskaya	910	N	558	Breitov
RO	Landrace	955	N	442	Romanian Landrace
SK	Slovenske biele mäsove	1004	N	446	Slovakian White

2 2 Local landraces

GB	Chester White	913	CE	540	Chester White
GB	Welsh	1018	ME	544	Welsh
F	Normand	982	CE	233	Normand
H	Mangalica	972	ME	306	Mangalitsa
RO	Mangalita	973	ME	443	Mangalitsa
CH	Schwalbenbauch Mangalitza	1020	PE	492	Swallow-Bellied Mangal.
CH	Wollschwein	1020	PE	492	Swallow-Bellied Mangal.

3 Saddlebacks

3 1 Saddlebacks with lop ears

GB	British Saddleback	912	PE	540	British Saddleback
D	Angler Sattelschwein	903	CE	281	Angeln Saddleback
D	Schwäbisch-Hällisches Schwein	997	PE	288	Swabian Hall Saddleback
D*	Deutsches Sattelschwein	924	ME	285	German Saddleback
CZ	Presticke	994	PE	158	Prestice
I	Cinta Senese	914	CE	376	Siena Belted
F	Pie noir du Pays Basque	987	CE	235	Basque Black Pied
SLO	Krskopoljski crnopasasti prasic	950	CE	449	Krskopolje Saddleback

3 2 Saddlebacks with erect ears

GB	Hampshire	945	CE	542	Hampshire
F	Hampshire (extinct)	941	E	230	Hampshire
I	Hampshire	943	CE	377	Hampshire
D*	Hampshire	942	CE	286	Hampshire
CS	Hampshire	940	N	155	Hampshire
RO	Hampshire	944	PE	442	Hampshire
F	Limousin	967	CE	232	Limousin
RO	Porcul de Banat	993	PE	444	Bazna

Table 19: Groups of similar breeds - PIGS -, continued

Coun- try	Local Breedname	Entry Number	ST. END.	BP page	International Breedname

4 Black breeds
4 1 Solid black breeds
GB	Large Black	959	ME	542	Large Black
P	Alentejana	902	N	434	Alentejana
E	Negra Iberica	981	N	475	Iberian Black
F	Gascon	935	CE	229	Gascony
SLO	Crna Slavonska	916		448	Black Slavonian
YU	Moravka	978		568	Morava

4 2 Berkshire group
GB	Berkshire	909	ME	539	Berkshire
USSR	Kemerovskaya	949	PE	559	Kemerovo
USSR	Severokavkazskaya	1000	PE	561	North Caucasus
UR	Ukrainskaya stepnaya ryabaya	1015	PE	499	Ukrainian Spotted Steppe
UR	Mirgorodskaya	976	N	498	Mirgorod
BEL	Belorusskaya cherno-pestraya	908	N	145	Byelorussian Black Pied
KAZ	Aksaiskaya cherno-pestraya	901	N	388	Aksai Black Pied

5 Red breeds
5 1 Duroc group
GB	Duroc	932	CE	541	Duroc
F	Duroc	927	CE	229	Duroc
I	Duroc	929	N	377	Duroc
CS	Duroc	926	N	154	Duroc
PL	Duroc	930	PE	420	Duroc
D*	Duroc	928	PE	286	Duroc
RO	Duroc	931	N	441	Duroc

5 2 Other red breeds
GB	Tamworth	1009	ME	543	Tamworth
E	Colorada	934	PE	474	Extremadura Red
E	Extremena retinta	934	PE	474	Extremadura Red
E	Olivenza	934	PE	474	Extremadura Red
I	Mora Romagnola	977	CE	379	Romagnola

6 Spotted breeds
6 1 Pietrain group
B	Pietrain	988	N	142	Pietrain
F	Pietrain	989	N	235	Pietrain
D	Pietrain	991	N	287	Pietrain
I	Pietrain	990		380	Pietrain

Table 19: Groups of similar breeds - PIGS -, continued

Coun-try	Local Breedname	Entry Number	ST. END.	BP page	International Breedname

6 2 Local spotted breeds

GB	Gloucestershire Old Spot	936	PE	541	Gloucestershire Old Spot
DK	Sortbroget	1005	CE	164	Danish Black Pied
D	Buntes Schwein	996	CE	288	Bentheim Black Pied
D	Schwarz-Weißes Bentheimer	996	CE	288	Bentheim Black Pied
I	Spotted	1006		380	Spotted
PL	Pulawska	995	ME	421	Pulawy
PL	Zlotnicka pstra	1025	ME	422	Zlotniki Black and White
HR	Turopolljac	1013	CE	150	Turopolje
YU	Slavenske ciernostrakate	1003		568	Slovakian Black Pied
E	Manchada de Jabugo	971	CE	474	Andalusian Spotted
USSR	Sibirskaya chernopestraya	1001	PE	561	Siberian Black Pied

7 Native unimproved breeds

F	Corse	915	E	228	Corsican
GO	Kakhetinskaya	948	ME	253	Kakhetian
ARM	Lesogornaya porodnaya gruppa	966	CE	131	Forest Mountain

8 Artificial or exotic breeds

F	Acadie P22	900	CE	228	Acadie P22
F	Chinois	974	CE	233	Meishan
F	Mei-Shan	974	CE	233	Meishan
F	Jia-Xing	947	CE	230	Black Jiaxing
F	Pen Ar Lan P 77	985	E	234	Pen Ar Lan P 77
F	Penshire P66	986	CE	234	Penshire P66
F	Tia Meslan P44	1011	CE	236	Tia Meslan P44
D*	Schwerfurter Fleischrasse	998	PE	289	Schwerfurt Meat Pig
D*	Leicoma	965	N	287	Leicoma

4.3.6 Groups of similar breeds - HORSES -

Horses are divided into five groups: Arab and Thouroughbred, Trotter, Halfbred (Warmblood) and Heavy horses (Coldblood) as large horses and into ponies as horses being smaller than 1,48 m. Large groups were subdivided into subgroups depending on the breed's history, genetic relationship or place of origin, according to the available information. Colours were not used for grouping since in most breeds a variety of colours is possible.

Arab/Thouroughbred are interbred intensively, and the relationship among them is quite close.

Trotter was developed in the second half of the 18th century. It is based on Arab, Thouroughbred and Halfbred. Trotters are distributed world-wide. Successful champions are used as sires in many different countries, e.g. in the listed Finnish and Norwegian Trotters, Swedish Trotter stallions were used.
Morgan is an American Trotter, and it is found in the U.K. and Canada as well as in the U.S.A.

Halfbred was developed from Arab and Thouroughbred by crossing in local horse populations. Many breeds resulted from this interbreeding.

Iberian halfbred: Andalusian and Lusitanian and their derivatives show the most distinct influence from Arab and Berb in Halfbreds. They were composed by these orientales and native Spanish and Portuguese horses. Some authors suppose also links between both Iberian breeds. Andalusian, Arab and Neapolitanian were incrossed into local Karst horses to form Lipitsa. Andalusian is also the ancestor of Kladruby and Senne.

Breeding of Anglo-Norman started in the 1830s. Into the native horse population of the Normandy, English Halfbreds and Thouroughbreds were introduced. In later times only carefully selected Thouroughbreds were used, but no other breeds. Anglo-Normans were used to form or to improve the other mentioned breeds of this group.

Hanoverian: They resulted from crossbreeding in 1755, and local mares with stallions from Mecklenburg and Trakehnen in about 1755. From 1830 to 1860 very frequently Thouroughbreds were incrossed. After this time this procedure was reduced to a minimum, because the foals became too light for agricultural purposes. After World War II Thouroughbreds were used again to produce a riding horse. Hanoverians were used to form Saxony Warmblood and Belgian Sport Horse.

British and Irish Halfbred were developed from local horses by crossbreeding with oriental and Thouroughbred in the 17th and 18th century. It resulted in a variety of riding, hunting and coachhorses but the Data Bank has information only on two breeds. Cleveland Bay is a long established breed, native to North Yorkshire, Thouroughbred is included in its history. Cob describes a type of a horse rather than a breed that is found mostly in the west of England and Ireland. The mentioned Hungarian breeds derived from British Halfbred. Irish Draught is an old local breed. Connemara ponies and imported Spanish horses had a great influence on this breed. Crossing Irish Draught with Thouroughbred produced Irish Hunter.

Heavy horses

This group is characterized by breeds with a deep, compact, heavily musculed body, large size and heavy weight, most breeds have feathered legs.

Ardennes-Flemish group: Ardennes is a native breed of the Maas-area. From there it spread out to other countries and influenced many local heavy horse breeds. Variations of Ardennes are Auxois and Northern Ardennes, who are larger and heavier than Ardennes because of Belgian ancestors. Flemish was included in the development of Belgian. Ardennes was included to form the breeds Freiburg and the related Cocutois and Yugoslawian Draft.

French heavy horses

French horses related to Ardennes are mentioned in that group. Boulonnais was derived from the North European heavy horse, Arab was incrossed - the head still shows the typical shape. Percheron was developed from local horse by incrossing Arab, Anglo-Norman and Boulonnais. Breton is represented by two types. The lighter variety, the Postier Breton, contains Norfolk Trotter. The heavier type, the Breton Heavy Draft, includes Percheron and Boulonnais. Italian Heavy Rapid Draft stems from Breton. Mulassier/Poitevin, based on a local horse and the Dutch horse, is used to produce mules.

Noric group: Noric, a native horse from the Salzburg area, is bred also in other Alpine areas and is included in South German Coldblood and in Black Forest.

Nordic heavy horses: Doele, a light coldblood, can be traced back to a local horse which was probably identical to the Fjord horse. This horse was incrossed by Danish (supposingly Frederikborg) and Thouroughbred stallions to produce Docle. North Swedish horse was created by crossing local horse with Docle. Jutland represents an old native draft horse being improved by Shire. Schleswig originated from Jutland being crossed with Suffolk. Frederiksborg Horse is a light draft horse originating from Andalusian but intercrossed since 1939 with Oldenburg and East Friesian. Finnhorse has a lighter and heavier variety; it was derived from a local forest horse, which was incrossed with several warmblood and coldblood breeds.

British breeds: Both, Clydesdale and Shire, originated from the Great Horse, which was similar to Flemish. Suffolk Punch is one of the oldest British coach horses and temporary crossed with Flemish and Yorkshire.

Pony breeds can be warmblood or coldblood types depending on which type of horse was used for incrossing during the breed's development or whether original pony type was maintained. Ponies were grouped according to the area of origin; in some cases the groups consist of an outstanding breed representing a certain region.

Nordic ponies represent breeds of the northern pony type, mainly purebred. Iceland ponies descended from Norwegian, Scottish and Irish horses introduced in the 11th and 12th century by early settlers.

British native ponies are subdivided into three groups. Exmoor is considered as the oldest native British breed. In Dartmoor other breeds were incrossed until the studbook was set up in 1899. Exmoor as well as Dartmoor were incrossed into New Forest among Arab and Hackney. Welsh developed from the Welsh Mountain pony; Arab was probably used in the breed history.
Connemara pony originated from Irish Hobby and it became popular in many countries.

French ponies: French Saddlebred Pony was developed from local ponies and Arab. Relationships among the other members of this group are not known.

Haflinger, an Alpine breed, was composed from local horse, Noric and Arab.

East European ponies: Hutsul originates directly from the Tarpan, but with considerable influence of Arab. The Konik is related to the Hutsul. The Bosnian Pony originated from the Busa-Pony, improved also by Arab.

In **South European** countries several native pony breeds can be found. They are well adapted to the harsh living conditions (high temperatures and low quality food).

Table 20: Groups of similar breeds - HORSES -
Group
    Subgroup

Coun-try	Local Breedname	Entry Number	ST. END.	BP page	International Breedname
1 Arab and Thoroughbred					
A	Vollblutaraber	815	N	136	Arab
SF	Arabialainen	706	CE	173	Arab
F	Arab	703	N	237	Arab.
IRL	Arab Horse	705	E	322	Arab
GB	Arab	704	N	545	Arab
F	Barbe	711	ME	239	Barb
H	Shagya arab	802	CE	309	Shagya Arab
F	Anglo-Arab	702	N	236	Anglo-Arab
I	Cavallo Anglo-Arabo-Sardo	717	N	382	Anglo-Arabo-Sarda
H	Gidran	751	CE	307	Gidran
SF	Täysverinen	811	CE	177	Thoroughbred
F	Pur-Sang	796	N	250	Thoroughbred
GR	Aglikos Katharohaemos	700	N	303	Thoroughbred
IRL	Thoroughbred	812	N	324	Thoroughbred
2 Trotter					
F	Trotteur Francais	813	N	251	French Trotter
SLO	Ljutomerski kasac	778		449	Ljutomer-Trotter
SF	Lämminverinen ravuri	773	N	175	Warm-blooded Trotter
N	Norsk Kaldblods Traver	789	N	413	Norwegian Heavy Trotter
GB	Morgan Horse	783	E	548	Morgan
3 Halfbred					
3 1 Iberian halfbreds and descendants					
E	Espanol-Andaluz	742	N	475	Andalusian
P	Lusitano	780	PE	435	Lusitanian
F	Lusitanien	779	N	246	Lusitanian
HR	Lipicanac	775	N	151	Lipitsa
H	Lipicai	774	E	308	Lipitsa
I	Lipizzano	777	CE	386	Lipitsa
F	Lipizzan	776	CE	246	Lipitsa
CZ	Kladrubsky	770	CE	159	Kladruby
D	Senner	801	CE	293	Senne
3 2 Anglo-Norman descendants					
D	Holsteiner Warmblut	760	N	291	Holstein
D	Altwürttemberger	701	CE	289	Altwuerttemberg
D	Zweibrücker	818	PE	294	Zweibruecken
H	Noniusz	785	PE	309	Nonius
D	Rottaler	797	CE	291	Rottal
NL	Gelders Paard	750	CE	404	Gelderland
NL	Groninger Paard	752	CE	405	Groningen
F	Cheval de Selle Francais	727	N	241	French Saddlebred
L	Cheval de selle	726	ME	395	Saddlebred
NL	Warmbloed Paard Nederlands	816	N	405	Netherlands Riding Horse
CH	Demi Sang Suisse	740	N	493	Halfbred
SF	Puoliverinen	795	PE	176	Halfbred

108

Table 20: Groups of similar breeds - HORSES -, continued

Coun-try	Local Breedname	Entry Number	ST. END.	BP page	International Breedname

3 3 Hanoverian group

D	Hannoveraner	758	N	290	Hanoverian
D	Sächsisches Warmblut	798	ME	292	Saxony Warmblood
B	Cheval de Sport Belge	728	N	143	Belgian Sport Horse

3 4 British and Irish halfbred

GB	Cleveland Bay Horse	732	N	545	Cleveland Bay
F	Cob	734	N	241	Cob
H	Kisberi felver	769	PE	307	Kisber Halfbred
H	Mezöhegyesi felver	782	PE	308	Mezoehegyes Halfbred
IRL	Irish Draught Horse	764	PE	323	Irish Draught
IRL	Irish Hunter	765	N	323	Irish Hunter
IRL	Irish Sport Horse	765	N	323	Irish Hunter

3 5 Local breeds with Oriental/Thoroughbred influence

I	Cavallo Sardo	724	E	385	Sardinian
I	Cavallo Siciliano	725	PE	386	Sicilian
I	Cavallo Maremmano	720	PE	383	Maremmana
I	Cavallo Sanfratellano	723	E	385	Sanfratellana
I	Cavallo Murgese	721	N	384	Murgese
F	Camargue	715	N	240	Camargue

4 Heavy-horses

4 1 Ardennes-Flemish group

B	Cheval de Trait Ardennais	729	N	143	Ardennes
L	Cheval de Trait Ardennais	730	ME	395	Ardennes
F	Ardennais	707	PE	237	Ardennes
F	Auxois	709	CE	238	Auxois
F	Ardennais du nord	708	PE	238	Northern Ardennes
F	Trait du nord	708	PE	238	Northern Ardennes
B	Cheval de Trait Belge	731	N	144	Flemish
CH	Franches-Montagnes	747	PE	494	Freiberg
F	Comtois	735	PE	242	Comtois
HR	Hrvatski Hladnokrvnjak	761	ME	150	Yugoslavian Draft

4 2 French heavy horses

F	Boulonnais	713	PE	239	Boulonnais
F	Percheron	790	PE	248	Percheron
F	Breton	714	PE	240	Breton
I	Cavallo Agricolo Italiano	716	PE	381	Rapid Heavy Draft
F	Mulassier	791	E	248	Poitou
F	Poitevin	791	E	248	Poitou

Table 20: Groups of similar breeds - HORSES -, continued

Coun-try	Local Breedname	Entry Number	ST. END.	BP page	International Breedname

4 3 Noric group
A	Norisches Kaltblut	788	N	136	Noric
I	Cavallo Norico	722	CE	384	Noric
D	Süddeutsches Kaltblut	810	N	294	South German Coldblood
D	Schwarzwälder Füchse	800	ME	293	Black Forest
D	St. Märgener Füchse	800	ME	293	Black Forest

4 4 Nordic heavy horses
N	Tyngre Doelehest	814	PE	413	Doele Draught Horse
S	Nordsvensk häst	787	N	479	North Swedish Horse
DK	Den Jydske Hest	741	ME	164	Jutland Horse
DK	Frederiksborgheste	748	ME	165	Frederiksborg Horse
D	Schleswiger Kaltblut	799	E	292	Schleswig Coldblood
SF	Suomenhevonen	809	N	177	Finnhorse

4 5 British heavy horses
GB	Shire Horse	804	N	549	Shire
GB	Clydesdale Horses	733	N	546	Clydesdale
GB	Suffolk Punch	808	PE	549	Suffolk

5 Ponies
5 1 Nordic ponies
N	Fjordhest	746	PE	412	Fjord
F	Fjord de Norvege	745	N	243	Fjord
S	Skogsruss	805	N	479	Gotland Pony
SF	Gotland Russ	820	CE	174	Gotland Pony
N	Lyngshest	786	ME	412	Nordland
N	Nordlandshest	786	ME	412	Nordland

5 2 Iceland ponies
IS	Islenski hesturinn	768	N	311	Iceland Pony
SF	Islannin hevonen	767	CE	174	Iceland Pony
F	Islandais	766	ME	245	Iceland Pony

5 3 British moor and forest ponies
GB	Dartmoor Pony	739	N	546	Dartmoor Pony
GB	Exmoor Pony	743	PE	547	Exmoor Pony
F	New Forest	784	PE	247	New Forest Pony
SF	New Forest Pony	821	ME	175	New Forest Pony
F	Dartmoor	738	ME	243	Dartmoor Pony
F	Welsh	817	ME	251	Welsh Pony
SF	Welsh Pony (A, B & D)	823	CE	178	Welsh Pony

5 4 British hill ponies
| GB | Fell Pony | 744 | N | 547 | Fell Pony |
| F | Highland | 759 | CE | 244 | Highland Pony |

110

```
Table 20: Groups of similar breeds - HORSES -, continued
Coun-  Local       Entry              ST.  BP   International
try    Breedname   Number             END. page Breedname
```

5 5 Shetland ponies

```
SF    Shetland Pony 822              PE 176 Shetland Pony
F     Shetland 803                  N  250 Shetland Pony
```

5 6 Connemara ponies

```
IRL   Connemara Pony 737            N  322 Connemara Pony
F     Connemara 736                 N  242 Connemara Pony
SF    Connemara Pony 819            CE 173 Connemara Pony
```

5 7 French ponies

```
F     Landais 772                   E  245 Landais
F     Merens 781                    N  247 Merens Pony
F     Poney Francais de Selle 792   N  249 French Saddlebred Pony
```

5 8 Haflinger group

```
D     Haflinger 754                 N  290 Haflinger
CH    Haflinger 756                 PE 494 Haflinger
I     Avelignese 710                N  381 Haflinger
F     Haflinger 753                 N  244 Haflinger
L     Haflinger 755                 N  396 Haflinger
GB    Haflinger 757                 E  548 Haflinger
```

5 9 East European ponies

```
CS    Hucul 762                     CE 156 Hutsul
PL    Hucul 763                     PE 423 Hutsul
PL    Koniki Polskie 771            N  423 Polish Konik
YU    Bosanski brdski konj 712         569 Bosnian Pony
```

5 10 South European ponies

```
P     Garrano 749                   ME 434 Garrano
P     Sorraia 807                   CE 435 Sorraia
F     Pottok 794                    PE 249 Pottok
I     Cavallo della Giara 719       PE 383 Giara Pony
I     Cavallo Bardigiano 718        N  382 Bardigiana
GR    Skyos Pony 806                E  304 Skyros Pony
```

4.4 Grouping of breeds according to specific factors

Breeds may be sorted according to specific factors if one is interested in the number of breeds which fulfil certain requirements or of which a certain amount of information is available. Examples with a few comments are given in the following tables 21-42:
In tables 43 to 47 the number of breeds is presented for which specific characteristics are reported.

Table 21: Origin of breed.
Goat breeds originate mostly from local breeds, in pigs 1/4 of the breeds result from imports.

Table 22: Breed is known since a given year.
266 of 877 breeds were known before 1900, 51 breeds before 1800.

Table 23: Herdbook has existed since a given year.
For 121 breeds a herdbook was set up before 1900, for 238 breeds later than 1960.

Table 24: Number of female breeding animals.
55 breeds have less than 100 females.

Table 25: Number of females in herdbook.
60 breeds have less than 100 females in herdbook.

Table 26: Number of male breeding animals.
63 of 877 breeds have less than 10 males.

Table 27: Trend in number of females based on year 1986:
Until 1986 the number of females was decreasing in 152 of 532 breeds, since 1986 the number has been decreasing in 169 breeds.

Table 28: Herd size.
A herd size of less than 5 is typical of more than half of the horse breeds and only of 2 percent of the sheep breeds.

Table 29: Number of herds of a breed.
This information is available only on 1/4 of the breeds.

Table 30: Cryoconservation of semen and embryos.
Semen is conserved of 2/3 of cattle breeds but only of 12 percent of sheep breeds. Embryos are conserved of 1/4 of cattle breeds, in 2 percent of sheep and horse breeds and not at all of goat and pig breeds.

Table 31: Number of males represented in conserved semen.
In 52 of 293 breeds less than 5 males are represented in cryoconserved semen.

Table 32: Number of males represented in conserved embryos.
In 11 of 24 cattle breeds less than 5 males are represented in cryoconserved embryos.

Table 33: Withers height of adults in cattle and horses.
In 8 of 277 cattle breeds females have a withers height of less than 110 cm.

Table 34: Withers height in sheep, goats and pigs.
In sheep the variation of withers height among breeds seems to be higher than in goats.

Table 35: Live weight of adults in cattle and horses.
           Females of 12 of 277 cattle breeds and of 7 of 123 horse breeds have a live weight of less than 300 kg.
Table 36: Coat colour in cattle, sheep, goats and pigs.
           Predominantly uni red coloured animals are typical of 11 of 126 pig breeds and of 5 of 283 sheep breeds.
Table 37: Coat colour in horses.
           Two horse breeds are black or predominantly black; in 35 horse breeds the colour black occurs either as only colour or besides other colours.
Table 38: Hair or wool of sheep and goats.
           16 of 283 of sheep breeds are hairbreeds.
Table 39: Number of horns in cattle, sheep and goats.
           4 of 283 sheep breeds have 4 horns in females, 21 of 277 cattle breeds are polled.
Table 40: 1st, 2nd, and 3rd main use in cattle, sheep and goats.
Table 41: 1st, 2nd and 3rd main use of breeds in pigs and horses.
           In horses meat production is the 1st main use of 12 breeds, tractive power the 1st main use of 15 breeds (of a total of 123 breeds).
Table 42: Specific management conditions.
           35 cattle breeds and 4 pig breeds are kept with no housing for 2 pig breeds, feeding conditions were reported as "total grazing".
Table 43: Special characteristics reported for cattle breeds.
Table 44: Special characteristics reported for sheep breeds.
Table 45: Special characteristics reported for goat breeds.
Table 46: Special characteristics reported for pig breeds.
Table 47: Special characteristics reported for horse breeds.

Table 21: Number of breeds by kind of origin

Origin of breed	Cattle	Sheep	Goats	Pigs	Horses	Total
From local breeds	168	207	51	65	62	553
Mainly from imports	30	24	7	33	21	115
From both sources	49	36	3	16	28	132
No information	30	16	7	12	12	77
Total	277	283	68	126	123	877

Table 22: Number of breeds by year since which breed is known by
its local name

Year	Cattle	Sheep	Goats	Pigs	Horses	Total
Before 1800	16	19	1	-	15	51
1800 - 1900	86	54	13	21	41	215
1901 - 1940	25	24	8	16	12	85
Later than 1940	31	39	5	46	11	132
No information	119	147	41	43	44	394
Total	277	283	68	126	123	877

Table 23: Number of breeds by year of herdbook setup

Year	Cattle	Sheep	Goats	Pigs	Horses	Total
Before 1850	6	2	-	1	12	21
1850 - 1899	51	17	2	6	24	100
1900 - 1929	55	34	8	15	17	129
1930 - 1960	32	27	12	29	14	114
Later than 1960	65	89	14	37	33	238
No information	68	114	32	38	23	275
Total	277	283	68	126	123	877

Table 24: Number of breeds by number of female breeding animals /
or - if number of females is unknown - number of males
plus number of females

Number of females	Cattle	Sheep	Goats	Pigs	Horses	Total
< 50	9	3/2	-/2	5	7	24/4
50 - 99	11	3/1	-/2	9	8	31/3
100 - 199	16	10/4	3/2	7	10	46/6
200 - 299	13	7/1	-/1	11	13	44/2
300 - 399	10	4	3	6	8	31
400 - 499	3	8	-/1	6	4	21/1
500 - 999	20	20/1	1/1	4	18	63/2
1000-1999	14	29/2	3	2	12	60/2
2000-2999	14	13/2	3	4	13	47/2
3000-3999	6	8/2	1/3	3	4	22/5
4000-4999	6	8	2/1	3	1	20/1
5000-5999	4	3	-/1	4	-	11/1
6000-7499	8	8	3/2	3	3	25/2
7500-9000	5	5	1/1	5	7	23/1
>9000	120/2	120/7	17/10	27	9	293/19
No information	16	12	4	27	6	65
Total	277	283	68	126	123	877

114

Table 25: Number of breeds by number of female breeding animals in
herdbook

Number of females	Cattle	Sheep	Goats	Pigs	Horses	Total
< 50	9	1	2	4	6	22
50 - 99	15	4	6	7	6	38
100 - 199	11	8	2	3	1	25
200 - 299	11	4	5	2	10	32
300 - 399	7	5	2	4	4	22
400 - 499	5	5	-	2	7	19
500 - 999	15	16	5	2	9	47
1000-1999	12	16	5	4	13	50
2000-2999	12	4	3	4	6	29
3000-3999	7	13	4	3	1	28
4000-4999	8	4	5	3	-	20
5000-5999	7	6	1	-	1	15
6000-7499	6	1	1	3	1	12
7500-9000	3	4	-	-	2	9
>9000	59	37	3	10	6	115
No information	90	155	24	75	50	394
Total	277	283	68	126	123	877

Table 26: Number of breeds by number of male breeding animals

Number of males	Cattle	Sheep	Goats	Pigs	Horses	Total
< 5	10	4	1	3	7	25
5 - 9	21	-	-	10	7	38
10 - 14	23	5	5	6	9	48
15 - 19	10	4	4	6	5	29
20 - 24	19	8	-	3	9	39
25 - 29	6	10	1	3	6	26
30 - 49	21	20	3	7	13	64
50 -100	28	31	8	16	30	113
>100	128	138	29	64	33	392
No information	11	63	17	8	4	103
Total	277	283	68	126	123	877

Table 27: Number of breeds with information on trend in
number of females since 1986

Trend	Cattle	Sheep	Goats	Pigs	Horses	Total
a) Until cited year						
increasing	46	46	9	14	33	148
stable	47	32	16	16	25	136
decreasing	62	39	16	17	18	152
No information	49	13	4	23	7	96
b) Since cited year						
increasing	64	57	4	14	45	184
stable	44	28	11	29	20	132
decreasing	84	32	10	25	18	169
No information	12	13	20	2	-	47
Total	204	130	45	70	83	532

Table 28: Number of breeds by average herd size total (T) or in
private herds (P)

Females per herd	Cattle T/P	Sheep T/P	Goats T/P	Pigs T/P	Horses T/P	Total T/P
1 - 4	30/16	4/-	5/4	11/6	56/27	106/53
5 - 9	34/10	15/11	12/2	4/5	3/-	68/28
10 - 14	28/8	11/8	4/4	1/-	-/1	44/21
15 - 19	6/-	6/5	-/-	-/-	1/2	13/7
20 - 29	18/6	23/14	-/-	11/1	3/-	55/21
30 - 49	27/10	12/6	-/-	8/2	6/1	53/19
50 - 69	12/7	10/5	1/1	5/3	1/-	29/16
70 -100	5/4	32/10	3/-	5/5	-/-	45/19
>100	8/5	44/6	6/5	15/5	2/-	75/21
No information	109/211	126/218	37/52	66/99	51/92	389/672
Total	277	283	68	126	123	877

Table 29: Number of breeds by number of herds (H)

Number of herds H	Cattle	Sheep	Goats	Pigs	Horses	Total
a) H > 10	65	54	8	14	19	160
No information	212	229	60	112	104	717
b) Number of H:						
< 5	8	14	3	11	7	43
5 - 9	7	5	1	-	2	15
10 - 14	9	7	1	4	3	24
15 - 19	9	9	-	-	1	19
20 - 29	8	8	-	1	2	19
30 - 49	11	4	3	2	2	22
50 - 69	8	5	-	2	-	15
70 -100	5	3	1	2	1	12
>100	14	18	3	5	7	47
No information	198	210	56	99	98	661
Total	277	283	68	126	123	877

Table 30: Number of breeds with cryoconservation of semen or embryos

Cryoconservation	Cattle	Sheep	Goats	Pigs	Horses
a) Semen					
Yes	184	34	16	35	24
No information	93	249	52	91	99
b) Embryos					
Yes	66	6	-	-	2
No information	211	277	68	126	121
Total	277	283	68	126	123

Table 31: Number of breeds by number of males represented in semen storage

Number of males	Cattle	Sheep	Goats	Pigs	Horses	Total
1 - 2	8	6	1	3	5	23
3 - 4	13	5	3	2	6	29
5 - 6	8	4	1	1	4	18
7 - 8	6	1	2	2	-	11
9 - 10	7	3	2	-	1	13
11 - 15	17	1	1	5	1	25
16 - 20	15	1	3	3	1	23
21 - 25	9	1	-	1	1	12
> 25	74	6	3	9	2	94
No information	27	6	-	9	3	45
Total	184	34	16	35	24	293

Table 32: Number of breeds by number of males represented in embryo storage

Number of males	Cattle	Sheep	Goats	Pigs	Horses	Total
1 - 2	7	-	-	-	1	8
3 - 4	4	1	-	-	-	5
5 - 6	9	1	-	-	-	10
7 - 8	7	-	-	-	-	7
9 - 10	4	1	-	-	-	5
11 - 15	4	-	-	-	-	4
16 - 20	4	-	-	-	-	4
21 - 25	-	-	-	-	-	-
> 25	9	-	-	-	-	9
No information	24	3	-	-	1	28
Total	72	6	-	-	2	80

Table 33: Number of breeds by withers height of
           adults (cm)

Height (cm)	Cattle		Horses	
	female	male	female	male
< 100	1	-	-	-
100 - 109	7	-	2	2
110 - 119	20	6	1	1
120 - 129	76	22	5	3
130 - 139	107	68	16	14
140 - 149	43	80	15	15
150 - 159	2	56	32	28
160 - 170	2	11	41	46
> 170	-	-	2	6
No information	19	34	9	8
Total	277		123	

Table 34: Number of breeds by withers height of adults (cm)

Withers height (cm)	Sheep		Goats		Pigs	
	female	male	female	male	female	male
< 40	1	-	-	-	-	-
40 - 49	4	2	-	-	3	-
50 - 59	23	8	1	-	-	3
60 - 69	96	38	23	5	6	1
70 - 79	65	86	32	23	16	10
80 - 89	21	47	6	29	22	11
90 - 99	2	18	-	4	8	18
100 - 110	-	1	-	1	6	13
> 110	-	1	-	-	1	5
No information	71	82	6	6	64	65
Total	283		68		126	

Table 35: Number of breeds by body weight of adults (kg)

Live weight (kg)	Cattle		Horses	
	female	male	female	male
< 250	3	-	4	2
250 - 299	9	-	3	3
300 - 349	6	1	4	1
350 - 399	12	5	9	6
400 - 449	20	6	11	11
450 - 499	32	4	12	6
500 - 549	36	8	16	14
550 - 599	34	3	8	11
600 - 649	41	16	13	8
650 - 699	31	11	1	9
700 - 749	24	16	6	11
750 - 799	8	18	2	1
800 - 849	6	25	3	3
850 - 899	5	17	1	3
900 - 949	2	25	4	5
950 - 999	-	12	-	1
1000 - 1049	1	25	-	2
1050 - 1100	-	33	-	-
> 1100	-	28	-	-
No information	7	24	26	26
Total	277		123	

Table 36: Number of breeds with specific coat colour
(More than one answer per breed is possible)

	Cattle	Sheep	Goats	Pigs
a) Predominantly unicoloured				
Black (b)	29	19	14	12
Grey (g)	23	12	7	2
Blue (bl)	6	4	2	-
Red (r)	61	5	5	11
Brown (br)	55	19	24	2
Yellow/Blond (y)	42	8	2	1
White (w)	19	228	28	64
No information	103	25	14	41
b) Colour combination				
b or bl and other	62	23	18	40
r and other	76	1	8	5
y or br and other	31	16	14	6
g or w and other	118	32	18	37
No information	156	251	44	85
Total	277	283	68	126

Table 37: Number of horse breeds of specific coat colour
            (More than one answer per breed is possible)

A) Horse breeds with only one or predominantly one colour
B) Horse breeds with predominantly more than one colour

	in A+B	in A
Grey	39	9
Light dapple-grey	1	1
Black	35	2
Brown	20	-
Bay	60	7
Chestnut	52	13
Sorrel	6	-
Roan	10	-
Dun	17	2
"Norwegian-" Dun	2	2
Isabelle	4	-
Piebald	5	-
Scewbald	1	-
Any colour	5	
Any colour except scewbald or piebald	6	
Any solid colour	16	
No information		10
Total		123

Table 38: Number of breeds with hair or
           wool classification

Classification	Sheep	Goats
a) Hair	16	55
b) Wool classification		
fine	21	-
medium/crossbred	52	-
coarse/carpet	38	-
mixed	4	-
not specified	106	1
No information	46	12
Total	283	68

Table 39: Number of breeds by number of horns
(More than one answer per breed is
possible)

Number of horns	Cattle	Sheep	Goats
a) Females			
4	–	4	–
2	256	56	59
0	21	224	23
Only knobs	3	5	2
No information	3	11	1
b) Males			
4	–	4	–
2	257	113	58
0	22	177	24
Only knobs	3	5	2
No information	2	4	1
Total	277	283	68

Table 40: Number of breeds by present 1st, 2nd, 3rd main use

Main use	Cattle			Sheep			Goats		
	1st	2nd	3rd	1st	2nd	3rd	1st	2nd	3rd
Milk	146	25	11	48	22	4	42	9	1
Tractive power	7	16	16	–	–	–	–	–	–
Meat	107	136	9	174	63	16	20	36	3
Wool	–	–	–	33	141	48	1	1	–
Fur	–	–	2	1	1	3	–	–	5
Veget. management	1	12	22	12	5	20	2	3	7
Sport, Hobby	3	7	5	4	8	9	1	1	8
Other	7	13	11	6	1	19	–	–	2
No information	6	68	201	5	42	164	2	18	42
Total		277			283			68	

Table 41: Number of breeds by present 1st, 2nd, 3rd main use

Main use	Pigs 1st	2nd	3rd	Horses 1st	2nd	3rd
Milk	-	-	-	-	-	-
Tractive power	-	-	-	15	31	7
Meat	88	8	-	12	9	5
Wool	-	-	-	-	-	-
Fur	-	1	1	-	-	-
Veget. management	-	1	-	1	6	10
Sport, Hobby	2	8	-	85	17	1
Other	32	13	1	6	9	13
No information	4	95	124	4	51	87
Total		126			123	

Table 42: Number of breeds with specific management conditions, 1st and 2nd indication

Management condition	Cattle 1st	2nd	Sheep 1st	2nd	Goats 1st	2nd	Pigs 1st	2nd	Horses 1st	2nd
a) _Type_										
Stationary	248	-	176	-	49	-	96	-	107	-
Transhumant	14	1	33	7	2	2	2	-	4	-
Nomadic	1	-	-	-	-	-	1	-	-	-
No information	14	276	74	276	17	66	27	126	12	123
b) _Housing period (months)_										
No housing	35	-	52	-	9	-	4	-	13	-
< 2	11	9	52	5	4	-	3	-	12	1
2 - 6	98	3	73	2	23	-	4	-	20	1
> 6	91	1	16	1	8	-	10	-	31	2
Total housing	27	3	12	1	7	-	76	-	6	2
No information	15	261	78	274	17	68	29	126	41	117
c) _Feeding conditions_										
Total grazing	22	-	32	-	13	-	2	-	6	-
Grazing+Fodder	100	6	97	6	32	3	26	-	29	2
Mixed	134	40	76	8	20	6	19	4	47	2
Concentrate	9	6	1	2	-	1	26	21	-	1
Total concentr.	-	1	-	-	-	-	24	1	-	-
No information	12	224	77	267	3	58	29	100	41	118
Total		277		283		68		126		123

Table 43: Special characteristics reported for cattle breeds

Characteristics (section D.3 in questionnaire)	Number of breeds
3.1 Quality of product for human nutrition	
Meat: high carcass quality, lean, marbling	31
Milk: high or special protein	14
Milk: colour of fat	8
3.2 Resistance against specific pathogens	
Tuberculosis	8
Leucosis	5
Anaplasmosis	4
Piroplasmosis	2
Brucellosis	2
Pneumonia	2
IBR/IBV	1
Trypanosoma	1
Limax	1
Mastitis	1
Foot and mouth diseases	1
Infections	8
3.3 Resistance against adverse environment	
Hardy, strong constitution	29
Climate: thermotolerance	21
Climate: heat, sunshine, tropical	15
Climate: cold	7
Climate: high rainfall	6
Stress resistant	1
3.4 Fertility	
High fertility and short calving interval	17
Longevity	17
Easy calving	15
Good maternal qualities	5
High twinning frequency	4
3.5 Utilization of by-prod. or marginal land	
Adaptation to wet lands	3
Ability to walk long distances	3
Eats lignified plants, fruits	1
High skin quality, fine leather	1
3.6 Others	
Hardy claws and good legs	18
Handling: ease/docile	6
Handling: difficult/aggressive	2
Quickness in learning	1

Table 44: Special characteristics reported for sheep breeds

Characteristics (section D.3 in questionnaire)	Number of breeds

3.1 Quality of product for human nutrition
Milk: special cheeses	24
Meat: game-like taste	5

3.2 Resistance against specific pathogens
Resistant against foot rot	6
High resistance against gastro-intestinal parasites	2
High resistance against parasites	1
Resistant against fasciolosis	1
Resistant against ovine mites	1

3.3 Resistance against adverse environment
Good for transhumance, transhumance even in winter	14
Good for poor vegetation	10
Climate: arid, dry	12
Climate: hot	8
Climate: humid	7
Climate: cold	6
Climate: resistant against rain	5

3.4 Fertility
Twinning	18
Inter- or aseasonal breeding	11
Long mating season	9
Seasonal breeding	5
Long sexual activity	4
More than 1 lambing per year	4
Litter size greater than 1	15
Low fertility, 1 lamb per year maximum	2

3.5 Utilization of by-prod. or marginal land
Mountains, steep zones	36
Difficult soils, very special soils (heath, dikes ...)	12
Marginal lands, pure pastures	11
Semi-desert	6
Humid soils, swamp, moorland	4
Arid soils	5
Marshy land	3
Diet of seaweed	1

3.6 Others
Able to walk long distances	11
Good mothering	4
Lambing successfully by frost	1
Gives much or special (curly, coloured) wool	14
4 teats in 20% of ewes	1

Table 45: Special characteristics reported for goat breeds

Characteristics (section D.3 in questionnaire)	Number of breeds
3.1 Quality of product for human nutrition	
Milk: used for allergy diet, used as medicine	7
Milk: special cheeses	4
3.2 Resistance against specific pathogens	
CAE-carrier without outbreak of the illness	1
CAE rehabilitated	1
3.3 Resistance against adverse environment	
Climate: semi-mountainous	13
Climate: mountainous	6
Climate: hot, sun	7
Very hardy, extreme climate conditions	4
Climate: humid	2
Climate: Mediterranean	2
Climate: cold	1
3.4 Fertility	
Twinning, more than 1 kid per year	6
High fertility, high prolificacy	5
Inter- and aseasonal breeding	2
Seasonal breeding	2
Reproduction up to high age	1
3.5 Utilization of by-prod. or marginal land	
Mountains, steep zones	10
Karst soils	5
Steppes	1
3.6 Others	
Robust, rustic, good for extensive systems	4
Long useful life	3
Able to walk long distances	2
Very good udder	2
Globular udder	1
Hard feet	2
Live with deer	1
Temperament with nerve	1

126

Table 46: Special characteristics reported for pig breeds

Characteristics (section D.3 in questionnaire)	Number of breeds
3.1 Quality of product for human nutrition	
Meat quality: "good", "high"	17
High fat content, extreme backfat thickness	7
High intramuscular fat content	3
Low frequency of halothan gene, little PSE	3
High PSE frequency	3
Meat quality: unsatisfactory	1
3.2 Resistance against specific pathogens	
Free of halothan gene	6
Low frequency of halothan gene	2
Stress resistant	3
Carrier of halothan gene	2
3.3 Resistance against adverse environment	
Climate: warm, heat	6
Climate: extreme	4
Adapted to poor feeding	4
Climate: cold	1
Climate: harsh North-Siberian	1
Good for outdoor management systems	2
3.4 Fertility	
High fertility, high prolificacy	12
Precocity	2
High and long fertility	1
Low fertility	1
Vitality	1
Piglet viability	1
3.5 Utilization of by-prod. or marginal land	
Adapted to extensive outdoor management systems	5
Adapted to rough feeding, fruits	1
Adapted to grazing in dehesa land	2
Adapted to wet land and marsh	2
3.6 Others	
No iron injection necessary	1
Good for extensive conditions	3
Hardiness, strong constitution	3
Sow hardiness	1
Halothane negative	1
Long body	1

Table 47: Special characteristics reported for horse breeds

Characteristics (section D.3 in questionnaire)	Number of breeds
3.1 Quality of product for human nutrition	
Special (high) meat quality	2
3.2 Resistance against specific pathogens	
Resistant against piroplasmosis	1
3.3 Resistance against adverse environment	
Climate: harsh, hardy, extreme	11
Climate: mountainous	3
Climate: northern seaside	1
Climate: cold	1
Climate: warm	1
Climate: windy and rainy	1
3.4 Fertility	
Reproductive up to high age	4
High prolificacy	2
Aseasonal breeding	1
Late maturity	1
3.5 Utilization of by-prod. or marginal land	
Steep zones, mountains	8
Marginal land, rough vegetation	4
Marshy land, humid soils	1
Arid soils	1
3.6 Others	
Living feral	3
Excellent timber horse	1
Very moveable	1
Hard hoofs	1
Surefooted	2
Good-natured	2
Very willing to work	1

5. Presentation of individual breeds

5.1 Explanation of structure of presentation

In this chapter each breed is presented - within country and species - with its main information which should be important for characterisation and for possible use of the breed and for decisions on conservation. In order to save space this information is presented in a structured form in bold letters in lines numbered from 1 to 24 as follows:

Line   Information

1   a) Local breed name
     b) EN = Entry number of breed, see page 1

2   a) International breed name; see page 1
     b) Main location of breed within country

3   a) Name of breed society or organisation looking after breed
     b) HB = Herdbook established:
       - (year)   = established in given year
       - "Yes"   = established, year is unknown
       - "miss"   = not established or no information

4   Address of breed society or organisation
     a) Town with postcode within country
     b) Street and number

5+6 Origin and development of breed (maximal 2 lines):
     a) "autochthon" or "composite of ..." (breeds, EN) or "imported as breed from...-"(breed, EN, country)
     b) If incrossing: "Incrossing since (year), from (breed)..., from (country)"

7   a) Number of breeding animals, reported in (year)
     b) Number of males/and number of females or total number of males and females or if no information: "miss"
     c) HB = number of females registered in herd book
     d) Trend of number of breeding animals : "decreasing", or "stable" or "increasing"
     e) Percentage of females mated pure
     f) Ne = effective population size, computed from number of males and females, see chapter 4.1.2

8   a) Withers height of adults, in cm: male, female
     b) Live weight of adults, in kg: male, female
     c) Number of herds in which breed is kept: number or " > 10" or "miss"
     d) AI = artificial insemination is used for reproduction: "Yes" or "miss"

9   Coat colour of animals
     a) Unicoloured: colour(s)
     b) Colour combination(s): colours

10   Exterior peculiarities of breed: e.g. number of horns in males/females

11   Main use of breed: (1) first, (2) second, (3) third ranking

12   Special abilities of breed .... (maximal one line)

13   Relative performance in specific traits compared with standard breed: International name and EN of standard breed

14   Absolute performance of breed is higher in given traits .. *)

15   Absolute performance of breed is equal in given traits .. *)

16   Absolute performance of breed is lower in given traits .. *)
      *) = ranked within each class of deviations

17   Conditions in
      a) management
      b) housing: number of months housing per year
      c) specific environment

18   Conservation programmes are under way:
      a) live animal conservation: "Yes" or "miss"
      b) Cryoconservation of semen: "Yes" or (number of males represented in conserved semen) or "miss"
      c) cryoconservation of embryos: "Yes" or (number of sires/number of dams represented in conserved embryos) or "miss"

19   Status of endangeredness of breed (see section 4.1.2)
      a) Status "critically endangered", "endangered", minimally endangered", "potentically endangered", "normal"
      b) Watch: criteria relevant to endangered status, for example: number of males, number of females in herdbook, trend, number of herds.

20   Number of group and subgroup of similar breeds within species, page number in chapter 4.3

21-24 Up to four similar breeds with local breed name, entry number, country and status of endangeredness are presented for possible cooperation with similar breeds, especially with the two least endangered and the two highest endangered similar breeds.

For countries and local breed names see also explanation on page 22.

5.2 Breed presentation by country and species

ARMENIA   **PIGS**

```
 1 - Lesogornaya porodnaya gruppa                        EN   966
 2   Forest Mountain; Forest-Mountain, Armenian SSR
 3   Food and Agriculture Organisation of the UN         HB:miss
 4   Rome 00100, Via delle Terme di Caracalla
 5 - Composite of local pigs of Armenia, Large White, Mangalica
 7   Numbers 1980: 16/105; HB: miss; decreasing; 100 %; Ne = 33
 8 - Height: miss/miss cm; Weight: 260/166 kg; Herd number: miss; AI:miss
 9   Colour: Uni black, grey
10   Pecularity: semi-lopped ears
11 - Main use: (1) general purpose,(2) miss,(3) miss
12   Spec. abilities: high meat quality, strong constitution
13   Performance compared with STB Large White 951:
14     higher: meat quality
15     equal: muscularity
16     lower:  litter size, feed conversion rate, daily gain
17 - Management: stationary; housing: miss m.;
18 - Conservation progr.: live animals: miss;Semen: miss;Embryos: miss
19   Status: critically endang.;Watch: ♂♂,HB♀♀,trend!
20 - Similar breeds (see group 7 on page 104)    EN  Country Status
21   Corse                                       915   F      endanger.
22   Kakhetinskaya                               948   GO     min. end.
```

AUSTRIA   **CATTLE**

```
 1 - Fleckvieh                                           EN    88
 2   Simmental; country-wide
 3   Arbeitsgemeinschaft Österreichischer Fleckviehzüchter   HB:1894
 4   Ried i. I. 4910, Volksfestplatz 1
 5 - Imported as breed from country Switzerland
 7   Numbers 1992: 2479/ miss; HB: 194557; increasing; 99 %; Ne = 9791
 8 - Height: 150/145 cm; Weight: 1250/800 kg; Herd number: 17151; AI: Yes
 9   Colour: Combination red, yellow, white
10   Pecularity: white head
11 - Main use: (1) milk,(2) meat,(3) miss
12   Spec. abilities: high protein content, hot climate adapted
13   Performance compared with STB Simmental 88:
14     higher: Breed is used
15     equal:  as standard breed,
16     lower:  no comparison possible.
17 - Management: stationary; housing: 2-6 m.; for extensive agriculture
18 - Conservation progr.: live animals: miss;Semen: Yes;Embryos: miss
19   Status: normal
20 - Similar breeds (see group 3/2 on page 77)   EN  Country Status
21   Ceske strakate                              61    CZ     crit.end.
22   Simentalska                                 237   PL     min. end.
23   Race d'Abondance                            213   F      normal
24   Montbeliard                                 176   F      normal
```

1 - Kärntner Blondvieh   EN   139
2   Austrian Blond; Kärnten
3   Kammer für Land- und Forstwirtschaft in Kärnten   HB:miss
4   Klagenfurt 9020, Museumgasse 5
5 - Composite of Keltenrinder, mitteldeutsches Bergvieh
6   Incrossing since 1950 from Fleckvieh 88 Austria
7   Numbers 1993: 5/80; HB: miss; increasing; 70 %; Ne = 8
8 - Height: 141/131 cm; Weight: 825/550 kg; Herd number: 19; AI: Yes
9   Colour: Uni yellow, white, blond
10 Pecularity: miss
11 - Main use: (1) meat,(2) milk,(3) vegetation management
12 Spec. abilities: excellent meat quality, fertility, stayability
13 Performance compared with STB Simmental 88:
14   higher: age of sexual maturity
15   equal: % fat, % protein, calving ease, calving interval
16   lower: milk yield, muscularity, daily gain
17 - Management: stationary; housing: 2-6 m.;
18 - Conservation progr.: live animals: Yes;Semen: 2;Embryos: miss
19 Status: critically endang.;Watch: ♂♂,HB♀♀,%pure,%incross!
20 - Similar breeds (see group 8/2 on page 81)   EN Country Status
21 Murbodner   178   A   crit.end.
22 Waldviertler Vieh   268   A   crit.end.
23 Murnau-Werdenfelser   180   D   endanger.
24 Gelbes Frankenvieh   100   D   normal

1 - Murbodner   EN   178
2   Murboden; Steiermark
3   Gelbviehzuchtgenossenschaft Steiermark   HB:miss
4   Waldbach, Schrimpf 21
5 - Composite of Bergschecken, Mürztaler Schlag
6   Incrossing since 1950 from Gelbvieh, Frankenvieh
7   Numbers 1993: 10/130; HB: miss; increasing; 50 %; Ne = 19
8 - Height: 141/135 cm; Weight: 950/600 kg; Herd number: 20; AI: Yes
9   Colour: Uni red, yellow
10 Pecularity: slate-blue muzzle with white surrounding
11 - Main use: (1) meat,(2) milk,(3) vegetation management
12 Spec. abilities: stayability
13 Performance compared with STB Simmental 88:
14   higher: miss
15   equal: muscularity, daily gain, % fat, % protein, calving ease
16   lower: milk yield
17 - Management: stationary; housing: 2-6 m.;
18 - Conservation progr.: live animals: Yes;Semen: 8;Embryos: 10/miss
19 Status: critically endang.;Watch: ♂♂,HB♀♀,%pure,%incross!
20 - Similar breeds (see group 8/2 on page 81)   EN Country Status
21 Kärntner Blondvieh   139   A   crit.end.
22 Waldviertler Vieh   268   A   crit.end.
23 Murnau-Werdenfelser   180   D   endanger.
24 Gelbes Frankenvieh   100   D   normal

```
 1 - Österreichisches Braunvieh                                    EN  190
 2   Austrian Brown; Vorarlberg, Tirol, Steiermark
 3   Arbeitsgemeinschaft österreichischer Braunviehzuchtverbände  HB:1990
 4   Innsbruck 6021, Brixner Strasse 1
 5 - Composite of Montafoner, Allgäuer Rind, Lechtaler, Oberinntaler
 6   Incrossing since 1950 from Braunvieh 40 Switzerland
 7   Numbers 1992: 1000/ miss; HB: 74437; stable; 100 %; Ne = 3947
 8 - Height: 155/140 cm; Weight: 1100/650 kg; Herd number: 9905; AI: Yes
 9   Colour: Uni brown
10   Pecularity: miss
11 - Main use: (1) milk,(2) meat,(3) vegetation management
12   Spec. abilities: long breeding season, for hot and cold climate
13   Performance compared with STB Holstein-Friesian:
14     higher: muscularity, % fat, % protein, handling ease
15     equal:  daily gain,calving ease,calving interval,age of sex. mat.
16     lower:  milk yield
17 - Management: stationary; housing: > 6 m.; mountain, semi desert
18 - Conservation progr.: live animals: miss;Semen: 350;Embryos: miss
19   Status: normal;            Watch: %incross!
```

20 - <u>Similar breeds</u> (see group 5/1 on page 79)	EN	Country	Status
21 Original Allgäuer Braunvieh	189	D	crit.end.
22 Agerolese	2	I	crit.end.
23 Bruna	46	I	normal
24 Aubrac	14	F	normal

```
 1 - Pinzgauer                                                     EN  202
 2   Pinzgau; Pinzgau (Salzburg)
 3   Organisation of Cattle Breeders in Maishofen,               HB:1921
 4   Maishofen 5751
 5 - Composite of Tiroler Rind (uni brown), Bergscheckenrind/spotted
 6   Incrossing since 1950 from Red Friesian Canada, USA
 7   Numbers 1992: 342/ miss; HB: 12651; decreasing; 25 %; Ne = 1332
 8 - Height: 147/138 cm; Weight: 1100/650 kg; Herd number: 1338; AI: Yes
 9   Colour: Combination brown, white
10   Pecularity: brown head, white stripe on back and belly
11 - Main use: (1) milk,(2) meat,(3) miss
12   Spec. abilities: calving ease, hard hoofs
13   Performance compared with STB Simmental 88:
14     higher: calving ease, handling ease, milkability
15     equal:  milk yield, calving interval, age of sexual maturity
16     lower:  muscularity, daily gain, % fat, % protein, calf mortality
17 - Management: stationary; housing: > 6 m.; mountainous country
18 - Conservation progr.: live animals: Yes;Semen: 80;Embryos: miss
19   Status: potential. endang.;Watch: trend,%pure,%incross!
```

20 - <u>Similar breeds</u> (see group 3/4 on page 77)	EN	Country	Status
21 Pustertaler Schecken	210	D	crit.end.
22 Pinzgauer	200	I	crit.end.
23 Pinzgauer	203	D	pot. end.
24 Slovenske pinzgavske	243	SK	normal

```
 1 - Tiroler Grauvieh                                          EN  256
 2   Tyrol Grey; Tirol
 3   Tiroler Grauviehzuchtverband                             HB:1926
 4   Innsbruck 6020, Brixner Strasse 1
 5 - Composite of native breed, Lechtaler, Wipptaler, Oberinntaler
 7   Numbers 1993: 40/ miss; HB: 3389; decreasing; 100 %; Ne = 158
 8 - Height: 130/125 cm; Weight: 950/550 kg; Herd number: 1054; AI: Yes
 9   Colour: Uni grey
10   Pecularity: males have white line on the dorsum
11 - Main use: (1) milk,(2) meat,(3) vegetation management
12   Spec. abilities: Kappa Kasein Type BB, heat, cold
13   Performance compared with STB Simmental 88:
14     higher: calving ease, calving rate
15     equal: muscularity, daily gain, %fat, %protein, calving interval
16     lower: milk yield, calf mortality
17 - Management: stationary; housing: > 6 m.; mountain
18 - Conservation progr.: live animals: miss;Semen: 125;Embryos: 1/1
19   Status: potential. endang.;Watch: trend!
```

20 - Similar breeds (see group 6/2 on page 81)	EN	Country	Status
21 Gascon Areole	99	F	crit.end.
22 Garfagnina	97	I	crit.end.
23 Grigia Alpina	105	I	normal
24 Gascon	98	F	normal

```
 1 - Tuxer                                                     EN  259
 2   Tux; Tirol (Zillertal)
 3   Landwirtschaftskammer für Tirol                          HB:miss
 4   Innsbruck 6020, Brixnerstr. 1
 5 - Autochthon, possibly originating from Herens 83 Switzerland
 7   Numbers 1993: 10/90; HB: miss; increasing; 80 %; Ne = 18
 8 - Height: 140/125 cm; Weight: 850/575 kg; Herd number: 28; AI: Yes
 9   Colour: Uni black, red, brown
10   Pecularity: short head, white at pelvis, belly, udder and tail
11 - Main use: (1) milk,(2) meat,(3) vegetation management
12   Spec. abilities: stayability
13   Performance compared with STB Simmental 88:
14     higher: age of sexual maturity
15     equal: % fat,% protein,calving ease,calving interval,calf mort.
16     lower: milk yield, daily gain, muscularity, handling ease
17 - Management: stationary; housing: 2-6 m.; mountainous country
18 - Conservation progr.: live animals: Yes;Semen: 10;Embryos: 15/miss
19   Status: critically endang.;Watch: ♂♂,HB♀♀,%pure!
```

20 - Similar breeds (see group 1/6 on page 76)	EN	Country	Status
21 Pohjoissuomenkarja	207	SF	crit.end.
22 Sidet tronderfe og nordland	235	N	crit.end.
23 Berrenda negra andaluza	29	E	min. end.
24 Gruzinskii gornyi skot	107	GO	normal

```
 1 - Waldviertler Vieh                                        EN  268
 2   Waldviertel; Niederösterreich
 3   ÖNGENE                                                   HB:1939
 4   Wien 1060, Gumpendorferstraße 15/II/2
 5 - Composite of Keltenrinder, mitteldeutsches Bergvieh; incrossing
 6   since 1950 from Glan-Donnersberger 101 Germany, Gelbvieh 100 Germany
 7   Numbers 1993: 8/40; HB: miss; increasing; 40 %; Ne = 12
 8 - Height: 140/132 cm; Weight: 900/575 kg; Herd number: 27; AI: Yes
 9   Colour: Uni red, brown, white, blond
10   Pecularity: wax coloured horns, flesh coloured muzzle
11 - Main use: (1) milk,(2) meat,(3) vegetation management
12   Spec. abilities: meat quality, hard hoofs, high stayability
13   Performance compared with STB Simmental 88:
14     higher: calving ease, age of sexual maturity
15     equal: % fat, % protein, calving interval, handling ease
16     lower: milk yield, daily gain, muscularity, calf mortality
17 - Management: stationary; housing: > 6 m.; rough climate
18 - Conservation progr.: live animals: Yes;Semen: 8;Embryos: 10/miss
19   Status: critically endang.;Watch: ♂♂,HB♀♀,%pure,%incross!
```

20 - Similar breeds (see group 8/2 on page 81)	EN	Country	Status
21 Kärntner Blondvieh	139	A	crit.end.
22 Murbodner	178	A	crit.end.
23 Murnau-Werdenfelser	180	D	endanger.
24 Gelbes Frankenvieh	100	D	normal

```
 1 - Kärntner Brillenschaf, Seeländer Schaf                  EN  521
 2   Carinthian; Kärnten
 3   Verein zur Förderung alter österreichischer Haustierrassen   HB:1988
 4   Klagenfurt 9020, Museumgasse 5
 5 - Composite of local breed, Paduaner, Bergamasca
 7   Numbers 1993: 19/162; HB: miss; increasing; 100 %; Ne = 45
 8 - Height: 75/65 cm; Weight: 85/65 kg; Herd number: 17; AI: miss
 9   Colour: Uni white, some uni black
10   Pecularity: horns 0/0; black spots around eyes and black ears
11 - Main use: (1) meat,(2) vegetation management,(3) wool
12   Spec. abilities: meat quality, game-like taste, hardy
13   Performance compared with STB German Merino 550:
14     higher: wool or fiber thickness
15     equal: carcass leanness, litter size, milk yield, wool yield
16     lower: age of sex. matur.,muscularity,daily gain,lambing interval
17 - Management: stationary; housing: 2-6 m.; mountainous country
18 - Conservation progr.: live animals: miss;Semen: 5;Embryos: miss
19   Status: endangered;        Watch: ♂♂,HB♀♀!
```

20 - Similar breeds (see group 7/2 on page 91)	EN	Country	Status
21 Braunes Bergschaf	431	D	crit.end.
22 Istriana	516	I	crit.end.
23 Bergamasca	415	I	normal
24 Weißes Bergschaf	416	D	normal

```
 1 - Norisches Kaltblut                                          EN   788
 2   Noric; Salzburg, Kärnten
 3   Arbeitsgemeinschaft Norischer Pferdezuchtverbände          HB:1898
 4   Österreichs, Maishofen 5751
 5 - Composite of heavy Roman war horses from Tessalien and
 6   autochthon varieties
 7   Numbers 1986: 110/6900; HB: 3000; decreasing; miss %; Ne = 424
 8 - Height: 157/154 cm; Weight: 800/700 kg; Herd number: miss; AI: miss
 9   Colour: usually chestnut, bay or brown
10   Pecularity:heavy head with convex profile
11 - Main use: (1) tractive power,(2) sport/hobby,(3) vegetation managem.
12   Spec. abilities: miss
13   Performance compared with STB Halfbred:
14     higher: pulling power, handling ease, daily gain
15     equal:  fertility
16     lower:  adaptability in dressage, jumping and in riding
17 - Management: stationary; housing: 2-6 m.;
18 - Conservation progr.: live animals: miss;Semen: 3;Embryos: miss
19   Status: normal;              Watch: trend!
```

```
20 - Similar breeds (see group 4/3 on page 110)   EN   Country Status
21   Cavallo Norico                               722   I      crit.end.
22   Schwarzwälder Füchse                         800   D      min. end.
23   Süddeutsches Kaltblut                        810   D      normal
```

```
 1 - Vollblutaraber                                              EN   815
 2   Arab; country-wide
 3   Verband der Vollblutaraberzüchter Österreichs              HB:1973
 4   Grubgütl 5302, Wankham 7
 5 - Imported as breed from Germany, Egypt, USA, Polen, USSR
 7   Numbers 1992: 83/289; HB: miss; increasing; 100 %; Ne = 258
 8 - Height: 155/155 cm; Weight: 450/450 kg; Herd number: miss; AI: miss
 9   Colour: grey, chestnut or bay
10   Pecularity: long fine mane and tail
11 - Main use: (1) sport/hobby,(2) miss,(3) miss
12   Spec. abilities: hardy
13   Performance compared with STB Arab 815:
14     higher: Breed is used
15     equal:  as standard breed,
16     lower:  no comparison possible.
17 - Management: stationary; housing: 12 m.; staying power
18 - Conservation progr.: live animals: Yes;Semen: miss;Embryos: miss
19   Status: normal;              Watch: HB♀♀!
```

```
20 - Similar breeds (see group 1 on page 108)     EN   Country Status
21   Arabialainen                                 706   SF     crit.end.
22   Täysverinen                                  811   SF     crit.end.
23   Arab                                         703   F      normal
24   Anglo-Arab                                   702   F      normal
```

```
 1 - Blanc Bleu Belge                                              EN   33
 2   Belgian Blue; country-wide
 3   Herd-Book de la race Blanc Bleu Belge                         HB:1993
 4   Ciney 5590, rue des Champs Elysees 4
 5 - Autochthon race de Moyenne et Haute Belgique
 7   Numbers 1991: 3500/529129; HB: 100518; increasing; 100 %; Ne = 13529
 8 - Height: 148/132 cm; Weight: 1200/700 kg; Herd number: miss; AI: Yes
 9   Colour: Combination black, blue, white
10   Pecularity: double musceling lumbar region
11 - Main use: (1) meat,(2) milk,(3) bulls for crossbreeding
12   Spec. abilities: miss
13   Performance compared with STB Charolais:
14     higher: muscularity, milk yield, daily gain, age of sex. maturity
15     equal:  calving interval, calf mortality
16     lower:  calving ease, calving rate
17 - Management: stationary; housing: 2-6 m.;
18 - Conservation progr.: live animals: miss;Semen: 400;Embryos: 100/1000
19   Status: normal
```

20 - Similar breeds (see group 7 on page 81)	EN	Country	Status
21 Belgian Blue	25	IRL	pot. end.
22 Blanc-Bleu-Belge	35	F	normal
23 Belgian Blue	26	GB	normal
24 Bleue du Nord	36	F	normal

```
 1 - Pie-Noire-Holstein                                           EN   198
 2   Holstein; Flandre - Wallone
 3   Herdbook Pie Noir-Holstein de Belgique                        HB:1973
 4   Bruxelles 1030, Avenue Suffrage Universel 49
 5 - Autochthon Pie-Rouge local; incrossing since 1950 from
 6   Holstein USA-Canada, 209 France, 277 Netherlands
 7   Numbers 1991: 25/240647; HB: 113319; decreasing; 100 %; Ne = 100
 8 - Height: 128/141 cm; Weight: 441/700 kg; Herd number: miss; AI: Yes
 9   Colour: Combination black, white
10   Pecularity: miss
11 - Main use: (1) milk,(2) miss,(3) miss
12   Spec. abilities: miss
13   Performance compared with STB Holstein 198:
14     higher: Breed is used
15     equal:  as standard breed,
16     lower:  no comparison possible.
17 - Management: stationary; housing: > 6 m.;
18 - Conservation progr.: live animals: miss;Semen: Yes;Embryos: miss
19   Status: normal;              Watch: %incross!
```

20 - Similar breeds (see group 1/1 on page 75)	EN	Country	Status
21 Sortbroget Dansk Malkekvaeg	245	DK	pot. end.
22 Nizinna-Czarno-Biala	185	PL	pot. end.
23 Deutsche Schwarzbunte	75	D	normal
24 Prim' Holstein	209	F	normal

```
 1 - Pie-Rouge, Roodbont                                        EN   199
 2   Belgian Red Pied; Provinces of Amvers, Limbourg and Liege
 3   Herd-Book Pie Rouge de Belgiqueu Belge                     HB:1973
 4   Bruxelles 1030, Avenue Suffrage Universel 49
 5 - Autochthon local Pie-Rouge; imported as breed from NL and Germany;
 6   Incross. since 1950 from Pie-Rouge 161 NL, Rotbunte 74 D, Red HF USA
 7   Numbers 1991: 150/211886; HB: 70982; decreasing; 60 %; Ne = 599
 8 - Height: 170/145 cm; Weight: 1000/700 kg; Herd number: miss; AI: Yes
 9   Colour: Combination red, white
10   Pecularity: miss
11 - Main use: (1) milk,(2) meat,(3) miss
12   Spec. abilities: miss
13   Performance compared with STB Holstein 198:
14     higher: muscularity, daily gain, % protein
15     equal: % fat,calving ease,calving interval,age of sexual maturity
16     lower:  milk yield
17 - Management: stationary; housing: > 6 m.;
18 - Conservation progr.: live animals: miss;Semen: Yes;Embryos: miss
19   Status: normal;             Watch: %pure,%incross!
```

20 - Similar breeds (see group 3/1 on page 76)	EN	Country	Status
21 Blanc-Rouge de Belgique	273	B	pot. end.
22 Ferrandais	85	F	pot. end.
23 Maine-Anjou	163	F	normal
24 Dansk Rodbroget Kvaeg	73	DK	normal

```
 1 - Rood Ras van Belgie                                        EN   224
 2   Belgian Red; western Flandre
 3   Roodvee Riindveestamboek                                   HB:1924
 4   Loppem Zedelgem 8210, Torhoutsesteenweg 48
 5 - Autochthon breed
 6   Incrossing since 1950 from Red Danish 222 Denmark
 7   Numbers 1991: 65/38953; HB: 8000; decreasing; 40 %; Ne = 258
 8 - Height: 150/140 cm; Weight: 1200/650 kg; Herd number: miss; AI: Yes
 9   Colour: Uni red, some combination red and white
10   Pecularity: miss
11 - Main use: (1) milk,(2) meat,(3) miss
12   Spec. abilities: miss
13   Performance compared with STB Simmental:
14     higher: milk yield
15     equal: muscularity, daily gain, % fat, % protein, calving ease
16     lower: miss
17 - Management: stationary; housing: miss m.;
18 - Conservation progr.: live animals: Yes;Semen: 50;Embryos: miss
19   Status: normal;             Watch: trend,%pure,%incross!
```

20 - Similar breeds (see group 4/3 on page 78)	EN	Country	Status
21 Donnersberger Rotvieh	101	D	crit.end.
22 Harzer Rotvieh	109	D	crit.end.
23 Czerwona Polska	72	PL	normal
24 Rod Dansk Malkerace	222	DK	normal

CATTLE

```
1 - Witrood Ras Van Belgie, Blanc-Rouge de Belgique          EN  273
2   Belgian White-and-Red; eastern Flandre
3   Herdbook de la race Blanc Rouge                          HB:1973
4   Oosterzele-Scheldewindeke 9860, Van Thorenburghlaan 14
5 - Old autochthon breed
6   Incrossing since 1950 from Holstein Red USA, Ayrshire 247 Finland
7   Numbers 1991: 575/95978; HB: 57266; decreasing; 92 %; Ne = 2277
8 - Height: 155/138 cm; Weight: 1300/750 kg; Herd number: miss; AI: Yes
9   Colour: Combination red, white
10  Pecularity: miss
11 - Main use: (1) milk,(2) meat,(3) miss
12  Spec. abilities: miss
13  Performance compared with STB Holstein 198:
14     higher: muscularity, daily gain, % fat, % protein, milkability
15     equal:  calving ease, calving interval, age of sexual maturity
16     lower:  milk yield
17 - Management: stationary; housing: 2-6 m.;
18 - Conservation progr.: live animals: miss;Semen: 120;Embryos: miss
19  Status: potential. endang.;Watch: trend,%pure,%incross!
```

20 - Similar breeds (see group 3/1 on page 76)	EN	Country	Status
21 Ferrandais	85	F	pot. end.
22 Deutsche Rotbunte	74	D	pot. end.
23 Dansk Rodbroget Kvaeg	73	DK	normal
24 Pie-Rouge	199	B	normal

SHEEP

```
1 - Mouton Laitier Belge                                     EN  561
2   Belgian Milk Sheep; country-wide
3   Federation Bationaledes Eleveurs de Chevres et           HB:miss
4   Moutons Laitiers; Beersel 1650, Kasteelstraat 40
5 - Autochthon
7   Numbers 1991: 19/ miss; HB: 114; stable; 100 %; Ne = 42
8 - Height: 95/85 cm; Weight: 113/75 kg; Herd number: miss; AI: miss
9   Colour: Uni white
10  Pecularity: horns 0/0, long thin tail without wool
11 - Main use: (1) milk,(2) meat,(3) wool
12  Spec. abilities: miss
13  Performance compared with STB miss:
14     higher: miss
15     equal:. miss
16     lower:  miss
17 - Management: stationary; housing: 2-6 m.;
18 - Conservation progr.: live animals: miss;Semen: miss;Embryos: miss
19  Status: minimally endang.; Watch: HB♀♀,herds!
```

20 - Similar breeds (see group 5/1 on page 89)	EN	Country	Status
21 Ostfriesisches Milchschaf	572	D*	normal
22 Ostfriesisches Milchschaf	573	D	normal
23 British Milksheep	438	GB	normal
24 Friese Melkschaap	493	NL	normal

```
 1 - Blanche                                                    EN   308
 2   Campine; northern Belgium
 3   Federation Bationaledes Eleveurs de Chevres et            HB:1930
 4   Moutons Laitiers; Beersel 1650, Kasteelstraat 40
 5 - Imported as breed from Switzerland
 7   Numbers 1991: 46/ miss; HB: 207; miss; 100 %; Ne = 151
 8 - Height: 75/65 cm; Weight: 60/60 kg; Herd number: miss; AI: miss
 9   Colour: Uni white
10   Pecularity: horns 2/2
11 - Main use: (1) milk,(2) meat,(3) fur
12   Spec. abilities: miss
13   Performance compared with STB Toggenburg 361:
14     higher: miss
15     equal: muscularity, daily gain, carcass leanness, litter size
16     lower: miss
17 - Management: stationary; housing: 2-6 m.;
18 - Conservation progr.: live animals: miss;Semen: miss;Embryos: miss
19   Status: potential. endang.;Watch: HB♀♀,herds,trend!
20 - Similar breeds (see group 1 on page 97)       EN  Country Status
21   Irish Goat                                    336  IRL   min. end.
22   Bila kratkosrsta                              306  CS    normal
23   Weiße Deutsche Edelziege                      367  D     normal
24   Gessenay                                      350  F     normal
```

```
 1 - Chamoisee                                                  EN   317
 2   Belgian Fawn
 3   Federation Bationaledes Eleveurs de Chevres et            HB:1930
 4   Moutons Laitiers; Beersel 1650, Kasteelstraat 40
 5 - Autochthon Chamois Coloured
 7   Numbers 1991: 37/ miss; HB: 138; miss; 100 %; Ne = 117
 8 - Height: 77/69 cm; Weight: 65/60 kg; Herd number: miss; AI: miss
 9   Colour: Uni brown, some combinations black and brown
10   Pecularity: horns 2/2
11 - Main use: (1) milk,(2) meat,(3) fur
12   Spec. abilities: miss
13   Performance compared with STB Toggenburg 361:
14     higher: miss
15     equal: muscularity, daily gain, carcass leanness, litter size
16     lower: miss
17 - Management: stationary; housing: 2-6 m.;
18 - Conservation progr.: live animals: miss;Semen: miss;Embryos: miss
19   Status: potential. endang.;Watch: HB♀♀,herds,trend!
20 - Similar breeds (see group 2 on page 97)       EN  Country Status
21   Erzgebirgsziege                               330  D     crit.end.
22   Hneda kratkosrsta                             334  CS    min. end.
23   Bunte Deutsche Edelziege                      310  D     normal
24   Alpine                                        301  F     normal
```

BELGIUM   GOATS

```
 1 - Toggenburger                                          EN  361
 2   Toggenburg
 3   Federation Bationaledes Eleveurs de Chevres et        HB:1930
 4   Moutons Laitiers; Beersel 1650, Kasteelstraat 40
 5 - Imported as breed from Switzerland
 7   Numbers 1991: 18/ miss; HB: 70; miss; 100 %; Ne = 34
 8 - Height: 73/65 cm; Weight: miss/miss kg; Herd number: miss; AI: miss
 9   Colour: Uni brown, combinations brown and white
10   Pecularity: horns 2/2
11 - Main use: (1) milk,(2) meat,(3) fur
12   Spec. abilities: miss
13   Performance compared with STB Campine 308:
14     higher: miss
15     equal:  muscularity, daily gain, carcass leanness, litter size
16     lower:  miss
17 - Management: stationary; housing: 2-6 m.;
18 - Conservation progr.: live animals: miss;Semen: miss;Embryos: miss
19   Status: endangered;        Watch: HB♀♀,herds,trend!
```

20 -	Similar breeds (see group 3 on page 97)	EN	Country	Status
21	Thüringer Waldziege	360	D	crit.end.
22	Poitevin	345	F	min. end.
23	Pure Toggenburg	346	GB	normal
24	Toggenburger	362	CH	normal

BELGIUM   PIGS

```
 1 - Belgisch Landvarken                                   EN  906
 2   Belgian Landrace
 3   Federation Nationale des Eleveurs de Porcs de Belgique  HB:1920
 4   Bruxelles 1030, Avenue Suffrage Universel 49
 5 - Autochthon local breed
 7   Numbers 1991: 4000/490000; HB: 18000; stable; 75 %; Ne = 13091
 8 - Height: 110/95 cm; Weight: 340/320 kg; Herd number: 399; AI: miss
 9   Colour: Uni white
10   Pecularity: lop ears
11 - Main use: (1) meat,(2) miss,(3) miss
12   Spec. abilities: lean meat
13   Performance compared with STB Pietrain 988:
14     higher: litter size, daily gain, meat quality, age of sex. matur.
15     equal:  feed conversion rate, farrowing interval, piglet mortality
16     lower:  % lean, muscularity
17 - Management: stationary; housing: 12 m.;
18 - Conservation progr.: live animals: miss;Semen: miss;Embryos: miss
19   Status: normal;           Watch: %pure!
```

20 -	Similar breeds (see group 2/1 on page 101)	EN	Country	Status
21	Belgische Landrasse	907	D*	crit.end.
22	Zlotnicka biala	1024	PL	crit.end.
23	Dansk Landrace	917	DK	normal
24	Landrace	952	CS	normal

```
 1 - Grand Yorkshire Belge                                    EN   937
 2   Large White; Provinces of Flandres, Anvers and Liege
 3   Federation Nationale des Eleveurs de Porcs de Belgique     HB:1928
 4   Bruxelles 1030, Avenue Suffrage Universel 49
 5 - Imported as breed from countries United Kingdom, Netherlands
 6   Incrossing since 1970 from Large White 960 France, 1023 GB, 938 NL
 7   Numbers 1991: 700/21500; HB: 350; stable; 66 %; Ne = 933
 8 - Height: 120/100 cm; Weight: 400/320 kg; Herd number: 12; AI: miss
 9   Colour: Uni white
10   Pecularity: erect ears
11 - Main use: (1) meat,(2) crossbreeding,(3) miss
12   Spec. abilities: prolificacy, hardy
13   Performance compared with STB Belgian Landrace 906:
14     higher: litter size, meat quality, daily gain, handling ease
15     equal:  feed convers. rate,age of sex. maturity,farrowing interval
16     lower:  % lean, muscularity
17 - Management: stationary; housing: 12 m.;
18 - Conservation progr.: live animals: miss;Semen: miss;Embryos: miss
19   Status: normal;              Watch: herds,%pure!
```

20 - <u>Similar breeds</u> (see group 1/1 on page 101)

	EN	Country	Status
21 Norsk Yorkshire	984	N	endanger.
22 Yorkshire	1021	SF	normal
23 Large White Pigs	963	IRL	normal
24 Large White	960	F	normal

```
 1 - Pietrain                                                 EN   988
 2   Pietrain
 3   Federation Nationale des Eleveurs de Porcs de Belgique     HB:1953
 4   Bruxelles 1030, Avenue Suffrage Universel 49
 5 - Composite of local breed, Large White, Bayeux
 6   Incrossing since 1970 from Pietrain 991 Germany
 7   Numbers 1991: 13000/43000; HB: 22000; increasing; 60 %; Ne = 32686
 8 - Height: 95/80 cm; Weight: 300/280 kg; Herd number: 207; AI: miss
 9   Colour: Combination black, white
10   Pecularity: black spots, short erect ears
11 - Main use: (1) meat,(2) miss,(3) miss
12   Spec. abilities: lean meat
13   Performance compared with STB Belgian Landrace 906:
14     higher: % lean, muscularity, age of sexual maturity
15     equal:  feed conversion rate, farrowing interval, handling ease
16     lower:  litter size, meat quality, daily gain, piglet mortality
17 - Management: stationary; housing: 12 m.;
18 - Conservation progr.: live animals: miss;Semen: miss;Embryos: miss
19   Status: normal;              Watch: %pure!
```

20 - <u>Similar breeds</u> (see group 6/1 on page 103)

	EN	Country	Status
21 Pietrain	989	F	normal
22 Pietrain	991	D	normal
23 Pietrain	990	I	miss

```
 1 - Cheval de Sport Belge                                      EN  728
 2   Belgian Sport Horse; country-wide
 3   Society Royale le Cheval de Sport Belge                    HB:miss
 4   Rhode St. Geneje 1640, Avenue Brassine 38
 5 - Composite of Cheval de Trait, Cheval Diarmes, Cheval de Demi-Sang
 6   Imported as breed from France, Ireland, United Kingdom
 7   Numbers 1992: 83/1400; HB: 960; increasing; miss %; Ne = 306
 8 - Height:miss/miss cm; Weight:miss/miss kg; Herd number:miss; AI:miss
 9   Colour: miss
10   Pecularity: miss
11 - Main use: (1) sport/hobby,(2) miss,(3) miss
12   Spec. abilities: miss
13   Performance compared with STB Halfbred:
14     higher: adaptability in jumping
15     equal:  handling ease, adaptability in dressage, speed in gallop
16     lower:  miss
17 - Management: stationary; housing: ≈ 2 m.;
18 - Conservation progr.: live animals: miss;Semen: miss;Embryos: miss
19   Status: normal;            Watch: %pure!
20 - Similar breeds (see group 3/3 on page 109)   EN  Country Status
21   Sächsisches Warmblut                         798  D      min. end.
22   Hannoveraner                                 758  D      normal
```

```
 1 - Cheval de Trait Ardennais                                  EN  729
 2   Ardennes; southern and eastern Belgium
 3   Societe Royale le Cheval de Trait Ardennais                HB:1926
 4   Marloie 6900, Rue de la gare
 5 - Autochthon local horse of Ardennes
 7   Numbers 1992: 244/1027; HB: 862; decreasing; 99 %; Ne = 761
 8 - Height: 158/155 cm; Weight: 700/600 kg; Herd number: 120; AI: miss
 9   Colour: usually bay, sometimes roan or chestnut
10   Pecularity: miss
11 - Main use: (1) sport/hobby,(2) tractive power,(3) meat
12   Spec. abilities: miss
13   Performance compared with STB Percheron:
14     higher: miss
15     equal:  handling ease, fertility, age of sexual maturity
16     lower:  speed in trotters,pulling power,speed in gallop,daily gain
17 - Management: stationary; housing: no
18 - Conservation progr.: live animals: miss;Semen: miss;Embryos: miss
19   Status: normal;            Watch: trend!
20 - Similar breeds (see group 4/1 on page 109)   EN  Country Status
21   Auxois                                       709  F      crit.end.
22   Cheval de Trait Ardennais                    730  L      min. end.
23   Ardennais                                    707  F      pot. end.
24   Cheval de Trait Belge                        731  B      normal
```

BELGIUM

HORSES

```
 1 - Cheval de Trait Belge                                          EN  731
 2   Flemish; central and northern Belgium
 3   Societe Royale Le Cheval de Trait Belge                        HB:1886
 4   Bruxelles 1030, Avenue Suffrage Universel 49
 5 - Autochthon local Flemish horse
 7   Numbers 1986: 65/10000; HB: 1500; decreasing; 99 %; Ne = 249
 8 - Height: 166/162 cm; Weight: 900/700 kg; Herd number: miss; AI: Yes
 9   Colour: sorrel, dun, red roan, chestnut
10   Pecularity: miss
11 - Main use: (1) sport/hobby,(2) tractive power,(3) meat
12   Spec. abilities: miss
13   Performance compared with STB Percheron:
14      higher: pulling power
15      equal:  handling ease,fertility,age of sexual maturity,daily gain
16      lower:  speed in gallop, speed in trotters
17 - Management: stationary; housing: no
18 - Conservation progr.: live animals: miss;Semen: miss;Embryos: miss
19   Status: normal;              Watch: trend!
```

20 - Similar breeds (see group 4/1 on page 109)	EN	Country	Status
21 Auxois	709	F	crit.end.
22 Cheval de Trait Ardennais	730	L	min. end.
23 Ardennais	707	F	pot. end.
24 Cheval de Trait Ardennais	729	B	normal

BELORUSSE

CATTLE

```
 1 - Krasnyi belorusskii skot                                       EN  149
 2   Byelorussian Red; Byelorussia: Grodno, Minsk regions
 3   Food and Agriculture Organisation of the UN                    HB:1967
 4   Rome 00100, Via delle Terme di Caracalla
 5 - Comp. of Angeln,German Red,Polish Red,Danish Red,local cattle; incr.
 6   since 1950 from Estonian Red 143, Latvian Brown 50, Danish Red 222
 7   Numbers 1990: miss /10400; HB: miss; decreasing; 42 %; Ne = 2498
 8 - Height: 135/129 cm; Weight: 750/460 kg; Herd number: miss; AI: miss
 9   Colour: Uni red
10   Pecularity: lean type, longevity
11 - Main use: (1) milk,(2) meat,(3) miss
12   Spec. abilities: miss
13   Performance compared with STB Russian Black Pied 64:
14      higher: miss
15      equal:  % fat
16      lower:  milk yield
17 - Management: stationary; housing: > 6 m.;
18 - Conservation progr.: live animals: Yes;Semen: Yes;Embryos: miss
19   Status: potential. endang.;Watch: ♂♂,HB♀♀,trend,%pure,%incross!
```

20 - Similar breeds (see group 4/3 on page 78)	EN	Country	Status
21 Donnersberger Rotvieh	101	D	crit.end.
22 Harzer Rotvieh	109	D	crit.end.
23 Rod Dansk Malkerace	222	DK	normal
24 Rood Ras van Belgie	224	B	normal

BELORUSSE   PIGS

```
 1 - Belorusskaya cherno-pestraya                                EN   908
 2   Byelorussian Black Pied; Minsk, Byelorussia
 3   Food and Agriculture Organisation of the UN              HB:1976
 4   Rome 00100, Via delle Terme di Caracalla
 5 - Composite of Large White, Large Black, Berkshire, Middle White,
 6   Tamworth, Yorkshire, local pigs
 7   Numbers 1990: 4600/7900; HB: miss; stable; 73 %; Ne = 11629
 8 - Height: miss/miss cm; Weight: 298/243 kg; Herd number: miss; AI:miss
 9   Colour: Combination black, white
10   Pecularity: lop ears, spotted
11 - Main use: (1) general purpose,(2) miss,(3) miss
12   Spec. abilities: resistant to stress
13   Performance compared with STB Large White 951:
14     higher: miss
15     equal: % lean, litter size, feed conversion rate, daily gain
16     lower: miss
17 - Management: stationary; housing: 12 m.;
18 - Conservation progr.: live animals: miss;Semen: miss;Embryos: miss
19   Status: normal;              Watch: HB♀♀,%pure!
20 - Similar breeds (see group 4/2 on page 103)    EN  Country Status
21   Berkshire                                     909  GB   min. end.
22   Kemerovskaya                                  949  USSR pot. end.
23   Mirgorodskaya                                 976  UR   normal
24   Aksaiskaya cherno-pestraya                    901  KAZ  normal
```

BULGARIA   CATTLE

```
 1 - Iskursko govedo                                            EN   104
 2   Iskar Grey; around the rivers Iskar, Vitt and Ossam
 3   National Breeders Service                                HB:1929
 4   Sofia 1756, Malinova Dolina, Shosse Bistritza 10
 5 - Autochthon local grey cattle
 7   Numbers 1986: 6/800; HB: 300; decreasing; 100 %; Ne = 11
 8 - Height: 140/118 cm; Weight: 750/350 kg; Herd number: 3; AI: Yes
 9   Colour: light to dark grey shading to black
10   Pecularity: horns 2/2, lyra formed horns, black muzzle and hoofs
11 - Main use: (1) milk,(2) meat,(3) vegetation management
12   Spec. abilities: miss
13   Performance compared with STB Holstein-Friesian:
14     higher: % fat, % protein, calving interval, handling ease
15     equal: calving ease, pulling power
16     lower: milk yield,daily gain,age of sexual maturity,calving rate
17 - Management: transhumant; housing: 2-6 m.;
18 - Conservation progr.: live animals: miss;Semen: 5;Embryos: miss
19   Status: critically endang.;Watch: ♂♂,trend,herds!
20 - Similar breeds (see group 6/1 on page 80)     EN  Country Status
21   Katerini                                      136  GR   crit.end.
22   Sykia                                         251  GR   crit.end.
23   Piemontese                                    197  I    normal
24   Maremmana                                     166  I    normal
```

BULGARIA   **CATTLE**

```
 1 - Rodopska kusoroga                                              EN  220
 2   Rodopi; Rhodopa region above 1800 m
 3   National Breeders Service                                      HB:1956
 4   Sofia 1756, Malinova Dolina, Shosse Bistritza 10
 5 - Autochthon breed
 7   Numbers 1986: 4/150; HB: 95; stable; 100 %; Ne = 7
 8 - Height: 115/97 cm; Weight: 350/240 kg; Herd number: 1; AI: miss
 9   Colour: Uni brown-black
10   Pecularity: horns 2/2, lyra formed horns, white eel-stripe
11 - Main use: (1) milk,(2) meat,(3) vegetation management
12   Spec. abilities: miss
13   Performance compared with STB Holstein-Friesian:
14      higher: calving rate, % fat, % protein
15      equal:  muscularity, calving interval, handling ease
16      lower:  milk yield, calving ease, calf mortality, pulling power
17 - Management: transhumant; housing: 2-6 m.;
18 - Conservation progr.: live animals: miss;Semen: miss;Embryos: miss
19   Status: critically endang.;Watch: ♂♂,HB♀♀,herds!
20 - Similar breeds (see group 5/5 on page 80)    EN  Country Status
21   Busha                                        52   YU   min. end.
22   Brachyceros                                  39   GR   pot. end.
```

CROATIA   **CATTLE**

```
 1 - Istarsko govedo                                                EN  126
 2   Istrian; central Istria
 3   Poljoprivredni Centar Hrvatske - Stocarski Selekcijski         HB:1988
 4   Centar, Kaciceva 9/III, 41000 Zagreb
 5 - Autochthon Podolian origin from Italy; incrossing since 1950 from
 6   Austrian Brown 190 Austria, German Brown 77 Germany, Brown-Swiss USA
 7   Numbers 1986: 15/500; HB: 50; decreasing; 70 %; Ne = 25
 8 - Height: 148/138 cm; Weight: 900/625 kg; Herd number: miss; AI: Yes
 9   Colour: Uni grey, light snout and rings around the eyes
10   Pecularity: horns 2/2, very long (about 1 m), black tongue
11 - Main use: (1) meat,(2) tractive power,(3) tourism
12   Spec. abilities: high heat tolerance, longevity
13   Performance compared with STB Slovenian Brown 221:
14      higher: handling ease,pulling power,% fat,% protein,calving ease
15      equal:  miss
16      lower:  milk yield, muscularity, daily gain, calving interval
17 - Management: stationary; housing: 2-6 m.; adapted to karst region
18 - Conservation progr.: live animals: Yes;Semen: 3;Embryos: miss
19   Status: critically endang.;Watch: ♂♂,HB♀♀,trend,%pure,%incross!
20 - Similar breeds (see group 6/1 on page 80)    EN  Country Status
21   Iskursko govedo                             104   BG   crit.end.
22   Katerini                                    136   GR   crit.end.
23   Piemontese                                  197   I    normal
24   Maremmana                                   166   I    normal
```

CROATIA   CATTLE

```
 1 - Simentalac                                              EN  236
 2   Simmental; Kontinentalna Hrvatska
 3   Poljoprivredni Centar Hrvatske - Stocarski Selekcijski      HB:1913
 4   Centar, Kaciceva 9/III, 41000 Zagreb
 5 - Imported as breed from Switzerland, Germany, Austria; incrossing
 6   since 1950 from Holstein Friesian (Red Holstein) USA, Canada
 7   Numbers 1986: 1170/383000; HB: 28078; decreasing; 98 %; Ne = 4493
 8 - Height: 152/137 cm; Weight: 1150/625 kg; Herd number: miss; AI: Yes
 9   Colour: Combination red, yellow, white, pied
10   Pecularity: white head
11 - Main use: (1) meat,(2) milk,(3) miss
12   Spec. abilities: marbled meat
13   Performance compared with STB Simmental 236:
14     higher: Breed is used
15     equal:  as standard breed,
16     lower:  no comparison possible.
17 - Management: stationary; housing: 12 m.;
18 - Conservation progr.: live animals: miss;Semen: 150;Embryos: miss
19   Status: normal;            Watch: trend!
```

20 - Similar breeds (see group 3/2 on page 77)	EN	Country	Status
21 Ceske strakate	61	CZ	crit.end.
22 Simentalska	237	PL	min. end.
23 Montbeliard	176	F	normal
24 Fleckvieh	88	A	normal

CROATIA   CATTLE

```
 1 - Sivo Govedo Dalmacije                                   EN  242
 2   Dalmatian Grey; Dalmatia
 3   Centar Hrvatske Stocarski Selekcijski Centar Hrvatske       HB:1945
 4   Kaciceva 9/III 41000 Zagreb
 5 - Autochthon Busa improved with Tyrol Grey Austria, Montafon
 7   Numbers 1986: 27/5500; HB: 350; decreasing; 60 %; Ne = 100
 8 - Height: 115/112 cm; Weight: 350/290 kg; Herd number: miss; AI: miss
 9   Colour: Uni grey
10   Pecularity: short and light horns, strong hooves
11 - Main use: (1) milk,(2) meat,(3) miss
12   Spec. abilities: high heat tolerance
13   Performance compared with STB Slovenian Brown 221:
14     higher: % fat, % protein, calving ease, age of sexual maturity
15     equal:  handling ease
16     lower:  milk yield, daily gain, muscularity, calving interval
17 - Management: miss; housing: miss m.; adapted to karst region
18 - Conservation progr.: live animals: miss;Semen: miss;Embryos: miss
19   Status: potential. endang.;Watch: trend,%pure!
```

20 - Similar breeds (see group 6/1 on page 80)	EN	Country	Status
21 Iskursko govedo	104	BG	crit.end.
22 Katerini	136	GR	crit.end.
23 Piemontese	197	I	normal
24 Maremmana	166	I	normal

```
 1 - Licka Ovca                                                    EN   530
 2   Lika; Lika and Gorski Kotar
 3   Poljoprivredni Centar Hrvatske - Stocarski Selekcijski        HB: Yes
 4   Centar, Kaciceva 9/III, 41000 Zagreb
 5 - Autochthon Pramenka
 7   Numbers 1986: miss /100000; HB: 1000; decreasing; 70 %; Ne = 181
 8 - Height: 65/63 cm; Weight: 40/35 kg; Herd number: miss; AI: miss
 9   Colour: Uni white
10   Pecularity: horns 2/2
11 - Main use: (1) meat,(2) milk,(3) wool
12   Spec. abilities: tolerance of heat, lack of water
13   Performance compared with STB Merino:
14      higher: miss
15      equal:  % fat, % protein, lambing interval
16      lower:  wool yield, thickness, daily gain
17 - Management: stationary; housing: 2-6 m.; adapted to mountain area
18 - Conservation progr.: live animals: miss;Semen: miss;Embryos: miss
19   Status: potential. endang.;Watch: ♂♂,trend,%pure!
20 - Similar breeds (see group 7/6 on page 92)      EN  Country Status
21   Florina                                        490   GR   endanger.
22   Ruda Dubrovacka Sheep                          611   HR   endanger.
23   Karagouniko                                    518   GR   normal
24   Sazakatsaniko                                  429   GR   normal
```

```
 1 - Paska Ovca                                                    EN   579
 2   Pag Island; Pag Island
 3   Poljoprivredni Centar Hrvatske - Stocarski Selekcijski        HB: Yes
 4   Centar, Kaciceva 9/III, 41000 Zagreb
 5 - Imported as breed from Spain and Italy, autochthon Pramenka
 7   Numbers 1986: miss /10000; HB: 4000; stable; 70 %; Ne = 724
 8 - Height: 53/50 cm; Weight: 35/30 kg; Herd number: miss; AI: miss
 9   Colour: Uni white
10   Pecularity: horns 0/0
11 - Main use: (1) milk and cheese,(2) meat,(3) wool
12   Spec. abilities: high heat tolerance, lack of water supply
13   Performance compared with STB Merino:
14      higher: miss
15      equal:  % fat, % protein, lambing interval, fiber thickness
16      lower:  milk yield,daily gain,litter size,age of sexual maturity
17 - Management: stationary; housing: no; adapted to karst area
18 - Conservation progr.: live animals: miss;Semen: miss;Embryos: miss
19   Status: potential. endang.;Watch: ♂♂,%pure!
20 - Similar breeds (see group 7/6 on page 92)      EN  Country Status
21   Florina                                        490   GR   endanger.
22   Ruda Dubrovacka Sheep                          611   HR   endanger.
23   Karagouniko                                    518   GR   normal
24   Sazakatsaniko                                  429   GR   normal
```

CROATIA   SHEEP

1 - **Ruda Dubrovacka Sheep**   EN   611
2   Dubrovnik; coastal area of Dubrovnik (Ston, Herceg Novi)
3   Stancia za Juzne Kulture   HB:miss
4   Dubrovnik
5 - Imported as breed from France, Spain, Italy; autochton Pramenka
7   Numbers 1986: **50/1000**; HB: **miss**; **decreasing**; **50 %**; Ne = **191**
8 - Height: **63/59** cm; Weight: **43/33** kg; Herd number: **miss**; AI: **miss**
9   Colour: **Uni white, about 10 % of the animals are spotted**
10 Pecularity: **horns 0/0**
11 - Main use: (1) **wool**,(2) **milk**,(3) **miss**
12 Spec. abilities: **high heat tolerance, tolerates lack of water**
13 Performance compared with STB **Merino**:
14   higher: **age of sexual maturity**
15   equal: **milk yield, % fat, lambing interval, fiber thickness**
16   lower: **daily gain, litter size, wool yield, muscularity**
17 - Management: **stationary**; housing: **2-6 m.**; adapted to arid area
18 - Conservation progr.: live animals: **Yes**;Semen: **miss**;Embryos: **miss**
19 Status: **endangered**;   Watch: **HB♀♀,trend,%pure**!
20 - <u>Similar breeds</u> (see group 7/6 on page 92)   <u>EN</u> <u>Country</u> <u>Status</u>
21 **Florina**   490 GR   endanger.
22 **Kymi**   523 GR   min. end.
23 **Karagouniko**   518 GR   normal
24 **Sazakatsaniko**   429 GR   normal

CROATIA   GOATS

1 - **Balkanska Koza**   EN   304
2   Balkan Goat; Sinj, Vrgovac, Benkovac, Obrovac
3   Poljoprivredni Centar Hrvatske - Stocarski Selekcijski   HB:miss
4   Centar, Kaciceva 9/III, 41000 Zagreb
5 - Composite of different local types
7   Numbers 1986: **miss /60000**; HB: **200**; **stable**; **70 %**; Ne = **18**
8 - Height: **67/61** cm; Weight: **50/35** kg; Herd number: **miss**; AI: **miss**
9   Colour: **Uni grey, spotted with various colous**
10 Pecularity: **horns 2/2**
11 - Main use: (1) **meat**,(2) **milk**,(3) **vegetation management**
12 Spec. abilities: **high heat tolerance**
13 Performance compared with STB **Saanen**:
14   higher: **wool yield**
15   equal: **% fat, % protein, lambing interval**
16   lower: **milk yield, litter size, leanness, age of sexual maturity**
17 - Management: **stationary**; housing: **2-6 m.**; adapted to arid area
18 - Conservation progr.: live animals: **miss**;Semen: **miss**;Embryos: **miss**
19 Status: **potential. endang.**;Watch: **♂♂,HB♀♀,%pure**!
20 - <u>Similar breeds</u> (see group 9 on page 98)   <u>EN</u> <u>Country</u> <u>Status</u>
21 **Roccaverano**   347 I   crit.end.
22 **Val di Livo (extinct)**   363 I   crit.end.
23 **Local breeds**   338 GR   normal
24 **Corse**   320 F   normal

CROATIA   PIGS

1 - Turopolljac   EN 1013
2   Turopolje; Turopolje and Posavina
3   Institute for Animal Husbandry and Dairy Science   HB:1800
4   Faculty of Agriculture Sciences University of Zagreb, Zagreb 41000
5 - Composite of Siska, Leichester
7   Numbers 1986: 10/250; HB: miss; decreasing; 50 %; Ne = 19
8 - Height: 147/148 cm; Weight: 246/242 kg; Herd number: miss; AI: miss
9   Colour: Combination black, yellow
10 Pecularity: miss
11 - Main use: (1) meat,(2) miss,(3) miss
12   Spec. abilities: extremely summer and winter temperature
13   Performance compared with STB Swedish Landrace:
14   higher: backfat thickness
15   equal: miss
16   lower: litter size, feed conversion rate, % lean, daily gain
17 - Management: transhumant; housing: ≈ 2 m.; wet land and marsh
18 - Conservation progr.: live animals: Yes;Semen: miss;Embryos: miss
19   Status: critically endang.;Watch: ♂♂,HB♀♀,trend,%pure!
20 - Similar breeds (see group 6/2 on page 104)   EN Country Status
21   Sortbroget   1005   DK   crit.end.
22   Schwarz-Weißes Bentheimer   996   D   crit.end.
23   Sibirskaya chernopestraya   1001   USSR pot. end.
24   Gloucestershire Old Spot   936   GB   pot. end.

CROATIA   HORSES

1 - Hrvatski Hladnokrvnjak   EN 761
2   Yugoslavian Draft; Medjimurje, Podravina, Baranja, Banija
3   Poljoprivredni entar Hrvatske - Stocarski Selekcijski   HB: Yes
4   Centar, Kaciceva 9/III, 41000 Zagreb
5 - Composite of different strains
6 - Imported as breed from Hungary, Austria, Belgium
7   Numbers 1986: 55/100; HB: 45; stable; 85 %; Ne = 97
8 - Height: 165/160 cm; Weight: 700/625 kg; Herd number: miss; AI: miss
9   Colour: usually black or brown, sometimes bay
10 Pecularity: miss
11 - Main use: (1) tractive power,(2) meat,(3) miss
12   Spec. abilities: miss
13   Performance compared with STB Percheron:
14   higher: speed in gallop, speed in trotters
15   equal: handling ease, fertility, age of sexual maturity
16   lower: pulling power, daily gain
17 - Management: stationary; housing: > 6 m.;
18 - Conservation progr.: live animals: miss;Semen: miss;Embryos: miss
19   Status: minimally endang.; Watch: HB♀♀,%pure!
20 - Similar breeds (see group 4/1 on page 109)   EN Country Status
21   Auxois   709   F   crit.end.
22   Cheval de Trait Ardennais   730   L   min. end.
23   Cheval de Trait Belge   731   B   normal
24   Cheval de Trait Ardennais   729   B   normal

CROATIA   HORSES

1 - Lipicanac   EN 775
2   Lipitsa; Slovenia
3   Poljoprivredni Centar Hrvatske - Stocarski Selekcijski   HB:1806
4   Centar, Kaciceva 9/III, 41000 Zagreb
5 - Imported as breed from Spain, Hungary, Italy, CSFR
7   Numbers 1986: 64/70; HB: 51; stable; 90 %; Ne = 114
8 - Height: 154/150 cm; Weight: 525/450 kg; Herd number: miss; AI: miss
9   Colour: grey, partial albinism
10 Pecularity: silky mane and tail
11 - Main use: (1) sport/hobby,(2) tractive power,(3) ceremonial
12 Spec. abilities: miss
13 Performance compared with STB Halfbred:
14   higher: handling ease, adaptability in dressage, fertility
15   equal: pulling power
16   lower: adapt. in jumping and in military, speed in gallop
17 - Management: stationary; housing: > 6 m.;
18 - Conservation progr.: live animals: miss;Semen: miss;Embryos: miss
19 Status: normal;   Watch: HB♀♀,%pure!
20 - Similar breeds (see group 3/1 on page 108)   EN Country Status
21 Lipizzan   776 F   crit.end.
22 Senner   801 D   crit.end.
23 Espanol-Andaluz   742 E   normal
24 Lusitanien   779 F   normal

CSFR   CATTLE

1 - Nizinne cernostrakate   EN 184
2   Czech Black Pied; country-wide
3   State Breeding Organization   HB:1980
4   Praha 2 12077, Vitezneho unora 64
5 - Composite of Bohemian Red Pied, HF 278 NL, 75 Germany, USA, Canada
6   Incrossing since 1950 from HF 75 Germany,278 Netherlands,Canada,USA
7   Numbers 1986: 300/33542; HB: 178; stable; 100 %; Ne = 447
8 - Height: 155/130 cm; Weight: 1100/575 kg; Herd number: miss; AI: Yes
9   Colour: Combination black, white, pied
10 Pecularity: miss
11 - Main use: (1) milk,(2) meat,(3) miss
12 Spec. abilities: miss
13 Performance compared with STB Bohemian Red Pied 61:
14   higher: milk yield, calf mortality
15   equal: calving ease, handling ease, milkability
16   lower: muscularity,daily gain,% fat,% protein,calving interval
17 - Management: stationary; housing: 12 m.;
18 - Conservation progr.: live animals: miss;Semen: 1500;Embryos: 15/100
19 Status: normal;   Watch: HB♀♀,%incross!
20 - Similar breeds (see group 1/4 on page 75)   EN Country Status
21 Schwarzbuntes Milchrind   229 D*   normal
22 Baltata cu negru romanesca   19 RO   normal
23 Crno-belo   71 YU   normal

151

```
 1 - Cigaja                                              EN   459
 2   Tsigai; mountain and submountain areas
 3   State Breeding Organization                        HB:1700
 4   Bratislava 85227, Starohajska cesta 29
 5 - Autochthon Tsigaia
 6   Incrossing since 1960 from East Friesian 573 Germany
 7   Numbers 1986: 3833/132861; HB: 13588; stable; 20 %; Ne = 11959
 8 - Height: 72/68 cm; Weight: 75/50 kg; Herd number: miss; AI: miss
 9   Colour: Uni white
10   Pecularity: horns 2/0, black head
11 - Main use: (1) wool,(2) milk,(3) meat
12   Spec. abilities: miss
13   Performance compared with STB Merino 475:
14     higher: milk yield, wool thickness, muscularity, daily gain
15     equal:  age of sex. matur., length of mating season, lambing int.
16     lower:  wool yield
17 - Management: transhumant; housing: 2-6 m.;
18 - Conservation progr.: live animals: miss;Semen: miss;Embryos: miss
19   Status: normal;              Watch: %pure!
```

20 - <u>Similar breeds</u> (see group 7/7 on page 93)

		<u>EN</u>	<u>Country</u>	<u>Status</u>
21	Cigaja	460	H	endanger.
22	Kivircik	654	GR	pot. end.
23	Cigaja	461	YU	normal
24	Tigaie	655	RO	normal

```
 1 - Zuslachtena valasska                                EN   658
 2   Valachian; submountain areas
 3   State Breeding Organisation                        HB:1956
 4   Bratislava 85227, Starohajska cesta 29
 5 - Autochthon native Valachian breed
 6   Incrossing since 1960 from Leicester 528, Lincoln 532 United Kingdom
 7   Numbers 1986: 3500/107000; HB: 24000; stable; 40 %; Ne = 12218
 8 - Height: 70/65 cm; Weight: 75/50 kg; Herd number: 254; AI: miss
 9   Colour: Uni white
10   Pecularity: horns 2/0
11 - Main use: (1) wool,(2) meat,(3) milk
12   Spec. abilities: miss
13   Performance compared with STB Merino 475:
14     higher: muscularity, daily gain, carcass leanness, litter size
15     equal:  age of sex. matur.,length of mating season,lambing interv.
16     lower:  wool or fiber yield
17 - Management: stationary; housing: > 6 m.; mountain
18 - Conservation progr.: live animals: miss;Semen: miss;Embryos: miss
19   Status: potential. endang.;Watch: %pure,%incross!
```

20 - <u>Similar breeds</u> (see group 7/6 on page 92)

		<u>EN</u>	<u>Country</u>	<u>Status</u>
21	Florina	490	GR	endanger.
22	Ruda Dubrovacka Sheep	611	HR	endanger.
23	Karagouniko	518	GR	normal
24	Sazakatsaniko	429	GR	normal

1 - Bila kratkosrsta   EN 306
2 White Shorteared Goat; country-wide
3 State Breeding Organization   HB:1928
4 Praha 2 12077, Vitezneho unora 64
5 - Autochthon origin white breed
7 Numbers 1986: 950/28000; HB: 1300; decreasing; 100 %; Ne = 2196
8 - Height: 85/80 cm; Weight: 70/50 kg; Herd number: miss; AI: Yes
9 Colour: Uni white
10 Pecularity: horns 2/2
11 - Main use: (1) milk,(2) meat,(3) miss
12 Spec. abilities: miss
13 Performance compared with STB Saanen:
14   higher: litter size,milk yield,muscularity,% fat,age of sex. mat.
15   equal: miss
16   lower: miss
17 - Management: stationary; housing: 12 m.;
18 - Conservation progr.: live animals: miss;Semen: 20;Embryos: miss
19 Status: normal;   Watch: trend!

20 - Similar breeds (see group 1 on page 97)	EN	Country	Status
21 Irish Goat	336	IRL	min. end.
22 Blanche	308	B	pot. end.
23 Weiße Deutsche Edelziege	367	D	normal
24 Gessenay	350	F	normal

1 - Hneda kratkosrsta   EN 334
2 Brown Shorteared Goat; submountain areas
3 State Breeding Organization   HB:1928
4 Praha 2 12077, Vitezneho unora 64
5 - Autochthon origin breed - brown
7 Numbers 1986: 70/2000; HB: 80; decreasing; 80 %; Ne = 149
8 - Height: 80/75 cm; Weight: 70/50 kg; Herd number: miss; AI: miss
9 Colour: Uni brown
10 Pecularity: horns 2/2
11 - Main use: (1) milk,(2) meat,(3) miss
12 Spec. abilities: miss
13 Performance compared with STB Saanen:
14   higher: litter size,muscularity,milk yield,% fat,age of sex. mat.
15   equal: miss
16   lower: miss
17 - Management: stationary; housing: 12 m.;
18 - Conservation progr.: live animals: miss;Semen: miss;Embryos: miss
19 Status: minimally endang.; Watch: HB♀♀,trend,%pure!

20 - Similar breeds (see group 2 on page 97)	EN	Country	Status
21 Erzgebirgsziege	330	D	crit.end.
22 Chamoisee	317	B	pot. end.
23 Bunte Deutsche Edelziege	310	D	normal
24 Alpine	301	F	normal

```
1 - Belgicka Landrase                                      EN   905
2   Belgian Landrace; country-wide
3   State Breeding Organization                            HB:1974
4   Praha 2 12077, Vitezneho unora 64
5 - Imported as breed from countries Belgium, Germany, France
6   Incrossing since 1970 from Belgian Landrace 906 Belgium, 919 Germany
7   Numbers 1986: 70/300; HB: 158; decreasing; 100 %; Ne = 194
8 - Height: 94/83 cm; Weight: 300/250 kg; Herd number: miss; AI: Yes
9   Colour: Uni white
10  Pecularity: lop ears
11 - Main use: (1) meat,(2) miss,(3) miss
12  Spec. abilities: miss
13  Performance compared with STB Large White 1017:
14    higher: % lean, muscularity
15    equal:  feed conversion rate,age of sexual mat.,farrowing interval
16    lower:  litter size, meat quality, daily gain, piglet mortality
17 - Management: stationary; housing: 12 m.;
18 - Conservation progr.: live animals: miss;Semen: 15;Embryos: miss
19  Status: potential. endang.;Watch: HB♀♀,trend!
```

20 - Similar breeds (see group 2/1 on page 101)	EN	Country	Status
21 Belgische Landrasse	907	D*	crit.end.
22 Zlotnicka biala	1024	PL	crit.end.
23 Landrace	952	CS	normal
24 Belgisch Landvarken	906	B	normal

```
1 - Duroc                                                  EN   926
2   Duroc; country-wide
3   State Breeding Organization                            HB:1973
4   Praha 2 12077, Vitezneho unora 64
5 - Imported as breed from countries USA, Canada
6   Incrossing since 1970 from Duroc 932 United Kingdom, USA, Canada
7   Numbers 1986: 860/500; HB: 332; stable; 100 %; Ne = 958
8 - Height: 96/86 cm; Weight: 300/260 kg; Herd number: miss; AI: Yes
9   Colour: Uni red
10  Pecularity: short lop ears
11 - Main use: (1) meat,(2) miss,(3) miss
12  Spec. abilities: miss
13  Performance compared with STB Large White 1017:
14    higher: piglet mortality
15    equal:  % lean,feed conversion rate,meat quality,age of sex. mat.
16    lower:  litter size, daily gain
17 - Management: stationary; housing: 12 m.;
18 - Conservation progr.: live animals: miss;Semen: 50;Embryos: miss
19  Status: normal
```

20 - Similar breeds (see group 5/1 on page 103)	EN	Country	Status
21 Duroc	927	F	crit.end.
22 Duroc	932	GB	crit.end.
23 Duroc	931	RO	normal
24 Duroc	929	I	normal

```
1 - Hampshire                                                    EN  940
2   Hampshire
3   State Breeding Organization                                  HB:1972
4   Praha 2 12077, Vitezneho unora 64
5 - Imported as breed from country USA
6   Incrossing since 1970 from Hampshire USA, Hampshire Canada
7   Numbers 1986: 600/400; HB: 286; stable; 100 %; Ne = 775
8 - Height: 96/86 cm; Weight: 300/270 kg; Herd number: miss; AI: Yes
9   Colour: Combination black, white
10  Pecularity: white belt, erect ears
11 - Main use: (1) meat,(2) miss,(3) miss
12  Spec. abilities: miss
13  Performance compared with STB Large White 1017:
14    higher: % lean, muscularity
15    equal:  litter size,meat quality,age of sexual mat.,farrowing int.
16    lower:  feed conversion rate, daily gain
17 - Management: stationary; housing: 12 m.;
18 - Conservation progr.: live animals: miss;Semen: 30;Embryos: miss
19  Status: normal
```

20 - Similar breeds (see group 3/2 on page 102)	EN	Country	Status
21 Limousin	967	F	crit.end.
22 Hampshire	942	D*	crit.end.
23 Porcul de Banat	993	RO	pot. end.
24 Hampshire	944	RO	pot. end.

```
1 - Landrace                                                     EN  952
2   Czech Landrace; country-wide
3   State Breeding Organization                                  HB:1961
4   Praha 2 12077, Vitezneho unora 64
5 - Imported as breed from countries Canada,Germany,Denmark,France,GB,S
6   Incross. since 1970 from Landrace 920 Germany,953 France,917 Denmark
7   Numbers 1986: 1260/6000; HB: 1816; stable; 37 %; Ne = 2976
8 - Height: 93/82 cm; Weight: 300/250 kg; Herd number: miss; AI: Yes
9   Colour: Uni white
10  Pecularity: lop ears
11 - Main use: (1) meat,(2) miss,(3) miss
12  Spec. abilities: miss
13  Performance compared with STB Large White 1017:
14    higher: miss
15    equal: % lean, litter size, meat quality, age of sexual maturity
16    lower:  feed conversion rate, daily gain, piglet mortality
17 - Management: stationary; housing: 12 m.;
18 - Conservation progr.: live animals: miss;Semen: 18;Embryos: miss
19  Status: normal              Watch: %pure!
```

20 - Similar breeds (see group 2/1 on page 101)	EN	Country	Status
21 Belgische Landrasse	907	D*	crit.end.
22 Zlotnicka biala	1024	PL	crit.end.
23 Dansk Landrace	917	DK	normal
24 Belgisch Landvarken	906	B	normal

```
 1 - Vile uslechtile                                            EN 1017
 2   Large White; country-wide
 3   State Breeding Organization                                HB:1927
 4   Praha 2 12077, Vitezneho unora 64
 5 - Composite of Old Czech Bristly Rychnow pig / Moravian Yorkshire
 6   Incrossing since 1970 from Large White BUL, 960 F, 1023 GB, 923 D
 7   Numbers 1986: 2430/64000; HB: 26000; stable; 23 %; Ne = 8889
 8 - Height: 100/85 cm; Weight: 320/250 kg; Herd number: miss; AI: Yes
 9   Colour: Uni white
10   Pecularity: erect ears
11 - Main use: (1) meat,(2) miss,(3) miss
12   Spec. abilities: miss
13   Performance compared with STB Large White 1017:
14     higher: Breed is used
15     equal:  as standard breed,
16     lower:  no comparison possible.
17 - Management: stationary; housing: 12 m.;
18 - Conservation progr.: live animals: miss;Semen: 48;Embryos: miss
19   Status: normal;              Watch: %pure,%incross!
20 - Similar breeds (see group 1/2 on page 101)    EN  Country Status
21   Bela Zlahtna                                  904  SLO   crit.end.
22   Middle White                                  975  GB    min. end.
23   Deutsches Edelschwein                         923  D     normal
24   Deutsches Edelschwein                         922  D*    normal
```

```
 1 - Hucul                                                      EN  762
 2   Hutsul; Topolcianky, Prag, Janova Hora
 3   Research Station for Horse Breeding                        HB:1922
 4   Slatinany 53821
 5 - Autochthon Carpatian type of Tarpan
 6   Incrossing since 1950 from Hucul Romania, Hucul 763 Poland
 7   Numbers 1992: 8/88; HB: miss; increasing; miss %; Ne = 14
 8 - Height: 150/145 cm; Weight: 360/340 kg; Herd number: 3; AI: miss
 9   Colour: usually dun or bay, sometimes chestnut or piebald
10   Pecularity: miss
11 - Main use: (1) tractive power,(2) sport/hobby,(3) miss
12   Spec. abilities: frugal, surefooted
13   Performance compared with STB Fjord:
14     higher: fertility
15     equal:  pulling power,handling ease,age of sexual mat.,daily gain
16     lower:  miss
17 - Management: transhumant; housing: 2-6 m.; mountain
18 - Conservation progr.: live animals: Yes;Semen: 2;Embryos: miss
19   Status: critically endang.;Watch: ♂♂,HB♀♀,herds,%pure,%incross!
20 - Similar breeds (see group 5/9 on page 111)    EN  Country Status
21   Hucul                                         763  PL    pot. end.
22   Koniki Polskie                                771  PL    normal
23   Bosanski brdski konj                          712  YU    miss
```

       <u>CATTLE</u>

```
 1 - Ceske strakate                                          EN   61
 2   Bohemian Red Pied; country-wide
 3   State Breeding Organization                            HB:1921
 4   Praha 2 12077, Vitezneho unora 64
 5 - Composite of Bohemian Red, Simmental, Bernese
 6   Incrossing since 1950 from Simmental 88 Austria, 78 Germany
 7   Numbers 1986: 220/263257; HB: 777; stable; 48 %; Ne = 686
 8 - Height: 150/132 cm; Weight: 1100/600 kg; Herd number: miss; AI: Yes
 9   Colour: Combination red, white, sometimes uni red
10   Pecularity: white head, spotted
11 - Main use: (1) milk,(2) meat,(3) miss
12   Spec. abilities: miss
13   Performance compared with STB Bohemian Red Pied 61:
14     higher: Breed is used
15     equal:  as standard breed,
16     lower:  no comparison possible.
17 - Management: stationary; housing: 12 m.;
18 - Conservation progr.: live animals: miss;Semen: 1700;Embryos: 30/1500
19   Status: critically endang.;Watch: %pure,%incross!
```

```
20 - Similar breeds (see group 3/2 on page 77)     EN  Country Status
21   Simentalska                                   237   PL    min. end.
22   Pie Rouge de l'Est                             89   F     pot. end.
23   Montbeliard                                   176   F     normal
24   Fleckvieh                                      88   A     normal
```

       <u>SHEEP</u>

```
 1 - Czech Merino                                           EN  475
 2   Merino; country-wide
 3   State Breeding Organization                            HB:1942
 4   Bratislava 85227, Starohajska cesta 29
 5 - Autochthon local Merino breeds
 6   Incrossing since 1960 from Mutton Merino 548 East Germany
 7   Numbers 1986: 8000/247000; HB: 41500; stable; 14 %; Ne = 26828
 8 - Height: 73/68 cm; Weight: 85/55 kg; Herd number: miss; AI: miss
 9   Colour: Uni white
10   Pecularity: horns 2/0
11 - Main use: (1) wool,(2) meat,(3) miss
12   Spec. abilities: miss
13   Performance compared with STB Merino 475:
14     higher: Breed is used
15     equal:  as standard breed,
16     lower:  no comparison possible.
17 - Management: stationary; housing: > 6 m.;
18 - Conservation progr.: live animals: miss;Semen: 5;Embryos: miss
19   Status: normal;            Watch: %pure,%incross!
```

```
20 - Similar breeds (see group 1/5 on page 87)     EN  Country Status
21   Polish Merino                                 583   PL    normal
22   Merinos de Palas                              552   RO    normal
23   Merinos Transilvanean                         556   RO    normal
```

SHEEP

1 - Sumavska   EN 643
2   Sumava; mountainous areas
3   State Breeding Organization   HB:1954
4   Praha 2 12077, Vitezneho unora 64
5 - Autochthon local breed
6   Incrossing since 1960 from Kent United Kingdom
7   Numbers 1986: 250/8500; HB: 3800; increasing; 40 %; Ne = 938
8 - Height: 69/65 cm; Weight: 80/50 kg; Herd number: miss; AI: miss
9   Colour: Uni white
10 Pecularity: horns 2/0
11 - Main use: (1) wool,(2) meat,(3) miss
12 Spec. abilities: humid conditions
13 Performance compared with STB Merino 475:
14   higher: wool or fiber thickness, litter size
15   equal: daily gain,age of sexual maturity,length of mating season
16   lower: wool or fiber yield, muscularity, carcass leanness
17 - Management: stationary; housing: > 6 m.;
18 - Conservation progr.: live animals: miss;Semen: miss;Embryos: miss
19 Status: potential. endang.;Watch: %pure,%incross!
20 - Similar breeds (see group 7/6 on page 92)   EN Country Status
21 Florina   490 GR   endanger.
22 Ruda Dubrovacka Sheep   611 HR   endanger.
23 Karagouniko   518 GR   normal
24 Sazakatsaniko   429 GR   normal

PIGS

1 - Presticke   EN 994
2   Prestice; western Bohemia
3   State Breeding Organization   HB:1964
4   Praha 2 12077, Vitezneho unora 64
5 - Composite of Old Czech Bristly Spotted, Black and Prestice Spotted
6   Incrossing since 1970 from Saddlebacks 903 D and 912 GB
7   Numbers 1986: 210/6000; HB: 1100; stable; 27 %; Ne = 705
8 - Height: 94/83 cm; Weight: 300/250 kg; Herd number: miss; AI: miss
9   Colour: Combination black, white
10 Pecularity: saddle, lop ears
11 - Main use: (1) meat,(2) miss,(3) miss
12 Spec. abilities: miss
13 Performance compared with STB Large White 1017:
14   higher: handling ease, litter size
15   equal: meat quality, age of sexual maturity, farrowing interval
16   lower: % lean, feed conversion rate, daily gain, muscularity
17 - Management: stationary; housing: 12 m.;
18 - Conservation progr.: live animals: miss;Semen: 17;Embryos: miss
19 Status: potential. endang.;Watch: %pure,%incross!
20 - Similar breeds (see group 3/1 on page 102)   EN Country Status
21 Pie noir du Pays Basque   987 F   crit.end.
22 Angler Sattelschwein   903 D   crit.end.
23 British Saddleback   912 GB   pot. end.
24 Schwäbisch-Hällisches Schwein   997 D   pot. end.

CZECH REPUBLIC   HORSES

```
 1 - Kladrubsky                                             EN  770
 2   Kladruby; Kladruby nad Labem/white, Slatinany/black
 3   Research Station for Horse Breeding                    HB:1579
 4   Slatinany 53821
 5 - Autochthon local horse + Span. Influence; incrossing since 1950 from
 6   Lipica 774 Hungary, Orlov trotter CSFR, Friesian NL, Andalusian P
 7   Numbers 1992: 11/153; HB: miss; stable; miss %; Ne = 21
 8 - Height: 166/162 cm; Weight: 595/570 kg; Herd number: 4; AI: miss
 9   Colour: 1 line grey and 1 line black
10   Pecularity: silky flowing mane and tail
11 - Main use: (1) sport/hobby,(2) tractive power,(3) coach horse
12   Spec. abilities: late maturing
13   Performance compared with STB Halfbred:
14     higher: pulling power
15     equal:  handling ease,fertility,age of sexual maturity,daily gain
16     lower:  miss
17 - Management: stationary; housing: 12 m.;
18 - Conservation progr.: live animals: Yes;Semen: 6;Embryos: miss
19   Status: critically endang.;Watch: ♂♂,HB♀♀,herds,%pure,%incross!
```

20 - Similar breeds (see group 3/1 on page 108)	EN	Country	Status
21 Lipizzan	776	F	crit.end.
22 Senner	801	D	crit.end.
23 Espanol-Andaluz	742	E	normal
24 Lusitanien	779	F	normal

DENMARK   CATTLE

```
 1 - Dansk Rodbroget Kvaeg                                  EN   73
 2   Danish Red Pied; Jutland
 3   Danish Red and White Breeding Society                  HB:1963
 4   Aarhus N 8200, Udkaersvej 15, Skejby
 5 - Composite of Shorthorn Denmark, 233 GB, D; incrossing since 1950
 6   from Meuse-Rhine-Yssel 161 Netherlands, Red Pied 74 Germany
 7   Numbers 1992: 40/22000; HB: 9200; increasing; 90 %; Ne = 159
 8 - Height: 150/135 cm; Weight: 900/600 kg; Herd number: miss; AI: Yes
 9   Colour: Combination red, white
10   Pecularity: miss
11 - Main use: (1) milk,(2) meat,(3) miss
12   Spec. abilities: miss
13   Performance compared with STB Holstein-Friesian 245:
14     higher: muscularity, % protein
15     equal:  % fat, calving ease, calving interval, age of sexual mat.
16     lower:  milk yield
17 - Management: stationary; housing: 2-6 m.;
18 - Conservation progr.: live animals: miss;Semen: 30;Embryos: miss
19   Status: normal;              Watch: %incross!
```

20 - Similar breeds (see group 3/1 on page 76)	EN	Country	Status
21 Blanc-Rouge de Belgique	273	B	pot. end.
22 Ferrandais	85	F	pot. end.
23 Maine-Anjou	163	F	normal
24 Pie-Rouge	199	B	normal

```
 1 - Jersey                                                    EN  130
 2   Jersey; country-wide
 3   Danmarks Jerseyforening                                   HB:1911
 4   Aarhus N 8200, Udkaersvej 15, Skejby
 5 - Imported as breed from countries Sweden, United Kingdom
 6   Incrossing since 1950 from Jersey USA, Jersey New Zealand
 7   Numbers 1992: 1900/210000; HB: 84000; decreasing; 89 %; Ne = 7432
 8 - Height: 130/120 cm; Weight: 500/400 kg; Herd number: miss; AI: Yes
 9   Colour: Uni yellow
10   Pecularity: miss
11 - Main use: (1) milk,(2) meat,(3) miss
12   Spec. abilities: high % fat
13   Performance compared with STB Holstein-Friesian 245:
14      higher: % fat, % protein
15      equal:  calving ease, calving interval, age of sexual maturity
16      lower:  milk yield, daily gain, muscularity
17 - Management: stationary; housing: 2-6 m.;
18 - Conservation progr.: live animals: miss;Semen: 500;Embryos: miss/90
19   Status: normal;              Watch: trend,%pure,%incross!
```

20 - <u>Similar breeds</u> (see group 8/4 on page 82)

		EN	Country	Status
21	Froment du Leon	93	F	endanger.
22	Jersey	132	IRL	pot. end.
23	Jersey	131	D	normal
24	Jersiais	134	F	normal

```
 1 - Rod Dansk Malkerace                                       EN  222
 2   Danish Red; country-wide
 3   Landsforeningen for Rod Dansk Malkerace                   HB:1885
 4   Aarhus N 8200, Udkaersvej 15, Skejby
 5 - Composite of Danish Cattle, Cattle from Schleswig Holstein
 6   Incrossing since 1950 from Brown Swiss USA, Red-and-White Sweden
 7   Numbers 1992: 400/170000; HB: 65000; decreasing; 97 %; Ne = 1590
 8 - Height: 154/137 cm; Weight: 800/600 kg; Herd number: miss; AI: Yes
 9   Colour: Uni red
10   Pecularity: muzzle and hoofs dark
11 - Main use: (1) milk,(2) meat,(3) miss
12   Spec. abilities: miss
13   Performance compared with STB Holstein-Friesian 245:
14      higher: muscularity, % fat, % protein
15      equal:  daily gain,calving ease,calving interval, age of sex. mat.
16      lower:  milk yield
17 - Management: stationary; housing: 2-6 m.;
18 - Conservation progr.: live animals: miss;Semen: 450;Embryos: miss/150
19   Status: normal;              Watch: trend,%incross!
```

20 - <u>Similar breeds</u> (see group 4/3 on page 78)

		EN	Country	Status
21	Donnersberger Rotvieh	101	D	crit.end.
22	Harzer Rotvieh	109	D	crit.end.
23	Czerwona Polska	72	PL	normal
24	Rood Ras van Belgie	224	B	normal

CATTLE

1 - Sortbroget Dansk Malkekvaeg   EN 245
2   Holstein-Friesian; mainly in Jutland
3   Avlsforeningen for Sortbroget Malkekvaeg i Danmark   HB:1891
4   Aarhus N 8200, Udkaersvej 15, Skejby
5 - Autochthon Black & White of Jutland; incrossing since 1950 from
6   Dutch Friesian 277 Netherlands, Holstein-Friesian USA
7   Numbers 1992: 2300/945000; HB: 368350; stable; 97 %; Ne = 9143
8 - Height: 150/140 cm; Weight: 850/600 kg; Herd number: miss; AI: Yes
9   Colour: Combination black, white
10 Pecularity: miss
11 - Main use: (1) milk,(2) meat,(3) protein production
12 Spec. abilities: milk breed
13 Performance compared with STB Holstein-Friesian 245:
14   higher: Breed is used
15   equal: as standard breed,
16   lower: no comparison possible.
17 - Management: stationary; housing: 2-6 m.;
18 - Conservation progr.:live animals: miss;Semen: 1800;Embryos: miss/550
19 Status: potential. endang.;Watch: %incross!
20 - Similar breeds (see group 1/1 on page 75)   EN Country Status
21 Nizinna-Czarno-Biala   185 PL   pot. end.
22 Pie-Noire-Holstein   198 B   normal
23 Deutsche Schwarzbunte   75 D   normal
24 Prim' Holstein   209 F   normal

SHEEP

1 - Dansk Landfar   EN 477
2   Danish Landrace; Jutland
3   Institute of Animal Science   HB:miss
4   Frederiksberg C 2000, Rolighedsvej 23
5 - miss
7   Numbers 1992: 20/200; HB: miss; increasing; 100 %; Ne = 51
8 - Height: 75/70 cm; Weight: 70/50 kg; Herd number: 20; AI: miss
9   Colour: Uni white
10 Pecularity: horns 0/0, grey head
11 - Main use: (1) meat,(2) wool,(3) sport/hobby
12 Spec. abilities: miss
13 Performance compared with STB Texel:
14   higher: litter size
15   equal: age of sex. matur., length of mating season, lambing int.
16   lower: muscularity, daily gain, carcass leanness, milk yield
17 - Management: stationary; housing: no
18 - Conservation progr.: live animals: Yes;Semen: miss;Embryos: miss
19 Status: critically endang.;Watch: ♂♂,HB♀♀!
20 - Similar breeds (see group 6/3 on page 90)   EN Country Status
21 Coburger Fuchsschaf   466 D   crit.end.
22 Utegangarsau   496 N   min. end.
23 Foroyskur Seydur   491 FR   normal
24 Gronlandsk Fär   504 DK   normal

```
1 - Gronlandsk Får                                           EN   504
2   Greenland Sheep; Greenland
3   The Greenland Sheep Breeders Association                 HB:miss
4   Upernaviarssuk, Greenland
5 - Imported as breed from countries Faeroe Island, Iceland
7   Numbers 1992: 1000/20000; HB: miss; decreasing; 100 %; Ne = 3810
8 - Height: 70/60 cm; Weight: 65/50 kg; Herd number: miss; AI: miss
9   Colour: Combination black, grey, brown, white
10  Pecularity: horns 2/2
11 - Main use: (1) meat,(2) wool,(3) miss
12  Spec. abilities: hardy weather resistant, walking long distances
13  Performance compared with STB Texel:
14    higher: wool or fiber thickness
15    equal:  carcass leanness, litter size, age of sexual maturity
16    lower:  muscularity,length of mating season,daily gain,milk yield
17 - Management: stationary; housing: 2-6 m.;
18 - Conservation progr.: live animals: miss;Semen: miss;Embryos: miss
19  Status: normal;              Watch: HB♀♀,trend!
20 - Similar breeds (see group 6/3 on page 90)
```

20	Similar breeds (see group 6/3 on page 90)	EN	Country	Status
21	Dansk Landfar	477	DK	crit.end.
22	Coburger Fuchsschaf	466	D	crit.end.
23	Suomenlammas	644	SF	normal
24	Foroyskur Seydur	491	FR	normal

```
1 - Hvidhovedet Marsk                                        EN   510
2   Marsh Sheep; Jutland
3   Dansk Fareavl                                            HB:miss
4   Brabrand 8220, Engdalvej 61
5 - Imported as breed from countries Germany, United Kingdom
6   Incrossing since 1960 from Texel 653 Netherlands
7   Numbers 1992: 225/1000; HB: miss; decreasing; miss %; Ne = 735
8 - Height: 80/75 cm; Weight: 60/75 kg; Herd number: 12; AI: miss
9   Colour: Uni white
10  Pecularity: horns 0/0
11 - Main use: (1) meat,(2) wool,(3) miss
12  Spec. abilities: weather resistant, high fertility
13  Performance compared with STB Texel:
14    higher: litter size, daily gain, wool yield, wool thickness
15    equal:  milk yield, age of sexual maturity, lambing interval
16    lower:  muscularity, carcass leanness
17 - Management: stationary; housing: no; marsh land
18 - Conservation progr.: live animals: miss;Semen: miss;Embryos: miss
19  Status: minimally endang.; Watch: HB♀♀,trend,herds,%pure!
20 - Similar breeds (see group 2/3 on page 88)
```

20	Similar breeds (see group 2/3 on page 88)	EN	Country	Status
21	Rauhwolliges Pommer. Landschaf	595	D*	crit.end.
22	Olkuska	571	PL	crit.end.
23	Pomorska	586	PL	normal
24	Kamieniecka	517	PL	normal

1 - Dansk Landrace   EN   322
2   Danish Landrace; country-wide
3   Danmarks Gedeavlerforening   HB:miss
4   Fuglebjerg 4250, Petersmindevej 15
5 - Imported as breed from Norway
6   Incrossing since 1960 from Dutch Landrace 341 Netherlands
7   Numbers 1992: 125/13000; HB: miss; increasing; 50 %; Ne = 495
8 - Height: **85/75** cm; Weight: **85/50** kg; Herd number: **miss**; AI: **miss**
9   Colour: **Combination black, grey, brown, white**
10   Pecularity: **horns 2/2**
11 - Main use: (1) **milk**,(2) **meat**,(3) **sport/hobby**
12   Spec. abilities: **very hardy, well adapted to humid and cold climate**
13   Performance compared with STB **Saanen**:
14   higher: **miss**
15   equal: **muscularity, daily gain, carc. leanness, % fat, % protein**
16   lower: **litter size, milk yield**
17 - Management: **stationary**; housing: **no**
18 - Conservation progr.: live animals: **Yes**;Semen: **miss**;Embryos: **miss**
19   Status: **normal**;   Watch: **HB♀♀,%pure!**
20 - <u>Similar breeds</u> (see group 10 on page 98)   <u>EN</u>   <u>Country</u>   <u>Status</u>
21   **Suomenvuohi**   358   SF   endanger.
22   **Nederlandse Landgeit**   341   NL   pot. end.
23   **Svensk Lantras**   359   S   normal
24   **Norsk Geit**   342   N   normal

1 - Dansk Landrace   EN   **917**
2   Danish Landrace; country-wide
3   Landsudvalget for Svin   HB:**1896**
4   Copenhageen V 1609, Axeltorv 3
5 - Autochthon Danish landpig
6   Incrossing since 1970 from Landrace 983 Norway, Landrace 970 Finland
7   Numbers 1992: 8000/60000; HB: 3300; increasing; 100 %; Ne = 9345
8 - Height: **90/90** cm; Weight: **325/225** kg; Herd number: **miss**; AI: **Yes**
9   Colour: **Uni white**
10   Pecularity: **lop ears**
11 - Main use: (1) **meat**,(2) **miss**,(3) **miss**
12   Spec. abilities: **miss**
13   Performance compared with STB **Large White**:
14   higher: **daily gain, age of sexual maturity**
15   equal: **% lean, litter size, meat quality, farrowing interval**
16   lower: **feed conversion rate**
17 - Management: **stationary**; housing: **12 m.**;
18 - Conservation progr.: live animals: **miss**;Semen: **25**;Embryos: **miss**
19   Status: **normal**
20 - <u>Similar breeds</u> (see group 2/1 on page 101)   <u>EN</u>   <u>Country</u>   <u>Status</u>
21   **Belgische Landrasse**   907   D*   crit.end.
22   **Zlotnicka biala**   1024   PL   crit.end.
23   **Landrace**   952   CS   normal
24   **Belgisch Landvarken**   906   B   normal

PIGS

```
 1 - Sortbroget                                              EN 1005
 2   Danish Black Pied; country-wide
 3   Landforeningen for opdraettere af Sortbrogede Svin       HB:1920
 4   Klippinge 4672, Vestermose
 5 - Autochthon local breed
 7   Numbers 1992: 20/100; HB: miss; decreasing; 80 %; Ne = 44
 8 - Height: 80/70 cm; Weight: 350/300 kg; Herd number: 20; AI: miss
 9   Colour: Uni black, white
10   Pecularity: miss
11 - Main use: (1) meat,(2) miss,(3) miss
12   Spec. abilities: miss
13   Performance compared with STB Danish Landrace 917:
14     higher: litter size, handling ease, piglet mortality
15     equal: meat quality, age of sexual maturity, farrowing interval
16     lower: % lean, feed conversion rate, daily gain, muscularity
17 - Management: stationary; housing: 12 m.;
18 - Conservation progr.: live animals: Yes;Semen: 2;Embryos: miss
19   Status: critically endang.;Watch: ♂♂,HB♀♀,trend,%pure!
```

20 - Similar breeds (see group 6/2 on page 104)   EN   Country Status

21	Schwarz-Weißes Bentheimer	996	D	crit.end.
22	Manchada de Jabugo	971	E	crit.end.
23	Sibirskaya chernopestraya	1001	USSR	pot. end.
24	Gloucestershire Old Spot	936	GB	pot. end.

HORSES

```
 1 - Den Jydske Hest                                          EN  741
 2   Jutland Horse; Jutland
 3   Avlsforeningen Den Jydske Hest                           HB:1881
 4   Aarhus N 8200, Udkaersvej 15, Skejby
 5 - Autochthon Danish country breed
 6   Incrossing since 1950 from Shire 804 and Suffolk 808 United Kingdom
 7   Numbers 1992: 45/350; HB: 36; stable; 100 %; Ne = 61
 8 - Height: 158/155 cm; Weight: 800/800 kg; Herd number: 150; AI: miss
 9   Colour: usually chestnut, sometimes sorrel or roan
10   Pecularity: often white markings on face and legs
11 - Main use: (1) sport/hobby,(2) meat,(3) vegetation management
12   Spec. abilities: miss
13   Performance compared with STB Percheron:
14     higher: miss
15     equal: pulling power,handling ease,fertility,age of sexual mat.
16     lower: miss
17 - Management: stationary; housing: 2-6 m.;
18 - Conservation progr.: live animals: Yes;Semen: 3;Embryos: miss
19   Status: minimally endang.; Watch: HB♀♀!
```

20 - Similar breeds (see group 4/4 on page 110)   EN   Country Status

21	Schleswiger Kaltblut	799	D	endanger.
22	Frederiksborgheste	748	DK	min. end.
23	Nordsvensk häst	787	S	normal
24	Suomenhevonen	809	SF	normal

DENMARK HORSES

```
1 - Frederiksborgheste                                        EN  748
2   Frederiksborg Horse; country-wide, mainly on Zealand & Funen
3   Frederiksborg Hesteavlsforeningen                         HB:1890
4   Aarhus N 8200, Udkaersvej 15, Skejby
5 - Autochthon Danish country breed derived from Andalusian and Neapo-
6   litanian horses; incrossing since 1950 from Warmblood DK, Arabian D
7   Numbers 1992: 37/500; HB: 42; increasing; 100 %; Ne = 59
8 - Height: 164/160 cm; Weight: 650/600 kg; Herd number: 200; AI: miss
9   Colour: almost invariably chestnut
10  Pecularity: miss
11 - Main use: (1) sport/hobby,(2) miss,(3) miss
12  Spec. abilities: miss
13  Performance compared with STB Halfbred:
14    higher: miss
15    equal:  pulling power,handling ease,fertility,age of sexual matur.
16    lower:  adaptability in dressage, jumping in military
17 - Management: stationary; housing: 2-6 m.;
18 - Conservation progr.: live animals: Yes;Semen: 3;Embryos: miss
19  Status: minimally endang.; Watch: HB♀♀!
```

```
20 - Similar breeds (see group 4/4 on page 110)    EN   Country  Status
21  Schleswiger Kaltblut                            799   D       endanger.
22  Den Jydske Hest                                 741   DK      min. end.
23  Nordsvensk häst                                 787   S       normal
24  Suomenhevonen                                   809   SF      normal
```

ESTONIA CATTLE

```
1 - Cherno-pestraya estonskaya                                EN   65
2   Estonian Black Pied; northwestern and northern Estonia
3   Food and Agriculture Organisation of the UN               HB:1885
4   Rome 00100, Via delle Terme di Caracalla
5 - Composite of Dutch Friesian, East Friesian, Estonian Native cattle
7   Numbers 1990: 500/129000; HB: miss; increasing; 95 %; Ne = 1992
8 - Height: 139/128 cm; Weight: 900/500 kg; Herd number: miss; AI: Yes
9   Colour: Combination black, white
10  Pecularity: black pied
11 - Main use: (1) milk,(2) meat,(3) miss
12  Spec. abilities: miss
13  Performance compared with STB Russian Black Pied 64:
14    higher: % fat
15    equal:  miss
16    lower:  milk yield
17 - Management: stationary; housing: > 6 m.;
18 - Conservation progr.: live animals: miss;Semen: miss;Embryos: miss
19  Status: normal;            Watch: HB♀♀!
```

```
20 - Similar breeds (see group 1/2 on page 75)     EN   Country  Status
21  Burlina                                         51    I       crit.end.
22  Breton Pie Noire                                42    F       endanger.
23  Deutsches Schwarzbuntes Rind                    79    D*      pot. end.
24  Cherno-pestraya litovskaya                      66    LT      normal
```

1 - Krasnaya estonskaya   EN   143
2   Estonian Red; southern central and eastern Estonia
3   Food and Agriculture Organisation of the UN   HB:1885
4   Rome 00100, Via delle Terme di Caracalla
5 - Composite of Angeln, Danish Red, Estonian Native cattle
6   Incrossing since 1950 from Danish Red 222 Denmark, Angeln 8 Germany
7   Numbers 1990: 757/168000; HB: miss; decreasing; 86 %; Ne = 3014
8 - Height: 135/128 cm; Weight: 850/480 kg; Herd number: miss; AI: Yes
9   Colour: Uni red
10   Pecularity: miss
11 - Main use: (1) milk,(2) miss,(3) miss
12   Spec. abilities: miss
13   Performance compared with STB Russian Black Pied 64:
14   higher: % fat
15   equal: miss
16   lower: milk yield
17 - Management: stationary; housing: > 6 m.;
18 - Conservation progr.: live animals: miss;Semen: miss;Embryos: miss
19   Status: minimally endang.; Watch: HB♀♀,trend,%pure,%incross!
20 - Similar breeds (see group 4/3 on page 78)   EN Country Status
21   Donnersberger Rotvieh   101 D   crit.end.
22   Harzer Rotvieh   109 D   crit.end.
23   Rod Dansk Malkerace   222 DK   normal
24   Rood Ras van Belgie   224 B   normal

1 - Mestnaya estonskaya   EN   171
2   Estonian Native; country-wide
3   Food and Agriculture Organisation of the UN   HB:1914
4   Rome 00100, Via delle Terme di Caracalla
5 - Autochthon
6   Incrossing since 1950 from West Finnish Cattle 153 Finland, Jersey
7   Numbers 1990: 5/620; HB: miss; decreasing; 92 %; Ne = 9
8 - Height: 134/125 cm; Weight: 800/500 kg; Herd number: miss; AI: miss
9   Colour: Uni red, brown, yellow
10   Pecularity: horns 0/0
11 - Main use: (1) milk,(2) miss,(3) miss
12   Spec. abilities: resistant to tuberculosis, leucosis; hardiness
13   Performance compared with STB Russian Black Pied 64:
14   higher: % fat
15   equal: miss
16   lower: milk yield
17 - Management: stationary; housing: > 6 m.; low food consumption / unit
18 - Conservation progr.: live animals: miss;Semen: miss;Embryos: miss
19   Status: critically endang.;Watch: ♂♂,HB♀♀,trend,%pure,%incross!
20 - Similar breeds (see group 4/4 on page 78)   EN Country Status
21   Länsisuomenkarja   153 SF   endanger.
22   Röd Kullig Lantras   225 S   min. end.
23   Norsk rodtfe   187 N   normal
24   Icelandic Dairy Cattle   118 IS   normal

ESTONIA   PIGS

```
1 - Estonskaya bekonnaya                                    EN  933
2   Estonian Bacon; country-wide
3   Food and Agriculture Organisation of the UN            HB:miss
4   Rome 00100, Via delle Terme di Caracalla
5 - Composite of native long-eared, Danish, Finnish, German Landraces,
6   Large White
7   Numbers 1990: 7400/19500; HB: miss; stable; 68 %; Ne = 21457
8 - Height: miss/miss cm; Weight: 323/244 kg; Herd number: miss; AI:miss
9   Colour: Uni white
10  Pecularity: lop-eared
11 - Main use: (1) meat,(2) crossbreeding dam line,(3) miss
12  Spec. abilities: miss
13  Performance compared with STB Large White 951:
14    higher: litter size
15    equal: % lean, feed conversion rate, daily gain
16    lower: miss
17 - Management: stationary; housing: 12 m.;
18 - Conservation progr.: live animals: miss;Semen: miss;Embryos: miss
19  Status: normal;              Watch: HB♀♀,%pure!
```

20 - Similar breeds (see group 2/1 on page 101)	EN	Country	Status
21 Belgische Landrasse	907	D*	crit.end.
22 Zlotnicka biala	1024	PL	crit.end.
23 Landrace	952	CS	normal
24 Belgisch Landvarken	906	B	normal

FAEROE ISLANDS   CATTLE

```
1 - Faeroesk                                                EN   84
2   Faeroes Cattle; Faroe Island
3   National Institute of Animal Science                   HB:miss
4   Tjele 8830, P.O. Box 39
5 - Imported as breed from Norway, Denmark
6   Incrossing since 1950 from Norwegian Red Friesian 187 Norway
7   Numbers 1992: 40/1200; HB: miss; decreasing; 100 %; Ne = 155
8 - Height: 130/120 cm; Weight: 410/350 kg; Herd number: miss; AI: miss
9   Colour: Uni or combination black, grey, red, brown, yellow, white
10  Pecularity: miss
11 - Main use: (1) milk,(2) meat,(3) miss
12  Spec. abilities: suitable of grazing on steep wet land
13  Performance compared with STB Holstein-Friesian:
14    higher: calf mortality
15    equal: % fat,% protein,calving ease and interval,age of sex. mat.
16    lower: pulling power,milk yield,muscularity,daily gain,milkabili.
17 - Management: stationary; housing: 12 m.;
18 - Conservation progr.: live animals: miss;Semen: 25;Embryos: miss
19  Status: minimally endang.; Watch: HB♀♀,trend,herds,%incross!
```

20 - Similar breeds (see group 10 on page 82)	EN	Country	Status
21 Albera	4	E	crit.end.
22 Mostrenca	177	E	endanger.
23 Inra 95	119	F	pot. end.
24 Corse	70	F	normal

FAEROE ISLANDS   SHEEP

```
 1 - Foroyskur Seydur                                        EN   491
 2   Faeroes Sheep
 3   Foroya Jardarrad                                        HB:miss
 4   Torshavn 110, B.O. Box 50
 5 - Imported as breed from countries Norway (Spaelsau 569)
 7   Numbers 1992: 3000/80000; HB: miss; increasing; 100 %; Ne = 11566
 8 - Height: 65/60 cm; Weight: 60/60 kg; Herd number: miss; AI: miss
 9   Colour: Uni blue, white
10   Pecularity: horns 0/0
11 - Main use: (1) meat,(2) wool,(3) fur
12   Spec. abilities: miss
13   Performance compared with STB Texel:
14      higher: wool or fiber thickness
15      equal:  carcass leanness, age of sexual maturity, lambing interval
16      lower:  litter size,muscularity,daily gain,length of mating season
17 - Management: stationary; housing: no
18 - Conservation progr.: live animals: miss;Semen: miss;Embryos: miss
19   Status: normal;              Watch: HB♀♀!
```

20 - Similar breeds (see group 6/3 on page 90)	EN	Country	Status
21 Dansk Landfar	477	DK	crit.end.
22 Coburger Fuchsschaf	466	D	crit.end.
23 Suomenlammas	644	SF	normal
24 Gronlandsk Fär	504	DK	normal

FINLAND   CATTLE

```
 1 - Itäsuomenkarja                                          EN   129
 2   East Finncattle; eastern Finland
 3   The Finnish Animal Breeding Association                 HB:1898
 4   Vantaa 01301, P.O. Box 40
 5 - Autochthon local breed
 6   Incrossing since 1950 from Friesian Sweden, Ayrshire 247 Finland
 7   Numbers 1993: 6/15; HB: miss; increasing; 100 %; Ne = 7
 8 - Height: 135/118 cm; Weight: 600/440 kg; Herd number: > 10; AI: Yes
 9   Colour: Combination red, white
10   Pecularity: horns 0/0, sides are red, the back is white
11 - Main use: (1) milk,(2) meat,(3) miss
12   Spec. abilities: frequency of k-kasein B is about 80%
13   Performance compared with STB Holstein-Friesian:
14      higher: % fat, % protein
15      equal:  calving ease and interval,age of sex. matur.,handling ease
16      lower:  daily gain,calf mort.,milk yield,muscularity,pulling power
17 - Management: stationary; housing: > 6 m.;
18 - Conservation progr.: live animals: Yes;Semen: 4;Embryos: 1/1
19   Status: critically endang.;Watch: ♂♂,♀♀,HB♀♀,%incross!
```

20 - Similar breeds (see group 3/7 on page 78)	EN	Country	Status
21 Telemark	254	N	crit.end.
22 Irish Moiled	123	GB	crit.end.
23 English Longhorn	82	GB	pot. end.
24 Vosgienne	267	F	pot. end.

```
1 - Länsisuomenkarja                                         EN   153
2   West Finncattle; country-wide
3   The Finnish Animal Breeding Association                  HB:1904
4   Vantaa 01301, P.O. Box 40
5 - Autochthon local breed
6   Incrossing since 1950 from Friesian Sweden, Ayrshire 247 Finland
7   Numbers 1986: 20/22600; HB: 360; decreasing; 80 %; Ne = 55
8 - Height: 140/123 cm; Weight: 850/470 kg; Herd number: miss; AI: Yes
9   Colour: Uni red
10  Pecularity: horns 0/0
11 - Main use: (1) milk,(2) meat,(3) miss
12  Spec. abilities: miss
13  Performance compared with STB Holstein-Friesian:
14    higher: % fat
15    equal: % protein,calving ease,calving interval,age of sexual mat.
16    lower:  daily gain, calf mortality, milk yield, muscularity
17 - Management: stationary; housing: > 6 m.;
18 - Conservation progr.: live animals: Yes;Semen: 15;Embryos: miss
19   Status: endangered;        Watch: HB♀♀,trend,%pure,%incross!
20 - Similar breeds (see group 4/4 on page 78)    EN  Country Status
21   Mestnaya estonskaya                          171   EW   crit.end.
22   Röd Kullig Lantras                           225   S    min. end.
23   Norsk rodtfe                                 187   N    normal
24   Icelandic Dairy Cattle                       118   IS   normal
```

```
1 - Pohjoissuomenkarja                                       EN   207
2   North Finncattle; northern Finland
3   The Finnish Animal Breeding Association                  HB:1905
4   Vantaa 01301, P.O. Box 40
5 - Autochthon white cattle of North Finland; incrossing since 1950 from
6   Friesian Sweden, Ayrshire 247 Finland, Fellbreed Sweden
7   Numbers 1993: 15/50; HB: miss; increasing; 100 %; Ne = 25
8 - Height: 128/118 cm; Weight: 650/400 kg; Herd number: > 10; AI: Yes
9   Colour: Combination white, black
10  Pecularity: horns 0/0, black spots
11 - Main use: (1) milk,(2) meat,(3) miss
12  Spec. abilities: frequency of k-kasein b is about 80%
13  Performance compared with STB Holstein-Friesian:
14    higher: % fat, % protein
15    equal: calving ease and interval,age of sexual maturity,handling
16    lower:  daily gain,calf mort.,milk yield,muscularity,pulling power
17 - Management: stationary; housing: > 6 m.;
18 - Conservation progr.: live animals: Yes;Semen: 2;Embryos: 2/1
19   Status: critically endang.;Watch: ♂♂,HB♀♀,herds,%incross!
20 - Similar breeds (see group 1/6 on page 76)    EN  Country Status
21   Tuxer                                        259   A    crit.end.
22   Sidet tronderfe og nordland                  235   N    crit.end.
23   Berrenda negra andaluza                       29   E    min. end.
24   Gruzinskii gornyi skot                       107   GO   normal
```

```
 1 - Suomen Ayrshire                                          EN   247
 2   Ayrshire; country-wide
 3   The Finnish Animal Breeding Association                  HB:1901
 4   Vantaa 01301, P.O. Box 40
 5 - Composite of Ayrshire 18 GB, S, local Finncattle; incrossing since
 6   1950 from Red and White Norway, Ayrshire 18 United Kingdom, USA
 7   Numbers 1986: 354/457800; HB: 35906; decreasing; 93 %; Ne = 1402
 8 - Height: 145/127 cm; Weight: 1000/500 kg; Herd number: miss; AI: Yes
 9   Colour: Combination red, white
10   Pecularity: miss
11 - Main use: (1) milk,(2) meat,(3) miss
12   Spec. abilities: one of the most prod. Ayrshire pop. of the world
13   Performance compared with STB Holstein-Friesian:
14     higher: % fat
15     equal:  milk yield,muscul.,% protein,calving ease,calving interval
16     lower:  daily gain
17 - Management: stationary; housing: > 6 m.;
18 - Conservation progr.: live animals: miss;Semen: 354;Embryos: Yes
19   Status: normal;              Watch: %incross!
20 - Similar breeds (see group 3/6 on page 78)    EN  Country Status
21   Ayrshire                                      17   IRL   endanger.
22   Ayrshire                                      18   GB    normal
```

```
 1 - Suomenlammas                                             EN   644
 2   Finnsheep; country-wide
 3   Finnish Sheep Breeders Assc.                             HB:1923
 4   Helsinki 00120, Lönnrotinkatu 13
 5 - Autochthon East-Finnish type of landrace sheep; incrossing
 6   since 1960 from Texel, Swedish Peltsheep Sweden, Rygja 614 Norway
 7   Numbers 1986: 6000/60000; HB: 282; stable; 95 %; Ne = 1077
 8 - Height: 72/65 cm; Weight: 87/66 kg; Herd number: miss; AI: Yes
 9   Colour: Uni black, brown, white
10   Pecularity: horns 0/0,4 teats in 20% ewes,functional in 25% of these
11 - Main use: (1) meat,(2) wool,(3) fur
12   Spec. abilities: mature young, long mating season, ∅ 2.7 littersize
13   Performance compared with STB Texel 648:
14     higher: litter size, length of mating season, lambing interval
15     equal:  miss
16     lower:  muscularity,age of sex. matur.,daily gain,carcass leanness
17 - Management: stationary; housing: > 6 m.;
18 - Conservation progr.: live animals: Yes;Semen: 6;Embryos: 5/20
19   Status: normal
20 - Similar breeds (see group 6/3 on page 90)    EN  Country Status
21   Dansk Landfar                                477   DK    crit.end.
22   Coburger Fuchsschaf                          466   D     crit.end.
23   Foroyskur Seydur                             491   FR    normal
24   Gronlandsk Fär                               504   DK    normal
```

FINLAND   SHEEP

```
 1 - Texel                                              EN   648
 2   Texel; southern Finland
 3   The Finnish Breeding Society for Sheep and Goat    HB:miss
 4   Helsinki 00120, Lönnrotinkatu 13
 5 - Imported as breed from countries Sweden, Denmark
 7   Numbers 1986: 30/400; HB: 150; increasing; 90 %; Ne = 100
 8 - Height: miss/miss cm; Weight: 105/80 kg; Herd number: miss; AI: miss
 9   Colour: Uni white
10   Pecularity: horns 0/0
11 - Main use: (1) meat,(2) wool,(3) miss
12   Spec. abilities: miss
13   Performance compared with STB miss:
14     higher: miss
15     equal:  miss
16     lower:  miss
17 - Management: stationary; housing: > 6 m.;
18 - Conservation progr.: live animals: miss;Semen: 3;Embryos: 3/3
19   Status: potential. endang.;Watch: HB♀♀,%pure!
20 - Similar breeds (see group 2/2 on page 88)    EN  Country Status
21   Texel                                        649  F    normal
22   Texel                                        650  D    normal
23   Texel                                        652  L    normal
24   Texel                                        651  IRL  normal
```

FINLAND   GOATS

```
 1 - Suomenvuohi                                         EN   358
 2   Finnish Landrace; western Finland
 3   Finnish Sheep Breeders Assc.                        HB:1932
 4   Helsinki 00120, Lönnrotinkatu 13
 5 - Autochthon Mixed Landrace
 6   Incrossing since 1960 from Norwegian 342 Norway
 7   Numbers 1986: 150/2250; HB: 18; stable; 100 %; Ne = 41
 8 - Height: 70/60 cm; Weight: 68/50 kg; Herd number: miss; AI: Yes
 9   Colour: Uni brown, white; combination black, grey, brown, white
10   Pecularity: horns 2/2, spotted, saddle
11 - Main use: (1) milk,(2) sport/hobby,(3) miss
12   Spec. abilities: miss
13   Performance compared with STB Saanen:
14     higher: miss
15     equal:  muscularity,carcass leanness,litter size,% fat,% protein
16     lower:  daily gain, milk yield
17 - Management: stationary; housing: > 6 m.;
18 - Conservation progr.: live animals: miss;Semen: 3;Embryos: miss
19   Status: endangered;        Watch: HB♀♀!
20 - Similar breeds (see group 10 on page 98)    EN  Country Status
21   Nederlandse Landgeit                         341  NL   pot. end.
22   Dansk Landrace                               322  DK   normal
23   Svensk Lantras                               359  S    normal
24   Norsk Geit                                   342  N    normal
```

```
 1 - Maatiaissika                                              EN  970
 2   Finnish Landrace; country-wide
 3   The Finnish Animal Breeding Association                  HB:1914
 4   Vantaa 01301, P.O. Box 40
 5 - Autochthon native domestic pig stock
 6   Incrossing since 1970 from Landrace 983 Norway
 7   Numbers 1986: 2500/20000; HB: 2500; stable; 100 %; Ne = 5000
 8 - Height: 100/75 cm; Weight: 250/200 kg; Herd number: miss; AI: Yes
 9   Colour: Uni white
10   Pecularity: lop ears
11 - Main use: (1) meat,(2) miss,(3) miss
12   Spec. abilities: very low frequency of halothane gene
13   Performance compared with STB Large White 1021:
14     higher: miss
15     equal: % lean,litter size,feed conv. rate,meat quality,daily gain
16     lower: miss
17 - Management: stationary; housing: 12 m.;
18 - Conservation progr.: live animals: miss;Semen: 500;Embryos: miss
19   Status: normal
```

20 - Similar breeds (see group 2/1 on page 101)	EN	Country	Status
21 Belgische Landrasse	907	D*	crit.end.
22 Zlotnicka biala	1024	PL	crit.end.
23 Landrace	952	CS	normal
24 Belgisch Landvarken	906	B	normal

```
 1 - Yorkshire                                                 EN 1021
 2   Large White; country-wide
 3   The Finnish Animal Breeding Association                  HB:1914
 4   Vantaa 01301, P.O. Box 40
 5 - Imported as breed from countries United Kingdom, Denmark
 6   Incrossing since 1970 from Yorkshire Sweden
 7   Numbers 1986: 3000/25000; HB: 2500; stable; 100 %; Ne = 5455
 8 - Height: 100/75 cm; Weight: 250/200 kg; Herd number: miss; AI: Yes
 9   Colour: Uni white
10   Pecularity: erect ears
11 - Main use: (1) meat,(2) miss,(3) miss
12   Spec. abilities: very low frequency of halothane gene
13   Performance compared with STB Finnish Landrace 970:
14     higher: miss
15     equal: % lean,litter size,feed conv. rate,meat quality,daily gain
16     lower: miss
17 - Management: stationary; housing: 12 m.;
18 - Conservation progr.: live animals: miss;Semen: 500;Embryos: miss
19   Status: normal
```

20 - Similar breeds (see group 1/1 on page 101)	EN	Country	Status
21 Norsk Yorkshire	984	N	endanger.
22 Grand Yorkshire Belge	937	B	normal
23 Large White Pigs	963	IRL	normal
24 Large White	960	F	normal

```
 1 - Arabialainen                                          EN  706
 2   Arab; southern Finland
 3   Suomen Hippos                                         HB:1955
 4   Espoo 02600, Tulkinkuja 3
 5 - Imported as breed from country Sweden
 6   Incrossing since 1950 from other Arabian breeds from Europe
 7   Numbers 1991: 4/120; HB: miss; increasing; 20 %; Ne = 7
 8 - Height: 155/150 cm; Weight: miss/miss kg; Herd number: miss; AI:miss
 9   Colour: grey, chestnut or bay
10   Pecularity: long fine mane and tail
11 - Main use: (1) sport/hobby,(2) miss,(3) miss
12   Spec. abilities: miss
13   Performance compared with STB miss:
14      higher: miss
15      equal:  miss
16      lower:  miss
17 - Management: stationary; housing: > 6 m.;
18 - Conservation progr.: live animals: miss;Semen: miss;Embryos: miss
19   Status: critically endang.;Watch: ♂♂,HB♀♀,herds,%pure!
20 - Similar breeds (see group 1 on page 108)    EN  Country Status
21   Täysverinen                                  811  SF   crit.end.
22   Gidran                                       751  H    crit.end.
23   Anglo-Arab                                   702  F    normal
24   Vollblutaraber                               815  A    normal
```

```
 1 - Connemara Pony                                        EN  819
 2   Connemara Pony
 3   Suomen Hippos                                         HB:miss
 4   Espoo 02600, Tulkinkuja 3
 5 - miss
 7   Numbers 1991: 3/220; HB: miss; increasing; miss %; Ne = 5
 8 - Height:miss/miss cm; Weight:miss/miss kg; Herd number:miss; AI:miss
 9   Colour: dun with dark legs, grey, bay, black, brown
10   Pecularity: few roan or chestnut
11 - Main use: (1) sport/hobby,(2) miss,(3) miss
12   Spec. abilities: miss
13   Performance compared with STB miss:
14      higher: miss
15      equal:  miss
16      lower:  miss
17 - Management: stationary; housing: > 6 m.;
18 - Conservation progr.: live animals: miss;Semen: miss;Embryos: miss
19   Status: critically endang.;Watch: ♂♂,HB♀♀!
20 - Similar breeds (see group 5/6 on page 111)  EN  Country Status
21   Connemara                                    736  F    normal
22   Connemara Pony                               737  IRL  normal
```

```
 1 - Gotland Russ                                                    EN   820
 2   Gotland Pony
 3   Suomen Hippos                                                   HB:miss
 4   Espoo 02600, Tulkinkuja 3
 5 - miss
 7   Numbers 1991: 6/350; HB: miss; stable; miss %; Ne = 11
 8 - Height:miss/miss cm; Weight:miss/miss kg; Herd number:miss; AI:miss
 9   Colour: commonly bay or black, all standard colours also
10   Pecularity: miss
11 - Main use: (1) sport/hobby,(2) miss,(3) miss
12   Spec. abilities: miss
13   Performance compared with STB miss:
14     higher: miss
15     equal: miss
16     lower: miss
17 - Management: stationary; housing: > 6 m.;
18 - Conservation progr.: live animals: miss;Semen: miss;Embryos: miss
19   Status: critically endang.;Watch: ♂♂,HB♀♀!
```

20 -	Similar breeds (see group 5/1 on page 110)	EN	Country	Status
21	Nordlandshest	786	N	min. end.
22	Fjordhest	746	N	pot. end.
23	Skogsruss	805	S	normal
24	Fjord de Norvege	745	F	normal

```
 1 - Islannin hevonen                                                EN   767
 2   Iceland Pony; southern Finland
 3   Suomen Hippos                                                   HB:1960
 4   Espoo 02600, Tulkinkuja 3
 5 - Imported as breed from country 768 Iceland
 6   Incrossing since 1950 from Iceland Pony 768 Iceland
 7   Numbers 1991: 4/250; HB: miss; increasing; 100 %; Ne = 7
 8 - Height: 135/135 cm; Weight: miss/miss kg; Herd number:miss; AI:miss
 9   Colour: usually grey or dun, sometimes bay or chestnut, few black
10   Pecularity: miss
11 - Main use: (1) sport/hobby,(2) miss,(3) miss
12   Spec. abilities: special gaits: amble and toelt
13   Performance compared with STB miss:
14     higher: miss
15     equal: miss
16     lower: miss
17 - Management: stationary; housing: > 6 m.;
18 - Conservation progr.: live animals: miss;Semen: miss;Embryos: miss
19   Status: critically endang.;Watch: ♂♂,HB♀♀,herds!
```

20 -	Similar breeds (see group 5/2 on page 110)	EN	Country	Status
21	Islandais	766	F	min. end.
22	Islenski hesturinn	768	IS	normal

```
 1 - Lämminverinen ravuri                                    EN   773
 2   Warm-blooded Trotter; country-wide
 3   Suomen Hippos                                           HB:1958
 4   Espoo 02600, Tulkinkuja 3
 5 - Imported from Sweden, Standardbreed USA, Orlov Trotter USSR
 6 - Incrossing since 1950 from Sweden
 7   Numbers 1991: 150/9000; HB: miss; increasing; 100 %; Ne = 590
 8 - Height: 157/157 cm; Weight: 500/510 kg; Herd number: miss; AI: miss
 9   Colour: bay, chestnut, black
10   Pecularity: miss
11 - Main use: (1) sport/hobby,(2) miss,(3) miss
12   Spec. abilities: miss
13   Performance compared with STB miss:
14     higher: miss
15     equal:  miss
16     lower:  miss
17 - Management: stationary; housing: > 6 m.;
18 - Conservation progr.: live animals: miss;Semen: miss;Embryos: miss
19   Status: normal
20 - Similar breeds (see group 2 on page 108)    EN  Country Status
21   Morgan Horse                                 783  GB    endanger.
22   Trotteur Francais                            813  F     normal
23   Norsk Kaldblods Traver                       789  N     normal
```

```
 1 - New Forest Pony                                         EN   821
 2   New Forest Pony
 3   Suomen Hippos                                           HB:miss
 4   Espoo 02600, Tulkinkuja 3
 5 - miss
 7   Numbers 1991: 12/700; HB: miss; increasing; miss %; Ne = 26
 8 - Height:miss/miss cm; Weight:miss/miss kg; Herd number: miss; AI:miss
 9   Colour: any colour except piebald or scewbald
10   Pecularity: miss
11 - Main use: (1) sport/hobby,(2) miss,(3) miss
12   Spec. abilities: miss
13   Performance compared with STB miss:
14     higher: miss
15     equal:  miss
16     lower:  miss
17 - Management: stationary; housing: > 6 m.;
18 - Conservation progr.: live animals: miss;Semen: miss;Embryos: miss
19   Status: minimally endang.; Watch: ♂♂,HB♀♀!
20 - Similar breeds (see group 5/3 on page 110)  EN  Country Status
21   Welsh Pony (A, B & D)                        823  SF    crit.end.
22   Dartmoor                                     738  F     min. end.
23   New Forest                                   784  F     pot. end.
24   Dartmoor Pony                                739  GB    normal
```

1 - Puoliverinen   EN 795
2   Halfbred; country-wide
3   Suomen Hippos   HB:1980
4   Espoo 02600, Tulkinkuja 3
5 - Imported as breed from Sweden and other European countries
7   Numbers 1991: 30/2300; HB: miss; increasing; 90 %; Ne = 118
8 - Height: 167/163 cm; Weight: miss/miss kg; Herd number: miss; AI:miss
9   Colour: mainly bay
10 Pecularity: miss
11 - Main use: (1) sport/hobby,(2) miss,(3) miss
12 Spec. abilities: miss
13 Performance compared with STB miss:
14   higher: miss
15   equal: miss
16   lower: miss
17 - Management: stationary; housing: > 6 m.;
18 - Conservation progr.: live animals: miss;Semen: miss;Embryos: miss
19 Status: potential. endang.;Watch: ♂♂,HB♀♀!
20 - Similar breeds (see group 3/2 on page 108)   EN Country Status
21 Altwürttemberger   701 D   crit.end.
22 Rottaler   797 D   crit.end.
23 Holsteiner Warmblut   760 D   normal
24 Cheval de Selle Francais   727 F   normal

1 - Shetland Pony   EN 822
2   Shetland Pony
3   Suomen Hippos   HB:miss
4   Espoo 02600, Tulkinkuja 3
5 - miss
7   Numbers 1991: 24/1500; HB: miss; increasing; miss %; Ne = 87
8 - Height:miss/miss cm; Weight:miss/miss kg; Herd number:miss; AI:miss
9   Colour: any colour
10 Pecularity: profuse mane and tail
11 - Main use: (1) sport/hobby,(2) miss,(3) miss
12 Spec. abilities: miss
13 Performance compared with STB miss:
14   higher: miss
15   equal: miss
16   lower: miss
17 - Management: stationary; housing: > 6 m.;
18 - Conservation progr.: live animals: miss;Semen: miss;Embryos: miss
19 Status: potential. endang.;Watch: ♂♂,HB♀♀!
20 - Similar breeds (see group 5/5 on page 111)   EN Country Status
21 Shetland   803 F   normal

1 - **Suomenhevonen** EN **809**
2   **Finnhorse; country-wide**
3   **Suomen Hippos r.y. (Finland's Hippos)** HB:**1907**
4   **Espoo 02600, Tulkinkuja 3**
5 - Autochthon North European domestic breeds
7   Numbers 1986: **235/8000**; HB: **300**; stable; **100 %**; Ne = **527**
8 - Height: **157/157** cm; Weight: **550/510** kg; Herd number: **miss**; AI: **Yes**
9   Colour: **usually chestnut, occasionally bay or black**
10 Pecularity: **white markings on the head and legs**
11 - Main use: (1) **sport/hobby**,(2) **tractive power**,(3) **vegetation manag.**
12 Spec. abilities: **all-round horse (trotter, riding horse, work horse)**
13 Performance compared with STB **Halfbred 795**:
14   higher: **pulling power, handl. ease, daily gain, speed in trotters**
15   equal: **adaptability in military**
16   lower: **adaptability in dressage and in jumping, speed in gallop**
17 - Management: **stationary**; housing: **> 6 m.**;
18 - Conservation progr.: live animals: **Yes**;Semen: **25**;Embryos: **miss**
19 Status: **normal**
20 - Similar breeds (see group 4/4 on page 110) EN Country Status
21 **Schleswiger Kaltblut**   799 D   endanger.
22 **Den Jydske Hest**   741 DK   min. end.
23 **Tyngre Doelehest**   814 N   pot. end.
24 **Nordsvensk häst**   787 S   normal

1 - **Täysverinen** EN **811**
2   **Thoroughbred; country-wide**
3   **Suomen Hippos** HB:**1960**
4   **Espoo 02600, Tulkinkuja 3**
5 - **Imported as breed from country Sweden**
6   **Incrossing since 1950 from Europe**
7   Numbers 1991: **1/30**; HB: **miss**; stable; **30 %**; Ne = **4**
8 - Height: **165/160** cm; Weight: **miss/miss** kg; Herd number: **miss**; AI:**miss**
9   Colour: **any solid colour**
10 Pecularity: **fine coat**
11 - Main use: (1) **sport/hobby**,(2) **miss**,(3) **miss**
12 Spec. abilities: **miss**
13 Performance compared with STB **miss**:
14   higher: **miss**
15   equal: **miss**
16   lower: **miss**
17 - Management: **miss**; housing: **miss** m.;
18 - Conservation progr.: live animals: **miss**;Semen: **miss**;Embryos: **miss**
19 Status: **critically endang.**;Watch: ♂♂,HB♀♀,herds,%pure!
20 - Similar breeds (see group 1 on page 108) EN Country Status
21 **Arabialainen**   706 SF   crit.end.
22 **Gidran**   751 H   crit.end.
23 **Anglo-Arab**   702 F   normal
24 **Vollblutaraber**   815 A   normal

HORSES

 1 - **Welsh Pony (A, B & D)**   EN   **823**
 2   **Welsh Pony**
 3   **Suomen Hippos**   HB:**miss**
 4   **Espoo 02600, Tulkinkuja 3**
 5 - **miss**
 7   Numbers 1991: **6/300**; HB: **miss**; **increasing**; **miss** %; Ne = **11**
 8 - Height:**miss/miss** cm; Weight:**miss/miss** kg; Herd number:**miss**; AI:**miss**
 9   Colour: **any colour except piebald or scewbald**
10   Pecularity: **miss**
11 - Main use: (1) **sport/hobby**,(2) **miss**,(3) **miss**
12   Spec. abilities: **miss**
13   Performance compared with STB **miss**:
14   higher: **miss**
15   equal: **miss**
16   lower: **miss**
17 - Management: **stationary**; housing: **> 6 m.**;
18 - Conservation progr.: live animals: **miss**;Semen: **miss**;Embryos: **miss**
19   Status: **critically endang.**;Watch: **♂♂,HB♀♀!**
20 - <u>Similar breeds</u> (see group 5/3 on page 110)   <u>EN</u> <u>Country</u> <u>Status</u>
21   **New Forest Pony**   821   SF   **min. end.**
22   **Dartmoor**   738   F   **min. end.**
23   **New Forest**   784   F   **pot. end.**
24   **Dartmoor Pony**   739   GB   **normal**

CATTLE

 1 - **Alpha 16 (terminated)**   EN   **6**
 2   **Alpha 16; Limousin**
 3   **Institut National Agronomique Paris-Grignon**   HB:**miss**
 4   **Paris Cedex 5 75231, rue Claude Bernard 16**
 5 - **Composite of Limousin, Charolais**
 7   Numbers 1986: **miss / miss**; HB: **miss**; **decreasing**; **miss** %; Ne = **miss**
 8 - Height: **145/135** cm; Weight: **1075/700** kg; Herd number: **miss**; AI: **miss**
 9   Colour: **Uni yellow**
10   Pecularity: **miss**
11 - Main use: (1) **meat**,(2) **crossbreeding easy calving**,(3) **miss**
12   Spec. abilities: **miss**
13   Performance compared with STB **Limousin 156**:
14   higher: **calving ease, calf mortality**
15   equal: **milk yield, muscularity, calving rate**
16   lower: **daily gain**
17 - Management: **stationary**; housing: **≈ 2 m.**;
18 - Conservation progr.: live animals: **miss**;Semen: **16**;Embryos: **miss**
19   Status: **terminated/critically endang.**;Watch: **♂♂,HB♀♀,trend,herds!**
20 - <u>Similar breeds</u> (see group 8/3 on page 81)   <u>EN</u> <u>Country</u> <u>Status</u>
21   **Limousin**   156   F   **normal**
22   **Parthenaise**   193   F   **normal**
23   **Limousin**   157   L   **normal**
24   **Irish Limousin**   122   IRL   **normal**

```
 1 - Alpine Herens                                              EN    7
 2   Herens; Chamonix Valley
 3   Institut Technique d'Elevage Bovin, Dpt. Amélioration      HB:miss
 4   Génétique, Paris Cedex 12 75595, rue de Bercy 149
 5 - Imported as breed from: Switzerland
 6   Incrossing since 1950 from Swiss Herens 83 Switzerland
 7   Numbers 1993: 3/120; HB: 120; stable; 60 %; Ne = 5
 8 - Height: miss/132 cm; Weight: miss/500 kg; Herd number: miss; AI: Yes
 9   Colour: Uni black, brown, dark red
10   Pecularity: miss
11 - Main use: (1) milk,(2) cow fights,(3) meat
12   Spec. abilities: miss
13   Performance compared with STB Tarentaise 253:
14      higher: muscularity, handling ease, pulling power
15      equal:  daily gain, % protein, calving ease, age of sex. maturity
16      lower:  milk yield, % fat, calving interval
17 - Management: stationary; housing: > 6 m.;
18 - Conservation progr.: live animals: Yes;Semen: Yes;Embryos: miss
19   Status: critically endang.;Watch: ♂♂,HB♀♀,herds,%pure,%incross!
20 - Similar breeds (see group 5/2 on page 80)     EN  Country Status
21   Tarentaise                                    253   F     normal
22   Valdostana Castana                            260   I     normal
23   Eringer Rind                                   83   CH    normal
```

```
 1 - Armoricaine                                              EN   10
 2   Armorican; central Bretagne
 3   Federation des races bovines bretonnes autochtones      HB:1919
 4   Quimper Cedex 29332, Allée Sully 5
 5 - Composite of Froment du Leon 93, Pie Rouge de Carhaix, Shorthorn
 6   Incrossing since 1950 from: Dairy Shorthorn 233 United Kingdom
 7   Numbers 1992: 6/20; HB: 20; decreasing; 50 %; Ne = 8
 8 - Height: miss /138 cm; Weight: miss /650 kg; Herd number: 7; AI: Yes
 9   Colour: Uni red, combination red, white
10   Pecularity: light muzzle, white belly
11 - Main use: (1) milk,(2) meat,(3) miss
12   Spec. abilities: miss
13   Performance compared with STB French Simmental 89:
14      higher: calving ease, calf mortality, calving rate
15      equal:  milk yield, musc., daily gain, % protein, calving interval
16      lower:  % fat, milkability, pulling power
17 - Management: stationary; housing: 2-6 m.;
18 - Conservation progr.: live animals: Yes;Semen: 9;Embryos: miss
19   Status: critically endang.;Watch:♂♂,HB♀♀,trend,herds,%pure,%incross!
20 - Similar breeds (see group 4/2 on page 78)     EN   Country Status
21   Kurganskaya                                   151   USSR  crit.end.
22   Irish Shorthorn                               124   IRL   normal
23   Lincoln Red                                   159   GB    normal
24   Beef Shorthorn Cattle                          24   GB    normal
```

```
 1 - Aubrac                                               EN    14
 2   Aubrac; southern Central Massif
 3   Union Aubrac                                         HB:1892
 4   Rodez 1200, rue du Terral 2
 5 - Autochthon Aubrac
 6   Incrossing since 1950 from Parthenaise 193 France
 7   Numbers 1988: 1000/54200; HB: 15000; increasing; 35 %; Ne = 3750
 8 - Height: 140/129 cm; Weight: 950/580 kg; Herd number: miss; AI: Yes
 9   Colour: Uni yellow to brown
10   Pecularity: black horn tips, light circle around muzzle
11 - Main use: (1) meat,(2) vegetation management,(3) milk
12   Spec. abilities: resist. to Trypanosoma, excel. fertility, longevity
13   Performance compared with STB Charolais 62:
14      higher: % fat, % protein, calving ease, pulling power, milk yield
15      equal:  age of sexual maturity, handling ease
16      lower:  muscularity, daily gain
17 - Management: stationary; housing: 2-6 m.; mountain
18 - Conservation progr.: live animals: miss;Semen: 25;Embryos: miss
19   Status: normal;            Watch: %pure,%incross!
20 - Similar breeds (see group 5/1 on page 79)    EN  Country Status
21   Original Allgäuer Braunvieh                 189    D    crit.end.
22   Agerolese                                     2    I    crit.end.
23   Bruna                                        46    I    normal
24   Österreichisches Braunvieh                  190    A    normal
```

```
 1 - Aure et Saint-Girons                                 EN    16
 2   Aure et Saint-Girons; upper regions of Pyrenees
 3   Institut Technique d'Elevage Bovin, Dpt. Amélioration  HB:1919
 4   Génétique, Paris Cedex 12 75595, rue de Bercy 149
 5 - Autochthon Pyrenean breed
 6   Incrossing since 1950 from Bazadais 23 France
 7   Numbers 1992: 20/84; HB: 84; stable; 80 %; Ne = 41
 8 - Height: miss /135 cm; Weight: miss /600 kg; Herd number: 19; AI: Yes
 9   Colour: Uni grey
10   Pecularity: miss
11 - Main use: (1) meat,(2) milk,(3) tractive power
12   Spec. abilities: marginal areas
13   Performance compared with STB Aubrac 14:
14      higher: % fat, % protein
15      equal:  milk yield,calving ease,calving interval,age of sex. mat.
16      lower:  muscularity, daily gain, handling ease, milkability
17 - Management: stationary; housing: 2-6 m.;
18 - Conservation progr.: live animals: Yes;Semen: miss;Embryos: miss
19   Status: minimally endang.; Watch: ♂♂,HB♀♀,%pure,%incross!
20 - Similar breeds (see group 5/3 on page 80)    EN  Country Status
21   Cabannina                                    54    I    crit.end.
22   Bazadais                                     23    F    normal
23   Salers                                      226    F    normal
```

```
 1 - Basco-Bearnaise                                          EN   22
 2   Basco-Bearnais; western Pyrenees
 3   Institut Technique d'Elevage Bovin, Dpt. Amélioration    HB:1981
 4   Génétique, Paris Cedex 12 75595, rue de Bercy 149
 5 - Autochthon Pyrenean breed
 6   Incrossing since 1950 from Blonde d'Aquitaine 37 France
 7   Numbers 1992: 11/74; HB: 74; decreasing; 80 %; Ne = 19
 8 - Height: miss /132 cm; Weight: miss /550 kg; Herd number: 22; AI: Yes
 9   Colour: Uni yellow
10   Pecularity: lyra-shaped horns
11 - Main use: (1) milk,(2) meat,(3) tractive power
12   Spec. abilities: stability, mountain grazing
13   Performance compared with STB Aubrac 14:
14     higher: miss
15     equal:  % fat,% protein,calving ease,calv. interval,calf mortality
16     lower:  daily gain,milk yield,muscularity,age of sexual maturity
17 - Management: stationary; housing: 2-6 m.; mountain
18 - Conservation progr.: live animals: Yes;Semen: miss;Embryos: miss
19   Status: critically endang.;Watch: ♂♂,HB♀♀,trend,%pure,%incross!
```

```
20 - Similar breeds (see group 8/1 on page 81)    EN  Country Status
21   Coopelso 93 (terminated)                      69   F    crit.end.
22   Villard de Lans                              264   F    pot. end.
23   Blonde d'Aquitaine                            38   GB   normal
24   Blonde d'Aquitaine                            37   F    normal
```

```
 1 - Bazadais                                                 EN   23
 2   Bazadais; Aquitaine
 3   Herd-book Bazadais, Maison du G.O.B.A.                   HB:1895
 4   Bazas 33430, Zone Industrielle, B.P. 15
 5 - Autochthon local breed
 7   Numbers 1988: 100/2100; HB: 1000; stable; 90 %; Ne = 364
 8 - Height: 145/136 cm; Weight: 900/650 kg; Herd number: miss; AI: Yes
 9   Colour: Uni brown
10   Pecularity: light muzzle
11 - Main use: (1) meat,(2) tractive power,(3) miss
12   Spec. abilities: Pyrenean heath (marginal), easy calving
13   Performance compared with STB Limousin 156:
14     higher: miss
15     equal:  milk yield,musc.,daily gain,calving ease,age of sex. mat.
16     lower:  miss
17 - Management: stationary; housing: 2-6 m.;
18 - Conservation progr.: live animals: miss;Semen: 40;Embryos: 4/5
19   Status: normal
```

```
20 - Similar breeds (see group 5/3 on page 80)    EN  Country Status
21   Cabannina                                     54   I    crit.end.
22   Aure et Saint-Girons                          16   F    min. end.
23   Salers                                       226   F    normal
```

```
1 - Blanc-Bleu-Belge                                      EN    35
2   Belgian Blue; northern France
3   Union Blanc Bleue                                     HB:1989
4   Artres 59259, Route Nationale 106, Querenaing
5 - Imported as breed from Belgium
6   Incrossing since 1950 from Belgian Blue 33 Belgium
7   Numbers 1988: 1000/10000; HB: 1000; increasing; 95 %; Ne = 2000
8 - Height: 148/140 cm; Weight: 1100/800 kg; Herd number: miss; AI: Yes
9   Colour: Combination black, blue, white
10  Pecularity: miss
11 - Main use: (1) meat,(2) miss,(3) miss
12  Spec. abilities: extreme beef type, double-muscling lumbar
13  Performance compared with STB Charolais 62:
14    higher: milk yield, muscularity
15    equal:  age of sexual maturity, handling ease
16    lower:  calving ease, daily gain, calv. interval, calf mortality
17 - Management: stationary; housing: > 6 m.;
18 - Conservation progr.: live animals: miss;Semen: miss;Embryos: miss
19  Status: normal;              Watch: %incross!
```

20 - Similar breeds (see group 7 on page 81)	EN	Country	Status
21 Belgian Blue	25	IRL	pot. end.
22 Blanc Bleu Belge	33	B	normal
23 Belgian Blue	26	GB	normal
24 Bleue du Nord	36	F	normal

```
1 - Bleue du Nord                                         EN    36
2   Bleue du Nord; Département du Nord
3   Union Blanc Bleue                                     HB:1982
4   Artres 59259, Route Nationale 106, Querenaing
5 - Autochthon Ardennaise, Durham, local breed
6   Incrossing since 1950 from Belgian Blue 33 Belgium
7   Numbers 1988: 200/8000; HB: 500; stable; 75 %; Ne = 571
8 - Height: miss/135 cm; Weight: miss/700 kg; Herd number: miss; AI: Yes
9   Colour: Combination black, blue, white
10  Pecularity: miss
11 - Main use: (1) milk,(2) meat,(3) miss
12  Spec. abilities: docile
13  Performance compared with STB Holstein-Friesian 209:
14    higher: muscularity, daily gain
15    equal:  % protein,calving interval,age of sex. mat.,handling ease
16    lower:  milk yield,calving ease,% fat,calf mortality,milkability
17 - Management: stationary; housing: 2-6 m.;
18 - Conservation progr.: live animals: miss;Semen: 11;Embryos: Yes
19  Status: normal;              Watch: %pure,%incross!
```

20 - Similar breeds (see group 7 on page 81)	EN	Country	Status
21 Belgian Blue	25	IRL	pot. end.
22 Blanc Bleu Belge	33	B	normal
23 Belgian Blue	26	GB	normal
24 Blanc-Bleu-Belge	35	F	normal

```
 1 - Blonde d'Aquitaine                                      EN    37
 2   Blonde d'Aquitaine; Atlantique Pyrenees, Garonne river
 3   Upra Blonde d'Aquitaine                                 HB:1898
 4   Agen-Bon-Encontre 47240, Route de Toulouse, B.P. 28
 5 - Composite of Garonnaise, Quercy, Blonde des Pyrénées
 7   Numbers 1988: 5500/256000; HB: 19000; increasing; 90 %; Ne = 17061
 8 - Height: 150/142 cm; Weight: 1100/800 kg; Herd number: miss; AI: Yes
 9   Colour: Uni blond
10   Pecularity: miss
11 - Main use: (1) meat,(2) crossbreeding f. beef prod.,(3) miss
12   Spec. abilities: miss
13   Performance compared with STB Charolais 62:
14     higher: calving ease, handling ease
15     equal:  milk yield,musc.,daily gain,calv. interv.,age of sex. mat.
16     lower:  miss
17 - Management: stationary; housing: 2-6 m.;
18 - Conservation progr.: live animals: miss;Semen: 60;Embryos: miss
19   Status: normal
```

20 - Similar breeds (see group 8/1 on page 81)	EN	Country	Status
21 Basco-Bearnaise	22	F	crit.end.
22 Coopelso 93 (terminated)	69	F	crit.end.
23 Villard de Lans	264	F	pot. end.
24 Blonde d'Aquitaine	38	GB	normal

```
 1 - Brava, Race Espagnole                                   EN    41
 2   Fighting Bull; Grande Camargue
 3   Ass. des Eleveurs de Taureaux de Race Espagnole, Park   HB:miss
 4   Naturel Régional de Camargue, Arles 13200, Mas du Pont de Rousty
 5 - Imported as breed from Spain
 6   Incrossing since 1950 from Brava Espagnole 257 Spain
 7   Numbers 1988: 40/1100; HB: miss; increasing; 100 %; Ne = 154
 8 - Height: 130/125 cm; Weight: 500/300 kg; Herd number: miss; AI: miss
 9   Colour: Uni black
10   Pecularity: miss
11 - Main use: (1) tourist attraction (corridas),(2) sport/hobby,(3) meat
12   Spec. abilities: feeding and climatic conditions of Camargue
13   Performance compared with STB miss:
14     higher: miss
15     equal:  miss
16     lower:  miss
17 - Management: stationary; housing: no
18 - Conservation progr.: live animals: Yes;Semen: miss;Embryos: miss
19   Status: potential. endang.;Watch: HB♀♀,%incross!
```

20 - Similar breeds (see group 2/1 on page 76)	EN	Country	Status
21 Cardena Andaluza	60	E	crit.end.
22 Serrana Negra	232	E	crit.end.
23 Camargue	58	F	pot. end.
24 Toro de Lidia	257	E	normal

```
 1 - Breton Pie Noire                                          EN   42
 2   Breton Black Pied; Bretagne
 3   Societe des eleveurs de la race Bretonne Pie Noire        HB:1886
 4   Quimper Cedex 29332, Allée Sully 5
 5 - Autochthon local Breton breed
 6   Incrossing since 1950 from Frisonne 209, Pie Noire France
 7   Numbers 1992: 18/512; HB: miss; increasing; 82 %; Ne = 47
 8 - Height: 123/117 cm; Weight: 600/400 kg; Herd number: 87; AI: Yes
 9   Colour: Combination black, white
10   Pecularity: miss
11 - Main use: (1) milk,(2) meat,(3) miss
12   Spec. abilities: marginal areas
13   Performance compared with STB Jersey 134:
14      higher: muscularity
15      equal:  daily gain,calving ease,calving interval,age of sex. mat.
16      lower:  % fat, milk yield, % protein, handling ease, milkability
17 - Management: stationary; housing: ≈ 2/2-6/> 6 m.;
18 - Conservation progr.: live animals: Yes;Semen: 22;Embryos: miss
19   Status: endangered;          Watch: ♂♂,HB♀♀,%pure,%incross!
```

20 - <u>Similar breeds</u> (see group 1/2 on page 75)

		EN	Country	Status
21	Burlina	51	I	crit.end.
22	Deutsche Schwarzbunte (Original)	76	D	endanger.
23	Cherno-pestraya litovskaya	66	LT	normal
24	Cherno-pestraya estonskaya	65	EW	normal

```
 1 - Brune des Alpes                                           EN   48
 2   French Brown; southern Pyrenees, Bourgogne
 3   Upra Brune                                                HB:1911
 4   Paris 75017, boulevard Péreire-Sud 95
 5 - Imported as breed from Switzerland; incrossing since 1950
 6   from Braunvieh Austria 191 and Germany 77,Brown Swiss 40 Switzerland
 7   Numbers 1988: 1000/42700; HB: 5500; decreasing; 70 %; Ne = 3385
 8 - Height: 145/138 cm; Weight: 1000/650 kg; Herd number: miss; AI: Yes
 9   Colour: Uni brown
10   Pecularity: light rim around dark muzzle
11 - Main use: (1) milk,(2) meat,(3) miss
12   Spec. abilities: mountain
13   Performance compared with STB Brown Swiss:
14      higher: miss
15      equal:  milk yield,musc.,daily gain,% fat,% protein,calving ease
16      lower:  miss
17 - Management: stationary; housing: 2-6 m.;
18 - Conservation progr.: live animals: miss;Semen: 198;Embryos: miss
19   Status: potential. endang.;Watch: trend,%pure,%incross!
```

20 - <u>Similar breeds</u> (see group 5/1 on page 79)

		EN	Country	Status
21	Original Allgäuer Braunvieh	189	D	crit.end.
22	Agerolese	2	I	crit.end.
23	Aubrac	14	F	normal
24	Österreichisches Braunvieh	190	A	normal

1 - **Camargue**   EN   **58**
2   Camargue; Grande Camargue
3   Association des Mauadrers de Taureaux Camargue, Parc   HB:miss
4   Naturel Régional de Camargue, Arles 13200, Mas du Pont de Rousty
5 - Autochthon local breed
6   Incrossing since 1950 from Brava 257 Spain
7   Numbers 1988: 100/2000; HB: miss; stable; 100 %; Ne = 381
8 - Height: **125/115** cm; Weight: **400/250** kg; Herd number: **miss**; AI: **miss**
9   Colour: **Uni black**
10 Pecularity: **miss**
11 - Main use: (1) **tourist attraction**,(2) **sport/hobby**,(3) **meat**
12 Spec. abilities: **feeding and climatic conditions of Camargue**
13 Performance compared with STB **miss**:
14   higher: **miss**
15   equal: **miss**
16   lower: **miss**
17 - Management: **stationary**; housing: **no**
18 - Conservation progr.: live animals: **miss**;Semen: **miss**;Embryos: **miss**
19 Status: **potential. endang.**;Watch: **HB♀♀,%incross!**
20 - <u>Similar breeds</u> (see group 2/1 on page 76)   <u>EN</u> <u>Country</u> <u>Status</u>
21 **Cardena Andaluza**   60   E   crit.end.
22 **Serrana Negra**   232   E   crit.end.
23 **Race Espagnole**   41   F   pot. end.
24 **Toro de Lidia**   257   E   normal

1 - **Charolais**   EN   **62**
2   Charolais; Bourgogne, Vendée
3   Herd-Book Charolais, Résidence Saint-Gildard   HB:1864
4   **Nevers Cedex 02 58002, rue de Lourdes 8, B.P. 107**
5 - **Autochthon Charolais and Nivernais**
7   Numbers 1988: 60000/1428000; HB: 110000; increasing; 95 %; Ne=155294
8 - Height: **146/139** cm; Weight: **1150/750** kg; Herd number: **miss**; AI: **Yes**
9   Colour: **Uni white**
10 Pecularity: **light muzzle**
11 - Main use: (1) **meat**,(2) **crossbreeding for beef prod.**,(3) **miss**
12 Spec. abilities: **meat quality and quantity, heat tolerant**
13 Performance compared with STB **Limousin 156**:
14   higher: **muscularity**
15   equal: **daily gain,calving ease,calving interval,age of sex. mat.**
16   lower: **miss**
17 - Management: **stationary**; housing: **2-6 m.**;
18 - Conservation progr.: live animals: **miss**;Semen: **250**;Embryos: **Yes**
19 Status: **normal**
20 - <u>Similar breeds</u> (see group 9/2 on page 82)   <u>EN</u> <u>Country</u> <u>Status</u>
21 **Irish Charolais**   121   IRL   normal
22 **Charolais**   63   L   normal
23 **British Charolais**   43   GB   normal

```
 1 - Coopelso 93 (terminated)                                        EN    69
 2   Coopelso 93; southwestern France
 3   MIDATEST                                                        HB:miss
 4   Soual 81580, Les Nauzes
 5 - Composite of Charolais 62, Blonde d'Aquitaine 37, Limousine 157
 7   Numbers 1991: 15/ miss; HB: miss; decreasing; miss %; Ne = miss
 8 - Height: 144/138 cm; Weight: 1000/700 kg; Herd number: miss; AI: Yes
 9   Colour: Uni yellow
10   Pecularity: miss
11 - Main use: (1) meat,(2) crossbreeding for beef prod.,(3) miss
12   Spec. abilities: miss
13   Performance compared with STB Charolais 62:
14     higher: muscularity
15     equal:  miss
16     lower:  daily gain, calving ease, calf mortality
17 - Management: miss; housing: miss m.;
18 - Conservation progr.: live animals: miss;Semen: 33;Embryos: 15/17
19   Status: terminated/critically endang.;Watch: ♂♂,HB♀♀,herds,%pure!
```

20 - Similar breeds (see group 8/1 on page 81)	EN	Country	Status
21 Basco-Bearnaise	22	F	crit.end.
22 Villard de Lans	264	F	pot. end.
23 Blonde d'Aquitaine	38	GB	normal
24 Blonde d'Aquitaine	37	F	normal

```
 1 - Corse                                                           EN    70
 2   Corsican; Corse
 3   Association de defense et promotion de la race bovine           HB:miss
 4   Corse, Ajaccio 20000, Cours Napoléon 60
 5 - Autochthon local breed; incrossing since 1950 from Limousine 156 F,
 6   Charolaise 62 France, Brune des Alpes 48 France, Aubrac 14 France
 7   Numbers 1988: 2000/42400; HB: miss; increasing; 60 %; Ne = 7640
 8 - Height: 120/115 cm; Weight: 350/280 kg; Herd number: miss; AI: Yes
 9   Colour: Uni black, grey, red, brown, yellow, blond
10   Pecularity: miss
11 - Main use: (1) meat,(3) miss,(2) vegetation management
12   Spec. abilities: poor feeding conditions
13   Performance compared with STB Charolais 62:
14     higher: calving ease, calving rate
15     equal:  calving interval, calf mortality
16     lower:  muscularity,daily gain,age of sex. maturity,handling ease
17 - Management: transhumant; housing: no; feral
18 - Conservation progr.: live animals: miss;Semen: 5;Embryos: miss
19   Status: normal;              Watch: HB♀♀,%pure,%incross!
```

20 - Similar breeds (see group 10 on page 82)	EN	Country	Status
21 Albera	4	E	crit.end.
22 Mostrenca	177	E	endanger.
23 Faeroesk	84	FR	min. end.
24 Inra 95	119	F	pot. end.

```
 1 - Ferrandais                                               EN    85
 2   Ferrandais; northern Central Massif
 3   Institut Technique d'Elevage Bovin, Dpt. Amélioration    HB:1905
 4   Génétique, Paris Cedex 12 75595, rue de Bercy 149
 5 - Autochthon breed of Auvergne
 7   Numbers 1992: 22/221; HB: 221; stable; 75 %; Ne = 61
 8 - Height: miss /138 cm; Weight: miss /650 kg; Herd number: 43; AI: Yes
 9   Colour: Combination black, red, white
10   Pecularity: miss
11 - Main use: (1) milk,(2) meat,(3) tractive power
12   Spec. abilities: miss
13   Performance compared with STB French Simmental 89:
14     higher: calving ease, calf mortality, calving rate, pulling power
15     equal:  muscularity, % protein, handling ease
16     lower:  milk yield, daily gain, % fat, milkability
17 - Management: stationary; housing: 2-6 m.;
18 - Conservation progr.: live animals: Yes;Semen: miss;Embryos: miss
19   Status: potential. endang.;Watch: %pure!
```

20 - Similar breeds (see group 3/1 on page 76)	EN	Country	Status
21 Blanc-Rouge de Belgique	273	B	pot. end.
22 Deutsche Rotbunte	74	D	pot. end.
23 Dansk Rodbroget Kvaeg	73	DK	normal
24 Pie-Rouge	199	B	normal

```
 1 - Flamande                                                 EN    87
 2   Flemish; northern France
 3   Upra Flamande                                            HB:1886
 4   Lille Cedex 59048, Cité Adminstrative
 5 - Autochthon local breed
 6   Incrossing since 1950 from Danish Red 223 DK, Belgian Red 225 B
 7   Numbers 1988: 60/3400; HB: 674; stable; 60 %; Ne = 220
 8 - Height: miss/135 cm; Weight: miss/650 kg; Herd number: miss; AI: Yes
 9   Colour: Uni black, red
10   Pecularity: miss
11 - Main use: (1) milk,(2) meat,(3) miss
12   Spec. abilities: miss
13   Performance compared with STB Holstein-Friesian 209:
14     higher: calving ease
15     equal:  muscularity,daily gain,% fat,% protein,age of sex. mat.
16     lower:  milk yield, milkability
17 - Management: stationary; housing: 2-6 m.;
18 - Conservation progr.: live animals: miss;Semen: 4;Embryos: miss
19   Status: potential. endang.;Watch: %pure,%incross!
```

20 - Similar breeds (see group 4/3 on page 78)	EN	Country	Status
21 Donnersberger Rotvieh	101	D	crit.end.
22 Harzer Rotvieh	109	D	crit.end.
23 Rod Dansk Malkerace	222	DK	normal
24 Rood Ras van Belgie	224	B	normal

1 - Froment du Leon   EN   93
2   Froment du Leon; northern Bretagne
3   Association des Eleveurs de la race Froment du Léon   HB:1907
4   Bulat-Pestivien 22160
5 - Autochthon local breed of North Bretagne
6   Incrossing since 1950 from Guernsey 109 United Kingdom
7   Numbers 1992: 9/59; HB: miss; increasing; 80 %; Ne = 15
8 - Height: miss /135 cm; Weight: miss /550 kg; Herd number: 15; AI: Yes
9   Colour: Uni yellow, white patches in some animals
10 Pecularity: miss
11 - Main use: (1) milk,(2) meat,(3) miss
12 Spec. abilities: high % fat, butter coloured milk
13 Performance compared with STB Jersey 134:
14   higher: milk yield, muscularity, daily gain
15   equal: calving ease,age of sex. mat.,calf mortality,calving rate
16   lower: % fat, % protein, handling ease
17 - Management: stationary; housing: 2-6 m.;
18 - Conservation progr.: live animals: Yes;Semen: miss;Embryos: miss
19 Status: endangered;   Watch: ♂♂,HB♀♀,herds,%pure,%incross!
20 - Similar breeds (see group 8/4 on page 82)   EN Country Status
21 Jersey   132 IRL pot. end.
22 Jersey   130 DK   normal
23 Jersey   131 D   normal
24 Jersiais   134 F   normal

1 - Gascon   EN   98
2   Gascon; Pyrenees, Piémont Pyrenees
3   Upra Gasconne   HB:1894
4   Foix 09000, avenue du General de Gaulle 32
5 - Autochthon Gasconne
6   Incrossing since 1950 from Piemontese 197 Italy
7   Numbers 1988: 800/17900; HB: 5000; decreasing; 85 %; Ne = 2759
8 - Height: 145/135 cm; Weight: 900/600 kg; Herd number: miss; AI: Yes
9   Colour: Uni grey
10 Pecularity: miss
11 - Main use: (1) meat,(2) vegetation management,(3) tractive power
12 Spec. abilities: excellent fertility, longevity
13 Performance compared with STB Charolais 62:
14   higher: calving ease,pulling power,age of sex. mat.,handling ease
15   equal: milk yield
16   lower: muscularity, daily gain
17 - Management: stationary/transhumant; housing: no/≈ 2/2-6 m.;
18 - Conservation progr.: live animals: Yes;Semen: 76;Embryos: miss
19 Status: normal;   Watch: %pure,trend,%incross!
20 - Similar breeds (see group 6/2 on page 81)   EN Country Status
21 Gascon Areole   99   F   crit.end.
22 Garfagnina   97   I   crit.end.
23 Tiroler Grauvieh   256 A   pot. end.
24 Grigia Alpina   105 I   normal

1 - Gascon Areole   EN   99
2   Gascon Areole; Département du Gers
3   Upra Gasconne   HB:1894
4   Foix 09000, avenue du General de Gaulle 32
5 - Autochthon Gasconne Aréolée
6   Incrossing since 1950 from Piemontese 197 Italy
7   Numbers 1992: 9/173; HB: 173; decreasing; 60 %; Ne = 17
8 - Height: 150/140 cm; Weight: 900/650 kg; Herd number: 29; AI: Yes
9   Colour: Combination grey, white, blond
10   Pecularity: calves born red, long horns
11 - Main use: (1) meat,(2) tractive power,(3) miss
12   Spec. abilities: excellent fertility, longevity
13   Performance compared with STB Charolais 62:
14   higher: calving ease,handling ease,pulling power,age of sex. mat.
15   equal: milk yield
16   lower: muscularity, daily gain
17 - Management: stationary; housing: 2-6 m.;
18 - Conservation progr.: live animals: Yes;Semen: miss;Embryos: miss
19   Status: critically endang.;Watch: ♂♂,trend,%pure,%incross!

20 - Similar breeds (see group 6/2 on page 81)	EN	Country	Status
21 Garfagnina	97	I	crit.end.
22 Tiroler Grauvieh	256	A	pot. end.
23 Grigia Alpina	105	I	normal
24 Gascon	98	F	normal

1 - Hereford   EN 110
2   Hereford; country-wide but rare
3   Association Hereford France   HB:1975
4   Breil 49490, Gaecr du Val d'or, Le chene brule
5 - Imported as breed from: USA, United Kingdom
6   Incrossing since 1950 from Hereford 112 United Kingdom, Canada, USA
7   Numbers 1988: 30/350; HB: 100; stable; 95 %; Ne = 82
8 - Height: 145/140 cm; Weight: 1000/600 kg; Herd number: miss; AI: Yes
9   Colour: Combination red, white
10   Pecularity: white head dominant
11 - Main use: (1) meat,(2) crossbreeding,(3) miss
12   Spec. abilities: easy calving, stability
13   Performance compared with STB Hereford 110:
14   higher: Breed is used
15   equal: as standard breed,
16   lower: no comparison possible.
17 - Management: stationary; housing: 2-6 m.; extensive conditions
18 - Conservation progr.: live animals: miss;Semen: miss;Embryos: miss
19   Status: potential. endang.;Watch: HB♀♀,herds,%pure,%incross!

20 - Similar breeds (see group 3/5 on page 77)	EN	Country	Status
21 Hereford	111	IRL	normal
22 Hereford	112	GB	normal
23 Kazakhskaya belogolovaya	138	KAZ	normal

```
 1 - Inra 95                                                    EN  119
 2   Inra 95; southwestern France
 3   INRA - Station de Génétique Quantitative et Appl.,        HB:miss
 4   Centre de Recherches de Jouy, Jouy en Josas 78352
 5 - Composite of Charolais 62, Blonde d'Aquitaine 37, Limousin 156,
 6   Maine-Anjou 163; incrossing since 1950 from: Piemontese 197 Italy
 7   Numbers 1991: 50/100; HB: 100; increasing; 80 %; Ne = 133
 8 - Height: 145/139 cm; Weight: 1050/740 kg; Herd number: miss; AI: Yes
 9   Colour: Uni white
 9   Colour: Combination black, blue, red, white
10   Pecularity: miss
11 - Main use: (1) meat,(2) crossbreeding,(3) miss
12   Spec. abilities: miss
13   Performance compared with STB Charolais 62:
14      higher: beef score (muscling), muscularity
15      equal:  daily gain, handling ease, calf mortality
16      lower:  calving interval,calving rate,calv. ease,age of sex. mat.
17 - Management: stationary; housing: 12 m.;
18 - Conservation progr.: live animals: miss;Semen: miss;Embryos: miss
19   Status: potential. endang.;Watch: HB♀♀,%pure,%incross,herds!
```

20 - <u>Similar breeds</u> (see group 10 on page 82)

		EN	Country	Status
21	Albera	4	E	crit.end.
22	Mostrenca	177	E	endanger.
23	Faeroesk	84	FR	min. end.
24	Corse	70	F	normal

```
 1 - Jersiais                                                   EN  134
 2   Jersey; western France
 3   Upra Jersiaise France
 4   Paris 75017, rue boulevard Pereire Sud 95                 HB:1903
 5 - Imported as breed from United Kingdom
 7   Numbers 1988: 100/3500; HB: 580; stable; 70 %; Ne = 341
 8 - Height: 130/123 cm; Weight: 650/400 kg; Herd number: miss; AI: Yes
 9   Colour: Uni red
10   Pecularity: miss
11 - Main use: (1) milk,(2) meat,(3) sport/hobby
12   Spec. abilities: high % fat
13   Performance compared with STB Jersey 134:
14      higher: Breed is used
15      equal:  as standard breed,
16      lower:  no comparison possible.
17 - Management: stationary; housing: 2-6 m.;
18 - Conservation progr.: live animals: miss;Semen: Yes;Embryos: miss
19   Status: normal;            Watch: %pure!
```

20 - <u>Similar breeds</u> (see group 8/4 on page 82)

		EN	Country	Status
21	Froment du Leon	93	F	endanger.
22	Jersey	132	IRL	pot. end.
23	Jersey	131	D	normal
24	Jersey	130	DK	normal

```
 1 - Limousin                                                      EN  156
 2   Limousin; western Central Massif / Limousin
 3   Herd-Book de la race Limousin                                HB:1886
 4   Limoges Cedex 87009, rue Soufflot 8, B.P. 331
 5 - Autochthon Limousin
 7   Numbers 1992: 21000/600000; HB: miss; increasing; 98 %; Ne = 81159
 8 - Height: 144/137 cm; Weight: 1050/670 kg; Herd number: miss; AI: Yes
 9   Colour: Uni yellow
10   Pecularity: miss
11 - Main use: (1) meat,(2) crossbreeding,(3) miss
12   Spec. abilities: extensive conditions
13   Performance compared with STB Limousin 156:
14      higher: Breed is used
15      equal:  as standard breed,
16      lower:  no comparison possible.
17 - Management: miss; housing: miss m.;
18 - Conservation progr.: live animals: miss;Semen: 31;Embryos: Yes
19   Status: normal;             Watch: HB♀♀!
20 - Similar breeds (see group 8/3 on page 81)     EN  Country Status
21   Alpha 16 (terminated)                           6   F      crit.end.
22   Parthenaise                                   193   F      normal
23   Limousin                                      157   L      normal
24   Irish Limousin                                122   IRL    normal
```

```
 1 - Lourdaise                                                     EN  160
 2   Lourdais; central Pyrenees
 3   Institut Technique d'Elevage Bovin, Dpt.                      HB:1981
 4   Amélioration Génétique, Paris Cedex 12 75595, rue de Bercy 149
 5 - Autochthon breed of Pyrenean
 6   Incrossing since 1950 from Limousin 156 France
 7   Numbers 1992: 10/45; HB: miss; increasing; 80 %; Ne = 16
 8 - Height: miss /135 cm; Weight: miss /600 kg; Herd number: 12; AI: Yes
 9   Colour: Uni yellow
10   Pecularity: pink mucosa
11 - Main use: (1) milk,(2) meat,(3) tractive power
12   Spec. abilities: miss
13   Performance compared with STB Aubrac 14:
14      higher: % fat, % protein, handling ease
15      equal:  milk yield,musc.,daily gain,calving ease,calv. interval
16      lower:  miss
17 - Management: stationary; housing: 2-6 m.;
18 - Conservation progr.: live animals: Yes;Semen: miss;Embryos: miss
19   Status: critically endang.;Watch: ♂♂,HB♀♀,herds,%pure,%incross!
20 - Similar breeds                                 EN  Country Status
21   miss                                         miss  miss    miss
```

```
 1 - Maine-Anjou                                                    EN  163
 2   Maine-Anjou; Pays de Loire
 3   Upra Maine Anjou                                              HB:1908
 4   Chateau Gontier 53204, rue de Razilly 36-38, B.P. 211
 5 - Composite of Mancelle, Shorthorn
 7   Numbers 1988: 2000/86900; HB: 6000; decreasing; 60 %; Ne = 6000
 8 - Height: 150/140 cm; Weight: 1350/850 kg; Herd number: miss; AI: Yes
 9   Colour: Combination red, white
10   Pecularity: miss
11 - Main use: (1) meat,(2) milk,(3) miss
12   Spec. abilities: twinning
13   Performance compared with STB Charolais 62:
14      higher: milk yield,handl. ease,milkability,prolificacy,daily gain
15      equal:  calving ease, calving interval, calf mortality
16      lower:  muscularity
17 - Management: stationary; housing: 2-6 m.;
18 - Conservation progr.: live animals: miss;Semen: 50;Embryos: 10/miss
19   Status: normal;               Watch: trend,%pure!
```

20 - Similar breeds (see group 3/1 on page 76)	EN	Country	Status
21 Blanc-Rouge de Belgique	273	B	pot. end.
22 Ferrandais	85	F	pot. end.
23 Dansk Rodbroget Kvaeg	73	DK	normal
24 Pie-Rouge	199	B	normal

```
 1 - Montbeliard                                                   EN  176
 2   Montbeliard; eastern France and eastern Central France
 3   Herd-Book de la race Montbeliard                              HB:1889
 4   Besancon Cedex 25015, rue Delarelle 3, B.P. 237
 5 - Composite of Comtoise, Tourache, Bernois
 6   Incrossing since 1950 from Red Holstein USA
 7   Numbers 1988: 2000/774000; HB: 124000; stable; 66 %; Ne = 7873
 8 - Height: 148/139 cm; Weight: 950/680 kg; Herd number: miss; AI: Yes
 9   Colour: Combination red, white
10   Pecularity: head and extremities white, light muzzle
11 - Main use: (1) milk,(2) meat,(3) miss
12   Spec. abilities: cheese "Comté"
13   Performance compared with STB French Simmental 89:
14      higher: milk yield, calving ease, milkability
15      equal:  daily gain,% fat,% protein,calv. interval,age of sex. mat.
16      lower:  muscularity
17 - Management: stationary; housing: 2-6 m.; mountain
18 - Conservation progr.: live animals: miss;Semen: 480;Embryos: 10/120
19   Status: normal;               Watch: %pure,%incross!
```

20 - Similar breeds (see group 3/2 on page 77)	EN	Country	Status
21 Ceske strakate	61	CZ	crit.end.
22 Simentalska	237	PL	min. end.
23 Race d'Abondance	213	F	normal
24 Fleckvieh	88	A	normal

```
 1 - Normande                                                    EN  186
 2   Normande; 90% in western France
 3   Upra Normande                                               HB:1883
 4   Caen 14300, rue des Carmélites 16-18
 5 - Autochthon local breed of Normandie
 7   Numbers 1988: 320/1072500; HB: 309000; decreasing; 85 %; Ne = 1279
 8 - Height: 155/140 cm; Weight: 1100/720 kg; Herd number: miss; AI: miss
 9   Colour: Combination black, red, white
10   Pecularity: dark muzzle
11 - Main use: (1) milk,(2) meat,(3) miss
12   Spec. abilities: extensive conditions
13   Performance compared with STB Holstein-Friesian 209:
14     higher: muscularity, % fat, % protein, handling ease
15     equal:  daily gain,calving ease,calving interval,age of sex. mat.
16     lower:  milk yield, milkability
17 - Management: stationary; housing: 2-6 m.;
18 - Conservation progr.: live animals: Yes;Semen: 300;Embryos: 1/9
19   Status: normal
```

20 - Similar breeds (see group 3/1 on page 76)	EN	Country	Status
21 Blanc-Rouge de Belgique	273	B	pot. end.
22 Ferrandais	85	F	pot. end.
23 Dansk Rodbroget Kvaeg	73	DK	normal
24 Pie-Rouge	199	B	normal

```
 1 - Parthenaise                                                 EN  193
 2   Parthenais; Poitou
 3   Upra Parthenaise                                            HB:1893
 4   Vouille 79230, "Les Ruralies", B.P. 4
 5 - Autochthon population of Vendee and Poitou
 7   Numbers 1988: 300/7070; HB: 2000; stable; 85 %; Ne = 1044
 8 - Height: 145/135 cm; Weight: 1050/750 kg; Herd number: miss; AI: Yes
 9   Colour: Uni, yellow to brown
10   Pecularity: black muzzle
11 - Main use: (1) meat,(2) miss,(3) miss
12   Spec. abilities: miss
13   Performance compared with STB Charolais 62:
14     higher: lean meat
15     equal:  daily gain, calving ease, calving interval, calf mortality
16     lower:  miss
17 - Management: stationary; housing: 2-6 m.;
18 - Conservation progr.: live animals: miss;Semen: 20;Embryos: 3/5
19   Status: normal;              Watch: %pure!
```

20 - Similar breeds (see group 8/3 on page 81)	EN	Country	Status
21 Alpha 16 (terminated)	6	F	crit.end.
22 Limousin	156	F	normal
23 Limousin	157	L	normal
24 Irish Limousin	122	IRL	normal

1 - **Pie Rouge de l'Est**   EN   **89**
2   French Simmental; northeastern France
3   Upra Pie Rouge de l'Est, Maison de l'Agriculture   HB:**1930**
4   Dijon 21100, rue de Mulhouse 42
5 - Composite breed of Jura Swiss, Simmental 241 Switzerland
6   Incrossing since 1950 from Simmental 241 Switzerland
7   Numbers 1988: **800/48600**; HB: **4400**; decreasing; **65 %**; Ne = **2708**
8 - Height: **148/139** cm; Weight: **1050/700** kg; Herd number: **miss**; AI: **Yes**
9   Colour: **Combination red, white**
10 Pecularity: **white extremities**
11 - Main use: (1) **milk**,(2) **meat**,(3) **miss**
12 Spec. abilities: **miss**
13 Performance compared with STB **French Simmental 89**:
14   higher: **Breed is used**
15   equal: **as standard breed,**
16   lower: **no comparison possible.**
17 - Management: **stationary**; housing: **2-6 m.**;
18 - Conservation progr.: live animals: **miss**;Semen: **198**;Embryos: **Yes**
19 Status: **potential. endang.**;Watch: **trend,%pure,%incross!**
20 - Similar breeds (see group 3/2 on page 77)   EN Country Status
21 **Ceske strakate**   61   CZ   crit.end.
22 **Simentalska**   237   PL   min. end.
23 **Montbeliard**   176   F   normal
24 **Fleckvieh**   88   A   normal

1 - **Pie Rouge des Plaines**   EN   **196**
2   Pie Rouge des Plaines; Bretagne
3   Upra Pie Rouge des Plaines   HB:**1970**
4   Quimper Cedex 29332, Allée Sully 5
5 - Autochthon Armoricaine 10 France, Meuse-Rhine-Yssel 161 Netherlands,
6   Rotbunt 74 Germany; incrossing since 1950 from Red Holstein USA
7   Numbers 1988: **300/39700**; HB: **4600**; decreasing; **90 %**; Ne = **1127**
8 - Height: **140/132** cm; Weight: **1000/650** kg; Herd number: **miss**; AI: **Yes**
9   Colour: **Combination red, white**
10 Pecularity: **light muzzle**
11 - Main use: (1) **milk**,(2) **meat**,(3) **miss**
12 Spec. abilities: **miss**
13 Performance compared with STB **French Simmental 89**:
14   higher: **milk yield, calving ease, age of sexual maturity**
15   equal: **muscularity,% fat,% protein,handling ease,calf mortality**
16   lower: **daily gain**
17 - Management: **stationary**; housing: **2-6 m.**;
18 - Conservation progr.: live animals: **miss**;Semen: **135**;Embryos: **miss**
19 Status: **normal**;   Watch: **trend,%pure!**
20 - Similar breeds (see group 3/1 on page 76)   EN Country Status
21 **Blanc-Rouge de Belgique**   273   B   pot. end.
22 **Ferrandais**   85   F   pot. end.
23 **Dansk Rodbroget Kvaeg**   73   DK   normal
24 **Pie-Rouge**   199   B   normal

```
 1 - Prim' Holstein                                                EN  209
 2   Holstein-Friesian; country-wide
 3   PRIM' Holstein France                                         HB:1922
 4   St Sylvain D'Anjou 49480, Le Montsoreau
 5 - Imported as breed from: Netherlands, USA
 6   Incrossing since 1950 from Holstein-Friesian USA
 7   Numbers 1991: 2000/3500000; HB: 411516; stable; 85 %; Ne = 7961
 8 - Height: 165/143 cm; Weight: 1100/700 kg; Herd number: miss; AI: Yes
 9   Colour: Combination black, white
10   Pecularity: miss
11 - Main use: (1) milk,(2) meat,(3) miss
12   Spec. abilities: miss
13   Performance compared with STB Holstein-Friesian 209:
14      higher: Breed is used
15      equal:  as standard breed,
16      lower:  no comparison possible.
17 - Management: stationary; housing: 2-6 m.;
18 - Conservation progr.: live animals: miss;Semen: 5000;Embryos: miss
19   Status: normal;           Watch: %incross!
20 - Similar breeds (see group 1/1 on page 75)   EN  Country Status
21   Sortbroget Dansk Malkekvaeg                  245  DK      pot. end.
22   Nizinna-Czarno-Biala                         185  PL      pot. end.
23   Deutsche Schwarzbunte                         75  D       normal
24   Pie-Noire-Holstein                           198  B       normal
```

```
 1 - Race d'Abondance                                              EN  213
 2   Abondance; northern Alpine Massif
 3   UPRA Abondance, Maison de l'Agriculture                       HB:1894
 4   Annecy Cedex 74010, avenue des Iles 52, B.P. 327
 5 - Autochthon Chablaisienne
 6   Incrossing since 1950 from Red Holstein USA
 7   Numbers 1988: 1000/66900; HB: 9600; decreasing; 75 %; Ne = 3623
 8 - Height: 146/133 cm; Weight: 1000/580 kg; Herd number: miss; AI: Yes
 9   Colour: Combination red, white
10   Pecularity: white head,red eye patch,white belly & lower extremities
11 - Main use: (1) milk,(2) meat,(3) vegetation management
12   Spec. abilities: mountain
13   Performance compared with STB French Simmental 89:
14      higher: calving ease, handling ease
15      equal:  milk yield, % fat, % protein, age of sex. mat., calf mort.
16      lower:  muscularity, daily gain
17 - Management: stationary; housing: > 6 m.;
18 - Conservation progr.: live animals: miss;Semen: 127;Embryos: 6/7
19   Status: normal;           Watch: trend,%pure,%incross!
20 - Similar breeds (see group 3/2 on page 77)   EN  Country Status
21   Ceske strakate                               61   CZ      crit.end.
22   Simentalska                                 237   PL      min. end.
23   Montbeliard                                 176   F       normal
24   Fleckvieh                                    88   A       normal
```

1 - Salers   EN   226
2   Salers; Central Massif
3   Herd-book de la race Salers   HB:1908
4   Aurillac Cedex 15002,rue du 139'Ri 26, B.P. 239
5 - Autochthon breed of Auvergne
7   Numbers 1988: 5000/163800; HB: 40000; stable; 40 %; Ne = 17778
8 - Height: 148/140 cm; Weight: 980/680 kg; Herd number: miss; AI: Yes
9   Colour: Uni red
10 Pecularity: miss
11 - Main use: (1) meat,(2) milk,(3) miss
12 Spec. abilities: extensive conditions, fertility
13 Performance compared with STB Charolais 62:
14   higher: milk yield,calv. ease,milkabil.,% protein,age of sex. mat.
15   equal: handling ease
16   lower: muscularity,daily gain,% fat,calving interval,calf mort.
17 - Management: stationary; housing: > 6 m.;
18 - Conservation progr.: live animals: miss;Semen: 35;Embryos: 5/10
19 Status: normal;   Watch: %pure!
20 - Similar breeds (see group 5/3 on page 80)   EN Country Status
21 Cabannina   54 I   crit.end.
22 Aure et Saint-Girons   16 F   min. end.
23 Bazadais   23 F   normal

1 - Tarentaise   EN   253
2   Tarentaise; Savoy, southeastern France
3   Upra Tarentaise   HB:1888
4   Chambery 73000, rue Métropole 11
5 - Autochthon breed of Savoyen
7   Numbers 1988: 500/17400; HB: 3927; decreasing; 75 %; Ne = 1774
8 - Height: 140/128 cm; Weight: 750/500 kg; Herd number: miss; AI: Yes
9   Colour: Uni light, yellowish brown
10 Pecularity: miss
11 - Main use: (1) milk,(2) meat,(3) vegetation management
12 Spec. abilities: cheese "Beaufort", mountains
13 Performance compared with STB French Simmental 89:
14   higher: calving ease, handling ease
15   equal: % fat, % protein, age of sexual maturity, calf mortality
16   lower: muscularity, daily gain, milk yield
17 - Management: stationary; housing: > 6 m.;
18 - Conservation progr.: live animals: miss;Semen: 95;Embryos: Yes
19 Status: normal;   Watch: trend,%pure!
20 - Similar breeds (see group 5/2 on page 80)   EN Country Status
21 Alpine Herens   7 F   crit.end.
22 Valdostana Castana   260 I   normal
23 Eringer Rind   83 CH   normal

1 - Villard de Lans   EN   264
2   Villard de Lans; Mountains of Vercors / Alps
3   Institut Technique d'Elevage Bovin, Dpt. Amélioration   HB:1978
4   Génétique, Paris Cedex 12 75595, rue de Bercy 149
5 - Composite of local: Femeline, Bressane
6   Incrossing since 1950 from Blonde d'Aquitaine 37 France
7   Numbers 1992: 25/144; HB: miss; stable; 80 %; Ne = 69
8 - Height: miss /140 cm; Weight: miss /700 kg; Herd number: 32; AI: Yes
9   Colour: Uni yellow
10 Pecularity: miss
11 - Main use: (1) milk,(2) meat,(3) tractive power
12 Spec. abilities: miss
13 Performance compared with STB French Simmental 89:
14   higher: pulling power, % fat
15   equal: musc.,daily gain,% protein,calving ease,calving interval
16   lower: milk yield, calf mortality, milkability
17 - Management: stationary; housing: 2-6 m.;
18 - Conservation progr.: live animals: Yes;Semen: 17;Embryos: miss
19 Status: potential. endang.;Watch: ♂♂,HB♀♀,%pure,%incross!
20 - Similar breeds (see group 8/1 on page 81)   EN Country Status
21 Basco-Bearnaise   22   F   crit.end.
22 Coopelso 93 (terminated)   69   F   crit.end.
23 Blonde d'Aquitaine   38   GB   normal
24 Blonde d'Aquitaine   37   F   normal

1 - Vosgienne   EN   267
2   Vosges; upper regions of Vosges
3   Livre Genealogique Vosgien   HB:1928
4   Mulhouse Cedex 68055, E.D.E. - rue de l'Est 4, B.P. 1266
5 - Autochthon breed of Vosges
6   Incrossing since 1950 from Telemark 254 Norway
7   Numbers 1988: 80/3180; HB: miss; stable; 80 %; Ne = 312
8 - Height: miss/135 cm; Weight: miss/600 kg; Herd number: miss; AI: Yes
9   Colour: Combination black, red, white
10 Pecularity: mottled white face, colour-sided, white back line
11 - Main use: (1) milk,(2) meat,(3) tractive power
12 Spec. abilities: fertility
13 Performance compared with STB Tarentaise 253:
14   higher: pulling power, muscularity, % protein
15   equal: daily gain,calving ease,calving interval,age of sex. mat.
16   lower: milk yield, % fat
17 - Management: stationary; housing: 2-6 m.;
18 - Conservation progr.: live animals: miss;Semen: 20;Embryos: Yes
19 Status: potential. endang.;Watch: HB♀♀,%pure,%incross!
20 - Similar breeds (see group 3/7 on page 78)   EN Country Status
21 Itäsuomenkarja   129   SF   crit.end.
22 Telemark   254   N   crit.end.
23 Irish Moiled   123   GB   crit.end.
24 English Longhorn   82   GB   pot. end.

```
 1 - Ardes (extinct)                                           EN   403
 2   Ardes; southeastern France / Puy de Dome
 3   I.N.R.A., Centre de Recherches de Jouy-en-Josas           HB:miss
 4   Jouy-en-Josas Cedex 78352
 5 - Composite of local, Lacaune 524 France
 7   Numbers miss: miss / miss; HB: miss; miss; miss %; Ne = miss
 8 - Height: 78/70 cm; Weight: 70/55 kg; Herd number: miss; AI: miss
 9   Colour: Uni white
10   Pecularity: horns 0/0
11 - Main use: (1) milk,(2) meat,(3) wool
12   Spec. abilities: miss
13   Performance compared with STB miss:
14      higher: miss
15      equal:  miss
16      lower:  miss
17 - Management: transhumant; housing: 2-6 m.;
18 - Conservation progr.: live animals: miss;Semen: miss;Embryos: miss
19   Status: extinct
```

20 - Similar breeds (see group 7/8 on page 93)	EN	Country	Status
21 Bizet	420	F	pot. end.
22 Grivette	503	F	pot. end.
23 Lacaune	524	F	normal
24 Blanc du Massif Central	423	F	normal

```
 1 - Aure et de Campan, Aurois                                 EN   404
 2   Aure-Campan; central Pyrenees
 3   Upra des races ovines des Pyrenees centrales              HB:1975
 4   Montrejeau 31210, rue des Pyrénées 28
 5 - Composite of local breed, Merino
 7   Numbers 1983: 600/23000; HB: miss; decreasing; 70 %; Ne = 2339
 8 - Height: 75/70 cm; Weight: 75/50 kg; Herd number: miss; AI: miss
 9   Colour: Uni white
10   Pecularity: horns 2/0
11 - Main use: (1) meat,(2) wool,(3) vegetation management
12   Spec. abilities: able to walk long distances, mountain
13   Performance compared with STB Limousin 531:
14      higher: wool or fiber thickness, wool or fiber yield
15      equal:  muscularity, lambing interval
16      lower:  litter size, milk yield
17 - Management: transhumant; housing: 2-6 m.;
18 - Conservation progr.: live animals: miss;Semen: miss;Embryos: miss
19   Status: potential. endang.;Watch: HB♀♀,trend,%pure!
```

20 - Similar breeds (see group 7/9 on page 93)	EN	Country	Status
21 Castillonnais	445	F	crit.end.
22 Baregeois	411	F	min. end.
23 Landais	526	F	min. end.
24 Tarasconnais	646	F	normal

```
 1 - Avranchin                                                    EN  405
 2   Avranchin; western Calvados
 3   Upra ovine Avranchin - Cotentin - Roussion, Maison de        HB:1928
 4   l'Agriculture, Saint Lo Cedex 50000, Avenue de Paris
 5 - Composite of local breed, Leicester 528, Kent, South Down 636 GB
 7   Numbers 1992: miss /8000; HB: miss; decreasing; 90 %; Ne = 1448
 8 - Height: miss/miss cm; Weight: 105/75 kg; Herd number: miss; AI: miss
 9   Colour: Uni white
10   Pecularity: brownish face and feet
11 - Main use: (1) meat,(2) wool,(3) crossbreeding
12   Spec. abilities: miss
13   Performance compared with STB Texel 649:
14      higher: litter size, age of sexual maturity
15      equal:  carcass leanness, lambing interval, wool yield
16      lower:  muscularity, daily gain, milk yield
17 - Management: miss; housing: miss m.;
18 - Conservation progr.: live animals: miss;Semen: miss;Embryos: miss
19   Status: potential. endang.;Watch: HB♀♀,trend,%pure!
```

```
20 - Similar breeds (see group 3 on page 88)      EN   Country  Status
21   Mouton Boulonnais                            559    F      crit.end.
22   Galway                                       495    IRL    endanger.
23   Mouton Charollais                            560    F      normal
24   Cotentin                                     473    F      normal
```

```
 1 - Baregeois                                                   EN  411
 2   Baregeois; central Pyrenees
 3   Upra des races ovines des Pyrenees centrales                HB:1975
 4   Montejeau 31210, rue des Pyrénées 28
 5 - Composite of local breed, Merino
 7   Numbers 1983: 100/3000; HB: miss; decreasing; 60 %; Ne = 387
 8 - Height: 78/70 cm; Weight: 90/60 kg; Herd number: miss; AI: miss
 9   Colour: Uni white, sometimes brown
10   Pecularity: horns 2/2
11 - Main use: (1) meat,(2) wool,(3) miss
12   Spec. abilities: able to walk long distances, mountain
13   Performance compared with STB Limousin 531:
14      higher: wool or fiber yield, wool or fiber thickness
15      equal:  lambing interval
16      lower:  age of sexual maturity
17 - Management: transhumant; housing: 2-6 m.;
18 - Conservation progr.: live animals: miss;Semen: miss;Embryos: miss
19   Status: minimally endang.; Watch: HB♀♀,trend,%pure!
```

```
20 - Similar breeds (see group 7/9 on page 93)    EN   Country  Status
21   Castillonnais                                445    F      crit.end.
22   Landais                                      526    F      min. end.
23   Aure et de Campan                            404    F      pot. end.
24   Tarasconnais                                 646    F      normal
```

```
 1 - Basco-Bearnaise                                          EN   412
 2   Basco-Bearnais; Bearnais Mountains
 3   Upra des races ovines laitieres des Pyrenees             HB:1975
 4   Mauleon Soule 64130, Ordiarp
 5 - Autochthon local breed of Basque and Béarnaises valleys
 7   Numbers 1983: 1200/60000; HB: miss; decreasing; 95 %; Ne = 4706
 8 - Height: miss /75 cm; Weight: 80/55 kg; Herd number: miss; AI: Yes
 9   Colour: Uni white
10   Pecularity: horns 2/2
11 - Main use: (1) milk,(2) meat,(3) wool
12   Spec. abilities: cheese
13   Performance compared with STB Lacaune 524:
14     higher: wool or fiber yield, % fat, % protein
15     equal:  carcass leanness
16     lower:  muscularity, daily gain, milk yield, wool thickness
17 - Management: transhumant; housing: miss m.;
18 - Conservation progr.: live animals: miss;Semen: miss;Embryos: miss
19   Status: normal;              Watch: HB♀♀,trend!
```

20 - Similar breeds (see group 5/2 on page 89)	EN	Country	Status
21 Caussenard des Garrigues	447	F	crit.end.
22 Altamurana	401	I	crit.end.
23 Manech (Tete Noire)	537	F	normal
24 Caussenard du Lot	448	F	normal

```
 1 - Berrichon de l'Indre                                     EN   417
 2   Berrichon de l'Indre; Champagne Berrichonne
 3   Upra de la race ovine Berrichon                          HB:1895
 4   Baugy 18800, Bois de Chaume
 5 - Autochthon Mouton Berrichon
 7   Numbers 1983: 34/4000; HB: miss; stable; 50 %; Ne = 135
 8 - Height: 83/78 cm; Weight: 90/60 kg; Herd number: 10; AI: miss
 9   Colour: Uni white
10   Pecularity: horns 0/0
11 - Main use: (1) meat,(2) wool,(3) miss
12   Spec. abilities: able to walk long distances
13   Performance compared with STB Limousin 531:
14     higher: litter size, wool or fiber thickness
15     equal:  muscularity,daily gain,carcass leanness,age of sex. matur.
16     lower:  milk yield
17 - Management: stationary; housing: 2-6 m.;
18 - Conservation progr.: live animals: Yes;Semen: miss;Embryos: miss
19   Status: minimally endang.; Watch: HB♀♀,herds,%pure!
```

20 - Similar breeds (see group 1/6 on page 87)	EN	Country	Status
21 Inra 401	515	F	pot. end.
22 Solognot	633	F	pot. end.
23 Charmoise	450	F	normal
24 Berrichon du Cher	418	F	normal

```
 1 - Berrichon du Cher                                      EN  418
 2   Berrichon du Cher; southwestern France and Central France
 3   Upra des races ovines Berrichonnes                     HB:1934
 4   Paris 75017, boulevard Péreire-Sud 95
 5 - Composite of local breed, Merino, Leicester 528 United Kingdom
 6   Incrossing since 1960 from Ile-de-France 513 France
 7   Numbers 1983: 11000/120000; HB: miss; decreasing; 90 %; Ne = 40305
 8 - Height: 73/68 cm; Weight: 110/70 kg; Herd number: miss; AI: Yes
 9   Colour: Uni white
10   Pecularity: horns 0/0
11 - Main use: (1) meat,(2) wool,(3) crossbreeding
12   Spec. abilities: miss
13   Performance compared with STB Suffolk 639:
14     higher: muscularity, wool or fiber thickness
15     equal: carcass leanness, age of sexual maturity, lambing interval
16     lower: milk yield, daily gain, litter size
17 - Management: stationary; housing: 2-6 m.;
18 - Conservation progr.: live animals: miss;Semen: 30;Embryos: miss
19   Status: normal;           Watch: HB♀♀,trend!
```

20 - Similar breeds (see group 1/6 on page 87)	EN	Country	Status
21 Berrichon de l'Indre	417	F	min. end.
22 Inra 401	515	F	pot. end.
23 Ile-de-France	513	F	normal
24 Charmoise	450	F	normal

```
 1 - Bizet                                                  EN  420
 2   Bizet; Haute Loire / Puy-de-Dome
 3   Upra des races ovines du Massif Central nord           HB:1946
 4   Lempdes 63370, Route de Thiers (RN 89) Marmilhat, B. P. 13
 5 - Autochthon local breed
 7   Numbers 1983: 120/10000; HB: miss; decreasing; 50 %; Ne = 474
 8 - Height: 80/75 cm; Weight: 75/50 kg; Herd number: miss; AI: miss
 9   Colour: Comb. black, white; grey-brown head with blacksided face
10   Pecularity: horns 2/0, brown legs
11 - Main use: (1) meat,(2) wool,(3) miss
12   Spec. abilities: miss
13   Performance compared with STB Limousin 531:
14     higher: lambing interval
15     equal: muscularity,carcass lean.,litter size,age of sex. maturity
16     lower: daily gain, milk yield
17 - Management: stationary; housing: 2-6 m.;
18 - Conservation progr.: live animals: miss;Semen: miss;Embryos: miss
19   Status: potential. endang.;Watch: HB♀♀,trend,%pure!
```

20 - Similar breeds (see group 7/8 on page 93)	EN	Country	Status
21 Grivette	503	F	pot. end.
22 Blanc du Massif Central	423	F	normal
23 Limousin	531	F	normal
24 Lacaune	524	F	normal

```
 1 - Blackface                                              EN   421
 2   Blackface; southern and southeastern France
 3   I.N.R.A., Centre de Recherches de Jouy-en-Josas        HB:miss
 4   Jouy-en-Josas Cedex, 78352
 5 - Imported as breed from country United Kingdom
 7   Numbers 1992: miss /1000; HB: miss; decreasing; miss %; Ne = 181
 8 - Height: miss/miss cm; Weight: miss/miss kg; Herd number:miss;AI:miss
 9   Colour: Uni white, black or black-white spotted head and legs
10   Pecularity: horns 2/2
11 - Main use: (1) meat,(2) wool,(3) vegetation management
12   Spec. abilities: miss
13   Performance compared with STB miss:
14      higher: miss
15      equal:  miss
16      lower:  miss
17 - Management: miss; housing: miss m.;
18 - Conservation progr.: live animals: miss;Semen: miss;Embryos: miss
19   Status: critically endang.;Watch: ♂♂,HB♀♀,trend,%pure!
20 - Similar breeds (see group 7/11 on page 94)    EN  Country Status
21   Whitefaced Woodland                           676  GB      pot. end.
22   Blackface Mountain                            422  IRL     normal
23   Dala                                          476  N       normal
24   Wicklow Cheviot                               677  IRL     normal
```

```
 1 - Blanc du Massif Central                                 EN   423
 2   Blanc du Massif Central; southeastern Central Massif
 3   Upra des eleveurs de la race ovine Blanc du Massif Central   HB:1967
 4   Mende 48000, avenue du Père Coudrin 1
 5 - Composite of local breed, Lacaune 524, Berrichon de l'Indre 417
 7   Numbers 1983: 4500/300000; HB: miss; decreasing; 75 %; Ne = 17734
 8 - Height: miss / miss cm; Weight: 95/60 kg; Herd number: miss; AI: Yes
 9   Colour: Uni white
10   Pecularity: horns 0/0
11 - Main use: (1) meat,(2) wool,(3) miss
12   Spec. abilities: able to walk long distances
13   Performance compared with STB Limousin 531:
14      higher: muscularity, daily gain, carcass leanness, milk yield
15      equal:  lambing interval, wool or fiber yield
16      lower:  litter size
17 - Management: miss; housing: miss m.;
18 - Conservation progr.: live animals: miss;Semen: miss;Embryos: miss
19   Status: normal;           Watch: HB♀♀,trend,%pure!
20 - Similar breeds (see group 7/8 on page 93)     EN  Country Status
21   Bizet                                         420  F       pot. end.
22   Grivette                                      503  F       pot. end.
23   Limousin                                      531  F       normal
24   Lacaune                                       524  F       normal
```

SHEEP

```
1 - Bleu du Maine                                           EN  425
2   Bleu du Maine; western and northern France
3   Upra des races ovines du Maine                         HB:1927
4   Allonnes 72700, La Futaie - Rouillon
5 - Composite of local breed, Bluefaced Leicester 427 United Kingdom
7   Numbers 1983: 7000/130000; HB: miss; stable; 75 %; Ne = 26569
8 - Height: 76/65 cm; Weight: 110/80 kg; Herd number: miss; AI: Yes
9   Colour: Uni white; dark blue face, blue mucosa
10  Pecularity: horns 0/0
11 - Main use: (1) meat,(2) wool,(3) miss
12  Spec. abilities: miss
13  Performance compared with STB Texel 649:
14     higher: litter size, age of sexual maturity
15     equal:  daily gain, carcass leanness, milk yield, lambing interval
16     lower:  muscularity
17 - Management: transhumant; housing: no
18 - Conservation progr.: live animals: miss;Semen: miss;Embryos: miss
19  Status: normal;              Watch: HB♀♀,%pure!
20 - Similar breeds (see group 2/1 on page 87)    EN  Country Status
21  Rouge de l'ouest                              605  GB   pot. end.
22  Rouge de l'ouest                              604  F    normal
23  Bleu du Maine                                 426  GB   normal
24  Blauköpfiges Fleischschaf                     424  D    normal
```

SHEEP

```
1 - Brigasque                                              EN  436
2   Brigasca; Maritime Alpes
3   I.N.R.A., Centre de Recherches de Jouy-en-Josas       HB:miss
4   Jouy-en-Josas Cedex, 78352
5 - Composite of moutons de pays,Langhe,Fabrosa 492 Italy,unknown others
7   Numbers 1993: miss /1000; HB: miss; stable; miss %; Ne = 181
8 - Height: 90/78 cm; Weight: 70/60 kg; Herd number: miss; AI: miss
9   Colour: Uni white, head and legs red marbled
10  Pecularity: horns 2/2
11 - Main use: (1) milk,(2) meat,(3) wool
12  Spec. abilities: steep mountain sides
13  Performance compared with STB Arles Merino 554:
14     higher: wool or fiber thickness,milk yield,length of mating season
15     equal:  age of sexual maturity, lambing interval
16     lower:  daily gain, litter size
17 - Management: transhumant; housing: 2-6 m.;
18 - Conservation progr.: live animals: miss;Semen: miss;Embryos: miss
19  Status: critically endang.;Watch: ♂♂,HB♀♀,%pure!
20 - Similar breeds (see group 7/3 on page 92)    EN  Country Status
21  Brigasca                                      435  I    crit.end.
22  Frabosana                                     492  I    crit.end.
23  Besch da pader                                485  CH   min. end.
24  Delle Langhe                                  478  I    normal
```

```
 1 - Castillonnais                                          EN   445
 2   Castillonnais; central Pyrenees (Ariège)
 3   Upra des races ovines des Pyrenees centrales           HB:1982
 4   Montrejeau 31210, rue des Pyrénées 28
 5 - Composite of local breed, South Down
 7   Numbers 1983: 20/500; HB: miss; decreasing; 40 %; Ne = 56
 8 - Height: 65/55 cm; Weight: 70/50 kg; Herd number: 12; AI: Yes
 9   Colour: Combination white with red spots on head and legs
10   Pecularity: horns 2/2,0
11 - Main use: (1) meat,(2) wool,(3) vegetation management
12   Spec. abilities: able to walk long distances
13   Performance compared with STB Limousin 531:
14      higher: miss
15      equal:  muscularity,carcass leanness,milk yield,age of sex. matur.
16      lower:  litter size, wool or fiber yield
17 - Management: transhumant; housing: 2-6 m.;
18 - Conservation progr.: live animals: miss;Semen: 7;Embryos: miss
19   Status: critically endang.;Watch: HB♀♀,trend,herds,%pure!
20 - Similar breeds (see group 7/9 on page 93)      EN  Country Status
21   Baregeois                                      411   F     min. end.
22   Landais                                        526   F     min. end.
23   Aure et de Campan                              404   F     pot. end.
24   Tarasconnais                                   646   F     normal
```

```
 1 - Caussenard des Garrigues                                EN   447
 2   Caussenard des Garrigues; Département du Gard et l'Hérault
 3   I.N.R.A., Centre de Recherches de Jouy-en-Josas         HB:miss
 4   Jouy-en-Josas Cedex, 78352
 5 - Autochthon variety of the south "Caussenarde"; incrossing since
 6   1960 from Blanc du Massif Central 423 France
 7   Numbers 1992: miss /1000; HB: miss; decreasing; miss %; Ne = 181
 8 - Height: miss/miss cm; Weight: 65/45 kg; Herd number: miss; AI: miss
 9   Colour: Uni white
10   Pecularity: horns 2/ miss
11 - Main use: (1) meat,(2) wool,(3) miss
12   Spec. abilities: marginal areas of Massif Central
13   Performance compared with STB miss:
14      higher: miss
15      equal:  miss
16      lower:  miss
17 - Management: transhumant; housing: miss m.;
18 - Conservation progr.: live animals: miss;Semen: miss;Embryos: miss
19   Status: critically endang.;Watch: ♂♂,HB♀♀,trend,%pure,%incross!
20 - Similar breeds (see group 5/2 on page 89)      EN  Country Status
21   Altamurana                                     401   I     crit.end.
22   Raiole                                         594   F     endanger.
23   Caussenard du Lot                              448   F     normal
24   Basco-Bearnaise                                412   F     normal
```

```
 1 - Caussenard du Lot                                    EN   448
 2   Caussenard du Lot; Département du Lot
 3   Upra de la race des Causses du Lot                   HB:1955
 4   Cahors Cedex 46004, avenue Jean Jaurès 430, B. P. 799
 5 - Autochthon local breed
 7   Numbers 1983: 2500/180000; HB: miss; stable; 50 %; Ne = 9863
 8 - Height: miss / miss cm; Weight: 90/60 kg; Herd number: miss; AI: Yes
 9   Colour: Uni white, black spectacles and ears
10   Pecularity: horns 0/0
11 - Main use: (1) meat,(2) wool,(3) miss
12   Spec. abilities: marginal areas
13   Performance compared with STB Limousin 531:
14      higher: lambing interval, milk yield, wool or fiber yield
15      equal:  muscularity, daily gain, carcass leanness, litter size
16      lower:  miss
17 - Management: miss; housing: miss m.;
18 - Conservation progr.: live animals: miss;Semen: miss;Embryos: miss
19   Status: normal;            Watch: HB♀♀,%pure!
```

20 -	Similar breeds (see group 5/2 on page 89)	EN	Country	Status
21	Caussenard des Garrigues	447	F	crit.end.
22	Altamurana	401	I	crit.end.
23	Manech (Tete Noire)	537	F	normal
24	Basco-Bearnaise	412	F	normal

```
 1 - Charmoise                                            EN   450
 2   Charmoise; western Central France
 3   Upra de la race ovine de la Charmoise                HB:1927
 4   Montmorillon 86500, Route de Chauvigny Toutefoie
 5 - Composite of mainly local breeds crossed with rams of Kent breed
 7   Numbers 1983: 2500/120000; HB: miss; decreasing; 75 %; Ne = 9796
 8 - Height: 65/60 cm; Weight: 70/45 kg; Herd number: miss; AI: Yes
 9   Colour: Uni white
10   Pecularity: horns 0/0
11 - Main use: (1) meat,(2) wool,(3) miss
12   Spec. abilities: miss
13   Performance compared with STB Limousin 531:
14      higher: muscularity, wool or fiber yield, wool or fiber thickness
15      equal:  carcass leanness, lambing interval
16      lower:  daily gain, litter size, milk yield, age of sex. maturity
17 - Management: miss; housing: miss m.;
18 - Conservation progr.: live animals: miss;Semen: miss;Embryos: miss
19   Status: normal;            Watch: HB♀♀,trend,%pure!
```

20 -	Similar breeds (see group 1/6 on page 87)	EN	Country	Status
21	Berrichon de l'Indre	417	F	min. end.
22	Inra 401	515	F	pot. end.
23	Ile-de-France	513	F	normal
24	Berrichon du Cher	418	F	normal

```
 1 - Clun Forest                                                  EN  464
 2   Clun Forest; western and southern Central Massif
 3   Association des eleveurs francais de Clun-Forest             HB:1970
 4   Paris Cedex 12 75595, rue de Bercy 149
 5 - Imported as breed from country United Kingdom
 6   Incrossing since 1960 from Clun Forest 465 United Kingdom
 7   Numbers 1983: 200/2500; HB: miss; stable; 40 %; Ne = 741
 8 - Height: miss/miss cm; Weight: 80/55 kg; Herd number: miss; AI: miss
 9   Colour: Uni white; brown head and legs
10   Pecularity: horns 0/0
11 - Main use: (1) meat,(2) wool,(3) miss
12   Spec. abilities: miss
13   Performance compared with STB Limousin 531:
14     higher: litter size, muscularity, milk yield, wool or fiber yield
15     equal:  daily gain, carcass leanness, age of sexual maturity
16     lower:  miss
17 - Management: miss; housing: miss m.; forest areas
18 - Conservation progr.: live animals: miss;Semen: miss;Embryos: miss
19   Status: potential. endang.;Watch: HB♀♀,%pure!
```

20 - <u>Similar breeds</u> (see group 4/1 on page 89)

		EN	Country	Status
21	Dorset Down	481	F	pot. end.
22	Shropshire	629	GB	pot. end.
23	Mouton Vendeen	562	F	normal
24	Hampshire	506	F	normal

```
 1 - Commun des Alpes, Alpine                                     EN  470
 2   French Alpine; "Hautes Alpes de l'Isère"
 3   Upra Prealpes du Sud                                         HB:miss
 4   Gap 05000, rue Capitaine de Bresson 8
 5 - Autochthon local population
 6   Incrossing since 1960 from Préalpes 589 France
 7   Numbers 1992: miss /2000; HB: miss; miss; miss %; Ne = 362
 8 - Height:miss/miss cm; Weight:miss/miss kg; Herd number:miss; AI:miss
 9   Colour: miss
10   Pecularity: miss
11 - Main use: (1) miss,(2) miss,(3) miss
12   Spec. abilities: miss
13   Performance compared with STB miss:
14     higher: miss
15     equal:  miss
16     lower:  miss
17 - Management: miss; housing: miss m.;
18 - Conservation progr.: live animals: miss;Semen: miss;Embryos: miss
19   Status: critically endang.;Watch: ♂♂,HB♀♀,trend,%pure,%incross!
```

20 - <u>Similar breeds</u> (see group 7/1 on page 91)

		EN	Country	Status
21	Alpagota	400	I	crit.end.
22	Bellunese	413	I	crit.end.
23	Biellese	419	I	normal
24	Prealpes du Sud	589	F	normal

```
1 - Corse                                                    EN  472
2   Corsican; Corse
3   Fédération Régionale Corse pour le Controle de performances  HB:1975
4   et la Sélection Ovine (FRECSOV), Corti 20250, Mairie de Corti
5 - Autochthon local population of Corse
6   Incrossing since 1960 from Sarde 618 Italy
7   Numbers 1983: 4000/110000; HB: miss; stable; 80 %; Ne = 15439
8 - Height: 60/55 cm; Weight: 50/35 kg; Herd number: miss; AI: miss
9   Colour: Uni white, some colour variants
10  Pecularity: horns 2/2
11 - Main use: (1) milk,(2) meat,(3) wool
12  Spec. abilities: production of cheese
13  Performance compared with STB Lacaune 524:
14    higher: lambing interval
15    equal:  miss
16    lower:  muscularity, daily gain, litter size, milk yield
17 - Management: transhumant; housing: miss m.; tending
18 - Conservation progr.: live animals: miss;Semen: miss;Embryos: miss
19  Status: normal;            Watch: HB♀♀,%pure,%incross!
20 - Similar breeds (see group 8/1 on page 94)    EN  Country  Status
21  Marrane                                        540  I       crit.end.
22  Rosset                                         603  I       crit.end.
23  Ouessant                                       574  F       pot. end.
24  Comisana                                       469  I       normal
```

```
1 - Cotentin                                                 EN  473
2   Cotentin; Normandie (Département du Calvados)
3   Upra ovine Avranchin, Cotentin et Roussin                   HB:1925
4   Saint Lo Cedex 50000, Maison de l'Agriculture, Avenue de Paris
5 - Composite of Cotentin, Kent, Leicester 528 United Kingdom
7   Numbers 1983: 300/6500; HB: miss; stable; 70 %; Ne = 1147
8 - Height: miss/miss cm; Weight: 115/75 kg; Herd number: miss; AI: miss
9   Colour: Uni white, head pink and white
10  Pecularity: horns 0/0
11 - Main use: (1) meat,(2) wool,(3) miss
12  Spec. abilities: miss
13  Performance compared with STB Texel 649:
14    higher: litter size, age of sexual maturity
15    equal:  carcass leanness, milk yield, lambing interval, wool yield
16    lower:  muscularity, daily gain
17 - Management: miss; housing: miss m.;
18 - Conservation progr.: live animals: miss;Semen: miss;Embryos: miss
19  Status: normal;            Watch: HB♀♀,%pure!
20 - Similar breeds (see group 3 on page 88)      EN  Country  Status
21  Mouton Boulonnais                              559  F       crit.end.
22  Galway                                         495  IRL     endanger.
23  Rouge de Hague                                 608  F       normal
24  Mouton Charollais                              560  F       normal
```

1 - Dorset Down   EN   481
2   Dorset Down; central and western France
3   Upra Suffolk-Hampshire-Dorset   HB:1966
4   Paris Cedex 12 75595, M.N.E. - rue de Bercy 149
5 - Imported as breed from country 482 United Kingdom
6   Incrossing since 1960 from Dorset Down 482 United Kingdom
7   Numbers 1983: 560/2000; HB: miss; decreasing; 95 %; Ne = 1750
8 - Height: miss / miss cm; Weight: 95/65 kg; Herd number: miss; AI: Yes
9   Colour: Uni white; brown face and legs
10 Pecularity: horns 0/0
11 - Main use: (1) meat,(2) wool,(3) terminal sires
12 Spec. abilities: miss
13 Performance compared with STB Suffolk 639:
14   higher: wool or fiber thickness
15   equal: muscularity, carcass leanness, age of sexual maturity
16   lower: milk yield, daily gain, litter size
17 - Management: miss; housing: miss m.;
18 - Conservation progr.: live animals: miss;Semen: miss;Embryos: miss
19 Status: potential. endang.;Watch: HB♀♀,trend,%incross!
20 - Similar breeds (see group 4/1 on page 89)   EN Country Status
21 Clun Forest   464 F   pot. end.
22 Shropshire   629 GB   pot. end.
23 Mouton Vendeen   562 F   normal
24 Hampshire   506 F   normal

1 - Finnois   EN   489
2   Finnsheep; Picardie, Champagne, Ardenn
3   Upra Finnois et Romanov   HB:1966
4   Montmorillon 86500, Route de Chauvigny
5 - Imported as breed from country 644 Finland
7   Numbers 1983: 80/120; HB: miss; stable; 90 %; Ne = 192
8 - Height: 70/60 cm; Weight: 80/60 kg; Herd number: miss; AI: miss
9   Colour: Uni white
10 Pecularity: horns 0/0
11 - Main use: (1) crossbreeding,(2) meat,(3) miss
12 Spec. abilities: high prolificacy
13 Performance compared with STB Limousin 531:
14   higher: litter size, age of sexual maturity, milk yield
15   equal: muscularity, daily gain, carcass leanness, lambing interv.
16   lower: miss
17 - Management: stationary; housing: 2-6 m.;
18 - Conservation progr.: live animals: miss;Semen: miss;Embryos: miss
19 Status: potential. endang.;Watch: HB♀♀,%pure!
20 - Similar breeds (see group 6/3 on page 90)   EN Country Status
21 Dansk Landfar   477 DK   crit.end.
22 Coburger Fuchsschaf   466 D   crit.end.
23 Foroyskur Seydur   491 FR   normal
24 Gronlandsk Fär   504 DK   normal

```
 1 - Grivette                                                    EN   503
 2   Grivette; Lyonesse region
 3   Association des éleveurs des moutons de race Grivette       HB:1982
 4   L'Arbresle 69210, avenue P. Sémard 6
 5 - Autochthon local population of Bas Dauphiné; incrossing since 1960
 6   from South Down 635 France, Rava 596 France
 7   Numbers 1983: 130/7000; HB: miss; stable; 70 %; Ne = 511
 8 - Height: 75/65 cm; Weight: 90/60 kg; Herd number: miss; AI: miss
 9   Colour: Uni white
10   Pecularity: horns 0/0, spots at birth
11 - Main use: (1) meat,(2) wool,(3) miss
12   Spec. abilities: miss
13   Performance compared with STB Limousin 531:
14      higher: litter size, milk yield, lambing interval
15      equal:  muscularity, carcass leanness, age of sexual maturity
16      lower:  daily gain
17 - Management: miss; housing: miss m.;
18 - Conservation progr.: live animals: miss;Semen: miss;Embryos: miss
19   Status: potential. endang.;Watch: HB♀♀,%pure,%incross,trend!
20 - Similar breeds (see group 7/8 on page 93)     EN  Country Status
21   Bizet                                        420   F    pot. end.
22   Blanc du Massif Central                      423   F    normal
23   Limousin                                     531   F    normal
24   Lacaune                                      524   F    normal
```

```
 1 - Hampshire                                                   EN   506
 2   Hampshire Down; country-wide
 3   Upra Suffolk-Hampshire-Dorset                              HB:1957
 4   Paris Cedex 12 75595, M.N.E. - rue de Bercy 149
 5 - Imported as breed from country 507 United Kingdom
 6   Incrossing since 1960 from Hampshire 507 United Kingdom
 7   Numbers 1983: 1000/9000; HB: miss; decreasing; 95 %; Ne = 3600
 8 - Height: miss/miss cm; Weight: 100/70 kg; Herd number: miss; AI: miss
 9   Colour: Uni white; black-brown face and legs
10   Pecularity: horns 0/0
11 - Main use: (1) meat,(2) wool,(3) crossbreeding
12   Spec. abilities: miss
13   Performance compared with STB Suffolk 639:
14      higher: wool or fiber yield, wool or fiber thickness
15      equal:  muscularity, carcass leanness, age of sexual maturity
16      lower:  daily gain, litter size, milk yield
17 - Management: miss; housing: miss m.;
18 - Conservation progr.: live animals: miss;Semen: miss;Embryos: miss
19   Status: normal;              Watch: HB♀♀,%pure!
20 - Similar breeds (see group 4/1 on page 89)     EN  Country Status
21   Clun Forest                                  464   F    pot. end.
22   Dorset Down                                  481   F    pot. end.
23   Southdown                                    635   F    normal
24   Mouton Vendeen                               562   F    normal
```

1 - **Ile-de-France**   EN **513**
2   **Ile-de-France; Parise Basin / eastern Central France**
3   **Upra Ile de France**   HB:**1922**
4   **Paris 75017, boulevard Péreire-Sud 95**
5 - **Composite of Merino 545 Spain, Leicester 528, Dishley United Kingdom**
7   Numbers 1983: **14000/350000**; HB: **miss**; **decreasing**; **80 %**; Ne = **53846**
8 - Height: **78/70** cm; Weight: **120/80** kg; Herd number: **miss**; AI: **Yes**
9   Colour: **Uni white**
10 Pecularity: **horns 0/0**
11 - Main use: (1) **meat**,(2) **wool**,(3) **crossbreeding**
12 Spec. abilities: **miss**
13 Performance compared with STB **Texel 649**:
14   higher: **wool or fiber thickness, lambing interval**
15   equal: **muscularity, daily gain, litter size, age of sexual matur.**
16   lower: **carcass leanness, milk yield, wool or fiber yield**
17 - Management: **stationary**; housing: **2-6 m.**;
18 - Conservation progr.: live animals: **miss**;Semen: **miss**;Embryos: **miss**
19 Status: **normal**;   Watch: **HB♀♀,%pure!**
20 - <u>Similar breeds</u> (see group 1/6 on page 87)   <u>EN</u> <u>Country</u> <u>Status</u>
21 **Berrichon de l'Indre**   **417** **F**   **min. end.**
22 **Inra 401**   **515** **F**   **pot. end.**
23 **Charmoise**   **450** **F**   **normal**
24 **Berrichon du Cher**   **418** **F**   **normal**

1 - **Inra 401**   EN **515**
2   **Inra 401; males disseminated country-wide**
3   **I.N.R.A., Centre de Rech. de Toulouse, Station d'Amerlio-**   HB:**miss**
4   **ration genet. des animaux, Castanet-Tolosan Cedex 31326, B. P. 27**
5 - **Composite of Romanov 601, Berrichon du Cher 418**
7   Numbers 1983: **50/900**; HB: **miss**; **stable**; **100 %**; Ne = **190**
8 - Height: **miss/miss** cm; Weight: **90/65** kg; Herd number: **miss**; AI: **miss**
9   Colour: **Combination black,brown,white;sometimes black or brown spots**
10 Pecularity: **horns 0/0**
11 - Main use: (1) **meat**,(2) **wool**,(3) **miss**
12 Spec. abilities: **prolificacy, aseasonal breeding**
13 Performance compared with STB **Limousin 531**:
14   higher: **litter size,age of sex. matur.,lambing interv.,muscularity**
15   equal: **carcass leanness, wool or fiber thickness**
16   lower: **miss**
17 - Management: **stationary**; housing: **> 6 m.**;
18 - Conservation progr.: live animals: **miss**;Semen: **miss**;Embryos: **miss**
19 Status: **potential. endang.**;Watch: **HB♀♀!**
20 - <u>Similar breeds</u> (see group 1/6 on page 87)   <u>EN</u> <u>Country</u> <u>Status</u>
21 **Berrichon de l'Indre**   **417** **F**   **min. end.**
22 **Solognot**   **633** **F**   **pot. end.**
23 **Charmoise**   **450** **F**   **normal**
24 **Berrichon du Cher**   **418** **F**   **normal**

```
 1 - Lacaune                                                      EN   524
 2   Lacaune; "Rayon de Roquefort"
 3   Upra de la race ovine de Lacaune, Maison de l'Agriculture    HB:1947
 4   Rodez 12009, Route de Moyrazès
 5 - Composite of local Sud du Massif Central, Ardes 403
 7   Numbers 1983: 8000/1100000; HB: miss; increasing; 90 %; Ne = 31769
 8 - Height: 76/ miss cm; Weight: 95/70 kg; Herd number: miss; AI: Yes
 9   Colour: Uni white
10   Pecularity: horns 0/0
11 - Main use: (1) milk,(2) meat,(3) wool (4) leather
12   Spec. abilities: Roquefort cheese
13   Performance compared with STB Limousin 531:
14      higher: daily gain, milk yield, muscularity, litter size
15      equal:  carcass leanness
16      lower:  wool or fiber yield
17 - Management: miss; housing: miss m.;
18 - Conservation progr.: live animals: miss;Semen: miss;Embryos: miss
19   Status: normal
```

20 - Similar breeds (see group 7/8 on page 93)	EN	Country	Status
21 Bizet	420	F	pot. end.
22 Grivette	503	F	pot. end.
23 Limousin	531	F	normal
24 Blanc du Massif Central	423	F	normal

```
 1 - Landais                                                      EN   526
 2   Landais; "Les Landes"
 3   Ecomusée de Marquèze                                         HB:miss
 4   Sabres 40630
 5 - Autochthon local population
 7   Numbers 1993: 20/205; HB: miss; stable; 100 %; Ne = 51
 8 - Height: 70/65 cm; Weight: 70/45 kg; Herd number: 3; AI: miss
 9   Colour: Comb. black,brown,white;mainly white;brown and black spots
10   Pecularity: horns 2/0
11 - Main use: (1) meat,(2) wool,(3) vegetation management
12   Spec. abilities: miss
13   Performance compared with STB miss:
14      higher: miss
15      equal:  miss
16      lower:  miss
17 - Management: stationary; housing: > 6 m.;
18 - Conservation progr.: live animals: Yes;Semen: miss;Embryos: miss
19   Status: minimally endang.; Watch: ♂♂,HB♀♀,herds!
```

20 - Similar breeds (see group 7/9 on page 93)	EN	Country	Status
21 Castillonnais	445	F	crit.end.
22 Baregeois	411	F	min. end.
23 Aure et de Campan	404	F	pot. end.
24 Tarasconnais	646	F	normal

```
 1 - Limousin                                                    EN   531
 2   Limousin; northern Central Massif
 3   Upra des races ovines du Massif Central nord                HB:1943
 4   Lempdes 63370, Route de Thiers (RN 89), Marmilhat, B. P. 13
 5 - Autochthon local breed of Massif Central
 7   Numbers 1983: 2400/180000; HB: miss; increasing; 65 %; Ne = 9474
 8 - Height: 80/72 cm; Weight: 85/55 kg; Herd number: miss; AI: Yes
 9   Colour: Uni white
10   Pecularity: horns 0/0
11 - Main use: (1) meat,(2) wool,(3) miss
12   Spec. abilities: miss
13   Performance compared with STB Arles Merino 554:
14     higher: daily gain, wool or fiber yield, length of mating season
15     equal:  litter size,milk yield,age of sex. matur.,lambing interval
16     lower:  miss
17 - Management: stationary; housing: ≈ 2 m.;
18 - Conservation progr.: live animals: miss;Semen: miss;Embryos: miss
19   Status: normal;              Watch: HB♀♀,%pure!
```

20 -	Similar breeds (see group 7/8 on page 93)	EN	Country	Status
21	Bizet	420	F	pot. end.
22	Grivette	503	F	pot. end.
23	Lacaune	524	F	normal
24	Blanc du Massif Central	423	F	normal

```
 1 - Lourdais                                                    EN   535
 2   Lourdais; Pyrenees
 3   Upra des races ovines des Pyrenees centrales                HB:1975
 4   Montrejeau 31210, rue des Pyrénées 28
 5 - Composite of ancient local breed, Mérinos
 7   Numbers 1983: 70/3000; HB: miss; decreasing; 40 %; Ne = 274
 8 - Height: 80/72 cm; Weight: 90/65 kg; Herd number: miss; AI: miss
 9   Colour: Uni white; 10% of animals brown or pied
10   Pecularity: horns 2/2
11 - Main use: (1) meat,(2) wool,(3) vegetation management
12   Spec. abilities: able to walk long distances, mountain climate
13   Performance compared with STB Limousin 531:
14     higher: milk yield
15     equal:  carcass leanness,lambing interval,wool yield and thickness
16     lower:  litter size, muscularity, age of sexual maturity
17 - Management: transhumant; housing: 2-6 m.;
18 - Conservation progr.: live animals: miss;Semen: 10;Embryos: miss
19   Status: minimally endang.; Watch: HB♀♀,trend,%pure!
```

20 -	Similar breeds (see group 7/9 on page 93)	EN	Country	Status
21	Castillonnais	445	F	crit.end.
22	Baregeois	411	F	min. end.
23	Aure et de Campan	404	F	pot. end.
24	Tarasconnais	646	F	normal

1 - **Manech (Tete Noire)**   EN   537
2   **Black-Face Manech; Euskadi (Basque Provinces)**
3   **Upra des races ovines laitieres des Pyrenees**   HB:1975
4   **Mauleon Soule 64130, Ordiarp**
5 - **Autochthon original local breed**
7   Numbers 1983: 4000/25000; HB: miss; increasing; 90 %; Ne = 13793
8 - Height: **miss /65 cm**; Weight: **75/50 kg**; Herd number: **miss**; AI: **Yes**
9   Colour: **Uni white; black face and legs**
10 Pecularity: **horns 2/2**
11 - Main use: (1) **milk**,(2) **meat**,(3) **wool**
12 Spec. abilities: **cheese production**
13 Performance compared with STB **Lacaune 524:**
14   higher: **% fat, % protein**
15   equal: **carcass leanness, wool or fiber yield**
16   lower: **muscularity, daily gain, litter size, milk yield**
17 - Management: **transhumant**; housing: **miss m.**; **tending**
18 - Conservation progr.: live animals: **miss**;Semen: **miss**;Embryos: **miss**
19 Status: **normal**;   Watch: **HB♀♀,%pure!**
20 - Similar breeds (see group 5/2 on page 89)   EN Country Status
21 **Caussenard des Garrigues**   447   F   crit.end.
22 **Altamurana**   401   I   crit.end.
23 **Caussenard du Lot**   448   F   normal
24 **Basco-Bearnaise**   412   F   normal

1 - **Manech (Tete Rousse)**   EN   538
2   **Red-Face Manech; Euskadi (Basque Provinces)**
3   **Upra des races ovines laitieres des Pyrenees**   HB:1975
4   **Mauleon Soule 64130, Ordiarp**
5 - **Autochthon original local breed**
7   Numbers 1983: 2400/150000; HB: miss; increasing; 90 %; Ne = **9449**
8 - Height: **miss /60 cm**; Weight: **70/45 kg**; Herd number: **miss**; AI: **Yes**
9   Colour: **Uni white; red spots; red face**
10 Pecularity: **horns 2/0**
11 - Main use: (1) **milk**,(2) **meat**,(3) **wool**
12 Spec. abilities: **cheese production**
13 Performance compared with STB **Lacaune 524:**
14   higher: **%fat, % protein**
15   equal: **carcass leanness, wool or fiber yield**
16   lower: **muscularity, daily gain, litter size, milk yield**
17 - Management: **miss**; housing: **miss m.**;
18 - Conservation progr.: live animals: **miss**;Semen: **miss**;Embryos: **miss**
19 Status: **normal**;   Watch: **HB♀♀,%pure!**
20 - Similar breeds (see group 5/2 on page 89)   EN Country Status
21 **Caussenard des Garrigues**   447   F   crit.end.
22 **Altamurana**   401   I   crit.end.
23 **Caussenard du Lot**   448   F   normal
24 **Basco-Bearnaise**   412   F   normal

```
 1 - Merinos de Rambouillet                                    EN   553
 2   Rambouillet; Bergerie Nat. Rambouillet
 3   Flock-Book Merinos de Rambouillet C.E.Z.                  HB:miss
 4   Rambouillet 78120, Bergerie Nationale
 5 - Composite of different Spanish Merino strains
 7   Numbers 1993: 15/90; HB: miss; stable; 100 %; Ne = 29
 8 - Height: 72/62 cm; Weight: 80/50 kg; Herd number: 1; AI: miss
 9   Colour: Uni white
10   Pecularity: horns 2/0
11 - Main use: (1) wool,(2) meat,(3) historic
12   Spec. abilities: excellent thermotolerance
13   Performance compared with STB Finnsheep 489:
14     higher: litter size, age of sexual maturity, daily gain
15     equal:  milk yield
16     lower:  lambing interval, wool or fiber yield, wool thickness
17 - Management: stationary; housing: > 6 m.;
18 - Conservation progr.: live animals: Yes;Semen: 40;Embryos: 10/17
19   Status: critically endang.;Watch: ♂♂,HB♀♀,herds!
```

20 - <u>Similar breeds</u> (see group 1/2 on page 87)

		EN	Country	Status
21	Merinos Precoce	555	F	pot. end.
22	Race de l'est a Laine Merinos	591	F	pot. end.
23	Merinos d'Arles	554	F	normal

```
 1 - Merinos d'Arles                                           EN   554
 2   Arles Merino; Provence
 3   Upra du Merinos d'Arles                                   HB:1946
 4   Salon de Provence 13300, Domaine du Merle
 5 - Composite of local, Merino, Merino Precoce; incrossing since 1960
 6   from Merino Precoce 555 France, Est a Laine Merino 591 France
 7   Numbers 1983: 4000/300000; HB: miss; decreasing; 75 %; Ne = 15790
 8 - Height: 70/60 cm; Weight: 80/50 kg; Herd number: miss; AI: miss
 9   Colour: Uni white
10   Pecularity: horns 2/0
11 - Main use: (1) meat,(2) wool,(3) vegetation management
12   Spec. abilities: able to walk long distances
13   Performance compared with STB Precoce 555:
14     higher: miss
15     equal:  carcass leanness, age of sexual maturity, lambing interval
16     lower:  muscularity,daily gain,wool yield,litter size,milk yield
17 - Management: miss; housing: miss m.; mountain
18 - Conservation progr.: live animals: miss;Semen: miss;Embryos: miss
19   Status: normal;              Watch: HB♀♀,%pure!
```

20 - <u>Similar breeds</u> (see group 1/2 on page 87)

		EN	Country	Status
21	Merinos de Rambouillet	553	F	crit.end.
22	Merinos Precoce	555	F	pot. end.
23	Race de l'est a Laine Merinos	591	F	pot. end.

```
 1 - Merinos Precoce                                      EN   555
 2   Precoce; eastern Parise Basin
 3   Flock-Book de la race Merinos Precoce                HB:1929
 4   Paris 75017, boulevard Péreire-Sud 95
 5 - Imported as breed from country Spain
 7   Numbers 1983: 150/1500; HB: miss; decreasing; 80 %; Ne = 546
 8 - Height: 80/73 cm; Weight: 100/65 kg; Herd number: miss; AI: miss
 9   Colour: Uni white
10   Pecularity: horns 2/0
11 - Main use: (1) meat,(2) wool,(3) crossbreeding
12   Spec. abilities: miss
13   Performance compared with STB Rambouillet 553:
14      higher: muscularity,daily gain,litter size,carc. leann.,milk yield
15      equal:  age of sexual maturity, lambing interval, wool thicknes
16      lower:  miss
17 - Management: stationary; housing: 2-6 m.;
18 - Conservation progr.: live animals: miss;Semen: miss;Embryos: miss
19   Status: potential. endang.;Watch: HB♀♀,trend,%pure!
```

```
20 - Similar breeds (see group 1/2 on page 87)      EN  Country Status
21   Merinos de Rambouillet                         553   F     crit.end.
22   Race de l'est a Laine Merinos                  591   F     pot. end.
23   Merinos d'Arles                                554   F     normal
```

```
 1 - Mourerous, Peone                                     EN   558
 2   Mourerous; southern Alps
 3   Syndicat de Défense et de Promot. de la race Mourerous    HB:1883
 4   Etabl. Dépt. de l'Elevage, Digne 04000, Boulevard Gassendi 66
 5 - Autochthon local of maritime Alpes
 6   Incrossing since 1960 from Prealpes 589 France
 7   Numbers 1983: 32/1500; HB: miss; stable; 60 %; Ne = 125
 8 - Height: miss /61 cm; Weight: 70/55 kg; Herd number: miss; AI: miss
 9   Colour: Combination brown, white; red to fawn head and legs
10   Pecularity: horns 0/0
11 - Main use: (1) meat,(2) wool,(3) miss
12   Spec. abilities: able to walk long distances
13   Performance compared with STB Arles Merino 554:
14      higher: muscularity, daily gain, milk yield
15      equal:  litter size, length of mating season, lambing interval
16      lower:  wool or fiber thickness
17 - Management: transhumant; housing: 2-6 m.; tending
18 - Conservation progr.: live animals: miss;Semen: miss;Embryos: miss
19   Status: minimally endang.; Watch: HB♀♀,%pure,%incross!
```

```
20 - Similar breeds (see group 7/1 on page 91)      EN  Country Status
21   Commun des Alpes                               470   F     crit.end.
22   Alpagota                                       400   I     crit.end.
23   Biellese                                       419   I     normal
24   Prealpes du Sud                                589   F     normal
```

```
 1 - Mouton Boulonnais                                              EN  559
 2   Boulonnais; northern French coast
 3   Association des Eleveurs de Mouton Boulonnais                   HB:miss
 4   Marchiennes 59870, rue Haute 164, Bouvignies
 5 - Composite of local, Leicester 528, New Kent, Dishley-Merino
 7   Numbers 1992: miss /1000; HB: miss; stable; miss %; Ne = 181
 8 - Height: miss /75 cm; Weight: 100/70 kg; Herd number: miss; AI: miss
 9   Colour: Uni white; face and legs blue or red, nose black
10   Pecularity: miss
11 - Main use: (1) meat,(2) wool,(3) miss
12   Spec. abilities: miss
13   Performance compared with STB Texel 649:
14     higher: miss
15     equal:  carcass leanness, wool or fiber thickness
16     lower:  litter size, wool or fiber yield
17 - Management: miss; housing: miss m.;
18 - Conservation progr.: live animals: miss;Semen: miss;Embryos: miss
19   Status: critically endang.;Watch: ♂♂,HB♀♀,%pure!
```

20 - <u>Similar breeds</u> (see group 3 on page 88)

20		EN	Country	Status
21	Galway	495	IRL	endanger.
22	Whiteface Dartmoor	675	GB	min. end.
23	Mouton Charollais	560	F	normal
24	Cotentin	473	F	normal

```
 1 - Mouton Charollais                                              EN  560
 2   Charollais; western and eastern Central France
 3   Upra de la race ovine Charollais                               HB:1963
 4   Charolles 71120, rue du Général Leclerc 36
 5 - Composite of local, Leicester Longwool 528, South Down 635
 7   Numbers 1983: 12000/110000; HB: miss; increasing; 95 %; Ne = 43279
 8 - Height: miss/miss cm; Weight: 105/75 kg; Herd number: miss; AI: Yes
 9   Colour: Uni white; face and legs brown with pink spots
10   Pecularity: horns 0/0
11 - Main use: (1) meat,(2) wool,(3) crossbreeding
12   Spec. abilities: miss
13   Performance compared with STB Texel 649:
14     higher: litter size, wool or fiber thickness
15     equal:  muscularity,daily gain,carcass leanness,age of sex. matur.
16     lower:  wool or fiber yield, milk yield
17 - Management: miss; housing: miss m.;
18 - Conservation progr.: live animals: miss;Semen: miss;Embryos: miss
19   Status: normal
```

20 - <u>Similar breeds</u> (see group 3 on page 88)

20		EN	Country	Status
21	Mouton Boulonnais	559	F	crit.end.
22	Galway	495	IRL	endanger.
23	Rouge de Hague	608	F	normal
24	Cotentin	473	F	normal

```
1 - Mouton Vendeen                                          EN  562
2   Vendeen; Atlantic coast
3   Upra de la race ovine Vendeen                           HB:1967
4   La Roche sur Yon 85001, Les Etablières, Route de Dompierre
5 - Composite of British and Flemish breeds
7   Numbers 1983: 7000/170000; HB: miss; stable; 75 %; Ne = 26893
8 - Height: miss/miss cm; Weight: 100/65 kg; Herd number: miss; AI: Yes
9   Colour: Uni white, grey face and legs
10  Pecularity: horns 0/0
11 - Main use: (1) meat,(2) wool,(3) crossbreeding
12  Spec. abilities: miss
13  Performance compared with STB Texel 649:
14    higher: litter size, age of sexual maturity, lambing interval
15    equal:  muscularity
16    lower:  wool yield, daily gain, carcass leanness, milk yield
17 - Management: miss; housing: miss m.;
18 - Conservation progr.: live animals: miss;Semen: miss;Embryos: miss
19  Status: normal;              Watch: HB♀♀,%pure!
```

20 - Similar breeds (see group 4/1 on page 89)	EN	Country	Status
21 Clun Forest	464	F	pot. end.
22 Dorset Down	481	F	pot. end.
23 Southdown	635	F	normal
24 Hampshire	506	F	normal

```
1 - Noir du Velay                                           EN  564
2   Velay Black; Departement Haute Loire
3   Upra des races ovines du Massif Central nord            HB:1970
4   Lempdes 63370, Route de Thiers (RN 89) Marmilhat, B. P. 13
5 - Autochthon local breed
7   Numbers 1983: 500/30000; HB: miss; stable; 75 %; Ne = 1967
8 - Height: 65/60 cm; Weight: 75/50 kg; Herd number: miss; AI: miss
9   Colour: Uni black, white spots on forehead and white tail-tip
10  Pecularity: horns 0/0
11 - Main use: (1) meat,(2) wool,(3) miss
12  Spec. abilities: miss
13  Performance compared with STB Limousin 531:
14    higher: lambing interval, wool or fiber thickness
15    equal:  muscularity,daily gain,carc. lean.,litter size,milk yield
16    lower:  wool or fiber yield
17 - Management: stationary; housing: 2-6 m.;
18 - Conservation progr.: live animals: miss;Semen: miss;Embryos: miss
19  Status: normal;              Watch: HB♀♀,%pure!
```

20 - Similar breeds (see group 7/8 on page 93)	EN	Country	Status
21 Bizet	420	F	pot. end.
22 Grivette	503	F	pot. end.
23 Lacaune	524	F	normal
24 Blanc du Massif Central	423	F	normal

1 - **Ouessant**   EN **574**
2   **Ushant**; western France, Pays de Loire
3   **Groupement des eleveurs de moutons d'Ouessant (G.E.M.O.)**   HB:**miss**
4   **Sautron 44880, Lande de Huaud**
5 - **Composite of Ouessant, Monts d'Arrée**
7   Numbers 1993: **140/1000**; HB: **miss**; **increasing**; **100 %**; Ne = **491**
8 - Height: **47/44** cm; Weight: **16/13** kg; Herd number: **miss**; AI: **miss**
9   Colour: **Uni black, red, brown, white**; sometimes spots on forehead
10 Pecularity: **horns 2/0**
11 - Main use:(1) **sport/hobby**,(2) **meat**,(3) **wool** (4) **vegetation management**
12 Spec. abilities: **miss**
13 Performance compared with STB **miss**:
14   higher: **miss**
15   equal: **miss**
16   lower: **miss**
17 - Management: **stationary**; housing: **no**
18 - Conservation progr.: live animals: **miss**;Semen: **miss**;Embryos: **miss**
19 Status: **potential. endang.**;Watch: **HB♀♀!**
20 - <u>Similar breeds</u> (see group 8/1 on page 94)   EN Country Status
21 **Marrane**   540   I   crit.end.
22 **Rosset**   603   I   crit.end.
23 **Comisana**   469   I   normal
24 **Corse**   472   F   normal

1 - **Prealpes du Sud**   EN **589**
2   **Prealpes du Sud**; southeastern France (Prèalpes)
3   **Upra de la race ovine des Prealpes du Sud, E.D.E.**   HB:**1947**
4   **Gap 05000, rue Capitaine de Bresson 8**
5 - **Autochthon local population**
7   Numbers 1983: **4500/250000**; HB: **miss**; **stable**; **70 %**; Ne = **17682**
8 - Height: **70/65** cm; Weight: **85/60** kg; Herd number: **miss**; AI: **Yes**
9   Colour: **Uni white**
10 Pecularity: **horns 0/0**
11 - Main use: (1) **meat**,(2) **wool**,(3) **miss**
12 Spec. abilities: **miss**
13 Performance compared with STB **Limousin 531**:
14   higher: **muscularity, lambing interval, wool or fiber thickness**
15   equal: **carcass leanness,litter size,milk yield,age of sex. matur.**
16   lower: **daily gain, wool or fiber yield**
17 - Management: **miss**; housing: **miss m.**; **tending**
18 - Conservation progr.: live animals: **miss**;Semen: **miss**;Embryos: **miss**
19 Status: **normal**;   Watch: **HB♀♀,%pure!**
20 - <u>Similar breeds</u> (see group 7/1 on page 91)   EN Country Status
21 **Commun des Alpes**   470   F   crit.end.
22 **Alpagota**   400   I   crit.end.
23 **Mourerous**   558   F   min. end.
24 **Biellese**   419   I   normal

SHEEP

1 - Race de l'est a Laine Merinos   EN 591
2   Merino de l'Est; eastern France (Lorraine)
3   Upra de la race ovine de L'Est a Laine Merinos   HB:1947
4   Paris Cedex 12 75595, M.N.E. - rue de Bercy 149
5 - Imported as breed from country Germany
6   Incrossing since 1960 from Merino Landschaf 550 Germany
7   Numbers 1983: 600/37000; HB: miss; stable; 35 %; Ne = 2362
8 - Height: miss/miss cm; Weight: 100/75 kg; Herd number: miss; AI: miss
9   Colour: Uni white
10 Pecularity: horns 0/0
11 - Main use: (1) meat,(2) wool,(3) vegetation management
12 Spec. abilities: able to walk long distances
13 Performance compared with STB Precoce 555:
14   higher: daily gain, milk yield
15   equal: carc. leann.,litter size,age of sex. mat.,lambing interv.
16   lower: muscularity
17 - Management: miss; housing: miss m.; extensive conditions
18 - Conservation progr.: live animals: miss;Semen: miss;Embryos: miss
19 Status: potential. endang.;Watch: HB♀♀,%pure,%incross!
20 - Similar breeds (see group 1/2 on page 87)   EN Country Status
21 Merinos de Rambouillet   553   F   crit.end.
22 Merinos Precoce   555   F   pot. end.
23 Merinos d'Arles   554   F   normal

FRANCE SHEEP

1 - Race de Thones et de Marthod   EN 592
2   Thones-Marthod; Savoy
3   Etablissement Départemental de l'Elevage   HB:miss
4   Chambery 73000, rue Métropole 11
5 - Autochthon local of Savoyen
7   Numbers 1983: 100/4000; HB: miss; stable; 50 %; Ne = 390
8 - Height: miss/miss cm; Weight: 80/60 kg; Herd number: miss; AI: miss
9   Colour: Uni white; black spectacles, nose tip, ears and feet
10 Pecularity: horns 2/2
11 - Main use: (1) meat,(2) wool,(3) cheese production
12 Spec. abilities: miss
13 Performance compared with STB Limousin 531:
14   higher: lambing interval, wool or fiber yield
15   equal: muscularity, carcass leanness, litter size, milk yield
16   lower: daily gain, wool or fiber thickness
17 - Management: miss; housing: miss m.; feral, extensive conditions
18 - Conservation progr.: live animals: miss;Semen: miss;Embryos: miss
19 Status: potential. endang.;Watch: HB♀♀,%pure!
20 - Similar breeds (see group 8/1 on page 94)   EN Country Status
21 Marrane   540   I   crit.end.
22 Rosset   603   I   crit.end.
23 Comisana   469   I   normal
24 Corse   472   F   normal

```
 1 - Raiole                                                   EN  594
 2   Raiole; Cévennes (southeastern Central Massif)
 3   Syndicat d'éleveurs de Brebis Raioles La Molière         HB:miss
 4   Valleraugue 30570
 5 - Autochthon strain of Caussenardes; incrossing since 1960 from
 6   Blanc du Massif Central 423 France, Tarasconnaise 646 France
 7   Numbers 1993: 20/1600; HB: miss; decreasing; 50 %; Ne = 59
 8 - Height: 63/73 cm; Weight: 90/60 kg; Herd number: miss; AI: miss
 9   Colour: Uni white; face and legs red spotted
10   Pecularity: horns 2/2
11 - Main use: (1) meat,(2) wool,(3) miss
12   Spec. abilities: miss
13   Performance compared with STB Finnsheep 489:
14     higher: daily gain,age of sex. matur.,lambing interval,wool yield
15     equal:  wool or fiber thickness
16     lower:  litter size,milk yield,% fat,% protein,l. of mating season
17 - Management: transhumant; housing: ≈ 2 m.; mountain
18 - Conservation progr.: live animals: Yes;Semen: miss;Embryos: miss
19   Status: endangered;       Watch: ♂♂,HB♀♀,%pure,%incros,trend!
```

20 - Similar breeds (see group 5/2 on page 89)	EN	Country	Status
21 Caussenard des Garrigues	447	F	crit.end.
22 Altamurana	401	I	crit.end.
23 Caussenard du Lot	448	F	normal
24 Basco-Bearnaise	412	F	normal

```
 1 - Rava                                                     EN  596
 2   Rava; Département du Puy-de-Dome
 3   Upra des races ovines du Massif Central nord             HB:1973
 4   Lempdes 63370, Route de Thiers (RN 89), Marmilhat, B. P. 13
 5 - Autochthon local population of Auvergne
 7   Numbers 1983: 550/30000; HB: miss; decreasing; 70 %; Ne = 2160
 8 - Height: 64/60 cm; Weight: 80/50 kg; Herd number: miss; AI: Yes
 9   Colour: Uni white; black spots on legs
10   Pecularity: horns 0/0
11 - Main use: (1) meat,(2) wool,(3) miss
12   Spec. abilities: miss
13   Performance compared with STB Limousin 531:
14     higher: daily gain, milk yield, lambing interval
15     equal:  muscularity,carc. leanness,litter size,age of sex. matur.
16     lower:  wool or fiber thickness
17 - Management: stationary; housing: 2-6 m.;
18 - Conservation progr.: live animals: miss;Semen: miss;Embryos: miss
19   Status: normal;          Watch: HB♀♀,trend,%pure!
```

20 - Similar breeds (see group 7/8 on page 93)	EN	Country	Status
21 Bizet	420	F	pot. end.
22 Grivette	503	F	pot. end.
23 Lacaune	524	F	normal
24 Blanc du Massif Central	423	F	normal

```
 1 - Romanov                                              EN  601
 2   Romanov; country-wide
 3   Upra Finnois et Romanov                              HB:1963
 4   Montmorillon 86500, Route de Chauvigny
 5 - Composite of Romanov from old Russia
 7   Numbers 1983: 500/6000; HB: miss; stable; 40 %; Ne = 1846
 8 - Height: miss / miss cm; Weight: 75/55 kg; Herd number: miss; AI: Yes
 9   Colour: Uni grey; black head and legs, white face-stripe
10   Pecularity: horns 2,0/2,0
11 - Main use: (1) crossbreeding,(2) meat,(3) miss
12   Spec. abilities: prolific
13   Performance compared with STB Limousin 531:
14     higher: litter size,age of sex. matur.,milk yield,lambing interval
15     equal:  carcass leanness, wool or fiber yield
16     lower:  wool or fiber thickness, muscularity, daily gain
17 - Management: miss; housing: miss m.;
18 - Conservation progr.: live animals: miss;Semen: miss;Embryos: miss
19   Status: potential. endang.;Watch: HB♀♀,%pure!
```

```
20 - Similar breeds (see group 6/3 on page 90)   EN  Country  Status
21   Dansk Landfar                               477  DK       crit.end.
22   Coburger Fuchsschaf                         466  D        crit.end.
23   Foroyskur Seydur                            491  FR       normal
24   Gronlandsk Fär                              504  DK       normal
```

```
 1 - Rouge de l'ouest                                     EN  604
 2   Rouge de l'Ouest; western France and western Central France
 3   Upra des races ovines du Maine                       HB:1968
 4   Allonnes 72700, La Futaie - Rouillon
 5 - Composite of local Poitevin,Blue Leicester 427 GB,Wensleydale 674 GB
 7   Numbers 1983: 10000/190000; HB: miss; increasing; 75 %; Ne = 38000
 8 - Height: miss/miss cm; Weight: 110/75 kg; Herd number: miss; AI: Yes
 9   Colour: Uni white; wine-red face, legs with grey-black spots
10   Pecularity: horns 0/0
11 - Main use: (1) meat,(2) wool,(3) crossbreeding
12   Spec. abilities: miss
13   Performance compared with STB Texel 649:
14     higher: litter size, age of sexual maturity
15     equal:  daily gain, carcass leanness, milk yield, lambing interval
16     lower:  muscularity, wool or fiber yield
17 - Management: miss; housing: miss m.;
18 - Conservation progr.: live animals: miss;Semen: miss;Embryos: miss
19   Status: normal
```

```
20 - Similar breeds (see group 2/1 on page 87)   EN  Country  Status
21   Rouge de l'ouest                            605  GB       pot. end.
22   Bleu du Maine                               425  F        normal
23   Bleu du Maine                               426  GB       normal
24   Blauköpfiges Fleischschaf                   424  D        normal
```

```
 1 - Rouge du Roussillon                                      EN  606
 2   Roussillon Red; Roussillon
 3   I.N.R.A., Centre de Recherches de Jouy-en-Josas         HB:miss
 4   Jouy-en-Josas Cedex, 78352
 5 - Composite of local breed (Merino, Barbary)
 7   Numbers 1993: miss /30; HB: miss; decreasing; miss %; Ne = 2
 8 - Height: miss / miss cm; Weight: 90/60 kg; Herd number: 2; AI: miss
 9   Colour: Uni white; red or spotted head and legs
10   Pecularity: 0/0
11 - Main use: (1) meat,(2) wool,(3) miss
12   Spec. abilities: poor feeding conditions
13   Performance compared with STB miss:
14     higher: miss
15     equal:  miss
16     lower:  miss
17 - Management: miss; housing: miss m.;
18 - Conservation progr.: live animals: miss;Semen: miss;Embryos: miss
19   Status: critically endang.;Watch: ♂♂,HB♀♀,trend,%pure,herds!
```

20 - <u>Similar breeds</u> (see group 8/3 on page 95)

		EN	Country	Status
21	Nostrana	570	I	endanger.
22	Coete	599	E	min. end.
23	Barbaresca Siciliana	410	I	normal
24	Barbaresca della Campania	409	I	normal

```
 1 - Roussin, Rouge de Hague                                  EN  608
 2   Roussin de la Hague; northern Département de la Manche
 3   Upra ovine Avranchin, Cotentin et Roussin               HB:1983
 4   Saint Lo Cedex 50000, Maison de l'Agriculture, Avenue de Paris
 5 - Composite of local breed, Suffolk 639 France, Leicester 528 United
 6   Kingdom, South Down 635 France
 7   Numbers 1983: 350/8000; HB: miss; increasing; 80 %; Ne = 1341
 8 - Height: miss/miss cm; Weight: 90/65 kg; Herd number: miss; AI: miss
 9   Colour: Uni white; head dark brown
10   Pecularity: horns 0/0, red at birth
11 - Main use: (1) meat,(2) wool,(3) miss
12   Spec. abilities: miss
13   Performance compared with STB Suffolk 639:
14     higher: litter size
15     equal:  carc. lean.,milk yield,age of sex. matur.,lambing interval
16     lower:  daily gain, muscularity, wool or fiber yield
17 - Management: miss; housing: miss m.;
18 - Conservation progr.: live animals: miss;Semen: miss;Embryos: miss
19   Status: normal;            Watch: HB♀♀,%pure!
```

20 - <u>Similar breeds</u> (see group 3 on page 88)

		EN	Country	Status
21	Mouton Boulonnais	559	F	crit.end.
22	Galway	495	IRL	endanger.
23	Mouton Charollais	560	F	normal
24	Cotentin	473	F	normal

```
 1 - Solognot                                              EN  633
 2   Solognot; Sologne and Touraine
 3   Flock-Book de la race ovine Solognot                  HB:1942
 4   Paris 75017, boulevard Péreire-Sud 95
 5 - Autochthon local population of Solognote
 7   Numbers 1983: 80/2300; HB: miss; increasing; 70 %; Ne = 309
 8 - Height: miss /65 cm; Weight: 85/55 kg; Herd number: miss; AI: miss
 9   Colour: Uni red
10   Pecularity: horns 0/0
11 - Main use: (1) meat,(2) wool,(3) vegetation management
12   Spec. abilities: resistance to gastro-intestinal parasites
13   Performance compared with STB Limousin 531:
14     higher: litter size, wool or fiber thickness
15     equal:  muscularity, carcass leanness, age of sexual maturity
16     lower:  daily gain, milk yield
17 - Management: miss; housing: miss m.; poor vegetation
18 - Conservation progr.: live animals: miss;Semen: miss;Embryos: miss
19   Status: potential. endang.;Watch: HB♀♀,%pure!
```

20 - Similar breeds (see group 1/6 on page 87)	EN	Country	Status
21 Berrichon de l'Indre	417	F	min. end.
22 Inra 401	515	F	pot. end.
23 Charmoise	450	F	normal
24 Berrichon du Cher	418	F	normal

```
 1 - Southdown                                             EN  635
 2   Southdown; Bourbonnais / country-wide
 3   Association des eleveurs du Southdown, Cidex 9058      HB:1947
 4   Domerat 03410, Bel Air - St Victor
 5 - Imported as breed from country 636 United Kingdom
 7   Numbers 1983: 3000/140000; HB: miss; decreasing; 70 %; Ne = 11748
 8 - Height: miss/miss cm; Weight: 90/60 kg; Herd number: miss; AI: miss
 9   Colour: Uni white; grey-brown face and legs
10   Pecularity: horns 0/0
11 - Main use: (1) meat,(2) wool,(3) miss
12   Spec. abilities: miss
13   Performance compared with STB Texel 649:
14     higher: wool or fiber thickness
15     equal:  muscularity, age of sexual maturity, lambing interval
16     lower:  daily gain,milk yield,wool or fiber yield,carcass leanness
17 - Management: miss; housing: miss m.;
18 - Conservation progr.: live animals: miss;Semen: miss;Embryos: miss
19   Status: normal
```

20 - Similar breeds (see group 4/1 on page 89)	EN	Country	Status
21 Clun Forest	464	F	pot. end.
22 Dorset Down	481	F	pot. end.
23 Mouton Vendeen	562	F	normal
24 Hampshire	506	F	normal

1 - **Suffolk**   EN **639**
2   **Suffolk; country-wide**
3   **Upra Suffolk-Hampshire-Dorset**   HB:**1957**
4   **Paris Cedex 12 75595, M.N.E. - rue de Bercy 149**
5 - **Imported as breed from country 642 United Kingdom**
6   **Incrossing since 1960 from Suffolk 642 United Kingdom**
7   Numbers **1983: 5000/50000**; HB: **miss**; **increasing**; **95 %**; Ne = **18182**
8 - Height: **miss/miss** cm; Weight: **105/75** kg; Herd number: **miss**; AI: **Yes**
9   Colour: **Uni white; head and legs black**
10 Pecularity: **horns 0/0**
11 - Main use: (1) **meat**,(2) **wool**,(3) **crossbreeding**
12 Spec. abilities: **miss**
13 Performance compared with STB **Texel 649**:
14   higher: **daily gain,milk yield,age of sexual maturity**
15   equal: **muscularity,carcass leanness,litter size,lambing interval**
16   lower: **wool or fiber yield**
17 - Management: **miss**; housing: **miss** m.;
18 - Conservation progr.: live animals: **miss**;Semen: **miss**;Embryos: **miss**
19 Status: **normal**
20 - <u>Similar breeds</u> (see group 4/2 on page 89)   <u>EN</u> <u>Country</u> <u>Status</u>
21 **Norfolk Horn**   565   GB   min. end.
22 **Suffolk**   640   D   normal
23 **Suffolk sheep**   642   GB   normal
24 **Suffolk**   641   IRL   normal

1 - **Tarasconnais**   EN **646**
2   **Tarasconnais; central Pyrenees**
3   **Upra des races ovines des Pyrenees centrales**   HB:**1975**
4   **Montrejeau 31210, rue des Pyrénées 28**
5 - **Autochthon local breed of Central Pyrenean**
7   Numbers **1983: 3000/100000**; HB: **miss**; **decreasing**; **80 %**; Ne = **11651**
8 - Height: **82/67** cm; Weight: **80/55** kg; Herd number: **miss**; AI: **Yes**
9   Colour: **Uni white; coloured spots on head and legs**
10 Pecularity: **horns 2/2**
11 - Main use: (1) **meat**,(2) **wool**,(3) **miss**
12 Spec. abilities: **able to walk long distances, mountain**
13 Performance compared with STB **Limousin 531**:
14   higher: **lambing interval**
15   equal: **muscularity,carcass leanness,wool yield,wool thickness**
16   lower: **daily gain,litter size,milk yield,age of sexual maturity**
17 - Management: **transhumant**; housing: **2-6** m.;
18 - Conservation progr.: live animals: **miss**;Semen: **miss**;Embryos: **miss**
19 Status: **normal**;   Watch: HB♀♀,**trend,%pure!**
20 - <u>Similar breeds</u> (see group 7/9 on page 93)   <u>EN</u> <u>Country</u> <u>Status</u>
21 **Castillonnais**   445   F   crit.end.
22 **Baregeois**   411   F   min. end.
23 **Landais**   526   F   min. end.
24 **Aure et de Campan**   404   F   pot. end.

SHEEP

```
 1 - Texel                                                    EN  649
 2   Texel; northeastern France
 3   Upra de la race ovine de Texel                           HB:1935
 4   Paris 75017, boulevard Péreire-Sud 95
 5 - Imported as breed from country 653 Netherlands
 6   Incrossing since 1960 from Texel 653 Netherlands
 7   Numbers 1983: 8000/180000; HB: miss; stable; 90 %; Ne = 30638
 8 - Height: 78/70 cm; Weight: 115/80 kg; Herd number: miss; AI: Yes
 9   Colour: Uni white; black nose and hoofs
10   Pecularity: horns 0/0
11 - Main use: (1) meat,(2) wool,(3) crossbreeding
12   Spec. abilities: miss
13   Performance compared with STB Texel 649:
14     higher: Breed is used
15     equal:  as standard breed,
16     lower:  no comparison possible.
17 - Management: miss; housing: miss m.;feral
18 - Conservation progr.: live animals: miss;Semen: miss;Embryos: miss
19   Status: normal
20 - Similar breeds (see group 2/2 on page 88)    EN  Country Status
21   Texel                                        648   SF   pot. end.
22   Texel                                        650   D    normal
23   Texel                                        652   L    normal
24   Texel                                        651   IRL  normal
```

GOATS

```
 1 - Alpine                                                   EN  301
 2   Alpine; every region with goat production
 3   Upra Caprine                                             HB:1930
 4   Blois Cedex 41018, Avenue de Vendome 15, B. P. 199
 5 - Autochthon origin breed of French-Swiss Alpine
 6   Incrossing since 1960 from British Alpine
 7   Numbers 1984: 33000/392000; HB: 120000; stable; 75 %; Ne = 103529
 8 - Height: 85/80 cm; Weight: 80/60 kg; Herd number: miss; AI: Yes
 9   Colour: Uni brown
10   Pecularity: horns 2/2, black dorsal stripe
11 - Main use: (1) milk,(2) meat,(3) miss
12   Spec. abilities: miss
13   Performance compared with STB Saanen 350:
14     higher: % fat, % protein
15     equal:  muscularity, daily gain, carcass leanness, litter size
16     lower:  miss
17 - Management: stationary; housing: > 6 m.;
18 - Conservation progr.: live animals: miss;Semen: 100;Embryos: miss
19   Status: normal;              Watch: %pure,%incross!
20 - Similar breeds (see group 2 on page 97)      EN  Country Status
21   Erzgebirgsziege                              330   D    crit.end.
22   Hneda kratkosrsta                            334   CS   min. end.
23   Camosciata delle Alpi                        314   I    normal
24   Bunte Deutsche Edelziege                     310   D    normal
```

```
 1 - Chevre du Rove                                              EN  319
 2   Rove; Provence
 3   Association de Défense des Caprins du Rove, Maison du       HB:miss
 4   Parc du Luberon, Apt 84400, Avenue des Druides
 5 - Autochthon local breed
 7   Numbers 1984: 100/1400; HB: miss; stable; 80 %; Ne = 373
 8 - Height: 85/72 cm; Weight: 80/55 kg; Herd number: miss; AI: miss
 9   Colour: Combination red, yellow
10   Pecularity: horns 2/2
11 - Main use: (1) milk,(2) meat,(3) vegetation management
12   Spec. abilities: adaptation on mediterranean conditions
13   Performance compared with STB Alpine 301:
14     higher: milk yield
15     equal:  daily gain, litter size, % protein, age of sexual maturity
16     lower:  % fat
17 - Management: stationary; housing: ≈ 2 m.;
18 - Conservation progr.: live animals: miss;Semen: miss;Embryos: miss
19   Status: potential. endang.;Watch: HB♀♀,%pure!
```

20 - Similar breeds (see group 8 on page 98)	EN	Country	Status
21 Derivata di Siria	323	I	crit.end.
22 Cabra Mallorquina	313	E	min. end.
23 Negra Serrana	316	E	normal
24 Charnequeira	318	P	normal

```
 1 - Corse                                                       EN  320
 2   Corsican; Corse, mainly in the upper regions
 3   INRA-LRDE                                                  HB:miss
 4   Corte 20250, B.P. 8
 5 - Autochthon local breed
 6   Incrossing since 1960 from Alpine 301 France
 7   Numbers 1986: 2100/39500; HB: miss; stable; 97 %; Ne = 7976
 8 - Height: miss/miss cm; Weight: 75/48 kg; Herd number: miss; AI: miss
 9   Colour: Combination black, grey, red, brown, yellow, white, blond
10   Pecularity: horns 2/2
11 - Main use: (1) milk,(2) meat,(3) miss
12   Spec. abilities: cheese production, mediterranean conditions
13   Performance compared with STB Alpine 301:
14     higher: % fat, % protein, length of mating season
15     equal:  miss
16     lower:  muscularity, milk yield, litter size, age of sexual matur.
17 - Management: transhumant; housing: no
18 - Conservation progr.: live animals: miss;Semen: miss;Embryos: miss
19   Status: normal;            Watch: HB♀♀,%incross!
```

20 - Similar breeds (see group 9 on page 98)	EN	Country	Status
21 Roccaverano	347	I	crit.end.
22 Val di Livo (extinct)	363	I	crit.end.
23 Sarda	351	I	normal
24 Local breeds	338	GR	normal

```
 1 - Poitevin                                                    EN  345
 2   Poitou; Poitou
 3   Upra Caprine                                                HB:1952
 4   Blois Cedex 41018, Avenue de Vendome 15, B. P. 199
 5 - Autochthon local breed
 6   Incrossing since 1960 from British Alpine United Kingdom
 7   Numbers 1992: 100/2000; HB: miss; decreasing; 90 %; Ne = 381
 8 - Height: 80/75 cm; Weight: 72/55 kg; Herd number: miss; AI: miss
 9   Colour: Uni brown
10   Pecularity: horns 2/2, long hair, white belly, head like Toggenburg
11 - Main use: (1) milk,(2) meat,(3) miss
12   Spec. abilities: miss
13   Performance compared with STB Saanen 350:
14     higher: % fat, % protein
15     equal: muscularity, carcass leanness, age of sexual maturity
16     lower:  daily gain, litter size, milk yield
17 - Management: stationary; housing: > 6 m.;
18 - Conservation progr.: live animals: miss;Semen: miss;Embryos: miss
19   Status: minimally endang.; Watch: HB♀♀,trend,%pure,%incross!
```

20 - Similar breeds (see group 3 on page 97)	EN	Country	Status
21 Thüringer Waldziege	360	D	crit.end.
22 Toggenburger	361	B	endanger.
23 Pure Toggenburg	346	GB	normal
24 Toggenburger	362	CH	normal

```
 1 - Saanen, Gessenay                                            EN  350
 2   Saanen; southeastern France
 3   Upra Caprine                                                HB:1959
 4   Blois 41002, Avenue de Vendome 15, B. P. 199
 5 - Imported as breed from country Switzerland; incrossing since 1960
 6   from Saanen 349 Switzerland, 367 Germany, United Kingdom
 7   Numbers 1983: 12000/181000; HB: miss; increasing; 90 %; Ne = 45016
 8 - Height: 85/80 cm; Weight: 92/70 kg; Herd number: miss; AI: Yes
 9   Colour: Uni white
10   Pecularity: horns 2/2
11 - Main use: (1) milk,(2) meat,(3) miss
12   Spec. abilities: miss
13   Performance compared with STB Alpine 301:
14     higher: miss
15     equal:  daily gain, litter size, milk yield, % fat, % protein
16     lower:  miss
17 - Management: stationary; housing: > 6 m.;
18 - Conservation progr.: live animals: miss;Semen: 80;Embryos: miss
19   Status: normal;          Watch: HB♀♀,%incross!
```

20 - Similar breeds (see group 1 on page 97)	EN	Country	Status
21 Irish Goat	336	IRL	min. end.
22 Blanche	308	B	pot. end.
23 Weiße Deutsche Edelziege	367	D	normal
24 Bila kratkosrsta	306	CS	normal

```
 1 - Acadie P22                                                    EN  900
 2   Acadie P22; Bretagne, Normandie
 3   Pen Ar Lan                                                    HB:miss
 4   Plelan le Grand 35380, B.P. 3, Maxent
 5 - Composite of Landrace, Duroc
 7   Numbers 1993: 8/70; HB: miss; stable; 100 %; Ne = 13
 8 - Height: miss / miss cm; Weight: 430/290 kg; Herd number: 1; AI: miss
 9   Colour: Combination grey, red, white
10   Pecularity: miss
11 - Main use: (1) meat,(2) miss,(3) miss
12   Spec. abilities: miss
13   Performance compared with STB Duroc 927:
14      higher: live weight at slaughter
15      equal: % lean, litter size, meat quality, daily gain
16      lower:  piglet mortality
17 - Management: stationary; housing: 12 m.;
18 - Conservation progr.: live animals: miss;Semen: miss;Embryos: miss
19   Status: critically endang.;Watch: ♂♂,HB♀♀,herds!
```

20 - Similar breeds (see group 8 on page 104)	EN	Country	Status
21 Jia-Xing	947	F	crit.end.
22 Mei-Shan	974	F	crit.end.
23 Schwerfurter Fleischrasse	998	D*	pot. end.
24 Leicoma	965	D*	normal

```
 1 - Corse                                                         EN  915
 2   Corsican; mountainous regions of Corsica
 3   I.N.R.A., Centre de Recherches de Jouy-en-Josas               HB:miss
 4   Jouy-en-Josas Cedex 78352
 5 - Autochthon local breed
 6   Incrossing since 1970 from Large White 960 France
 7   Numbers 1983: 150/2500; HB: miss; stable; 20 %; Ne = 566
 8 - Height: 68/63 cm; Weight: 150/150 kg; Herd number: miss; AI: miss
 9   Colour: Combination black, red, blond
10   Pecularity: miss
11 - Main use: (1) meat,(2) miss,(3) miss
12   Spec. abilities: adapted to local basic feed
13   Performance compared with STB Large White 960:
14      higher: meat quality, live weight at slaughter
15      equal:  age of sexual maturity
16      lower:  % lean,feed conversion rate,daily gain,farrowing interval
17 - Management: stationary; housing: ≈ 2 m.; extensive conditions
18 - Conservation progr.: live animals: miss;Semen: miss;Embryos: miss
19   Status: endangered;        Watch: HB♀♀,%pure,%incross!
```

20 - Similar breeds (see group 7 on page 104)	EN	Country	Status
21 Lesogornaya porodnaya gruppa	966	ARM	crit.end.
22 Kakhetinskaya	948	GO	min. end.

```
 1 - Duroc                                                      EN  927
 2   Duroc; some special farms
 3   Upra Porcine                                               HB:miss
 4   Paris 75017, Boulevard Péreire Sud 95
 5 - Imported as breed from countries USA, Hungary
 7   Numbers 1993: 6/100; HB: miss; stable; 100 %; Ne = 10
 8 - Height: miss / miss cm; Weight: 350/300 kg; Herd number: 1; AI: miss
 9   Colour: Uni red
10   Pecularity: miss
11 - Main use: (1) meat,(2) crossbreeding,(3) miss
12   Spec. abilities: rusticity
13   Performance compared with STB Large White 960:
14     higher: meat quality, % lean, piglet mortality, muscularity
15     equal:  age of sexual maturity, farrowing interval, handling ease
16     lower:  litter size, feed conversion rate, daily gain
17 - Management: stationary; housing: 12 m.;
18 - Conservation progr.: live animals: Yes;Semen: miss;Embryos: miss
19   Status: critically endang.;Watch: ♂♂,HB♀♀,herds!
```

20 - Similar breeds (see group 5/1 on page 103)	EN	Country	Status
21 Duroc	932	GB	crit.end.
22 Duroc	928	D*	pot. end.
23 Duroc	929	I	normal
24 Duroc	926	CS	normal

```
 1 - Gascon                                                     EN  935
 2   Gascony; Pyrenees
 3   Institut Technique du Porc                                 HB:miss
 4   Paris 75595 Cedex 12, rue de Bercy 149
 5 - Autochthon breed Gasconne
 7   Numbers 1983: 15/80; HB: miss; increasing; 25 %; Ne = 28
 8 - Height: 75/75 cm; Weight: 200/180 kg; Herd number: miss; AI: Yes
 9   Colour: Uni black
10   Pecularity: miss
11 - Main use: (1) meat,(2) sport/hobby,(3) miss
12   Spec. abilities: miss
13   Performance compared with STB Large White 960:
14     higher: feed conversion rate, piglet mortality
15     equal:  meat quality, muscularity
16     lower:  % lean, litter size, daily gain
17 - Management: stationary; housing: 12 m.;
18 - Conservation progr.: live animals: Yes;Semen: 12;Embryos: miss
19   Status: critically endang.;Watch: ♂♂,HB♀♀,%pure!
```

20 - Similar breeds (see group 4/1 on page 103)	EN	Country	Status
21 Large Black	959	GB	min. end.
22 Alentejana	902	P	normal
23 Negra Iberica	981	E	normal

1 - Hampshire (extinct)   EN   941
2   Hampshire; some special farms
3   Upra Porcine   HB:miss
4   Paris 75017, Boulevard Péreire Sud 95
5 - Imported as breed from countries 945 United Kingdom, USA
6   Incrossing since 1970 from Hampshire USA
7   Numbers 1983: miss /270; HB: miss; decreasing; 100 %; Ne = 27
8 - Height: miss/miss cm; Weight: 310/270 kg; Herd number: miss; AI:miss
9   Colour: Combination white, black
10   Pecularity: white belt, erect ears
11 - Main use: (1) meat,(2) crossbreeding,(3) miss
12   Spec. abilities: miss
13   Performance compared with STB Large White 960:
14   higher: % lean, muscularity
15   equal: age of sexual maturity, farrowing interval, handling ease
16   lower: litter size, meat quality, daily gain
17 - Management: miss; housing: miss m.;
18 - Conservation progr.: live animals: miss;Semen: miss;Embryos: miss
19   Status: extinct/endangered;Watch: ♂♂,HB♀♀,trend!

20 - Similar breeds (see group 3/2 on page 102)	EN	Country	Status
21 Limousin	967	F	crit.end.
22 Hampshire	942	D*	crit.end.
23 Hampshire	944	RO	pot. end.
24 Hampshire	940	CS	normal

1 - Jia-Xing   EN   947
2   Black Jiaxing; Charente (INRA)
3   I.N.R.A., Centre de Recherches de Jouy-en-Josas   HB:miss
4   Jouy-en-Josas Cedex 78352
5 - Imported as breed from country China
7   Numbers 1993: 5/12; HB: miss; stable; 100 %; Ne = 6
8 - Height: miss / miss cm; Weight: 170/200 kg; Herd number: 1; AI: miss
9   Colour: Uni black
10   Pecularity: miss
11 - Main use: (1) experimental use,(2) miss,(3) miss
12   Spec. abilities: early maturity, fertility, 20 teats per sow
13   Performance compared with STB Large White 960:
14   higher: age of sexual maturity, litter size, piglet mortality
15   equal: meat quality, farrowing interval, handling ease
16   lower: % lean, daily gain, muscularity, feed conversion rate
17 - Management: miss; housing: miss m.;
18 - Conservation progr.: live animals: miss;Semen: miss;Embryos: miss
19   Status: critically endang.;Watch: ♂♂,HB♀♀,herds!

20 - Similar breeds (see group 8 on page 104)	EN	Country	Status
21 Acadie P22	900	F	crit.end.
22 Mei-Shan	974	F	crit.end.
23 Schwerfurter Fleischrasse	998	D*	pot. end.
24 Leicoma	965	D*	normal

```
1 - Landrace                                                  EN  953
2   French Landrace; all regions with pig production
3   Upra Porcine                                             HB:1952
4   Paris 75017, Boulevard Péreire Sud 95
5 - Imported as breed from countries Denmark, Sweden; incrossing since
6   1970 from Landrace 980 Netherlands, 911 United Kingdom, 920 Germany
7   Numbers 1983: 600/5085; HB: miss; stable; 76 %; Ne = 2147
8 - Height: 95/90 cm; Weight: 350/300 kg; Herd number: miss; AI: Yes
9   Colour: Uni white
10  Pecularity: lop ears
11 - Main use: (1) meat,(2) crossbreeding,(3) miss
12  Spec. abilities: meat quality
13  Performance compared with STB Large White 960:
14    higher: miss
15    equal: % lean, litter size, feed conversion rate, meat quality
16    lower: miss
17 - Management: stationary; housing: 12 m.;
18 - Conservation progr.: live animals: miss;Semen: miss;Embryos: miss
19  Status: potential. endang.;Watch: HB♀♀!
```

20 - Similar breeds (see group 2/1 on page 101)	EN	Country	Status
21 Belgische Landrasse	907	D*	crit.end.
22 Zlotnicka biala	1024	PL	crit.end.
23 Landrace	952	CS	normal
24 Belgisch Landvarken	906	B	normal

```
1 - Landrace Belge                                            EN  957
2   Belgian Landrace; mainly northern France
3   Upra Porcine                                             HB:1972
4   Paris 75017, Boulevard Péreire Sud 95
5 - Imported as breed from country Belgium
6   Incrossing since 1970 from Belgian Landrace 906 Belgium
7   Numbers 1983: 180/1415; HB: miss; stable; 99 %; Ne = 639
8 - Height: 90/85 cm; Weight: 330/280 kg; Herd number: miss; AI: Yes
9   Colour: Uni white
10  Pecularity: lop ears
11 - Main use: (1) meat,(2) crossbreeding,(3) miss
12  Spec. abilities: halothane positive
13  Performance compared with STB Large White 960:
14    higher: % lean, muscularity
15    equal: feed conversion rate,age of sex. matur.,farrowing interval
16    lower: litter size, meat quality, daily gain, handling ease
17 - Management: stationary; housing: 12 m.;
18 - Conservation progr.: live animals: miss;Semen: miss;Embryos: miss
19  Status: normal;              Watch: HB♀♀!
```

20 - Similar breeds (see group 2/1 on page 101)	EN	Country	Status
21 Belgische Landrasse	907	D*	crit.end.
22 Zlotnicka biala	1024	PL	crit.end.
23 Landrace	952	CS	normal
24 Belgisch Landvarken	906	B	normal

1 - **Large White**   EN **960**
2   **Large White; all regions with pig production**
3   **Upra Porcine**   HB:**1926**
4   **Paris 75017, Boulevard Péreire Sud 95**
5 - Imported as breed from countries United Kingdom; incrossing since
6   1970 from Large White 1023 United Kingdom, 938 Netherlands
7   Numbers 1983: 1250/11438; HB: **miss**; stable; 80 %; Ne = **4507**
8 - Height: **105/100** cm; Weight: **380/320** kg; Herd number: **miss**; AI: **Yes**
9   Colour: **Uni white**
10 Pecularity: **erect ears**
11 - Main use: (1) **meat**,(2) **crossbreeding**,(3) **miss**
12 Spec. abilities: **meat quality**
13 Performance compared with STB **Belgian Landrace 957**:
14   higher: **meat quality**
15   equal: **% lean, litter size, feed conversion rate**
16   lower: **piglet mortality**
17 - Management: **stationary**; housing: **12 m.**;
18 - Conservation progr.: live animals: **miss**;Semen: **miss**;Embryos: **miss**
19 Status: **normal**;   Watch: **HB♀♀,%pure!**
20 - <u>Similar breeds</u> (see group 1/1 on page 101)   <u>EN</u> <u>Country</u> <u>Status</u>
21 **Norsk Yorkshire**   984 **N**   endanger.
22 **Grand Yorkshire Belge**   937 **B**   normal
23 **Large White Pigs**   963 **IRL** normal
24 **Yorkshire**   1021 **SF**   normal

1 - **Limousin**   EN **967**
2   **Limousin; Limousin**
3   **Institut Technique du Porc**   HB:**1935**
4   **Paris 75595 Cedex 12, rue de Bercy 149**
5 - Autochthon, also named Porc de Saint Yriex
7   Numbers 1983: 8/70; HB: **miss**; stable; 70 %; Ne = **13**
8 - Height: **75/75** cm; Weight: **180/150** kg; Herd number: **miss**; AI: **Yes**
9   Colour: **Combination black, white**
10 Pecularity: **white saddle, black head, erect ears**
11 - Main use: (1) **meat**,(2) **sport/hobby**,(3) **miss**
12 Spec. abilities: **miss**
13 Performance compared with STB **Large White 960**:
14   higher: **live weight at slaughter,feed conversion rate,meat quality**
15   equal: **miss**
16   lower: **% lean, daily gain, litter size, muscularity**
17 - Management: **stationary**; housing: **> 6 m.**; **extensive conditions**
18 - Conservation progr.: live animals: **Yes**;Semen: **12**;Embryos: **miss**
19 Status: **critically endang.**;Watch: **♂♂,HB♀♀,%pure!**
20 - <u>Similar breeds</u> (see group 3/2 on page 102)   <u>EN</u> <u>Country</u> <u>Status</u>
21 **Hampshire**   942 **D***   crit.end.
22 **Hampshire**   943 **I**   crit.end.
23 **Hampshire**   944 **RO**   pot. end.
24 **Hampshire**   940 **CS**   normal

```
 1 - Mei-Shan, Chinois                                      EN  974
 2   Meishan; Charent (INRA)
 3   INRA, Dépt. de Génétique Animale-CNRZ                  HB:miss
 4   Jouy-en-Josas 78350, Domaine de Villvert
 5 - Imported as breed from country China
 6   Incrossing since 1970 from Mei-Shan China
 7   Numbers 1991: 20/80; HB: miss; decreasing; 100 %; Ne = 41
 8 - Height: miss/miss cm; Weight: 200/240 kg; Herd number: miss; AI:miss
 9   Colour: Combination black, white; spotted
10   Pecularity: miss
11 - Main use: (1) experimental use,(2) miss,(3) miss
12   Spec. abilities: early maturity, fertility, meat quality
13   Performance compared with STB Large White 960:
14      higher: litter size, age of sexual maturity, piglet mortality
15      equal:  meat quality, farrowing interval, handling ease
16      lower:  % lean, daily gain, muscularity, feed conversion rate
17 - Management: miss; housing: miss m.;
18 - Conservation progr.: live animals: miss;Semen: miss;Embryos: miss
19   Status: critically endang.;Watch: HB♀♀,trend!
```

20 - Similar breeds (see group 8 on page 104)	EN	Country	Status
21 Acadie P22	900	F	crit.end.
22 Jia-Xing	947	F	crit.end.
23 Schwerfurter Fleischrasse	998	D*	pot. end.
24 Leicoma	965	D*	normal

```
 1 - Normand                                               EN  982
 2   Normand; Normandie
 3   Institut Technique du Porc                            HB:1937
 4   Paris 75595 Cedex 12, rue de Bercy 149
 5 - Autochthon Craonnaise
 7   Numbers 1983: 15/200; HB: miss; decreasing; 40 %; Ne = 33
 8 - Height: 100/100 cm; Weight: 350/300 kg; Herd number: miss; AI: Yes
 9   Colour: Uni white
10   Pecularity: miss
11 - Main use: (1) meat,(2) miss,(3) miss
12   Spec. abilities: miss
13   Performance compared with STB Large White 960:
14      higher: feed conversion rate, meat quality, piglet mortality
15      equal:  muscularity
16      lower:  % lean, litter size, daily gain
17 - Management: stationary; housing: 12 m.;
18 - Conservation progr.: live animals: Yes;Semen: 12;Embryos: miss
19   Status: critically endang.;Watch: ♂♂,HB♀♀,trend,%pure!
```

20 - Similar breeds (see group 2/2 on page 102)	EN	Country	Status
21 Chester White	913	GB	crit.end.
22 Mangalica	972	H	min. end.
23 Mangalita	973	RO	min. end.
24 Schwalbenbauch Mangalitza	1020	CH	pot. end.

```
 1 - Pen Ar Lan P 77                                          EN  985
 2   Pen Ar Lan P 77; around Ille river and Vilaine river (Bretagne)
 3   Pen Ar Lan                                               HB:miss
 4   Plelan le Grand 35380, B. P. 3, Maxent
 5 - Composite of Large White 960, Hampshire 941, Pietrain 989
 7   Numbers 1993: 18/250; HB: miss; increasing; 100 %; Ne = 44
 8 - Height: miss / miss cm; Weight: 430/290 kg; Herd number: 1; AI: miss
 9   Colour: Combination black, brown, white
10   Pecularity: miss
11 - Main use: (1) meat,(2) miss,(3) miss
12   Spec. abilities: stress-resistant
13   Performance compared with STB Large White 960:
14      higher: % lean, muscularity
15      equal:  litter size, feed conversion rate, daily gain
16      lower:  meat quality
17 - Management: stationary; housing: 12 m.;
18 - Conservation progr.: live animals: miss;Semen: miss;Embryos: miss
19   Status: endangered;        Watch: ♂♂,HB♀♀,herds!
```

20 - <u>Similar breeds</u> (see group 8 on page 104)

		EN	Country	Status
21	Acadie P22	900	F	crit.end.
22	Jia-Xing	947	F	crit.end.
23	Schwerfurter Fleischrasse	998	D*	pot. end.
24	Leicoma	965	D*	normal

```
 1 - Penshire P66                                             EN  986
 2   Penshire P66; around Ille river and Vilaine river (Bretagne)
 3   Pen Ar Lan                                               HB: Yes
 4   Plelan le Grand 35380, B. P. 3, Maxent
 5 - Composite of Hampshire 941 ,Large White 960, Duroc 927
 7   Numbers 1993: 15/150; HB: miss; stable; 100 %; Ne = 32
 8 - Height: miss / miss cm; Weight: 430/290 kg; Herd number: 1; AI: miss
 9   Colour: Combination black, brown, white
10   Pecularity: belt, spots
11 - Main use: (1) meat,(2) miss,(3) miss
12   Spec. abilities: stress-resistant
13   Performance compared with STB Large White 960:
14      higher: % lean, muscularity
15      equal:  feed conversion rate, daily gain, age of sexual maturity
16      lower:  litter size, meat quality
17 - Management: stationary; housing: 12 m.;
18 - Conservation progr.: live animals: miss;Semen: miss;Embryos: miss
19   Status: critically endang.;Watch: ♂♂,HB♀♀,herds!
```

20 - <u>Similar breeds</u> (see group 8 on page 104)

		EN	Country	Status
21	Acadie P22	900	F	crit.end.
22	Jia-Xing	947	F	crit.end.
23	Schwerfurter Fleischrasse	998	D*	pot. end.
24	Leicoma	965	D*	normal

```
 1 - Pie noir du Pays Basque                                       EN   987
 2   Basque Black Pied; Euskadi (Basque Provinces): Pyrenees
 3   Institut Technique du Porc                                    HB:miss
 4   Paris 75595 Cedex 12, rue de Bercy 149
 5 - Autochthon var. Bearnaise, var. Basque
 7   Numbers 1983: 8/70; HB: miss; stable; 40 %; Ne = 13
 8 - Height: 75/75 cm; Weight: 180/150 kg; Herd number: miss; AI: Yes
 9   Colour: Combination black, white
10   Pecularity: white saddle, black head, lop ears
11 - Main use: (1) meat,(2) sport/hobby,(3) miss
12   Spec. abilities: miss
13   Performance compared with STB Large White 960:
14     higher: feed conversion rate, meat quality, piglet mortality
15     equal:  muscularity
16     lower: % lean, litter size, daily gain
17 - Management: stationary; housing: no
18 - Conservation progr.: live animals:  Yes;Semen: 12;Embryos: miss
19   Status: critically endang.;Watch: ♂♂,HB♀♀,%pure!
20 - Similar breeds (see group 3/1 on page 102)    EN  Country Status
21   Angler Sattelschwein                          903   D    crit.end.
22   Cinta Senese                                  914   I    crit.end.
23   British Saddleback                            912   GB   pot. end.
24   Schwäbisch-Hällisches Schwein                 997   D    pot. end.
```

```
 1 - Pietrain                                                      EN   989
 2   Pietrain; mainly northern France
 3   Upra Porcine                                                  HB:1958
 4   Paris 75017, Boulevard Pereire Sud 95
 5 - Imported as breed from country Belgium
 6   Incrossing since 1970 from Pietrain 988 Belgium, 991 Germany
 7   Numbers 1983: 90/665; HB: miss; increasing; 100 %; Ne = 317
 8 - Height: 85/80 cm; Weight: 280/250 kg; Herd number: miss; AI: Yes
 9   Colour: Combination black, white
10   Pecularity: black spots, short erect ears
11 - Main use: (1) meat,(2) crossbreeding,(3) miss
12   Spec. abilities: halothane-positive,meat quantity,poor meat quality
13   Performance compared with STB Large White 960:
14     higher: % lean, muscularity
15     equal:  feed conversion rate, farrowing interval
16     lower:  daily gain, litter size, meat quality, age of sex. matur.
17 - Management: stationary; housing: 12 m.;
18 - Conservation progr.: live animals: miss;Semen: miss;Embryos: miss
19   Status: normal;              Watch: HB♀♀!
20 - Similar breeds (see group 6/1 on page 103)    EN  Country Status
21   Pietrain                                      988   B    normal
22   Pietrain                                      991   D    normal
23   Pietrain                                      990   I    miss
```

PIGS

```
 1 - Tia Meslan P44                                            EN 1011
 2    Tia Meslan P44; around Ille river and Vilaine river (Bretagne)
 3    I.N.R.A., Centre de Recherches de Jouy-en-Josas           HB:miss
 4    Jouy-en-Josas Cedex 78352
 5 - Composite of Pen Ar Lan P77 985, Meishan 974, Jia Xing 947
 7    Numbers 1993: 5/70; HB: miss; stable; 100 %; Ne = 8
 8 - Height: miss/miss cm; Weight: miss/miss kg; Herd number: 1; AI: miss
 9    Colour: Uni white
10    Pecularity: miss
11 - Main use: (1) experimental,(2) miss,(3) miss
12    Spec. abilities: miss
13    Performance compared with STB Large White 960:
14      higher: age of sexual maturity, litter size, meat quality
15      equal:  feed conversion rate, farrowing interval, handling ease
16      lower:  daily gain, % lean, muscularity, live weight at slaughter
17 - Management: stationary; housing: 12 m.;
18 - Conservation progr.: live animals: miss;Semen: miss;Embryos: miss
19    Status: critically endang.;Watch: ♂♂,HB♀♀,herds!
```

```
20 - Similar breeds (see group 8 on page 104)      EN   Country  Status
21    Acadie P22                                   900   F       crit.end.
22    Jia-Xing                                     947   F       crit.end.
23    Schwerfurter Fleischrasse                    998   D*      pot. end.
24    Leicoma                                      965   D*      normal
```

HORSES

```
 1 - Anglo-Arab                                               EN  702
 2    Anglo-Arab; Limousin, southern Pyrenees, Aquitaine, Languedoc, Prov.
 3    Stud-Book des races francaises de cheveaux de selle,     HB:1941
 4    Section: Arabe et Anglo-Arabe, Institut du cheval, Pompadour 19230
 5 - Composite of Arab, Thoroughbred
 6    Incrossing since 1950 from Thoroughbred, Arab Europe
 7    Numbers 1991: 258/3390; HB: miss; increasing; 79 %; Ne = 959
 8 - Height: 168/160 cm; Weight: 550/500 kg; Herd number: 2984; AI: Yes
 9    Colour: bay, chestnut, grey
10    Pecularity: miss
11 - Main use: (1) sport/hobby,(2) courses,(3) miss
12    Spec. abilities: miss
13    Performance compared with STB Halfbred:
14      higher: speed in gallop
15      equal:  speed in trotters
16      lower:  adaptability in dressage, adaptability in jumping
17 - Management: stationary; housing: miss m.;
18 - Conservation progr.: live animals: miss;Semen: 15;Embryos: miss
19    Status: normal
```

```
20 - Similar breeds (see group 1 on page 108)      EN   Country  Status
21    Arabialainen                                 706   SF      crit.end.
22    Täysverinen                                  811   SF      crit.end.
23    Arab                                         703   F       normal
24    Vollblutaraber                               815   A       normal
```

HORSES

1 - **Arab**   EN **703**
2   **Arab; southern France**
3   **Association francaise des eleveurs de chevaux Arabes**   HB:**1833**
4   **- ACA -, Paris 75008, rue de Penthieure 22**
5 - **Imported as breed from Middle-Orient, incrossing since 1950 from**
6   **Arab Tunisia, Maroc, Spain, USSR**
7   Numbers 1990: **324/1108**; HB: **1108**; **increasing**; **98 %**; Ne = **1003**
8 - Height: **154/152** cm; Weight: **450/450** kg; Herd number: **miss**; AI: **Yes**
9   Colour: **grey, chestnut, bay**
10 Pecularity: **long fine mane and tail**
11 - Main use: (1) **sport/hobby**,(2) **courses**,(3) **miss**
12 Spec. abilities: **miss**
13 Performance compared with STB **Halfbred**:
14   higher: **miss**
15   equal: **handling ease,adapt. in dress.,fertility,age of sex. mat.**
16   lower: **adaptability in jumping**
17 - Management: **stationary**; housing: **miss** m.;
18 - Conservation progr.: live animals: **miss**;Semen: **1**;Embryos: **miss**
19 Status: **normal**;   Watch: **%incross!**
20 - Similar breeds (see group 1 on page 108)   EN Country Status
21 **Arabialainen**   706   SF   **crit.end.**
22 **Täysverinen**   811   SF   **crit.end.**
23 **Anglo-Arab**   702   F   **normal**
24 **Vollblutaraber**   815   A   **normal**

FRANCE   HORSES

1 - **Ardennais**   EN **707**
2   **Ardennes; Lorraine, Alsace, northern Picardi**
3   **Syndicat d'elevage du cheval Ardennais**   HB:**1929**
4   **Bouxieres aux Dames 54132, Hameau des Noisetiers 23**
5 - **Autochthon Ardennais**
6   **Incrossing since 1950 from Trait Belge 731 Belgium**
7   Numbers 1990: **228/2850**; HB: **1458**; **decreasing**; **48 %**; Ne = **789**
8 - Height: **160/158** cm; Weight: **700/700** kg; Herd number: **miss**; AI: **miss**
9   Colour: **usually bay or roan, sometimes grey,chestnut,dun or isabelle**
10 Pecularity: **miss**
11 - Main use: (1) **meat**,(2) **tractive power**,(3) **vegetation management**
12 Spec. abilities: **miss**
13 Performance compared with STB **Breton 714**:
14   higher: **miss**
15   equal: **daily gain, sexual maturity**
16   lower: **fertility**
17 - Management: **stationary**; housing: **miss** m.;
18 - Conservation progr.: live animals: **miss**;Semen: **miss**;Embryos: **miss**
19 Status: **potential. endang.**;Watch: **trend,%pure,%incross!**
20 - Similar breeds (see group 4/1 on page 109)   EN Country Status
21 **Auxois**   709   F   **crit.end.**
22 **Cheval de Trait Ardennais**   730   L   **min. end.**
23 **Cheval de Trait Belge**   731   B   **normal**
24 **Cheval de Trait Ardennais**   729   B   **normal**

```
 1 - Ardennais du nord, Trait du nord                            EN  708
 2   Northern Ardennes; northern Picardie
 3   Syndicat central d'elevage du cheval Ardennais du Nord      HB:1913
 4   Cambrai 59407, Hotel de Ville
 5 - Autochthon Trait du Nord
 6   Incrossing since 1950 from Trait Belge 731 Belgium
 7   Numbers 1990: 40/662; HB: 339; decreasing; 47 %; Ne = 143
 8 - Height: 165/160 cm; Weight: 1000/775 kg; Herd number: miss; AI: Yes
 9   Colour: bay, roan, dun, more rarely chestnut
10   Pecularity: miss
11 - Main use: (1) meat,(2) tractive power,(3) miss
12   Spec. abilities: miss
13   Performance compared with STB Percheron 790:
14     higher: miss
15     equal:  pulling power,handling ease,fertility,age of sex. maturity
16     lower:  miss
17 - Management: stationary; housing: miss m.;
18 - Conservation progr.: live animals: miss;Semen: miss;Embryos: miss
19   Status: potential. endang.;Watch: trend,%pure!
20 - Similar breeds (see group 4/1 on page 109)   EN  Country Status
21   Auxois                                        709   F     crit.end.
22   Cheval de Trait Ardennais                     730   L     min. end.
23   Cheval de Trait Belge                         731   B     normal
24   Cheval de Trait Ardennais                     729   B     normal
```

```
 1 - Auxois                                                      EN  709
 2   Auxois; Bourgogne
 3   Syndicat du cheval de Trait Ardennais de l'Auxois,          HB:1913
 4   Direction des Services Vétérinaires, Dijon 21000, rue Hoche 2
 5 - Autochthon Auxois
 7   Numbers 1991: 16/82; HB: miss; decreasing; 100 %; Ne = 31
 8 - Height: 164/164 cm; Weight: 900/900 kg; Herd number: 20; AI: miss
 9   Colour: usually bay or roan, sometimes dun or chestnut
10   Pecularity: miss
11 - Main use: (1) meat,(2) tractive power,(3) miss
12   Spec. abilities: miss
13   Performance compared with STB Percheron 790:
14     higher: miss
15     equal:  pulling power
16     lower:  miss
17 - Management: stationary; housing: miss m.;
18 - Conservation progr.: live animals: miss;Semen: miss;Embryos: miss
19   Status: critically endang.;Watch: ♂♂,HB♀♀,trend!
20 - Similar breeds (see group 4/1 on page 109)   EN  Country Status
21   Cheval de Trait Ardennais                     730   L     min. end.
22   Hrvatski Hladnokrvnjak                        761   HR    min. end.
23   Cheval de Trait Belge                         731   B     normal
24   Cheval de Trait Ardennais                     729   B     normal
```

1 - **Barbe**   EN 711
2   **Barb; country-wide**
3   **Association Francaise du Cheval Barbe**   HB:1988
4   **Le Mans 72000, rue du Cirque 18**
5 - **Imported as breed from countries Algeria, Tunisia, Morocco**
6   **Incrossing since 1950 from Barbe Algeria, Tunisia, Morocco**
7   **Numbers 1991: 22/198; HB: miss; increasing; 100 %; Ne = 59**
8 - Height: **155/miss** cm; Weight: **miss/miss** kg; Herd number: **86**; AI: **miss**
9   Colour: **grey, chestnut or bay**
10 Pecularity: **profuse mane and flowing low-set tail**
11 - Main use: (1) **sport/hobby**,(2) **miss**,(3) **miss**
12 Spec. abilities: **miss**
13 Performance compared with STB **Anglo-Arab 702**:
14   higher: **adaptability in jumping**
15   equal: **miss**
16   lower: **adaptability in dressage**
17 - Management: **stationary**; housing: **miss** m.;
18 - Conservation progr.: live animals: **miss**;Semen: **miss**;Embryos: **miss**
19 Status: **minimally endang.**; Watch: **HB♀♀!**
20 - <u>Similar breeds</u> (see group 1 on page 108)   <u>EN</u> <u>Country</u> <u>Status</u>
21 **Arabialainen**   706 SF   crit.end.
22 **Täysverinen**   811 SF   crit.end.
23 **Anglo-Arab**   702 F   normal
24 **Vollblutaraber**   815 A   normal

1 - **Boulonnais**   EN 713
2   **Boulonnais; northern Picardie**
3   **Syndicat hippique Boulonnais**   HB:1886
4   **Wimereux 62930, Rue Sainte Adrienne**
5 - **Autochthon Boulonnais**
7   **Numbers 1990: 37/655; HB: 472; decreasing; 70 %; Ne = 137**
8 - Height: **163/163** cm; Weight: **900/900** kg; Herd number: **miss**; AI: **miss**
9   Colour: **usually light dapple-grey, sometimes chestnut**
10 Pecularity: **small Arabic-type head**
11 - Main use: (1) **meat**,(2) **tractive power**,(3) **miss**
12 Spec. abilities: **miss**
13 Performance compared with STB **Breton 714**:
14   higher: **fertility**
15   equal: **daily gain**
16   lower: **age of sexual maturity**
17 - Management: **stationary**; housing: **miss** m.;
18 - Conservation progr.: live animals: **miss**;Semen: **miss**;Embryos: **miss**
19 Status: **potential. endang.**;Watch: **trend,%pure!**
20 - <u>Similar breeds</u> (see group 4/2 on page 109)   <u>EN</u> <u>Country</u> <u>Status</u>
21 **Poitevin**   791 F   endanger.
22 **Breton**   714 F   pot. end.
23 **Cavallo Agricolo Italiano**   716 I   pot. end.
24 **Percheron**   790 F   pot. end.

```
 1 - Breton                                                          EN  714
 2   Breton; Bretagne, Pays de Loire
 3   Syndicat des eleveurs du cheval Breton                         HB:1909
 4   Landerneau 29220, B. P. 24-22, rue de la Libération
 5 - Composite of Trait Breton, Petit Trait Breton, Postier Breton
 7   Numbers 1990: 530/11524; HB: 2920; decreasing; 24 %; Ne = 1794
 8 - Height: 158/158 cm; Weight: 850/850 kg; Herd number: miss; AI: miss
 9   Colour: chestnut or dun, rarely bay or roan
10   Pecularity: miss
11 - Main use: (1) meat,(2) tractive power,(3) vegetation management
12   Spec. abilities: stability
13   Performance compared with STB Percheron 790:
14      higher: miss
15      equal:  miss
16      lower:  pulling power
17 - Management: stationary; housing: miss m.;
18 - Conservation progr.: live animals: miss;Semen: miss;Embryos: miss
19   Status: potential. endang.;Watch: trend,%pure!
```

20 - Similar breeds (see group 4/2 on page 109)	EN	Country	Status
21 Poitevin	791	F	endanger.
22 Boulonnais	713	F	pot. end.
23 Cavallo Agricolo Italiano	716	I	pot. end.
24 Percheron	790	F	pot. end.

```
 1 - Camargue                                                        EN  715
 2   Camargue; Camargue
 3   Association des eleveurs de chevaux Camargue                   HB:1978
 4   Arles 13200, Mas du Pont du Rousty
 5 - Autochthon Camargue
 7   Numbers 1990: 67/500; HB: 500; increasing; 96 %; Ne = 236
 8 - Height: 140/140 cm; Weight: 350/350 kg; Herd number: miss; AI: miss
 9   Colour: light grey
10   Pecularity: miss
11 - Main use: (1) herdsman horse,(2) sport/hobby,(3) vegetation managem.
12   Spec. abilities: stability
13   Performance compared with STB Halfbred:
14      higher: handling ease
15      equal:  miss
16      lower:  adaptability in dressage and in jumping, speed in gallop
17 - Management: feral; housing: miss m.;
18 - Conservation progr.: live animals: miss;Semen: miss;Embryos: miss
19   Status: normal
```

20 - Similar breeds (see group 3/5 on page 109)	EN	Country	Status
21 Cavallo Sanfratellano	723	I	endanger.
22 Cavallo Sardo	724	I	endanger.
23 Cavallo Maremmano	720	I	pot. end.
24 Cavallo Murgese	721	I	normal

```
 1 - Cheval de Selle Francais                              EN  727
 2   French Saddlebred; Normandie/northern Picardie/Bourgogne/Rhone/Alpes
 3   Federation Francaise des Syndicats d'Eleveurs de      HB:1963
 4   chevaux de Selle paris 75008, rue de Penthievre 22
 5 - Composite of old French halfbred
 7   Numbers 1990: 461/13974; HB: 13974; increasing; 67 %; Ne = 1785
 8 - Height: 170/165 cm; Weight: 575/525 kg; Herd number: miss; AI: miss
 9   Colour: chestnut, bay, grey
10   Pecularity: miss
11 - Main use: (1) sport/hobby,(2) courses,(3) miss
12   Spec. abilities: miss
13   Performance compared with STB Halfbred:
14     higher: handling ease, adaptability in jumping
15     equal:  pulling power, adaptability in dressage, speed in gallop
16     lower:  miss
17 - Management: stationary; housing: miss m.;
18 - Conservation progr.: live animals: miss;Semen: 120;Embryos: Yes
19   Status: normal;           Watch: %pure!
```

20 - Similar breeds (see group 3/2 on page 108)	EN	Country	Status
21 Altwürttemberger	701	D	crit.end.
22 Rottaler	797	D	crit.end.
23 Warmbloed Paard Nederlands	816	NL	normal
24 Holsteiner Warmblut	760	D	normal

```
 1 - Cob                                                   EN  734
 2   Cob; Normandie
 3   Syndicat d'elevage des chevaux de race Cob Normand,   HB:miss
 4   Maison de l'Agriculture, Saint Lo 50000, Avenue de Paris
 5 - Composite of Norman coach horse (Hackney, Thoroughbred, native)
 7   Numbers 1990: 59/1371; HB: 753; decreasing; 97 %; Ne = 219
 8 - Height: 164/164 cm; Weight: 600/600 kg; Herd number: miss; AI: miss
 9   Colour: bay, chestnut
10   Pecularity: miss
11 - Main use: (1) meat,(2) tractive power,(3) coach-horse, tourism
12   Spec. abilities: meat quality (fine fiber)
13   Performance compared with STB Percheron 790:
14     higher: miss
15     equal:  miss
16     lower:  pulling power
17 - Management: stationary; housing: miss m.;
18 - Conservation progr.: live animals: miss;Semen: miss;Embryos: miss
19   Status: normal;           Watch: trend!
```

20 - Similar breeds (see group 3/4 on page 109)	EN	Country	Status
21 Kisberi felver	769	H	pot. end.
22 Mezöhegyesi felver	782	H	pot. end.
23 Cleveland Bay Horse	732	GB	normal
24 Irish Sport Horse	765	IRL	normal

```
 1 - Comtois                                                    EN  735
 2   Comtois; Franche-Comté, southern France
 3   Syndicat d'elevage du cheval Comtois Haras National        HB:1919
 4   de Besancon, Besancon 25000, rue de Dole 52
 5 - Autochthon Comtois
 7   Numbers 1990: 397/8008; HB: 2024; decreasing; 25 %; Ne = 1328
 8 - Height: 155/155 cm; Weight: 700/700 kg; Herd number: miss; AI: Yes
 9   Colour: dark chestnut or copper-coloured, rarely bay
10   Pecularity: miss
11 - Main use: (1) meat,(2) tractive power,(3) coach-horse, tourism
12   Spec. abilities: stability
13   Performance compared with STB Percheron 790:
14      higher: miss
15      equal:  miss
16      lower:  pulling power
17 - Management: stationary; housing: miss m.;
18 - Conservation progr.: live animals: miss;Semen: miss;Embryos: miss
19   Status: potential. endang.;Watch: trend,%pure!
20 - Similar breeds (see group 4/1 on page 109)    EN  Country Status
21   Auxois                                          709  F       crit.end.
22   Cheval de Trait Ardennais                       730  L       min. end.
23   Cheval de Trait Belge                           731  B       normal
24   Cheval de Trait Ardennais                       729  B       normal
```

FRANCE   HORSES

```
 1 - Connemara                                                  EN  736
 2   Connemara Pony; country-wide
 3   Association francaise du Poney Connemara                    HB:1969
 4   Chateauneuf 18190, Le Preuil
 5 - Imported as breed from country 737 Ireland
 6   Incrossing since 1950 from Connemara 737 Ireland
 7   Numbers 1991: 142/596; HB: miss; increasing; 89 %; Ne = 459
 8 - Height: 142/142 cm; Weight: 450/400 kg; Herd number: miss; AI: miss
 9   Colour: mainly grey, sometimes black,bay,chestnut,roan or isabelle
10   Pecularity: miss
11 - Main use: (1) sport/hobby,(2) miss,(3) miss
12   Spec. abilities: miss
13   Performance compared with STB Fjord 745:
14      higher: adaptability in dressage and in jumping, speed in gallop
15      equal:  miss
16      lower:  pulling power
17 - Management: stationary; housing: miss m.;
18 - Conservation progr.: live animals: miss;Semen: Yes;Embryos: miss
19   Status: normal;            Watch: HB♀♀,%pure,%incross!
20 - Similar breeds (see group 5/6 on page 111)    EN  Country Status
21   Connemara Pony                                  819  SF      crit.end.
22   Connemara Pony                                  737  IRL     normal
```

1 - Dartmoor   EN   738
2   Dartmoor Pony; northern Picardie, Central France, Bretagne
3   Association francaise du Poney Dartmmor   HB:1969
4   Auray 56400, Kerourio Brech
5 - Imported as breed from country United Kingdom
6   Incrossing since 1950 from Dartmoor 739 United Kingdom
7   Numbers 1991: 24/113; HB: miss; stable; 92 %; Ne = 59
8 - Height: 117/117 cm; Weight: 300/280 kg; Herd number: > 10; AI: miss
9   Colour: usually bay, also all colours except piebald or scewbald
10 Pecularity: miss
11 - Main use: (1) sport/hobby,(2) miss,(3) miss
12 Spec. abilities: miss
13 Performance compared with STB Fjord 745:
14   higher: adaptability in jumping,speed in gallop,speed in trotters
15   equal: miss
16   lower: pulling power
17 - Management: stationary; housing: miss m.;
18 - Conservation progr.: live animals: miss;Semen: miss;Embryos: miss
19 Status: minimally endang.; Watch: HB♀♀,%pure!
20 - Similar breeds (see group 5/3 on page 110)   EN Country Status
21 Welsh Pony (A, B & D)   823   SF   crit.end.
22 New Forest Pony   821   SF   min. end.
23 New Forest   784   F   pot. end.
24 Dartmoor Pony   739   GB   normal

1 - Fjord de Norvege   EN   745
2   Fjord; Alsace
3   Association francaise du Poney Fjord   HB:1969
4   Lembach 67510, B. P. 9
5 - Imported as breed from countries Netherlands, Switzerland
6   Incrossing since 1950 from Fjord Netherlands and Switzerland
7   Numbers 1986: 70/590; HB: 590; stable; 83 %; Ne = 250
8 - Height: 140/140 cm; Weight: 580/520 kg; Herd number: miss; AI: miss
9   Colour: dun with dark legs
10 Pecularity: tail and erect mane: central black and outward silver
11 - Main use: (1) sport/hobby,(2) tractive power,(3) miss
12 Spec. abilities: miss
13 Performance compared with STB Fjord 745:
14   higher: Breed is used
15   equal: as standard breed,
16   lower: no comparison possible.
17 - Management: stationary; housing: miss m.;
18 - Conservation progr.: live animals: miss;Semen: miss;Embryos: miss
19 Status: normal;   Watch: %pure!
20 - Similar breeds (see group 5/1 on page 110)   EN Country Status
21 Gotland Russ   820   SF   crit.end.
22 Nordlandshest   786   N   min. end.
23 Fjordhest   746   N   pot. end.
24 Skogsruss   805   S   normal

```
 1 - Haflinger                                                EN  753
 2   Haflinger; Alsace, Rhones-Alps, Normandie
 3   Association francaise du Poney Haflinger                  HB:1970
 4   St Splice Lauriere 87370, Avenue de la gare
 5 - Imported as breed from Austria, 757 United Kingdom
 6   Incrossing since 1950 from Haflinger Austria, 757 United Kingdom
 7   Numbers 1990: 48/500; HB: 450; increasing; 90 %; Ne = 174
 8 - Height: 143/138 cm; Weight: 580/520 kg; Herd number: miss; AI: miss
 9   Colour: light to dark chestnut
10   Pecularity: full flaxen mane and tail
11 - Main use: (1) sport/hobby,(2) tractive power,(3) miss
12   Spec. abilities: miss
13   Performance compared with STB Fjord 745:
14     higher: miss
15     equal:  pulling power, adaptability in dressage and jumping
16     lower:  miss
17 - Management: stationary; housing: miss m.;
18 - Conservation progr.: live animals: miss;Semen: miss;Embryos: miss
19   Status: normal
```

20 - Similar breeds (see group 5/8 on page 111)	EN	Country	Status
21 Haflinger	757	GB	endanger.
22 Haflinger	756	CH	pot. end.
23 Avelignese	710	I	normal
24 Haflinger	754	D	normal

```
 1 - Highland                                                 EN  759
 2   Highland Pony; Bretagne, Normandie
 3   Association francaise du Poney Highland                   HB:1969
 4   Saint Omer 62500, rue de Dunkerque 157, fond de cour 3
 5 - Imported as breed from United Kingdom
 6   Incrossing since 1950 from Highland United Kingdom
 7   Numbers 1991: 12/64; HB: 64; stable; 88 %; Ne = 21
 8 - Height: 134/134 cm; Weight: 550/500 kg; Herd number: miss; AI: miss
 9   Colour: grey, sorrel, chestnut, isabelle
10   Pecularity: rarely dun with zebra-striped legs
11 - Main use: (1) sport/hobby,(2) miss,(3) miss
12   Spec. abilities: miss
13   Performance compared with STB Fjord 745:
14     higher: adaptability in dressage, adaptability in jumping
15     equal:  speed in gallop, speed in trotters
16     lower:  pulling power
17 - Management: stationary; housing: miss m.;
18 - Conservation progr.: live animals: miss;Semen: miss;Embryos: miss
19   Status: critically endang.;Watch: ♂♂,HB♀♀,%pure!
```

20 - Similar breeds (see group 5/4 on page 110)	EN	Country	Status
21 Fell Pony	744	GB	normal

```
 1 - Islandais                                          EN  766
 2   Iceland Pony; Alsace, Lorraine, Auvergne
 3   Association francaise du Poney Islandais            HB:1969
 4   Paris 75013, Avenue de Choisy 137
 5 - Imported as breed from country Netherlands
 6   Incrossing since 1950 from Islandais Germany,Switzerland,768 Iceland
 7   Numbers 1990: 16/222; HB: 222; increasing; 93 %; Ne = 36
 8 - Height: 134/134 cm; Weight: 420/380 kg; Herd number: miss; AI: miss
 9   Colour: all colours admissible
10   Pecularity: miss
11 - Main use: (1) sport/hobby,(2) miss,(3) miss
12   Spec. abilities: miss
13   Performance compared with STB Fjord 745:
14     higher: miss
15     equal:  miss
16     lower:  pulling power
17 - Management: stationary; housing: miss m.;
18 - Conservation progr.: live animals: miss;Semen: miss;Embryos: miss
19   Status: minimally endang.; Watch: ♂♂,%pure,%incross!
20 - Similar breeds (see group 5/2 on page 110)    EN  Country Status
21   Islannin hevonen                               767  SF    crit.end.
22   Islenski hesturinn                             768  IS    normal
```

```
 1 - Landais                                            EN  772
 2   Landais; Aquitaine
 3   Association francaise du Poney Landais              HB:1967
 4   St Paul les Dax 40180, Saubusse
 5 - Autochthon Landais
 7   Numbers 1991: 21/78; HB: miss; decreasing; 65 %; Ne = 43
 8 - Height: 128/128 cm; Weight: miss/miss kg; Herd number: miss; AI:miss
 9   Colour: bay, black, brown, chestnut
10   Pecularity: grey, piebald and scewbald are refused
11 - Main use: (1) sport/hobby,(2) miss,(3) miss
12   Spec. abilities: miss
13   Performance compared with STB Fjord 745:
14     higher: adaptability in jumping,speed in gallop,speed in trotters
15     equal:  adaptability in dressage
16     lower:  pulling power
17 - Management: stationary; housing: miss m.;
18 - Conservation progr.: live animals: miss;Semen: miss;Embryos: miss
19   Status: endangered;          Watch: HB♀♀,trend,%pure!
20 - Similar breeds (see group 5/7 on page 111)    EN  Country Status
21   Merens                                         781  F     normal
22   Poney Francais de Selle                        792  F     normal
```

```
 1 - Lipizzan                                              EN   776
 2   Lipitsa; country-wide
 3   Association francaise du Lipizzan                      HB:1989
 4   Luzarches 95270, Haras de Thimecourt
 5 - Imported as breed from country Austria
 6   Incrossing since 1950 from Lipitsa Austria
 7   Numbers 1991: 5/15; HB: miss; increasing; 100 %; Ne = 6
 8 - Height: 160/150 cm; Weight: 650/550 kg; Herd number: 15; AI: miss
 9   Colour: usually grey with a sleek coat
10   Pecularity: silky mane and tail
11 - Main use: (1) sport/hobby,(2) dressage,(3) miss
12   Spec. abilities: miss
13   Performance compared with STB Halfbred:
14      higher: adaptability in dressage
15      equal:  adaptability in jumping,speed in gallop,speed in trotters
16      lower:  miss
17 - Management: stationary; housing: miss m.;
18 - Conservation progr.: live animals: miss;Semen: miss;Embryos: miss
19   Status: critically endang.;Watch: ♂♂,HB♀♀!
```

20 - Similar breeds (see group 3/1 on page 108)	EN	Country	Status
21 Senner	801	D	crit.end.
22 Lipizzano	777	I	crit.end.
23 Espanol-Andaluz	742	E	normal
24 Lusitanien	779	F	normal

```
 1 - Lusitanien                                            EN   779
 2   Lusitanian; country-wide
 3   Association francaise du Cheval Lusitanien             HB:1987
 4   Antony 92160, 49 rue de Chatenay-sterel 5
 5 - Imported as breed from country 780 Portugal
 6   Incrossing since 1950 from Lusitanian 780 Portugal
 7   Numbers 1990: 48/210; HB: 210; increasing; 99 %; Ne = 156
 8 - Height: 175/155 cm; Weight: 650/550 kg; Herd number: miss; AI: miss
 9   Colour: grey, any solid colour also
10   Pecularity: miss
11 - Main use: (1) sport/hobby,(2) bull fighting,(3) miss
12   Spec. abilities: miss
13   Performance compared with STB Halfbred:
14      higher: adaptability in dressage
15      equal:  speed in gallop, speed in trotters
16      lower:  adaptability in jumping
17 - Management: stationary; housing: miss m.;
18 - Conservation progr.: live animals: miss;Semen: miss;Embryos: miss
19   Status: normal
```

20 - Similar breeds (see group 3/1 on page 108)	EN	Country	Status
21 Lipizzan	776	F	crit.end.
22 Senner	801	D	crit.end.
23 Lipicanac	775	HR	normal
24 Espanol-Andaluz	742	E	normal

246

```
1 - Merens                                                        EN   781
2   Merens Pony; Ariege, Alps
3   Syndicat hippique d'elevage de la race Merens, Chambre        HB:1945
4   d'Agriculture de l'Ariége, Foix 090000, av. du Général de Gaulle 32
5 - Autochthon Ariégeois
7   Numbers 1990: 60/617; HB: 617; stable; 97 %; Ne = 219
8 - Height: 142/142 cm; Weight: 600/550 kg; Herd number: miss; AI: miss
9   Colour: thick hairy black coats
10  Pecularity: no markings at all
11 - Main use: (1) sport/hobby,(2) tractive power,(3) vegetation manag.
12  Spec. abilities: stability
13  Performance compared with STB Fjord 745:
14     higher: miss
15     equal:  pulling power, adaptability in dressage and in jumping
16     lower:  miss
17 - Management: stationary; housing: miss m.; extensive system
18 - Conservation progr.: live animals: miss;Semen: miss;Embryos: miss
19  Status: normal
```

20 - Similar breeds (see group 5/7 on page 111)	EN	Country	Status
21 Landais	772	F	endanger.
22 Poney Francais de Selle	792	F	normal

```
1 - New Forest                                                    EN   784
2   New Forest Pony; Normandie, Pays de Loire
3   Association francaise du Poney New Forest                     HB: Yes
4   Chateauroux 36000, avenue de Verdun 365
5 - Imported as breed from country United Kingdom
6   Incrossing since 1950 from New Forest United Kingdom
7   Numbers 1990: 55/345; HB: 345; decreasing; 54 %; Ne = 190
8 - Height: 134/134 cm; Weight: 430/380 kg; Herd number: miss; AI: miss
9   Colour: usually bay or grey
10  Pecularity: piebald or scewbald are not accepted
11 - Main use: (1) sport/hobby,(2) miss,(3) miss
12  Spec. abilities: miss
13  Performance compared with STB Fjord 745:
14     higher: adaptability in jumping,speed in gallop,speed in trotters
15     equal:  adaptability in dressage
16     lower:  pulling power
17 - Management: stationary; housing: miss m.;
18 - Conservation progr.: live animals: miss;Semen: miss;Embryos: miss
19  Status: potential. endang.;Watch: trend,%pure!
```

20 - Similar breeds (see group 5/3 on page 110)	EN	Country	Status
21 Welsh Pony (A, B & D)	823	SF	crit.end.
22 New Forest Pony	821	SF	min. end.
23 Exmoor Pony	743	GB	pot. end.
24 Dartmoor Pony	739	GB	normal

1 - Percheron   EN   790
2   Percheron; Pays de Loire, Normandie
3   Societe hippique Percheronne   HB:1883
4   Nogent le Rotrou 28400, rue Doullay 1
5 - Autochthon Percheron
7   Numbers 1986: 175/3480; HB: 1641; decreasing; 44 %; Ne = 633
8 - Height: 165/165 cm; Weight: 950/900 kg; Herd number: miss; AI: miss
9   Colour: grey or black
10   Pecularity: bluish hoofs, small Arabic-type head
11 - Main use: (1) meat,(2) tractive power,(3) miss
12   Spec. abilities: tractive power
13   Performance compared with STB Breton 714:
14   higher: miss
15   equal: daily gain
16   lower: fertility, age of sexual maturity
17 - Management: stationary; housing: miss m.;
18 - Conservation progr.: live animals: miss;Semen: miss;Embryos: miss
19   Status: potential. endang.;Watch: trend,%pure!
20 - Similar breeds (see group 4/2 on page 109)   EN   Country   Status

21	Poitevin	791	F	endanger.
22	Boulonnais	713	F	pot. end.
23	Cavallo Agricolo Italiano	716	I	pot. end.
24	Breton	714	F	pot. end.

1 - Poitevin, Mulassier   EN   791
2   Poitou; Pays de Loire, Poitou-Charentes
3   Haras National   HB:1884
4   Saintes 17017, B.P. 174, Avenue Jourdan
5 - Composite of Poitou, Friesian
7   Numbers 1990: 22/224; HB: 224; decreasing; 40 %; Ne = 61
8 - Height: 168/168 cm; Weight: 900/800 kg; Herd number: miss; AI: Yes
9   Colour: mainly dun, any solid colour also
10   Pecularity: miss
11 - Main use: (1) meat,(2) tractive power,(3) production of mules
12   Spec. abilities: miss
13   Performance compared with STB Percheron 790:
14   higher: miss
15   equal: pulling power
16   lower: miss
17 - Management: stationary; housing: miss m.;
18 - Conservation progr.: live animals: miss;Semen: miss;Embryos: miss
19   Status: endangered;   Watch: trend,%pure!
20 - Similar breeds (see group 4/2 on page 109)   EN   Country   Status

21	Boulonnais	713	F	pot. end.
22	Breton	714	F	pot. end.
23	Cavallo Agricolo Italiano	716	I	pot. end.
24	Percheron	790	F	pot. end.

1 - **Poney Francais de Selle**   EN   **792**
2   French Saddlebred Pony; country-wide
3   Association francaise du Poney Francais de Selle   HB:1969
4   **Voutre 53600, Touchevallier**
5 - **Composite of local pony, Arab, Connemara, Welsh, New Forest pony**
7   Numbers 1990: **50/827**; HB: **482**; **increasing**; **25 %**; Ne = **181**
8 - Height: **136/136** cm; Weight: **420/400** kg; Herd number: **miss**; AI: **miss**
9   Colour: **all colours admissible**
10   Pecularity: **miss**
11 - Main use: (1) **sport/hobby**,(2) **miss**,(3) **miss**
12   Spec. abilities: **miss**
13   Performance compared with STB **Fjord 745**:
14   higher: **adaptability in dressage and in jumping, speed in gallop**
15   equal: **miss**
16   lower: **pulling power**
17 - Management: **stationary**; housing: **miss m.**;
18 - Conservation progr.: live animals: **miss**;Semen: **miss**;Embryos: **miss**
19   Status: **normal**;   Watch: **%pure!**
20 - <u>Similar breeds</u> (see group 5/7 on page 111)   <u>EN</u>   <u>Country</u> <u>Status</u>
21   **Landais**   772   F   **endanger.**
22   **Merens**   781   F   **normal**

1 - **Pottok**   EN   **794**
2   Pottok; Euskadi (Basque Provinces)
3   Association Nationale du Pottok   HB:1971
4   **Espelette 64250, Maison Armanenia**
5 - **Autochthon Pottok**
7   Numbers 1990: **27/205**; HB: **205**; **stable**; **74 %**; Ne = **89**
8 - Height: **134/130** cm; Weight: **350/300** kg; Herd number: **miss**; AI: **miss**
9   Colour: **bay, brown, chestnut, piebald, scewbald**
10   Pecularity: **miss**
11 - Main use: (1) **sport/hobby**,(2) **meat**,(3) **miss**
12   Spec. abilities: **resistant against piroplasmosis**
13   Performance compared with STB **Fjord 745**:
14   higher: **miss**
15   equal: **miss**
16   lower: **pulling power**
17 - Management: **stationary**; housing: **no; extensive conditions**
18 - Conservation progr.: live animals: **miss**;Semen: **miss**;Embryos: **miss**
19   Status: **potential. endang.**;Watch: **%pure!**
20 - <u>Similar breeds</u> (see group 5/10 on page 111)   <u>EN</u>   <u>Country</u> <u>Status</u>
21   **Sorraia**   807   P   **crit.end.**
22   **Skyos Pony**   806   GR   **endanger.**
23   **Cavallo della Giara**   719   I   **pot. end.**
24   **Cavallo Bardigiano**   718   I   **normal**

```
 1 - Pur-Sang                                                      EN  796
 2   Thoroughbred; Normandie
 3   Syndicat des eleveurs de chevaux de Sang de France           HB:1833
 4   Boulogne 92100, avenue le tour se leve 257
 5 - Imported as breed from country United kingdom; incrossing since 1950
 6   from Thoroughbred USA, United Kingdom, 812 Ireland
 7   Numbers 1990: 486/8454; HB: 8454; decreasing; 80 %; Ne = 1838
 8 - Height: 165/175 cm; Weight: 500/450 kg; Herd number: miss; AI: miss
 9   Colour: usually bay, sometimes chestnut or grey
10   Pecularity: miss
11 - Main use: (1) horse race,(2) sport/hobby,(3) miss
12   Spec. abilities: miss
13   Performance compared with STB Thoroughbred 796:
14     higher: Breed is used
15     equal:  as standard breed,
16     lower:  no comparison possible.
17 - Management: stationary; housing: miss m.;
18 - Conservation progr.: live animals: miss;Semen: miss;Embryos: miss
19   Status: normal;              Watch: trend,%pure,%incross!
20 - Similar breeds (see group 1 on page 108)   EN  Country Status
21   Arabialainen                               706   SF    crit.end.
22   Täysverinen                                811   SF    crit.end.
23   Anglo-Arab                                 702   F     normal
24   Vollblutaraber                             815   A     normal
```

```
 1 - Shetland                                                     EN  803
 2   Shetland Pony; country-wide
 3   Groupement des eleveurs du Poney Shetland                    HB:1966
 4   Paris 75014, rue de la Tombe Issoire 112
 5 - Imported as breed from country United Kingdom
 6   Incrossing since 1950 from Shetland Netherlands, Shetland Belgium
 7   Numbers 1986: 450/4000; HB: miss; miss; 100 %; Ne = 1618
 8 - Height: 107/107 cm; Weight: miss/miss kg; Herd number: miss; AI:miss
 9   Colour: all colours admissible
10   Pecularity: profuse mane and tail
11 - Main use: (1) sport/hobby,(2) miss,(3) miss
12   Spec. abilities: miss
13   Performance compared with STB Fjord 745:
14     higher: miss
15     equal:  miss
16     lower:  pulling power
17 - Management: stationary; housing: miss m.;
18 - Conservation progr.: live animals: miss;Semen: miss;Embryos: miss
19   Status: normal;              Watch: HB♀♀,%incross!
20 - Similar breeds (see group 5/5 on page 111)   EN  Country Status
21   Shetland Pony                                 822   SF    pot. end.
```

```
 1 - Trotteur Francais                                        EN  813
 2   French Trotter; Normandie, northern Picardie, Pays de Loir
 3   Groupement pour l'amelioration de l'elevage Trotteur (GAET)  HB:1922
 4   Paris 75008, rue de Penthievre 20
 5 - Composite of Anglo-Normand,Norman coach-horse,Thoroughbred,Hackney
 7   Numbers 1990: 788/20230; HB: 20230; increasing; 91 %; Ne = 3034
 8 - Height: 160/160 cm; Weight: 525/525 kg; Herd number: miss; AI: miss
 9   Colour: any solid colour
10   Pecularity: often with white markings
11 - Main use: (1) courses,(2) sport/hobby,(3) miss
12   Spec. abilities: miss
13   Performance compared with STB Thoroughbred 796:
14     higher: speed in trotters, pulling power
15     equal:  adaptability in jumping
16     lower:  adaptability in dressage, speed in gallop
17 - Management: stationary; housing: miss m.;
18 - Conservation progr.: live animals: miss;Semen: 1;Embryos: 1/1
19   Status: normal
```

20 - Similar breeds (see group 2 on page 108)	EN	Country	Status
21 Morgan Horse	783	GB	endanger.
22 Lämminverinen ravuri	773	SF	normal
23 Norsk Kaldblods Traver	789	N	normal

```
 1 - Welsh                                                    EN  817
 2   Welsh Pony; country-wide
 3   Association francaise du Poney Welsh                      HB:1969
 4   Montaigu Cedex 85601, B. P. 2
 5 - Imported as breed from country United Kingdom
 6   Incrossing since 1950 from Welsh United Kingdom,Belgium,Netherlands
 7   Numbers 1991: 88/248; HB: miss; decreasing; 66 %; Ne = 260
 8 - Height: 135/135 cm; Weight: 400/350 kg; Herd number: miss; AI: miss
 9   Colour: all colours admissible except piebald or scewbald
10   Pecularity: miss
11 - Main use: (1) sport/hobby,(2) miss,(3) miss
12   Spec. abilities: miss
13   Performance compared with STB Fjord 745:
14     higher: adaptability in jumping,speed in gallop,speed in trotters
15     equal:  miss
16     lower:  pulling power
17 - Management: stationary; housing: miss m.;
18 - Conservation progr.: live animals: miss;Semen: miss;Embryos: miss
19   Status: minimally endang.; Watch: HB♀♀,trend,%pure,%incross!
```

20 - Similar breeds (see group 5/3 on page 110)	EN	Country	Status
21 Welsh Pony (A, B & D)	823	SF	crit.end.
22 New Forest Pony	821	SF	min. end.
23 New Forest	784	F	pot. end.
24 Dartmoor Pony	739	GB	normal

```
 1 - Dagestanskii and Gruzinskii gornyi skot                      EN   107
 2   Dagestan/Georgian Mountain;Georgia,south of Tiflis (Caucasus) region
 3   Food and Agriculture Organisation of the UN               HB:miss
 4   Rome 00100, Via delle Terme di Caracalla
 5 - Autochthon
 7   Numbers 1990: 573/28000; HB: miss; decreasing; 33 %; Ne = 2246
 8 - Height: 112/108 cm; Weight: 420/290 kg; Herd number: miss; AI: miss
 9   Colour: Uni black
 9   Colour: Combination black, red, white
10   Pecularity: miss
11 - Main use: (1) milk; meat,(2) miss,(3) miss
12   Spec. abilities: adap. to temperature fluctuations of south. climate
13   Performance compared with STB Russian Simmental 241:
14      higher: % fat
15      equal:  miss
16      lower:  milk yield
17 - Management: stationary; housing: no/≈ 2/2-6 m.; high mount. grazing
18 - Conservation progr.: live animals: miss;Semen: miss;Embryos: miss
19   Status: normal;             Watch: HB♀♀,trend,%pure!
20 - Similar breeds (see group 1/6 on page 76)    EN  Country Status
21   Tuxer                                        259  A    crit.end.
22   Pohjoissuomenkarja                           207  SF   crit.end.
23   Fjällras                                      86  S    endanger.
24   Berrenda negra andaluza                       29  E    min. end.
```

```
 1 - Kavkazskaya buraya                                           EN   137
 2   Caucasian Brown; Azerbaijan
 3   Food and Agriculture Organisation of the UN               HB:miss
 4   Rome 00100, Via delle Terme di Caracalla
 5 - Composite of Lesser Caucasus breed, Swiss Brown, Kastroma, Lebedin
 6   Incrossing since 1950 from Brown Swiss USA
 7   Numbers 1990: 2700/251000; HB: miss; decreasing; 39 %; Ne = 10685
 8 - Height: 129/123 cm; Weight: 750/450 kg; Herd number: miss; AI: Yes
 9   Colour: Uni brown
10   Pecularity: miss
11 - Main use: (1) milk; meat,(2) miss,(3) miss
12   Spec. abilities: miss
13   Performance compared with STB Russian Simmental 241:
14      higher: miss
15      equal:  % fat
16      lower:  milk yield
17 - Management: stationary; housing: 2-6 m.;
18 - Conservation progr.: live animals: miss;Semen: miss;Embryos: miss
19   Status: normal;             Watch: HB♀♀,trend,%pure,%incross!
20 - Similar breeds (see group 5/1 on page 79)    EN  Country Status
21   Original Allgäuer Braunvieh                  189  D    crit.end.
22   Agerolese                                      2  I    crit.end.
23   Aubrac                                        14  F    normal
24   Österreichisches Braunvieh                   190  A    normal
```

CATTLE

```
1 - Krasnyi megrelskii skot                                    EN  150
2   Mingrelian Red; western Georgia
3   Food and Agriculture Organisation of the UN                HB:miss
4   Rome 00100, Via delle Terme di Caracalla
5 - Autochthon
7   Numbers 1990: 41/862; HB: miss; decreasing; 43 %; Ne = 157
8 - Height: 124/115 cm; Weight: 450/300 kg; Herd number: miss; AI: Yes
9   Colour: Uni red
10  Pecularity: colour shades brown, grey
11 - Main use: (1) milk; meat,(2) miss,(3) miss
12  Spec. abilities: adap. to water logged-meadows+poor alpine pastures
13  Performance compared with STB Russian Simmental 241:
14    higher: % fat
15    equal:  miss
16    lower:  milk yield
17 - Management: stationary; housing: no/≈ 2/2-6 m.;
18 - Conservation progr.: live animals: miss;Semen: miss;Embryos: miss
19  Status: endangered;        Watch: HB♀♀,trend,%pure!
20 - Similar breeds (see group 4/5 on page 79)    EN   Country Status
21  Yurinskaya                                    276  USSR    crit.end.
22  Krasnaya tambovskaya                          148  USSR    min. end.
23  Kalmytskaya                                   135  USSR    normal
24  Bestuzhevskaya                                 31  USSR    normal
```

PIGS

```
1 - Kakhetinskaya                                               EN  948
2   Kakhetian; eastern Georgia: Akhmeta, Telavi, Gurjaam, Dushet
3   Food and Agriculture Organisation of the UN                HB:miss
4   Rome 00100, Via delle Terme di Caracalla
5 - Autochthon
7   Numbers 1990: 38/429; HB: miss; stable; 99 %; Ne = 140
8 - Height: miss/miss cm; Weight: 250/155 kg; Herd number: miss; AI:miss
9   Colour: Uni grey, piglets have striped patterns
10  Pecularity: erect ears, close to wild boar
11 - Main use: (1) general purpose,(2) miss,(3) miss
12  Spec. abilities: strong constitution
13  Performance compared with STB Large White 951:
14    higher: miss
15    equal:  miss
16    lower:  litter size
17 - Management: stationary; housing: 12 m.;
18 - Conservation progr.: live animals: miss;Semen: miss;Embryos: miss
19  Status: minimally endang.; Watch: HB♀♀!
20 - Similar breeds (see group 7 on page 104)     EN   Country Status
21  Lesogornaya porodnaya gruppa                  966  ARM     crit.end.
22  Corse                                         915  F       endanger.
```

CATTLE

1 - **Angler** EN **8**
2   **Angeln; Schleswig-Holstein**
3   **Verband Angler Rinderzüchter e.V.** HB:**1879**
4   **Süderbrarup 24392, Angeln-Halle**
5 - **Autochthon Angler; incrossing since 1950 from Red Danish 222**
6   **Denmark, Red and White Sweden, Finnish Ayrshire 247 Finland**
7   **Numbers 1986: 226/36000; HB: 15000; stable; 100 %; Ne = 891**
8 - Height: **150/135** cm; Weight: **1100/600** kg; Herd number: **miss**; AI: **Yes**
9   Colour: **Uni red, brown**
10   Pecularity: **black hoofs, black muzzle**
11 - Main use: (1) **milk**,(2) **meat**,(3) **miss**
12   Spec. abilities: **heat resistance, short calving interval**
13   Performance compared with STB **Holstein-Friesian 75**:
14   higher: **calving ease, % fat, % protein of milk**
15   equal: **muscularity, calving interval, handling ease, calving rate**
16   lower: **calf mortality, milk yield, age of sexual maturity**
17 - Management: **stationary**; housing: **2-6 m.**;
18 - Conservation progr.: live animals: **miss**;Semen: **120**;Embryos: **6/12**
19   Status: **potential. endang.**;Watch: **%incross!**
20 - <u>Similar breeds</u> (see group 4/3 on page 78) <u>EN</u> <u>Country</u> <u>Status</u>
21   **Donnersberger Rotvieh** 101 D crit.end.
22   **Harzer Rotvieh** 109 D crit.end.
23   **Rod Dansk Malkerace** 222 DK normal
24   **Rood Ras van Belgie** 224 B normal

CATTLE

1 - **Deutsche Angus** EN **80**
2   **German Angus; country-wide**
3   **Bundesverband Deutscher Angushalter e.V.** HB:**1956**
4   **Kassel 34117, Thomeestr.3**
5 - **Composite of Aberdeen Angus, Deutsche Schwarzbunte 75,**
6   **Deutsches Fleckvieh 78, Deutsche Rotbunte 74**
7   **Numbers 1992: 130/10000; HB: 2000; stable; miss %; Ne = 488**
8 - Height: **140/130** cm; Weight: **1100/600** kg; Herd number: **miss**; AI: **miss**
9   Colour: **Uni black, blue, red, brown; some colour combinations**
10   Pecularity: **polled**
11 - Main use: (1) **meat**,(2) **vegetation management**,(3) **miss**
12   Spec. abilities: **miss**
13   Performance compared with STB **German Simmental 78**:
14   higher: **calving ease, age of sexual maturity**
15   equal: **muscularity, daily gain, handling ease**
16   lower: **calf mortality**
17 - Management: **stationary**; housing: **2-6 m.**;
18 - Conservation progr.: live animals: **miss**;Semen: **miss**;Embryos: **miss**
19   Status: **normal**
20 - <u>Similar breeds</u> (see group 2/2 on page 76) <u>EN</u> <u>Country</u> <u>Status</u>
21   **Kerry Cattle** 140 IRL min. end.
22   **Murray Grey** 181 GB pot. end.
23   **Angus** 9 IRL normal
24   **Galloway** 94 D normal

1 - Deutsche Rotbunte   EN   74
2   German Red Pied; central and western FRG
3   Verband Deutscher Rotbuntzüchter   HB:1892
4   Münster 48143, Engelstr. 97
5 - Composite of Rot- und Schwarzbuntes Niederungsrind 76; incrossing
6   since 1950 from MRY 161 NL, Holstein-Friesian USA/Canada
7   Numbers 1991: 2303/ miss; HB: 170071; increasing; miss %; Ne = 9089
8 - Height: 157/140 cm; Weight: 1150/650 kg; Herd number: miss; AI: miss
9   Colour: Combination red, white
10 Pecularity: miss
11 - Main use: (1) milk,(2) meat,(3) miss
12 Spec. abilities: miss
13 Performance compared with STB Holstein-Friesian 75:
14   higher: muscularity, % protein, daily gain
15   equal: age of sexual maturity, handling ease, calf mortality
16   lower: milk yield, % fat, calving ease
17 - Management: stationary; housing: 2-6 m.;
18 - Conservation progr.: live animals: miss;Semen: 20;Embryos: miss
19   Status: potential. endang.;Watch: %incross!

20 - Similar breeds (see group 3/1 on page 76)	EN	Country	Status
21 Blanc-Rouge de Belgique	273	B	pot. end.
22 Ferrandais	85	F	pot. end.
23 Dansk Rodbroget Kvaeg	73	DK	normal
24 Pie-Rouge	199	B	normal

1 - Deutsche Schwarzbunte   EN   75
2   Holstein-Friesian; country-wide
3   Verband Deutscher Schwarzbuntzüchter e.V.   HB:1878
4   Bonn 53113, Adenauerallee 174
5 - Composite of local breeds from Germany and The Netherlands
6   Incrossing continuously since 1950 from Holstein Friesian USA/CDN
7   Numbers 1986: 7350/3100000; HB: 805649; stable; 95 %; Ne = 29134
8 - Height: 160/145 cm; Weight: 1100/670 kg; Herd number: miss; AI: Yes
9   Colour: Combination black and white
10 Pecularity: miss
11 - Main use: (1) milk,(2) miss,(3) miss
12 Spec. abilities: miss
13 Performance compared with STB Brown Swiss:
14   higher: milk yield, % fat, calving ease, age of sexual maturity
15   equal: muscularity, daily gain, handling ease, calving rate
16   lower: % protein
17 - Management: stationary; housing: > 6 m.;
18 - Conservation progr.: live animals: miss;Semen: Yes;Embryos: Yes
19   Status: normal

20 - Similar breeds (see group 1/1 on page 75)	EN	Country	Status
21 Sortbroget Dansk Malkekvaeg	245	DK	pot. end.
22 Nizinna-Czarno-Biala	185	PL	pot. end.
23 Prim' Holstein	209	F	normal
24 Pie-Noire-Holstein	198	B	normal

```
 1 - Deutsche Schwarzbunte (Original)                              EN   76
 2   German Original Black Pied;Schleswig-H.,Nds.,Brandenb.,NRW,Rhld.-Pf.
 3   Landwirtschaftsministerium Berlin - Brandenburg              HB:1876
 4   Schwalmtal-Rainrod 41366, Schulstr.8
 5 - Composite of local breeds from Germany and The Netherlands
 6   Incrossing since 1950 from other Original Black Pied 76
 7   Numbers 1990: 12/500; HB: 400; stable; 70 %; Ne = 25
 8 - Height: 155/136 cm; Weight: 900/600 kg; Herd number: miss; AI: Yes
 9   Colour: Combinat. black and white; some red spots at muzzle and anus
10   Pecularity: no HF-incrossing
11 - Main use: (1) milk,(2) meat,(3) vegetation management
12   Spec. abilities: rare milk proteine genes
13   Performance compared with STB Holstein-Friesian 75:
14     higher: muscularity, daily gain, age of sexual maturity, % protein
15     equal:  calving interval, calf mortality, calving rate
16     lower:  % fat, milk yield
17 - Management: stationary; housing: > 6 m.; adapted to wet soil
18 - Conservation progr.: live animals: Yes;Semen: 140;Embryos: Yes
19   Status: endangered;         Watch: ♂♂,%pure,%incross!
```

20 - Similar breeds (see group 1/2 on page 75)	EN	Country	Status
21 Burlina	51	I	crit.end.
22 Breton Pie Noire	42	F	endanger.
23 Cherno-pestraya litovskaya	66	LT	normal
24 Cherno-pestraya estonskaya	65	EW	normal

```
 1 - Deutsches Braunvieh                                          EN   77
 2   German Brown; southern Germany
 3   Allgäuer Herdbuchgesellschaft (AHG)                         HB:1893
 4   Kempten 87435, Kotternerstr. 36
 5 - Autochthon Schweizer Torfrind
 6   Incrossing since 1950 from Brown Swiss USA
 7   Numbers 1991: 3000/340000; HB: 176391; decreasing; miss %; Ne=11799
 8 - Height: 152/138 cm; Weight: 1000/650 kg; Herd number: miss; AI: miss
 9   Colour: Uni brown
10   Pecularity: black muzzle, white surrounded; black horn tips
11 - Main use: (1) milk,(2) meat,(3) vegetation management
12   Spec. abilities: stayability, for rough climate
13   Performance compared with STB German Simmental 78:
14     higher: calving ease, milk yield, age of sexual maturity
15     equal:  daily gain, % fat, % protein, handling ease, calving rate
16     lower:  muscularity, pulling power, calf mortality
17 - Management: stationary; housing: > 6 m.; mountainous country
18 - Conservation progr.: live animals: miss;Semen: 150;Embryos: miss
19   Status: potential. endang.;Watch: %incross!
```

20 - Similar breeds (see group 5/1 on page 79)	EN	Country	Status
21 Original Allgäuer Braunvieh	189	D	crit.end.
22 Agerolese	2	I	crit.end.
23 Aubrac	14	F	normal
24 Österreichisches Braunvieh	190	A	normal

1 - Deutsches Fleckvieh   EN   78
2   German Simmental; Baden-Württemberg, Bayern, Hessen
3   Arbeitsgemeinschaft Süddeutscher Rinderzuchtverbände e.V.   HB:1892
4   München 80336, Haydnstr.11
5 - Composite of Simmental cattle local breed; incrossing since 1950
6   from Fleckvieh 88 Austria and Simmental 240 Switzerland
7   Numbers 1991: miss/1653250; HB: 610270; decreasing;miss %; Ne=835297
8 - Height: 154/140 cm; Weight: 1200/750 kg; Herd number: miss; AI: miss
9   Colour: Combination red, brown, yellow, white; spotted
10 Pecularity: dominant white head; some genetically polled
11 - Main use: (1) milk,(2) meat,(3) miss
12 Spec. abilities: carcass quality
13 Performance compared with STB Holstein-Friesian 75:
14   higher: muscularity, daily gain, % protein, calf mortality
15   equal: age of sexual maturity, handling ease, calving rate
16   lower: milk yield, % fat, calving ease
17 - Management: stationary; housing: > 6 m.;
18 - Conservation progr.: live animals: miss;Semen: 3061;Embryos: miss
19 Status: normal

20 - Similar breeds (see group 3/2 on page 77)	EN	Country	Status
21 Ceske strakate	61	CZ	crit.end.
22 Simentalska	237	PL	min. end.
23 Montbeliard	176	F	normal
24 Fleckvieh	88	A	normal

1 - Deutsches Schwarzbuntes Rind   EN   79
2   German Black Pied; District of Cottbus
3   Lehr- und Versuchsanstalt für Tierzucht und Tierhaltung   HB:1876
4   Paretz 14669, Parkring 13
5 - Autochthon; incrossing since 1950 from Schwarzbunte Schweden,
6   Schwarzbunte 64 USSR, Schwarzbunte 185 Poland
7   Numbers 1986: 20/3900; HB: 2700; stable; 70 %; Ne = 60
8 - Height: 145/130 cm; Weight: 1000/650 kg; Herd number: 7; AI: Yes
9   Colour: Combination black, white
10 Pecularity: white on forehead
11 - Main use: (1) milk,(2) meat,(3) miss
12 Spec. abilities: miss
13 Performance compared with STB Holstein-Friesian 75:
14   higher: muscularity, % fat, % protein
15   equal: daily gain,calving ease,calving interval,age of sex. mat.
16   lower: milk yield, milkability
17 - Management: stationary; housing: > 6 m.;
18 - Conservation progr.: live animals: Yes;Semen: 60;Embryos: miss
19 Status: potential. endang.;Watch: herds,%pure,%incross!

20 - Similar breeds (see group 1/2 on page 75)	EN	Country	Status
21 Burlina	51	I	crit.end.
22 Breton Pie Noire	42	F	endanger.
23 Cherno-pestraya litovskaya	66	LT	normal
24 Cherno-pestraya estonskaya	65	EW	normal

GERMANY   CATTLE

```
 1 - Donnersberger Rotvieh                                    EN  101
 2   Donnersberg; Administrative District of Rheinhessen-Pfalz
 3   Bezirkszüchtervereinigung Rheinhessen-Pfalz              HB:1898
 4   Kaiserslautern 67655, Fischerstr.1
 5 - Autochthon local red cattle, Simmentaler, Braunvieh
 6   Incrossing since 1950 from Danish Red 222 Denmark, Angler 8 Germany
 7   Numbers 1986: 10/1500; HB: 500; stable; 90 %; Ne = 20
 8 - Height: 150/138 cm; Weight: 1106/ miss kg; Herd number: 20; AI: Yes
 9   Colour: Uni red
10   Pecularity: black hoofs and muzzle
11 - Main use: (1) milk,(2) meat,(3) miss
12   Spec. abilities: miss
13   Performance compared with STB German Red Pied 74:
14      higher: % fat, % protein, calving ease, calving rate
15      equal:  milk yield, calving interval, handling ease, milkability
16      lower:  muscular., daily gain, age of sexual maturity, calf mort.
17 - Management: miss; housing: miss m.; highlands
18 - Conservation progr.: live animals: miss;Semen: 120;Embryos: 6/12
19   Status: critically endang.;Watch: ♂♂,%incross,%pure!
```

20 - Similar breeds (see group 4/3 on page 78)	EN	Country	Status
21 Harzer Rotvieh	109	D	crit.end.
22 Vogelsberger Rind	265	D	crit.end.
23 Rod Dansk Malkerace	222	DK	normal
24 Rood Ras van Belgie	224	B	normal

GERMANY   CATTLE

```
 1 - Galloway                                                 EN   94
 2   Galloway
 3   Bundesverband Deutscher Gallowayzüchter e.V.            HB:1982
 4   Bonn 53175, Godesberger Allee 142-148
 5 - Imported as breed from United Kingdom and Canada
 6   Incrossing since 1950 from Galloway 96 United Kingdom
 7   Numbers 1992: 1099/ miss; HB: 5619; increasing; 90 %; Ne = 3677
 8 - Height: 135/128 cm; Weight: 700/450 kg; Herd number: 1229; AI: Yes
 9   Colour: Uni black
10   Pecularity: horns 0/0, straggly coat, white belt in Belted Galloway
11 - Main use: (1) vegetation management,(2) hobby,(3) meat
12   Spec. abilities: good meat taste; for outdoor keeping
13   Performance compared with STB Charolais:
14      higher: calving ease, calving rate, calf mortality
15      equal:  calving interval, handling ease
16      lower:  milk yield, muscularity, daily gain, age of sexual mat.
17 - Management: stationary; housing: no; for hilly and wet country
18 - Conservation progr.: live animals: miss;Semen: Yes;Embryos: Yes
19   Status: normal
```

20 - Similar breeds (see group 2/2 on page 76)	EN	Country	Status
21 Kerry Cattle	140	IRL	min. end.
22 Murray Grey	181	GB	pot. end.
23 Angus	9	IRL	normal
24 Deutsche Angus	80	D	normal

1 - Gelbes Frankenvieh   EN 100
2   German Yellow; Lower Franken
3   Rinderzuchtverband Würzburg e.V.   HB:1897
4   Würzburg 97080, P.B. 6646, Veitshöchheimer Str. 14
5 - Composite of yellow and red local breeds
6   Incrossing since 1950 from Danish Red 222, Red Flemisch 224 Belgium
7   Numbers 1991: miss /40000; HB: 17000; increasing; miss %; Ne = 21720
8 - Height: 152/137 cm; Weight: 1225/725 kg; Herd number: miss; AI: miss
9   Colour: Uni red, yellow
10 Pecularity: miss
11 - Main use: (1) milk,(2) meat,(3) sire line for beef production
12 Spec. abilities: cows suitable for suckling calves for beef product.
13 Performance compared with STB German Simmental 78:
14   higher: muscularity, daily gain
15   equal: % fat, % protein, calving ease, age of sexual maturity
16   lower: milk yield
17 - Management: stationary; housing: 12 m.;
18 - Conservation progr.: live animals: miss;Semen: 18;Embryos: miss
19 Status: normal;   Watch: %incross!

20 - Similar breeds (see group 8/2 on page 81)	EN	Country	Status
21 Kärntner Blondvieh	139	A	crit.end.
22 Murbodner	178	A	crit.end.
23 Waldviertler Vieh	268	A	crit.end.
24 Murnau-Werdenfelser	180	D	endanger.

1 - Glanrind   EN 102
2   Glan; Rheinland-Pfalz, Saarland
3   Verein zur Erhaltung und Förderung des Glanrindes   HB:1898
4   Idar-Oberstein 55743, Unterm Wald 2
5 - Composite of local red cattle, Berner Vieh, Limpurger
6   Incrossing since 1950 from Angler 8, Deutsches Gelbvieh 100
7   Numbers 1990: 11/158; HB: 62; increasing; 90 %; Ne = 19
8 - Height: 148/140 cm; Weight: 1000/650 kg; Herd number: miss; AI: Yes
9   Colour: Uni yellow
10 Pecularity: light mouth and nose
11 - Main use: (1) meat,(2) milk,(3) tractive power
12 Spec. abilities: good meat quality with high % of red muscle fibres
13 Performance compared with STB German Simmental 78:
14   higher: calving rate, pulling power, handling ease
15   equal: muscularity,daily gain,% fat,calving ease,calving interv.
16   lower: milk yield, % protein
17 - Management: stationary; housing: > 6 m.;
18 - Conservation progr.: live animals: Yes;Semen: 3;Embryos: miss
19 Status: critically endang.;Watch: ♂♂,HB♀♀,%incross,%pure!

20 - Similar breeds (see group 8/2 on page 81)	EN	Country	Status
21 Kärntner Blondvieh	139	A	crit.end.
22 Murbodner	178	A	crit.end.
23 Murnau-Werdenfelser	180	D	endanger.
24 Gelbes Frankenvieh	100	D	normal

CATTLE

1 - Harzer Rotvieh   EN 109
2   Harz; Niedersachsen
3   Verband der Harz- und Rotviehzüchter in Niedersachsen   HB: Yes
4   Süderbrarup 24392, Angeln-Halle
5 - Autochthon Harzer Rotvieh
6   Incrossing since 1950 from Angler 8 Germany
7   Numbers 1986: 7/360; HB: 360; stable; 100 %; Ne = 13
8 - Height: 150/135 cm; Weight: 1100/600 kg; Herd number: 14; AI: Yes
9   Colour: Uni red, brown
10 Pecularity: black hoof, black muzzle
11 - Main use: (1) milk,(2) meat,(3) tourist attraction
12 Spec. abilities: high fat % and protein %
13 Performance compared with STB Holstein-Friesian 75:
14   higher: calving ease, % fat, % protein, daily gain
15   equal: muscularity, calving interval, handling ease, calving rate
16   lower: calf mortality, milk yield, age of sexual maturity
17 - Management: miss; housing: miss m.; highlands
18 - Conservation progr.: live animals: miss;Semen: 120;Embryos: 6/12
19 Status: critically endang.;Watch: ♂♂,herds,%incross!
20 - Similar breeds (see group 4/3 on page 78)   EN Country Status
21 Donnersberger Rotvieh   101 D   crit.end.
22 Vogelsberger Rind   265 D   crit.end.
23 Rod Dansk Malkerace   222 DK   normal
24 Rood Ras van Belgie   224 B   normal

CATTLE

1 - Hessisches Rotvieh   EN 113
2   Hessian Red; Hessen
3   Hessische Zucht- und Absatzgenossenschaft, Abteilung   HB: Yes
4   Rotvieh, Kassel 34117, Thomeestr.3
5 - Autochthon Hessisches Rotvieh
6   Incrossing since 1950 from Angler 8 Germany
7   Numbers 1988: 21/2537; HB: 946; decreasing; 100 %; Ne = 64
8 - Height: 150/135 cm; Weight: 1100/600 kg; Herd number: miss; AI: Yes
9   Colour: Uni red
10 Pecularity: miss
11 - Main use: (1) milk,(2) meat,(3) miss
12 Spec. abilities: high fat % (5%) and protein % (3.7%), vitality
13 Performance compared with STB Holstein-Friesian 75:
14   higher: calving ease, % fat, % protein, daily gain, meat quality
15   equal: muscularity, calving interval, handling ease, calving rate
16   lower: calf mortality, milk yield, age of sexual maturity
17 - Management: stationary; housing: > 6 m.;
18 - Conservation progr.: live animals: Yes;Semen: 120;Embryos: 6/12
19 Status: minimally endang.; Watch: ♂♂,trend,%incross!
20 - Similar breeds (see group 4/3 on page 78)   EN Country Status
21 Donnersberger Rotvieh   101 D   crit.end.
22 Harzer Rotvieh   109 D   crit.end.
23 Rod Dansk Malkerace   222 DK   normal
24 Rood Ras van Belgie   224 B   normal

```
 1 - Hinterwälder                                              EN  115
 2   Hinterwald; Baden-Württemberg, southern Schwarzwald
 3   Zuchtverband für Fleckvieh und Wäldervieh e.V.          HB:1889
 4   Titisee-Neustadt 79822, Walter-Göbel-Weg 4
 5 - Autochthon originating from Keltenrind
 6   Incrossing since 1950 from Vorderwälder 266
 7   Numbers 1990: 55/2100; HB: 301; stable; 85 %; Ne = 186
 8 - Height: 133/120 cm; Weight: 725/450 kg; Herd number: 200; AI: Yes
 9   Colour: Combination red, yellow, white; similar to Fleckvieh
10   Pecularity: Lyra-formed horns, genetically white head
11 - Main use: (1) milk,(2) meat,(3) vegetation management
12   Spec. abilities: no IBR/IPV, hard hoofs
13   Performance compared with STB German Simmental 78:
14      higher: calving ease, calving rate, stayability
15      equal: % fat, % protein, calving interval, age of sexual maturity
16      lower: milk yield, daily gain, muscularity, calf mortality
17 - Management: stationary; housing: > 6 m.; mountainous country
18 - Conservation progr.: live animals: Yes;Semen: 35;Embryos: miss
19   Status: minimally endang.; Watch: HB♀♀,%pure,%incross!
20 - Similar breeds (see group 3/3 on page 77)    EN Country Status
21   Vorderwälder                                  266   D    min. end.
22   Hinterwälder                                  116   CH   pot. end.
```

```
 1 - Jersey                                                    EN  131
 2   Jersey
 3   Verband Deutscher Jerseyzüchter e.V.                    HB:1961
 4   Hörstel 48477, Uferstr.10
 5 - Imported as breed from Denmark
 6   Incrossing since 1950 from Jersey 130 Denmark continously
 7   Numbers 1991: 38/ miss; HB: 2844; increasing; miss %; Ne = 150
 8 - Height: 129/125 cm; Weight: 515/415 kg; Herd number: miss; AI: miss
 9   Colour: Uni red, brown
10   Pecularity: miss
11 - Main use: (1) milk,(2) miss,(3) miss
12   Spec. abilities: % fat very high
13   Performance compared with STB Holstein-Friesian 75:
14      higher: % fat, % protein, calving ease, calving rate
15      equal: handling ease, milkability
16      lower: milk yield,muscularity,daily gain,age of sexual maturity
17 - Management: stationary; housing: 2-6/> 6/12 m.;
18 - Conservation progr.: live animals: miss;Semen: miss;Embryos: miss
19   Status: normal;              Watch: HB♀♀!
20 - Similar breeds (see group 8/4 on page 82)    EN Country Status
21   Froment du Leon                                93   F    endanger.
22   Jersey                                        132   IRL  pot. end.
23   Jersiais                                      134   F    normal
24   Jersey                                        130   DK   normal
```

```
1 - Limpurger                                                        EN  158
2   Limpurger; Baden-Württemberg(Aalen,Schwäbisch Gmünd,Gaildorf)
3   Züchtervereinigung Limpurger Rind                              HB:1987
4   Schwäbisch-Hall 74523, Alte Reifensteige 16
5 - Autochthon red local breed and Allgäuer cattle 77; incrossing since
6   1950 from Gelbvieh 100, Fleckvieh 78, Glan-Donnersberger 101
7   Numbers 1993: 18/125; HB: miss; increasing; miss %; Ne = 40
8 - Height: 145/135 cm; Weight: 1050/625 kg; Herd number: 30; AI: Yes
9   Colour: Uni yellow
10  Pecularity: light muzzle and hoofs, light back stripe
11 - Main use: (1) milk,(2) meat,(3) vegetation management
12  Spec. abilities: meat quality, hard hoofs
13  Performance compared with STB German Simmental 78:
14    higher: miss
15    equal:  daily gain,% fat,% protein,calving ease,calving interval
16    lower:  milk yield, muscularity
17 - Management: stationary; housing: > 6 m.;
18 - Conservation progr.: live animals: Yes;Semen: 11;Embryos: miss
19  Status: critically endang.;Watch: ♂♂,HB♀♀,%pure,%incross!
```

20 - Similar breeds (see group 8/2 on page 81)	EN	Country	Status
21 Kärntner Blondvieh	139	A	crit.end.
22 Murbodner	178	A	crit.end.
23 Murnau-Werdenfelser	180	D	endanger.
24 Gelbes Frankenvieh	100	D	normal

```
1 - Murnau-Werdenfelser                                             EN  180
2   Murnau-Werdenfels; "Werdenfelser Land" in Bayern
3   Zuchtverband für Murnau-Werdenfelser Vieh                     HB:1927
4   Weilheim 82362, Waisenhausstr.5
5 - Composite of Oberinntal Grey, Brown Swiss, Murboden
7   Numbers 1993: 13/700; HB: 112; increasing; miss %; Ne = 25
8 - Height: 138/128 cm; Weight: 925/525 kg; Herd number: 30; AI: Yes
9   Colour: Uni yellow
10  Pecularity: white rim around dark muzzle; black pigmented mucosa
11 - Main use: (1) milk,(2) meat,(3) miss
12  Spec. abilities: miss
13  Performance compared with STB German Simmental 78:
14    higher: longevity, calving ease, age of sexual maturity
15    equal:  daily gain, % protein, handling ease, calving rate
16    lower:  milk yield, muscularity, % fat, calf mortality
17 - Management: miss; housing: miss m.; wet and mountainous country
18 - Conservation progr.: live animals: Yes;Semen: 11;Embryos: Yes
19  Status: endangered;        Watch: ♂♂,HB♀♀,%pure!
```

20 - Similar breeds (see group 8/2 on page 81)	EN	Country	Status
21 Kärntner Blondvieh	139	A	crit.end.
22 Murbodner	178	A	crit.end.
23 Waldviertler Vieh	268	A	crit.end.
24 Gelbes Frankenvieh	100	D	normal

```
 1 - Original Allgäuer Braunvieh                                    EN   189
 2   Original German Brown; Allgäu, s.w. Baden-Württemberg, s.e. Bayern
 3   Allgäuer Herdbuchgesellschaft                                  HB:1893
 4   Kempten 87435, Kotternerstr.36
 5 - Autochthon Allgäuer cattle and Schweizer Torfrind
 6   Incrossing since 1950 from Brown Swiss 40 Switzerland
 7   Numbers 1986: 12/400; HB: 200; decreasing; 80 %; Ne = 24
 8 - Height: 145/135 cm; Weight: 900/550 kg; Herd number: miss; AI: Yes
 9   Colour: Uni brown, white rounded dark muzzle
10   Pecularity: dark muzzle, hoofs and horn tips
11 - Main use: (1) milk,(2) meat,(3) vegetation management
12   Spec. abilities: Kappa Kasein PB
13   Performance compared with STB German Brown 77:
14     higher: age of sexual maturity, stayability, muscularity
15     equal: % fat, % protein, calving interval, handling ease
16     lower:  calving ease, milk yield, daily gain
17 - Management: stationary; housing: > 6 m.; mountainous country
18 - Conservation progr.: live animals: Yes;Semen: 14;Embryos: miss
19   Status: critically endang.;Watch: ♂♂,HB♀♀,trend,%pure,%incross!
```

20 - Similar breeds (see group 5/1 on page 79)	EN	Country	Status
21 Agerolese	2	I	crit.end.
22 Pisana	205	I	crit.end.
23 Aubrac	14	F	normal
24 Österreichisches Braunvieh	190	A	normal

```
 1 - Pinzgauer                                                      EN   203
 2   Pinzgau; Bayern, Österreich
 3   Rinderzuchtverband Traunstein, Abteilung Pinzgauer             HB:1896
 4   Traunstein 83278, Kardinal-Faulhaber Str.15
 5 - Composite of some local cattle before 1850 and Pinzgauer 202 Austria
 6   Incrossing since 1950 from Pinzgauer 202 Austria
 7   Numbers 1992: 22/1300; HB: 279; increasing; miss %; Ne = 63
 8 - Height: 144/135 cm; Weight: 1000/700 kg; Herd number: 60; AI: Yes
 9   Colour: Combination red, brown, white
10   Pecularity: white back and belly
11 - Main use: (1) milk,(2) meat,(3) miss
12   Spec. abilities: hard hoofs
13   Performance compared with STB German Simmental 78:
14     higher: age of sexual maturity
15     equal: % protein, handling ease, calf mortality, calving rate
16     lower:  milk yield, muscularity, daily gain, % fat, calving ease
17 - Management: stationary; housing: > 6 m.;
18 - Conservation progr.: live animals: Yes;Semen: 14;Embryos: miss
19   Status: potential. endang.;Watch: ♂♂,%pure,%incross!
```

20 - Similar breeds (see group 3/4 on page 77)	EN	Country	Status
21 Pustertaler Schecken	210	D	crit.end.
22 Pinzgauer	200	I	crit.end.
23 Pinzgauer	202	A	pot. end.
24 Slovenske pinzgavske	243	SK	normal

1 - Pustertaler Schecken   EN   210
2   Pustertaler Sprinzen; southern Bayern
3   Gesellschaft zur Erhaltung alter und gefährdeter   HB:miss
4   Haustierrassen e.V., Witzenhausen 37215, Gelsterstr. 2
5 - Composite of Raetian grey 214 CH, local red, Herens 83 CH,
6   Pinzgauer 200 Italy; imported as breed from South-Tyrol/Italy
7   Numbers 1993: 6/24; HB: miss; increasing; 100 %; Ne = 8
8 - Height: 137/128 cm; Weight: 900/550 kg; Herd number: miss; AI: Yes
9   Colour: Combination black, red, brown, white
10 Pecularity: white flanks pied brown or black,broad white back stripe
11 - Main use: (1) meat,(2) milk,(3) miss
12 Spec. abilities: miss
13 Performance compared with STB German Simmental 78:
14   higher: calving ease, handling ease
15   equal: muscularity, daily gain, % protein, age of sexual maturity
16   lower: milk yield, % fat, calf mortality
17 - Management: miss; housing: miss m.;
18 - Conservation progr.: live animals: miss;Semen: miss;Embryos: miss
19 Status: critically endang.;Watch: ♂♂,HB♀♀,herds!
20 - Similar breeds (see group 3/4 on page 77)   EN Country Status
21 Pinzgauer   200   I   crit.end.
22 Pustertaler Sprinzen   211   I   crit.end.
23 Pinzgauer   202   A   pot. end.
24 Slovenske pinzgavske   243   SK   normal

1 - Schwarzbuntes Milchrind   EN   229
2   German Black Pied Dairy; country-wide
3   Lehr- und Versuchsanstalt für Tierzucht und Tierhaltung   HB:1970
4   Paretz 14669, Parkring 13
5 - Composite of Deutsche Schwarzbunte 79 German Democratic Republic
6   Jersey 130 Denmark, Holstein Friesian
7   Numbers 1986: 700/2010000; HB: 356000; stable; 80 %; Ne = 2795
8 - Height: 150/138 cm; Weight: 1050/650 kg; Herd number: miss; AI: Yes
9   Colour: Combination black, white
10 Pecularity: miss
11 - Main use: (1) milk,(2) meat,(3) miss
12 Spec. abilities: miss
13 Performance compared with STB Holstein-Friesian 75:
14   higher: % fat, % protein, calving ease
15   equal: muscularity, daily gain, age of sexual maturity, handling
16   lower: milk yield, calving interval
17 - Management: stationary; housing: > 6 m.;
18 - Conservation progr.: live animals: miss;Semen: 1800;Embryos: miss
19 Status: normal;   Watch: %pure!
20 - Similar breeds (see group 1/4 on page 75)   EN Country Status
21 Nizinne cernostrakate   184   CS   normal
22 Baltata cu negru romanesca   19   RO   normal
23 Crno-belo   71   YU   normal

1 - **Vogelsberger Rind**   EN **265**
2   **Vogelsberg; Vogelsberg / Hessen**
3   **Verein zur Erhaltung und Förderung des roten Höhenviehs e.V.** HB:miss
4   **Leun-Biskirchen 35368, Handstr.12**
5 - **Autochthon local red cattle**
6   **Incrossing since 1950 from Angler 8 Germany**
7   Numbers 1990: 9/180; HB: 180; increasing; 95 %; Ne = 17
8 - Height: **138/128** cm; Weight: **600/500** kg; Herd number: 30; AI: **Yes**
9   Colour: **Uni red**
10 Pecularity: **light muzzle, light horns with black tips**
11 - Main use: (1) **milk**,(2) **meat**,(3) **vegetation management**
12 Spec. abilities: **hard hoofs**
13 Performance compared with STB **German Simmental** 78:
14   higher: **% fat, % protein, calving ease, milkability**
15   equal: **daily gain, calving rate**
16   lower: **milk yield, muscularity**
17 - Management: **stationary**; housing: **> 6 m.**;
18 - Conservation progr.: live animals: **Yes**;Semen: **7**;Embryos: **1/1**
19 Status: **critically endang.**;Watch: **♂♂,HB♀♀,%pure,%incross!**
20 - <u>Similar breeds</u> (see group 4/3 on page 78)   <u>EN</u> <u>Country</u> <u>Status</u>
21 **Donnersberger Rotvieh**   101 D   crit.end.
22 **Harzer Rotvieh**   109 D   crit.end.
23 **Rod Dansk Malkerace**   222 DK   normal
24 **Rood Ras van Belgie**   224 B   normal

1 - **Vorderwälder**   EN **266**
2   **Vorderwald; Baden-Württemberg, southern Schwarzwald**
3   **Zuchtverband für Fleckvieh und Wäldervieh e.V.**   HB:1896
4   **Titisee-Neustadt 79822, Walter-Göbel-Weg 4**
5 - **Autochthon local cattle known before 1850**
6   **Incrossing since 1950 from Ayrshire 18 United Kingdom**
7   Numbers 1990: 355/17500; HB: 5694; stable; 60 %; Ne = 1337
8 - Height: **150/135** cm; Weight: **1050/600** kg; Herd number: 1800; AI: **Yes**
9   Colour: **Combination red, yellow, white, spotted**
10 Pecularity: **lyra formed horns, white head**
11 - Main use: (1) **milk**,(2) **meat**,(3) **vegetation management**
12 Spec. abilities: **miss**
13 Performance compared with STB **German Simmental** 78:
14   higher: **calving ease, calving rate, stayability**
15   equal: **% fat, % protein, calving interval, age of sexual maturity**
16   lower: **milk yield, muscularity, daily gain, calf mortality**
17 - Management: **stationary**; housing: **> 6 m.**; **mountainous country**
18 - Conservation progr.: live animals: **Yes**;Semen: **120**;Embryos: miss
19 Status: **minimally endang.**; Watch: **%pure,%incross!**
20 - <u>Similar breeds</u> (see group 3/3 on page 77)   <u>EN</u> <u>Country</u> <u>Status</u>
21 **Hinterwälder**   115 D   min. end.
22 **Hinterwälder**   116 CH   pot. end.

```
 1 - Westfälisches Rotvieh                                          EN  270
 2   Westphalian Red; Westfalen
 3   Verband Westfälischer Rotviehzüchter e.V.                      HB:1890
 4   Erndtebrück 57339, Hauptmühle 7
 5 - Autochthon Westfälisches Rotvieh; incrossing since 1950
 6   from Angler 8 Germany, Danish Red 222 Denmark
 7   Numbers 1986: 20/2000; HB: 1000; decreasing; 100 %; Ne = 58
 8 - Height: 152/136 cm; Weight: 1100/650 kg; Herd number: miss; AI: Yes
 9   Colour: Uni red, brown
10   Pecularity: black hoof, black muzzle
11 - Main use: (1) milk,(2) meat,(3) miss
12   Spec. abilities: miss
13   Performance compared with STB Holstein-Friesian 75:
14     higher: calving ease, % fat, % protein, daily gain
15     equal:  muscularity, calving interval, handling ease, calving rate
16     lower:  calf mortality, milk yield, age of sexual maturity
17 - Management: stationary; housing: > 6 m.; highlands
18 - Conservation progr.: live animals: Yes;Semen: 120;Embryos: 6/12
19   Status: minimally endang.; Watch: trend,%incross!
20 - Similar breeds (see group 4/3 on page 78)    EN  Country Status
21   Donnersberger Rotvieh                        101  D      crit.end.
22   Harzer Rotvieh                               109  D      crit.end.
23   Rod Dansk Malkerace                          222  DK     normal
24   Rood Ras van Belgie                          224  B      normal
```

```
 1 - Bentheimer Landschaf                                          EN  414
 2   Bentheim; Districts of Bentheim and Lingen, Diepholz Moorland
 3   Landes-Schafzuchtverband Weser-Ems e.V.                       HB:1934
 4   Oldenburg 26121, Mars-La-Tour-Str.13
 5 - Composite of local heather/marsh sheep, Drenthe Heath 484 NL
 6   Incrossing since 1960 from Causses du Lot 448 France
 7   Numbers 1990: 45/1000; HB: 590; increasing; 90 %; Ne = 167
 8 - Height: 72/67 cm; Weight: 80/60 kg; Herd number: miss; AI: miss
 9   Colour: Uni white, black eyes and ears, pigmented legs
10   Pecularity: horns 0/0, hardy
11 - Main use: (1) meat,(2) vegetation management,(3) wool
12   Spec. abilities: game like taste of meat
13   Performance compared with STB German Merino 550:
14     higher: lambing interval, wool or fiber thickness
15     equal:  carcass leanness
16     lower:  litter size,muscularity,daily gain,age of sexual maturity
17 - Management: stationary; housing: 2-6 m.;
18 - Conservation progr.: live animals: Yes;Semen: 2;Embryos: miss
19   Status: normal;              Watch: %incross!
20 - Similar breeds (see group 6/2 on page 90)    EN  Country Status
21   Schoonebeker Heideschaap                     620  NL     min. end.
22   Veluwse Heideschaap                          660  NL     min. end.
23   Drentse Heideschaap                          484  NL     pot. end.
24   Mergelland Schaap                            544  NL     normal
```

```
 1 - Blauköpfiges Fleischschaf                              EN   424
 2   Bleu du Maine; country-wide
 3   Vereinigung Rheinischer Schafzüchter                   HB:1975
 4   Bonn 53115, Endenicher Allee 60
 5 - Imported as breed from France and United Kingdom
 7   Numbers 1986: 300/4000; HB: 1400; increasing; 100 %; Ne = 988
 8 - Height: 78/68 cm; Weight: 120/80 kg; Herd number: miss; AI: miss
 9   Colour: Combination blue, white, blue head and legs
10   Pecularity: horns 0/0, some brown body
11 - Main use: (1) meat,(2) wool,(3) miss
12   Spec. abilities: miss
13   Performance compared with STB German Merino 550:
14     higher: lambing interval,muscularity,litter size,fiber thickness
15     equal:  daily gain, carcass leanness, milk yield, fiber yield
16     lower:  age of sexual maturity
17 - Management: stationary; housing: 2-6 m.;
18 - Conservation progr.: live animals: miss;Semen: miss;Embryos: miss
19   Status: normal
```

20 - Similar breeds (see group 2/1 on page 87)	EN	Country	Status
21 Rouge de l'ouest	605	GB	pot. end.
22 Bleu du Maine	425	F	normal
23 Bleu du Maine	426	GB	normal
24 Rouge de l'ouest	604	F	normal

```
 1 - Braunes Bergschaf                                      EN   431
 2   Brown Mountain; Bavarian Alps and Prealps
 3   Bayerische Herdbuchgesellschaft für Schafzucht         HB:1977
 4   München 80336, Haydnstr.11
 5 - Composite of Zaupelschaf and Steinschaf
 6   Incrossing since 1960 from Bergschaf Italy and Bergschaf Austria
 7   Numbers 1990: 12/500; HB: 270; stable; 100 %; Ne = 25
 8 - Height: 75/65 cm; Weight: 95/65 kg; Herd number: miss; AI: miss
 9   Colour: Uni brown
10   Pecularity: horns 0/0
11 - Main use: (1) meat,(2) vegetation manegement,(3) living cell therapy
12   Spec. abilities: high fertility, asaisonal breeding
13   Performance compared with STB German Merino 550:
14     higher: fiber thickness, litter size, milk yield
15     equal:  carcass leanness
16     lower:  age of sexual maturity, muscularity, daily gain
17 - Management: stationary; housing: 2-6 m.; mountainous country
18 - Conservation progr.: live animals: Yes;Semen: miss;Embryos: miss
19   Status: critically endang.;Watch: ♂♂,HB♀♀!
```

20 - Similar breeds (see group 7/2 on page 91)	EN	Country	Status
21 Istriana	516	I	crit.end.
22 Lamon	525	I	crit.end.
23 Bergamasca	415	I	normal
24 Weißes Bergschaf	416	D	normal

```
 1 - Coburger Fuchsschaf                                              EN  466
 2   Coburg; Highlands in Bayern and Hessen
 3   Bayerische Herdbuchgesellschaft für Schafzucht                   HB:1966
 4   München 80336, Haydnstr.11
 5 - Autochthon brown headed local sheep; imports from GB and France
 6   Incrossing since 1960 from Solognot 633, Rouge de West 604 France
 7   Numbers 1993: 11/1500; HB: 1050; increasing; 100 %; Ne = 23
 8 - Height: 77/65 cm; Weight: 95/70 kg; Herd number: 50; AI: miss
 9   Colour: Uni brown body
10   Pecularity: horns 0/0, red head
11 - Main use: (1) meat,(2) wool,(3) vegetation management
12   Spec. abilities: game-like taste of meat; robust
13   Performance compared with STB German Merino 550:
14     higher: lambing interval, fiber thickness
15     equal: carcass leanness, milk yield, age of sexual maturity
16     lower: muscularity, daily gain, litter size, fiber yield
17 - Management: stationary; housing: ≈ 2 m.; hilly country
18 - Conservation progr.: live animals: Yes;Semen: miss;Embryos: miss
19   Status: critically endang.;Watch: ♂♂!
20 - Similar breeds (see group 6/3 on page 90)     EN  Country Status
21   Dansk Landfar                                 477   DK    crit.end.
22   Utegangarsau                                  496   N     min. end.
23   Foroyskur Seydur                              491   FR    normal
24   Gronlandsk Fär                                504   DK    normal
```

```
 1 - Graue gehörnte Heidschnucke                                     EN  501
 2   German Grey Heath; Niedersachsen, specially Lüneburger Heide
 3   Verband Lüneburger Heidschnuckenzüchter e.V.                     HB:1923
 4   Uelzen 29525, Wilhelm-Seedorf-Str.3, P.B. 509
 5 - Autochthon local heather sheep (Heidschnucke)
 7   Numbers 1993: 68/ miss; HB: 1387; stable; 100 %; Ne = 259
 8 - Height: 73/62 cm; Weight: 75/47 kg; Herd number: miss; AI: miss
 9   Colour: Uni grey, head bare and black
10   Pecularity: horns 2/2, in males spiral formed; short tail
11 - Main use: (1) vegetation management,(2) meat,(3) hobby
12   Spec. abilities: game like taste of meat, vegetation management
13   Performance compared with STB German Blackheaded Mutton 622:
14     higher: wool or fiber thickness, vegetation management
15     equal: lambing interval
16     lower: muscularity, daily gain, carcass leanness, litter size
17 - Management: stationary; housing: 2-6 m.; heath land
18 - Conservation progr.: live animals: miss;Semen: miss;Embryos: miss
19   Status: normal
20 - Similar breeds (see group 6/1 on page 90)     EN  Country Status
21   Weiße gehörnte Heidschnucke                   667   D     min. end.
22   Weiße hornlose Heidschnucke                   668   D     pot. end.
```

```
 1 - Kärntner Brillenschaf                                    EN  520
 2   Carinthian; Districts of Berchtesgaden and Traunstein
 3   Gesellschaft zur Erhaltung alter und gefährdeter          HB:1989
 4   Haustierrassen e.V., Witzenhausen 37215, Gelsterstr.2
 5 - Composite of Zaupelschaf, Steinschaf, Vilnößer Schaf; imports from
 6   Austria, Italy; incrossing since 1960 from Weißes Bergschaf 416 D
 7   Numbers 1993: 15/250; HB: 93; stable; 100 %; Ne = 29
 8 - Height: 75/65 cm; Weight: 85/65 kg; Herd number: 18; AI: miss
 9   Colour: Uni white head and body
10   Pecularity: horns 0/0; black ears and rims around eyes, hard hoofs
11 - Main use: (1) meat,(2) wool,(3) vegetation management
12   Spec. abilities: asaisonal breeding, robust
13   Performance compared with STB German Merino 550:
14     higher: fiber thickness
15     equal:  carcass leanness, litter size, milk yield, fiber yield
16     lower:  age of sex. matur.,muscularity,daily gain,lambing interval
17 - Management: transhumant; housing: 2-6 m.; mountainous country
18 - Conservation progr.: live animals: Yes;Semen: 3;Embryos: miss
19   Status: endangered;          Watch: ♂♂,HB♀♀,herds!
```

20 - Similar breeds (see group 7/2 on page 91)	EN	Country	Status
21 Braunes Bergschaf	431	D	crit.end.
22 Istriana	516	I	crit.end.
23 Bergamasca	415	I	normal
24 Weißes Bergschaf	416	D	normal

```
 1 - Leineschaf                                              EN  529
 2   Leine; Niedersachsen
 3   Landesschafzuchtverband Niedersachsen e.V.               HB:1906
 4   Hannover 30159, Johannssenstr.10
 5 - Autochthon local breed; incrossing since 1960 from Texel 653
 6   Netherlands, Ostfriesisches Milchschaf 573 Germany
 7   Numbers 1986: 80/1500; HB: 520; increasing; 100 %; Ne = 277
 8 - Height: 82/72 cm; Weight: 110/75 kg; Herd number: miss; AI: miss
 9   Colour: Uni white
10   Pecularity: horns 0/0
11 - Main use: (1) meat,(2) wool,(3) miss
12   Spec. abilities: twinning, seasonal, good mothering abilities
13   Performance compared with STB Texel 650:
14     higher: litter size, milk yield
15     equal:  daily gain, carcass leanness, age of sexual maturity
16     lower:  muscularity, fiber thickness
17 - Management: stationary; housing: 2-6 m.;
18 - Conservation progr.: live animals: Yes;Semen: miss;Embryos: miss
19   Status: potential. endang.;Watch: %incross!
```

20 - Similar breeds (see group 2/3 on page 88)	EN	Country	Status
21 Rauhwolliges Pommer. Landschaf	595	D*	crit.end.
22 Olkuska	571	PL	crit.end.
23 Pomorska	586	PL	normal
24 Kamieniecka	517	PL	normal

```
 1 - Merinofleischschaf                                           EN   548
 2   German Mutton Merino; country-wide
 3   Landesschafzuchtverband Sachsen-Anhalt e.V.                  HB:1903
 4   Halle 06118, Angerstr.3a
 5 - Autochthon Merinokammwollschaf
 6   Incrossing since 1960 from Merinoprecose 555 F, Leicester 528 GB
 7   Numbers 1986: 8000/350000; HB: 90062; decreasing; 90 %; Ne = 29389
 8 - Height: 81/77 cm; Weight: 100/65 kg; Herd number: miss; AI: Yes
 9   Colour: Uni white
10   Pecularity: horns 0/0
11 - Main use: (1) wool,(2) meat,(3) miss
12   Spec. abilities: carcass quality, 60 % twinning
13   Performance compared with STB German Merino 550:
14     higher: wool or fiber yield, litter size, wool or fiber thickness
15     equal:  muscularity,daily gain,carcass leanness,age of sex. matur.
16     lower:  miss
17 - Management: stationary; housing: 2-6 m.; arid climate
18 - Conservation progr.: live animals: miss;Semen: Yes;Embryos: miss
19   Status: normal;              Watch: trend,%incross!
```

20 - <u>Similar breeds</u> (see group 1/4 on page 87)

		EN	Country	Status
21	Merinolangwollschaf	551	D*	normal
22	Merinofleischschaf	549	D	normal
23	Merinolandschaf	550	D	normal

```
 1 - Merinofleischschaf                                           EN   549
 2   German Mutton Merino; Niedersachsen
 3   Landesschafzuchtverband Niedersachsen                        HB:1919
 4   Hannover 30159, Johanssenstr.10
 5 - Imported as breed from Spain, France, United Kingdom
 7   Numbers 1993: 48/ miss; HB: 1400; decreasing; 100 %; Ne = 186
 8 - Height: 82/75 cm; Weight: 130/75 kg; Herd number: miss; AI: miss
 9   Colour: Uni white
10   Pecularity: horns 0/0
11 - Main use: (1) meat,(2) wool,(3) miss
12   Spec. abilities: off season breeding, doing well under dryer climate
13   Performance compared with STB German Merino 550:
14     higher: muscularity, litter size
15     equal:  daily gain,carcass leanness,milk yield,age of sexual mat.
16     lower:  fiber thickness
17 - Management: stationary; housing: 2-6 m.;
18 - Conservation progr.: live animals: miss;Semen: miss;Embryos: miss
19   Status: normal
```

20 - <u>Similar breeds</u> (see group 1/4 on page 87)

		EN	Country	Status
21	Merinofleischschaf	548	D*	normal
22	Merinolangwollschaf	551	D*	normal
23	Merinolandschaf	550	D	normal

```
1 - Merinolandschaf                                        EN  550
2   German Merino; western Germany
3   Vereinigung Deutscher Landesschafzuchtverbände e.V.         HB:1922
4   Bonn 53175, Godesberger Allee 142-148
5 - Composite of Franken-, Württembergisches Bastard-, Marsch- and
6   Zaupelschaf; imports as breed from contries Spain, United Kingdom
7   Numbers 1987: 1640/573590; HB: 9940; increasing; 80 %; Ne = 5631
8 - Height: 95/80 cm; Weight: 130/80 kg; Herd number: miss; AI: miss
9   Colour: Uni white
10  Pecularity: horns 0/0, long distance walker
11 - Main use: (1) meat,(2) wool,(3) vegetation management
12  Spec. abilities: aseasonal breeding
13  Performance compared with STB German Merino 550:
14    higher: Breed is used
15    equal:  as standard breed,
16    lower:  no comparison possible.
17 - Management: tending; housing: ≈ 2 m.; also for semi desert
18 - Conservation progr.: live animals: miss;Semen: 2;Embryos: miss
19  Status: normal
```

20 - <u>Similar breeds</u> (see group 1/4 on page 87)

		EN	Country	Status
21	Merinofleischschaf	548	D*	normal
22	Merinolangwollschaf	551	D*	normal
23	Merinofleischschaf	549	D	normal

```
1 - Merinolangwollschaf                                    EN  551
2   Merino Longwool; Thüringen, Sachsen
3   Landesverband Thüringer Schafzüchter e.V.                  HB:1972
4   Erfurt 99089, Mittelhäuser Str.74
5 - Composite of Nordkamkas, Fleischwollschaf, Lincoln 532 GB,
6   Corriedale; imported as breed from USSR, Canada
7   Numbers 1986: 2500/200000; HB: 44840; stable; 80 %; Ne = 9472
8 - Height: 84/80 cm; Weight: 100/70 kg; Herd number: miss; AI: Yes
9   Colour: Uni white
10  Pecularity: horns 0/0
11 - Main use: (1) wool,(2) meat,(3) vegetation management
12  Spec. abilities: 40-60 % twinning
13  Performance compared with STB German Merino 550:
14    higher: wool or fiber thickness, wool or fiber yield
15    equal:  daily gain,age of sexual maturity,length of mating season
16    lower:  muscularity, carcass leanness, litter size
17 - Management: stationary; housing: ≈ 2 m.; hilly country
18 - Conservation progr.: live animals: miss;Semen: Yes;Embryos: miss
19  Status: normal;                Watch: %pure!
```

20 - <u>Similar breeds</u> (see group 1/4 on page 87)

		EN	Country	Status
21	Merinofleischschaf	548	D*	normal
22	Merinofleischschaf	549	D	normal
23	Merinolandschaf	550	D	normal

```
1 - Ostfriesisches Milchschaf                              EN  572
2   East Friesian; Sachsen
3   Sächsischer Schaf- und Ziegenzuchtverband e.V.        HB: Yes
4   Markkleeberg 04416, Bornaische Str. 31-33
5 - Autochthon Marschschafschläge
7   Numbers 1986: 1500/50000; HB: 3500; decreasing; 80 %; Ne = 4200
8 - Height: 86/80 cm; Weight: 110/80 kg; Herd number: miss; AI: Yes
9   Colour: Uni white
10  Pecularity: horns 0/0, long hairless tail
11 - Main use: (1) milk,(2) meat,(3) wool
12  Spec. abilities: milk, 100 % twinning
13  Performance compared with STB East Friesian 572:
14    higher: Breed is used
15    equal:  as standard breed,
16    lower:  no comparison possible.
17 - Management: stationary; housing: 2-6 m.; humid climate
18 - Conservation progr.: live animals: miss;Semen: miss;Embryos: miss
19  Status: normal;            Watch: %pure,trend!
20 - Similar breeds (see group 5/1 on page 89)    EN  Country Status
21  Mouton Laitier Belge                           561  B    min. end.
22  Ostfriesisches Milchschaf                      573  D    normal
23  British Milksheep                              438  GB   normal
24  Friese Melkschaap                              493  NL   normal
```

```
1 - Ostfriesisches Milchschaf                              EN  573
2   East Friesian; northern Germany
3   Vereinigung Deutscher Landesschafzuchtverbände e.V.   HB:1890
4   Bonn 53175, Godesberger Allee 142-148
5 - Autochthon Ostfriesisches Milchschaf
7   Numbers 1986: 3000/27000; HB: 3800; increasing; 95 %; Ne = 6706
8 - Height: 85/78 cm; Weight: 125/80 kg; Herd number: miss; AI: miss
9   Colour: Mostly uni white, some black or brown
10  Pecularity: horns 0/0, long bare tail
11 - Main use: (1) milk,(2) meat,(3) wool
12  Spec. abilities: high nutritional value of milk, twinning
13  Performance compared with STB East Friesian 573:
14    higher: Breed is used
15    equal:  as standard breed,
16    lower:  no comparison possible.
17 - Management: stationary; housing: 2-6 m.;
18 - Conservation progr.: live animals: miss;Semen: miss;Embryos: miss
19  Status: normal
20 - Similar breeds (see group 5/1 on page 89)    EN  Country Status
21  Mouton Laitier Belge                           561  B    min. end.
22  Ostfriesisches Milchschaf                      572  D*   normal
23  British Milksheep                              438  GB   normal
24  Friese Melkschaap                              493  NL   normal
```

```
 1 - Rauhwolliges Pommersches Landschaf                        EN  595
 2   Pomeranian Coarsewool; Mecklenburg-Vorpommern
 3   Institut für Schafwirtschaft                              HB: Yes
 4   Klockow 17291, Kreis Prenzlau
 5 - Composite of Zaupelschaf, Skudde, local coarse wool breeds
 7   Numbers 1986: 13/208; HB: miss; increasing; 100 %; Ne = 27
 8 - Height: 75/70 cm; Weight: 65/50 kg; Herd number: 15; AI: miss
 9   Colour: Uni grey, blue
10   Pecularity: horns 0/0; black head and black legs
11 - Main use: (1) vegetation management,(2) wool,(3) hobby
12   Spec. abilities: 40 % twinning, foot rot resistance
13   Performance compared with STB German Grey Heath 501:
14      higher: muscularity, daily gain, carcass leanness, wool yield
15      equal:  litter size,age of sexual maturity,length of mating season
16      lower:  miss
17 - Management:stationary;housing:≈2 m.;poor pastures:sandy+boggy soils
18 - Conservation progr.: live animals: Yes;Semen: miss;Embryos: miss
19   Status: critically endang.;Watch: ♂♂,HB♀♀,herds!
```

20 - Similar breeds (see group 2/3 on page 88)	EN	Country	Status
21 Olkuska	571	PL	crit.end.
22 Hvidhovedet Marsk	510	DK	min. end.
23 Pomorska	586	PL	normal
24 Kamieniecka	517	PL	normal

```
 1 - Rhönschaf                                                  EN  597
 2   Rhoen; Rhoen Highlands in Bayern, Hessen and Thüringen
 3   Vereinigung Deutscher Landesschafzuchtverbände e.V.       HB:1890
 4   Bonn 53175, Godesberger Allee 142-148
 5 - Autochthon local breed of hilly areas (Rhön, Thüringen, Harz)
 7   Numbers 1990: 65/13500; HB: 1665; increasing; 90 %; Ne = 250
 8 - Height: 82/75 cm; Weight: 90/65 kg; Herd number: 15; AI: miss
 9   Colour: White body and legs, black head
10   Pecularity: horns 0/0, long distance walker
11 - Main use: (1) meat,(2) wool,(3) vegetation management
12   Spec. abilities: rainy climate in mountain-region
13   Performance compared with STB Scottish Blackface:
14      higher: fiber yield, fiber thickness
15      equal:  carcass leanness, litter size, milk yield
16      lower:  muscularity, daily gain, age of sexual maturity
17 - Management: transhumant; housing: ≈ 2 m.; hilly country
18 - Conservation progr.: live animals: Yes;Semen: miss;Embryos: miss
19   Status: normal;              Watch: HB♀♀,herds!
```

20 - Similar breeds (see group 6/3 on page 90)	EN	Country	Status
21 Dansk Landfar	477	DK	crit.end.
22 Coburger Fuchsschaf	466	D	crit.end.
23 Foroyskur Seydur	491	FR	normal
24 Gronlandsk Fär	504	DK	normal

```
 1 - Schwarzköpfiges Fleischschaf                              EN   623
 2   German Blackheaded Mutton; Mecklenburg-Vorpommern
 3   Landesschafzuchtverband Mecklenburg-Vorpommern e.V.        HB:1920
 4   Rostock 18069, Krischanweg 21
 5 - Composite of local breeds,Oxfordshire,Hampshire 507,Suffolk 642 GB
 6   Incrossing since 1960 from Suffolk 642 GB
 7   Numbers 1986: miss /4000; HB: 3100; miss; 60 %; Ne = 561
 8 - Height: 77/73 cm; Weight: 120/75 kg; Herd number: 15; AI: miss
 9   Colour: Uni white
10   Pecularity: horns 0/0; black head and legs
11 - Main use: (1) meat,(2) wool,(3) vegetation management
12   Spec. abilities: meat quality, 40 % twinning
13   Performance compared with STB Suffolk 640:
14     higher: litter size, wool or fiber yield, wool or fiber thickness
15     equal: muscularity,daily gain,carcass leanness,age of sexual mat.
16     lower: miss
17 - Management: stationary; housing: 2-6 m.;low land
18 - Conservation progr.: live animals: Yes;Semen: miss;Embryos: miss
19   Status: endangered;        Watch: ♂♂,trend,%pure,%incross!
```

20 -	<u>Similar breeds</u> (see group 4/3 on page 89)	<u>EN</u>	<u>Country</u>	<u>Status</u>
21	Schwarzköpfiges Fleischschaf	622	D	normal
22	Braunköpfiges Fleischschaf	432	CH	normal
23	Oxford Down	575	GB	normal

```
 1 - Schwarzköpfiges Fleischschaf                              EN   622
 2   German Blackheaded Mutton; northern and western Germany, Hessen
 3   Vereinigung Deutscher Landesschafzuchtverbände e.V.        HB:1922
 4   Bonn 53175, Godesberger Allee 142-148
 5 - Composite of local breeds, German Oxford and Hampshire
 6 - Imported as breed from United Kingdom
 7   Numbers 1986: 6500/325000; HB: 16000; increasing; 95 %; Ne = 18489
 8 - Height: 85/77 cm; Weight: 120/75 kg; Herd number: miss; AI: Yes
 9   Colour: White body, black head and legs
10   Pecularity: horns 0/0
11 - Main use: (1) meat,(2) wool,(3) vegetation management
12   Spec. abilities: long mating season
13   Performance compared with STB German Merino 550:
14     higher: carcass leanness, fiber thickness
15     equal: muscularity, daily gain, litter size, milk yield
16     lower: age of sexual maturity
17 - Management: stationary/tending; housing: 2-6 m.; rainy country
18 - Conservation progr.: live animals: miss;Semen: miss;Embryos: miss
19   Status: normal
```

20 -	<u>Similar breeds</u> (see group 4/3 on page 89)	<u>EN</u>	<u>Country</u>	<u>Status</u>
21	Schwarzköpfiges Fleischschaf	623	D*	endanger.
22	Braunköpfiges Fleischschaf	432	CH	normal
23	Oxford Down	575	GB	normal

```
 1 - Suffolk                                                 EN   640
 2   Suffolk; western Germany / Hessen
 3   Hessischer Schafzuchtverband e.V.                       HB:1973
 4   Kassel 34117, Kölnische Str.48-50
 5 - Imported as breed from USA and France
 6   Incrossing since 1960 from Suffolk USA, Suffolk France
 7   Numbers 1986: 40/3000; HB: 700; increasing; 100 %; Ne = 151
 8 - Height: 85/75 cm; Weight: 120/85 kg; Herd number: 12; AI: miss
 9   Colour: Combination grey, white; black head, black legs
10   Pecularity: horns 0/0
11 - Main use: (1) meat,(2) wool,(3) sire line
12   Spec. abilities: miss
13   Performance compared with STB German Merino 550:
14      higher: daily gain,muscularity,lambing interval,carcass leanness
15      equal:  milk yield, age of sexual maturity, length of mat. season
16      lower:  miss
17 - Management: stationary; housing: 2-6 m.;
18 - Conservation progr.: live animals: miss;Semen: 10;Embryos: miss
19   Status: normal;              Watch: herds,%incross!
20 - Similar breeds (see group 4/2 on page 89)      EN  Country Status
21   Norfolk Horn                                   565   GB    min. end.
22   Suffolk                                        639   F     normal
23   Suffolk sheep                                  642   GB    normal
24   Suffolk                                        641   IRL   normal
```

```
 1 - Texel                                                   EN   650
 2   Texel; northern former FRG
 3   Vereinigung Deutscher Landesschafzuchtverbände e.V.     HB:1962
 4   Bonn 53175, Godesberger Allee 142-148
 5 - Imported as breed from Netherlands and France
 7   Numbers 1986: 2500/130000; HB: 8000; increasing; 90 %; Ne = 7619
 8 - Height: 80/75 cm; Weight: 120/80 kg; Herd number: miss; AI: miss
 9   Colour: Uni white
10   Pecularity: horns 0/0, dark nostrils
11 - Main use: (1) meat,(2) wool,(3) miss
12   Spec. abilities: best carcass quality, seasonal breeding
13   Performance compared with STB Texel 650:
14      higher: Breed is used
15      equal:  as standard breed,
16      lower:  no comparison possible.
17 - Management: stationary; housing: 2-6 m.;
18 - Conservation progr.: live animals: miss;Semen: miss;Embryos: miss
19   Status: normal
20 - Similar breeds (see group 2/2 on page 88)      EN  Country Status
21   Texel                                          648   SF    pot. end.
22   Texel                                          649   F     normal
23   Texel                                          652   L     normal
24   Texel                                          651   IRL   normal
```

```
 1 - Vierhornschaf                                               EN   662
 2   Jacob Sheep; Rheinland, Niederrhein
 3   Jacob Sheep Society - United Kingdom, Registered Office:     HB:miss
 4   The Pines, Hants BH24 2SB, Ringwood Road 242
 5 - Imported as breed from United Kingdom; incrossing since
 6   1960 from Jacob sheep of United Kingdom and Netherlands
 7   Numbers 1986: 5/20; HB: miss; increasing; 100 %; Ne = 7
 8 - Height: 85/70 cm; Weight: 60/50 kg; Herd number: 1; AI: miss
 9   Colour: Combination of black, grey, brown, white
10   Pecularity: horns 4,2/4,2 various numbers of horns, robust
11 - Main use: (1) hobby,(2) wool,(3) meat
12   Spec. abilities: twinning
13   Performance compared with STB German Merino 550:
14     higher: age of sexual maturity, carcass leanness, litter size
15     equal:  length of mating season, fiber thickness
16     lower:  muscularity, daily gain, fiber yield
17 - Management: stationary; housing: ≈ 2 m.; extensive agriculture
18 - Conservation progr.: live animals: miss;Semen: miss;Embryos: miss
19   Status: critically endang.;Watch: ♂♂,HB♀♀,herds,%incross!
```

20 - Similar breeds (see group 6/4 on page 91)	EN	Country	Status
21 Manx Loaghtan	539	GB	min. end.
22 Castlemilk Moorit Sheep	446	GB	pot. end.
23 Soay	631	GB	normal
24 Hebridean	508	GB	normal

```
 1 - Waldschaf, Bayernwaldschaf                                  EN   665
 2   Bavarian Forest; Bayrischer Wald, Niederbayern, partly Oberbayern
 3   AG zur Erhaltung von Waldschaf und Steinschaf               HB:1988
 4   Tierzuchtamt, Pfaffenhofen 74397
 5 - Composite of Zaupelschaf, Bergschaf, Merinolandschaf
 6   Incrossing since 1960 from Böhmerwaldschaf CSFR
 7   Numbers 1993: 12/250; HB: 177; increasing; 90 %; Ne = 24
 8 - Height: 70/62 cm; Weight: 65/47 kg; Herd number: 15; AI: miss
 9   Colour: Uni white
10   Pecularity: horns 0/0
11 - Main use: (1) meat,(2) wool,(3) vegetation management
12   Spec. abilities: miss
13   Performance compared with STB German Merino 550:
14     higher: fiber thickness, carcass leanness
15     equal:  milk yield
16     lower:  muscularity,daily gain,litter size,age of sexual maturity
17 - Management: stationary; housing: 2-6 m.;
18 - Conservation progr.: live animals: Yes;Semen: 4;Embryos: miss
19   Status: critically endang.;Watch: ♂♂,HB♀♀,herds,%pure,%incross!
```

20 - Similar breeds (see group 7/4 on page 92)	EN	Country	Status
21 Cikta	462	H	endanger.
22 Bündner Oberländerschaf	441	CH	min. end.
23 Schwarzbraunes Bergschaf	621	CH	normal

```
 1 - Weiße gehörnte Heidschnucke                           EN  667
 2   White Horned Heath; Region of Weser-Ems / Niedersachsen
 3   Landes-Schafzuchtverband Weser-Ems e.V.                HB:1936
 4   Oldenburg 26121, Mars-La-Tour-Str.13, P.B. 2549
 5 - Autochthon Heidschnucke (grey and white)
 7   Numbers 1992: 25/450; HB: 100; stable; 80 %; Ne = 61
 8 - Height: 53/55 cm; Weight: 73/45 kg; Herd number: 20; AI: miss
 9   Colour: Uni white
10   Pecularity: horns 2/2, winding
11 - Main use: (1) vegetation management,(2) meat,(3) wool
12   Spec. abilities: miss
13   Performance compared with STB German Merino 550:
14      higher: lambing interval, fiber thickness, carcass leanness
15      equal:  miss
16      lower:  muscularity,daily gain,litter size,length of mating season
17 - Management: tending; housing: 2-6 m.; swamp and heath land
18 - Conservation progr.: live animals: Yes;Semen: 1;Embryos: miss
19   Status: minimally endang.; Watch: HB♀♀,%pure!
20 - Similar breeds (see group 6/1 on page 90)    EN  Country Status
21   Weiße hornlose Heidschnucke                  668   D    pot. end.
22   Graue gehörnte Heidschnucke                  501   D    normal
```

```
 1 - Weiße hornlose Heidschnucke, Moorschnucke              EN  668
 2   White Polled Heath; Niedersachsen
 3   Landesschafzuchtverband Niedersachsen e.V.             HB:1920
 4   Hannover 30159, Johannssenstr.10
 5 - Autochthon Heidschnucke - Varieties
 6   Incrossing since 1960 from w. gehörnte Heidschnucke 667 Germany
 7   Numbers 1992: 61/1110; HB: miss; decreasing; 100 %; Ne = 231
 8 - Height: 55/50 cm; Weight: 70/42 kg; Herd number: miss; AI: Yes
 9   Colour: Uni white
10   Pecularity: horns 0/0
11 - Main use: (1) vegetation management,(2) meat,(3) wool
12   Spec. abilities: seasonal, mainly single birth
13   Performance compared with STB German Merino 550:
14      higher: lambing interval, fiber thickness, carcass leanness
15      equal:  age of sexual maturity
16      lower:  daily gain, muscularity, litter size, wool yield
17 - Management: stationary; housing: ≈ 2 m.; moorland, heather land
18 - Conservation progr.: live animals: Yes;Semen: miss;Embryos: miss
19   Status: potential. endang.;Watch: trend,%incross!
20 - Similar breeds (see group 6/1 on page 90)    EN  Country Status
21   Weiße gehörnte Heidschnucke                  667   D    min. end.
22   Graue gehörnte Heidschnucke                  501   D    normal
```

```
 1 - Weißes Bergschaf                                              EN   416
 2   White Mountain; Bavarian Alps and Prealps
 3   Bayerische Herdbuchgesellschaft für Schafzucht              HB:1938
 4   München 80336, Haydnstr.11
 5 - Composite of Zaupelschaf and Steinschaf
 6   Incrossing since 1960 from Italian and Austrian Bergschaf
 7   Numbers 1987: 55/28000; HB: 900; increasing; 95 %; Ne = 207
 8 - Height: 82/72 cm; Weight: 105/75 kg; Herd number: miss; AI: miss
 9   Colour: Uni white
10   Pecularity: horns 0/0
11 - Main use: (1) meat,(2) vegetation management,(3) living cell therapy
12   Spec. abilities: high fertility, aseasonal breeding
13   Performance compared with STB German Merino 550:
14     higher: wool or fiber thickness, litter size, milk yield
15     equal:  carcass leanness
16     lower:  age of sexual maturity, muscularity,daily gain
17 - Management: stationary; housing: 2-6 m.; mountainous country
18 - Conservation progr.: live animals: Yes;Semen: miss;Embryos: miss
19   Status: normal
```

20 - Similar breeds (see group 7/2 on page 91)	EN	Country	Status
21 Braunes Bergschaf	431	D	crit.end.
22 Istriana	516	I	crit.end.
23 Fabrianese	487	I	normal
24 Bergamasca	415	I	normal

```
 1 - Weißköpfiges Fleischschaf                                    EN   670
 2   German Whiteheaded Mutton; northwestern Germany
 3   Landesverband Schleswig-Holsteinischer Schafzüchter e.V.    HB:1885
 4   Kiel 24106, Steenbeker Weg 151
 5 - Autochthon Marschschaf; incrossing since 1960 from
 6   Berrichon du Cher 418 France, some imports from United Kingdom
 7   Numbers 1986: 800/98000; HB: 2800; decreasing; 15 %; Ne = 2489
 8 - Height: miss/miss cm; Weight: 125/80 kg; Herd number: miss; AI: miss
 9   Colour: Uni white
10   Pecularity: horns 0/0
11 - Main use: (1) meat,(2) wool,(3) vegetation management
12   Spec. abilities: carcass quality, twinning
13   Performance compared with STB Texel 650:
14     higher: daily gain, length of mating season, wool yield
15     equal:  litter size, age of sexual maturity, lambing interval
16     lower:  muscularity
17 - Management: stationary; housing: ≈ 2 m.;
18 - Conservation progr.: live animals: miss;Semen: miss;Embryos: miss
19   Status: normal;            Watch: trend,%pure,%incross!
```

20 - Similar breeds (see group 3 on page 88)	EN	Country	Status
21 Mouton Boulonnais	559	F	crit.end.
22 Galway	495	IRL	endanger.
23 Mouton Charollais	560	F	normal
24 Cotentin	473	F	normal

1 - Bunte Deutsche Edelziege, Alpen-Ziege   EN   310
2   German Improved Fawn; country-wide
3   Arbeitsgemeinschaft Deutscher Ziegenzüchter   HB:1928
4   Stuttgart 70190, Heinrich-Baumann-Str. 1-3
5 - Composite of Rehfarbene Schwarzwaldziege, Frankenziege 334 CS,
6   332 CH, Sächsische Ziege; incrossing since 1960 from Brown Fawn
7   Numbers 1986: 1000/30000; HB: 5000; increasing; 95 %; Ne = 3333
8 - Height: 85/75 cm; Weight: 75/65 kg; Herd number: miss; AI: miss
9   Colour: Uni brown, black back stripe, light or dark brown belly
10 Pecularity: horns 2,0/2,0
11 - Main use: (1) milk,(2) meat,(3) hobby
12 Spec. abilities: hard hoofs, adapted to hot clima
13 Performance compared with STB German Improved White 367:
14   higher: miss
15   equal: miss
16   lower: miss
17 - Management: stationary; housing: > 6 m.; hilly and dry country
18 - Conservation progr.: live animals: miss;Semen: 10;Embryos: miss
19 Status: normal

20 - Similar breeds (see group 2 on page 97)	EN	Country	Status
21 Erzgebirgsziege	330	D	crit.end.
22 Hneda kratkosrsta	334	CS	min. end.
23 Camosciata delle Alpi	314	I	normal
24 Alpine	301	F	normal

1 - Burenziege   EN   311
2   Boer; western Germany (former FRG)
3   Arbeitsgemeinschaft Deutscher Ziegenzüchter   HB:1980
4   Stuttgart 70190, Heinrich-Baumann-Str. 1-3
5 - Imported as breed from Namibia, South Africa
6   Incrossing since 1960 from Boer Namibia, Boer South Africa
7   Numbers 1986: 200/3000; HB: 1500; increasing; 95 %; Ne = 706
8 - Height:miss/miss cm; Weight:miss/miss kg; Herd number:miss; AI:miss
9   Colour: Uni white, some combination of red and white
10 Pecularity: horns 2/2, some red spots on chest and head
11 - Main use: (1) meat,(2) vegetation management,(3) miss
12 Spec. abilities: hardy, aseasonality, 1.8 lambs
13 Performance compared with STB German Improved White 367:
14   higher: muscular.,daily gain,carc. leanness,length of mating seas.
15   equal: litter size
16   lower: age of sexual maturity
17 - Management: stationary; housing: 2-6 m.; semi desert, hot climate
18 - Conservation progr.: live animals: miss;Semen: miss;Embryos: miss
19 Status: normal

20 - Similar breeds	EN	Country	Status
21 miss	miss	miss	miss

```
 1 - Erzgebirgsziege                                              EN   330
 2   Erzgebirg Goat; Sachsen, mainly higher Erzgebirge / Vogtland
 3   Sächsischer Schaf- und Ziegenzuchtverband e. V.             HB:1936
 4   Markkleeberg 04416, Bornaische Str.31-33
 5 - Autochthon
 7   Numbers 1986: 12/650; HB: 38; miss; 100 %; Ne = 18
 8 - Height: miss/miss cm; Weight: 73/53 kg; Herd number: miss; AI: miss
 9   Colour: Combination red, brown
10   Pecularity: horns 0/0, black face and back stripe, black legs
11 - Main use: (1) milk,(2) miss,(3) miss
12   Spec. abilities: dietary value of milk
13   Performance compared with STB German Improved Fawn 310:
14     higher: % fat
15     equal: carcass leanness, litter size, age of sexual maturity
16     lower: muscularity, daily gain, milk yield
17 - Management: stationary; housing: 2-6 m.;
18 - Conservation progr.: live animals: miss;Semen: miss;Embryos: miss
19   Status: critically endang.;Watch: ♂♂,HB♀♀,trend,herds!
20 - Similar breeds (see group 2 on page 97)     EN  Country Status
21   Hneda kratkosrsta                          334  CS   min. end.
22   Chamoisee                                  317  B    pot. end.
23   Bunte Deutsche Edelziege                   310  D    normal
24   Alpine                                     301  F    normal
```

```
 1 - Thüringer Waldziege                                          EN   360
 2   Thuringian Forest; Thüringen
 3   Thüringerwald-Ziegenzucht-Verein e.V.                       HB:1935
 4   Burglemnitz 07356
 5 - Composite of Toggenburger-, Harzer-, Rhönziege, Thüringer Landziege
 6   Incrossing since 1960 from Toggenburger 362 Switzerland
 7   Numbers 1993: 10/150; HB: 80; stable; 90 %; Ne = 18
 8 - Height: 78/74 cm; Weight: 55/48 kg; Herd number: 3; AI: miss
 9   Colour: Uni brown, white flecks on head and legs, light face
10   Pecularity: horns 2,0/2,0
11 - Main use: (1) milk,(2) meat,(3) vegetation management
12   Spec. abilities: dietary value of milk, good legs
13   Performance compared with STB German Improved Fawn 310:
14     higher: litter size (2.2), longevity
15     equal: muscularity, carcass leanness, milk yield, % fat
16     lower: daily gain
17 - Management: stationary; housing: 2-6 m.; hilly country
18 - Conservation progr.: live animals: miss;Semen: miss;Embryos: miss
19   Status: critically endang.;Watch: ♂♂,HB♀♀,herds,%incross,%pure!
20 - Similar breeds (see group 3 on page 97)     EN  Country Status
21   Toggenburger                               361  B    endanger.
22   Poitevin                                   345  F    min. end.
23   Pure Toggenburg                            346  GB   normal
24   Toggenburger                               362  CH   normal
```

GERMANY   GOATS

```
 1 - Weiße Deutsche Edelziege, Saanenziege              EN   367
 2   German Improved White; country-wide
 3   Landesverband Bayerischer Ziegenzüchter            HB:1927
 4   München 80336, Haydnstr.8
 5 - Composite of local white breeds and Saanen 349 Switzerland
 6   Incrossing since 1960 from Saanen 349 Switzerland
 7   Numbers 1986: 700/15000; HB: 3000; increasing; 95 %; Ne = 2270
 8 - Height: 85/75 cm; Weight: 75/65 kg; Herd number: miss; AI: miss
 9   Colour: Uni white
10   Pecularity: horns 2,0/2,0, good udder, hard hoofs
11 - Main use: (1) milk,(2) meat,(3) hobby
12   Spec. abilities: diet. value of milk,saisonality,1.8 lambs,longevity
13   Performance compared with STB German Improved Fawn 310:
14     higher: muscularity, daily gain, carcass leanness, milk yield
15     equal: litter size, % protein, age of sexual maturity
16     lower: % fat
17 - Management: stationary; housing: > 6 m.;
18 - Conservation progr.: live animals: Yes;Semen: 5;Embryos: miss
19   Status: normal
20 - Similar breeds (see group 1 on page 97)     EN  Country Status
21   Irish Goat                                  336  IRL   min. end.
22   Blanche                                     308  B     pot. end.
23   Gessenay                                    350  F     normal
24   Bila kratkosrsta                            306  CS    normal
```

GERMANY   PIGS

```
 1 - Angler Sattelschwein                                EN   903
 2   Angeln Saddleback; Schleswig-Holstein
 3   Schweineherdbuchzucht Schleswig-Holstein e.V.       HB:1937
 4   Neumünster 24537, Rendsburgerstr. 178
 5 - Composite of Landraces and Wessex Saddleback; incrossing since 1970
 6   from Hampshire 945 GB, Saddleback H, Deutsches Sattelschwein 924 D
 7   Numbers 1993: 9/281; HB: 73; increasing; 30 %; Ne = 26
 8 - Height: 90/85 cm; Weight: 350/300 kg; Herd number: 11; AI: Yes
 9   Colour: Combination black and white
10   Pecularity: white saddle
11 - Main use: (1) meat,(2) hobby,(3) dam line
12   Spec. abilities: adapted to outdoor management systems
13   Performance compared with STB German Landrace/universal 920:
14     higher: feed conversion rate,meat quality,litter size,daily gain
15     equal: age of sexual maturity, handling ease
16     lower: % lean, piglet mortality, muscularity, farrowing interval
17 - Management: stationary; housing: 12 m.;
18 - Conservation progr.: live animals: Yes;Semen: miss;Embryos: miss
19   Status: critically endang.;Watch: ♂♂,HB♀♀,%pure,%incross,herds!
20 - Similar breeds (see group 3/1 on page 102)  EN  Country Status
21   Pie noir du Pays Basque                     987  F     crit.end.
22   Cinta Senese                                914  I     crit.end.
23   British Saddleback                          912  GB    pot. end.
24   Schwäbisch-Hällisches Schwein               997  D     pot. end.
```

1 - Belgische Landrasse   EN   907
2   Belgian Landrace; Brandenburg
3   WTZ Schweinezucht und Schweineproduktion   HB:1972
4   Ruhlsdorf 16348, Dorfstr.1
5 - Imported as breed from Belgium, Germany, CSFR
7   Numbers 1986: 22/123; HB: miss; stable; miss %; Ne = 53
8 - Height: 95/87 cm; Weight: 290/220 kg; Herd number: 2; AI: Yes
9   Colour: Uni white
10 Pecularity: lop ears
11 - Main use: (1) sire line,(2) meat,(3) miss
12 Spec. abilities: lean carcass
13 Performance compared with STB Belgian Landrace 907:
14   higher: Breed is used
15   equal: as standard breed,
16   lower: no comparison possible.
17 - Management: stationary; housing: > 6 m.;
18 - Conservation progr.: live animals: Yes;Semen: 2;Embryos: miss
19 Status: critically endang.;Watch: HB♀♀,herds,%pure!
20 - <u>Similar breeds</u> (see group 2/1 on page 101)   <u>EN</u> <u>Country</u> <u>Status</u>
21 Zlotnicka biala   1024   PL   crit.end.
22 Landrace Belga   956   I   endanger.
23 Landrace   952   CS   normal
24 Belgisch Landvarken   906   B   normal

1 - Deutsche Landrasse   EN   918
2   German Landrace
3   WTZ Schweinezucht und Schweineproduktion   HB:1954
4   Ruhlsdorf 16348, Dorfstr. 1
5 - Composite of Landrace from D, NL, YU, S, PL, DK
6   Incrossing since 1970 from Landrace 980 Netherlands, 983 Norway
7   Numbers 1986: 509/ miss; HB: 4704; stable; miss %; Ne = 1837
8 - Height: 98/88 cm; Weight: 290/230 kg; Herd number: miss; AI: Yes
9   Colour: Uni white
10 Pecularity: lop ears
11 - Main use: (1) dam line,(2) meat,(3) miss
12 Spec. abilities: 90 % halothane - negative
13 Performance compared with STB Large White 922:
14   higher: litter size, piglet mortality
15   equal: % lean, muscularity, live weight at slaughter
16   lower: feed conversion rate, daily gain
17 - Management: stationary; housing: 12 m.;
18 - Conservation progr.: live animals: miss;Semen: 16;Embryos: miss
19 Status: normal;   Watch: %pure!
20 - <u>Similar breeds</u> (see group 2/1 on page 101)   <u>EN</u> <u>Country</u> <u>Status</u>
21 Belgische Landrasse   907   D*   crit.end.
22 Zlotnicka biala   1024   PL   crit.end.
23 Landrace   952   CS   normal
24 Belgisch Landvarken   906   B   normal

1 - Deutsche Landrasse B   EN 919
2   Belgian Landrace; 10 regions
3   Zentralverband der Deutschen Schweineproduktion   HB:1971
4   Bonn 53113, Adenauerallee 174
5 - Imported as breed from Belgium
6   Incrossing since 1970 from Pietrain of several countries
7   Numbers 1990: 70/ miss; HB: 785; decreasing; miss %; Ne = 257
8 - Height: 82/79 cm; Weight: 290/270 kg; Herd number: miss; AI: Yes
9   Colour: Uni white
10 Pecularity: highly stress susceptible in warm climate
11 - Main use: (1) meat,(2) miss,(3) miss
12 Spec. abilities: high lean content+muscular type, high PSE-frequency
13 Performance compared with STB German Landrace/universal 920:
14   higher: piglet mortality, muscularity, % lean
15   equal: feed conversion rate, age of sexual maturity
16   lower: litter size, meat quality, daily gain
17 - Management: stationary; housing: 12 m.;
18 - Conservation progr.: live animals: miss;Semen: miss;Embryos: miss
19 Status: potential. endang.;Watch: %pure,%incross,trend!

20 - Similar breeds (see group 2/1 on page 101)	EN	Country	Status
21 Belgische Landrasse	907	D*	crit.end.
22 Zlotnicka biala	1024	PL	crit.end.
23 Landrace	952	CS	normal
24 Belgisch Landvarken	906	B	normal

1 - Deutsche Landrasse/Sauenlinie   EN 921
2   German Landrace/dam line; 13 regions
3   Zentralverband der Deutschen Schweineproduktion   HB:1985
4   Bonn 53113, Adenauerallee 174
5 - Composite of German Landrace DL(U) 920, Swiss Edelschwein 1007,
6   Large White from DK, S, 984 N, 1021 SF and incrossing of Large White
7   Numbers 1990: 969/ miss; HB: 14308; increasing; 100 %; Ne = 3630
8 - Height: 85/80 cm; Weight: 275/250 kg; Herd number: miss; AI: Yes
9   Colour: Uni white
10 Pecularity: low frequency of Halothane stress gene, lop ears
11 - Main use: (1) meat,(2) miss,(3) miss
12 Spec. abilities: good meat quality (little PSE)
13 Performance compared with STB German Landrace/universal 920:
14   higher: litter size, meat quality
15   equal: feed conversion rate, age of sexual maturity
16   lower: % lean, daily gain, muscularity
17 - Management: stationary; housing: > 6 m.;
18 - Conservation progr.: live animals: miss;Semen: Yes;Embryos: miss
19 Status: normal

20 - Similar breeds (see group 2/1 on page 101)	EN	Country	Status
21 Belgische Landrasse	907	D*	crit.end.
22 Zlotnicka biala	1024	PL	crit.end.
23 Landrace	952	CS	normal
24 Belgisch Landvarken	906	B	normal

1 - Deutsche Landrasse/Universal   EN   920
2   German Landrace/universal; 3 regions
3   Zentralverband der Deutschen Schweineproduktion   HB:1904
4   Bonn 53113, Adenauerallee 174
5 - Composite of Dt.veredelt.Landschw.(DVL)+Nederl.Landvorken NL;imports
6   from NL; incrossing since 1970 from Belgian Landrace 919 Germany
7   Numbers 1990: 115/ miss; HB: 1777; decreasing; 100 %; Ne = 432
8 - Height: 85/80 cm; Weight: 275/250 kg; Herd number: miss; AI: Yes
9   Colour: Uni white
10 Pecularity: lop ears
11 - Main use: (1) meat,(2) miss,(3) miss
12 Spec. abilities: high lean content; PSE is common
13 Performance compared with STB German Landrace/universal 920:
14   higher: Breed is used
15   equal: as standard breed,
16   lower: no comparison possible.
17 - Management: stationary; housing: > 6 m.;
18 - Conservation progr.: live animals: miss;Semen: Yes;Embryos: miss
19 Status: normal;   Watch: %incross,trend!
20 - Similar breeds (see group 2/1 on page 101)   EN Country Status
21 Belgische Landrasse   907 D*   crit.end.
22 Zlotnicka biala   1024 PL   crit.end.
23 Landrace   952 CS   normal
24 Belgisch Landvarken   906 B   normal

1 - Deutsches Edelschwein   EN   922
2   Large White; Mecklenburg, Thüringen, Sachsen-Anhalt
3   WTZ Schweinezucht und Schweineproduktion   HB:1954
4   Ruhlsdorf 16348, Dorfstr. 1
5 - Composite of Large White type 923 from Germany, 951 USSR, Hungary
6   Incrossing since 1970 from Latvian White 964 Latvia
7   Numbers 1986: 351/4330; HB: miss; stable; miss %; Ne = 1299
8 - Height: 102/92 cm; Weight: 300/240 kg; Herd number: miss; AI: Yes
9   Colour: Uni white
10 Pecularity: erect ears
11 - Main use: (1) dam line,(2) meat,(3) miss
12 Spec. abilities: halothane negative
13 Performance compared with STB Belgian Landrace 907:
14   higher: daily gain, vitality
15   equal: % lean, muscularity, live weight at slaughter
16   lower: litter size, feed conversion rate, piglet mortality
17 - Management: stationary; housing: 12 m.;
18 - Conservation progr.: live animals: miss;Semen: 7;Embryos: miss
19 Status: normal;   Watch: HB♀♀,%pure,%incross!
20 - Similar breeds (see group 1/2 on page 101)   EN Country Status
21 Bela Zlahtna   904 SLO   crit.end.
22 Middle White   975 GB   min. end.
23 Deutsches Edelschwein   923 D   normal
24 Vile uslechtile   1017 CS   normal

1 - Deutsches Edelschwein   EN 923
2   Large White; 12 regions, mainly in Ammerland
3   Zentralverband der Deutschen Schweineproduktion   HB:1904
4   Bonn 53113, Adenauerallee 174
5 - Composite of Landraces, Large White, Middle White United Kingdom
6   Incrossing since 1970 from Groote Yorkshire 939 Netherlands
7   Numbers 1990: 483/ miss; HB: 2733; increasing; miss %; Ne = 1642
8 - Height: 85/80 cm; Weight: 320/280 kg; Herd number: miss; AI: Yes
9   Colour: Uni white
10 Pecularity: erect ears
11 - Main use: (1) meat,(2) dam line for crossbreeding,(3) miss
12 Spec. abilities: free of Halothane stress gene
13 Performance compared with STB German Landrace/universal 920:
14   higher: meat quality, litter size, daily gain
15   equal: handling ease, piglet mortality, live weight at slaughter
16   lower: % lean, feed conversion rate, age of sexual
17 - Management: stationary; housing: > 6 m.;
18 - Conservation progr.: live animals: miss;Semen: Yes;Embryos: miss
19 Status: normal;   Watch: %incross!
20 - <u>Similar breeds</u> (see group 1/2 on page 101)   EN Country Status
21 Bela Zlahtna   904   SLO   crit.end.
22 Middle White   975   GB   min. end.
23 Deutsches Edelschwein   922   D*   normal
24 Vile uslechtile   1017 CS   normal

1 - Deutsches Sattelschwein   EN 924
2   German Saddleback;Sachsen, Thüringen, Brandenburg, Meckl.-Vorpommern
3   WTZ Schweinezucht und Schweineproduktion   HB:1970
4   Ruhlsdorf 16348, Dorfstr.1
5 - Composite of Angler Sattelschwein 903 D, Schwäb.-Häll. Schwein 997 D
6   Incross. since 1970 from Angler Sattelschwein 903 D,Presticke 994 CZ
7   Numbers 1993: 26/292; HB: 107; stable; 40 %; Ne = 66
8 - Height: 92/86 cm; Weight: 350/300 kg; Herd number: miss; AI: Yes
9   Colour: black and white, white saddle
10 Pecularity: lop ears
11 - Main use: (1) meat,(2) miss,(3) miss
12 Spec. abilities: higher fat and intramusc. fat cont., halothane neg.
13 Performance compared with STB German Landrace/universal 920:
14   higher: meat quality, litter size, feed conversion, vitality
15   equal: age of sexual maturity, farrowing interval, handling ease
16   lower: % lean, daily gain, muscularity, live weight at slaughter
17 - Management: stationary; housing: > 6 m.; outdoor systems
18 - Conservation progr.: live animals: Yes;Semen: miss;Embryos: miss
19 Status: minimally endang.; Watch: HB♀♀,%pure,%incross,herds!
20 - <u>Similar breeds</u> (see group 3/1 on page 102)   EN Country Status
21 Pie noir du Pays Basque   987   F   crit.end.
22 Angler Sattelschwein   903   D   crit.end.
23 British Saddleback   912   GB   pot. end.
24 Schwäbisch-Hällisches Schwein   997   D   pot. end.

```
 1 - Duroc                                                       EN  928
 2   Duroc; Brandenburg, Thüringen
 3   WTZ Schweinezucht und Schweineproduktion                    HB:1974
 4   Ruhlsdorf 16348, Dorfstr. 1
 5 - Imported as breed from USA, CSFR
 6   Incrossing since 1970 from Duroc USA, Duroc Semen USA (1982)
 7   Numbers 1986: 70/290; HB: miss; stable; miss %; Ne = 226
 8 - Height: 100/90 cm; Weight: 290/220 kg; Herd number: miss; AI: Yes
 9   Colour: Uni red, brown
10   Pecularity: short lop ears
11 - Main use: (1) sire line,(2) miss,(3) miss
12   Spec. abilities: Halothane - negative
13   Performance compared with STB Belgian Landrace 907:
14     higher: meat quality, piglet mortality
15     equal:  miss
16     lower:  litter size, % lean, daily gain
17 - Management: stationary; housing: 12 m.;
18 - Conservation progr.: live animals: miss;Semen: 4;Embryos: miss
19   Status: potential. endang.;Watch: HB♀♀,%pure!
20 - Similar breeds (see group 5/1 on page 103)   EN  Country Status
21   Duroc                                        927  F       crit.end.
22   Duroc                                        932  GB      crit.end.
23   Duroc                                        929  I       normal
24   Duroc                                        926  CS      normal
```

```
 1 - Hampshire                                                   EN  942
 2   Hampshire; Thüringen
 3   WTZ Schweinezucht und Schweineproduktion                    HB:1974
 4   Ruhlsdorf 16348, Dorfstr. 1
 5 - Imported as breed from USA, CSFR
 6   Incrossing since 1970 from Hampshire USA
 7   Numbers 1986: 4/25; HB: miss; decreasing; miss %; Ne = 6
 8 - Height: 97/85 cm; Weight: 260/200 kg; Herd number: 1; AI: miss
 9   Colour: black, white saddle
10   Pecularity: erect ears, white forelegs
11 - Main use: (1) sire line,(2) miss,(3) miss
12   Spec. abilities: miss
13   Performance compared with STB Belgian Landrace 907:
14     higher: muscularity, meat quality, piglet mortality
15     equal:  % lean
16     lower:  litter size, feed conversion rate, daily gain
17 - Management: stationary; housing: > 6 m.;
18 - Conservation progr.: live animals: Yes;Semen: 1;Embryos: miss
19   Status: critically endang.;Watch: ♂♂,HB♀♀,trend,herds!
20 - Similar breeds (see group 3/2 on page 102)   EN  Country Status
21   Limousin                                     967  F       crit.end.
22   Hampshire                                    943  I       crit.end.
23   Hampshire                                    944  RO      pot. end.
24   Hampshire                                    940  CS      normal
```

```
1 - Leicoma                                                    EN  965
2   Leicoma; Sachsen-Anhalt, Brandenburg, Sachsen
3   WTZ Schweinezucht und Schweineproduktion                  HB:1971
4   Ruhlsdorf 16348, Dorfstr. 1
5 - Composite of Landrace 920 D and 980 NL, Duroc 928, Saddleback 924,
6   Estonian Bacon 933; incrossing since 1970 from all 5 breeds
7   Numbers 1986: 324/3933; HB: miss; increasing; miss %; Ne = 1197
8 - Height: 100/90 cm; Weight: 290/220 kg; Herd number: miss; AI: Yes
9   Colour: Uni white, some pigmentation possible
10  Pecularity: lop ears
11 - Main use: (1) dam line,(2) meat,(3) miss
12  Spec. abilities: mostly halothane negative
13  Performance compared with STB Belgian Landrace 907:
14    higher: litter size, daily gain, muscularity, live weight
15    equal: % lean
16    lower:  feed conversion rate, piglet mortality
17 - Management: stationary; housing: 12 m.;
18 - Conservation progr.: live animals: miss;Semen: 6;Embryos: miss
19  Status: normal;            Watch: HB♀♀,%pure,%incross!
20 - Similar breeds (see group 8 on page 104)    EN  Country Status
21  Acadie P22                                   900  F    crit.end.
22  Jia-Xing                                     947  F    crit.end.
23  Pen Ar Lan P 77                              985  F    endanger.
24  Schwerfurter Fleischrasse                    998  D*   pot. end.
```

```
1 - Pietrain                                                   EN  991
2   Pietrain; all regions / 13 societies
3   Zentralverband der Deutschen Schweineproduktion           HB:1961
4   Bonn 53113, Adenauerallee 174
5 - Imported as breed from Belgium
6   Incrossing since 1970 from Landrasse B 919 Germany
7   Numbers 1990: 1266/ miss; HB: 10431; decreasing; miss %; Ne = 4516
8 - Height: 80/75 cm; Weight: 270/250 kg; Herd number: miss; AI: Yes
9   Colour: Combination black and white, sometimes red
10  Pecularity: spotted, high frequency of Halothane stress gene
11 - Main use: (1) meat,(2) miss,(3) miss
12  Spec. abilities: extreme lean content+muscular type,high prop. PSE
13  Performance compared with STB German Landrace/universal 920:
14    higher: piglet mortality, muscularity, % lean
15    equal:  feed conversion rate, farrowing interval, handling ease
16    lower:  daily gain,litter size,meat quality,live weight at slaugh.
17 - Management: miss; housing: miss m.;
18 - Conservation progr.: live animals: miss;Semen: Yes;Embryos: miss
19  Status: normal,            Watch: %incross!
20 - Similar breeds (see group 6/1 on page 103)  EN  Country Status
21  Pietrain                                     988  B    normal
22  Pietrain                                     989  F    normal
23  Pietrain                                     990  I    miss
```

```
1 - Schwarz-Weißes Bentheimer, Buntes Schwein                    EN   996
2   Bentheim Black Pied; Shire of Bentheim / Emsland
3   Schweinezuchtverband Weser-Ems e. G.                         HB:1987
4   Oldenburg 26123, Europaplatz 14-16
5 - Autochthon local landrace in Emsland
6   Incrossing since 1970 from Pietrain 991 Germany
7   Numbers 1992: 10/90; HB: 59; decreasing; 100 %; Ne = 17
8 - Height: 75/70 cm; Weight: 250/180 kg; Herd number: 10; AI: Yes
9   Colour: Uni black, white; combination of black and white; spotted
10  Pecularity: lop ears
11 - Main use: (1) meat,(2) miss,(3) miss
12  Spec. abilities: no additional iron supply necessary for piglets
13  Performance compared with STB German Landrace/universal 920:
14     higher: meat quality, litter size
15     equal:  handling ease
16     lower: % lean, feed conversion rate, muscularity, daily gain
17 - Management: stationary; housing: > 6 m.;
18 - Conservation progr.: live animals:  Yes;Semen: miss;Embryos: miss
19   Status: critically endang.;Watch: ♂♂,HB♀♀,trend,herds,%incross!
```

20 - Similar breeds (see group 6/2 on page 104)	EN	Country	Status
21 Sortbroget	1005	DK	crit.end.
22 Manchada de Jabugo	971	E	crit.end.
23 Sibirskaya chernopestraya	1001	USSR	pot. end.
24 Gloucestershire Old Spot	936	GB	pot. end.

```
1 - Schwäbisch-Hällisches Schwein                                EN   997
2   Swabian Hall Saddleback; Baden-Württemberg,Bayern,Rhld.-Pfalz,Hessen
3   Schweinezuchtverband Baden-Württemberg                       HB:1925
4   Stuttgart 70190, Heinrich-Baumann-Str.1-3
5 - Composite of Landraces, Old Saddlebacks (Asian Origin)
7   Numbers 1993: 35/4199; HB: 199; increasing; 9 %; Ne = 128
8 - Height: 90/80 cm; Weight: 350/280 kg; Herd number: miss; AI: Yes
9   Colour: Combination black and white, lop ears
10  Pecularity: white saddle, low frequency of Halothane stress gene
11 - Main use: (1) dam line for crossing,(2) hobby,(3) miss
12  Spec. abilities: high intramuscular fat content, meat quality
13  Performance compared with STB German Landrace/universal 920:
14     higher: meat quality, litter size, feed conversion rate
15     equal:  farrowing interval
16     lower: % lean, daily gain, age of sexual maturity
17 - Management: stationary; housing: > 6 m.; outdoor management systems
18 - Conservation progr.: live animals:  Yes;Semen: miss;Embryos: miss
19   Status: potential. endang.;Watch: HB♀♀,%pure!
```

20 - Similar breeds (see group 3/1 on page 102)	EN	Country	Status
21 Pie noir du Pays Basque	987	F	crit.end.
22 Angler Sattelschwein	903	D	crit.end.
23 Presticke	994	CZ	pot. end.
24 British Saddleback	912	GB	pot. end.

```
 1 - Schwerfurter Fleischrasse                                    EN  998
 2   Schwerfurt Meat Pig; Mecklenburg, Thüringen
 3   WTZ Schweinezucht und Schweineproduktion                     HB:1970
 4   Ruhlsdorf 16348, Dorfstr.1
 5 - Composite of Belgian Landrace, Pietrain, Lacombe
 7   Numbers 1986: 210/4147; HB: miss; decreasing; miss %; Ne = 800
 8 - Height: 98/85 cm; Weight: 290/220 kg; Herd number: miss; AI: Yes
 9   Colour: Uni white, some pigmentation possible
10   Pecularity: lop ears
11 - Main use: (1) sire line,(2) meat,(3) miss
12   Spec. abilities: miss
13   Performance compared with STB Belgian Landrace 907:
14     higher: % lean, daily gain, muscularity, piglet mortality
15     equal:  live weight at slaughter
16     lower:  litter size, feed conversion rate
17 - Management: stationary; housing: 12 m.;
18 - Conservation progr.: live animals: miss;Semen: 7;Embryos: miss
19   Status: potential. endang.;Watch: HB♀♀,trend!
20 - Similar breeds (see group 8 on page 104)     EN  Country Status
21   Acadie P22                                    900  F      crit.end.
22   Jia-Xing                                      947  F      crit.end.
23   Pen Ar Lan P 77                               985  F      endanger.
24   Leicoma                                       965  D*     normal
```

```
 1 - Altwürttemberger                                             EN  701
 2   Altwuerttemberg; Baden-Württemberg
 3   Verein zur Erhaltung des Altwürttemberger Pferdes im         HB:1907
 4   PZV B.-W., Stuttgart 70190, Heinrich-Baumann-Str.1-3
 5 - Autochthon local breed and Anglo-Norman stallions
 6   Incrossing since 1950 from Trakehner Germany
 7   Numbers 1993: 4/35; HB: miss; increasing; 100 %; Ne = 6
 8 - Height: 165/159 cm; Weight: 600/550 kg; Herd number: miss; AI: miss
 9   Colour: predominantly chestnut, bay, brown or black
10   Pecularity: often white markings on face and limbs
11 - Main use: (1) sport/hobby,(2) tractive power,(3) vegetat. management
12   Spec. abilities: reproductive up to high age
13   Performance compared with STB Halfbred:
14     higher: pulling power, fertility, daily gain
15     equal:  handling ease, age of sexual maturity
16     lower:  adaptability in jumping and military, speed in gallop
17 - Management: stationary; housing: > 6 m.;
18 - Conservation progr.: live animals: Yes;Semen: miss;Embryos: miss
19   Status: critically endang.;Watch: ♂♂,HB♀♀,herds,%incross!
20 - Similar breeds (see group 3/2 on page 108)   EN  Country Status
21   Rottaler                                      797  D      crit.end.
22   Gelders Paard                                 750  NL     crit.end.
23   Holsteiner Warmblut                           760  D      normal
24   Cheval de Selle Francais                      727  F      normal
```

```
 1 - Haflinger                                              EN   754
 2   Haflinger; Bayern
 3   Landesverband Bayerischer Pferdezüchter              HB:1895
 4   München 81929, Landshammer Str.11
 5 - Composite of Heavy Horse, OX Arab
 6   Imported as breed from country Austria
 7   Numbers 1986: 348/6682; HB: miss; stable; 100 %; Ne = 1323
 8 - Height: 160/156 cm; Weight: 500/400 kg; Herd number: miss; AI: miss
 9   Colour: light to dark chestnut
10   Pecularity: full flaxen mane and tail
11 - Main use: (1) sport/hobby,(2) tractive power,(3) meat
12   Spec. abilities: miss
13   Performance compared with STB Fjord:
14     higher: adaptability in dressage and jumping, speed in gallop
15     equal:  pulling power,handling ease,fertility,age of sexual matur.
16     lower:  miss
17 - Management: miss; housing: miss m.; mountainous country
18 - Conservation progr.: live animals: miss;Semen: miss;Embryos: miss
19   Status: normal;               Watch: HB♀♀!
20 - Similar breeds (see group 5/8 on page 111)    EN  Country Status
21   Haflinger                                     757   GB    endanger.
22   Haflinger                                     756   CH    pot. end.
23   Avelignese                                    710   I     normal
24   Haflinger                                     753   F     normal
```

```
 1 - Hannoveraner                                          EN   758
 2   Hanoverian; Niedersachsen
 3   Verband hannoverscher Warmblutzüchter e.V.           HB:1888
 4   Verden / Aller 27283, Lindhooper Str.92
 5 - Composite of autochthon breed, Thoroughbred, Trakehner; incrossing
 6   since 1950 from Thoroughbred D, GB, USA, Trakehner D, Anglo-Arab F
 7   Numbers 1986: 326/15031; HB: 11497; increasing; 90 %; Ne = 1268
 8 - Height: 165/163 cm; Weight: 600/500 kg; Herd number: miss; AI: Yes
 9   Colour: any solid colour
10   Pecularity: some white markings
11 - Main use: (1) sport/hobby,(2) tractive power,(3) miss
12   Spec. abilities: popular riding horse
13   Performance compared with STB Holstein 760:
14     higher: miss
15     equal:  pulling power, handling ease, adaptability in dressage
16     lower:  miss
17 - Management: stationary; housing: 2-6 m.;
18 - Conservation progr.: live animals: miss;Semen: 80;Embryos: miss
19   Status: normal
20 - Similar breeds (see group 3/3 on page 109)    EN  Country Status
21   Sächsisches Warmblut                          798   D     min. end.
22   Cheval de Sport Belge                         728   B     normal
```

1 - Holsteiner Warmblut EN 760
2   Holstein; Schleswig-Holstein
3   Verband der Züchter des Holsteiner Pferdes e. V. HB:1886
4   Elmshorn 25336, Westerstr. 93
5 - Autochthon Marschpferde
6   Incrossing since 1950 from Thoroughbred United Kingdom
7   Numbers 1986: 71/2643; HB: 2427; increasing; miss %; Ne = 276
8 - Height: 168/165 cm; Weight: 650/600 kg; Herd number: miss; AI: Yes
9   Colour: any solid colour
10 Pecularity: white markings
11 - Main use: (1) sport/hobby,(2) miss,(3) miss
12 Spec. abilities:
13 Performance compared with STB Thoroughbred:
14   higher: pulling power, handling ease, adaptability in dressage
15   equal: fertility, age of sexual maturity, daily gain
16   lower: speed in gallop,adaptability in military,speed in trotters
17 - Management: stationary; housing: ≈ 2 m.;
18 - Conservation progr.: live animals: miss;Semen: 4;Embryos: miss
19 Status: normal
20 - Similar breeds (see group 3/2 on page 108)   EN Country Status
21 Altwürttemberger   701 D   crit.end.
22 Rottaler   797 D   crit.end.
23 Warmbloed Paard Nederlands   816 NL   normal
24 Cheval de Selle Francais   727 F   normal

1 - Rottaler EN 797
2   Rottal; Bayern
3   Gesellschaft zur Erhaltung alter und gefährdeter HB:miss
4   Haustierrassen e.V., Witzenhausen 37215, Gelsterstr. 2
5 - Autochthon Rottaler
7   Numbers 1993: 2/20; HB: miss; decreasing; miss %; Ne = 3
8 - Height: 175/170 cm; Weight: miss/miss kg; Herd number: miss; AI: Yes
9   Colour: mainly bay with few marks, sometimes black or chestnut
10 Pecularity: miss
11 - Main use: (1) sport/hobby,(2) miss,(3) miss
12 Spec. abilities: miss
13 Performance compared with STB Holstein 760:
14   higher: handling ease, fertility, pulling power
15   equal: adaptability in dressage, adaptability in jumping
16   lower: miss
17 - Management: stationary; housing: miss m.;
18 - Conservation progr.: live animals: Yes;Semen: 2;Embryos: miss
19 Status: critically endang.;Watch: ♂♂,HB♀♀,trend,%pure,herds!
20 - Similar breeds (see group 3/2 on page 108)   EN Country Status
21 Altwürttemberger   701 D   crit.end.
22 Gelders Paard   750 NL   crit.end.
23 Holsteiner Warmblut   760 D   normal
24 Cheval de Selle Francais   727 F   normal

1 - Sächsisches Warmblut   EN 798
2   Saxony Warmblood; Thüringen, Sachsen
3   Pferdezuchtverband Sachsen e.V.   HB:1872
4   Dresden 01237, Winterbergstr.98
5 - Composite of Alt-Oldenburger / Ostfriesen
6   Incrossing since 1950 from Alt-Oldenburger Germany
7   Numbers 1990: 20/450; HB: 400; decreasing; 95 %; Ne = 55
8 - Height: 163/160 cm; Weight: 650/600 kg; Herd number: miss; AI: miss
9   Colour: any solid colour
10 Pecularity: miss
11 - Main use: (1) sport/hobby,(2) tractive power,(3) vegetation managem.
12 Spec. abilities: longevity
13 Performance compared with STB Deutsches Reitpferd:
14   higher: handling ease,pulling power,fertility,coach driving sport
15   equal: adaptability in dressage and jumping, speed in gallop
16   lower: adaptability in military
17 - Management: stationary; housing: 2-6 m.;
18 - Conservation progr.: live animals: Yes;Semen: miss;Embryos: miss
19 Status: minimally endang.; Watch: trend,%pure,%incross!
20 - Similar breeds (see group 3/3 on page 109)   EN Country Status
21 Cheval de Sport Belge   728 B   normal
22 Hannoveraner   758 D   normal

1 - Schleswiger Kaltblut   EN 799
2   Schleswig Coldblood;Hamburg/Schleswig-Hostein,northern Niedersachsen
3   Pferdestammbuch Schleswig-Holstein   HB:1891
4   Kiel 24106, Steenbeckerweg 151
5 - Composite of Bauernlandpferd with Jütisches Kaltblut; some
6   imports from Denmark; incrossing since 1950 from Jütland 741 Denmark
7   Numbers 1993: 10/130; HB: miss; increasing; miss %; Ne = 19
8 - Height: 163/158 cm; Weight: 850/700 kg; Herd number: 12; AI: miss
9   Colour: chestnut, black, grey
10 Pecularity: miss
11 - Main use: (1) miss,(2) miss,(3) miss
12 Spec. abilities: miss
13 Performance compared with STB miss:
14   higher: miss
15   equal: miss
16   lower: miss
17 - Management: miss; housing: miss m.; wet country
18 - Conservation progr.: live animals: miss;Semen: miss;Embryos: miss
19 Status: endangered;   Watch: ♂♂,HB♀♀,herds,%pure,%incross!
20 - Similar breeds (see group 4/4 on page 110)   EN Country Status
21 Den Jydske Hest   741 DK   min. end.
22 Frederiksborgheste   748 DK   min. end.
23 Nordsvensk häst   787 S   normal
24 Suomenhevonen   809 SF   normal

```
 1 - Schwarzwälder Füchse, St. Märgener Füchse                    EN  800
 2   Black Forest; Baden-Wuerttemberg
 3   Pferdezuchtverband Baden-Württemberg e. V.                  HB:1896
 4   Titisee-Neustadt 79822, Walter-Göbel-Weg 4
 5 - Autochthon breed with some imports (1890)
 6   Incrossing since 1950 from Noriker 788 Austria
 7   Numbers 1991: 14/320; HB: 280; increasing; 100 %; Ne = 31
 8 - Height: 156/152 cm; Weight: 680/610 kg; Herd number: miss; AI: Yes
 9   Colour: usually (dark) chestnut,few bay,1 grey family; often blazes
10   Pecularity: light mane + tail,sometimes stitched white hairs on body
11 - Main use: (1) tractive power,(2) sport/hobby,(3) vegetation managem.
12   Spec. abilities: longevity
13   Performance compared with STB Halfbred:
14     higher: pulling power, handling ease, fertility
15     equal:  age of sexual maturity
16     lower:  adaptability in jumping, military and dressage
17 - Management: stationary; housing: > 6 m.; hilly country
18 - Conservation progr.: live animals: Yes;Semen: 5;Embryos: miss
19   Status: minimally endang.; Watch: ♂♂,HB♀♀,herds,%incross!
20 - Similar breeds (see group 4/3 on page 110)   EN  Country Status
21   Cavallo Norico                                722  I     crit.end.
22   Norisches Kaltblut                            788  A     normal
23   Süddeutsches Kaltblut                         810  D     normal
```

```
 1 - Senner                                                       EN  801
 2   Senne; eastern Westfalen
 3   Gesellschaft zur Erhaltung alter und gefährdeter            HB:1710
 4   Haustierrassen e.V., Witzenhausen 37215, Gelsterstr. 2
 5 - Composite of Thoroughbred United Kingdom, Arab, Anglo-Arabs
 6   Incrossing since 1950 from Anglo-Arab 702 France
 7   Numbers 1993: 0/15; HB: miss; increasing; miss %; Ne = 0
 8 - Height: 165/162 cm; Weight: 550/510 kg; Herd number: miss; AI: miss
 9   Colour: predominantly bay or grey
10   Pecularity: miss
11 - Main use: (1) sport/hobby,(2) vegetat. management,(3) tractive power
12   Spec. abilities: longevity
13   Performance compared with STB Anglo-Arab:
14     higher: adaptability in jumping,adaptability in military,fertility
15     equal:  pull. power,handl. ease,speed in gallop,age of sex. matur.
16     lower:  miss
17 - Management: stationary; housing: ≈ 2 m.;
18 - Conservation progr.: live animals: miss;Semen: miss;Embryos: miss
19   Status: critically endang.;Watch: ♂♂,HB♀♀,herds,%incross!
20 - Similar breeds (see group 3/1 on page 108)   EN  Country Status
21   Lipizzan                                      776  F     crit.end.
22   Lipizzano                                     777  I     crit.end.
23   Espanol-Andaluz                               742  E     normal
24   Lusitanien                                    779  F     normal
```

```
 1 - Süddeutsches Kaltblut                                        EN  810
 2   South German Coldblood; Bayern
 3   Pferdezuchtverband Baden-Württemberg e.V.                    HB:1750
 4   Stuttgart 70190, Heinrich-Baumann-Str. 1-3
 5 - Imported as breed Pinzgauer from country Austria
 6   Incrossing since 1950 from Percheron 790 France
 7   Numbers 1990: 61/1165; HB: 1041; increasing; 95 %; Ne = 231
 8 - Height: 162/156 cm; Weight: 700/500 kg; Herd number: miss; AI: miss
 9   Colour: often bay or chestnut, greatcolour variety
10   Pecularity: sometimes piebalds: e.g. Harlekin-Tiger
11 - Main use: (1) tractive power,(2) sport/hobby,(3) meat
12   Spec. abilities: good working horse
13   Performance compared with STB Fjord:
14     higher: pulling power, daily gain
15     equal:  handling ease, adaptability in dressage and in jumping
16     lower:  speed in gallop, speed in trotters
17 - Management: stationary; housing: 2-6 m.;
18 - Conservation progr.: live animals: Yes;Semen: miss;Embryos: miss
19   Status: normal;              Watch: %incross!
```

20 - Similar breeds (see group 4/3 on page 110)	EN	Country	Status
21 Cavallo Norico	722	I	crit.end.
22 Schwarzwälder Füchse	800	D	min. end.
23 Norisches Kaltblut	788	A	normal

```
 1 - Zweibrücker                                                  EN  818
 2   Zweibruecken; Rheinland-Pfalz, Saarland
 3   Pferdezuchtverband Rheinland-Pfalz-Saar e.V.                 HB:1906
 4   Bad Kreuznach 55543, Burgenlandstr. 7
 5 - Composite of Arab, Anglo-Norman
 6   Incrossing since 1970 from Arab Germany, Hannoverian 758 Germany
 7   Numbers 1986: 140/1900; HB: 1280; stable; 100 %; Ne = 505
 8 - Height: 168/165 cm; Weight: 650/600 kg; Herd number: 1300; AI: miss
 9   Colour: any solid colour
10   Pecularity: miss
11 - Main use: (1) sport/hobby,(2) miss,(3) miss
12   Spec. abilities: miss
13   Performance compared with STB Holstein 760:
14     higher: miss
15     equal:  pulling power, handling ease, adaptability in dressage
16     lower:  miss
17 - Management: stationary; housing: 12 m.;
18 - Conservation progr.: live animals: miss;Semen: 3;Embryos: miss
19   Status: potential. endang.;Watch: %incross!
```

20 - Similar breeds (see group 3/2 on page 108)	EN	Country	Status
21 Altwürttemberger	701	D	crit.end.
22 Rottaler	797	D	crit.end.
23 Holsteiner Warmblut	760	D	normal
24 Cheval de Selle Francais	727	F	normal

1 - **Brachyceros**   EN **39**
2   Greek Shorthorn; mountains and highlands of central Greece
3   Laboratory of Animal Husbandry, Aristotle University   HB:miss
4   Thessaloniki, Thessaloniki 54006
5 - Autochthon descended from Illyrian cattle with character of brach
7   Numbers 1986: miss /10000; HB: miss; decreasing; miss %; Ne = 1810
8 - Height: miss/106 cm; Weight: miss/240 kg; Herd number: miss; AI:miss
9   Colour: Uni black, grey, brown
10 Pecularity: short horns
11 - Main use: (1) meat,(2) tractive power,(3) milk
12 Spec. abilities: miss
13 Performance compared with STB Local breed:
14   higher: % fat,age of sexual maturity,pulling power
15   equal: calving ease,calving interval,calf mortality,calving rate
16   lower: milk yield, muscularity, daily gain, handling ease
17 - Management: stationary; housing: ≈ 2 m.; low feeding requirements
18 - Conservation progr.: live animals: miss;Semen: miss;Embryos: miss
19 Status: potential. endang.;Watch: ♂♂,HB♀♀,trend!
20 - Similar breeds (see group 5/5 on page 80)   EN Country Status
21 **Rodopska kusoroga**   220   BG   crit.end.
22 **Busha**   52   YU   min. end.

1 - **Katerini**   EN **136**
2   Katerini; Macedonia and Thrace
3   Laboratory of Animal Husbandry, Aristotle University   HB:miss
4   Thessaloniki, Thessaloniki 54006
5 - Autochthon local breed with charact. of Bos Taurus primigenius
7   Numbers 1993: 10/450; HB: miss; decreasing; miss %; Ne = 20
8 - Height: 123/113 cm; Weight: 400/285 kg; Herd number: miss; AI: miss
9   Colour: Uni grey, brown
10 Pecularity: lyra-shaped horns
11 - Main use: (1) meat,(2) tractive power,(3) milk
12 Spec. abilities: miss
13 Performance compared with STB Local breed:
14   higher: % fat, age of sexual maturity, pulling power
15   equal: calving ease,calving interval,calf mortality,calving rate
16   lower: milk yield, muscularity, daily gain, handling ease
17 - Management: stationary; housing: ≈ 2 m.; low feeding requirements
18 - Conservation progr.: live animals: miss;Semen: miss;Embryos: miss
19 Status: critically endang.;Watch: ♂♂,HB♀♀,trend,%pure!
20 - Similar breeds (see group 6/1 on page 80)   EN Country Status
21 **Iskursko govedo**   104   BG   crit.end.
22 **Sykia**   251   GR   crit.end.
23 **Piemontese**   197   I   normal
24 **Maremmana**   166   I   normal

1 - **Sykia**   EN **251**
2   Sykia; Sykia village in Halkidiki-Macedonia
3   Laboratory of Animal Husbandry, Aristotle University   HB:miss
4   Thessaloniki, Thessaloniki 54006
5 - Autochthon local breed being derived from Bos Taurus primigenius
7   Numbers 1993: 5/120; HB: miss; decreasing; miss %; Ne = **8**
8 - Height: miss/116 cm; Weight: miss/miss kg; Herd number:miss; AI:miss
9   Colour: **Uni grey**
10 Pecularity: **lyra shaped horns**
11 - Main use: (1) **meat**,(2) tractive power,(3) milk
12 Spec. abilities: **miss**
13 Performance compared with STB **Local breed:**
14   higher: **% fat, age of sexual maturity, pulling power**
15   equal: **calving ease,calving interval,calf mortality,calving rate**
16   lower: **milk yield, muscularity, daily gain, handling ease**
17 - Management: **stationary**; housing: ≈ 2 m.; **low feeding requirements**
18 - Conservation progr.: live animals: miss;Semen: miss;Embryos: miss
19 Status: **critically endang.**;Watch: ♂♂,HB♀♀,**trend,%pure!**
20 - <u>Similar breeds</u> (see group 6/1 on page 80)   <u>EN</u> <u>Country</u> <u>Status</u>
21 Iskursko govedo   104 BG   crit.end.
22 Katerini   136 GR   crit.end.
23 Piemontese   197 I   normal
24 **Maremmana**   166 I   normal

1 - **Boutsiko, Sazakatsaniko, Vlahiko, Siteia**   EN **429**
2   Mountain breeds; Greek mountains and highlands
3   Laboratory of Animal Husbandry, Aristotle University   HB:miss
4   Thessaloniki, Thessaloniki 54006
5 - Autochthon indigenous breeds of Zackel origin
7   Numbers 1986: miss /1500000; HB: miss; increasing; miss %; Ne=271500
8 - Height: miss/58 cm; Weight: miss/33 kg; Herd number: miss; AI: miss
9   Colour: **Uni black, brown, white; brown and black spots**
10 Pecularity: **horns 2/0, spiral horns, some females have small horns**
11 - Main use: (1) **milk**,(2) **meat**,(3) **wool**
12 Spec. abilities: **white cheeses, harsh conditions**
13 Performance compared with STB **Chios 453:**
14   higher: **carcass leanness, % fat, age of sexual maturity**
15   equal: **wool yield**
16   lower: **litter size, milk yield, muscularity, daily gain**
17 - Management: **stationary/transh.**; housing: ≈ 2 m.; **mountainous country**
18 - Conservation progr.: live animals: miss;Semen: miss;Embryos: miss
19 Status: **normal**;   Watch: ♂♂,HB♀♀,**%pure!**
20 - <u>Similar breeds</u> (see group 7/6 on page 92)   <u>EN</u> <u>Country</u> <u>Status</u>
21 Florina   490 GR   endanger.
22 **Ruda Dubrovacka Sheep**   611 HR   endanger.
23 **Mytilini**   563 GR   normal
24 **Karagouniko**   518 GR   normal

```
 1 - Chios                                                        EN  453
 2   Chios; Island of Chios (original nucleous), country-wide
 3   Laboratory of Animal Husbandry, Aristotle University        HB:miss
 4   Thessaloniki, Thessaloniki 54006
 5 - Autochthon indigenous breed of eastern origin
 7   Numbers 1986: miss /16000; HB: 2000; stable; 95 %; Ne = 362
 8 - Height: 81/73 cm; Weight: 72/50 kg; Herd number: miss; AI: miss
 9   Colour: Uni white, dark spots on the head, belly and feet
10   Pecularity: horns 2/0, spiral horns, some females have small horns
11 - Main use: (1) milk,(2) meat,(3) wool
12   Spec. abilities: two period breeding season, twinning
13   Performance compared with STB Chios 453:
14     higher: Breed is used
15     equal:  as standard breed,
16     lower:  no comparison possible.
17 - Management: stationary; housing: ≈ 2 m.; mild maritime conditions
18 - Conservation progr.: live animals: miss;Semen: miss;Embryos: miss
19   Status: potential. endang.;Watch: ♂♂,%pure!
```

20 - Similar breeds (see group 5/2 on page 89)	EN	Country	Status
21 Caussenard des Garrigues	447	F	crit.end.
22 Altamurana	401	I	crit.end.
23 Caussenard du Lot	448	F	normal
24 Basco-Bearnaise	412	F	normal

```
 1 - Florina, Pellagonia                                         EN  490
 2   Pellagonia; northwestern Macedonia
 3   Laboratory of Animal Husbandry, Aristotle University        HB:miss
 4   Thessaloniki, Thessaloniki 54006
 5 - Composite of indigenous breed, perhaps cross between mountain
 6   and lowland local breed
 7   Numbers 1993: 20/400; HB: miss; decreasing; miss %; Ne = 55
 8 - Height: miss/67 cm; Weight: miss/43 kg; Herd number: miss; AI: miss
 9   Colour: Uni white, black spots around the eyes and the nose
10   Pecularity: horns 2/0, spiral horns, thin tail
11 - Main use: (1) milk,(2) meat,(3) wool
12   Spec. abilities: cheese production
13   Performance compared with STB Chios 453:
14     higher: carcass leanness, % fat, age of sexual maturity
15     equal:  wool yield
16     lower:  litter size, milk yield, muscularity, daily gain
17 - Management: stationary; housing: ≈ 2 m.;  mountainous conditions
18 - Conservation progr.: live animals: miss;Semen: miss;Embryos: miss
19   Status: endangered;        Watch: HB♀♀,trend,%pure,herds!
```

20 - Similar breeds (see group 7/6 on page 92)	EN	Country	Status
21 Ruda Dubrovacka Sheep	611	HR	endanger.
22 Kymi	523	GR	min. end.
23 Karagouniko	518	GR	normal
24 Sazakatsaniko	429	GR	normal

```
 1 - Karagouniko                                                    EN  518
 2   Karagouniko; Thessaly
 3   Laboratory of Animal Husbandry, Aristotle University          HB:miss
 4   Thessaloniki, Thessaloniki 54006
 5 - Autochthon breed of initial Zackel origin
 7   Numbers 1986: 20/200000; HB: 18000; increasing; 95 %; Ne = 60
 8 - Height: 78/69 cm; Weight: 80/60 kg; Herd number: miss; AI: miss
 9   Colour: Uni white, black spots on head and feet
10   Pecularity: horns 2/0, spiral horns, thin tail
11 - Main use: (1) milk,(2) meat,(3) wool
12   Spec. abilities: high quality white cheeses
13   Performance compared with STB Chios 453:
14      higher: muscularity, carcass leanness, % fat
15      equal:  daily gain, % protein, age of sexual maturity
16      lower:  litter size,milk yield,length of mat. season,wool thickn.
17 - Management: stationary; housing: ≈ 2 m.; dry hot conditions
18 - Conservation progr.: live animals: miss;Semen: miss;Embryos: miss
19   Status: normal;              Watch: ♂♂!
20 - Similar breeds (see group 7/6 on page 92)      EN  Country Status
21   Florina                                        490   GR    endanger.
22   Ruda Dubrovacka Sheep                          611   HR    endanger.
23   Mytilini                                       563   GR    normal
24   Sazakatsaniko                                  429   GR    normal
```

```
 1 - Kymi                                                           EN  523
 2   Kymi; around Kymi village on the Island of Euboea
 3   Laboratory of Animal Husbandry, Aristotle University          HB:miss
 4   Thessaloniki, Thessaloniki 54006
 5 - Autochthon local breed originating from the Skopelos breed
 7   Numbers 1993: 50/900; HB: 500; decreasing; 95 %; Ne = 182
 8 - Height: miss /64 cm; Weight: miss /55 kg; Herd number: >10; AI: miss
 9   Colour: Uni white, brown and black spots at face and feet
10   Pecularity: horns 2/0, spiral horns, thin tail
11 - Main use: (1) milk,(2) meat,(3) wool
12   Spec. abilities: twinning, long breeding season
13   Performance compared with STB Chios 453:
14      higher: muscularity, carcass leanness
15      equal:  daily gain, litter size, % fat, age of sexual maturity
16      lower:  milk yield, wool thickness
17 - Management: stationary; housing: ≈ 2 m.; insular conditions
18 - Conservation progr.: live animals: miss;Semen: miss;Embryos: miss
19   Status: minimally endang.; Watch: trend!
20 - Similar breeds (see group 7/6 on page 92)      EN  Country Status
21   Florina                                        490   GR    endanger.
22   Ruda Dubrovacka Sheep                          611   HR    endanger.
23   Karagouniko                                    518   GR    normal
24   Sazakatsaniko                                  429   GR    normal
```

```
 1 - Mytilini, Lesvos                                         EN   563
 2   Mytilene; Islands of Lesvos and Limnos
 3   Laboratory of Animal Husbandry, Aristotle University         HB:miss
 4   Thessaloniki, Thessaloniki 54006
 5 - Autochthon breed of eastern origin
 7   Numbers 1986: miss /95000; HB: 10000; stable; 90 %; Ne = 1810
 8 - Height: 67/64 cm; Weight: 61/42 kg; Herd number: miss; AI: miss
 9   Colour: Uni brown, white; black or brown spots on nose, ears, feet
10   Pecularity: horns 2/0, some females with small horns, long tail
11 - Main use: (1) milk,(2) meat,(3) wool
12   Spec. abilities: special type of hard cheese
13   Performance compared with STB Chios 453:
14     higher: age of sexual maturity, % fat, lambing interval
15     equal:  muscularity, daily gain, carcass leanness
16     lower:  litter size, milk yield, length of mating season
17 - Management: stationary; housing: ≈ 2 m.; insular conditions
18 - Conservation progr.: live animals: miss;Semen: miss;Embryos: miss
19   Status: normal;           Watch: ♂♂!
20 - Similar breeds (see group 7/6 on page 92)     EN  Country Status
21   Florina                                       490   GR    endanger.
22   Ruda Dubrovacka Sheep                         611   HR    endanger.
23   Karagouniko                                   518   GR    normal
24   Sazakatsaniko                                 429   GR    normal
```

```
 1 - Serres                                                   EN   627
 2   Serrai; Plains of Serres (eastern Macedonia)
 3   Laboratory of Animal Husbandry, Aristotle University         HB:miss
 4   Thessaloniki, Thessaloniki 54006
 5 - Autochthon breed of Tsigai origin
 7   Numbers 1986: miss /25000; HB: 3000; stable; miss %; Ne = 543
 8 - Height: 70/67 cm; Weight: 63/50 kg; Herd number: miss; AI: miss
 9   Colour: Uni white; black head and legs
10   Pecularity: horns 2/2, spiral horns, thin tail
11 - Main use: (1) milk,(2) meat,(3) wool
12   Spec. abilities: local cheeses, long breeding season
13   Performance compared with STB Chios 453:
14     higher: muscularity, daily gain, carcass leanness, % fat
15     equal:  age of sexual maturity, wool yield
16     lower:  litter size, milk yield, length of mating season
17 - Management: stationary; housing: ≈ 2 m.;
18 - Conservation progr.: live animals: miss;Semen: miss;Embryos: miss
19   Status: normal;           Watch: ♂♂,%pure!
20 - Similar breeds (see group 7/6 on page 92)     EN  Country Status
21   Florina                                       490   GR    endanger.
22   Ruda Dubrovacka Sheep                         611   HR    endanger.
23   Karagouniko                                   518   GR    normal
24   Sazakatsaniko                                 429   GR    normal
```

```
 1 - Sfakia                                                          EN   628
 2   Sfakia; Island of Grete (Chania)
 3   Laboratory of Animal Husbandry, Aristotle University          HB:miss
 4   Thessaloniki, Thessaloniki 54006
 5 - Autochthon breed with Zackel origin and Italian sheep
 7   Numbers 1986: miss /60000; HB: 7000; stable; 95 %; Ne = 1267
 8 - Height: 65/58 cm; Weight: 42/33 kg; Herd number: miss; AI: miss
 9   Colour: Uni white; dark spots around the eyes and the feet
10   Pecularity: horns 2/0, spiral horns, thin tail, roman nose
11 - Main use: (1) milk,(2) meat,(3) wool
12   Spec. abilities: cheese production
13   Performance compared with STB Chios 453:
14     higher: carcass lean., % fat, age of sex. matur., lambing interval
15     equal:  wool yield
16     lower:  muscularity, daily gain, litter size, milk yield
17 - Management: stationary/transh.; housing: ≈ 2 m.; harsh conditions
18 - Conservation progr.: live animals: miss;Semen: miss;Embryos: miss
19   Status: normal;              Watch: ♂♂!
```

20 - <u>Similar breeds</u> (see group 7/6 on page 92)

	EN	Country	Status
21 Florina	490	GR	endanger.
22 Ruda Dubrovacka Sheep	611	HR	endanger.
23 Karagouniko	518	GR	normal
24 Sazakatsaniko	429	GR	normal

```
 1 - Skopelos, Glossa                                               EN   630
 2   Skopelos; Island of Skopelos & Magnissia (mainland)
 3   Laboratory of Animal Husbandry, Aristotle University          HB:miss
 4   Thessaloniki, Thessaloniki 54006
 5 - Autochthon local breed possibly originating form Halkidiki
 7   Numbers 1993: 70/1800; HB: miss; stable; 95 %; Ne = 270
 8 - Height: 71/63 cm; Weight: 59/45 kg; Herd number: > 10; AI: miss
 9   Colour: Uni white; black spots around the eyes
10   Pecularity: horns 2/0, spiral horns, thin tail
11 - Main use: (1) milk,(2) meat,(3) wool
12   Spec. abilities: white cheese, twinning, long breeding season
13   Performance compared with STB Chios 453:
14     higher: miss
15     equal:  muscularity, daily gain, carcass leanness, litter size
16     lower:  fiber thickness
17 - Management: stationary; housing: ≈ 2 m.; insular condidtions
18 - Conservation progr.: live animals: miss;Semen: miss;Embryos: miss
19   Status: potential. endang.;Watch: HB♀♀!
```

20 - <u>Similar breeds</u> (see group 7/6 on page 92)

	EN	Country	Status
21 Florina	490	GR	endanger.
22 Ruda Dubrovacka Sheep	611	HR	endanger.
23 Karagouniko	518	GR	normal
24 Sazakatsaniko	429	GR	normal

1 - **Thraki, Kivircik**   EN **654**
2   **Kivircik; Thrace (northeastern Greece)**
3   Laboratory of Animal Husbandry, Aristotle University   HB:**miss**
4   Thessaloniki, Thessaloniki 54006
5 - Autochthon breed belonging to the Cuda group (Tsigai origin)
7   Numbers 1986: **miss** /**20000**; HB: **miss**; **decreasing**; **miss** %; Ne = **3620**
8 - Height: **63/55** cm; Weight: **miss** /**38** kg; Herd number: **miss**; AI: **miss**
9   Colour: **Uni white; brown and black spots around the head and feet**
10 Pecularity: **horns 2/2, spiral horn, thin tail**
11 - Main use: (1) **milk**,(2) **meat**,(3) **wool**
12 Spec. abilities: **miss**
13 Performance compared with STB **Chios 453**:
14   higher: **carcass leanness, % fat, age of sexual maturity**
15   equal: **wool yield**
16   lower: **litter size, milk yield, muscularity, daily gain**
17 - Management: **stationary**; housing: ≈ **2** m.; **semi mountain conditions**
18 - Conservation progr.: live animals: **miss**;Semen: **miss**;Embryos: **miss**
19 Status: **potential. endang.**;Watch: ♂♂,HB♀♀,trend,%pure!
20 - <u>Similar breeds</u> (see group 7/7 on page 93)   <u>EN</u> <u>Country</u> <u>Status</u>
21 **Cigaja**   460   H   endanger.
22 **Cigaja**   459   CS   normal
23 **Cigaja**   461   YU   normal
24 **Tigaie**   655   RO   normal

1 - **Vlahiko, Sarakatsaniko**   EN **664**
2   **Greek Zackel; mountainous regions of Greece**
3   Laboratory of Animal Husbandry, Aristotle University   HB:**miss**
4   Thessaloniki, Thessaloniki 54006
5 - **miss**
7   Numbers 1983: **50000/1000000**; HB: **miss**; **decreasing**; **50** %; Ne = **190476**
8 - Height: **58/53** cm; Weight: **45/34** kg; Herd number: **miss**; AI: **miss**
9   Colour: **Uni black, brown, white; colour combinations**
10 Pecularity: **horns 2/0**
11 - Main use: (1) **milk**,(2) **meat**,(3) **miss**
12 Spec. abilities: **miss**
13 Performance compared with STB **miss**:
14   higher: **miss**
15   equal: **miss**
16   lower: **miss**
17 - Management: **miss**; housing: **miss** m.;
18 - Conservation progr.: live animals: **miss**;Semen: **miss**;Embryos: **miss**
19 Status: **normal**;   Watch: HB♀♀,trend,%pure!
20 - <u>Similar breeds</u> (see group 7/6 on page 92)   <u>EN</u> <u>Country</u> <u>Status</u>
21 **Florina**   490   GR   endanger.
22 **Ruda Dubrovacka Sheep**   611   HR   endanger.
23 **Karagouniko**   518   GR   normal
24 **Sazakatsaniko**   429   GR   normal

SHEEP

1 - Zakynthos   EN 681
2   Zakynthos; Island of Zakynthos
3   Laboratory of Animal Husbandry, Aristotle University   HB:miss
4   Thessaloniki, Thessaloniki 54006
5 - Autochthon local breed possibly related to Italian
6   Bergamaska breed 415
7   Numbers 1993: 25/450; HB: miss; decreasing; 95 %; Ne = 87
8 - Height: miss /70 cm; Weight: 63/50 kg; Herd number: miss; AI: miss
9   Colour: Uni white
10 Pecularity: horns 2/0, spiral horns, thin long tail, roman nose
11 - Main use: (1) milk,(2) meat,(3) wool
12 Spec. abilities: twinning, long breeding season
13 Performance compared with STB Chios 453:
14   higher: fiber thickness
15   equal: muscularity, daily gain, carcass leanness, litter size
16   lower: milk yield
17 - Management: stationary; housing: ≈ 2 m.; insular conditions
18 - Conservation progr.: live animals: miss;Semen: miss;Embryos: miss
19 Status: minimally endang.; Watch: HB♀♀,trend!
20 - Similar breeds (see group 7/2 on page 91)   EN Country Status
21 Braunes Bergschaf   431 D   crit.end.
22 Istriana   516 I   crit.end.
23 Bergamasca   415 I   normal
24 Weißes Bergschaf   416 D   normal

GOATS

1 - Local breeds   EN 338
2   Local breeds; Greek mountains and highlands
3   Laboratory of Animal Husbandry, Aristotle University   HB:miss
4   Thessaloniki, Thessaloniki 54006
5 - Autochthon indigenous breed
7   Numbers 1986: miss /6000000; HB: miss; increasing; 80 %; Ne=1086000
8 - Height: 74/66 cm; Weight: 48/40 kg; Herd number: miss; AI: miss
9   Colour: Uni black, brown, combination black, grey, brown, white
10 Pecularity: horns 2/2, great variation in shape and size
11 - Main use: (1) milk,(2) meat,(3) hair production
12 Spec. abilities: various types of cheese, milk fed kids
13 Performance compared with STB Local breeds 338:
14   higher: Breed is used
15   equal: as standard breed;
16   lower: no comparison possible
17 - Management: stationary/transh.; housing: ≈ 2 m.; mountainous country
18 - Conservation progr.: live animals: miss;Semen: miss;Embryos: miss
19 Status: normal;   Watch: HB♀♀!
20 - Similar breeds (see group 9 on page 98)   EN Country Status
21 Roccaverano   347 I   crit.end.
22 Val di Livo (extinct)   363 I   crit.end.
23 Sarda   351 I   normal
24 Corse   320 F   normal

GOATS

```
 1 - Skopelos                                                    EN  356
 2   Skopelos; Island of Skopelos and Magnissia (mainland)
 3   Laboratory of Animal Husbandry, Aristotle University          HB:miss
 4   Thessaloniki, Thessaloniki 54006
 5 - Autochthon indigenous breed
 7   Numbers 1986: miss /8000; HB: miss; increasing; 95 %; Ne = 1448
 8 - Height: 73/64 cm; Weight: 57/45 kg; Herd number: miss; AI: miss
 9   Colour: Uni red, brown, some combinations black, red, brown, white
10   Pecularity: horns 2/2, great variation in shape and size
11 - Main use: (1) milk,(2) meat,(3) hair production
12   Spec. abilities: various types of cheese
13   Performance compared with STB Local breeds 338:
14      higher: milk yield, litter size
15      equal:  muscularity, daily gain, carcass leanness, % fat
16      lower:  age of sexual maturity
17 - Management: stationary; housing: ≈ 2 m.; insular maritime conditions
18 - Conservation progr.: live animals: miss;Semen: miss;Embryos: miss
19   Status: potential. endang.;Watch: ♂♂,HB♀♀!
```

20 - Similar breeds (see group 9 on page 98)	EN	Country	Status
21 Roccaverano	347	I	crit.end.
22 Val di Livo (extinct)	363	I	crit.end.
23 Local breeds	338	GR	normal
24 Corse	320	F	normal

HORSES

```
 1 - Aglikos Katharohaemos                                       EN  700
 2   Thoroughbred; Attica, Thessaly, Macedonia, Peleponnese, etc.
 3   Jockey Club of Greece                                         HB:1954
 4   Athens 10673, Pl. Filikis Etaerias 18
 5 - Imported as breed from United Kingdom
 6   Incrossing since 1950 from Thoroughbred United Kingdom and Hungary
 7   Numbers 1986: 120/490; HB: 490; increasing; 100 %; Ne = 386
 8 - Height: 170/170 cm; Weight: 550/520 kg; Herd number: miss; AI: miss
 9   Colour: any solid colour
10   Pecularity: fine coat
11 - Main use: (1) sport/hobby,(2) miss,(3) miss
12   Spec. abilities: miss
13   Performance compared with STB Thoroughbred 700:
14      higher: Breed is used
15      equal:  as standard breed,
16      lower:  no comparison possible.
17 - Management: stationary; housing: 12 m.;
18 - Conservation progr.: live animals: miss;Semen: miss;Embryos: miss
19   Status: normal
```

20 - Similar breeds (see group 1 on page 108)	EN	Country	Status
21 Arabialainen	706	SF	crit.end.
22 Täysverinen	811	SF	crit.end.
23 Anglo-Arab	702	F	normal
24 Vollblutaraber	815	A	normal

GREECE   HORSES

1 - Skyos Pony   EN 806
2   Skyros Pony; Skyros Island
3   Hippikos Homilos Skyrou   HB:miss
4   Equine Club of Skyros, GR-Skyros
5 - Autochthon local breed
7   Numbers 1993: 26/53; HB: miss; stable; miss %; Ne = 47
8 - Height: 104/104 cm; Weight: 130/120 kg; Herd number: 3; AI: miss
9   Colour: grey, dun, chestnut, bay
10 Pecularity: miss
11 - Main use: (1) sport/hobby,(2) tractive power,(3) miss
12 Spec. abilities: miss
13 Performance compared with STB Arab:
14   higher: handling ease
15   equal: fertility, age of sexual maturity
16   lower: pulling power, daily gain
17 - Management: transhumant; housing: 2-6 m.;
18 - Conservation progr.: live animals: Yes;Semen: miss;Embryos: miss
19 Status: endangered;   Watch: HB♀♀,herds,%pure!
20 - Similar breeds (see group 5/10 on page 111)   EN Country Status
21 Sorraia   807   P   crit.end.
22 Garrano   749   P   min. end.
23 Pottok   794   F   pot. end.
24 Cavallo Bardigiano   718   I   normal

HUNGARY   CATTLE

1 - Magyar szürke   EN 162
2   Hungarian Grey; Great Hungarian Plain
3   Institute for Agricultural Qualification   HB:1900
4   Budapest 1024, Keleti K. U. 24
5 - Autochthon Native breeds of Podolic origin; incrossing since
6   1950 from Maremmana 166 Italy, Podolian Yugoslavia
7   Numbers 1993: 55/1200; HB: miss; stable; 100 %; Ne = 210
8 - Height: 150/136 cm; Weight: 800/525 kg; Herd number: 8; AI: miss
9   Colour: Uni blue, grey; males are darker
10 Pecularity: horns 2/2, long, 70-80 cm; res. to foot and mouth d.
11 - Main use: (1) genetic resource,(2) tractive power,(3) meat
12 Spec. abilities: adaptability to extreme climate, easy calving
13 Performance compared with STB Hereford:
14   higher: pulling power, calving ease, milk yield, meat quality
15   equal: % fat, % protein, calving interval
16   lower: muscularity, handling ease, calf mortality
17 - Management: transhumant; housing: no; poor pastures
18 - Conservation progr.: live animals: Yes;Semen: 15;Embryos: 5/80
19 Status: minimally endang.; Watch: HB♀♀,herds,%incross!
20 - Similar breeds (see group 6/1 on page 80)   EN Country Status
21 Iskursko govedo   104   BG   crit.end.
22 Katerini   136   GR   crit.end.
23 Piemontese   197   I   normal
24 Maremmana   166   I   normal

304

```
1 - Cigaja                                                   EN   460
2   Tsigai; Szalkszentmarton, Oroshaza
3   Institute for Agricultural Qualification                HB:1974
4   Budapest 1024, Keleti K. U. 24
5 - Autochthon unknown local breed
7   Numbers 1986: 25/350; HB: miss; stable; 100 %; Ne = 84
8 - Height: 60/50 cm; Weight: 60/50 kg; Herd number: 2; AI: miss
9   Colour: Uni white, colour combinations, black face and feet
10  Pecularity: horns 0/0
11 - Main use: (1) milk,(2) meat,(3) genetic resource
12  Spec. abilities: milk, adaptability to extreme climate
13  Performance compared with STB Merino:
14    higher: milk yield
15    equal:  daily gain,litter size,% fat,% protein,age of sexual mat.
16    lower:  muscularity, carcass leanness, wool yield
17 - Management: transhumant; housing: > 6 m.;
18 - Conservation progr.: live animals: Yes;Semen: miss;Embryos: miss
19  Status: endangered;        Watch: HB♀♀,herds!
```

20 - <u>Similar breeds</u> (see group 7/7 on page 93)	<u>EN</u>	<u>Country</u>	<u>Status</u>
21 Kivircik	654	GR	pot. end.
22 Cigaja	459	CS	normal
23 Cigaja	461	YU	normal
24 Tigaie	655	RO	normal

```
1 - Cikta                                                    EN   462
2   Cikta; Nagydorog
3   Institute for Agricultural Qualification                HB:1974
4   Budapest 1024, Keleti K. U. 24
5 - Imported as breed from Germany
7   Numbers 1993: 22/350; HB: miss; increasing; 100 %; Ne = 65
8 - Height: 55/47 cm; Weight: 37/45 kg; Herd number: 1; AI: miss
9   Colour: Uni white
10  Pecularity: horns 2/0; merino - like
11 - Main use: (1) genetic resources,(2) miss,(3) miss
12  Spec. abilities: adaptability to extreme climate
13  Performance compared with STB Merino:
14    higher: miss
15    equal:  litter size,milk yield,% fat,% protein,age of sexual mat.
16    lower:  muscularity, daily gain, carcass leanness, wool yield
17 - Management: transhumant; housing: > 6 m.;
18 - Conservation progr.: live animals: Yes;Semen: miss;Embryos: miss
19  Status: endangered;        Watch: HB♀♀,herds!
```

20 - <u>Similar breeds</u> (see group 7/4 on page 92)	<u>EN</u>	<u>Country</u>	<u>Status</u>
21 Bayernwaldschaf	665	D	crit.end.
22 Bündner Oberländerschaf	441	CH	min. end.
23 Schwarzbraunes Bergschaf	621	CH	normal

1 - Racka   EN 593
2   Racka; Hortobagy, Debrecen, Bugac
3   Institute for Agricultural Qualification   HB:1800
4   Budapest 1024, Keleti K. U. 24.
5 - Autochthon
7   Numbers 1986: 100/1600; HB: miss; increasing; 100 %; Ne = 377
8 - Height: 57/50 cm; Weight: 35/40 kg; Herd number: miss; AI: miss
9   Colour: Uni black, white
10 Pecularity: horns 2/2, corkscrew - shaped
11 - Main use: (1) wool,(2) meat,(3) milk
12 Spec. abilities: adaptability to extreme climate
13 Performance compared with STB Merino:
14   higher: milk yield
15   equal: litter size, % fat, % protein, age of sexual maturity
16   lower: wool yield, wool thickness, muscularity, daily gain
17 - Management: transhumant; housing: > 6 m.;
18 - Conservation progr.: live animals: Yes;Semen: miss;Embryos: miss
19 Status: potential. endang.;Watch: HB♀♀!
20 - Similar breeds (see group 7/6 on page 92)   EN Country Status
21 Florina   490 GR   endanger.
22 Ruda Dubrovacka Sheep   611 HR   endanger.
23 Karagouniko   518 GR   normal
24 Sazakatsaniko   429 GR   normal

1 - Mangalica   EN 972
2   Mangalitsa; Pusztaegres, B. szentgyörgy, Szalkszentmarton
3   Institute of Agricultural Qualification   HB:1922
4   Budapest 1024, Keleti K. U. 24.
5 - Composite of Sumadia and native Hungarian local breeds
6   Incrossing since 1970 from Sumadia Yugoslavia
7   Numbers 1986: 50/400; HB: miss; increasing; 100 %; Ne = 178
8 - Height: 75/65 cm; Weight: 350/300 kg; Herd number: miss; AI: miss
9   Colour: Uni black, red, blond; some swallow-bellied
10 Pecularity: wool coat, lop ears
11 - Main use: (1) meat,(2) genetic resource,(3) miss
12 Spec. abilities: generally resistant to harsh environment
13 Performance compared with STB Large White:
14   higher: fat, meat quality, age of sexual maturity
15   equal: farrowing interval, handling ease, piglet mortality
16   lower: % lean, litter size, feed conversion rate, daily gain
17 - Management: stationary; housing: ≈ 2 m.;
18 - Conservation progr.: live animals: Yes;Semen: miss;Embryos: miss
19 Status: minimally endang.; Watch: HB♀♀!
20 - Similar breeds (see group 2/2 on page 102)   EN Country Status
21 Normand   982 F   crit.end.
22 Chester White   913 GB   crit.end.
23 Mangalita   973 RO   min. end.
24 Schwalbenbauch Mangalitza   1020 CH   pot. end.

1 - **Gidran**   EN   751
2   **Gidran; Kaposvar**
3   **Institute for Agricultural Qualification**   HB:1785
4   **Budapest 1024, Keleti K. U. 24**
5 - **Composite of local breeds + one Arab Halfbred stallion; incrossing**
6   **since 1950 from Shagya-Araber 802 Hungary, Englisches Vollblut**
7   Numbers 1986: **20/200**; HB: **60**; **stable**; **80 %**; Ne = **37**
8 - Height: **170/160** cm; Weight: **500/400** kg; Herd number: **1**; AI: **miss**
9   Colour: **sorrel, chestnut**
10 Pecularity: **miss**
11 - Main use: (1) **genetic resource**,(2) **sport/hobby**,(3) **tractive power**
12 Spec. abilities: **good adaptability to extreme factors**
13 Performance compared with STB **Shagya Arab 802**:
14   higher: **pulling power,adaptability in jumping,age of sexual matur.**
15   equal: **fertility**
16   lower: **handling ease**
17 - Management: **transhumant**; housing: **> 6 m.**;
18 - Conservation progr.: live animals: **Yes**;Semen: **miss**;Embryos: **miss**
19 Status: **critically endang.**;Watch: **HB♀♀,herds,%pure,%incross**!
20 - <u>Similar breeds</u> (see group 1 on page 108)   <u>EN</u> <u>Country</u> <u>Status</u>
21 **Arabialainen**   706   SF   crit.end.
22 **Täysverinen**   811   SF   crit.end.
23 **Anglo-Arab**   702   F   normal
24 **Vollblutaraber**   815   A   normal

1 - **Kisberi felver**   EN   769
2   **Kisber Halfbred; eastern and western Hungary**
3   **Institute for Agricultural Qualification**   HB:1860
4   **Budapest 1024, Keleti K. U. 24.**
5 - **Composite of Hungarian local horses and English Thoroughbred**
6   **Incrossing since 1950 from Holsteiner 760 Germany**
7   Numbers 1986: **80/1000**; HB: **miss**; **stable**; **80 %**; Ne = **296**
8 - Height: **163/161** cm; Weight: **500/450** kg; Herd number: **miss**; AI: **Yes**
9   Colour: **bay, sorrel**
10 Pecularity: **miss**
11 - Main use: (1) **sport/hobby**,(2) **tractive power**,(3)
12 Spec. abilities: **for coach and riding**
13 Performance compared with STB **Kisber Halfbred 769**:
14   higher: **Breed is used**
15   equal: **as standard breed,**
16   lower: **no comparison possible.**
17 - Management: **stationary**; housing: **> 6 m.**;
18 - Conservation progr.: live animals: **Yes**;Semen: **6**;Embryos: **miss**
19 Status: **potential. endang.**;Watch: **HB♀♀,%pure,%incross**!
20 - <u>Similar breeds</u> (see group 3/4 on page 109)   <u>EN</u> <u>Country</u> <u>Status</u>
21 **Mezöhegyesi felver**   782   H   pot. end.
22 **Irish Draught Horse**   764   IRL   pot. end.
23 **Irish Sport Horse**   765   IRL   normal
24 **Cob**   734   F   normal

1 - Lipicai   EN 774
2   Lipitsa; northern Hungary
3   Institute for Agricultural Qualification   HB:1580
4   Budapest 1024, Keleti K. U. 24
5 - Composite of Neapolitan and other Spanish lines
7   Numbers 1986: 25/600; HB: miss; decreasing; 100 %; Ne = 90
8 - Height: 159/156 cm; Weight: 500/420 kg; Herd number: 5; AI: miss
9   Colour: grey with a sleek coat and silky mane and tail
10 Pecularity: foals born black, brown or grey, become white at 7 years
11 - Main use: (1) tractive power,(2) sport/hobby,(3) miss
12 Spec. abilities: miss
13 Performance compared with STB Shagya Arab 802:
14   higher: pulling power,adaptability in dressage,daily gain, speed
15   equal: fertility, age of sexual maturity
16   lower: handling ease, adaptability in jumping and in military
17 - Management: stationary; housing: > 6 m.;
18 - Conservation progr.: live animals: Yes;Semen: miss;Embryos: miss
19 Status: endangered;   Watch: HB♀♀,trend,herds!
20 - Similar breeds (see group 3/1 on page 108)

	EN	Country	Status
21 Lipizzan	776	F	crit.end.
22 Senner	801	D	crit.end.
23 Espanol-Andaluz	742	E	normal
24 Lusitanien	779	F	normal

1 - Mezöhegyesi felver   EN 782
2   Mezoehegyes Halfbred; country-wide
3   Institute for Agricultural Qualification   HB:1850
4   Budapest 1024, Keleti K. U. 24
5 - Composite of local breeds and Thoroughbred; incrossing since 1950
6   from Hannoveraner 758 Germany, Throroughbred United Kingdom
7   Numbers 1986: 50/800; HB: 60; decreasing; 80 %; Ne = 109
8 - Height: 165/161 cm; Weight: 520/480 kg; Herd number: miss; AI: miss
9   Colour: bay
10 Pecularity: miss
11 - Main use: (1) sport/hobby,(2) tractive power,(3) miss
12 Spec. abilities: miss
13 Performance compared with STB Kisber Halfbred 769:
14   higher: adaptability in dressage, daily gain
15   equal: pulling power, handling ease, adaptability in jumping
16   lower: miss
17 - Management: stationary; housing: > 6 m.;
18 - Conservation progr.: live animals: Yes;Semen: 2;Embryos: miss
19 Status: potential. endang.;Watch: HB♀♀,trend,%pure,%incross!
20 - Similar breeds (see group 3/4 on page 109)

	EN	Country	Status
21 Kisberi felver	769	H	pot. end.
22 Irish Draught Horse	764	IRL	pot. end.
23 Irish Sport Horse	765	IRL	normal
24 Cob	734	F	normal

```
 1 - Noniusz                                              EN  785
 2   Nonius; eastern Hungary
 3   Institute for Agricultural Qualification            HB:1785
 4   Budapest 1024, Keleti K. U. 24
 5 - Composite of local breeds and Anglonorman and Thoroughbred GB
 6   Incrossing since 1950 from Thoroughbred GB and Holsteiner 760 D
 7   Numbers 1986: 82/3000; HB: miss; decreasing; 60 %; Ne = 319
 8 - Height: 165/162 cm; Weight: 600/55 kg; Herd number: miss; AI: miss
 9   Colour: black or brown
10   Pecularity: without any markings
11 - Main use: (1) tractive power,(2) miss,(3) miss
12   Spec. abilities: miss
13   Performance compared with STB Kisber Halfbred 769:
14      higher: pulling power, daily gain, handling ease
15      equal:  fertility, age of sexual maturity, speed in trotters
16      lower:  adaptability in jumping, military and in dressage
17 - Management: stationary; housing: > 6 m.;
18 - Conservation progr.: live animals: Yes;Semen: miss;Embryos: miss
19   Status: potential. endang.;Watch: HB♀♀,trend,%pure!
```

20 - Similar breeds (see group 3/2 on page 108)	EN	Country	Status
21 Altwürttemberger	701	D	crit.end.
22 Rottaler	797	D	crit.end.
23 Holsteiner Warmblut	760	D	normal
24 Cheval de Selle Francais	727	F	normal

```
 1 - Shagya arab                                         EN  802
 2   Shagya Arab; western Hungary
 3   Institute for Agricultural Qualification            HB:1850
 4   Budapest 1024, Keleti K. U. 24
 5 - Composite of local breed and Arab
 7   Numbers 1986: 10/60; HB: miss; decreasing; 70 %; Ne = 17
 8 - Height: 155/152 cm; Weight: 450/400 kg; Herd number: 4; AI: miss
 9   Colour: usually grey
10   Pecularity: silky mane and tail, fine coat
11 - Main use: (1) sport/hobby,(2) miss,(3) miss
12   Spec. abilities: miss
13   Performance compared with STB Shagya Arab 802:
14      higher: Breed is used
15      equal:  as standard breed,
16      lower:  no comparison possible.
17 - Management: stationary; housing: > 6 m.;
18 - Conservation progr.: live animals: Yes;Semen: miss;Embryos: miss
19   Status: critically endang.;Watch: ♂♂,HB♀♀,trend,herds,%pure!
```

20 - Similar breeds (see group 1 on page 108)	EN	Country	Status
21 Arabialainen	706	SF	crit.end.
22 Täysverinen	811	SF	crit.end.
23 Anglo-Arab	702	F	normal
24 Vollblutaraber	815	A	normal

1 - Galloway   EN   95
2   Galloway; country-wide
3   Bunadarfelag Islands (The Agricultural Society of   HB:miss
4   Iceland), Reykjavik 127, Baendahöllinni, P.B.7080
5 - Imported as breed from Scotland
6   Incrossing since 1950 from Dun & Belted Galloway Scotland
7   Numbers 1986: miss /20; HB: 20; stable; 100 %; Ne = 4
8 - Height: 123/ miss cm; Weight: 780/560 kg; Herd number: 1; AI: miss
9   Colour: Uni black, grey, some belted
10 Pecularity: horns 0/0, polled
11 - Main use: (1) meat,(2) miss,(3) miss
12 Spec. abilities: flavour of meat, hardiness
13 Performance compared with STB miss:
14   higher: miss
15   equal: miss
16   lower: miss
17 - Management: stationary; housing: > 6 m.;
18 - Conservation progr.: live animals: miss;Semen: miss;Embryos: miss
19 Status: critically endang.;Watch: ♂♂,HB♀♀,herds!
20 - Similar breeds (see group 1/5 on page 75)   EN Country Status
21 Galloway   95   IS   crit.end.
22 Murray Grey   181   GB   pot. end.
23 Deutsche Angus   80   D   normal
24 Angus   9   IRL normal

1 - Icelandic Dairy Cattle   EN   118
2   Icelandic Cattle
3   Bunadarfelag Islands (The Agricultural Society of   HB:miss
4   Iceland), Reykjavik 127, Baendahöllinni, P.B.7080
5 - Autochthon native breed
7   Numbers 1986: 20/33000; HB: miss; miss; 88 %; Ne = 61
8 - Height: miss/130 cm; Weight: miss/430 kg; Herd number: miss; AI:miss
9   Colour: Combination black, grey, red, brown
10 Pecularity: horns 2,0/2,0
11 - Main use: (1) milk,(2) meat,(3) miss
12 Spec. abilities: miss
13 Performance compared with STB Icelandic Cattle 118:
14   higher: Breed is used
15   equal: as standard breed,
16   lower: no comparison possible.
17 - Management: stationary; housing: > 6 m.;
18 - Conservation progr.: live animals: miss;Semen: Yes;Embryos: miss
19 Status: normal;   Watch: HB♀♀,%pure!
20 - Similar breeds (see group 4/4 on page 78)   EN Country Status
21 Mestnaya estonskaya   171   EW   crit.end.
22 Länsisuomenkarja   153   SF   endanger.
23 Röd Kullig Lantras   225   S   min. end.
24 Norsk rodtfe   187   N   normal

```
 1 - Icelandic Sheep                                                EN  512
 2   Icelandic Sheep; country-wide
 3   Bunadarfelag Islands (The Agricultural Society of             HB:miss
 4   Iceland), Reykjavik 127, Baendahöllinni, P.B.7080
 5 - Autochthon native breed
 7   Numbers 1986: 15000/700000; HB: miss; decreasing; 100 %; Ne = 58741
 8 - Height: 78/68 cm; Weight: 95/63 kg; Herd number: miss; AI: Yes
 9   Colour: Combination black, grey, brown, white
10   Pecularity: horns 4,2,0/4,2,0
11 - Main use: (1) meat,(2) wool,(3) miss
12   Spec. abilities: high fertility gene (Thoka-gene)
13   Performance compared with STB Icelandic Sheep 512:
14     higher: Breed is used
15     equal:  as standard breed,
16     lower:  no comparison possible.
17 - Management: stationary; housing: 2-6/> 6 m.;
18 - Conservation progr.: live animals: miss;Semen: miss;Embryos: miss
19   Status: normal
```

		EN	Country	Status
20 -	Similar breeds (see group 6/3 on page 90)			
21	Dansk Landfar	477	DK	crit.end.
22	Coburger Fuchsschaf	466	D	crit.end.
23	Foroyskur Seydur	491	FR	normal
24	Gronlandsk Fär	504	DK	normal

```
 1 - Islenski hesturinn                                             EN  768
 2   Iceland Pony; country-wide
 3   Bunadarfelag Islands (The Agricultural Society of             HB:1923
 4   Iceland), Reykjavik 127, Baendahöllinni, P.B.7080
 5 - Autochthon native breed of Nordic origin
 6 - Imported as breed from Norway, Great Britain
 7   Numbers 1986: 400/25000; HB: 12000; increasing; 100 %; Ne = 1548
 8 - Height: 135/132 cm; Weight: 380/340 kg; Herd number: miss; AI: miss
 9   Colour: usually grey or dun, sometimes bay or chestnut
10   Pecularity: rarely black or piebald; special gaits: amble and toelt
11 - Main use: (1) sport/hobby,(2) meat,(3) miss
12   Spec. abilities: meat quality,hardy in cold climate,conception rate
13   Performance compared with STB miss:
14     higher: miss
15     equal:  miss
16     lower:  miss
17 - Management: stationary; housing: no/≈ 2/2-6 m.; rough vegetation
18 - Conservation progr.: live animals: miss;Semen: miss;Embryos: miss
19   Status: normal
```

		EN	Country	Status
20 -	Similar breeds (see group 5/2 on page 110)			
21	Islannin hevonen	767	SF	crit.end.
22	Islandais	766	F	min. end.

 1 - **Angus**   EN   **9**
 2   **Angus; country-wide**
 3   **Department of Agriculture and Food**   HB:**1967**
 4   **Dublin 2, Kildare Street**
 5 - Imported as breed from Scotland, Canada; incrossing since 1950
 6   from Aberdeen Angus 1 United Kingdom, Angus Canada, New Zealand
 7   Numbers 1992: **120/1400**; HB: **1400**; **increasing**; **100 %**; Ne = **442**
 8 - Height: **135/112** cm; Weight: **800/500** kg; Herd number: **300**; AI: **Yes**
 9   Colour: **Uni black**
10   Pecularity: **horns 0/0, polled**
11 - Main use: (1) **meat**,(2) **miss**,(3) **miss**
12   Spec. abilities: **hardy breed surviving outdoor in winter**
13   Performance compared with STB **Hereford 111**:
14   higher: **miss**
15   equal: **miss**
16   lower: **daily gain, calving ease, calf mortality**
17 - Management: **stationary**; housing: **2-6 m.**;
18 - Conservation progr.: live animals: **miss**;Semen: **miss**;Embryos: **miss**
19   Status: **normal**
20 - <u>Similar breeds</u> (see group 2/2 on page 76)   <u>EN</u> <u>Country</u> <u>Status</u>
21   **Kerry Cattle**   140   IRL   min. end.
22   **Murray Grey**   181   GB   pot. end.
23   **Galloway**   94   D   normal
24   **Deutsche Angus**   80   D   normal

 1 - **Ayrshire**   EN   **17**
 2   **Ayrshire; country-wide**
 3   **Ayrshire Cattle Society of Great Britain & Ireland**   HB:**1877**
 4   **Racecourse Road 1, Ayr, Scotland, KA7 2DE**
 5 - Imported as breed from **18** United Kingdom
 6   Incrossing since 1950 from Ayrshire **18** United Kingdom
 7   Numbers 1992: **15/1600**; HB: **1600**; **decreasing**; **60 %**; Ne = **36**
 8 - Height: **137/127** cm; Weight: **900/700** kg; Herd number: **60**; AI: **miss**
 9   Colour: **Combination red, white**
10   Pecularity: **miss**
11 - Main use: (1) **milk**,(2) **meat**,(3) **miss**
12   Spec. abilities: **miss**
13   Performance compared with STB **Holstein-Friesian 91**:
14   higher: **miss**
15   equal: **% fat, % protein**
16   lower: **milk yield**
17 - Management: **stationary**; housing: **2-6 m.**;
18 - Conservation progr.: live animals: **miss**;Semen: **miss**;Embryos: **miss**
19   Status: **endangered**;   Watch: **♂♂,trend,%pure!**
20 - <u>Similar breeds</u> (see group 3/6 on page 78)   <u>EN</u> <u>Country</u> <u>Status</u>
21   **Suomen Ayrshire**   247   SF   normal
22   **Ayrshire**   18   GB   normal

```
 1 - Belgian Blue                                       EN    25
 2   Belgian Blue; country-wide
 3   Belgian Blue Society                               HB:1980
 4   Samakend, Gorey, Co. Wexford
 5 - Imported as breed from Belgium; incrossing since 1950
 6   continously from Belgian Blue 33 Belgium
 7   Numbers 1992: 25/200; HB: 200; increasing; 100 %; Ne = 76
 8 - Height: 140/130 cm; Weight: 1249/700 kg; Herd number: 80; AI: Yes
 9   Colour: Combination blue, white
10   Pecularity: miss
11 - Main use: (1) meat,(2) miss,(3) miss
12   Spec. abilities: double muscel
13   Performance compared with STB Hereford 111:
14     higher: calf mortality
15     equal:  daily gain, age of sexual maturity, pulling power
16     lower:  calving ease
17 - Management: stationary; housing: 2-6 m.;
18 - Conservation progr.: live animals: miss;Semen: 20;Embryos: miss
19   Status: potential. endang.;Watch: ♂♂!
```

20 - Similar breeds (see group 7 on page 81)	EN	Country	Status
21 Blanc Bleu Belge	33	B	normal
22 Blanc-Bleu-Belge	35	F	normal
23 Belgian Blue	26	GB	normal
24 Bleue du Nord	36	F	normal

```
 1 - Friesian                                           EN    91
 2   Holstein-Friesian; country-wide
 3   Holstein Friesian Cattle Society of Great Britain and     HB:1909
 4   Ireland, Scotsbridge House, Rickmansworth, Herts, United Kingdom
 5 - Imported as breed from United Kingdom, Netherlands; incrossing since
 6   1950 from Friesian New Zealand, Canada and 117 United Kingdom
 7   Numbers 1992: 3000/1320000; HB: 100000; stable; 50 %; Ne = 11651
 8 - Height: 150/140 cm; Weight: 1200/700 kg; Herd number: 2100; AI: Yes
 9   Colour: Combination black, white
10   Pecularity: miss
11 - Main use: (1) milk,(2) meat,(3) miss
12   Spec. abilities: miss
13   Performance compared with STB Holstein-Friesian 117:
14     higher: miss
15     equal:  milk yield,muscularity,daily gain,% fat,% protein,calving
16     lower:  miss
17 - Management: stationary; housing: 2-6 m.;
18 - Conservation progr.: live animals: miss;Semen: miss;Embryos: miss
19   Status: normal;          Watch: %pure,%incross!
```

20 - Similar breeds (see group 1/1 on page 75)	EN	Country	Status
21 Sortbroget Dansk Malkekvaeg	245	DK	pot. end.
22 Nizinna-Czarno-Biala	185	PL	pot. end.
23 Prim' Holstein	209	F	normal
24 Pie-Noire-Holstein	198	B	normal

```
1 - Hereford                                          EN  111
2   Hereford; country-wide
3   Irish Hereford Breed Society                      HB:1850
4   Mespil Road 27, Dublin 4
5 - Composite of White and red/brown cattle from Wales, imported as breed
6   from 112 GB; incrossing since 1950 from Hereford (each year) 112 GB
7   Numbers 1992: 300/5000; HB: 5000; stable; 100 %; Ne = 1132
8 - Height: 137/127 cm; Weight: 900/650 kg; Herd number: 600; AI: Yes
9   Colour: Combination red, white
10  Pecularity: white head
11 - Main use: (1) meat,(2) miss,(3) miss
12  Spec. abilities: survive winter well outdoor, poor feed
13  Performance compared with STB Hereford 111:
14    higher: Breed is used
15    equal:  as standard breed,
16    lower:  no comparison possible.
17 - Management: stationary; housing: 2-6 m.;
18 - Conservation progr.: live animals: miss;Semen: 100;Embryos: miss
19  Status: normal
```

20 - Similar breeds (see group 3/5 on page 77)	EN	Country	Status
21 Hereford	110	F	pot. end.
22 Hereford	112	GB	normal
23 Kazakhskaya belogolovaya	138	KAZ	normal

```
1 - Irish Blonde d'Aquitaine                          EN  120
2   Blonde d'Aquitaine; country-wide
3   Irish Blonde d'Aquitaine Cattle Society           HB:1975
4   Lough House, Duncormick, Co. Wexford
5 - Imported as breed from 37 France
6   Incrossing since 1950 from Blonde d'Aquitaine (cont.) 37 France
7   Numbers 1992: 30/250; HB: 250; stable; 100 %; Ne = 107
8 - Height: 152/145 cm; Weight: 1218/1002 kg; Herd number: 100; AI: Yes
9   Colour: Uni blond
10  Pecularity: miss
11 - Main use: (1) meat,(2) miss,(3) miss
12  Spec. abilities: miss
13  Performance compared with STB Hereford 111:
14    higher: calf mortality, daily gain
15    equal:  age of sexual maturity
16    lower:  calving ease
17 - Management: stationary; housing: 2-6 m.;
18 - Conservation progr.: live animals: miss;Semen: 20;Embryos: miss
19  Status: potential. endang.;Watch: ♂♂,HB♀♀!
```

20 - Similar breeds (see group 8/1 on page 81)	EN	Country	Status
21 Basco-Bearnaise	22	F	crit.end.
22 Coopelso 93 (terminated)	69	F	crit.end.
23 Blonde d'Aquitaine	38	GB	normal
24 Blonde d'Aquitaine	37	F	normal

```
 1 - Irish Charolais                                      EN  121
 2   Charolais; country-wide
 3   Irish Charolais Cattle Society Ltd.                  HB:1967
 4   Irish Farm Centre, Blue Bell, Dublin 12
 5 - Imported as breed from 62 France
 6   Incrossing since 1950 from Charolais (continously) 62 France
 7   Numbers 1992: 300/3200; HB: 3200; increasing; 100 %; Ne = 1097
 8 - Height: 150/140 cm; Weight: 910/750 kg; Herd number: 850; AI: Yes
 9   Colour: Uni white
10   Pecularity: miss
11 - Main use: (1) meat,(2) miss,(3) miss
12   Spec. abilities: muscularity
13   Performance compared with STB Hereford 111:
14     higher: calf mortality, daily gain
15     equal:  age of sexual maturity
16     lower:  calving ease
17 - Management: stationary; housing: 2-6 m.;
18 - Conservation progr.: live animals: miss;Semen: 100;Embryos: miss
19   Status: normal
```

20 - <u>Similar breeds</u> (see group 9/2 on page 82)

		EN	Country	Status
21	Charolais	62	F	normal
22	Charolais	63	L	normal
23	British Charolais	43	GB	normal

```
 1 - Irish Limousin                                       EN  122
 2   Limousin; country-wide
 3   Irish Limousin Cattle Society                        HB:1971
 4   Castle Grace, Cloltheen Co. Tipperary
 5 - Imported as breed from 156 France
 6   Incrossing since 1950 from Limousin (each year) 156 France
 7   Numbers 1992: 80/1600; HB: 1600; increasing; 100 %; Ne = 305
 8 - Height: 137/127 cm; Weight: 900/600 kg; Herd number: 300; AI: Yes
 9   Colour: Uni red
10   Pecularity: miss
11 - Main use: (1) meat,(2) miss,(3) miss
12   Spec. abilities: miss
13   Performance compared with STB Hereford 111:
14     higher: calf mortality, muscularity
15     equal:  daily gain, age of sexual maturity
16     lower:  calving ease
17 - Management: stationary; housing: 2-6 m.;
18 - Conservation progr.: live animals: miss;Semen: 100;Embryos: miss
19   Status: normal
```

20 - <u>Similar breeds</u> (see group 8/3 on page 81)

		EN	Country	Status
21	Alpha 16 (terminated)	6	F	crit.end.
22	Limousin	156	F	normal
23	Limousin	157	L	normal
24	Parthenaise	193	F	normal

```
 1 - Irish Shorthorn                                      EN  124
 2   Shorthorn; country-wide
 3   Shorthorn Society of Great Britain and Ireland       HB:1822
 4   4th Street, NAC, Stoneleigh Park, Kenilworth, Warwickshire
 5 - Imported as breed 233 from United Kingdom
 7   Numbers 1991: 500/7000; HB: 2000; increasing; 50 %; Ne = 1600
 8 - Height: 148/138 cm; Weight: 1000/600 kg; Herd number: miss; AI: Yes
 9   Colour: Combination grey, red, white
10   Pecularity: miss
11 - Main use: (1) meat,(2) milk,(3) miss
12   Spec. abilities: miss
13   Performance compared with STB Holstein-Friesian 91:
14      higher: miss
15      equal: % fat, % protein, age of sexual maturity
16      lower:  milk yield
17 - Management: stationary; housing: 2-6 m.; for hilly country
18 - Conservation progr.: live animals: miss;Semen: 20;Embryos: miss
19   Status: normal;                 Watch: %pure!
```

20 - Similar breeds (see group 4/2 on page 78)	EN	Country	Status
21 Armoricaine	10	F	crit.end.
22 Kurganskaya	151	USSR	crit.end.
23 Lincoln Red	159	GB	normal
24 Beef Shorthorn Cattle	24	GB	normal

```
 1 - Irish Simmental                                      EN  125
 2   Simmental; country-wide
 3   Irish Simmental Cattle Society Ltd.                  HB:1971
 4   6 Bridge Street, Arklow, Co Wicklow
 5 - Imported as breed 88 from Austria, 240 Switzerland
 6   Incrossing since 1950 from Fleckvieh 88 Austria
 7   Numbers 1992: 140/3000; HB: 3000; increasing; 100 %; Ne = 535
 8 - Height: 150/140 cm; Weight: 1150/700 kg; Herd number: 500; AI: Yes
 9   Colour: Combination red, white
10   Pecularity: white head
11 - Main use: (1) meat,(2) miss,(3) miss
12   Spec. abilities: miss
13   Performance compared with STB Hereford 111:
14      higher: calf mortality, muscularity, daily gain
15      equal:  age of sexual maturity
16      lower:  calving ease
17 - Management: stationary; housing: 2-6 m.;
18 - Conservation progr.: live animals: miss;Semen: 100;Embryos: miss
19   Status: normal
```

20 - Similar breeds (see group 3/2 on page 77)	EN	Country	Status
21 Ceske strakate	61	CZ	crit.end.
22 Simentalska	237	PL	min. end.
23 Montbeliard	176	F	normal
24 Fleckvieh	88	A	normal

1 - Jersey   EN 132
2   Jersey; Leinster
3   Jersey Cattle Society of United Kingdom   HB: Yes
4   Jersey House, 154 Castle Hill, Reading, Berks RGI 7RP
5 - Imported as breed from 133 United Kingdom; incrossing since 1950
6   from 133 United Kingdom, Jersey 130 Denmark, New Zealand, Canada
7   Numbers 1992: 20/2500; HB: 2300; decreasing; 60 %; Ne = 60
8 - Height: 140/120 cm; Weight: 600/400 kg; Herd number: 36; AI: miss
9   Colour: Uni brown
10 Pecularity: white ring around muzzle
11 - Main use: (1) milk,(2) meat,(3) miss
12 Spec. abilities: miss
13 Performance compared with STB Holstein-Friesian 91:
14   higher: % fat, % protein, calving ease, handling ease
15   equal: age of sexual maturity, calf mortality, calving rate
16   lower: milk yield, muscularity, daily gain
17 - Management: stationary; housing: 2-6 m.;
18 - Conservation progr.: live animals: miss;Semen: miss;Embryos: miss
19 Status: potential. endang.;Watch: trend,%pure!
20 - Similar breeds (see group 8/4 on page 82)   EN Country Status
21 Froment du Leon   93   F   endanger.
22 Jersey   130   DK   normal
23 Jersey   131   D   normal
24 Jersiais   134   F   normal

1 - Kerry Cattle   EN 140
2   Kerry; Kerry
3   The Kerry Cattle Society of Ireland   HB:1887
4   Cahirnane, Killarney, Co Kerry
5 - Autochthon, precise origins are not known
6   Incrossing since 1950 from Kerry United Kingdom
7   Numbers 1991: 33/550; HB: 320; increasing; 65 %; Ne = 120
8 - Height: 140/122 cm; Weight: 590/375 kg; Herd number: 50; AI: Yes
9   Colour: Uni black, occasional white marking on udder
10 Pecularity: white horns tipped with black
11 - Main use: (1) milk,(2) meat,(3) miss
12 Spec. abilities: hardy, low feeding
13 Performance compared with STB Holstein-Friesian 91:
14   higher: % fat
15   equal: % protein
16   lower: milk yield
17 - Management: stationary; housing: 2-6 m.; wet hilly country
18 - Conservation progr.: live animals: miss;Semen: Yes;Embryos: miss
19 Status: minimally endang.; Watch: %pure!
20 - Similar breeds (see group 2/2 on page 76)   EN Country Status
21 Murray Grey   181   GB   pot. end.
22 Deutsche Angus   80   D   normal
23 Angus   9   IRL normal
24 Galloway   94   D   normal

```
 1 - Blackface Mountain                                          EN  422
 2   Blackfaced Mountain;Regions of Kerry,Galway/Mayo,Donegal & Waterford
 3   Department of Agriculture and Food, 6e Agriculture House,    HB:miss
 4   Dublin 2, Kildare Street
 5 - Autochthon Scottish Blackface
 7   Numbers 1991: 25000/1000000; HB: miss; increasing; 25 %; Ne = 97561
 8 - Height: 55/50 cm; Weight: 80/60 kg; Herd number: miss; AI: miss
 9   Colour: Combination black, white; black face with white markings
10   Pecularity: horns 2/2, hardy
11 - Main use: (1) meat,(2) wool,(3) miss
12   Spec. abilities: miss
13   Performance compared with STB miss:
14     higher: miss
15     equal:  miss
16     lower:  miss
17 - Management: stationary; housing: no; mountainous country
18 - Conservation progr.: live animals: miss;Semen: miss;Embryos: miss
19   Status: normal;              Watch: %pure!
```

20 - Similar breeds (see group 7/11 on page 94)	EN	Country	Status
21 Blackface	421	F	crit.end.
22 Whitefaced Woodland	676	GB	pot. end.
23 Dala	476	N	normal
24 Wicklow Cheviot	677	IRL	normal

```
 1 - Galway                                                      EN  495
 2   Galway; western Ireland
 3   Galway Sheep Breeders Society                                HB:1923
 4   Boyhill, Co. Galway, Atlenry
 5 - Autochthon native Irish breed
 7   Numbers 1991: 50/25000; HB: 381; decreasing; 10 %; Ne = 177
 8 - Height: 80/72 cm; Weight: 100/74 kg; Herd number: 14; AI: miss
 9   Colour: Uni white; white head
10   Pecularity: horns 0/0
11 - Main use: (1) meat,(2) wool,(3) miss
12   Spec. abilities: miss
13   Performance compared with STB Suffolk 641:
14     higher: age of sexual maturity, wool yield
15     equal:  carcass leanness, milk yield, wool thickness
16     lower:  muscularity, daily gain, litter size
17 - Management: stationary; housing: no
18 - Conservation progr.: live animals: miss;Semen: miss;Embryos: miss
19   Status: endangered;          Watch: trend,herds,%pure!
```

20 - Similar breeds (see group 3 on page 88)	EN	Country	Status
21 Mouton Boulonnais	559	F	crit.end.
22 Whiteface Dartmoor	675	GB	min. end.
23 Mouton Charollais	560	F	normal
24 Cotentin	473	F	normal

1 - Suffolk   EN 641
2   Suffolk; country-wide
3   Suffolk Sheep Society   HB: Yes
4   Glenor, Doneraile, Co Co RK
5 - Imported as breed 642 from United Kingdom
6   Incrossing since 1960 from Suffolk (continously) 642 United Kingdom
7   Numbers 1991: 50000/2000000; HB: 300000; increasing; 75 %; Ne=171429
8 - Height: 75/70 cm; Weight: 120/85 kg; Herd number: miss; AI: miss
9   Colour: Uni white; black head and legs
10 Pecularity: horns 0/0
11 - Main use: (1) meat,(2) wool,(3) sire line
12 Spec. abilities: miss
13 Performance compared with STB Texel 651:
14   higher: daily gain, litter size
15   equal: milk yield, age of sexual maturity, lambing interval
16   lower: muscularity, carcass leanness
17 - Management: stationary; housing: no
18 - Conservation progr.: live animals: miss;Semen: miss;Embryos: miss
19 Status: normal

20 - Similar breeds (see group 4/2 on page 89)	EN	Country	Status
21 Norfolk Horn	565	GB	min. end.
22 Suffolk	639	F	normal
23 Suffolk sheep	642	GB	normal
24 Suffolk	640	D	normal

1 - Texel   EN 651
2   Texel; country-wide
3   Irish Texel Society   HB:1976
4   Dublin 15, 9 Hawthorn Lawn, Castleknock
5 - Imported as breed from 653 Netherlands
7   Numbers 1991: 3500/120000; HB: 5000; stable; 15 %; Ne = 8235
8 - Height: 73/68 cm; Weight: 110/75 kg; Herd number: miss; AI: miss
9   Colour: Uni white
10 Pecularity: horns 0/0
11 - Main use: (1) meat,(2) wool,(3) sire line
12 Spec. abilities: high lean meat content
13 Performance compared with STB Suffolk 641:
14   higher: muscularity, carcass leanness, conformation
15   equal: milk yield, age of sexual maturity, lambing interval
16   lower: daily gain, litter size
17 - Management: stationary; housing: no
19 Status: normal;   Watch: %pure!
18 - Conservation progr.: live animals: miss;Semen: miss;Embryos: miss

20 - Similar breeds (see group 2/2 on page 88)	EN	Country	Status
21 Texel	648	SF	pot. end.
22 Texel	649	F	normal
23 Texel	652	L	normal
24 Texel	650	D	normal

```
1 - Wicklow Cheviot                                          EN  677
2   Wicklow Cheviot; Co. Wicklow
3   Wicklow Mountain Sheep Breeders Society                  HB:1926
4   Ashford, Co. Wicklow
5 - Autochthon breed from Wicklow mountains (United Kingdom)
6 - Imported as breed from United Kingdom
7   Numbers 1991: 1800/400000; HB: 8000; increasing; 20 %; Ne = 5878
8 - Height: 70/60 cm; Weight: 90/70 kg; Herd number: miss; AI: miss
9   Colour: Uni white
10  Pecularity: horns 0/0
11 - Main use: (1) meat,(2) wool,(3) crossbreeding
12  Spec. abilities: hardy breed, suited to hill type condition
13  Performance compared with STB Scottish Blackface:
14     higher: wool yield, muscularity, daily gain
15     equal:  carcass leanness,litter size,milk yield,age of sex. matur.
16     lower:  miss
17 - Management: stationary; housing: no
18 - Conservation progr.: live animals: miss;Semen: miss;Embryos: miss
19  Status: normal
```

20 - Similar breeds (see group 7/11 on page 94)	EN	Country	Status
21 Blackface	421	F	crit.end.
22 Whitefaced Woodland	676	GB	pot. end.
23 Dala	476	N	normal
24 Blackface Mountain	422	IRL	normal

```
1 - Irish Goat                                               EN  336
2   Irish Goat; country-wide
3   Irish Goat Clubations, Irish Goat Producers or Irish     HB:1918
4   Angora Goat Society, Ballymachd, Kilmacahogue, Co. Wicklow
5 - Autochthon Irish fernal
7   Numbers 1991: 150/6500; HB: 700; decreasing; 20 %; Ne = 494
8 - Height: 90/80 cm; Weight: 85/55 kg; Herd number: miss; AI: miss
9   Colour: Uni grey, white
10  Pecularity: horns 2/2
11 - Main use: (1) milk,(2) wool,(3) meat
12  Spec. abilities: hardy
13  Performance compared with STB miss:
14     higher: miss
15     equal: miss
16     lower: miss
17 - Management: stationary; housing: no; mountainous country
18 - Conservation progr.: live animals: miss;Semen: miss;Embryos: miss
19  Status: minimally endang.; Watch: trend,%pure!
```

20 - Similar breeds (see group 1 on page 97)	EN	Country	Status
21 Blanche	308	B	pot. end.
22 Bila kratkosrsta	306	CS	normal
23 Weiße Deutsche Edelziege	367	D	normal
24 Gessenay	350	F	normal

```
1 - Irish Landrace                                        EN  946
2   Irish Landrace; country-wide
3   Irish Pig Breeders Society                            HB:1969
4   Dublin 2, 84 Merrion Square
5 - Imported as breed from United Kingdom, Norway
6   Incrossing since 1970 from 911 United Kingdom, 983 Norway, Sweden
7   Numbers 1992: 3200/85500; HB: 450; increasing; 7 %; Ne = 1578
8 - Height: 80/70 cm; Weight: 235/200 kg; Herd number: miss; AI: Yes
9   Colour: Uni white
10  Pecularity: lop ears
11 - Main use: (1) meat,(2) miss,(3) miss
12  Spec. abilities: miss
13  Performance compared with STB Large White 963:
14     higher: % lean, muscularity
15     equal:  litter size,feed conversion,daily gain,age of sexual mat.
16     lower:  meat quality
17 - Management: stationary; housing: 12 m.;
18 - Conservation progr.: live animals: miss;Semen: miss;Embryos: miss
19  Status: normal;           Watch: %pure!
```

		EN	Country	Status
20 -	Similar breeds (see group 2/1 on page 101)			
21	Belgische Landrasse	907	D*	crit.end.
22	Zlotnicka biala	1024	PL	crit.end.
23	Landrace	952	CS	normal
24	Belgisch Landvarken	906	B	normal

```
1 - Large White Pigs                                      EN  963
2   Large White; country-wide
3   Irish Pig Breeders Society                            HB:1969
4   Dublin 2, 84 Merrion Square
5 - Imported as breed 1023 from United Kingdom, Sweden
6   Incrossing since 1970 from Yorkshire Sweden, Large White 1023 GB
7   Numbers 1992: 3200/85500; HB: 350; increasing; 7 %; Ne = 1262
8 - Height: 80/70 cm; Weight: 250/210 kg; Herd number: miss; AI: Yes
9   Colour: Uni white
10  Pecularity: erect ears
11 - Main use: (1) meat,(2) miss,(3) miss
12  Spec. abilities: miss
13  Performance compared with STB Irish Landrace 946:
14     higher: meat quality
15     equal:  litter size,feed conversion,daily gain,age of sexual mat.
16     lower:  % lean, muscularity
17 - Management: stationary; housing: 12 m.;
18 - Conservation progr.: live animals: miss;Semen: miss;Embryos: miss
19  Status: normal;           Watch: %pure!
```

		EN	Country	Status
20 -	Similar breeds (see group 1/1 on page 101)			
21	Norsk Yorkshire	984	N	endanger.
22	Grand Yorkshire Belge	937	B	normal
23	Large White	960	F	normal
24	Yorkshire	1021	SF	normal

```
 1 - Arab Horse                                             EN  705
 2   Arab; eastern and southeastern Ireland
 3   Irish Regional Group of the Arab Horse Society         HB: Yes
 4   Summerhill. Village Co. Meath
 5 - Imported as breed 704 from United Kingdom and USA
 7   Numbers 1991: 15/100; HB: 40; decreasing; 50 %; Ne = 23
 8 - Height: 150/145 cm; Weight: 400/350 kg; Herd number: 12; AI: miss
 9   Colour: grey, chestnut, bay
10   Pecularity: long fine mane and tail
11 - Main use: (1) sport/hobby,(2) miss,(3) miss
12   Spec. abilities: miss
13   Performance compared with STB Thoroughbred 812:
14     higher: pulling power, handling ease, fertility
15     equal:  age of sexual maturity, daily gain
16     lower:  miss
17 - Management: stationary; housing: ≈ 2 m.;
18 - Conservation progr.: live animals: miss;Semen: miss;Embryos: miss
19   Status: endangered;        Watch: ♂♂,HB♀♀,trend,herds,%pure!
```

20 - Similar breeds (see group 1 on page 108)	EN	Country	Status
21 Arabialainen	706	SF	crit.end.
22 Täysverinen	811	SF	crit.end.
23 Anglo-Arab	702	F	normal
24 Vollblutaraber	815	A	normal

```
 1 - Connemara Pony                                         EN  737
 2   Connemara Pony; Connemara, Co. Galway
 3   Connemara Pony Breeders' Society                       HB:1926
 4   73 Dalysfort Road, Hill, Co. Galway
 5 - Autochthon Celtic Pony
 7   Numbers 1991: 168/2500; HB: 1500; increasing; 95 %; Ne = 604
 8 - Height: 145/138 cm; Weight: 430/400 kg; Herd number: miss; AI: miss
 9   Colour: dun with dark legs, grey, bay, black, brown
10   Pecularity: few roan or chestnut
11 - Main use: (1) sport/hobby,(2) miss,(3) miss
12   Spec. abilities: hardy; resistant to wind and rain
13   Performance compared with STB Welsh pony:
14     higher: pulling power, adaptability in dressage and in jumping
15     equal:  handling ease, fertility, age of sexual maturity
16     lower:  miss
17 - Management: stationary; housing: no; low quality vegetation
18 - Conservation progr.: live animals: miss;Semen: miss;Embryos: miss
19   Status: normal
```

20 - Similar breeds (see group 5/6 on page 111)	EN	Country	Status
21 Connemara Pony	819	SF	crit.end.
22 Connemara	736	F	normal

1 - Irish Draught Horse   EN 764
2   Irish Draught; country-wide
3   Irish Draught Horse Society   HB:1918
4   Dublin 4, Ballsbridge
5 - Composite of "Irish Hobby" and Great Horse
7   Numbers 1991: 90/2200; HB: 1260; increasing; 40 %; Ne = 336
8 - Height: 165/160 cm; Weight: 750/600 kg; Herd number: miss; AI: miss
9   Colour: predominantly grey, goltured by by and chestnut
10 Pecularity: miss
11 - Main use: (1) sport/hobby,(2) tractive power,(3) farm work
12 Spec. abilities: hardy, no cold-blooded horse
13 Performance compared with STB Halfbred:
14   higher: pulling power, handling ease, adaptability in jumping
15   equal: adaptability in dressage,fertility,age of sexual maturity
16   lower: miss
17 - Management: stationary; housing: ≈ 2 m.;
18 - Conservation progr.: live animals: miss;Semen: miss;Embryos: miss
19 Status: potential. endang.;Watch: %pure!
20 - Similar breeds (see group 3/4 on page 109)   EN Country Status
21 Kisberi felver   769   H   pot. end.
22 Mezöhegyesi felver   782   H   pot. end.
23 Irish Sport Horse   765   IRL   normal
24 Cob   734   F   normal

1 - Irish Sport Horse, Irish Hunter   EN 765
2   Irish Hunter; country-wide
3   Irish Horse Register, Agriculture House   HB:1974
4   Dublin 2, Kildare Street
5 - Composite of Irish Draught 764 and Thoroughbred 812
7   Numbers 1991: 50/9000; HB: 7000; increasing; 15 %; Ne = 199
8 - Height: 170/165 cm; Weight: 650/550 kg; Herd number: miss; AI: miss
9   Colour: any solid colour
10 Pecularity: miss
11 - Main use: (1) sport/hobby,(2) miss,(3) miss
12 Spec. abilities: miss
13 Performance compared with STB Thoroughbred 812:
14   higher: adaptability in jumping and in military, handling ease
15   equal: pulling power, fertility, age of sexual maturity
16   lower: speed in gallop, speed in trotters
17 - Management: stationary; housing: ≈ 2 m.;
18 - Conservation progr.: live animals: miss;Semen: 10;Embryos: miss
19 Status: normal;   Watch: %pure!
20 - Similar breeds (see group 3/4 on page 109)   EN Country Status
21 Kisberi felver   769   H   pot. end.
22 Mezöhegyesi felver   782   H   pot. end.
23 Cleveland Bay Horse   732   GB   normal
24 Cob   734   F   normal

```
 1 - Thoroughbred                                              EN  812
 2   Thoroughbred; country-wide
 3   Weatherbys Studbook                                      HB:1791
 4   NAAS, Co. Kildare
 5 - Imported as breed from United Kingdom
 6   Incrossing since 1950 from Thoroughbred USA, United Kingdom, 796 F
 7   Numbers 1991: 380/12100; HB: 12100; increasing; 95 %; Ne = 1474
 8 - Height: 169/160 cm; Weight: 500/475 kg; Herd number: miss; AI: miss
 9   Colour: any solid colour
10   Pecularity: miss
11 - Main use: (1) sport/hobby,(2) miss,(3) miss
12   Spec. abilities: miss
13   Performance compared with STB Thoroughbred 812:
14      higher: Breed is used
15      equal:  as standard breed,
16      lower:  no comparison possible.
17 - Management: stationary; housing: ≈ 2 m.;
18 - Conservation progr.: live animals: miss;Semen: miss;Embryos: miss
19   Status: normal
```

20 - Similar breeds (see group 1 on page 108)	EN	Country	Status
21 Arabialainen	706	SF	crit.end.
22 Täysverinen	811	SF	crit.end.
23 Anglo-Arab	702	F	normal
24 Vollblutaraber	815	A	normal

```
 1 - Agerolese                                                 EN   2
 2   Agerose; Province of Naples (Campania)
 3   Provincial Breeders Association                          HB:miss
 4   Naples, Cesare Battisti Street 15
 5 - Composite of Italian Brown 46, Jersey, Friesian, Podolian 206
 6   Incrossing since 1950 from: Friesian Italy 92
 7   Numbers 1992: 8/190; HB: miss; decreasing; 100 %; Ne = 15
 8 - Height: 135/125 cm; Weight: 650/450 kg; Herd number: miss; AI: miss
 9   Colour: Uni brown, chestnut to almost black
10   Pecularity: light rim around dark muzzle
11 - Main use: (1) milk,(2) meat,(3) miss
12   Spec. abilities: mountain
13   Performance compared with STB miss:
14      higher: miss
15      equal:  miss
16      lower:  miss
17 - Management: stationary; housing: 12 m.;
18 - Conservation progr.: live animals: Yes;Semen: miss;Embryos: miss
19   Status: critically endang.;Watch: ♂♂,HB♀♀,trend,herds,%incross!
```

20 - Similar breeds (see group 5/1 on page 79)	EN	Country	Status
21 Original Allgäuer Braunvieh	189	D	crit.end.
22 Pisana	205	I	crit.end.
23 Aubrac	14	F	normal
24 Österreichisches Braunvieh	190	A	normal

```
 1 - Bruna                                                    EN    46
 2   Brown Mountain; country-wide
 3   Ass. Naz. All. bovini azza Bruna                        HB:1954
 4   Bussolengo (Verona) 37012, Loc Ferlina 204
 5 - Incrossing since 1950 from Brown Mountain 190 Austria,
 6   Brown Swiss USA
 7   Numbers 1991: 1024/547441; HB: 157038; decreasing; 85 %; Ne = 4070
 8 - Height: 145/135 cm; Weight: 825/550 kg; Herd number: miss; AI: Yes
 9   Colour: Uni brown
10   Pecularity: miss
11 - Main use: (1) milk,(2) meat,(3) miss
12   Spec. abilities: miss
13   Performance compared with STB Holstein-Friesian 92:
14     higher: % fat, % protein, age of sexual maturity
15     equal:  calving interval
16     lower:  milk yield
17 - Management: stationary; housing: 12 m.;
18 - Conservation progr.: live animals: miss;Semen: miss;Embryos: miss
19   Status: normal;              Watch: %incross!
```

20 - Similar breeds (see group 5/1 on page 79)	EN	Country	Status
21 Original Allgäuer Braunvieh	189	D	crit.end.
22 Agerolese	2	I	crit.end.
23 Aubrac	14	F	normal
24 Österreichisches Braunvieh	190	A	normal

ITALY   CATTLE

```
 1 - Burlina                                                  EN    51
 2   Burlina; Province of Vicenza, Treviso
 3   Ente di Sviluppo Agricolo del Veneto                    HB:1985
 4   Venice 30125, Via S. Croce 1187
 5 - Autochthon local breed
 6   Incrossing since 1950 from Frisona 92 Italy
 7   Numbers 1991: 6/214; HB: 214; increasing; miss %; Ne = 11
 8 - Height: 130/120 cm; Weight: 625/525 kg; Herd number: miss; AI: Yes
 9   Colour: Combination black, white
10   Pecularity:light rim around black muzzle,calves up to 2 m. red/blond
11 - Main use: (1) milk,(2) meat,(3) miss
12   Spec. abilities: miss
13   Performance compared with STB Holstein-Friesian 92:
14     higher: miss
15     equal:  % fat, % protein, age of sexual maturity
16     lower:  milk yield, calving interval
17 - Management: stationary; housing: > 6 m.;
18 - Conservation progr.: live animals: Yes;Semen: 6;Embryos: miss
19   Status: critically endang.;Watch: ♂♂,herds,%incross!
```

20 - Similar breeds (see group 1/2 on page 75)	EN	Country	Status
21 Breton Pie Noire	42	F	endanger.
22 Deutsche Schwarzbunte (Original)	76	D	endanger.
23 Cherno-pestraya litovskaya	66	LT	normal
24 Cherno-pestraya estonskaya	65	EW	normal

1 - Cabannina   EN   54
2   Cabannina; Province of Genova
3   Provincial Breeders Association   HB:1985
4   Genova, Via De Amicis 2
5 - Incrossing since 1950 from: Brown Mountain 46
7   Numbers 1992: 10/262; HB: 235; increasing; 60 %; Ne = 19
8 - Height: 125/120 cm; Weight: 500/375 kg; Herd number: miss; AI: miss
9   Colour: Uni brown
10 Pecularity: pale dorsal stripe
11 - Main use: (1) milk,(2) miss,(3) miss
12 Spec. abilities: mountain, marginal areas
13 Performance compared with STB Holstein-Friesian 92:
14   higher: miss
15   equal: % fat, % protein
16   lower: milk yield, calving interval, age of sexual maturity
17 - Management: stationary; housing: 12 m.;
18 - Conservation progr.: live animals: Yes;Semen: 8;Embryos: miss
19 Status: critically endang.;Watch: ♂♂,%pure,%incross!
20 - Similar breeds (see group 5/3 on page 80)   EN Country Status
21 Aure et Saint-Girons   16   F   min. end.
22 Bazadais   23   F   normal
23 Salers   226 F   normal

1 - Calvana   EN   57
2   Calvana; Province of Florence
3   Comunita Montana "Val di Bisenzio"   HB:1985
4   Vernio-Firenze 50048, Via della Piaggia 5
5 - Autochthon Chiana
6   Incrossing since 1950 from Chianina 67 Italy
7   Numbers 1991: 5/50; HB: 50; stable; 100 %; Ne = 8
8 - Height: 155/145 cm; Weight: 1025/700 kg; Herd number: 7; AI: miss
9   Colour: Uni white; skin and mucosae dark pigmented
10 Pecularity: hoofs, horn tips and tail switch dark
11 - Main use: (1) meat,(2) miss,(3) miss
12 Spec. abilities: mountain, marginal areas
13 Performance compared with STB miss:
14   higher: miss
15   equal: miss
16   lower: miss
17 - Management: stationary; housing: 12 m.;
18 - Conservation progr.: live animals: Yes;Semen: 1;Embryos: miss
19 Status: critically endang.;Watch: ♂♂,HB♀♀,herds,%incross!
20 - Similar breeds (see group 9/3 on page 82)   EN Country Status
21 Bianca val padana   173 I   pot. end.
22 Chianina   67   I   normal
23 Marchigiana   165 I   normal

```
1 - Chianina                                                    EN   67
2   Chianina; Tuscany and Umbria
3   Ass. Naz. Allevatori Bovini Italiani da Carne              HB:1963
4   Roma 00161, Via Bosio 22
5 - miss
7   Numbers 1991: 515/66000; HB: 18000; decreasing; 100 %; Ne = 2003
8 - Height: 160/148 cm; Weight: 1350/900 kg; Herd number: miss; AI: Yes
9   Colour: Uni white
10  Pecularity: pigmented skin, dark muzzle, hoofs and tail switch
11 - Main use: (1) meat,(2) miss,(3) miss
12  Spec. abilities: miss
13  Performance compared with STB miss:
14     higher: miss
15     equal:  miss
16     lower:  miss
17 - Management: stationary; housing: 2-6/12 m.;
18 - Conservation progr.: live animals: miss;Semen: 13;Embryos: miss
19  Status: normal;              Watch: trend!
```

20 - Similar breeds (see group 9/3 on page 82)	EN	Country	Status
21 Calvana	57	I	crit.end.
22 Bianca val padana	173	I	pot. end.
23 Marchigiana	165	I	normal

```
1 - Cinisara                                                    EN   68
2   Cinisara; Province of Palermo
3   Associazione Regionale Allevatori Della Sicilia            HB:miss
4   Palermo 90139, Via P. pe Belmonte 55
5 - Incrossing since 1950 from Frisona 92 Italy
7   Numbers 1991: 400/7000; HB: miss; increasing; 75 %; Ne = 1514
8 - Height: 140/135 cm; Weight: 750/400 kg; Herd number: miss; AI: miss
9   Colour: Uni black
10  Pecularity: miss
11 - Main use: (1) milk,(2) miss,(3) miss
12  Spec. abilities: resist. to anaplasmosis,piroplasmosis,tuberculosis
13  Performance compared with STB Holstein-Friesian 92:
14     higher: % fat,% protein, calving ease, handling ease, calving rate
15     equal:  muscularity, age of sexual maturity
16     lower:  milkability,pulling power,milk yield,daily gain,calf mort.
17 - Management: stationary; housing: 12 m.;
18 - Conservation progr.: live animals: miss;Semen: miss;Embryos: miss
19  Status: potential. endang.;Watch: HB♀♀,%pure,%incross!
```

20 - Similar breeds (see group 6/1 on page 80)	EN	Country	Status
21 Iskursko govedo	104	BG	crit.end.
22 Katerini	136	GR	crit.end.
23 Piemontese	197	I	normal
24 Maremmana	166	I	normal

```
 1 - Frisona                                                      EN    92
 2   Holstein-Friesian; country-wide
 3   Ass. Naz. All. bovini Razza Frisona Italiana                 HB:1952
 4   Cremona 26100, Via Bergamo 292
 5 - Incrossing since 1950 from Friesian 277 NL, Holstein CND, USA
 7   Numbers 1991: 4200/2150000; HB: 1101000; miss; 90 %; Ne = 16736
 8 - Height: 160/140 cm; Weight: 1150/700 kg; Herd number: miss; AI: Yes
 9   Colour: Combination black, white
10   Pecularity: miss
11 - Main use: (1) milk,(2) meat,(3) miss
12   Spec. abilities: miss
13   Performance compared with STB Holstein-Friesian 92:
14     higher: Breed is used
15     equal:  as standard breed,
16     lower:  no comparison possible.
17 - Management: stationary; housing: 12 m.;
18 - Conservation progr.: live animals: miss;Semen: miss;Embryos: miss
19   Status: normal;              Watch: %incross!
20 - Similar breeds (see group 1/1 on page 75)    EN  Country Status
21   Sortbroget Dansk Malkekvaeg                   245  DK    pot. end.
22   Nizinna-Czarno-Biala                          185  PL    pot. end.
23   Prim' Holstein                                209  F     normal
24   Pie-Noire-Holstein                            198  B     normal
```

```
 1 - Garfagnina                                                   EN    97
 2   Garfagnina; Province of Lucca
 3   Comunita Montana della Garfagnana                            HB:1985
 4   Castel Nuovo di Garfagnana (LU)
 5 - Incrossing since 1950 from Brown Mountain 46 Italy
 7   Numbers 1992: 8/86; HB: 86; increasing; 50 %; Ne = 14
 8 - Height: 140/125 cm; Weight: 600/425 kg; Herd number: miss; AI: miss
 9   Colour: Uni blue
10   Pecularity: miss
11 - Main use: (1) milk,(2) meat,(3) miss
12   Spec. abilities: mountain
13   Performance compared with STB miss:
14     higher: miss
15     equal:  miss
16     lower:  miss
17 - Management: stationary; housing: 12 m.;
18 - Conservation progr.: live animals: Yes;Semen: 6;Embryos: miss
19   Status: critically endang.;Watch: ♂♂,HB♀♀,%pure,%incross!
20 - Similar breeds (see group 6/2 on page 81)    EN  Country Status
21   Gascon Areole                                  99  F     crit.end.
22   Tiroler Grauvieh                              256  A     pot. end.
23   Grigia Alpina                                 105  I     normal
24   Gascon                                         98  F     normal
```

```
 1 - Grigia Alpina                                             EN   105
 2   Grey Alpine; Provinces of Bolzano and Trento
 3   Ass. Naz. Allevatori Bovini Razza Grigio Alpina          HB:1949
 4   Bolzano 39100, Via Raiffeisen 2
 5 - Composite of local Grigia, Ultimo, Isarco, Passiria, Sare,
 6   Brown 190 Austria
 7   Numbers 1991: 67/25430; HB: 9661; increasing; 100 %; Ne = 266
 8 - Height: 133/126 cm; Weight: 950/575 kg; Herd number: miss; AI: Yes
 9   Colour: Uni grey
10   Pecularity: miss
11 - Main use: (1) milk,(2) meat,(3) miss
12   Spec. abilities: mountain
13   Performance compared with STB Brown Mountain 46:
14     higher: miss
15     equal: % fat, % protein
16     lower:  milk yield
17 - Management: stationary; housing: > 6 m.;
18 - Conservation progr.: live animals: miss;Semen: 100;Embryos: miss
19   Status: normal
```

20 - Similar breeds (see group 6/2 on page 81)	EN	Country	Status
21 Gascon Areole	99	F	crit.end.
22 Garfagnina	97	I	crit.end.
23 Tiroler Grauvieh	256	A	pot. end.
24 Gascon	98	F	normal

```
 1 - Marchigiana                                               EN   165
 2   Marchigiana; Dis. Marche-Abruzzo-Molise
 3   Ass. Naz. Allevatori Bovini Italiani da Carne            HB:1957
 4   Roma 00161, Via Bosio 22
 5 - Composite of Apulian Podolian 207, Chian, Chianina
 7   Numbers 1991: 258/77000; HB: 28600; decreasing; 100 %; Ne = 1023
 8 - Height: 150/140 cm; Weight: 1300/800 kg; Herd number: miss; AI: Yes
 9   Colour: Uni white
10   Pecularity: pigmented skin, black-tipped horns, dark muzzle
11 - Main use: (1) meat,(2) miss,(3) miss
12   Spec. abilities: miss
13   Performance compared with STB miss:
14     higher: miss
15     equal:  miss
16     lower:  miss
17 - Management: stationary; housing: 12 m.;
18 - Conservation progr.: live animals: miss;Semen: 21;Embryos: miss
19   Status: normal;              Watch: trend!
```

20 - Similar breeds (see group 9/3 on page 82)	EN	Country	Status
21 Calvana	57	I	crit.end.
22 Bianca val padana	173	I	pot. end.
23 Chianina	67	I	normal

1 - **Maremmana**   EN   166
2   **Maremmana**; Tuscany and Latium
3   Ass. Naz. Allevatori Bovini Italiani da Carne   HB:1935
4   Roma 00161, Via Bosio 22
5 - Incrossing since 1950 from Chianina 67 Italy, Charolais 62 France
7   Numbers 1991: 120/10000; HB: 4000; decreasing; 100 %; Ne = **466**
8 - Height: **150/125** cm; Weight: **800/550** kg; Herd number: **miss**; AI: **miss**
9   Colour: **Uni medium grey**
10 Pecularity: **very long lyra-shaped horns**
11 - Main use: (1) **meat**,(2) **miss**,(3) **miss**
12 Spec. abilities: **marginal areas**
13 Performance compared with STB **miss**:
14   higher: **miss**
15   equal: **miss**
16   lower: **miss**
17 - Management: **stationary**; housing: **no**
18 - Conservation progr.: live animals: **miss**;Semen: **miss**;Embryos: **miss**
19 Status: **normal**;   Watch: **%incross,trend!**
20 - <u>Similar breeds</u> (see group 6/1 on page 80)   <u>EN</u> <u>Country</u> <u>Status</u>
21 Iskursko govedo   104   BG   crit.end.
22 Katerini   136   GR   crit.end.
23 Podolica   206   I   normal
24 Piemontese   197   I   normal

1 - **Modenese, Bianca val padana**   EN   173
2   **Modenese**; Province of Modena
3   Ass. Provinciale Allevatori   HB:1963
4   Modena 41100, Corso Canal Grande 16
5 - miss
7   Numbers 1992: 36/350; HB: 250; decreasing; 90 %; Ne = **126**
8 - Height: **155/145** cm; Weight: **1050/650** kg; Herd number: **miss**; AI: **Yes**
9   Colour: **Uni white**
10 Pecularity: **black hoofs, black muzzle, white horns black-tipped**
11 - Main use: (1) **milk**,(2) **meat**,(3) **miss**
12 Spec. abilities: **hill**
13 Performance compared with STB **Brown Mountain 46**:
14   higher: **miss**
15   equal: **milk yield, % fat, % protein, calving ease, calving rate**
16   lower: **miss**
17 - Management: **stationary**; housing: **12 m.**;
18 - Conservation progr.: live animals: **Yes**;Semen: **28**;Embryos: **miss**
19 Status: **potential. endang.**;Watch: **%pure,trend!**
20 - <u>Similar breeds</u> (see group 9/3 on page 82)   <u>EN</u> <u>Country</u> <u>Status</u>
21 Calvana   57   I   crit.end.
22 Chianina   67   I   normal
23 **Marchigiana**   165   I   normal

```
 1 - Modicana                                                    EN  174
 2   Modicana; Sicilia
 3   Associazione regionale allevatori della Sicilia            HB:miss
 4   Palermo 90139, Via P.pe Belmonte 55
 5 - Autochthon; Incrossing since 1950 from Brown Mountain 46 Italy,
 6   Charolais 62 France, Limousin 156 France
 7   Numbers 1983: 1600/170000; HB: miss; decreasing; 70 %; Ne = 6340
 8 - Height: 155/140 cm; Weight: 900/550 kg; Herd number: miss; AI: Yes
 9   Colour: Uni red
10   Pecularity: dark muzzle, dark-tipped horns
11 - Main use: (1) milk,(2) meat,(3) miss
12   Spec. abilities: resist. to anaplasmosis,piroplasmosis,tuberculosis
13   Performance compared with STB Brown Mountain 46:
14      higher: % fat,% protein, calving ease, handling ease, calving rate
15      equal:  muscularity, age of sexual maturity
16      lower:  milkability, pulling power, milk yield, daily gain
17 - Management: stationary; housing: 12 m.;
18 - Conservation progr.: live animals: miss;Semen: 3;Embryos: miss
19   Status: potential. endang.;Watch: HB♀♀,trend,%pure,%incross!
```

20 - Similar breeds (see group 6/1 on page 80)	EN	Country	Status
21 Iskursko govedo	104	BG	crit.end.
22 Katerini	136	GR	crit.end.
23 Piemontese	197	I	normal
24 Maremmana	166	I	normal

```
 1 - Pezzata rossa d'Oropa                                       EN  194
 2   Oropa; Province of Vercelli
 3   Provincial Breeders Association                            HB:1964
 4   Vercelli 13100, Via Carducci 4
 5 - Composite of Aosta, Simmental
 6   Incrossing since 1950 from Simmental
 7   Numbers 1992: 65/4600; HB: 931; decreasing; 100 %; Ne = 243
 8 - Height: 135/125 cm; Weight: 850/625 kg; Herd number: miss; AI: Yes
 9   Colour: Combination red, white
10   Pecularity: white head, occasionally black-pied
11 - Main use: (1) milk,(2) meat,(3) miss
12   Spec. abilities: mountain
13   Performance compared with STB Italian Red Pied 195:
14      higher: calving ease, calving rate
15      equal: % fat, % protein
16      lower:  milk yield
17 - Management: stationary; housing: > 6 m.;
18 - Conservation progr.: live animals: miss;Semen: 7;Embryos: miss
19   Status: potential. endang.;Watch: trend,%incross!
```

20 - Similar breeds (see group 3/2 on page 77)	EN	Country	Status
21 Ceske strakate	61	CZ	crit.end.
22 Simentalska	237	PL	min. end.
23 Montbeliard	176	F	normal
24 Fleckvieh	88	A	normal

```
 1 - Pezzata Rossa Italiana                                       EN   195
 2   Italian Red Pied; country-wide
 3   Ass. Naz. All. bovini Razza Pezzata Rossa Italiana            HB:1964
 4   Udine 33100, Via Baltistini 28
 5 - Incrossing since 1950 from Simmental 88 Austria,Simmental 78 Germany
 6   Simmental 240 Switzerland, Simmental 89 France
 7   Numbers 1991: 380/564000; HB: 180000; miss; 60 %; Ne = 1517
 8 - Height: miss/miss cm; Weight: miss/miss kg; Herd number: miss;AI:Yes
 9   Colour: Combination red, white
10   Pecularity: miss
11 - Main use: (1) meat,(2) milk,(3) miss
12   Spec. abilities: miss
13   Performance compared with STB Holstein-Friesian 92:
14     higher: age of sexual maturity, % fat, % protein
15     equal:  miss
16     lower:  milk yield, calving interval
17 - Management: stationary; housing: 12 m.;
18 - Conservation progr.: live animals: miss;Semen: miss;Embryos: miss
19   Status: potential. endang.;Watch: %pure,%incross!
20 - Similar breeds (see group 3/2 on page 77)    EN  Country Status
21   Ceske strakate                               61   CZ   crit.end.
22   Simentalska                                 237   PL   min. end.
23   Montbeliard                                 176   F    normal
24   Fleckvieh                                    88   A    normal
```

```
 1 - Piemontese                                                   EN   197
 2   Piedmont; District of Piedmont
 3   Ass. Naz. Allevatori Bovini Razza Piemontese                  HB:1963
 4   Torino 10151, Via Valeggio 22
 5 - miss
 7   Numbers 1991: 921/180000; HB: 42000; decreasing; 100 %; Ne = 3605
 8 - Height: 150/145 cm; Weight: 950/600 kg; Herd number: miss; AI: Yes
 9   Colour: Uni blue, light brownish grey to white
10   Pecularity: black tail switch, eyelashes, muzzle, ears, hoofs
11 - Main use: (1) meat,(2) miss,(3) miss
12   Spec. abilities: miss
13   Performance compared with STB Holstein-Friesian 92:
14     higher: % protein, age of sexual maturity, % fat
15     equal:  miss
16     lower:  milk yield
17 - Management: stationary; housing: 12 m.;
18 - Conservation progr.: live animals: miss;Semen: Yes;Embryos: miss
19   Status: normal
20 - Similar breeds (see group 6/1 on page 80)    EN  Country Status
21   Iskursko govedo                             104   BG   crit.end.
22   Katerini                                    136   GR   crit.end.
23   Podolica                                    206   I    normal
24   Maremmana                                   166   I    normal
```

1 - **Pinzgauer**   EN **200**
2   **Pinzgau; Province of Bolzano**
3   **Ass. Naz. Allevatori Bovini Razza Grigio Alpina**   HB: **Yes**
4   **Bolzano 39100, Via Raiffeisen 2**
5 - miss
7   Numbers 1991: **4/2620**; HB: **1240**; **decreasing**; **80 %**; Ne = **7**
8 - Height: **140/132** cm; Weight: **1150/675** kg; Herd number: **miss**; AI: **Yes**
9   Colour: **Combination red, white**
10 Pecularity: **broad white back-stripe, coloursided with coloured head**
11 - Main use: (1) **milk**,(2) **meat**,(3) **miss**
12 Spec. abilities: **mountain**
13 Performance compared with STB **Holstein-Friesian 92**:
14   higher: **handling ease, % fat, % protein**
15   equal: **calving interval**
16   lower: **milk yield**
17 - Management: **stationary**; housing: **> 6 m.**; **pastures, woods**
18 - Conservation progr.: live animals: **Yes**;Semen: **15**;Embryos: **miss**
19 Status: **critically endang.**;Watch: **♂♂,trend,%pure!**
20 - <u>Similar breeds</u> (see group 3/4 on page 77)   <u>EN</u> <u>Country</u> <u>Status</u>
21 **Pustertaler Schecken**   210   D   crit.end.
22 **Pustertaler Sprinzen**   211   I   crit.end.
23 **Pinzgauer**   202   A   pot. end.
24 **Slovenske pinzgavske**   243   SK   normal

1 - **Pisana**   EN **205**
2   **Pisana; Province of Pisa**
3   **Provincial Breeders Association**   HB:**1985**
4   **Pisa 56100, Via Benedetto Croce**
5 - **Composite of Italian Brown, Chianina**
6   **Incrossing since 1950 from Brown Mountain 46 Italy**
7   Numbers 1991: **4/154**; HB: **154**; **decreasing**; **30 %**; Ne = **7**
8 - Height: **150/145** cm; Weight: **800/525** kg; Herd number: **miss**; AI: **Yes**
9   Colour: **Uni brown, chestnut to black**
10 Pecularity: **miss**
11 - Main use: (1) **milk, meat**,(2) **miss**,(3) **miss**
12 Spec. abilities: **miss**
13 Performance compared with STB **miss**:
14   higher: **miss**
15   equal: **miss**
16   lower: **miss**
17 - Management: **stationary**; housing: **12 m.**;
18 - Conservation progr.: live animals: **Yes**;Semen: **21**;Embryos: **miss**
19 Status: **critically endang.**;Watch: **♂♂,HB♀♀,trend,%pure,%incross!**
20 - <u>Similar breeds</u> (see group 5/1 on page 79)   <u>EN</u> <u>Country</u> <u>Status</u>
21 **Original Allgäuer Braunvieh**   189   D   crit.end.
22 **Agerolese**   2   I   crit.end.
23 **Aubrac**   14   F   normal
24 **Österreichisches Braunvieh**   190   A   normal

1 - **Podolica**   EN   206
2   **Podolian**; Basilicata, Calabria, Pugli
3   Ass. Naz. Allevatori Bovini Italiani da carne   HB:1937
4   Roma 00161, Via Bosio 22
5 - Composite of local and old Podolian breeds
7   Numbers 1991: **437/53000**; HB: **20000**; **increasing**; miss %; Ne = **1711**
8 - Height: **152/128** cm; Weight: **700/400** kg; Herd number: **miss**; AI: **miss**
9   Colour: **Uni medium grey**
10 Pecularity: **calves born red; lyra-shaped hornes**
11 - Main use: (1) **meat**,(2) **miss**,(3) **miss**
12 Spec. abilities: **miss**
13 Performance compared with STB **miss**:
14   higher: **miss**
15   equal: **miss**
16   lower: **miss**
17 - Management: **stationary**; housing: **no**; **arid hill, mediterr. scrub**
18 - Conservation progr.: live animals: **miss**;Semen: **miss**;Embryos: **miss**
19 Status: **normal**;   Watch: **%pure!**
20 - Similar breeds (see group 6/1 on page 80)   EN   Country   Status
21   **Iskursko govedo**   104   BG   crit.end.
22   **Katerini**   136   GR   crit.end.
23   **Piemontese**   197   I   normal
24   **Maremmana**   166   I   normal

1 - **Pontremolese**   EN   208
2   **Pontremolese**; Province of Lucca
3   Associazione Italiana Allovatoria   HB:1935
4   Rome 00161, Via G. Tomanetti 9
5 - Incrossing since 1950 from Brown Mountain 46 Italy
7   Numbers 1992: **7/27**; HB: **27**; **increasing**; 50 %; Ne = **10**
8 - Height: **145/125** cm; Weight: **750/500** kg; Herd number: **1**; AI: **Yes**
9   Colour: **Uni yellow, corn coloured**
10 Pecularity: **miss**
11 - Main use: (1) **milk; meat**,(2) **miss**,(3) **miss**
12 Spec. abilities: **mountain**
13 Performance compared with STB **miss**:
14   higher: **miss**
15   equal: **miss**
16   lower: **miss**
17 - Management: **stationary**; housing: **> 6 m.**; **pastures - woods**
18 - Conservation progr.: live animals: **Yes**;Semen: **6**;Embryos: **miss**
19 Status: **critically endang.**;Watch: **♂♂,HB♀♀,herds,%pure,%incross!**
20 - Similar breeds (see group 8/5 on page 82)   EN   Country   Status
21   **Tortonese**   258   I   crit.end.
22   **Reggiana**   217   I   pot. end.

CATTLE

```
 1 - Pustertaler Sprinzen                                    EN  211
 2   Pustertaler Sprinzen; Province of Bolzano
 3   Ass. Naz. Allevatori Bovini Razza Grigio Alpina         HB:miss
 4   Bolzano 39100, Via Raiffeisen 2
 5 - Incrossing since 1950 from Pinzgauer 200 Italy
 7   Numbers 1991: 3/60; HB: miss; increasing; 80 %; Ne = 5
 8 - Height: 140/130 cm; Weight: 800/500 kg; Herd number: 1; AI: miss
 9   Colour: Combination black, red, white, with red or black pied sides
10   Pecularity: miss
11 - Main use: (1) milk; meat,(2) miss,(3) miss
12   Spec. abilities: mountain
13   Performance compared with STB miss:
14     higher: miss
15     equal:  miss
16     lower:  miss
17 - Management: stationary; housing: > 6 m.; poor pastures
18 - Conservation progr.: live animals: Yes;Semen: 2;Embryos: miss
19   Status: critically endang.;Watch: ♂♂,HB♀♀,herds,%pure,%incross!
20 - Similar breeds (see group 3/4 on page 77)    EN  Country Status
21   Pustertaler Schecken                          210   D     crit.end.
22   Pinzgauer                                     200   I     crit.end.
23   Pinzgauer                                     202   A     pot. end.
24   Slovenske pinzgavske                          243   SK    normal
```

CATTLE

```
 1 - Reggiana                                                EN  217
 2   Reggiana; Province of Reggio Emilia
 3   Provincial Breeders Association                         HB:1935
 4   Reggio Emilia 421, Via Bojardi 4/a
 5 - miss
 7   Numbers 1992: 49/1024; HB: 473; decreasing; 70 %; Ne = 178
 8 - Height: 145/140 cm; Weight: 650/500 kg; Herd number: miss; AI: Yes
 9   Colour: Uni red, brown, yellow
10   Pecularity: light muzzle, black-tipped horns
11 - Main use: (1) milk,(2) miss,(3) miss
12   Spec. abilities: miss
13   Performance compared with STB Brown Mountain 46:
14     higher: milkability, calving rate
15     equal:  milk yield, % fat, % protein
16     lower:  miss
17 - Management: stationary; housing: 12 m.;
18 - Conservation progr.: live animals: Yes;Semen: 57;Embryos: miss
19   Status: potential. endang.;Watch: trend,%pure!
20 - Similar breeds (see group 8/5 on page 82)    EN  Country Status
21   Pontremolese                                  208   I     crit.end.
22   Tortonese                                     258   I     crit.end.
```

```
1 - Rendena                                                          EN  218
2   Rendena; Prov. of Trento, Vicenza and Padov
3   Ass. Naz. Allevatori Bovini Razza Rendena                       HB:1982
4   Trento 381, Via Lavisotto 125
5 - Incrossing since 1950 from Brown Mountain 46 Italy
7   Numbers 1992: 36/10500; HB: 4200; decreasing; 70 %; Ne = 143
8 - Height: 130/125 cm; Weight: 600/475 kg; Herd number: miss; AI: Yes
9   Colour: Uni dark chestnut-brown, nearly black
10  Pecularity: pale muzzle ring and dorsal stripe
11 - Main use: (1) milk,(2) miss,(3) miss
12  Spec. abilities: mountain
13  Performance compared with STB Holstein-Friesian 92:
14    higher: age of sexual maturity
15    equal: % fat, % protein
16    lower: milk yield, calving interval
17 - Management: stationary; housing: > 6 m.; poor pastures
18 - Conservation progr.: live animals: miss;Semen: Yes;Embryos: miss
19  Status: minimally endang.; Watch: trend,%pure,%incross!
20 - Similar breeds (see group 5/1 on page 79)      EN  Country Status
21  Original Allgäuer Braunvieh                     189    D    crit.end.
22  Agerolese                                         2    I    crit.end.
23  Aubrac                                           14    F    normal
24  Österreichisches Braunvieh                      190    A    normal
```

```
1 - Romagnola                                                        EN  223
2   Romagnola; Dis. Emilia Romagna / Marche
3   Ass. Naz. Allevatori Bovini Italiani da carne                   HB:1963
4   Roma 00161, Via Bosio 22
5 - Autochthon
7   Numbers 1991: 235/11000; HB: 9200; decreasing; 100 %; Ne = 917
8 - Height: 145/135 cm; Weight: 1150/800 kg; Herd number: miss; AI: Yes
9   Colour: Uni light grey to white
10  Pecularity: pigmented skin, dark muzzle and horns, calves brown
11 - Main use: (1) meat,(2) miss,(3) miss
12  Spec. abilities: miss
13  Performance compared with STB miss:
14    higher: miss
15    equal: miss
16    lower: miss
17 - Management: stationary; housing: 2-6/12 m.; hill - pastures
18 - Conservation progr.: live animals: miss;Semen: 16;Embryos: miss
19  Status: normal;              Watch: trend!
20 - Similar breeds (see group 6/1 on page 80)      EN  Country Status
21  Iskursko govedo                                 104   BG    crit.end.
22  Katerini                                        136   GR    crit.end.
23  Piemontese                                      197    I    normal
24  Maremmana                                       166    I    normal
```

1 - **Sarda**   EN **227**
2   Sardinian; Sardinia
3   Ass. Reg. Allevatori della Sardegna   HB:miss
4   Cagliari 9100, Via Mameli 115
5 - Incrossing since 1950 from Brown Mountain 46 Italy
7   Numbers 1991: **200/** miss; HB: **3685**; decreasing; miss %; Ne = **759**
8 - Height: **110/105** cm; Weight: **300/250** kg; Herd number: miss; AI: miss
9   Colour: **Uni yellow, solid-coloured, pied, brindle**
10   Pecularity: miss
11 - Main use: (1) **meat,**(2) miss,(3) miss
12   Spec. abilities: **mountain**
13   Performance compared with STB miss:
14   higher: miss
15   equal: miss
16   lower: miss
17 - Management: **stationary**; housing: miss m.; **arid soils**
18 - Conservation progr.: live animals: **Yes;**Semen: miss;Embryos: miss
19   Status: **minimally endang.**; Watch: **trend,%pure,%incross!**
20 - Similar breeds (see group 5/1 on page 79)   EN Country Status
21   **Original Allgäuer Braunvieh**   189 D   crit.end.
22   **Agerolese**   2 I   crit.end.
23   **Aubrac**   14 F   normal
24   **Österreichisches Braunvieh**   190 A   normal

1 - **Sardo-Modicana**   EN **228**
2   Sardo-Modicana; Cagliari, Oristano (Sardi)
3   Ass. Reg. Allevatori della Sardegna   HB:miss
4   Cagliari 9100, Via Mamelia 115
5 - Composite of Sardinian 227 Italy, Modicana 174 Italy
6   Incrossing since 1950 from Brown Mountain 46 Italy
7   Numbers 1991: **324/** miss; HB: **1557**; increasing; miss %; Ne = **1073**
8 - Height: **140/135** cm; Weight: **600/525** kg; Herd number: miss; AI: miss
9   Colour: **Uni red, yellow-brown to dark red**
10   Pecularity: miss
11 - Main use: (1) **meat,**(2) miss,(3) miss
12   Spec. abilities: miss
13   Performance compared with STB miss:
14   higher: miss
15   equal: miss
16   lower: miss
17 - Management: **stationary**; housing: miss m.; **arid soils**
18 - Conservation progr.: live animals: miss;Semen: miss;Embryos: miss
19   Status: **normal**;   Watch: **%pure,%incross!**
20 - Similar breeds (see group 6/1 on page 80)   EN Country Status
21   **Iskursko govedo**   104 BG   crit.end.
22   **Katerini**   136 GR   crit.end.
23   **Piemontese**   197 I   normal
24   **Maremmana**   166 I   normal

337

```
 1 - Tortonese, Varzese, Ottonese                                    EN   258
 2   Montana; Alessandria,Pavia,Piacenz
 3   Ass. Italiana Allevatori                                        HB:miss
 4   Roma 00161, Via Tomassetti 9
 5 - Incrossing since 1950 from Reggiana 217 Italy, Brown Mountain 46 I
 7   Numbers 1992: 3/100; HB: 32; decreasing; 50 %; Ne = 5
 8 - Height: 140/130 cm; Weight: 700/500 kg; Herd number: miss; AI: miss
 9   Colour: Uni yellow
10   Pecularity: light muzzle
11 - Main use: (1) milk,(2) meat,(3) miss
12   Spec. abilities: mountain
13   Performance compared with STB miss:
14     higher: miss
15     equal:  miss
16     lower:  miss
17 - Management: stationary; housing: 12 m.;
18 - Conservation progr.: live animals: Yes;Semen: Yes;Embryos: miss
19   Status: critically endang.;Watch: ♂♂,HB♀♀,trend,%pure,%incross!
20 - Similar breeds (see group 8/5 on page 82)     EN  Country Status
21   Pontremolese                                  208    I    crit.end.
22   Reggiana                                      217    I    pot. end.
```

```
 1 - Valdostana Castana                                              EN   260
 2   Aosta Chestnut; Aosta Valley
 3   Ass. Naz. Allevaturi Bovini Razza Valdostana                    HB:1985
 4   Aosta 11100, Piazza Arco d'Augusto 10
 5 - Composite of Aosta Black Pied 261 Italy, Herens 83 Switzerland
 6   Incrossing since 1950 from Herens 83 Switzerland
 7   Numbers 1992: 108/5000; HB: 4800; stable; 98 %; Ne = 423
 8 - Height: 130/120 cm; Weight: 600/500 kg; Herd number: miss; AI: Yes
 9   Colour: Uni, chestnut predominant or combination chestnut and white
10   Pecularity: miss
11 - Main use: (1) milk; meat,(2) cow fihgting,(3) miss
12   Spec. abilities: mountain
13   Performance compared with STB Holstein-Friesian 92:
14     higher: age of sexual maturity, % protein
15     equal:  % fat
16     lower:  milk yield, calving interval
17 - Management: stationary; housing: > 6 m.;
18 - Conservation progr.: live animals: miss;Semen: Yes;Embryos: miss
19   Status: normal;              Watch: %incross!
20 - Similar breeds (see group 5/2 on page 80)     EN  Country Status
21   Alpine Herens                                   7    F    crit.end.
22   Tarentaise                                    253    F    normal
23   Eringer Rind                                   83    CH   normal
```

1 - **Valdostana Pezzata Nera**   EN 261
2   **Aosta Black Pied; Province of Aosta (Aosta Valley)**
3   **Ass. Naz. Allevatori Bovini Razza Valdostana**   HB:1985
4   **Aosta 11100, Piazza Arco d'Augusto 10**
5 - **Autochthon derived from Illyrian Celtic**
7   Numbers 1992: 21/2500; HB: 2200; decreasing; 98 %; Ne = 66
8 - Height: **130/120** cm; Weight: **600/500** kg; Herd number: **miss**; AI: **Yes**
9   Colour: **Combination black, white**
10   Pecularity: **miss**
11 - Main use: (1) **milk; meat**,(2) **cow fighting**,(3) **miss**
12   Spec. abilities: **mountain**
13   Performance compared with STB **Holstein-Friesian 92**:
14   higher: **age of sexual maturity, % protein**
15   equal: **% fat**
16   lower: **milk yield, calving interval**
17 - Management: **stationary**; housing: **> 6 m.**;
18 - Conservation progr.: live animals: **miss**;Semen: **Yes**;Embryos: **miss**
19   Status: **potential. endang.**;Watch: **♂♂,trend!**
20 - <u>Similar breeds</u> (see group 1/2 on page 75)   <u>EN</u> <u>Country</u> <u>Status</u>
21   **Burlina**   51   I   crit.end.
22   **Breton Pie Noire**   42   F   endanger.
23   **Cherno-pestraya litovskaya**   66   LT   normal
24   **Cherno-pestraya estonskaya**   65   EW   normal

1 - **Valdostana Pezzata Rossa**   EN 262
2   **Aosta Red Pied; Aosta, Torino, Vercel.Cuneo**
3   **Ass. Naz. Allevatori Bovini Razza Valdostana**   HB:1958
4   **Aosta 11100, Piazza Arco d'Augusto 10**
5 - **miss**
7   Numbers 1992: 189/50000; HB: 14752; decreasing; 98 %; Ne = 746
8 - Height: **135/130** cm; Weight: **650/500** kg; Herd number: **miss**; AI: **Yes**
9   Colour: **Combination red, white**
10   Pecularity: **white head, light muzzle**
11 - Main use: (1) **milk**,(2) **meat**,(3) **miss**
12   Spec. abilities: **mountain**
13   Performance compared with STB **Holstein-Friesian 92**:
14   higher: **age of sexual maturity, % protein**
15   equal: **% fat**
16   lower: **milk yield, calving interval**
17 - Management: **stationary**; housing: **> 6 m.**;
18 - Conservation progr.: live animals: **miss**;Semen: **Yes**;Embryos: **miss**
19   Status: **normal**;   Watch: **trend!**
20 - <u>Similar breeds</u> (see group 3/2 on page 77)   <u>EN</u> <u>Country</u> <u>Status</u>
21   **Ceske strakate**   61   CZ   crit.end.
22   **Simentalska**   237 PL   min. end.
23   **Montbeliard**   176 F   normal
24   **Fleckvieh**   88   A   normal

```
 1 - Alpagota                                                    EN   400
 2   Alpagota; Province of Belluno (Venezia)
 3   ESAV                                                        HB: Yes
 4   Venezia 30125, Via S. Cruce 1187
 5 - Composite of Lamon 525, Vicentina, Istriana 516
 7   Numbers 1991: miss /600; HB: miss; decreasing; miss %; Ne = 109
 8 - Height: 67/57 cm; Weight: 52/42 kg; Herd number: miss; AI: miss
 9   Colour: Uni white, dark spots on face and legs
10   Pecularity: horns 0/0
11 - Main use: (1) meat,(2) milk,(3) wool
12   Spec. abilities: miss
13   Performance compared with STB miss:
14      higher: miss
15      equal:  miss
16      lower:  miss
17 - Management: stationary/transhumant; housing: 2-6 m.;
18 - Conservation progr.: live animals: miss;Semen: miss;Embryos: miss
19   Status: critically endang.;Watch: ♂♂,HB♀♀,trend,herds,%pure!
20 - Similar breeds (see group 7/1 on page 91)      EN  Country Status
21   Commun des Alpes                               470   F     crit.end.
22   Bellunese                                      413   I     crit.end.
23   Biellese                                       419   I     normal
24   Prealpes du Sud                                589   F     normal
```

```
 1 - Altamurana                                                  EN   401
 2   Altamurana; Provinces of Bari and Foggia (Apulia)
 3   Assonapa                                                    HB:1972
 4   Roma 00161, Via Ravenna 9/c
 5 - Autochthon local breed
 7   Numbers 1991: 8/900; HB: 134; decreasing; miss %; Ne = 14
 8 - Height: 70/65 cm; Weight: 52/37 kg; Herd number: 1; AI: miss
 9   Colour: Uni white, occasionally dark spots on face
10   Pecularity: horns 0/0
11 - Main use: (1) milk,(2) wool,(3) miss
12   Spec. abilities: arid soils
13   Performance compared with STB miss:
14      higher: miss
15      equal:  miss
16      lower:  miss
17 - Management: stationary; housing: 12 m.;
18 - Conservation progr.: live animals: miss;Semen: miss;Embryos: miss
19   Status: critically endang.;Watch: ♂♂,HB♀♀,trend,herds,%pure!
20 - Similar breeds (see group 5/2 on page 89)      EN  Country Status
21   Caussenard des Garrigues                       447   F     crit.end.
22   Raiole                                         594   F     endanger.
23   Caussenard du Lot                              448   F     normal
24   Basco-Bearnaise                                412   F     normal
```

1 - **Appenninica**   EN   **402**
2   **Apennine; Apennine Mountain, Emilia, Abruzzi**
3   **Assonapa**   HB:**1981**
4   **Roma 00161, Via Ravenna 9/c**
5 - **Autochthon local breed**
7   Numbers 1991: **264/114000**; HB: **13422**; **stable**; miss %; Ne = **1036**
8 - Height: **80/70** cm; Weight: **80/60** kg; Herd number: **miss**; AI: **miss**
9   Colour: **Uni white**
10   Pecularity: **horns 0/0**
11 - Main use: (1) **meat**,(2) **miss**,(3) **miss**
12   Spec. abilities: **hill**
13   Performance compared with STB **miss**:
14   higher: **miss**
15   equal: **miss**
16   lower: **miss**
17 - Management: **stationary**; housing: **12** m.;
18 - Conservation progr.: live animals: **miss**;Semen: **miss**;Embryos: **miss**
19   Status: **normal**
20 - <u>Similar breeds</u> (see group 7/5 on page 92)   <u>EN</u> <u>Country</u> <u>Status</u>
21   **Cornella bianca**   471   I   crit.end.
22   **Garfagnina bianca**   498   I   crit.end.
23   **Pagliarola**   576   I   normal
24   **Massese**   541   I   normal

1 - **Bagnolese**   EN   **408**
2   **Bagnolese; Province of Avellino (Campania)**
3   **Assonapa**   HB:**miss**
4   **Roma 00161, Via Ravenna 9/c**
5 - **Composite of Comisana and local breed**
6   **Incrossing since 1960 from Comisana 469, Sicilian Barbary 410**
7   Numbers 1991: **35000**; HB: **miss**; **increasing**; miss %; Ne = **6335**
8 - Height: **70/50** cm; Weight: **85/60** kg; Herd number: **miss**; AI: **miss**
9   Colour: **Combination brown, white**
10   Pecularity: **horns 0/0**
11 - Main use: (1) **meat**,(2) **wool**,(3) **miss**
12   Spec. abilities: **hill**
13   Performance compared with STB **miss**:
14   higher: **miss**
15   equal: **miss**
16   lower: **miss**
17 - Management: **miss**; housing: **miss** m.;
18 - Conservation progr.: live animals: **miss**;Semen: **miss**;Embryos: **miss**
19   Status: **potential. endang.**;Watch: ♂♂,HB♀♀,**%pure,%incross**!
20 - <u>Similar breeds</u> (see group 8/1 on page 94)   <u>EN</u> <u>Country</u> <u>Status</u>
21   **Marrane**   540   I   crit.end.
22   **Rosset**   603   I   crit.end.
23   **Comisana**   469   I   normal
24   **Corse**   472   F   normal

```
 1 - Barbaresca della Campania                                    EN   409
 2   Campanian Barbary; Campania
 3   Assonapa                                                     HB:1971
 4   Roma 00161, Via Ravenna 9/c
 5 - Composite of Tunisian Barbary, local breeds
 7   Numbers 1991: 42/30000; HB: 1672; stable; miss %; Ne = 164
 8 - Height: 97/72 cm; Weight: 95/67 kg; Herd number: miss; AI: miss
 9   Colour: Uni white, often dark spots on face and legs
10   Pecularity: horns 0/0
11 - Main use: (1) meat,(2) milk,(3) miss
12   Spec. abilities: hill
13   Performance compared with STB miss:
14     higher: miss
15     equal:  miss
16     lower:  miss
17 - Management: stationary; housing: 12 m.;
18 - Conservation progr.: live animals: miss;Semen: miss;Embryos: miss
19   Status: normal;              Watch: ♂♂,%pure!
```

20 - Similar breeds (see group 8/3 on page 95)	EN	Country	Status
21 Rouge du Roussillon	606	F	crit.end.
22 Nostrana	570	I	endanger.
23 Pinzirita	581	I	normal
24 Barbaresca Siciliana	410	I	normal

```
 1 - Barbaresca Siciliana                                         EN   410
 2   Sicilian Barbary; Sicily
 3   Assonapa                                                     HB:1977
 4   Roma 00161, Via Ravenna 9/c
 5 - Composite of Pinzirita 581, Barbaresca from Africa
 7   Numbers 1991: 215/25800; HB: 7830; stable; miss %; Ne = 837
 8 - Height: 85/80 cm; Weight: 105/67 kg; Herd number: miss; AI: miss
 9   Colour: Uni white, sometimes pied, neck black or brown
10   Pecularity: horns 0/0
11 - Main use: (1) meat,(2) miss,(3) miss
12   Spec. abilities: arid hill
13   Performance compared with STB Sardinian 618:
14     higher: age of sexual maturity
15     equal:  miss
16     lower:  milk yield
17 - Management: stationary; housing: 12 m.;
18 - Conservation progr.: live animals: miss;Semen: miss;Embryos: miss
19   Status: normal;              Watch: %pure!
```

20 - Similar breeds (see group 8/3 on page 95)	EN	Country	Status
21 Rouge du Roussillon	606	F	crit.end.
22 Nostrana	570	I	endanger.
23 Pinzirita	581	I	normal
24 Barbaresca della Campania	409	I	normal

```
 1 - Bellunese                                              EN  413
 2   Bellunese; Province of Treviso (Venetia)
 3   Assonapa                                              HB:miss
 4   Roma 00161, Via Ravenna 9/c
 5 - Composite of Alpagota 400, Lamon 525
 7   Numbers 1991: 25; HB: miss; decreasing; miss %; Ne = 2
 8 - Height: 65/57 cm; Weight: 52/42 kg; Herd number: 1; AI: miss
 9   Colour: Uni white, occasionally dark spots on face
10   Pecularity: horns 0/0
11 - Main use: (1) milk; meat,(2) miss,(3) miss
12   Spec. abilities: miss
13   Performance compared with STB miss:
14     higher: miss
15     equal:  miss
16     lower:  miss
17 - Management: miss; housing: 2-6 m.;
18 - Conservation progr.: live animals: miss;Semen: miss;Embryos: miss
19   Status: critically endang.;Watch: ♂♂,HB♀♀,trend,herds,%pure!
```

20 - <u>Similar breeds</u> (see group 7/1 on page 91)	<u>EN</u>	<u>Country</u>	<u>Status</u>
21 Commun des Alpes	470	F	crit.end.
22 Alpagota	400	I	crit.end.
23 Biellese	419	I	normal
24 Prealpes du Sud	589	F	normal

```
 1 - Bergamasca                                            EN  415
 2   Bergamasca; Lombardy
 3   Assonapa                                             HB:1976
 4   Roma 00161, Via Ravenna 9/c
 5 - Composite of Ovis Aries Sudanica
 7   Numbers 1991: 215/30000; HB: 13884; stable; miss %; Ne = 847
 8 - Height: 90/80 cm; Weight: 105/82 kg; Herd number: miss; AI: miss
 9   Colour: Uni white
10   Pecularity: horns 0/0
11 - Main use: (1) milk,(2) wool,(3) miss
12   Spec. abilities: miss
13   Performance compared with STB miss:
14     higher: miss
15     equal:  miss
16     lower:  miss
17 - Management: transhumant; housing: 2-6 m.;
18 - Conservation progr.: live animals: miss;Semen: miss;Embryos: miss
19   Status: normal;          Watch: %pure!
```

20 - <u>Similar breeds</u> (see group 7/2 on page 91)	<u>EN</u>	<u>Country</u>	<u>Status</u>
21 Braunes Bergschaf	431	D	crit.end.
22 Istriana	516	I	crit.end.
23 Fabrianese	487	I	normal
24 Weißes Bergschaf	416	D	normal

```
1 - Biellese                                                    EN   419
2   Biellese; Piedmont
3   Assonapa                                                    HB:1986
4   Roma 00161, Via Ravenna 9/c
5 - miss
7   Numbers 1991: 46/24000; HB: 863; increasing; miss %; Ne = 175
8 - Height: 90/82 cm; Weight: 85/72 kg; Herd number: miss; AI: miss
9   Colour: Uni white
10  Pecularity: horns 0/0
11 - Main use: (1) meat,(2) wool,(3) miss
12  Spec. abilities: miss
13  Performance compared with STB miss:
14    higher: miss
15    equal: miss
16    lower: miss
17 - Management: stationary/transhumant; housing: 2-6/12 m.;
18 - Conservation progr.: live animals: miss;Semen: miss;Embryos: miss
19  Status: normal;              Watch: %pure!
```

20 - Similar breeds (see group 7/1 on page 91)	EN	Country	Status
21 Commun des Alpes	470	F	crit.end.
22 Alpagota	400	I	crit.end.
23 Mourerous	558	F	min. end.
24 Prealpes du Sud	589	F	normal

```
1 - Brentegana                                                  EN   433
2   Brentegana; Province of Verona (Venetia)
3   Assonapa                                                    HB:miss
4   Roma 00161, Via Ravenna 9/c
5 - Autochthon derivative of Lamon (Alpine group)
7   Numbers 1983: 3000; HB: miss; stable; miss %; Ne = 543
8 - Height: 92/82 cm; Weight: 95/75 kg; Herd number: miss; AI: miss
9   Colour: Uni white
10  Pecularity: horns 0/0
11 - Main use: (1) meat,(2) wool,(3) miss
12  Spec. abilities: miss
13  Performance compared with STB miss:
14    higher: miss
15    equal: miss
16    lower: miss
17 - Management: miss; housing: miss m.;
18 - Conservation progr.: live animals: miss;Semen: miss;Embryos: miss
19  Status: minimally endang.; Watch: ♂♂,HB♀♀,%pure!
```

20 - Similar breeds (see group 7/1 on page 91)	EN	Country	Status
21 Commun des Alpes	470	F	crit.end.
22 Alpagota	400	I	crit.end.
23 Biellese	419	I	normal
24 Prealpes du Sud	589	F	normal

1 - **Brianzola**   EN **434**
2   Brianzola; Province of Como (Lombardy)
3   Assonapa   HB:miss
4   Roma 00161, Via Ravenna 9/c
5 - Composite of Bergamasca 415, Varesina 659
7   Numbers 1983: 20; HB: miss; decreasing; miss %; Ne = 4
8 - Height: **90/85** cm; Weight: **85/77** kg; Herd number: 1; AI: miss
9   Colour: **Uni white**
10 Pecularity: **horns 0/0**
11 - Main use: (1) **milk**,(2) miss,(3) miss
12 Spec. abilities: miss
13 Performance compared with STB miss:
14   higher: miss
15   equal: miss
16   lower: miss
17 - Management: miss; housing: miss m.;
18 - Conservation progr.: live animals: miss;Semen: miss;Embryos: miss
19 Status: **critically endang.**;Watch: ♂♂,HB♀♀,trend,herds,**%pure**!
20 - <u>Similar breeds</u> (see group 7/1 on page 91)   <u>EN</u> <u>Country</u> <u>Status</u>
21 **Commun des Alpes**   470   F   crit.end.
22 **Alpagota**   400   I   crit.end.
23 **Biellese**   419   I   normal
24 **Prealpes du Sud**   589   F   normal

1 - **Brigasca**   EN **435**
2   Brigasca; Province of Imperia (Liguria)
3   Assessorato Agricoltura Regione Liguria   HB:miss
4   Genova 16121, Via Fieschi 15
5 - Autochthon local population
7   Numbers 1991: miss /200; HB: miss; decreasing; miss %; Ne = 18
8 - Height: **80/67** cm; Weight: **67/57** kg; Herd number: miss; AI: miss
9   Colour: **Uni white**
10 Pecularity: **horns 2/2**
11 - Main use: (1) **milk; meat; wool**,(2) miss,(3) miss
12 Spec. abilities: **mountain**
13 Performance compared with STB miss:
14   higher: miss
15   equal: miss
16   lower: miss
17 - Management: miss; housing: miss m.;
18 - Conservation progr.: live animals: miss;Semen: miss;Embryos: miss
19 Status: **critically endang.**;Watch: ♂♂,HB♀♀,trend,**%pure**!
20 - <u>Similar breeds</u> (see group 7/3 on page 92)   <u>EN</u> <u>Country</u> <u>Status</u>
21 **Brigasque**   436   F   crit.end.
22 **Frabosana**   492   I   crit.end.
23 **Besch da pader**   485   CH   min. end.
24 **Delle Langhe**   478   I   normal

```
 1 - Brogne                                                    EN  440
 2   Brogne; Province of Verona (Venetia)
 3   Assonapa                                                  HB:miss
 4   Roma 00161, Via Ravenna 9/c
 5 - Composite of Bergamasca 415, Lamon 525
 7   Numbers 1991: miss /600; HB: miss; increasing; miss %; Ne = 109
 8 - Height: 67/57 cm; Weight: 60/47 kg; Herd number: 1; AI: miss
 9   Colour: Uni white
10   Pecularity: horns 0/0
11 - Main use: (1) milk,(2) wool,(3) miss
12   Spec. abilities: hill
13   Performance compared with STB miss:
14      higher: miss
15      equal:  miss
16      lower:  miss
17 - Management: miss; housing: miss m.;
18 - Conservation progr.: live animals: miss;Semen: miss;Embryos: miss
19   Status: critically endang.;Watch: ♂♂,HB♀♀,herds,%pure!
```

20 -	Similar breeds (see group 7/1 on page 91)	EN	Country	Status
21	Commun des Alpes	470	F	crit.end.
22	Alpagota	400	I	crit.end.
23	Biellese	419	I	normal
24	Prealpes du Sud	589	F	normal

```
 1 - Ciavenasca                                                EN  458
 2   Ciavenasca; Province of Sondrio (Lombardy)
 3   Assonapa                                                  HB:miss
 4   Roma 00161, Via Ravenna 9/c
 5 - Autochthon local population
 7   Numbers 1983: 3000; HB: miss; stable; miss %; Ne = 543
 8 - Height: 60/52 cm; Weight: 50/42 kg; Herd number: miss; AI: miss
 9   Colour: Uni white
10   Pecularity: horns 0/0
11 - Main use: (1) meat,(2) miss,(3) miss
12   Spec. abilities: highlands - mountains
13   Performance compared with STB miss:
14      higher: miss
15      equal:  miss
16      lower:  miss
17 - Management: miss; housing: miss m.;
18 - Conservation progr.: live animals: miss;Semen: miss;Embryos: miss
19   Status: minimally endang.; Watch: ♂♂,HB♀♀,%pure!
```

20 -	Similar breeds (see group 8/1 on page 94)	EN	Country	Status
21	Marrane	540	I	crit.end.
22	Rosset	603	I	crit.end.
23	Comisana	469	I	normal
24	Corse	472	F	normal

```
 1 - Ciuta (extinct)                                    EN  463
 2   Ciuta; Province of Sondrio (Lombardy)
 3   Assonapa                                           HB:miss
 4   Roma 00161, Via Ravenna 9/c
 5 - Composite of Ciavenasca 458, local breed
 7   Numbers 1983: miss / miss; HB: miss; decreasing; miss %; Ne = miss
 8 - Height: 47/47 cm; Weight: 37/32 kg; Herd number: miss; AI: miss
 9   Colour: Uni white
10   Pecularity: horns 2/2
11 - Main use: (1) meat,(2) miss,(3) miss
12   Spec. abilities: mountain
13   Performance compared with STB miss:
14     higher: miss
15     equal: miss
16     lower: miss
17 - Management: miss; housing: miss m.;
18 - Conservation progr.: live animals: miss;Semen: miss;Embryos: miss
19   Status: extinct
20 - Similar breeds (see group 8/1 on page 94)    EN  Country Status
21   Marrane                                      540   I    crit.end.
22   Rosset                                       603   I    crit.end.
23   Comisana                                     469   I    normal
24   Corse                                        472   F    normal
```

```
 1 - Comisana                                           EN  469
 2   Comisana; Sicily
 3   Assonapa                                           HB:1976
 4   Roma 00161, Via Ravenna 9/c
 5 - Composite of Maltese, Sicilian 410
 7   Numbers 1991: 3380/450000; HB: 158676; stable; miss %; Ne = 13238
 8 - Height: 75/60 cm; Weight: 65/40 kg; Herd number: miss; AI: miss
 9   Colour: Uni white
10   Pecularity: horns 0/0
11 - Main use: (1) milk,(2) meat,(3) miss
12   Spec. abilities: miss
13   Performance compared with STB Sardinian 618:
14     higher: age of sexual maturity
15     equal: miss
16     lower: milk yield
17 - Management: stationary; housing: 12 m.;
18 - Conservation progr.: live animals: miss;Semen: miss;Embryos: miss
19   Status: normal
20 - Similar breeds (see group 8/1 on page 94)    EN  Country Status
21   Marrane                                      540   I    crit.end.
22   Rosset                                       603   I    crit.end.
23   Ouessant                                     574   F    pot. end.
24   Corse                                        472   F    normal
```

```
1 - Cornella bianca                                      EN   471
2   Cornella White; Province of Bologna, Emilia Romagna
3   Assonapa                                             HB:miss
4   Roma 00161, Via Ravenna 9/c
5 - Autochthon local breed
7   Numbers 1991: miss /35; HB: miss; decreasing; miss %; Ne = 3
8 - Height: 87/77 cm; Weight: 82/67 kg; Herd number: 1; AI: miss
9   Colour: Uni white
10  Pecularity: horns 2/2
11 - Main use: (1) milk,(2) meat,(3) miss
12  Spec. abilities: miss
13  Performance compared with STB Sardinian 618:
14     higher: age of sexual maturity
15     equal:  miss
16     lower:  milk yield
17 - Management: stationary; housing: miss m.;
18 - Conservation progr.: live animals: miss;Semen: miss;Embryos: miss
19  Status: critically endang.;Watch: ♂♂,HB♀♀,trend,herds,%pure!
```

20 - Similar breeds (see group 7/5 on page 92)	EN	Country	Status
21 Garfagnina bianca	498	I	crit.end.
22 Pomarancina	585	I	crit.end.
23 Massese	541	I	normal
24 Appenninica	402	I	normal

```
1 - Delle Langhe                                         EN   478
2   Langhe; Prov. of Cuneo, Asti and Savona
3   Assonapa                                             HB:1974
4   Roma 00161, Via Ravenna 9/c
5 - Autochthon local breed
7   Numbers 1991: 214/16200; HB: 4773; stable; miss %; Ne = 819
8 - Height: 80/75 cm; Weight: 82/67 kg; Herd number: miss; AI: miss
9   Colour: Uni white
10  Pecularity: horns 0/0
11 - Main use: (1) milk,(2) meat,(3) miss
12  Spec. abilities: hill
13  Performance compared with STB miss:
14     higher: miss
15     equal:  miss
16     lower:  miss
17 - Management: stationary; housing: 12 m.;
18 - Conservation progr.: live animals: miss;Semen: miss;Embryos: miss
19  Status: normal;             Watch: %pure!
```

20 - Similar breeds (see group 7/3 on page 92)	EN	Country	Status
21 Brigasque	436	F	crit.end.
22 Brigasca	435	I	crit.end.
23 Frabosana	492	I	crit.end.
24 Besch da pader	485	CH	min. end.

```
1 - Di Corteno                                          EN  480
2   Corteno; Province of Brescia (Lombardy)
3   Assonapa                                           HB:miss
4   Roma 00161, Via Ravenna 9/c
5 - Autochthon derivative of Bergamasca (Alpine group)
7   Numbers 1991: miss /2000; HB: miss; increasing; miss %; Ne = 362
8 - Height: 70/60 cm; Weight: 67/57 kg; Herd number: miss; AI: miss
9   Colour: Uni white
10  Pecularity: horns 0/0
11 - Main use: (1) meat,(2) miss,(3) miss
12  Spec. abilities: miss
13  Performance compared with STB miss:
14    higher: miss
15    equal:  miss
16    lower:  miss
17 - Management: miss; housing: miss m.;
18 - Conservation progr.: live animals: miss;Semen: miss;Embryos: miss
19  Status: minimally endang.; Watch: ♂♂,HB♀♀,%pure!
```

20 - Similar breeds (see group 7/2 on page 91)	EN	Country	Status
21 Braunes Bergschaf	431	D	crit.end.
22 Istriana	516	I	crit.end.
23 Bergamasca	415	I	normal
24 Weißes Bergschaf	416	D	normal

ITALY   SHEEP

```
1 - Fabrianese                                         EN  487
2   Fabrianese; Province of Ancona (Marche)
3   Assonapa                                           HB:1974
4   Roma 00161, Via Ravenna 9/c
5 - Composite of Bergamasca 415, local breeds
7   Numbers 1991: 81/15000; HB: 3152; decreasing; miss %; Ne = 316
8 - Height: 80/70 cm; Weight: 80/60 kg; Herd number: miss; AI: miss
9   Colour: Uni white
10  Pecularity: horns 0/0
11 - Main use: (1) meat,(2) milk,(3) miss
12  Spec. abilities: mountain
13  Performance compared with STB miss:
14    higher: miss
15    equal:  miss
16    lower:  miss
17 - Management: stationary; housing: 12 m.;
18 - Conservation progr.: live animals: miss;Semen: miss;Embryos: miss
19  Status: normal;          Watch: trend,%pure!
```

20 - Similar breeds (see group 7/2 on page 91)	EN	Country	Status
21 Braunes Bergschaf	431	D	crit.end.
22 Istriana	516	I	crit.end.
23 Bergamasca	415	I	normal
24 Weißes Bergschaf	416	D	normal

```
 1 - Finarda                                              EN  488
 2   Finarda; Piedmont, Lombardy
 3   Assonapa                                             HB:miss
 4   Roma 00161, Via Ravenna 9/c
 5 - Composite of Bergamasca 415, Biellese 419
 7   Numbers 1991: miss /5000; HB: miss; stable; miss %; Ne = 905
 8 - Height: 95/87 cm; Weight: 110/90 kg; Herd number: miss; AI: miss
 9   Colour: Uni white
10   Pecularity: horns 0/0
11 - Main use: (1) meat,(2) miss,(3) miss
12   Spec. abilities: miss
13   Performance compared with STB miss:
14     higher: miss
15     equal:  miss
16     lower:  miss
17 - Management: miss; housing: miss m.;
18 - Conservation progr.: live animals: miss;Semen: miss;Embryos: miss
19   Status: minimally endang.; Watch: ♂♂,HB♀♀,%pure!
```

20 - Similar breeds (see group 7/2 on page 91)	EN	Country	Status
21 Braunes Bergschaf	431	D	crit.end.
22 Istriana	516	I	crit.end.
23 Bergamasca	415	I	normal
24 Weißes Bergschaf	416	D	normal

```
 1 - Frabosana                                            EN  492
 2   Frabosana; Ligurian Alps, Province of Cuneo
 3   Assonapa                                             HB:miss
 4   Roma 00161, Via Ravenna 9/c
 5 - Autochthon local population
 7   Numbers 1991: miss /1100; HB: miss; miss; miss %; Ne = 199
 8 - Height: 77/70 cm; Weight: 70/62 kg; Herd number: 10; AI: miss
 9   Colour: Uni white, sometimes brown
10   Pecularity: horns 2/2
11 - Main use: (1) meat,(2) milk,(3) miss
12   Spec. abilities: miss
13   Performance compared with STB miss:
14     higher: miss
15     equal:  miss
16     lower:  miss
17 - Management: miss; housing: miss m.;
18 - Conservation progr.: live animals: miss;Semen: miss;Embryos: miss
19   Status: critically endang.;Watch: ♂♂,HB♀♀,trend,herds,%pure!
```

20 - Similar breeds (see group 7/3 on page 92)	EN	Country	Status
21 Brigasque	436	F	crit.end.
22 Brigasca	435	I	crit.end.
23 Besch da pader	485	CH	min. end.
24 Delle Langhe	478	I	normal

```
1 - Garessina                                               EN   497
2   Garessina; Ligurian Alps, Piedmont
3   Assonapa                                                 HB:miss
4   Roma 00161, Via Ravenna 9/c
5 - Composite of Appenninica 402 and local breed
7   Numbers 1991: miss /100; HB: miss; decreasing; miss %; Ne = 8
8 - Height: 62/57 cm; Weight: 52/47 kg; Herd number: miss; AI: miss
9   Colour: Uni white
10  Pecularity: horns 0/0
11 - Main use: (1) meat; wool,(2) miss,(3) miss
12  Spec. abilities: miss
13  Performance compared with STB miss:
14    higher: miss
15    equal:  miss
16    lower:  miss
17 - Management: miss; housing: miss m.;
18 - Conservation progr.: live animals: miss;Semen: miss;Embryos: miss
19  Status: critically endang.;Watch: ♂♂,HB♀♀,trend,herds,%pure!
20 - Similar breeds (see group 7/1 on page 91)     EN  Country Status
21  Commun des Alpes                               470   F    crit.end.
22  Alpagota                                       400   I    crit.end.
23  Biellese                                       419   I    normal
24  Prealpes du Sud                                589   F    normal
```

```
1 - Garfagnina bianca                                       EN   498
2   Garfagnina White; northwestern Tuscany
3   Assessorato Agricoltura Regione Tuscana                  HB:miss
4   Firenze 50127, Via Di Novoli 26
5 - Composite of Apennine-group
7   Numbers 1991: miss /180; HB: miss; increasing; miss %; Ne = 16
8 - Height: 67/62 cm; Weight: 52/42 kg; Herd number: 1; AI: miss
9   Colour: Uni white
10  Pecularity: horns 2/2
11 - Main use: (1) milk,(2) miss,(3) miss
12  Spec. abilities: miss
13  Performance compared with STB miss:
14    higher: miss
15    equal:  miss
16    lower:  miss
17 - Management: miss; housing: miss m.;
18 - Conservation progr.: live animals: Yes;Semen: miss;Embryos: miss
19  Status: critically endang.;Watch: ♂♂,HB♀♀,herds,%pure!
20 - Similar breeds (see group 7/5 on page 92)     EN  Country Status
21  Cornella bianca                                471   I    crit.end.
22  Pomarancina                                    585   I    crit.end.
23  Massese                                        541   I    normal
24  Appenninica                                    402   I    normal
```

```
 1 - Gentile di Puglia                                          EN  499
 2   Gentile di Puglia; southern Italy
 3   Assonapa                                                   HB:1971
 4   Roma 00161, Via Ravenna 9/c
 5 - Composite of Spanish Merino 545 Spain, local, Saxony and Rambouillet
 7   Numbers 1991: 398/210000; HB: 11161; decreasing; miss %; Ne = 1537
 8 - Height: 70/60 cm; Weight: 65/40 kg; Herd number: miss; AI: miss
 9   Colour: Uni white
10   Pecularity: horns 2/0
11 - Main use: (1) wool,(2) meat,(3) miss
12   Spec. abilities: miss
13   Performance compared with STB miss:
14     higher: miss
15     equal:  miss
16     lower:  miss
17 - Management: transhumant; housing: 2-6 m.;
18 - Conservation progr.: live animals: miss;Semen: miss;Embryos: miss
19   Status: normal;              Watch: trend,%pure!
```

20 - Similar breeds (see group 1/3 on page 87)	EN	Country	Status
21 Matesina	542	I	crit.end.
22 Trimeticcia di Segezia	657	I	min. end.
23 Sopravissana	634	I	normal

```
 1 - Istriana                                                   EN  516
 2   Istrian; Udine, Gorizia, Trieste
 3   Assonapa                                                   HB:miss
 4   Roma 00161, Via Ravenna 9/c
 5 - Composite of probably Lamon 525, Istrian
 7   Numbers 1991: 10/150; HB: miss; decreasing; miss %; Ne = 19
 8 - Height: 80/65 cm; Weight: 65/52 kg; Herd number: 1; AI: miss
 9   Colour: Uni white
10   Pecularity: horns 2/2
11 - Main use: (1) milk; meat,(2) miss,(3) miss
12   Spec. abilities: karst - soils
13   Performance compared with STB miss:
14     higher: miss
15     equal:  miss
16     lower:  miss
17 - Management: miss; housing: miss m.;
18 - Conservation progr.: live animals: miss;Semen: miss;Embryos: miss
19   Status: critically endang.;Watch: ♂♂,HB♀♀,trend,herds,%pure!
```

20 - Similar breeds (see group 7/2 on page 91)	EN	Country	Status
21 Braunes Bergschaf	431	D	crit.end.
22 Lamon	525	I	crit.end.
23 Bergamasca	415	I	normal
24 Weißes Bergschaf	416	D	normal

```
1 - Lamon                                                    EN  525
2   Lamon; Belluno (Venetia)
3   Assonapa                                                 HB:miss
4   Roma 00161, Via Ravenna 9/c
5 - Autochthon derivative of Bergamasca 415
7   Numbers 1991: miss /60; HB: miss; decreasing; miss %; Ne = 5
8 - Height: 82/72 cm; Weight: 77/67 kg; Herd number: 4; AI: miss
9   Colour: Uni white, dark spots on face and legs
10  Pecularity: horns 0/0
11 - Main use: (1) meat,(2) milk,(3) miss
12  Spec. abilities: miss
13  Performance compared with STB miss:
14    higher: miss
15    equal:  miss
16    lower:  miss
17 - Management: miss; housing: miss m.;
18 - Conservation progr.: live animals: miss;Semen: miss;Embryos: miss
19  Status: critically endang.;Watch: ♂♂,HB♀♀,trend,herds,%pure!
```

20 - Similar breeds (see group 7/2 on page 91)	EN	Country	Status
21 Braunes Bergschaf	431	D	crit.end.
22 Istriana	516	I	crit.end.
23 Bergamasca	415	I	normal
24 Weißes Bergschaf	416	D	normal

```
1 - Leccese                                                  EN  527
2   Leccese; Apulia
3   Assonapa                                                 HB:1972
4   Roma 00161, Via Ravenna 9/c
5 - Autochthon local breed
7   Numbers 1991: 326/108000; HB: 9066; stable; miss %; Ne = 1259
8 - Height: 75/65 cm; Weight: 60/45 kg; Herd number: miss; AI: miss
9   Colour: Uni white, black face and legs, occasionally black
10  Pecularity: horns 2/0
11 - Main use: (1) milk; meat; wool,(2) miss,(3) miss
12  Spec. abilities: miss
13  Performance compared with STB Sardinian 618:
14    higher: miss
15    equal:  miss
16    lower:  milk yield
17 - Management: stationary; housing: 12 m.;
18 - Conservation progr.: live animals: miss;Semen: miss;Embryos: miss
19  Status: normal
```

20 - Similar breeds (see group 5/2 on page 89)	EN	Country	Status
21 Caussenard des Garrigues	447	F	crit.end.
22 Altamurana	401	I	crit.end.
23 Caussenard du Lot	448	F	normal
24 Basco-Bearnaise	412	F	normal

1 - **Livo**   EN **533**
2   **Livo; Province of Como (Lombardy)**
3   **Assonapa**   HB:**miss**
4   **Roma 00161, Via Ravenna 9/c**
5 - **Autochthon local population**
7   Numbers 1983: **500**; HB: **miss**; **stable**; **miss** %; Ne = **79**
8 - Height: **72/67** cm; Weight: **70/52** kg; Herd number: **miss**; AI: **miss**
9   Colour: **Uni yellow**
10 Pecularity: **horns 0/0**
11 - Main use: (1) **meat**,(2) **milk**,(3) **miss**
12 Spec. abilities: **hill**
13 Performance compared with STB **miss**:
14   higher: **miss**
15   equal: **miss**
16   lower: **miss**
17 - Management: **miss**; housing: **miss** m.;
18 - Conservation progr.: live animals: **miss**;Semen: **miss**;Embryos: **miss**
19 Status: **minimally endang.**; Watch: ♂♂,**HB♀♀,herds,%pure!**
20 - <u>Similar breeds</u> (see group 7/1 on page 91)   <u>EN</u> <u>Country</u> <u>Status</u>
21 **Commun des Alpes**   470   F   crit.end.
22 **Alpagota**   400   I   crit.end.
23 **Biellese**   419   I   normal
24 **Prealpes du Sud**   589   F   normal

1 - **Locale**   EN **534**
2   **Locale; Ligurian Alps, Massa Carra**
3   **A.I.A.**   HB:**miss**
4   **Roma 00161, Via Tomassetti 9c**
5 - **Composite of Appenninica 402 and local breed**
7   Numbers 1983: **1500**; HB: **miss**; **stable**; **miss** %; Ne = **272**
8 - Height: **75/70** cm; Weight: **62/52** kg; Herd number: **miss**; AI: **miss**
9   Colour: **Combination grey, white**
10 Pecularity: **horns 0/0**
11 - Main use: (1) **milk; meat; wool**,(2) **miss**,(3) **miss**
12 Spec. abilities: **hill**
13 Performance compared with STB **miss**:
14   higher: **miss**
15   equal: **miss**
16   lower: **miss**
17 - Management: **miss**; housing: **miss** m.;
18 - Conservation progr.: live animals: **miss**;Semen: **miss**;Embryos: **miss**
19 Status: **potential. endang.**;Watch: ♂♂,**HB♀♀,%pure!**
20 - <u>Similar breeds</u> (see group 7/5 on page 92)   <u>EN</u> <u>Country</u> <u>Status</u>
21 **Cornella bianca**   471   I   crit.end.
22 **Garfagnina bianca**   498   I   crit.end.
23 **Massese**   541   I   normal
24 **Appenninica**   402   I   normal

1 - Marrane   EN 540
2   Marrane; Genova (Ligurian Alps)
3   Assonapa   HB:miss
4   Roma 00161, Via Ravenna 9/c
5 - Composite of Appenninica 402 and local breed
7   Numbers 1983: 150; HB: miss; decreasing; miss %; Ne = 13
8 - Height: 65/60 cm; Weight: 52/42 kg; Herd number: miss; AI: miss
9   Colour: Uni yellow, sometimes light brown
10 Pecularity: horns 0/0
11 - Main use: (1) meat,(2) wool,(3) miss
12 Spec. abilities: hill
13 Performance compared with STB miss:
14   higher: miss
15   equal: miss
16   lower: miss
17 - Management: miss; housing: miss m.;
18 - Conservation progr.: live animals: miss;Semen: miss;Embryos: miss
19 Status: critically endang.;Watch: ♂♂,HB♀♀,trend,herds,%pure!
20 - Similar breeds (see group 8/1 on page 94)   EN Country Status
21 Rosset   603   I   crit.end.
22 Savoiarda   619   I   crit.end.
23 Comisana   469   I   normal
24 Corse   472   F   normal

1 - Massese   EN 541
2   Massese; Versilia, northwestern Tuscany
3   Assonapa   HB:1971
4   Roma 00161, Via Ravenna 9/c
5 - Composite of Apennine type 402
7   Numbers 1991: 277/108000; HB: 14184; decreasing; miss %; Ne = 1087
8 - Height: 80/70 cm; Weight: 70/50 kg; Herd number: miss; AI: miss
9   Colour: Uni black, grey, brown, darker head
10 Pecularity: horns 2/2
11 - Main use: (1) milk,(2) miss,(3) miss
12 Spec. abilities: hill - mountain
13 Performance compared with STB Sardinian 618:
14   higher: age of sexual maturity
15   equal: miss
16   lower: milk yield
17 - Management: stationary; housing: 12 m.;
18 - Conservation progr.: live animals: miss;Semen: miss;Embryos: miss
19 Status: normal;   Watch: trend!
20 - Similar breeds (see group 7/5 on page 92)   EN Country Status
21 Cornella bianca   471   I   crit.end.
22 Garfagnina bianca   498   I   crit.end.
23 Pagliarola   576   I   normal
24 Appenninica   402   I   normal

```
1 - Matesina                                              EN   542
2   Matesina; Province of Caserta (Campania)
3   Assonapa                                              HB:miss
4   Roma 00161, Via Ravenna 9/c
5 - Autochthon derivative of Gentile di Puglia 499
7   Numbers 1991: miss /300; HB: miss; decreasing; miss %; Ne = 31
8 - Height: 65/60 cm; Weight: 70/60 kg; Herd number: miss; AI: miss
9   Colour: Uni brown
10  Pecularity: horns 2/0
11 - Main use: (1) meat,(2) wool,(3) miss
12  Spec. abilities: hill
13  Performance compared with STB miss:
14    higher: miss
15    equal:  miss
16    lower:  miss
17 - Management: miss; housing: miss m.;
18 - Conservation progr.: live animals: miss;Semen: miss;Embryos: miss
19  Status: critically endang.;Watch: ♂♂,HB♀♀,trend,herds,%pure!
20 - Similar breeds (see group 1/3 on page 87)    EN  Country Status
21    Trimeticcia di Segezia                      657   I    min. end.
22    Gentile di Puglia                           499   I    normal
23    Sopravissana                                634   I    normal
```

```
1 - Nostrana                                              EN   570
2   Nostrana; Province of Massa, Carrara-Parma
3   Assonapa                                              HB:miss
4   Roma 00161, Via Ravenna 9/c
5 - Autochthon derivative of Garfagnina (Apennine group)
7   Numbers 1991: miss /1500; HB: miss; increasing; miss %; Ne = 272
8 - Height: 70/65 cm; Weight: 60/52 kg; Herd number: miss; AI: miss
9   Colour: Uni white
10  Pecularity: horns 0/0
11 - Main use: (1) meat,(2) wool,(3) miss
12  Spec. abilities: hill
13  Performance compared with STB miss:
14    higher: miss
15    equal:  miss
16    lower:  miss
17 - Management: miss; housing: miss m.;
18 - Conservation progr.: live animals: miss;Semen: miss;Embryos: miss
19  Status: endangered;        Watch: ♂♂,HB♀♀,%pure!
20 - Similar breeds (see group 8/3 on page 95)    EN  Country Status
21    Rouge du Roussillon                         606   F    crit.end.
22    Coete                                       599   E    min. end.
23    Barbaresca Siciliana                        410   I    normal
24    Barbaresca della Campania                   409   I    normal
```

1 - **Pagliarola**   EN **576**
2   **Pagliarola; Abruzzi and Molise**
3   **Assonapa**   HB:miss
4   **Roma 00161, Via Ravenna 9/c**
5 - **Composite of Appenninica 402, Merinos**
7   Numbers 1983: **200000**; HB: **miss**; **stable**; **miss** %; Ne = **36200**
8 - Height: **67/62** cm; Weight: **60/47** kg; Herd number: **miss**; AI: **miss**
9   Colour: **Uni yellow, also reddish - black**
10 Pecularity: **horns 0/0**
11 - Main use: (1) **meat**,(2) **wool**,(3) **miss**
12 Spec. abilities: **hill**
13 Performance compared with STB **miss**:
14   higher: **miss**
15   equal: **miss**
16   lower: **miss**
17 - Management: **miss**; housing: **miss** m.;
18 - Conservation progr.: live animals: **miss**;Semen: **miss**;Embryos: **miss**
19 Status: **normal**;   Watch: ♂♂,HB♀♀,**%pure**!
20 - <u>Similar breeds</u> (see group 7/5 on page 92)   <u>EN</u> <u>Country</u> <u>Status</u>
21 **Cornella bianca**   471   I   crit.end.
22 **Garfagnina bianca**   498   I   crit.end.
23 **Massese**   541   I   normal
24 **Appenninica**   402   I   normal

1 - **Pinzirita**   EN **581**
2   **Pinzirita; Sicily**
3   **Assonapa**   HB: **Yes**
4   **Roma 00161, Via Ravenna 9/c**
5 - **Autochthon local population**
7   Numbers 1991: **29**/ miss; HB: **1215**; **increasing**; **miss** %; Ne = **113**
8 - Height: **52/42** cm; Weight: **47/37** kg; Herd number: **miss**; AI: **miss**
9   Colour: **Uni white**
10 Pecularity: **horns 2/0**
11 - Main use: (1) **milk; meat; wool**,(2) **miss**,(3) **miss**
12 Spec. abilities: **miss**
13 Performance compared with STB **miss**:
14   higher: **miss**
15   equal: **miss**
16   lower: **miss**
17 - Management: **miss**; housing: **miss** m.;
18 - Conservation progr.: live animals: **miss**;Semen: **miss**;Embryos: **miss**
19 Status: **normal**;   Watch: **%pure**!
20 - <u>Similar breeds</u> (see group 8/3 on page 95)   <u>EN</u> <u>Country</u> <u>Status</u>
21 **Rouge du Roussillon**   606   F   crit.end.
22 **Nostrana**   570   I   endanger.
23 **Barbaresca Siciliana**   410   I   normal
24 **Barbaresca della Campania**   409   I   normal

```
 1 - Pomarancina                                        EN   585
 2   Pomarancina; Province of Pisa (Tuscany)
 3   Assonapa                                          HB:miss
 4   Roma 00161, Via Ravenna 9/c
 5 - Composite of the Apennine group
 7   Numbers 1991: miss /800; HB: miss; decreasing; miss %; Ne = 145
 8 - Height: 72/60 cm; Weight: 57/47 kg; Herd number: miss; AI: miss
 9   Colour: Uni white
10   Pecularity: horns 0/0
11 - Main use: (1) milk; meat; wool,(2) miss,(3) miss
12   Spec. abilities: hill
13   Performance compared with STB miss:
14     higher: miss
15     equal:  miss
16     lower:  miss
17 - Management: miss; housing: miss m.;
18 - Conservation progr.: live animals: miss;Semen: miss;Embryos: miss
19   Status: critically endang.;Watch: ♂♂,HB♀♀,trend,herds,%pure!
```

20 - Similar breeds (see group 7/5 on page 92)	EN	Country	Status
21 Cornella bianca	471	I	crit.end.
22 Garfagnina bianca	498	I	crit.end.
23 Massese	541	I	normal
24 Appenninica	402	I	normal

```
 1 - Pusterese                                          EN   590
 2   Pusterese; Province of Bolzano
 3   Assonapa                                          HB:miss
 4   Roma 00161, Via Ravenna 9/c
 5 - Composite of Tirolese 656, Lamon 525
 7   Numbers 1983: 50; HB: miss; decreasing; miss %; Ne = 4
 8 - Height: 75/67 cm; Weight: 57/50 kg; Herd number: miss; AI: miss
 9   Colour: Uni yellow
10   Pecularity: horns 0/0
11 - Main use: (1) meat,(2) milk,(3) miss
12   Spec. abilities: miss
13   Performance compared with STB miss:
14     higher: miss
15     equal:  miss
16     lower:  miss
17 - Management: miss; housing: miss m.;
18 - Conservation progr.: live animals: miss;Semen: miss;Embryos: miss
19   Status: critically endang.;Watch: ♂♂,HB♀♀,trend,herds,%pure!
```

20 - Similar breeds (see group 7/3 on page 92)	EN	Country	Status
21 Brigasque	436	F	crit.end.
22 Brigasca	435	I	crit.end.
23 Besch da pader	485	CH	min. end.
24 Delle Langhe	478	I	normal

```
 1 - Rosset                                              EN  603
 2   Rosset; Aosta Valley
 3   Assonapa                                            HB:miss
 4   Roma 00161, Via Ravenna 9/c
 5 - Autochthon common origin with Savoiarda 619
 7   Numbers 1983: 250; HB: miss; decreasing; miss %; Ne = 24
 8 - Height: 62/55 cm; Weight: 57/47 kg; Herd number: miss; AI: miss
 9   Colour: Uni yellow, dark spots on face and legs
10   Pecularity: horns 2,0/2,0
11 - Main use: (1) meat,(2) wool,(3) miss
12   Spec. abilities: miss
13   Performance compared with STB miss:
14     higher: miss
15     equal:  miss
16     lower:  miss
17 - Management: miss; housing: miss m.;
18 - Conservation progr.: live animals: miss;Semen: miss;Embryos: miss
19   Status: critically endang.;Watch: ♂♂,HB♀♀,trend,herds,%pure!
```

20 - <u>Similar breeds</u> (see group 8/1 on page 94)   <u>EN</u> <u>Country</u> <u>Status</u>

21	Marrane	540	I	crit.end.
22	Savoiarda	619	I	crit.end.
23	Comisana	469	I	normal
24	Corse	472	F	normal

```
 1 - Saltasassi                                          EN  616
 2   Saltasassi; Province of Novara (Piedmont)
 3   Assonapa                                            HB:miss
 4   Roma 00161, Via Ravenna 9/c
 5 - Autochthon local population
 7   Numbers 1983: 2500; HB: miss; stable; miss %; Ne = 453
 8 - Height: 62/55 cm; Weight: 60/46 kg; Herd number: miss; AI: miss
 9   Colour: Uni white
10   Pecularity: horns 0/0
11 - Main use: (1) meat,(2) miss,(3) miss
12   Spec. abilities: hill, mountain
13   Performance compared with STB miss:
14     higher: miss
15     equal:  miss
16     lower:  miss
17 - Management: miss; housing: miss m.;
18 - Conservation progr.: live animals: miss;Semen: miss;Embryos: miss
19   Status: minimally endang.; Watch: ♂♂,HB♀♀,%pure!
```

20 - <u>Similar breeds</u> (see group 7/1 on page 91)   <u>EN</u> <u>Country</u> <u>Status</u>

21	Commun des Alpes	470	F	crit.end.
22	Alpagota	400	I	crit.end.
23	Biellese	419	I	normal
24	Prealpes du Sud	589	F	normal

```
 1 - Sambucana, Demontina                                    EN   617
 2   Sambucana; Province of Cuneo (Piedmont)
 3   Assonapa                                                HB:miss
 4   Roma 00161, Via Ravenna 9/c
 5 - Autochthon, probably derivative of Garessio 497
 7   Numbers 1991: 2000; HB: miss; increasing; miss %; Ne = 362
 8 - Height: 67/63 cm; Weight: 65/60 kg; Herd number: miss; AI: miss
 9   Colour: Uni white
10   Pecularity: horns 0/0
11 - Main use: (1) meat,(2) miss,(3) miss
12   Spec. abilities: mountain
13   Performance compared with STB miss:
14      higher: miss
15      equal:  miss
16      lower:  miss
17 - Management: miss; housing: miss m.;
18 - Conservation progr.: live animals: miss;Semen: miss;Embryos: miss
19   Status: minimally endang.; Watch: ♂♂,HB♀♀,%pure!
```

20 - Similar breeds (see group 7/1 on page 91)	EN	Country	Status
21 Commun des Alpes	470	F	crit.end.
22 Alpagota	400	I	crit.end.
23 Biellese	419	I	normal
24 Prealpes du Sud	589	F	normal

```
 1 - Sarda                                                   EN   618
 2   Sardinian; Sardinia
 3   Assonapa                                                HB:1971
 4   Roma 00161, Via Ravenna 9/c
 5 - Autochthon local breed
 7   Numbers 1991: 2252/2820000; HB: 152259; increasing; miss %; Ne=8877
 8 - Height: 72/62 cm; Weight: 57/42 kg; Herd number: miss; AI: miss
 9   Colour: Uni white, occasionally black
10   Pecularity: horns 2/0
11 - Main use: (1) milk,(2) miss,(3) miss
12   Spec. abilities: miss
13   Performance compared with STB miss:
14      higher: miss
15      equal:  miss
16      lower:  miss
17 - Management: stationary; housing: 12 m.;
18 - Conservation progr.: live animals: miss;Semen: miss;Embryos: miss
19   Status: normal;              Watch: %pure!
```

20 - Similar breeds (see group 8/3 on page 95)	EN	Country	Status
21 Rouge du Roussillon	606	F	crit.end.
22 Nostrana	570	I	endanger.
23 Barbaresca Siciliana	410	I	normal
24 Barbaresca della Campania	409	I	normal

1 - **Savoiarda**   EN **619**
2   **Savoiarda; Province of Turin (Piedmont)**
3   **Assonapa**   HB:miss
4   **Roma 00161, Via Ravenna 9/c**
5 - **Autochthon local population**
7   Numbers 1983: **100**; HB: **miss**; **decreasing**; miss %; Ne = **8**
8 - Height: **77/67** cm; Weight: **67/60** kg; Herd number: **miss**; AI: **miss**
9   Colour: **Uni white, black spots on face and legs**
10 Pecularity: **horns 2/2**
11 - Main use: (1) **milk; meat; wool**,(2) **miss**,(3) **miss**
12 Spec. abilities: **miss**
13 Performance compared with STB **miss**:
14   higher: **miss**
15   equal: **miss**
16   lower: **miss**
17 - Management: **miss**; housing: **miss** m.;
18 - Conservation progr.: live animals: **miss**;Semen: **miss**;Embryos: **miss**
19 Status: **critically endang.**;Watch: ♂♂,HB♀♀,trend,herds,%pure!
20 - <u>Similar breeds</u> (see group 8/1 on page 94)   <u>EN</u> <u>Country</u> <u>Status</u>
21 **Marrane**   540   I   crit.end.
22 **Rosset**   603   I   crit.end.
23 **Comisana**   469   I   normal
24 **Corse**   472   F   normal

1 - **Sciara, Moscia Calabrese**   EN **624**
2   **Sciara; Prov. of Cosenza and Catanzaro**
3   **Assonapa**   HB:miss
4   **Roma 00161, Via Ravenna 9/c**
5 - **Autochthon local breed**
7   Numbers 1983: **15000**; HB: **miss**; **decreasing**; miss %; Ne = **2715**
8 - Height: **72/62** cm; Weight: **57/47** kg; Herd number: **miss**; AI: **miss**
9   Colour: **Uni white**
10 Pecularity: **horns 0/0**
11 - Main use: (1) **milk**,(2) **miss**,(3) **miss**
12 Spec. abilities: **hill**
13 Performance compared with STB **miss**:
14   higher: **miss**
15   equal: **miss**
16   lower: **miss**
17 - Management: **miss**; housing: **miss** m.;
18 - Conservation progr.: live animals: **miss**;Semen: **miss**;Embryos: **miss**
19 Status: **potential. endang.**;Watch: ♂♂,HB♀♀,trend,%pure!
20 - <u>Similar breeds</u> (see group 5/2 on page 89)   <u>EN</u> <u>Country</u> <u>Status</u>
21 **Caussenard des Garrigues**   447   F   crit.end.
22 **Altamurana**   401   I   crit.end.
23 **Caussenard du Lot**   448   F   normal
24 **Basco-Bearnaise**   412   F   normal

1 - Sopravissana   EN   634
2   Sopravissana; central Apennines / Latium
3   Assonapa   HB:1972
4   Roma 00161, Via Ravenna 9/c
5 - Composite of Visso 663, Spanish Merino 545, Rambouillet
7   Numbers 1991: 290/192000; HB: 13446; decreasing; miss %; Ne = 1136
8 - Height: 70/60 cm; Weight: 65/50 kg; Herd number: miss; AI: miss
9   Colour: Uni white
10 Pecularity: horns 2/0
11 - Main use: (1) milk; meat; wool,(2) miss,(3) miss
12 Spec. abilities: miss
13 Performance compared with STB miss:
14   higher: miss
15   equal: miss
16   lower: miss
17 - Management: transhumant; housing: 2-6 m.;
18 - Conservation progr.: live animals: miss;Semen: miss;Embryos: miss
19 Status: normal;   Watch: trend,%pure!
20 - Similar breeds (see group 1/3 on page 87)   EN   Country Status
21 Matesina   542   I   crit.end.
22 Trimeticcia di Segezia   657   I   min. end.
23 Gentile di Puglia   499   I   normal

1 - Tacola   EN   645
2   Tacola; Province of Vercelli (Piedmont)
3   Assonapa   HB:miss
4   Roma 00161, Via Ravenna 9/c
5 - Autochthon derivative of Biellese (Alpine group)
7   Numbers 1983: 100; HB: miss; decreasing; miss %; Ne = 8
8 - Height:miss/miss cm; Weight:miss/miss kg; Herd number: miss;AI: miss
9   Colour: Uni white
10 Pecularity: horns 0/0
11 - Main use: (1) meat,(2) miss,(3) miss
12 Spec. abilities: miss
13 Performance compared with STB miss:
14   higher: miss
15   equal: miss
16   lower: miss
17 - Management: miss; housing: miss m.;
18 - Conservation progr.: live animals: miss;Semen: miss;Embryos: miss
19 Status: critically endang.;Watch: ♂♂,HB♀♀,trend,herds,%pure!
20 - Similar breeds (see group 7/1 on page 91)   EN   Country Status
21 Commun des Alpes   470   F   crit.end.
22 Alpagota   400   I   crit.end.
23 Biellese   419   I   normal
24 Prealpes du Sud   589   F   normal

1 - Tiroler Bergschaf   EN 656
2   Tyrol Mountain; Province of Bolzano
3   A.P.A.   HB:miss
4   Bolzano 39100, Via Renon 33a
5 - Imported as breed from Austria, Germany
7   Numbers 1983: 24000; HB: miss; increasing; miss %; Ne = 4344
8 - Height: 82/70 cm; Weight: 85/75 kg; Herd number: miss; AI: miss
9   Colour: Uni white, occsionaly black pied
10 Pecularity: horns 2/0
11 - Main use: (1) meat,(2) wool,(3) miss
12 Spec. abilities: mountain
13 Performance compared with STB miss:
14   higher: miss
15   equal: miss
16   lower: miss
17 - Management: miss; housing: miss m.;
18 - Conservation progr.: live animals: miss;Semen: miss;Embryos: miss
19 Status: normal;   Watch: ♂♂,HB♀♀,%pure!
20 - Similar breeds (see group 7/2 on page 91)   EN Country Status
21 Braunes Bergschaf   431   D   crit.end.
22 Istriana   516   I   crit.end.
23 Bergamasca   415   I   normal
24 Weißes Bergschaf   416   D   normal

1 - Trimeticcia di Segezia   EN 657
2   Segezia Triple Cross; Apulia
3   Istituto Sperimentale per la Zootecnia   HB:miss
4   Segezia - Foggia 71020
5 - Composite of Ile de France 513 France, Gentile di Puglia 499 Italy,
6   Württemberger 550 Germany
7   Numbers 1991: miss /600; HB: miss; increasing; miss %; Ne = 109
8 - Height: 72/67 cm; Weight: 100/65 kg; Herd number: miss; AI: miss
9   Colour: Uni white
10 Pecularity: horns 0/0
11 - Main use: (1) milk; meat; wool,(2) miss,(3) miss
12 Spec. abilities: miss
13 Performance compared with STB miss:
14   higher: miss
15   equal: miss
16   lower: miss
17 - Management: miss; housing: miss m.;
18 - Conservation progr.: live animals: miss;Semen: miss;Embryos: miss
19 Status: minimally endang.; Watch: ♂♂,HB♀♀,herds,%pure!
20 - Similar breeds (see group 1/3 on page 87)   EN Country Status
21 Matesina   542   I   crit.end.
22 Gentile di Puglia   499   I   normal
23 Sopravissana   634   I   normal

```
 1 - Varesina                                                    EN   659
 2   Varesina; Province of Varese (Lombardy)
 3   Assessorato Agricoltura Regione Lombardia                   HB: Yes
 4   Milano 20129, Viale Premuda 27
 5 - Autochthon derivative of Bergamo 415
 7   Numbers 1991: miss /900; HB: miss; increasing; miss %; Ne = 163
 8 - Height: 82/77 cm; Weight: 87/73 kg; Herd number: miss; AI: miss
 9   Colour: Uni white
10   Pecularity: horns 0/0
11 - Main use: (1) meat,(2) wool,(3) miss
12   Spec. abilities: miss
13   Performance compared with STB miss:
14     higher: miss
15     equal:  miss
16     lower:  miss
17 - Management: miss; housing: miss m.;
18 - Conservation progr.: live animals: miss;Semen: miss;Embryos: miss
19   Status: minimally endang.; Watch: ♂♂,HB♀♀,herds,%pure!
```

20 - <u>Similar breeds</u> (see group 7/2 on page 91)	<u>EN</u>	<u>Country</u>	<u>Status</u>
21 Braunes Bergschaf	431	D	crit.end.
22 Istriana	516	I	crit.end.
23 Bergamasca	415	I	normal
24 Weißes Bergschaf	416	D	normal

```
 1 - Vissana                                                     EN   663
 2   Vissana; Marche
 3   Assonapa                                                    HB:miss
 4   Roma 00161, Via Ravenna 9/c
 5 - Composite of Apennine group
 7   Numbers 1991: 1000; HB: miss; stable; miss %; Ne = 181
 8 - Height: 70/60 cm; Weight: 52/42 kg; Herd number: miss; AI: miss
 9   Colour: Uni white
10   Pecularity: horns 2,0/0
11 - Main use: (1) milk; meat; wool,(2) miss,(3) miss
12   Spec. abilities: hill
13   Performance compared with STB miss:
14     higher: miss
15     equal:  miss
16     lower:  miss
17 - Management: miss; housing: miss m.;
18 - Conservation progr.: live animals: miss;Semen: miss;Embryos: miss
19   Status: minimally endang.; Watch: ♂♂,HB♀♀,%pure!
```

20 - <u>Similar breeds</u> (see group 7/5 on page 92)	<u>EN</u>	<u>Country</u>	<u>Status</u>
21 Cornella bianca	471	I	crit.end.
22 Garfagnina bianca	498	I	crit.end.
23 Massese	541	I	normal
24 Appenninica	402	I	normal

```
 1 - Zucca Modenese                                          EN   682
 2   Zucca Modenese; Emilia Romagna
 3   Assonapa                                                HB:miss
 4   Roma 00161, Via Ravenna 9/c
 5 - Composite of Apennine group
 7   Numbers 1983: 150; HB: miss; decreasing; miss %; Ne = 13
 8 - Height: 85/72 cm; Weight: 77/57 kg; Herd number: miss; AI: miss
 9   Colour: Uni white
10   Pecularity: horns 0/0
11 - Main use: (1) milk,(2) meat,(3) wool
12   Spec. abilities: miss
13   Performance compared with STB miss:
14     higher: miss
15     equal:  miss
16     lower:  miss
17 - Management: miss; housing: miss m.;
18 - Conservation progr.: live animals: miss;Semen: miss;Embryos: miss
19   Status: critically endang.;Watch: ♂♂,HB♀♀,trend,herds,%pure!
```

20 - Similar breeds (see group 7/5 on page 92)	EN	Country	Status
21 Cornella bianca	471	I	crit.end.
22 Garfagnina bianca	498	I	crit.end.
23 Massese	541	I	normal
24 Appenninica	402	I	normal

ITALY   GOATS

```
 1 - Alpina                                                  EN   300
 2   Alpine; Alps (northern Italy)
 3   Assonapa                                                HB:miss
 4   Roma 00161, Via Ravenna 9/c
 5 - Autochthon heterogenous population
 7   Numbers 1991: 6000; HB: miss; stable; miss %; Ne = 1086
 8 - Height: 77/67 cm; Weight: 62/52 kg; Herd number: miss; AI: miss
 9   Colour: Uni black, brown, white, also pied colour
10   Pecularity: horns 2,0/2,0
11 - Main use: (1) milk; meat,(2) miss,(3) miss
12   Spec. abilities: mountain
13   Performance compared with STB miss:
14     higher: miss
15     equal:  miss
16     lower:  miss
17 - Management: miss; housing: miss m.;
18 - Conservation progr.: live animals: miss;Semen: miss;Embryos: miss
19   Status: potential. endang.;Watch: ♂♂,HB♀♀,%pure!
```

20 - Similar breeds (see group 2 on page 97)	EN	Country	Status
21 Erzgebirgsziege	330	D	crit.end.
22 Hneda kratkosrsta	334	CS	min. end.
23 Bunte Deutsche Edelziege	310	D	normal
24 Alpine	301	F	normal

1 - Bastarda, Di Benevento   EN   305
2   Benevento; Province of Benevento (Campania)
3   Assonapa   HB:miss
4   Roma 00161, Via Ravenna 9/c
5 - Composite of local breeds, Maltese 339, Garganica 331, Alpina 300
7   Numbers 1991: 50; HB: miss; decreasing; miss %; Ne = 4
8 - Height: 85/75 cm; Weight: 70/60 kg; Herd number: 2; AI: miss
9   Colour: Combination red, white
10 Pecularity: horns 0/0
11 - Main use: (1) milk; meat,(2) miss,(3) miss
12 Spec. abilities: arid hill
13 Performance compared with STB miss:
14   higher: miss
15   equal: miss
16   lower: miss
17 - Management: miss; housing: miss m.;
18 - Conservation progr.: live animals: miss;Semen: miss;Embryos: miss
19 Status: critically endang.;Watch: ♂♂,HB♀♀,trend,herds,%pure!
20 - <u>Similar breeds</u> (see group 5 on page 97)   <u>EN</u> <u>Country</u> <u>Status</u>
21 Di Campobasso   324   I   crit.end.
22 Cilentana Grigia   328   I   crit.end.
23 Maltese   339   I   normal
24 Ionica   335   I   normal

1 - Camosciata delle Alpi   EN   314
2   Camosciata Alpine; Alps (northern Italy)
3   Assonapa   HB:1986
4   Roma 00161, Via Ravenna 9/c
5 - miss
7   Numbers 1991: 156/ miss; HB: 4275; stable; miss %; Ne = 602
8 - Height: 70/65 cm; Weight: 57/47 kg; Herd number: miss; AI: miss
9   Colour: Uni brown
10 Pecularity: horns 2/2
11 - Main use: (1) milk,(2) meat,(3) miss
12 Spec. abilities: Mountain
13 Performance compared with STB Saanen 348:
14   higher: age of sexual maturity
15   equal: miss
16   lower: milk yield
17 - Management: stationary; housing: 12 m.;
18 - Conservation progr.: live animals: miss;Semen: miss;Embryos: miss
19 Status: normal;   Watch: %pure!
20 - <u>Similar breeds</u> (see group 2 on page 97)   <u>EN</u> <u>Country</u> <u>Status</u>
21 Erzgebirgsziege   330   D   crit.end.
22 Hneda kratkosrsta   334   CS   min. end.
23 Bunte Deutsche Edelziege   310   D   normal
24 Alpine   301   F   normal

```
 1 - Derivata di Siria                                    EN   323
 2     Syrian Derivative; Sicily
 3     Assonapa                                           HB:miss
 4     Roma 00161, Via Ravenna 9/c
 5 - Autochthon local population
 7     Numbers 1991: 50000; HB: 236; decreasing; miss %; Ne = 22
 8 - Height: 80/65 cm; Weight: 50/42 kg; Herd number: 4; AI: miss
 9     Colour: Uni red
10     Pecularity: horns 2/0
11 - Main use: (1) milk; meat,(2) miss,(3) miss
12     Spec. abilities: arid hill
13     Performance compared with STB miss:
14       higher: miss
15       equal:  miss
16       lower:  miss
17 - Management: miss; housing: miss m.;
18 - Conservation progr.: live animals: miss;Semen: miss;Embryos: miss
19     Status: critically endang.;Watch: ♂♂,HB♀♀,trend,herds,%pure!
20 - Similar breeds (see group 8 on page 98)       EN  Country Status
21     Cabra Mallorquina                            313   E     min. end.
22     Chevre du Rove                               319   F     pot. end.
23     Negra Serrana                                316   E     normal
24     Charnequeira                                 318   P     normal
```

```
 1 - Di Campobasso                                        EN   324
 2     Campobasso; Province of Campobasso (Molise)
 3     Assonapa                                           HB:miss
 4     Roma 00161, Via Ravenna 9/c
 5 - Composite of local breeds, Maltese 339, Garganica 331, Alpina 300
 7     Numbers 1991: 100; HB: miss; decreasing; miss %; Ne = 8
 8 - Height: 70/60 cm; Weight: 60/47 kg; Herd number: miss; AI: miss
 9     Colour: Uni brown, white, many colours are possible
10     Pecularity: horns 2/2
11 - Main use: (1) milk; meat,(2) miss,(3) miss
12     Spec. abilities: mountain
13     Performance compared with STB miss:
14       higher: miss
15       equal:  miss
16       lower:  miss
17 - Management: miss; housing: miss m.;
18 - Conservation progr.: live animals: miss;Semen: miss;Embryos: miss
19     Status: critically endang.;Watch: ♂♂,HB♀♀,trend,herds,%pure!
20 - Similar breeds (see group 5 on page 97)       EN  Country Status
21     Di Benevento                                 305   I     crit.end.
22     Cilentana Grigia                             328   I     crit.end.
23     Maltese                                      339   I     normal
24     Ionica                                       335   I     normal
```

1 - **Di Cosenza**   EN **325**
2   **Cosenza; Calabria**
3   **Assonapa**   HB:miss
4   **Roma 00161, Via Ravenna 9/c**
5 - **Composite of local breeds, Maltese 339, Garganica 331**
7   Numbers 1983: **40000**; HB: **miss**; **stable**; **miss** %; Ne = **7240**
8 - Height: **77/60** cm; Weight: **67/47** kg; Herd number: **miss**; AI: **miss**
9   Colour: **Uni black, brown, white, many colours are possible**
10   Pecularity: **horns 2/2**
11 - Main use: (1) **milk; meat**,(2) **miss**,(3) **miss**
12   Spec. abilities: **mountain**
13   Performance compared with STB **miss**:
14   higher: **miss**
15   equal: **miss**
16   lower: **miss**
17 - Management: **miss**; housing: **miss** m.;
18 - Conservation progr.: live animals: **miss**;Semen: **miss**;Embryos: **miss**
19   Status: **potential. endang.**;Watch: **♂♂,HB♀♀,%pure!**
20 - <u>Similar breeds</u> (see group 5 on page 97)   <u>EN</u> <u>Country</u> <u>Status</u>
21   **Di Benevento**   305   I   crit.end.
22   **Di Campobasso**   324   I   crit.end.
23   **Maltese**   339   I   normal
24   **Ionica**   335   I   normal

1 - **Di L' Aquila**   EN **326**
2   **Aquila; Province of L'Aquila (Abruzzi)**
3   **Assonapa**   HB:miss
4   **Roma 00161, Via Ravenna 9/c**
5 - **Composite of local breeds, Toggenburg 362 Switzerland, Alpina 300**
6   **Italy, Maltese 339 Italy, Girgentana 333 Italy**
7   Numbers 1991: **3000**; HB: **miss**; **decreasing**; **miss** %; Ne = **543**
8 - Height: **77/67** cm; Weight: **70/57** kg; Herd number: **miss**; AI: **miss**
9   Colour: **Uni black, brown, white, many colours are possible**
10   Pecularity: **horns 2,0/2,0**
11 - Main use: (1) **milk; meat**,(2) **miss**,(3) **miss**
12   Spec. abilities: **mountain**
13   Performance compared with STB **miss**:
14   higher: **miss**
15   equal: **miss**
16   lower: **miss**
17 - Management: **miss**; housing: **miss** m.;
18 - Conservation progr.: live animals: **miss**;Semen: **miss**;Embryos: **miss**
19   Status: **potential. endang.**;Watch: **♂♂,HB♀♀,trend,%pure!**
20 - <u>Similar breeds</u> (see group 5 on page 97)   <u>EN</u> <u>Country</u> <u>Status</u>
21   **Di Benevento**   305   I   crit.end.
22   **Di Campobasso**   324   I   crit.end.
23   **Maltese**   339   I   normal
24   **Ionica**   335   I   normal

```
1 - Di Potenza                                               EN  327
2   Potenza; Province of Potenza (Basilicata)
3   Assonapa                                                 HB:miss
4   Roma 00161, Via Ravenna 9/c
5 - Composite of local breeds, Maltese 339 Italy, Alpina 301 Italy,
6   Garganica 331 Italy
7   Numbers 1991: 500; HB: miss; decreasing; miss %; Ne = 79
8 - Height: 80/70 cm; Weight: 75/50 kg; Herd number: miss; AI: miss
9   Colour: Uni black, brown, many colours are possible
10  Pecularity: horns 2/2
11 - Main use: (1) milk; meat,(2) miss,(3) miss
12  Spec. abilities: hill
13  Performance compared with STB miss:
14    higher: miss
15    equal:  miss
16    lower:  miss
17 - Management: miss; housing: miss m.;
18 - Conservation progr.: live animals: miss;Semen: miss;Embryos: miss
19  Status: endangered;          Watch: ♂♂,HB♀♀,trend,herds,%pure!
20 - Similar breeds (see group 5 on page 97)     EN  Country Status
21  Di Benevento                                305   I    crit.end.
22  Di Campobasso                               324   I    crit.end.
23  Maltese                                     339   I    normal
24  Ionica                                      335   I    normal
```

```
1 - Di Salerno, Cilentana Grigia                             EN  328
2   Salerno; Province of Salerno (Campania)
3   Assonapa                                                 HB:miss
4   Roma 00161, Via Ravenna 9/c
5 - Autochthon local population
7   Numbers 1991: 30; HB: miss; decreasing; miss %; Ne = 2
8 - Height: 65/55 cm; Weight: 60/40 kg; Herd number: miss; AI: miss
9   Colour: Uni black, brown
10  Pecularity: miss
11 - Main use: (1) milk; meat,(2) miss,(3) miss
12  Spec. abilities: hill
13  Performance compared with STB miss:
14    higher: miss
15    equal:  miss
16    lower:  miss
17 - Management: miss; housing: miss m.;
18 - Conservation progr.: live animals: miss;Semen: miss;Embryos: miss
19  Status: critically endang.;Watch: ♂♂,HB♀♀,trend,herds,%pure!
20 - Similar breeds (see group 5 on page 97)     EN  Country Status
21  Di Benevento                                305   I    crit.end.
22  Di Campobasso                               324   I    crit.end.
23  Maltese                                     339   I    normal
24  Ionica                                      335   I    normal
```

```
 1 - Di Teramo                                              EN   329
 2   Teramo; Province of Teramo (Abruzzi)
 3   Assonapa                                               HB:miss
 4   Roma 00161, Via Ravenna 9/c
 5 - Autochthon local population
 7   Numbers 1991: 400; HB: miss; decreasing; miss %; Ne = 50
 8 - Height: 72/65 cm; Weight: 70/45 kg; Herd number: miss; AI: miss
 9   Colour: Uni black, brown, many colours are possible
10   Pecularity: horns 2/2
11 - Main use: (1) milk,(2) miss,(3) miss
12   Spec. abilities: hill
13   Performance compared with STB miss:
14     higher: miss
15     equal: miss
16     lower: miss
17 - Management: miss; housing: miss m.;
18 - Conservation progr.: live animals: miss;Semen: miss;Embryos: miss
19   Status: critically endang.;Watch: ♂♂,HB♀♀,trend,herds,%pure!
```

20 - Similar breeds (see group 5 on page 97)	EN	Country	Status
21 Di Benevento	305	I	crit.end.
22 Di Campobasso	324	I	crit.end.
23 Maltese	339	I	normal
24 Ionica	335	I	normal

```
 1 - Garganica                                              EN   331
 2   Garganica; Province of Foggia (Apulia)
 3   Assonapa                                               HB:1976
 4   Roma 00161, Via Ravenna 9/c
 5 - miss
 7   Numbers 1991: 12/ miss; HB: 280; decreasing; miss %; Ne = 25
 8 - Height: 85/75 cm; Weight: 65/50 kg; Herd number: miss; AI: miss
 9   Colour: Uni black
10   Pecularity: horns 2/2, screw-shaped horns
11 - Main use: (1) milk; meat,(2) miss,(3) miss
12   Spec. abilities: hill
13   Performance compared with STB miss:
14     higher: miss
15     equal: miss
16     lower: miss
17 - Management: stationary; housing: 12 m.;
18 - Conservation progr.: live animals: miss;Semen: miss;Embryos: miss
19   Status: critically endang.;Watch: ♂♂,HB♀♀,trend,%pure!
```

20 - Similar breeds (see group 5 on page 97)	EN	Country	Status
21 Di Benevento	305	I	crit.end.
22 Di Campobasso	324	I	crit.end.
23 Maltese	339	I	normal
24 Ionica	335	I	normal

1 - **Girgentana**   EN 333
2   **Girgentana**; Province of Agrigento (Sicily)
3   **Assonapa**   HB:1976
4   **Roma 00161, Via Ravenna 9/c**
5 - **Autochthon from Markhor**
7   Numbers 1991: **14**/ miss; HB: **258**; **decreasing**; miss %; Ne = **30**
8 - Height: **80/70** cm; Weight: **65/50** kg; Herd number: miss; AI: miss
9   Colour: **Uni white, occasionally brown spotted face**
10 Pecularity: **horns 2/2, big screw-shaped horns**
11 - Main use: (1) **milk; meat**,(2) miss,(3) miss
12 Spec. abilities: **hill**
13 Performance compared with STB **Saanen 348**:
14   higher: **age of sexual maturity, milk yield**
15   equal: miss
16   lower: miss
17 - Management: **stationary**; housing: **2-6 m.**;
18 - Conservation progr.: live animals: miss;Semen: miss;Embryos: miss
19 Status: **critically endang.**;Watch: ♂♂,HB♀♀,trend,**%pure!**
20 - <u>Similar breeds</u> (see group 6 on page 98)   <u>EN</u> <u>Country</u> <u>Status</u>
21 **Istriana**   337   I   crit.end.
22 **Sempione**   353   I   crit.end.
23 **Blanca Serrana Andaluza**   307   E   pot. end.

1 - **Ionica**   EN 335
2   **Ionica**; Province of Taranto (Apulia)
3   **Assonapa**   HB:1981
4   **Roma 00161, Via Ravenna 9/c**
5 - **Composite of local breeds, Maltese 339**
7   Numbers 1991: **66**/ miss; HB: **1868**; **stable**; miss %; Ne = **255**
8 - Height: **80/70** cm; Weight: **70/50** kg; Herd number: miss; AI: miss
9   Colour: **Uni white, sometimes black head**
10 Pecularity: **horns 2,0/2,0, big screw-shaped horns**
11 - Main use: (1) **milk**,(2) **meat**,(3) miss
12 Spec. abilities: **arid soils**
13 Performance compared with STB **Saanen 348**:
14   higher: **age of sexual maturity**
15   equal: miss
16   lower: **milk yield**
17 - Management: **stationary**; housing: **12 m.**;
18 - Conservation progr.: live animals: miss;Semen: miss;Embryos: miss
19 Status: **normal**;   Watch: **%pure!**
20 - <u>Similar breeds</u> (see group 5 on page 97)   <u>EN</u> <u>Country</u> <u>Status</u>
21 **Di Benevento**   305   I   crit.end.
22 **Di Campobasso**   324   I   crit.end.
23 **Malaguena**   321   E   normal
24 **Maltese**   339   I   normal

```
 1 - Istriana                                              EN   337
 2   Istrian Goat; Province of Gorizia (Friuli)
 3   Assonapa                                            HB:miss
 4   Roma 00161, Via Ravenna 9/c
 5 - Autochthon local population
 7   Numbers 1991: 20; HB: miss; decreasing; miss %; Ne = 4
 8 - Height: 65/60 cm; Weight: 55/55 kg; Herd number: miss; AI: miss
 9   Colour: Uni white
10   Pecularity: horns 0/0
11 - Main use: (1) milk,(2) meat,(3) miss
12   Spec. abilities: karst soils
13   Performance compared with STB miss:
14     higher: miss
15     equal:  miss
16     lower:  miss
17 - Management: miss; housing: miss m.;
18 - Conservation progr.: live animals: miss;Semen: miss;Embryos: miss
19   Status: critically endang.;Watch: ♂♂,HB♀♀,trend,herds,%pure!
20 - Similar breeds (see group 6 on page 98)    EN  Country Status
21   Girgentana                                  333   I    crit.end.
22   Sempione                                    353   I    crit.end.
23   Blanca Serrana Andaluza                     307   E    pot. end.
```

```
 1 - Maltese                                              EN   339
 2   Maltese; Sicily, Calabria, Basilicat
 3   Assonapa                                            HB:1976
 4   Roma 00161, Via Ravenna 9/c
 5 - miss
 7   Numbers 1991: 132/ miss; HB: 4084; stable; miss %; Ne = 512
 8 - Height: 90/70 cm; Weight: 70/50 kg; Herd number: miss; AI: miss
 9   Colour: Uni white, black forehead, lower jaw, neck, ears
10   Pecularity: horns 0/0
11 - Main use: (1) milk,(2) meat,(3) miss
12   Spec. abilities: hill
13   Performance compared with STB Saanen 348:
14     higher: age of sexual maturity
15     equal:  miss
16     lower:  milk yield
17 - Management: stationary; housing: 12 m.;
18 - Conservation progr.: live animals: miss;Semen: miss;Embryos: miss
19   Status: normal;              Watch: %pure!
20 - Similar breeds (see group 5 on page 97)    EN  Country Status
21   Di Benevento                                305   I    crit.end.
22   Di Campobasso                               324   I    crit.end.
23   Malaguena                                   321   E    normal
24   Ionica                                      335   I    normal
```

```
1 - Roccaverano                                                    EN  347
2   Roccaverano; Province of Asti (Piedmont)
3   Assonapa                                                       HB:miss
4   Roma 00161, Via Ravenna 9/c
5 - Autochthon local population
7   Numbers 1991: 200; HB: miss; decreasing; miss %; Ne = 18
8 - Height: 82/72 cm; Weight: 75/57 kg; Herd number: miss; AI: miss
9   Colour: Uni brown, white
10  Pecularity: horns 0/0
11 - Main use: (1) milk,(2) meat,(3) miss
12  Spec. abilities: hill
13  Performance compared with STB miss:
14    higher: miss
15    equal:  miss
16    lower:  miss
17 - Management: miss; housing: miss m.;
18 - Conservation progr.: live animals: miss;Semen: miss;Embryos: miss
19  Status: critically endang.;Watch: ♂♂,HB♀♀,trend,herds,%pure!
```

20 - Similar breeds (see group 9 on page 98)	EN	Country	Status
21 Val di Livo (extinct)	363	I	crit.end.
22 Skopelos	356	GR	pot. end.
23 Local breeds	338	GR	normal
24 Corse	320	F	normal

```
1 - Saanen                                                         EN  348
2   Saanen; Piedmont, Emilia Romagna, Apulia
3   Assonapa                                                       HB:1981
4   Roma 00161, Via Ravenna 9/c
5 - miss
7   Numbers 1991: 137/ miss; HB: 4184; decreasing; miss %; Ne = 531
8 - Height: 87/72 cm; Weight: 90/60 kg; Herd number: miss; AI: miss
9   Colour: Uni white
10  Pecularity: horns 2,0/2,0
11 - Main use: (1) milk,(2) meat,(3) miss
12  Spec. abilities: miss
13  Performance compared with STB Saanen 348:
14    higher: Breed is used
15    equal:  as standard breed,
16    lower:  no comparison possible.
17 - Management: stationary; housing: 12 m.;
18 - Conservation progr.: live animals: miss;Semen: miss;Embryos: miss
19  Status: normal;              Watch: trend,%pure!
```

20 - Similar breeds (see group 1 on page 97)	EN	Country	Status
21 Irish Goat	336	IRL	min. end.
22 Blanche	308	B	pot. end.
23 Gessenay	350	F	normal
24 Bila kratkosrsta	306	CS	normal

```
 1 - Sarda                                              EN   351
 2   Sardinian; Sardinia
 3   Assonapa                                           HB:1981
 4   Roma 00161, Via Ravenna 9/c
 5 - miss
 7   Numbers 1991: 165/ miss; HB: 3990; increasing; miss %; Ne = 634
 8 - Height: 67/60 cm; Weight: 60/47 kg; Herd number: miss; AI: miss
 9   Colour: Uni white, combination black, white
10   Pecularity: horns 2/2
11 - Main use: (1) milk; meat,(2) miss,(3) miss
12   Spec. abilities: arid soils
13   Performance compared with STB Saanen 348:
14     higher: age of sexual maturity
15     equal:  miss
16     lower:  milk yield
17 - Management: stationary; housing: 2-6 m.;
18 - Conservation progr.: live animals: miss;Semen: miss;Embryos: miss
19   Status: normal;              Watch: %pure!
20 - Similar breeds (see group 9 on page 98)    EN  Country Status
21   Roccaverano                                 347   I    crit.end.
22   Val di Livo (extinct)                       363   I    crit.end.
23   Local breeds                                338  GR    normal
24   Corse                                       320   F    normal
```

```
 1 - Sempione                                           EN   353
 2   Sempione; Province of Vercelle (Piedmont)
 3   Assonapa                                           HB:miss
 4   Roma 00161, Via Ravenna 9/c
 5 - Composite of local population, highly crossed
 7   Numbers 1991: 80; HB: miss; increasing; miss %; Ne = 6
 8 - Height: 75/60 cm; Weight: 62/52 kg; Herd number: miss; AI: miss
 9   Colour: Uni white
10   Pecularity: horns 2/2
11 - Main use: (1) meat,(2) miss,(3) miss
12   Spec. abilities: mountain
13   Performance compared with STB miss:
14     higher: miss
15     equal:  miss
16     lower:  miss
17 - Management: miss; housing: miss m.;
18 - Conservation progr.: live animals: miss;Semen: miss;Embryos: miss
19   Status: critically endang.;Watch: ♂♂,HB♀♀,herds,%pure!
20 - Similar breeds (see group 6 on page 98)    EN  Country Status
21   Girgentana                                  333   I    crit.end.
22   Istriana                                    337   I    crit.end.
23   Blanca Serrana Andaluza                     307   E    pot. end.
```

1 - **Val di Livo (extinct)**   EN **363**
2   **Val di Livo; Province of Coma (Lombaroy)**
3   **Assonapa**   HB:miss
4   **Roma 00161, Via Ravenna 9/c**
5 - **Composite of heterogenous population**
7   Numbers 1983: **150**; HB: **miss**; **decreasing**; **miss %**; Ne = **13**
8 - Height: **70/60** cm; Weight: **60/47** kg; Herd number: **miss**; AI: **miss**
9   Colour: **very heterogeneous in colour**
10 Pecularity: **horns 2,0/2,0**
11 - Main use: (1) **milk**,(2) **miss**,(3) **miss**
12 Spec. abilities: **hill**
13 Performance compared with STB **miss**:
14   higher: **miss**
15   equal: **miss**
16   lower: **miss**
17 - Management: **miss**; housing: **miss m.**;
18 - Conservation progr.: live animals: **miss**;Semen: **miss**;Embryos: **miss**
19 Status: **extinct/critically endang.**;Watch: ♂♂,HB♀♀,**trend,herds,%pure**!
20 - <u>Similar breeds</u> (see group 9 on page 98)   <u>EN</u> <u>Country</u> <u>Status</u>
21 **Roccaverano**   347   I   crit.end.
22 **Skopelos**   356   GR   pot. end.
23 **Local breeds**   338   GR   normal
24 **Corse**   320   F   normal

1 - **Valgerola**   EN **364**
2   **Valgerola; Province of Sondrio (Lombardy)**
3   **Assonapa**   HB:miss
4   **Roma 00161, Via Ravenna 9/c**
5 - **Autochthon local population**
7   Numbers 1989: **miss /4300**; HB: **700**; **increasing**; **miss %**; Ne = **127**
8 - Height: **95/72** cm; Weight: **80/60** kg; Herd number: **miss**; AI: **miss**
9   Colour: **Uni black,combination white/black,many colours are possible**
10 Pecularity: **horns 2/2, big horns**
11 - Main use: (1) **milk**,(2) **meat**,(3) **miss**
12 Spec. abilities: **hill**
13 Performance compared with STB **miss**:
14   higher: **miss**
15   equal: **miss**
16   lower: **miss**
17 - Management: **miss**; housing: **miss m.**;
18 - Conservation progr.: live animals: **miss**;Semen: **miss**;Embryos: **miss**
19 Status: **potential. endang.**;Watch: ♂♂,**%pure**!
20 - <u>Similar breeds</u> (see group 9 on page 98)   <u>EN</u> <u>Country</u> <u>Status</u>
21 **Roccaverano**   347   I   crit.end.
22 **Val di Livo (extinct)**   363   I   crit.end.
23 **Local breeds**   338   GR   normal
24 **Corse**   320   F   normal

GOATS

1 - Vallesana   EN   365
2   Vallesana; Province of Novara (Piedmont)
3   Assonapa   HB:miss
4   Roma 00161, Via Ravenna 9/c
5 - Imported as breed Walliser Schwarz-Halsziege 366 from Switzerland
7   Numbers 1991: 2/300; HB: 60; decreasing; miss %; Ne = 3
8 - Height: 82/65 cm; Weight: 72/55 kg; Herd number: miss; AI: miss
9   Colour: Combination black/white, black fore- and white hindquarters
10 Pecularity: horns 2/2
11 - Main use: (1) meat,(2) milk,(3) miss
12 Spec. abilities: hill
13 Performance compared with STB miss:
14   higher: miss
15   equal: miss
16   lower: miss
17 - Management: miss; housing: miss m.;
18 - Conservation progr.: live animals: miss;Semen: miss;Embryos: miss
19 Status: critically endang.;Watch: ♂♂,HB♀♀,trend,herds,%pure!
20 - Similar breeds (see group 7 on page 98)   EN Country Status
21 Serpentina   354 P   normal
22 Walliser Schwarzhalsziege   366 CH   normal

PIGS

1 - Cinta Senese   EN   914
2   Siena Belted; Tuscany
3   Ass. Prov. Allevatori   HB:miss
4   Siena 17100, Via Montanini 140
5 - miss
7   Numbers 1992: 8/50; HB: 50; decreasing; 40 %; Ne = 13
8 - Height: miss/miss cm; Weight: miss/miss kg; Herd number: 10; AI:miss
9   Colour: Combination black, white
10 Pecularity: white belt, lop ears
11 - Main use: (1) meat,(2) miss,(3) miss
12 Spec. abilities: miss
13 Performance compared with STB miss:
14   higher: miss
15   equal: miss
16   lower: miss
17 - Management: stationary; housing: no
18 - Conservation progr.: live animals: miss;Semen: miss;Embryos: miss
19 Status: critically endang.;Watch: ♂♂,HB♀♀,trend,%pure!
20 - Similar breeds (see group 3/1 on page 102)   EN Country Status
21 Pie noir du Pays Basque   987 F   crit.end.
22 Angler Sattelschwein   903 D   crit.end.
23 British Saddleback   912 GB   pot. end.
24 Schwäbisch-Hällisches Schwein   997 D   pot. end.

```
1 - Duroc                                               EN  929
2   Duroc
3   ANAS                                                HB: Yes
4   Rome 00161, via G.B. de Rossi 3
5 - miss
7   Numbers 1991: 337/ miss; HB: 410; stable; miss %; Ne = 740
8 - Height:miss/miss cm; Weight:miss/miss kg; Herd number:miss; AI:miss
9   Colour: Uni red
10  Pecularity: miss
11 - Main use: (1) meat,(2) miss,(3) miss
12  Spec. abilities: miss
13  Performance compared with STB miss:
14    higher: miss
15    equal:  miss
16    lower:  miss
17 - Management: stationary; housing: 12 m.;
18 - Conservation progr.: live animals: miss;Semen: miss;Embryos: miss
19  Status: normal;              Watch: %pure!
```

20 - Similar breeds (see group 5/1 on page 103)	EN	Country	Status
21 Duroc	927	F	crit.end.
22 Duroc	932	GB	crit.end.
23 Duroc	931	RO	normal
24 Duroc	926	CS	normal

```
1 - Hampshire                                           EN  943
2   Hampshire; country-wide
3   ANAS                                                HB: Yes
4   Rome 00161, via G.B. de Rossi 3
5 - miss
7   Numbers 1991: 10/ miss; HB: 24; miss; miss %; Ne = 13
8 - Height:miss/miss cm; Weight:miss/miss kg; Herd number:miss; AI:miss
9   Colour: Combination black, white
10  Pecularity: white belt, erect ears
11 - Main use: (1) meat,(2) miss,(3) miss
12  Spec. abilities: miss
13  Performance compared with STB miss:
14    higher: miss
15    equal:  miss
16    lower:  miss
17 - Management: stationary; housing: 12 m.;
18 - Conservation progr.: live animals: miss;Semen: miss;Embryos: miss
19  Status: critically endang.;Watch: ♂♂,HB♀♀,herds,%pure!
```

20 - Similar breeds (see group 3/2 on page 102)	EN	Country	Status
21 Limousin	967	F	crit.end.
22 Hampshire	942	D*	crit.end.
23 Hampshire	944	RO	pot. end.
24 Hampshire	940	CS	normal

```
1 - Landrace                                           EN   954
2   Italian Landrace; country-wide
3   ANAS                                                HB: Yes
4   Rome 00161, via G.B. de Rossi 3
5 - miss
7   Numbers 1991: 725/ miss; HB: 1942; stable; miss %; Ne = 2112
8 - Height: miss/miss cm; Weight: miss/miss kg; Herd number:miss; AI:Yes
9   Colour: Uni white
10  Pecularity: lop ears
11 - Main use: (1) meat,(2) miss,(3) miss
12  Spec. abilities: miss
13  Performance compared with STB miss:
14     higher: miss
15     equal:  miss
16     lower:  miss
17 - Management: stationary; housing: 12 m.;
18 - Conservation progr.: live animals: miss;Semen: miss;Embryos: miss
19  Status: normal;              Watch: %pure!
20 - Similar breeds (see group 2/1 on page 101)    EN  Country Status
21  Belgische Landrasse                             907  D*    crit.end.
22  Zlotnicka biala                                 1024 PL    crit.end.
23  Landrace                                        952  CS    normal
24  Belgisch Landvarken                             906  B     normal
```

```
1 - Landrace Belga                                     EN   956
2   Belgian Landrace; country-wide
3   ANAS                                                HB: Yes
4   Rome 00161, via G.B. de Rossi 3
5 - miss
7   Numbers 1991: 38/ miss; HB: 72; decreasing; miss %; Ne = 99
8 - Height:miss/miss cm; Weight:miss/miss kg; Herd number:miss; AI:miss
9   Colour: Uni white
10  Pecularity: lop ears
11 - Main use: (1) meat,(2) miss,(3) miss
12  Spec. abilities: miss
13  Performance compared with STB miss:
14     higher: miss
15     equal:  miss
16     lower:  miss
17 - Management: stationary; housing: 12 m.;
18 - Conservation progr.: live animals: miss;Semen: miss;Embryos: miss
19  Status: endangered;          Watch: HB♀♀,trend,%pure!
20 - Similar breeds (see group 2/1 on page 101)    EN  Country Status
21  Belgische Landrasse                             907  D*    crit.end.
22  Zlotnicka biala                                 1024 PL    crit.end.
23  Landrace                                        952  CS    normal
24  Belgisch Landvarken                             906  B     normal
```

1 - **Large White**   EN **961**
2   **Large White**
3   **ANAS**   HB: **Yes**
4   **Rome 00161, via G.B. de Rossi 3**
5 - **miss**
7   Numbers 1991: 2212/ miss; HB: 14205; miss; miss %; Ne = 7656
8 - Height:**miss/miss** cm; Weight:**miss/miss** kg; Herd number:**miss**; AI:**Yes**
9   Colour: **Uni white**
10 Pecularity: **erect ears**
11 - Main use: (1) **miss**,(2) **miss**,(3) **miss**
12 Spec. abilities: **miss**
13 Performance compared with STB **miss**:
14   higher: **miss**
15   equal: **miss**
16   lower: **miss**
17 - Management: **stationary**; housing: **12 m.**;
18 - Conservation progr.: live animals: **miss**;Semen: **miss**;Embryos: **miss**
19 Status: **normal**
20 - <u>Similar breeds</u> (see group 1/1 on page 101)   <u>EN</u> <u>Country</u> <u>Status</u>
21 **Norsk Yorkshire**   984   N   endanger.
22 **Grand Yorkshire Belge**   937   B   normal
23 **Large White**   960   F   normal
24 **Yorkshire**   1021 SF   normal

1 - **Mora Romagnola**   EN **977**
2   **Romagnola; Romagna**
3   **Ass. Prov. Allevatori**   HB: **Yes**
4   **Ravenna 48100, Via Diaz 69**
5 - **miss**
7   Numbers 1992: 2/6; HB: 3; decreasing; miss %; Ne = 2
8 - Height: **miss/miss** cm; Weight: **miss/miss** kg; Herd number: **2**; AI: **miss**
7   Numbers 1992: 2/6; HB: 3; decreasing; miss %; AI: **miss**
8 - Height: **miss / miss** cm; Weight: **miss / miss** kg; Herd number: **2**
9   Colour: **miss**
10 Pecularity: **miss**
11 - Main use: (1) **meat**,(2) **miss**,(3) **miss**
12 Spec. abilities: **miss**
13 Performance compared with STB **miss**:
14   higher: **miss**
15   equal: **miss**
16   lower: **miss**
17 - Management: **stationary**; housing: **no**
18 - Conservation progr.: live animals: **miss**;Semen: **miss**;Embryos: **miss**
19 Status: **critically endang.**;Watch: ♂♂,HB♀♀,trend,herds,**%pure!**
20 - <u>Similar breeds</u> (see group 5/2 on page 103)   <u>EN</u> <u>Country</u> <u>Status</u>
21 **Tamworth**   1009 GB   min. end.
22 **Colorada**   934   E   pot. end.

```
1 - Pietrain                                              EN  990
2   Pietrain; country-wide
3   ANAS                                                  HB:miss
4   Rome 00161, via G.B. de Rossi 3
5 - miss
7   Numbers miss: miss / miss; HB: miss; miss; miss %; Ne = miss
8 - Height:miss/miss cm; Weight:miss/miss kg; Herd number:miss; AI:miss
9   Colour: Combination white, black, reddish
10  Pecularity: black or reddish spots, short erect ears
11 - Main use: (1) meat,(2) miss,(3) miss
12  Spec. abilities: miss
13  Performance compared with STB miss:
14    higher: miss
15    equal:  miss
16    lower:  miss
17 - Management: stationary; housing: 12 m.;
18 - Conservation progr.: live animals: miss;Semen: miss;Embryos: miss
19  Status: miss
```

20 - Similar breeds (see group 6/1 on page 103)	EN	Country	Status
21 Pietrain	988	B	normal
22 Pietrain	989	F	normal
23 Pietrain	991	D	normal

```
1 - Spotted                                               EN 1006
2   Spotted
3   ANAS                                                  HB:miss
4   Rome 00161, via G.B. de Rossi 3
5 - miss
7   Numbers miss: miss / miss; HB: miss; miss; miss %; Ne = miss
8 - Height:miss/miss cm; Weight:miss/miss kg; Herd number:miss; AI:miss
9   Colour: Combination black, white
10  Pecularity: white spots
11 - Main use: (1) miss,(2) miss,(3) miss
12  Spec. abilities: miss
13  Performance compared with STB miss:
14    higher: miss
15    equal:  miss
16    lower:  miss
17 - Management: miss; housing: miss m.;
18 - Conservation progr.: live animals: miss;Semen: miss;Embryos: miss
19  Status: miss
```

20 - Similar breeds (see group 6/2 on page 104)	EN	Country	Status
21 Sortbroget	1005	DK	crit.end.
22 Schwarz-Weißes Bentheimer	996	D	crit.end.
23 Sibirskaya chernopestraya	1001	USSR	pot. end.
24 Gloucestershire Old Spot	936	GB	pot. end.

```
 1 - Avelignese                                              EN  710
 2   Haflinger; country-wide
 3   Associazione Nazionale Allevatori Cavallo Razza         HB:1973
 4   Avelignese Firenze 50129, Via Cavour 106
 5 - Incrossing since 1950 from Haflinger Austria
 7   Numbers 1992: 331/8600; HB: 7778; increasing; miss %; Ne = 1270
 8 - Height: 138/135 cm; Weight: miss/miss kg; Herd number: miss; AI:miss
 9   Colour: light to dark chestnut
10   Pecularity: full flaxen mane and tail
11 - Main use: (1) sport/hobby,(2) meat,(3) tractive power
12   Spec. abilities: mountain
13   Performance compared with STB miss:
14     higher: miss
15     equal:  miss
16     lower:  miss
17 - Management: stationary; housing: ≈ 2/> 6 m.;
18 - Conservation progr.: live animals: miss;Semen: miss;Embryos: miss
19   Status: normal
```

20 - Similar breeds (see group 5/8 on page 111)	EN	Country	Status
21 Haflinger	757	GB	endanger.
22 Haflinger	756	CH	pot. end.
23 Haflinger	754	D	normal
24 Haflinger	753	F	normal

```
 1 - Cavallo Agricolo Italiano                               EN  716
 2   Rapid Heavy Draft; Emilia Romagna
 3   Ass. Nazionale Allevatori del Cavallo, Agricolo         HB:1981
 4   Italiano da Tiro Pesante Rapido, Verona, Via Locatelli 20
 5 - Autochthon local breed
 6   Incrossing since 1950 from Breton 714 France, Belgian
 7   Numbers 1991: 355/8000; HB: 1937; increasing; miss %; Ne = 1200
 8 - Height: 160/155 cm; Weight: 700/570 kg; Herd number: miss; AI: miss
 9   Colour: bay
10   Pecularity: miss
11 - Main use: (1) meat,(2) tractive power,(3) miss
12   Spec. abilities: miss
13   Performance compared with STB miss:
14     higher: miss
15     equal:  miss
16     lower:  miss
17 - Management: stationary; housing: 2-6/12 m.;
18 - Conservation progr.: live animals: miss;Semen: miss;Embryos: miss
19   Status: potential. endang.;Watch: %pure,%incross!
```

20 - Similar breeds (see group 4/2 on page 109)	EN	Country	Status
21 Poitevin	791	F	endanger.
22 Boulonnais	713	F	pot. end.
23 Percheron	790	F	pot. end.
24 Breton	714	F	pot. end.

```
1 - Cavallo Anglo-Arabo-Sardo                                    EN  717
2   Anglo-Arabo-Sarda; Sardinia
3   Istituto Incremento Ippico di Ozieri,                       HB:1981
4   Ozieri (SS), Piazza Duchessa Borgia 4
5 - Composite of Sardinian 724, Thoroughbred, Arab (required >= 25%
6   Arab "blood"); incrossing since 1950 from Thoroughbred
7   Numbers 1991: 62/1081; HB: 1081; stable; 100 %; Ne = 235
8 - Height: 163/160 cm; Weight: miss/miss kg; Herd number: miss; AI:miss
9   Colour: grey, bay, chestnut
10  Pecularity: miss
11 - Main use: (1) sport/hobby,(2) miss,(3) miss
12  Spec. abilities: miss
13  Performance compared with STB miss:
14    higher: miss
15    equal:  miss
16    lower:  miss
17 - Management: stationary; housing: 12 m.;
18 - Conservation progr.: live animals: miss;Semen: miss;Embryos: miss
19  Status: normal;              Watch: %incross!
```

		EN	Country	Status
20 - Similar breeds (see group 1 on page 108)				
21	Arabialainen	706	SF	crit.end.
22	Täysverinen	811	SF	crit.end.
23	Anglo-Arab	702	F	normal
24	Vollblutaraber	815	A	normal

```
1 - Cavallo Bardigiano                                           EN  718
2   Bardigiana; Emilia Romagna, Liguria
3   Associazione Nazionale degli Allevatori di Cavalli di       HB:1977
4   Razza Bardigiana, Parma, Via Salnitrara 3
5 - Autochthon local breed
6   Incrossing since 1950 from Haflinger 710 Italy
7   Numbers 1992: 90/1600; HB: 1250; increasing; 100 %; Ne = 336
8 - Height: 143/142 cm; Weight: miss/miss kg; Herd number: miss; AI:miss
9   Colour: bay, brown, black
10  Pecularity: miss
11 - Main use: (1) meat,(2) sport/hobby,(3) miss
12  Spec. abilities: miss
13  Performance compared with STB miss:
14    higher: miss
15    equal:  miss
16    lower:  miss
17 - Management: stationary; housing: 2-6 m.;
18 - Conservation progr.: live animals: miss;Semen: miss;Embryos: miss
19  Status: normal;              Watch: %incross!
```

		EN	Country	Status
20 - Similar breeds (see group 5/10 on page 111)				
21	Sorraia	807	P	crit.end.
22	Skyos Pony	806	GR	endanger.
23	Cavallo della Giara	719	I	pot. end.
24	Pottok	794	F	pot. end.

382

1 - Cavallo della Giara   EN 719
2   Giara Pony; Sardinia (Tableland of Giara)
3   Istituto Incremento Ippico di Ozieri   HB:miss
4   Ozieri (SS), Piazza Duchessa Borgia 4
5 - Autochthon local breed
7   Numbers 1992: 40/350; HB: miss; stable; miss %; Ne = 144
8 - Height: 135/130 cm; Weight: miss/miss kg; Herd number: 40; AI: miss
9   Colour: bay, brown, black
10 Pecularity: miss
11 - Main use: (1) sport/hobby,(2) meat,(3) miss
12 Spec. abilities: harsh dry environment, feral population
13 Performance compared with STB miss:
14   higher: miss
15   equal: miss
16   lower: miss
17 - Management: stationary; housing: no
18 - Conservation progr.: live animals: miss;Semen: miss;Embryos: miss
19 Status: potential. endang.;Watch: HB♀♀,%pure!
20 - Similar breeds (see group 5/10 on page 111)   EN Country Status
21 Sorraia   807 P   crit.end.
22 Skyos Pony   806 GR   endanger.
23 Pottok   794 F   pot. end.
24 Cavallo Bardigiano   718 I   normal

1 - Cavallo Maremmano   EN 720
2   Maremmana; Tuscany
3   Associazione Nazionale Allevatori Cavallo di Razza   HB:1980
4   Maremmana Grosetto, Via Monterosa 16
5 - Autochthon local breed
6   Incrossing since 1950 from Thoroughbred
7   Numbers 1992: 142/ miss; HB: 1500; increasing; miss %; Ne = 519
8 - Height: 165/162 cm; Weight: miss/miss kg; Herd number: 801; AI: miss
9   Colour: bay, brown, black
10 Pecularity: miss
11 - Main use: (1) sport/hobby,(2) tractive power,(3) miss
12 Spec. abilities: miss
13 Performance compared with STB miss:
14   higher: miss
15   equal: miss
16   lower: miss
17 - Management: stationary; housing: no/12 m.;
18 - Conservation progr.: live animals: miss;Semen: miss;Embryos: miss
19 Status: potential. endang.;Watch: %incross!
20 - Similar breeds (see group 3/5 on page 109)   EN Country Status
21 Cavallo Sanfratellano   723 I   endanger.
22 Cavallo Sardo   724 I   endanger.
23 Cavallo Murgese   721 I   normal
24 Camargue   715 F   normal

```
1 - Cavallo Murgese                                              EN  721
2   Murgese; Puglia
3   Ass. Regionale Allevatori dell'Asino di Martina Franca e     HB:1948
4   del Cavallo delle Murge, Martina Franca, Piazza Filippo D'Angiò 53
5 - miss
7   Numbers 1991: 50/742; HB: 742; decreasing; 100 %; Ne = 187
8 - Height: 164/162 cm; Weight: 550/480 kg; Herd number: miss; AI: miss
9   Colour: grey, black
10  Pecularity: miss
11 - Main use: (1) sport/hobby,(2) tractive power,(3) miss
12  Spec. abilities: miss
13  Performance compared with STB miss:
14    higher: miss
15    equal: miss
16    lower: miss
17 - Management: stationary; housing: no/2-6 m.;
18 - Conservation progr.: live animals: miss;Semen: miss;Embryos: miss
19  Status: normal;              Watch: trend!
```

20 - Similar breeds (see group 3/5 on page 109)

	EN	Country	Status
21 Cavallo Sanfratellano	723	I	endanger.
22 Cavallo Sardo	724	I	endanger.
23 Cavallo Maremmano	720	I	pot. end.
24 Camargue	715	F	normal

```
1 - Cavallo Norico                                               EN  722
2   Noric; "Alto Adige"
3   Federazione Allevatori Cavalli di Razza Avelignese           HB: Yes
4   dell'Alto-Adige, Bolzano, Via Crispi 15
5 - Autochthon local breed
6   Incrossing since 1950 from Noric 788 Austria
7   Numbers 1992: 3/ miss; HB: 65; stable; miss %; Ne = 5
8 - Height: 155/153 cm; Weight: miss/miss kg; Herd number: miss; AI:miss
9   Colour: bay, chestnut, brown, grey
10  Pecularity: miss
11 - Main use: (1) tractive power,(2) sport/hobby,(3) meat
12  Spec. abilities: mountain
13  Performance compared with STB miss:
14    higher: miss
15    equal: miss
16    lower: miss
17 - Management: stationary; housing: > 6 m.;
18 - Conservation progr.: live animals: miss;Semen: miss;Embryos: miss
19  Status: critically endang.;Watch: ♂♂,HB♀♀,herds,%pure!
```

20 - Similar breeds (see group 4/3 on page 110)

	EN	Country	Status
21 Schwarzwälder Füchse	800	D	min. end.
22 Norisches Kaltblut	788	A	normal
23 Süddeutsches Kaltblut	810	D	normal

```
 1 - Cavallo Sanfratellano                              EN   723
 2   Sanfratellana; Sicily
 3   Istituto Incremento Ippico di Catania             HB:miss
 4   Catania, Via Vittorio Emanuele 508
 5 - Autochthon local breed
 6   Incrossing since 1950 from Thoroughbred
 7   Numbers 1992: 13/ miss; HB: 297; decreasing; miss %; Ne = 28
 8 - Height: 156/156 cm; Weight: miss/miss kg; Herd number: 240; AI: miss
 9   Colour: bay, brown, black
10   Pecularity: miss
11 - Main use: (1) sport/hobby,(2) meat,(3) tractive power
12   Spec. abilities: miss
13   Performance compared with STB miss:
14      higher: miss
15      equal: miss
16      lower: miss
17 - Management: stationary; housing: no
18 - Conservation progr.: live animals: miss;Semen: miss;Embryos: miss
19   Status: endangered;        Watch: ♂♂,HB♀♀,trend,%pure,%incross!
```

20 - <u>Similar breeds</u> (see group 3/5 on page 109)

20	Similar breeds (see group 3/5 on page 109)	EN	Country	Status
21	Cavallo Sardo	724	I	endanger.
22	Cavallo Maremmano	720	I	pot. end.
23	Cavallo Murgese	721	I	normal
24	Camargue	715	F	normal

```
 1 - Cavallo Sardo                                      EN   724
 2   Sardinian; Sardinia
 3   Istituto Incremento Ippico di Ozieri             HB:miss
 4   Ozieri (SS), Piazza Duchessa Borgia 4
 5 - Autochthon local breed
 6   Incrossing since 1950 from Thoroughbred, Arab, Anglo-Arabo-Sarda 717
 7   Numbers 1986: miss /1500; HB: miss; stable; miss %; Ne = 272
 8 - Height: 159/157 cm; Weight: miss/miss kg; Herd number: miss; AI:miss
 9   Colour: bay, brown, black , grey
10   Pecularity: miss
11 - Main use: (1) meat,(2) sport/hobby,(3) miss
12   Spec. abilities: miss
13   Performance compared with STB miss:
14      higher: miss
15      equal: miss
16      lower: miss
17 - Management: stationary; housing: no
18 - Conservation progr.: live animals: miss;Semen: miss;Embryos: miss
19   Status: endangered;        Watch: ♂♂,HB♀♀,%pure,%incross!
```

20 - <u>Similar breeds</u> (see group 3/5 on page 109)

20	Similar breeds (see group 3/5 on page 109)	EN	Country	Status
21	Cavallo Sanfratellano	723	I	endanger.
22	Cavallo Maremmano	720	I	pot. end.
23	Cavallo Murgese	721	I	normal
24	Camargue	715	F	normal

```
 1 - Cavallo Siciliano                                           EN   725
 2   Sicilian; Sicilia
 3   Istituto Incremento Ippico di Catania                       HB: Yes
 4   Catania, Via Vittorio Emanuele 508
 5 - Autochthon local breed
 6   Incrossing since 1950 from Thoroughbred, Arab
 7   Numbers 1988: 45/2323; HB: 160; stable; miss %; Ne = 141
 8 - Height: 164/164 cm; Weight: miss/miss kg; Herd number: miss; AI:miss
 9   Colour: bay
10   Pecularity: miss
11 - Main use: (1) sport/hobby,(2) meat,(3) miss
12   Spec. abilities: miss
13   Performance compared with STB miss:
14     higher: miss
15     equal:  miss
16     lower:  miss
17 - Management: stationary; housing: > 6 m.;
18 - Conservation progr.: live animals: miss;Semen: miss;Embryos: miss
19   Status: potential. endang.;Watch: %incross,%pure!
```

20 - Similar breeds (see group 3/5 on page 109)	EN	Country	Status
21 Cavallo Sanfratellano	723	I	endanger.
22 Cavallo Sardo	724	I	endanger.
23 Cavallo Murgese	721	I	normal
24 Camargue	715	F	normal

```
 1 - Lipizzano                                                   EN   777
 2   Lipitsa; Lazio (Tormancina, Roma)
 3   Istituto Sperimentale per la Zootecnia, Azenda Agraria      HB:1984
 4   Sperimentale Tormancina, Monterotondo (Roma) 00016, Via Salaria 31
 5 - miss
 7   Numbers 1992: 6/ miss; HB: 54; increasing; 100 %; Ne = 10
 8 - Height: 158/156 cm; Weight: miss/miss kg; Herd number: miss; AI:miss
 9   Colour: grey
10   Pecularity: sleek coat, silky mane and tail
11 - Main use: (1) sport/hobby,(2) miss,(3) miss
12   Spec. abilities: miss
13   Performance compared with STB miss:
14     higher: miss
15     equal:  miss
16     lower:  miss
17 - Management: stationary; housing: 12 m.;
18 - Conservation progr.: live animals: miss;Semen: miss;Embryos: miss
19   Status: critically endang.;Watch: ♂♂,HB♀♀,herds!
```

20 - Similar breeds (see group 3/1 on page 108)	EN	Country	Status
21 Lipizzan	776	F	crit.end.
22 Senner	801	D	crit.end.
23 Espanol-Andaluz	742	E	normal
24 Lusitanien	779	F	normal

```
 1 - Alatauskaya                                              EN    3
 2   Ala-Tau; southeastern Kazakhstan, northeastern Kirgizia
 3   Food and Agriculture Organisation of the UN              HB:1950
 4   Rome 00100, Via delle Terme di Caracalla
 5 - Composite of Swiss Brown, Kirgiz, Kazakh
 6   Incrossing since 1950 from Kostroma 142 and Jersey USSR
 7   Numbers 1990: 4700/376600; HB: miss; decreasing; 54 %; Ne = 18568
 8 - Height: 136/127 cm; Weight: 800/500 kg; Herd number: miss; AI: Yes
 9   Colour: Uni brown
10   Pecularity: miss
11 - Main use: (1) milk,(2) meat,(3) miss
12   Spec. abilities: some cows produce 13-14 healthy calves
13   Performance compared with STB Russian Simmental 241:
14     higher: miss
15     equal: % fat
16     lower: milk yield
17 - Management: stationary; housing: 2-6 m.; some cows 15-17 years old
18 - Conservation progr.: live animals: miss;Semen: miss;Embryos: miss
19   Status: potential. endang.;Watch: HB♀♀,trend,%pure,%incross!
```

20 - Similar breeds (see group 5/1 on page 79)	EN	Country	Status
21 Original Allgäuer Braunvieh	189	D	crit.end.
22 Agerolese	2	I	crit.end.
23 Aubrac	14	F	normal
24 Österreichisches Braunvieh	190	A	normal

```
 1 - Aulieatinskaya                                           EN   15
 2   Aulie-Ata; southern Kazakhstan, northern Kirgizia
 3   Food and Agriculture Organisation of the UN              HB:1935
 4   Rome 00100, Via delle Terme di Caracalla
 5 - Composite of Friesian, Kazakh
 7   Numbers 1990: 1000/82000; HB: miss; decreasing; 59 %; Ne = 3952
 8 - Height: 139/129 cm; Weight: 900/510 kg; Herd number: miss; AI: Yes
 9   Colour: Uni black, occasionally grey
10   Pecularity: usually black with white markings on underside
11 - Main use: (1) milk; meat,(2) miss,(3) miss
12   Spec. abilities: resist. to theileriosis,piroplasmosis,hot climate
13   Performance compared with STB Russian Simmental 241:
14     higher: miss
15     equal: % fat
16     lower: milk yield
17 - Management: stationary; housing: 2-6 m.;
18 - Conservation progr.: live animals: miss;Semen: miss;Embryos: miss
19   Status: normal;          Watch: HB♀♀,trend,%pure!
```

20 - Similar breeds (see group 1/3 on page 75)	EN	Country	Status
21 Yakutskii skot	274	USSR	min. end.
22 Istobenskaya	128	USSR	pot. end.
23 Kholmogorskaya	141	USSR	normal
24 Cherno-pestraya	64	USSR	normal

CATTLE

1 - Kazakhskaya belogolovaya   EN 138
2   Kazakh Whiteheaded; northern Kazakhstan
3   Food and Agriculture Organisation of the UN   HB: Yes
4   Rome 00100, Via delle Terme di Caracalla
5 - Composite of Hereford, local Kazakh, Kalmyk 135
7   Numbers 1990: 31600/572600; HB: miss; stable; 28 %; Ne = 119789
8 - Height: 133/124 cm; Weight: 820/550 kg; Herd number: miss; AI: miss
9   Colour: Combination red, white
10 Pecularity: white head
11 - Main use: (1) meat,(2) milk,(3) miss
12 Spec. abilities: tolerate cold and hot weather, high weight gains
13 Performance compared with STB Russian Simmental 241:
14   higher: % fat
15   equal: miss
16   lower: milk yield
17 - Management: stationary; housing: > 6 m.;
18 - Conservation progr.: live animals: miss;Semen: miss;Embryos: miss
19 Status: normal;   Watch: HB♀♀,%pure!
20 - Similar breeds (see group 3/5 on page 77)   EN Country Status
21 Hereford   110   F   pot. end.
22 Hereford   111   IRL normal
23 Hereford   112   GB   normal

PIGS

1 - Aksaiskaya cherno-pestraya   EN 901
2   Aksai Black Pied; Alma Ata, southeastern Kazakhstan
3   Food and Agriculture Organisation of the UN   HB:miss
4   Rome 00100, Via delle Terme di Caracalla
5 - Composite of native breed, Large White, Berkshire
7   Numbers 1990: 96/450; HB: miss; stable; 100 %; Ne = 317
8 - Height: miss/miss cm; Weight: 317/245 kg; Herd number: miss; AI:miss
9   Colour: Combination black, white
10 Pecularity: erect ears, black pied
11 - Main use: (1) general purpose,(2) miss,(3) miss
12 Spec. abilities: miss
13 Performance compared with STB Large White 951:
14   higher: feed conversion rate
15   equal: litter size
16   lower: daily gain
17 - Management: stationary; housing: 12 m.;
18 - Conservation progr.: live animals: miss;Semen: miss;Embryos: miss
19 Status: normal;   Watch: HB♀♀!
20 - Similar breeds (see group 4/2 on page 103)   EN Country Status
21 Berkshire   909   GB   min. end.
22 Kemerovskaya   949   USSR pot. end.
23 Mirgorodskaya   976   UR   normal
24 Belorusskaya cherno-pestraya   908   BEL normal

PIGS

1 - **Semirechenskaya**   EN **999**
2   **Semirechensk; southeastern Kazakhstan**
3   Food and Agriculture Organisation of the UN   HB:miss
4   Rome 00100, Via delle Terme di Caracalla
5 - Composite of Asiatic wild, Large White, Kemerovo
7   Numbers 1990: 505/2900; HB: miss; decreasing; 93 %; Ne = 1720
8 - Height: miss/miss cm; Weight: 275/222 kg; Herd number: miss; AI:miss
9   Colour: **Uni white**
10 Pecularity: **erect ears, occasionally black-pied, dark brown or tan**
11 - Main use: (1) **general purpose**,(2) **miss**,(3) **miss**
12 Spec. abilities: **piglet viability**
13 Performance compared with STB **Large White 951:**
14   higher: **miss**
15   equal: **% lean, litter size, feed conversion rate**
16   lower: **daily gain**
17 - Management: **stationary**; housing: **12 m.; sow hardiness**
18 - Conservation progr.: live animals: **miss**;Semen: **miss**;Embryos: **miss**
19 Status: **potential. endang.**;Watch: **HB♀♀,trend,%pure!**
20 - <u>Similar breeds</u> (see group 1/2 on page 101)   <u>EN</u> <u>Country</u> <u>Status</u>
21 **Bela Zlahtna**   904   SLO   crit.end.
22 **Middle White**   975   GB   min. end.
23 **Deutsches Edelschwein**   922   D*   normal
24 **Vile uslechtile**   1017 CS   normal

CATTLE

1 - **Buraya latviiskaya**   EN **50**
2   **Latvian Brown; country-wide**
3   Food and Agriculture Organisation of the UN   HB:1885
4   Rome 00100, Via delle Terme di Caracalla
5 - Composite of Angeln, local
6   **Incrossing since 1950 from Danish Red 222 Denmark**
7   Numbers 1990: 3500/556000; HB: miss; decreasing; 77 %; Ne = 13912
8 - Height: 140/130 cm; Weight: 800/520 kg; Herd number: miss; AI: **Yes**
9   Colour: **Uni red, brown, dark red**
10 Pecularity: **miss**
11 - Main use: (1) **milk**,(2) **miss**,(3) **miss**
12 Spec. abilities: **miss**
13 Performance compared with STB **Russian Black Pied 64:**
14   higher: **% fat**
15   equal: **miss**
16   lower: **milk yield**
17 - Management: **stationary**; housing: **> 6 m.;**
18 - Conservation progr.: live animals: **miss**;Semen: **miss**;Embryos: **miss**
19 Status: **normal**;   Watch: **HB♀♀,trend,%pure,%incross!**
20 - <u>Similar breeds</u> (see group 4/3 on page 78)   <u>EN</u> <u>Country</u> <u>Status</u>
21 **Donnersberger Rotvieh**   101   D   crit.end.
22 **Harzer Rotvieh**   109   D   crit.end.
23 **Rod Dansk Malkerace**   222   DK   normal
24 **Rood Ras van Belgie**   224   B   normal

LATVIA — PIGS

1 - Latviiskaya belaya   EN 964
2   Latvian White; country-wide
3   Food and Agriculture Organisation of the UN   HB:miss
4   Rome 00100, Via delle Terme di Caracalla
5 - Composite of Russian White, Latvian native, Large White, Edelschwein
7   Numbers 1990: 3400/72500; HB: miss; decreasing; 78 %; Ne = 12991
8 - Height: miss/miss cm; Weight: 321/251 kg; Herd number: miss; AI:miss
9   Colour: Uni white
10 Pecularity: erect ears
11 - Main use: (1) general purpose,(2) miss,(3) miss
12 Spec. abilities: miss
13 Performance compared with STB Large White 951:
14   higher: miss
15   equal: % lean, litter size, feed conversion rate
16   lower: daily gain
17 - Management: stationary; housing: 12 m.;
18 - Conservation progr.: live animals: miss;Semen: miss;Embryos: miss
19 Status: normal;   Watch: HB♀♀,trend,%pure!
20 - Similar breeds (see group 1/2 on page 101)   EN Country Status
21 Bela Zlahtna   904 SLO crit.end.
22 Middle White   975 GB   min. end.
23 Deutsches Edelschwein   922 D*   normal
24 Vile uslechtile   1017 CS   normal

LITHUANIA — CATTLE

1 - Cherno-pestraya litovskaya   EN   66
2   Lithuanian Black Pied; country-wide
3   Food and Agriculture Organisation of the UN   HB:1951
4   Rome 00100, Via delle Terme di Caracalla
5 - Composite of Dutch Black Pied,Swedish+East Friesian,local Lithuanian
6   Incrossing since 1950 from Holstein Friesian 277 NL
7   Numbers 1990: 100/311000; HB: miss; stable; 93 %; Ne = 400
8 - Height: 140/129 cm; Weight: 950/550 kg; Herd number: miss; AI: Yes
9   Colour: Combination black, white
10 Pecularity: miss
11 - Main use: (1) milk,(2) meat,(3) miss
12 Spec. abilities: strong constitution
13 Performance compared with STB Russian Black Pied 64:
14   higher: % fat
15   equal: miss
16   lower: milk yield
17 - Management: stationary; housing: > 6 m.
18 - Conservation progr.: live animals: miss;Semen: miss;Embryos: miss
19 Status: normal;   Watch: HB♀♀,%incross!
20 - Similar breeds (see group 1/2 on page 75)   EN Country Status
21 Burlina   51   I   crit.end.
22 Breton Pie Noire   42   F   endanger.
23 Deutsches Schwarzbuntes Rind   79   D*   pot. end.
24 Cherno-pestraya estonskaya   65   EW   normal

LITHUANIA   CATTLE

```
 1 - Krasnaya litovskaya                                    EN   145
 2   Lithuanian Red; country-wide
 3   Food and Agriculture Organisation of the UN           HB: Yes
 4   Rome 00100, Via delle Terme di Caracalla
 5 - Composite of Ayrshire, Swiss Brown, Angeln, Dutch and Danish Red,
 6   Shorthorn, local; incrossing since 1950 from Danish Red 222 Denmark
 7   Numbers 1990: 227/233000; HB: miss; stable; 90 %; Ne = 907
 8 - Height: 135/126 cm; Weight: 750/490 kg; Herd number: miss; AI: Yes
 9   Colour: Uni red
10   Pecularity: miss
11 - Main use: (1) milk,(2) meat,(3) miss
12   Spec. abilities: miss
13   Performance compared with STB Russian Black Pied 64:
14     higher: % fat
15     equal:  miss
16     lower:  milk yield
17 - Management: stationary; housing: > 6 m.;
18 - Conservation progr.: live animals: miss;Semen: miss;Embryos: miss
19   Status: normal;          Watch: HB♀♀,%pure,%incross!
20 - Similar breeds (see group 4/3 on page 78)    EN  Country Status
21   Donnersberger Rotvieh                         101   D     crit.end.
22   Harzer Rotvieh                                109   D     crit.end.
23   Rod Dansk Malkerace                           222   DK    normal
24   Rood Ras van Belgie                           224   B     normal
```

LITHUANIA   PIGS

```
 1 - Litovskaya belaya                                      EN   968
 2   Lithuanian White; country-wide
 3   Food and Agriculture Organisation of the UN           HB:1967
 4   Rome 00100, Via delle Terme di Caracalla
 5 - Composite of Large White, Edelschwein, local Lithuanian
 6   Incrossing since 1970 from Yorkshire Sweden, Landrace 920 Germany
 7   Numbers 1990: 8600/83500; HB: miss; stable; 95 %; Ne = 31188
 8 - Height: miss/miss cm; Weight: 313/248 kg; Herd number: miss; AI:miss
 9   Colour: Uni white
10   Pecularity: erect or semi-erect ears
11 - Main use: (1) general purpose,(2) miss,(3) miss
12   Spec. abilities: miss
13   Performance compared with STB Large White 951:
14     higher: litter size
15     equal:  feed conversion rate
16     lower:  % lean, daily gain
17 - Management: stationary; housing: 12 m.;
18 - Conservation progr.: live animals: miss;Semen: miss;Embryos: miss
19   Status: normal;          Watch: HB♀♀,%pure,%incross!
20 - Similar breeds (see group 1/2 on page 101)   EN  Country Status
21   Bela Zlahtna                                  904   SLO   crit.end.
22   Middle White                                  975   GB    min. end.
23   Deutsches Edelschwein                         922   D*    normal
24   Vile uslechtile                               1017  CS    normal
```

```
 1 - Black and White                                          EN   32
 2   Holstein-Friesian; southern Luxembourg
 3   Federation des Herdbooks Luxembourgeois               HB:1923
 4   Cap 8328, rue du Kiem 55
 5 - Imported as breed from countries 277 Netherlands, 76 Germany, USA
 6   Incrossing since 1950 from Holstein-Friesian 277 NL, 76 Germany,USA
 7   Numbers 1986: miss /40000; HB: 8000; decreasing; 75 %; Ne = 1448
 8 - Height: miss/140 cm; Weight: miss/700 kg; Herd number: miss; AI:miss
 9   Colour: Combination black, white
10   Pecularity: miss
11 - Main use: (1) milk,(2) meat,(3) miss
12   Spec. abilities: miss
13   Performance compared with STB Holstein-Friesian 32:
14     higher: Breed is used
15     equal:  as standard breed,
16     lower:  no comparison possible.
17 - Management: stationary; housing: 2-6 m.;
18 - Conservation progr.: live animals: miss;Semen: 50;Embryos: miss
19   Status: normal;              Watch: %pure,%incross!
20 - Similar breeds (see group 1/1 on page 75)    EN  Country Status
21   Sortbroget Dansk Malkekvaeg                  245   DK   pot. end.
22   Nizinna-Czarno-Biala                         185   PL   pot. end.
23   Prim' Holstein                               209   F    normal
24   Pie-Noire-Holstein                           198   B    normal
```

```
 1 - Charolais                                                EN   63
 2   Charolais; country-wide
 3   Federation des Herdbooks Luxembourgeois               HB:1967
 4   Cap 8328, Rue du Kiem 55
 5 - Imported as breed from country 62 France
 6   Incrossing since 1950 from Charolais 62 France
 7   Numbers 1986: 100/1500; HB: 900; increasing; 100 %; Ne = 360
 8 - Height: 160/135 cm; Weight: 1100/800 kg; Herd number: miss; AI: miss
 9   Colour: Uni white
10   Pecularity: miss
11 - Main use: (1) meat,(2) miss,(3) miss
12   Spec. abilities: miss
13   Performance compared with STB Charolais 63:
14     higher: Breed is used
15     equal:  as standard breed,
16     lower:  no comparison possible.
17 - Management: stationary; housing: 2-6 m.;
18 - Conservation progr.: live animals: miss;Semen: 10;Embryos: miss
19   Status: normal
20 - Similar breeds (see group 9/2 on page 82)    EN  Country Status
21   Charolais                                     62   F    normal
22   Irish Charolais                              121   IRL  normal
23   British Charolais                             43   GB   normal
```

```
1 - Limousin                                                    EN  157
2   Limousin; country-wide
3   Federation des Herdbooks Luxembourgeois                     HB:1971
4   Cap 8328, rue du Kiem 55
5 - Imported as breed from country 156 France
6   Incrossing since 1950 from Limousin 156 France
7   Numbers 1986: 200/2500; HB: 1500; increasing; 100 %; Ne = 706
8 - Height: 155/125 cm; Weight: 1000/700 kg; Herd number: miss; AI: miss
9   Colour: Uni blond
10  Pecularity: miss
11 - Main use: (1) meat,(2) miss,(3) miss
12  Spec. abilities: miss
13  Performance compared with STB Charolais 63:
14    higher: calving ease, calving rate, % fat, % protein, handl. ease
15    equal:  muscularity
16    lower:  milk yield, daily gain, calving interval, age of sex. mat.
17 - Management: stationary; housing: 2-6 m.;
18 - Conservation progr.: live animals: Yes;Semen: 15;Embryos: miss
19  Status: normal
```

20 - Similar breeds (see group 8/3 on page 81)	EN	Country	Status
21 Alpha 16 (terminated)	6	F	crit.end.
22 Limousin	156	F	normal
23 Irish Limousin	122	IRL	normal
24 Parthenaise	193	F	normal

```
1 - Meuse-Rhine-Yssel                                          EN  215
2   Red and White; northern Luxembourg
3   Federation des Herdbooks Luxembourgeois                    HB:1923
4   Cap 8328, rue du Kiem 55
5 - Imported as breed from countries Netherlands, Germany; incrossing
6   since 1950 from MRY 161 Netherlands, Deutsche Rotbunte 74 Germany
7   Numbers 1986: miss /25000; HB: 6000; stable; 80 %; Ne = 1086
8 - Height: miss/142 cm; Weight: miss/600 kg; Herd number: miss; AI:miss
9   Colour: Combination red, white
10  Pecularity: miss
11 - Main use: (1) milk,(2) meat,(3) miss
12  Spec. abilities: miss
13  Performance compared with STB Holstein-Friesian 32:
14    higher: muscularity, daily gain, age of sexual maturity
15    equal:  % fat, % protein, calving ease and interval, handling ease
16    lower:  milk yield
17 - Management: stationary; housing: 2-6 m.;
18 - Conservation progr.: live animals: Yes;Semen: 30;Embryos: miss
19  Status: normal;            Watch: %incross!
```

20 - Similar breeds (see group 3/1 on page 76)	EN	Country	Status
21 Blanc-Rouge de Belgique	273	B	pot. end.
22 Ferrandais	85	F	pot. end.
23 Dansk Rodbroget Kvaeg	73	DK	normal
24 Pie-Rouge	199	B	normal

```
1  - Texel                                                         EN   652
2    Texel; country-wide
3    Flockbook Luxembourgeois, ASTA                                HB:1968
4    Luxembourg 1019, B. P. 1904
5  - Imported as breed from countries Netherlands, France; incrossing
6    since 1960 from Texel 653 Netherlands, Texel 649 France
7    Numbers 1986: 400/7000; HB: 1000; increasing; 100 %; Ne = 1143
8  - Height: 97/80 cm; Weight: 110/85 kg; Herd number: miss; AI: miss
9    Colour: Uni blond
10   Pecularity: horns 0/0, white head
11 - Main use: (1) meat,(2) vegetation management,(3) wool
12   Spec. abilities: miss
13   Performance compared with STB Texel 652:
14     higher: Breed is used
15     equal:  as standard breed,
16     lower:  no comparison possible.
17 - Management: stationary; housing: ≈ 2 m.;
18 - Conservation progr.: live animals: miss;Semen: miss;Embryos: miss
19   Status: normal
```

20 - Similar breeds (see group 2/2 on page 88)	EN	Country	Status
21 Texel	648	SF	pot. end.
22 Texel	649	F	normal
23 Texel	651	IRL	normal
24 Texel	650	D	normal

```
1  - Landrace belge                                                EN   958
2    Belgian Landrace; country-wide
3    Federation des Herdbooks Luxembourgeois                       HB:1955
4    Cap 8328, rue du Kiem 55
5  - Imported as breed from country Belgium
6    Incrossing since 1970 from Belgian Landrace 906 Belgium
7    Numbers 1986: 500/11000; HB: 200; decreasing; 60 %; Ne = 571
8  - Height: 93/85 cm; Weight: 225/175 kg; Herd number: miss; AI: miss
9    Colour: Uni white
10   Pecularity: lop ears
11 - Main use: (1) meat,(2) miss,(3) miss
12   Spec. abilities: miss
13   Performance compared with STB Belgian Landrace 958:
14     higher: Breed is used
15     equal:  as standard breed,
16     lower:  no comparison possible.
17 - Management: stationary; housing: 12 m.;
18 - Conservation progr.: live animals: miss;Semen: Yes;Embryos: miss
19   Status: normal;                 Watch: %incross,trend!
```

20 - Similar breeds (see group 2/1 on page 101)	EN	Country	Status
21 Belgische Landrasse	907	D*	crit.end.
22 Zlotnicka biala	1024	PL	crit.end.
23 Landrace	952	CS	normal
24 Belgisch Landvarken	906	B	normal

```
1 - Cheval de selle                                        EN   726
2   Saddlebred; country-wide
3   Federation des Studbooks                               HB:1970
4   Bettembourg 3254, rue de Luxembrourg 231
5 - Imported as breed from countries Germany, France
7   Numbers 1986: 15/600; HB: 300; stable; 100 %; Ne = 34
8 - Height: 168/162 cm; Weight: 600/500 kg; Herd number: miss; AI: miss
9   Colour: mainly bay or chestnut
10  Pecularity: miss
11 - Main use: (1) sport/hobby,(2) miss,(3) miss
12  Spec. abilities: miss
13  Performance compared with STB Halfbred:
14     higher: miss
15     equal:  handling ease, adaptability in dressage and jumping
16     lower:  miss
17 - Management: stationary; housing: 2-6/> 6 m.;
18 - Conservation progr.: live animals: miss;Semen: miss;Embryos: miss
19  Status: minimally endang.; Watch: ♂♂!
20 - Similar breeds (see group 3/2 on page 108)   EN  Country Status
21  Altwürttemberger                              701   D    crit.end.
22  Rottaler                                      797   D    crit.end.
23  Holsteiner Warmblut                           760   D    normal
24  Cheval de Selle Francais                      727   F    normal
```

```
1 - Cheval de Trait Ardennais                              EN   730
2   Ardennes; country-wide
3   Federation des Studbooks                               HB:1930
4   Bettembourg 3254, rue de Luxembourg 231
5 - Imported as breed from country Belgium
6   Incrossing since 1950 from 729 Belgium
7   Numbers 1986: 15/350; HB: 200; stable; 100 %; Ne = 33
8 - Height: 160/155 cm; Weight: 900/800 kg; Herd number: miss; AI: miss
9   Colour: bay, grey, roan, chestnut
10  Pecularity: miss
11 - Main use: (1) sport/hobby,(2) meat,(3) tractive power
12  Spec. abilities: miss
13  Performance compared with STB Percheron:
14     higher: handling ease
15     equal:  pulling power, fertility, daily gain
16     lower:  age of sexual maturity
17 - Management: stationary; housing: ≈ 2 m.;
18 - Conservation progr.: live animals: Yes;Semen: miss;Embryos: miss
19  Status: minimally endang.; Watch: ♂♂,HB♀♀!
20 - Similar breeds (see group 4/1 on page 109)   EN  Country Status
21  Auxois                                        709   F    crit.end.
22  Hrvatski Hladnokrvnjak                        761   HR   min. end.
23  Cheval de Trait Belge                         731   B    normal
24  Cheval de Trait Ardennais                     729   B    normal
```

HORSES

1 - Haflinger   EN 755
2   Haflinger; country-wide
3   Federation des Studbooks   HB:1970
4   Bettembourg 3254, rue de Luxembourg 231
5 - Imported as breed from countries Austria, 754 Germany
7   Numbers 1986: 30/400; HB: 250; increasing; 100 %; Ne = 107
8 - Height: 145/138 cm; Weight: 500/450 kg; Herd number: miss; AI: miss
9   Colour: light to dark chestnut
10 Pecularity: full flaxen mane and tail
11 - Main use: (1) sport/hobby,(2) tractive power,(3) meat
12 Spec. abilities: miss
13 Performance compared with STB Fjord:
14   higher: adapt. in jumping and military, fertility, handling ease
15   equal: pulling power, age of sexual maturity, daily gain
16   lower: miss
17 - Management: stationary; housing: ≈ 2 m.;
18 - Conservation progr.: live animals: miss;Semen: miss;Embryos: miss
19 Status: normal
20 - Similar breeds (see group 5/8 on page 111)   EN Country Status
21 Haflinger   757 GB   endanger.
22 Haflinger   756 CH   pot. end.
23 Haflinger   754 D   normal
24 Haflinger   753 F   normal

CATTLE

1 - Groninger Blaarkop   EN 106
2   Groningen Whiteheaded; mainly northern and western Netherlands
3   Netherlands Rundvee Syndicaat   HB:1907
4   AL Arnhem 6800, Postbus 454
5 - Autochthon original Dutch: Groninger Blaarkop
6   Incrossing since 1950 from Holstein-Friesian USA
7   Numbers 1990: 15/12000; HB: 4000; decreasing; 25 %; Ne = 36
8 - Height: 138/132 cm; Weight: 800/600 kg; Herd number: miss; AI: Yes
9   Colour: Combination black/white, red/white
10 Pecularity: white face with dark eye-rings
11 - Main use: (1) milk,(2) meat,(3) sport/hobby
12 Spec. abilities: strong legs and feet
13 Performance compared with STB Holstein-Friesian 277:
14   higher: miss
15   equal: muscul.,daily gain,% protein,calving ease,calving interval
16   lower: milk yield, % fat
17 - Management: stationary; housing: 2-6 m.;
18 - Conservation progr.: live animals: miss;Semen: 20;Embryos: miss
19 Status: endangered;   Watch: ♂♂,trend,%pure,%incross!
20 - Similar breeds (see group 1/7 on page 76)   EN Country Status
21 Belogolovaya ukrainskaya   27   UR   crit.end.

1 - **Lakenvelder**   EN **152**
2   **Dutch Belted; scattered country-wide**
3   **Fokkersclub voor Lakenvelders**   HB:**1979**
4   **DJ Wageningen 6702, p.o. Nude 25**
5 - **Autochthon original Dutch Belted (= Lakenvelder)**
6   **Incrossing since 1950 from Belted Galloway 28 United Kingdom**
7   **Numbers 1990: 30/550; HB: 500; stable; 90 %; Ne = 113**
8 - **Height: 137/132 cm; Weight: 700/550 kg; Herd number: 10; AI: Yes**
9   **Colour: Combination black/white, red/white**
10   **Pecularity: fore and hind quarters black resp; white belt**
11 - **Main use: (1) appear. attractive,(2) milk,(3) vegetation management**
12   **Spec. abilities: miss**
13   **Performance compared with STB Holstein-Friesian 277:**
14   **higher: calving ease, calving rate**
15   **equal: muscularity,daily gain,% prot.,calv.inter.,age of sex.mat.**
16   **lower: milk yield, % fat**
17 - **Management: stationary; housing: 2-6 m.; hoof quality, easy calving**
18 - **Conservation progr.: live animals: Yes;Semen: 9;Embryos: miss**
19   **Status: minimally endang.; Watch: herds,%pure,%incross!**
20 - <u>Similar breeds</u> (see group 1/5 on page 75)   <u>EN</u> <u>Country</u> <u>Status</u>
21   **Belted Galloway**   28   GB   **normal**

1 - **Maas-Rijn-Yssel, Roodbont**   EN **161**
2   **Meuse-Rhine-Yssel; southern and eastern Netherlands**
3   **Royal Dutch Cattle Syndicat**   HB:**miss**
4   **AL Arnhem 6800, Postbus 454**
5 - **Autochthon breed**
7   **Numbers 1990: 50/400000; HB: 200000; stable; 60 %; Ne = 200**
8 - **Height: 150/135 cm; Weight: 1000/600 kg; Herd number: miss; AI: miss**
9   **Colour: Combination red, white**
10   **Pecularity: miss**
11 - **Main use: (1) milk,(2) meat,(3) miss**
12   **Spec. abilities: miss**
13   **Performance compared with STB Holstein-Friesian 277:**
14   **higher: muscularity, % protein**
15   **equal: % fat,calving ease,calv. interval,handling ease,calf mort.**
16   **lower: milk yield,daily gain,age of sexual maturity,milkability**
17 - **Management: stationary; housing: > 6 m.;**
18 - **Conservation progr.: live animals: miss;Semen: Yes;Embryos: miss**
19   **Status: potential. endang.;Watch: ♂♂,%pure!**
20 - <u>Similar breeds</u> (see group 3/1 on page 76)   <u>EN</u> <u>Country</u> <u>Status</u>
21   **Blanc-Rouge de Belgique**   273   B   **pot. end.**
22   **Ferrandais**   85   F   **pot. end.**
23   **Dansk Rodbroget Kvaeg**   73   DK   **normal**
24   **Pie-Rouge**   199   B   **normal**

CATTLE

1 - Zwartbont   EN 277
2   Holstein-Friesian
3   Royal Dutch Cattle Syndicat   HB:miss
4   AL Arnhem 6800, Postbus 454
5 - Composite of Dutch Friesian, Holstein-Friesian USA
7   Numbers 1990: 100/2000000; HB: 1000000; stable; 100 %; Ne = 400
8 - Height: miss/140 cm; Weight: miss/650 kg; Herd number: miss; AI:miss
9   Colour: Combination black, white
10 Pecularity: miss
11 - Main use: (1) milk,(2) miss,(3) miss
12 Spec. abilities: miss
13 Performance compared with STB Holstein-Friesian 277:
14   higher: Breed is used
15   equal: as standard breed,
16   lower: no comparison possible.
17 - Management: stationary; housing: > 6 m.;
18 - Conservation progr.: live animals: miss;Semen: Yes;Embryos: Yes
19 Status: normal
20 - Similar breeds (see group 1/1 on page 75)   EN Country Status
21 Sortbroget Dansk Malkekvaeg   245 DK   pot. end.
22 Nizinna-Czarno-Biala   185 PL   pot. end.
23 Prim' Holstein   209 F   normal
24 Pie-Noire-Holstein   198 B   normal

SHEEP

1 - Drentse Heideschaap   EN 484
2   Drenthe Heath Sheep; northern and southern Netherlands
3   Fokkersclub Drentze en Schoonebeker Heideschapen   HB:1986
4   NH Heythuysen 6093, Bosscherkampweg 11
5 - Autochthon Orgigin Drente Heath Sheep and Schoonebeker 620
7   Numbers 1990: 150/3500; HB: 500; stable; 75 %; Ne = 462
8 - Height: 65/60 cm; Weight: 55/45 kg; Herd number: miss; AI: miss
9   Colour: Combination black, grey, brown, yellow, white
10 Pecularity: horns 2/2, spotted on a white basis
11 - Main use: (1) vegetation management,(2) sport/hobby,(3) meat
12 Spec. abilities: miss
13 Performance compared with STB Texel 653:
14   higher: carcass leanness, wool or fiber thickness
15   equal: age of sexual mat.,length of mating season,lambing interv.
16   lower: daily gain, litter size, milk yield,muscularity,wool yield
17 - Management: stationary; housing: no
18 - Conservation progr.: live animals: Yes;Semen: miss;Embryos: miss
19 Status: potential. endang.;Watch: HB♀♀,%pure!
20 - Similar breeds (see group 6/2 on page 90)   EN Country Status
21 Schoonebeker Heideschaap   620 NL   min. end.
22 Veluwse Heideschaap   660 NL   min. end.
23 Mergelland Schaap   544 NL   normal
24 Bentheimer Landschaf   414 D   normal

```
 1 - Friese Melkschaap                                          EN  493
 2   Friesian Milksheep; coast provinces and central Netherlands
 3   Fries Melkschapen stamboek                                 HB:1908
 4   TA Makkusga 8423, Buter heideveld 16
 5 - Autochthon local coast sheep, Friesian, Zealand, East Friesian
 6   573 D,Flemish sheep; incrossing since 1960 from East Friesian 573 D
 7   Numbers 1986: 120/2500; HB: 2100; increasing; 80 %; Ne = 454
 8 - Height: 90/85 cm; Weight: 85/75 kg; Herd number: miss; AI: miss
 9   Colour: Uni white
10   Pecularity: horns 0/0, naked tail
11 - Main use: (1) milk,(2) wool,(3) sport/hobby
12   Spec. abilities: miss
13   Performance compared with STB Texel 653:
14     higher: milk yield, litter size
15     equal: % fat,% protein,age of sexual mat.,length of mating season
16     lower:  muscularity, daily gain, carcass leanness, wool yield
17 - Management: stationary; housing: ≈ 2 m.;
18 - Conservation progr.: live animals: miss;Semen: miss;Embryos: miss
19   Status: normal;              Watch: %pure,%incross!
```

20 - Similar breeds (see group 5/1 on page 89)	EN	Country	Status
21 Mouton Laitier Belge	561	B	min. end.
22 Ostfriesisches Milchschaf	572	D*	normal
23 British Milksheep	438	GB	normal
24 Ostfriesisches Milchschaf	573	D	normal

```
 1 - Kempische Heideschaap                                      EN  522
 2   Kempen Heath Sheep; Province of Brabant, southern Netherlands
 3   Stichting "Het Kempisch Heideschaap"                       HB:1967
 4   PL Sterksel 6029, Vlaamse weg 20
 5 - Autochthon local breed of heath, probably crossed with Mergelland
 7   Numbers 1986: 35/800; HB: 600; stable; 75 %; Ne = 132
 8 - Height: 72/66 cm; Weight: 65/55 kg; Herd number: 10; AI: miss
 9   Colour: Uni white
10   Pecularity: horns 0/0
11 - Main use: (1) vegetation management,(2) meat,(3) wool
12   Spec. abilities: miss
13   Performance compared with STB Texel 653:
14     higher: carcass leanness, wool or fiber thickness
15     equal:  age of sexual mat.,length of mating season,lambing interv.
16     lower:  daily gain, litter size, milk yield,muscularity,wool yield
17 - Management: stationary; housing: no; extensive conditions
18 - Conservation progr.: live animals: Yes;Semen: miss;Embryos: miss
19   Status: potential. endang.;Watch: HB♀♀,%pure!
```

20 - Similar breeds (see group 6/2 on page 90)	EN	Country	Status
21 Schoonebeker Heideschaap	620	NL	min. end.
22 Veluwse Heideschaap	660	NL	min. end.
23 Mergelland Schaap	544	NL	normal
24 Bentheimer Landschaf	414	D	normal

```
 1 - Mergelland Schaap                                              EN  544
 2   Mergelland; Province of Limburg / mainly southern Netherlands
 3   Vereniging "Oos Mergelland Sjoap"                             HB:1980
 4   RN Meerssen 6231, Lange Raarberg 32
 5 - Autochthon Meuse sheep
 6   Incrossing since 1960 from Kempen Heath Sheep 522 Netherlands
 7   Numbers 1990: 70/400; HB: 350; increasing; 90 %; Ne = 233
 8 - Height: 72/68 cm; Weight: 70/60 kg; Herd number: miss; AI: miss
 9   Colour: Uni white
10   Pecularity: horns 0/0
11 - Main use: (1) vegetation management,(2) sport/hobby,(3) wool
12   Spec. abilities: miss
13   Performance compared with STB Texel 653:
14     higher: carcass leanness, wool or fiber thickness
15     equal:  age of sexual mat.,length of mating season,lambing interv.
16     lower:  daily gain,litter size,milk yield,muscularity,wool yield
17 - Management: stationary; housing: ≈ 2 m.; extensive conditions
18 - Conservation progr.: live animals: miss;Semen: miss;Embryos: miss
19   Status: normal;                Watch: %pure,%incross!
```

20 - Similar breeds (see group 6/2 on page 90)	EN	Country	Status
21 Schoonebeker Heideschaap	620	NL	min. end.
22 Veluwse Heideschaap	660	NL	min. end.
23 Drentse Heideschaap	484	NL	pot. end.
24 Bentheimer Landschaf	414	D	normal

```
 1 - Schoonebeker Heideschaap                                      EN  620
 2   Schoonebeker; mainly Prov. of Drente (northern Netherlands)
 3   Fokkersclub Drentse en Schoonebeker Heideschapen             HB:1990
 4   NH Heyrhuysen 6093, Bosscherkampweg 11
 5 - Autochthon local breed of N. Holland mixed with Drente Heath Sheep
 7   Numbers 1990: 50/1000; HB: 60; increasing; 80 %; Ne = 109
 8 - Height: 74/68 cm; Weight: 68/60 kg; Herd number: 5; AI: miss
 9   Colour: Combination black, grey, brown, white
10   Pecularity: horns 0/0, spotted on a white basis
11 - Main use: (1) vegetation management,(2) sport/hobby,(3) meat
12   Spec. abilities: miss
13   Performance compared with STB Texel 653:
14     higher: carcass leanness, wool or fiber thickness
15     equal:  age of sexual mat.,length of mating season,lambing interv.
16     lower:  daily gain,litter size,milk yield,muscularity,wool yield
17 - Management: stationary; housing: no/≈ 2 m.; extensive condition
18 - Conservation progr.: live animals: Yes;Semen: miss;Embryos: miss
19   Status: minimally endang.; Watch: HB♀♀,herds,%pure!
```

20 - Similar breeds (see group 6/2 on page 90)	EN	Country	Status
21 Veluwse Heideschaap	660	NL	min. end.
22 Drentse Heideschaap	484	NL	pot. end.
23 Mergelland Schaap	544	NL	normal
24 Bentheimer Landschaf	414	D	normal

```
1 - Texelaar                                                    EN   653
2   Texel
3   N.T.S.                                                      HB:1909
4   AL Zwolle 8000, Postbus 490
5 - Composite of autochthon Texel, Lincoln 532, Leicester 528 GB
7   Numbers 1990: 30000/800000; HB: 50000; stable; 80 %; Ne = 75000
8 - Height: miss/miss cm; Weight: 120/90 kg; Herd number: miss; AI: Yes
9   Colour: Uni white, blond
10  Pecularity: horns 0/0
11 - Main use: (1) meat,(2) wool,(3) miss
12  Spec. abilities: very good conformation/muscularity, good meat qual.
13  Performance compared with STB Texel 653:
14     higher: Breed is used
15     equal:  as standard breed,
16     lower:  no comparison possible.
17 - Management: stationary; housing: ≈ 2 m.;
18 - Conservation progr.: live animals: miss;Semen: miss;Embryos: miss
19  Status: normal
```

20 - Similar breeds (see group 2/2 on page 88)	EN	Country	Status
21 Texel	648	SF	pot. end.
22 Texel	649	F	normal
23 Texel	651	IRL	normal
24 Texel	650	D	normal

```
1 - Veluwse Heideschaap                                         EN   660
2   Veluwe Heath; central and eastern Netherlands
3   Stichting Zeldzame Huisdierrassen                           HB:miss
4   Groningen 9712, Poststraat 6
5 - Autochthon original local breed of heath sheep
7   Numbers 1990: 25/1000; HB: miss; stable; 70 %; Ne = 94
8 - Height: 78/72 cm; Weight: 70/60 kg; Herd number: 8; AI: miss
9   Colour: Uni white
10  Pecularity: horns 0/0
11 - Main use: (1) vegetation management,(2) sport/hobby,(3) meat
12  Spec. abilities: miss
13  Performance compared with STB Texel 653:
14     higher: carcass leanness, wool or fiber thickness
15     equal:  age of sexual mat.,length of mating season,lambing interv.
16     lower:  daily gain, litter size, milk yield,muscularity,wool yield
17 - Management: stationary; housing: no/≈ 2 m.; extensive conditions
18 - Conservation progr.: live animals: Yes;Semen: miss;Embryos: miss
19  Status: minimally endang.; Watch: HB♀♀,herds,%pure!
```

20 - Similar breeds (see group 6/2 on page 90)	EN	Country	Status
21 Schoonebeker Heideschaap	620	NL	min. end.
22 Drentse Heideschaap	484	NL	pot. end.
23 Mergelland Schaap	544	NL	normal
24 Bentheimer Landschaf	414	D	normal

1 - **Bonte geit (extinct)**   EN **309**
2   **Dutch Pied Original**
3   **Nederlands Organisatie u. Geitenfokkery**   HB:**miss**
4   **CS Lunteren 6741, Secr. Tolhuisweg 2**
5 - **miss**
7   Numbers miss: miss / miss; HB: miss; miss; miss %; Ne = miss
8 - Height:**miss**/**miss** cm; Weight:**miss**/**miss** kg; Herd number:**miss**; AI:**miss**
9   Colour: **Combination black, grey, brown, white**
10 Pecularity: **horns 2/2**
11 - Main use: (1) **miss**,(2) **miss**,(3) **miss**
12 Spec. abilities: **miss**
13 Performance compared with STB **miss**:
14   higher: **miss**
15   equal: **miss**
16   lower: **miss**
17 - Management: **miss**; housing: **miss** m.;
18 - Conservation progr.: live animals: **Yes**;Semen: **miss**;Embryos: **miss**
19 Status: **extinct**
20 - <u>Similar breeds</u> (see group 3 on page 97)   <u>EN</u> <u>Country</u> <u>Status</u>
21 **Thüringer Waldziege**   360   D   crit.end.
22 **Toggenburger**   361   B   endanger.
23 **Pure Toggenburg**   346   GB   normal
24 **Toggenburger**   362   CH   normal

1 - **Nederlandse Landgeit**   EN **341**
2   **Dutch Landrace; scattered country-wide**
3   **Landelijke Fokkersclub, Nederlandse Landgeiten**   HB:**1972**
4   **AK Zevenbergen 4762, Hazeldonkse zandweg 49**
5 - **Autochthon original Dutch Landrace**
7   Numbers 1990: 42/360; HB: 346; stable; 90 %; Ne = 150
8 - Height: **79/67** cm; Weight: **55/35** kg; Herd number: **6**; AI: **miss**
9   Colour: **Uni grey,blue,white,combinations possible,sometimes spotted**
10 Pecularity: **horns 2/2, males always, females sometimes long hair**
11 - Main use: (1) **sport/hobby**,(2) **milk**,(3) **vegetation management**
12 Spec. abilities: **miss**
13 Performance compared with STB **Saanen**:
14   higher: **miss**
15   equal: **muscularity, daily gain, carcass leanness, litter size**
16   lower: **milk yield**
17 - Management: **stationary**; housing: **≈ 2 m.; extensive conditions**
18 - Conservation progr.: live animals: **Yes**;Semen: **miss**;Embryos: **miss**
19 Status: **potential. endang.**;Watch: **herds,%pure!**
20 - <u>Similar breeds</u> (see group 10 on page 98)   <u>EN</u> <u>Country</u> <u>Status</u>
21 **Suomenvuohi**   358   SF   endanger.
22 **Dansk Landrace**   322   DK   normal
23 **Svensk Lantras**   359   S   normal
24 **Norsk Geit**   342   N   normal

1 - Groot Yorkshire-S   EN 938
2   Large White / sire line; southern and eastern Netherlands
3   The Dutch Pig Herdbook Societies   HB:1930
4   BD Nijmegen 6501, P. B. 1159
5 - Imported as breed from country United Kingdom
7   Numbers 1986: 2500/8000; HB: 7000; decreasing; 60 %; Ne = 7368
8 - Height: 120/100 cm; Weight: 350/300 kg; Herd number: miss; AI: Yes
9   Colour: Uni white
10 Pecularity: erect ears
11 - Main use: (1) reproduction,(2) meat,(3) miss
12 Spec. abilities: miss
13 Performance compared with STB Dutch Landrace 980:
14   higher: % lean, muscularity, meat quality, daily gain
15   equal: age of sexual maturity,farrowing interval,piglet mortality
16   lower: litter size, feed conversion rate
17 - Management: stationary; housing: 12 m.;
18 - Conservation progr.: live animals: miss;Semen: miss;Embryos: miss
19 Status: normal;   Watch: trend!
20 - Similar breeds (see group 1/2 on page 101)   EN Country Status
21 Bela Zlahtna   904 SLO   crit.end.
22 Middle White   975 GB   min. end.
23 Deutsches Edelschwein   922 D*   normal
24 Vile uslechtile   1017 CS   normal

1 - Groot Yorkshire-Z   EN 939
2   Large White / dam line; southern and eastern Netherlands
3   The Dutch Pig Herdbook Societies   HB:1930
4   BD Nijmegen 6501, P. B. 1159
5 - Composite of Dutch Yorkshire, Yorkshire 1023 United Kingdom,
4   Yorkshire 960 France
7   Numbers 1986: 100/5000; HB: 4500; increasing; 15 %; Ne = 391
8 - Height: 120/100 cm; Weight: 350/300 kg; Herd number: miss; AI: Yes
9   Colour: Uni white
10 Pecularity: erect ears
11 - Main use: (1) reproduction,(2) meat,(3) miss
12 Spec. abilities: miss
13 Performance compared with STB Dutch Landrace 980:
14   higher: % lean, litter size, daily gain, muscularity
15   equal: meat quality, age of sexual maturity, farrowing interval
16   lower: feed conversion rate, handling ease
17 - Management: stationary; housing: 12 m.;
18 - Conservation progr.: live animals: miss;Semen: miss;Embryos: miss
19 Status: normal;   Watch: %pure!
20 - Similar breeds (see group 1/2 on page 101)   EN Country Status
21 Bela Zlahtna   904 SLO   crit.end.
22 Middle White   975 GB   min. end.
23 Deutsches Edelschwein   922 D*   normal
24 Vile uslechtile   1017 CS   normal

1 - **Nederlands Landras**   EN **980**
2   **Dutch Landrace; southern and eastern Netherlans**
3   **The Dutch Pig Herdbook Societies**   HB:**1930**
4   **BD Nijmegen 6501, P. B. 1159**
5 - **Composite of local Dutch pigs, old Danish and old German Landrace**
7   Numbers 1986: **100/50000**; HB: **40000**; **decreasing**; **15 %**; Ne = **399**
8 - Height: **120/100** cm; Weight: **350/300** kg; Herd number: **miss**; AI: **Yes**
9   Colour: **Uni white**
10 Pecularity: **lop ears**
11 - Main use: (1) **reproduction**,(2) **meat**,(3) **miss**
12 Spec. abilities: **miss**
13 Performance compared with STB **Dutch Landrace 980**:
14   higher: **Breed is used**
15   equal: **as standard breed,**
16   lower: **no comparison possible.**
17 - Management: **stationary**; housing: **12 m.**;
18 - Conservation progr.: live animals: **miss**;Semen: **miss**;Embryos: **miss**
19 Status: **normal**;   Watch: **trend,%pure!**
20 - <u>Similar breeds</u> (see group 2/1 on page 101)   <u>EN</u> <u>Country</u> <u>Status</u>
21 **Belgische Landrasse**   **907** **D***   **crit.end.**
22 **Zlotnicka biala**   **1024** **PL**   **crit.end.**
23 **Landrace**   **952** **CS**   **normal**
24 **Belgisch Landvarken**   **906** **B**   **normal**

1 - **Gelders Paard**   EN **750**
2   **Gelderland; scattered country-wide**
3   **Vereniging van Fokkers en liefhebbers van het Gelders** HB:**1979**
4   **basispaard, DK Babberich 6909, c.o. Veldhuizenseweg 2**
5 - **Composite of original local Gelderland Horse, Anglo Normans France,**
6   **Holstein 760 Germany, Oldenburger East Friesian Germany**
7   Numbers 1990: **9/500**; HB: **450**; **stable**; **20 %**; Ne = **17**
8 - Height: **175/165** cm; Weight: **700/600** kg; Herd number: **> 10**; AI: **miss**
9   Colour: **commonly chestnut with white markings or grey**
10 Pecularity: **miss**
11 - Main use:(1) **basic mares f. sport h.**,(2) **sport/hobby**,(3) **tract.power**
12 Spec. abilities: **miss**
13 Performance compared with STB **Halfbred**:
14   higher: **pulling power**
15   equal: **handling ease, adaptability in dressage and in jumping**
16   lower: **speed in gallop**
17 - Management: **stationary**; housing: **2-6 m.**;
18 - Conservation progr.: live animals: **Yes**;Semen: **4**;Embryos: **miss**
19 Status: **critically endang.**;Watch: **♂♂,herds,%pure!**
20 - <u>Similar breeds</u> (see group 3/2 on page 108)   <u>EN</u> Country <u>Status</u>
21 **Altwürttemberger**   **701** **D**   **crit.end.**
22 **Rottaler**   **797** **D**   **crit.end.**
23 **Holsteiner Warmblut**   **760** **D**   **normal**
24 **Cheval de Selle Francais**   **727** **F**   **normal**

1 - Groninger Paard   EN 752
2   Groningen; northern and eastern Netherlands
3   Vereniging Het Groninger paard   HB:1985
4   AZ Delft 2622, c.o Chilipad 1
5 - Composite of local Friesian Horse, Thoroughbred, Cleveland 732 GB,
6   Oldenburger; incrossing since 1950 from Holstein 760 D, Oldenburg D
7   Numbers 1990: 12/75; HB: 45; stable; 75 %; Ne = 19
8 - Height: 175/160 cm; Weight: 700/600 kg; Herd number: miss; AI: miss
9   Colour: preferably black or brown
10   Pecularity: miss
11 - Main use: (1) sport/hobby,(2) tractive power,(3) for halfbred breed.
12   Spec. abilities: miss
13   Performance compared with STB Halfbred:
14   higher: pulling power, handling ease
15   equal: adaptability in jumping, fertility, age of sexual maturity
16   lower: adaptability in dressage and in military, speed in gallop
17 - Management: stationary; housing: 2-6 m.;
18 - Conservation progr.: live animals: Yes;Semen: Yes;Embryos: miss
19   Status: critically endang.;Watch: ♂♂,HB♀♀,%pure,%incross!
20 - Similar breeds (see group 3/2 on page 108)   EN Country Status
21   Altwürttemberger   701   D   crit.end.
22   Rottaler   797   D   crit.end.
23   Holsteiner Warmblut   760   D   normal
24   Cheval de Selle Francais   727   F   normal

1 - Warmbloed Paard Nederlands   EN 816
2   Netherlands Riding Horse
3   Uoninklyhe Vereniging Warmbloed Paardenstamboek   HB: Yes
4   AJ Zeist 3700, Postbus 382
5 - miss
7   Numbers 1990: 200/25000; HB: 20000; stable; 100 %; Ne = 792
8 - Height: 170/165 cm; Weight: 700/600 kg; Herd number: miss; AI: miss
9   Colour: all solid colours
10   Pecularity: miss
11 - Main use: (1) sport/hobby,(2) miss,(3) miss
12   Spec. abilities: miss
13   Performance compared with STB Thoroughbred:
14   higher: handl. ease, pulling power, adapt. in dressage and jumping
15   equal: adaptability in military,fertility,age of sexual maturity
16   lower: speed in gallop
17 - Management: stationary; housing: > 6 m.;
18 - Conservation progr.: live animals: miss;Semen: miss;Embryos: miss
19   Status: normal
20 - Similar breeds (see group 3/2 on page 108)   EN Country Status
21   Altwürttemberger   701   D   crit.end.
22   Rottaler   797   D   crit.end.
23   Holsteiner Warmblut   760   D   normal
24   Cheval de Selle Francais   727   F   normal

1 - Norsk rodtfe   EN 187
2   Norwegian Red Cattle; country-wide
3   Avlslaget for Norsk Rodt Fe   HB:1935
4   Hamar 2300, Vangsveien 121
5 - Composite of Swedish Red (SRB), local Norwegian breeds; incrossing
6   since 1950 from Swedish Red 225 Sweden, Finish Ayrshire 247 Finland
7   Numbers 1983: 170/470000; HB: miss; stable; 95 %; Ne = 680
8 - Height: 142/130 cm; Weight: 1000/575 kg; Herd number: miss; AI: Yes
9   Colour: Combination black, red, white
10 Pecularity: horns 2/2
11 - Main use: (1) milk,(2) meat,(3) miss
12 Spec. abilities: good results on Madagascar, Afrika
13 Performance compared with STB Holstein-Friesian:
14   higher: calving ease, muscularity, % fat, % protein, calving rate
15   equal: milk yield, daily gain, age of sex. maturity, milkability
16   lower: miss
17 - Management: stationary; housing: > 6 m.; high quality of skin
18 - Conservation progr.: live animals: miss;Semen: 3500;Embryos: 46/167
19   Status: normal;   Watch: HB♀♀,%incross!
20 - Similar breeds (see group 4/4 on page 78)   EN Country Status
21   Mestnaya estonskaya   171   EW   crit.end.
22   Länsisuomenkarja   153   SF   endanger.
23   Röd Kullig Lantras   225   S   min. end.
24   Icelandic Dairy Cattle   118   IS   normal

1 - Sidet tronderfe og nordland   EN 235
2   Blacksided Trondheim; County of Sor-Trondelag
3   Avlslaget for Sidet Tronder og Nordlandsfe   HB:1952
4   Fagerhaug 7416
5 - Composite of Sidet Tronderfe og nordland, Roros Cattle, Nordland
6   Cattle; incrossing since 1950 from Swedish Mountain 86 Sweden
7   Numbers 1983: 10/650; HB: miss; decreasing; 100 %; Ne = 20
8 - Height: 140/119 cm; Weight: 650/350 kg; Herd number: miss; AI: Yes
9   Colour: Combination black, white; black side - white back
10 Pecularity: horns 0/0
11 - Main use: (1) milk,(2) meat,(3) miss
12 Spec. abilities: miss
13 Performance compared with STB Holstein-Friesian:
14   higher: % fat, % protein, calving ease
15   equal: age of sex. mat.,handling ease,calf mortality,calving rate
16   lower: milk yield, muscularity, daily gain, pulling power
17 - Management: stationary; housing: > 6 m.;
18 - Conservation progr.: live animals: miss;Semen: 60;Embryos: miss
19   Status: critically endang.;Watch: ♂♂,HB♀♀,trend,%incross!
20 - Similar breeds (see group 1/6 on page 76)   EN Country Status
21   Tuxer   259   A   crit.end.
22   Pohjoissuomenkarja   207   SF   crit.end.
23   Berrenda negra andaluza   29   E   min. end.
24   Gruzinskii gornyi skot   107   GO   normal

CATTLE

1 - Telemark   EN 254
2   Telemark; Telemark
3   Avlslaget for Telemarksfe   HB:1926
4   Skien 3700, Fylkeshuset
5 - Autochthon Telemarksfe
6   Incrossing since 1950 from Norwegian Red Cattle 187 Norway
7   Numbers 1983: 6/200; HB: miss; decreasing; 100 %; Ne = 11
8 - Height: 140/121 cm; Weight: 700/400 kg; Herd number: miss; AI: Yes
9   Colour: Combination red, white; red sided, white back
10 Pecularity: red muzzle, colours brindled
11 - Main use: (1) milk,(2) meat,(3) miss
12 Spec. abilities: miss
13 Performance compared with STB Hostein-Friesian:
14   higher: % fat, % protein, calving ease
15   equal: age of sex. mat.,handling ease,calf mortality,calving rate
16   lower: milk yield, muscularity, daily gain, pulling power
17 - Management: stationary; housing: > 6 m.;
18 - Conservation progr.: live animals: miss;Semen: 41;Embryos: 1/1
19 Status: critically endang.;Watch: ♂♂,HB♀♀,trend,%incross!
20 - Similar breeds (see group 3/7 on page 78)   EN Country Status
21 Itäsuomenkarja   129   SF   crit.end.
22 Irish Moiled   123   GB   crit.end.
23 English Longhorn   82   GB   pot. end.
24 Vosgienne   267   F   pot. end.

SHEEP

1 - Dala   EN 476
2   Dala; country-wide
3   Stiftelsen Norsk Landbruks Museum   HB:1926
4   Norges landbrukshogskole, Circus, As 1432, P.B.104
5 - Composite of Norsk Landrace 569, Leicester 528 GB, Sheviot 452 GB
6   Incrossing since 1960 from Texel Denmark, Finnish Landrace 644 SF
7   Numbers 1992: 150000; HB: miss; decreasing; miss %; Ne = 27150
8 - Height: miss/miss cm; Weight: 115/80 kg; Herd number: miss; AI: Yes
9   Colour: Uni white
10 Pecularity: horns 0/0
11 - Main use: (1) meat,(2) wool,(3) miss
12 Spec. abilities: 1,9 lambs per adult winterfed ewe
13 Performance compared with STB Suffolk:
14   higher: age of sexual maturity, wool yield, wool thickness
15   equal: daily gain, litter size, milk yield, lambing interval
16   lower: muscularity
17 - Management: stationary; housing: > 6 m.; pasture on Morentorn ranges
18 - Conservation progr.: live animals: miss;Semen: 45;Embryos: miss
19 Status: normal;   Watch: ♂♂,HB♀♀,trend,%pure,%incross!
20 - Similar breeds (see group 7/11 on page 94)   EN Country Status
21 Blackface   421   F   crit.end.
22 Whitefaced Woodland   676   GB   pot. end.
23 Wicklow Cheviot   677   IRL   normal
24 Blackface Mountain   422   IRL   normal

1 - Gammelnorsk, Utegangarsau   EN   496
2   Old Norwegian; Selbjorn, Austevoll, Horda
3   Stiftelsen Norsk Landbruks Museum   HB:miss
4   Norges landbrukshogskole, Circus, As 1432, P.B.104
5 - Autochthon old local breed
7   Numbers 1983: 40/450; HB: miss; stable; 100 %; Ne = 147
8 - Height: miss / miss cm; Weight: 43/32 kg; Herd number: 15; AI: miss
9   Colour: Uni black, grey, brown, white, combinations are possible
10 Pecularity: horns 2/2
11 - Main use: (1) meat,(2) wool,(3) miss
12 Spec. abilities: very hardy
13 Performance compared with STB Old Norwegian Short Tailed 569:
14   higher: miss
15   equal: age of sexual maturity, lambing interval
16   lower: muscularity, daily gain
17 - Management: stationary; housing: no; extensive conditions
18 - Conservation progr.: live animals: miss;Semen: 1;Embryos: miss
19 Status: minimally endang.; Watch: HB♀♀,herds!
20 - Similar breeds (see group 6/3 on page 90)   EN Country Status
21 Dansk Landfar   477   DK   crit.end.
22 Coburger Fuchsschaf   466   D   crit.end.
23 Foroyskur Seydur   491   FR   normal
24 Gronlandsk Fär   504   DK   normal

1 - Norsk Pels-Sau   EN   566
2   Norwegian Fur Sheep; southern Norway
3   Norsk sau og geitalslag   HB:1968
4   Oslo 2 0254, Parkv.72
5 - Composite of Norwegian Short Tailed Landrace 569, Swedish
6   Pälsfar 580; incrossing since 1960 from Swedish Fur Sheep 580 Sweden
7   Numbers 1983: 8000/15000; HB: miss; stable; 80 %; Ne = 20870
8 - Height: miss/miss cm; Weight: 90/62 kg; Herd number: miss; AI: miss
9   Colour: Uni grey, white
10 Pecularity: horns 0/0
11 - Main use: (1) meat,(2) fur,(3) wool
12 Spec. abilities: miss
13 Performance compared with STB Old Norwegian Short Tailed 569:
14   higher: miss
15   equal: muscularity,daily gain,litter size,age of sexual maturity
16   lower: wool or fiber yield
17 - Management: stationary; housing: > 6 m.;
18 - Conservation progr.: live animals: miss;Semen: 4;Embryos: miss
19 Status: normal;   Watch: HB♀♀,%pure,%incross!
20 - Similar breeds (see group 6/3 on page 90)   EN Country Status
21 Dansk Landfar   477   DK   crit.end.
22 Coburger Fuchsschaf   466   D   crit.end.
23 Foroyskur Seydur   491   FR   normal
24 Gronlandsk Fär   504   DK   normal

```
1 - Rygja sau                                              EN  614
2   Rygja sheep; western coast
3   Stiftelsen Norsk Landbruks Museum                      HB:1926
4   Norges landbrukshogskole, Circus, As 1432, P.B.104
5 - Composite of local landrace, Cheviot 452 GB, Leicester 528 GB
6   Incrossing since 1960 from Texel Denmark, Finsk 644 Finland
7   Numbers 1992: 35000; HB: miss; decreasing; 89 %; Ne = 6335
8 - Height: miss/miss cm; Weight: 110/75 kg; Herd number: miss; AI: Yes
9   Colour: Uni black, white
10  Pecularity: horns 0/0, badger face
11 - Main use: (1) meat,(2) wool,(3) miss
12  Spec. abilities: wool free of medullated fibers
13  Performance compared with STB Texel:
14     higher: litter size, wool or fiber yield
15     equal:  carcass leanness,age of sexual mat.,length of mating seas.
16     lower:  muscularity
17 - Management: stationary; housing: > 6 m.;
18 - Conservation progr.: live animals: miss;Semen: 4;Embryos: miss
19  Status: potential. endang.;Watch: ♂♂,HB♀♀,trend,%pure,%incross!
```

20 - Similar breeds (see group 6/3 on page 90)	EN	Country	Status
21 Dansk Landfar	477	DK	crit.end.
22 Coburger Fuchsschaf	466	D	crit.end.
23 Foroyskur Seydur	491	FR	normal
24 Gronlandsk Fär	504	DK	normal

```
1 - Spaelsau                                               EN  569
2   Old Norwegian Short Tailed; country-wide
3   Stiftelsen Norsk Landbruks Museum                      HB:1947
4   Norges landbrukshogskole, Circus, As 1432, P.B.104
5 - Autochthon old landrace; incrossing since 1960 from Icelandic
6   Landrace 512 Iceland, Finnish Landrace 644 Finland
7   Numbers 1983: 7000/212000; HB: miss; increasing; 100 %; Ne = 27105
8 - Height: miss / miss cm; Weight: 90/57 kg; Herd number: miss; AI: Yes
9   Colour: Uni black, grey, brown, white, combinations are possible
10  Pecularity: horns 2/0, only a few males are horned
11 - Main use: (1) meat,(2) wool,(3) fur (4) vegetation management
12  Spec. abilities: miss
13  Performance compared with STB Dala 476:
14     higher: litter size, age of sexual maturity, lambing interval
15     equal:  miss
16     lower:  muscularity, daily gain, wool or fiber yield
17 - Management: stationary; housing: > 6 m.;
18 - Conservation progr.: live animals: miss;Semen: 18;Embryos: miss
19  Status: normal;            Watch: %incross!
```

20 - Similar breeds (see group 6/3 on page 90)	EN	Country	Status
21 Dansk Landfar	477	DK	crit.end.
22 Coburger Fuchsschaf	466	D	crit.end.
23 Foroyskur Seydur	491	FR	normal
24 Gronlandsk Fär	504	DK	normal

```
 1 - Steigar sau                                                    EN  638
 2   Steigar sheep; northern Norway
 3   Stiftelsen Norsk Landbruks Museum                             HB:1925
 4   Norges landbrukshogskole, Circus, As 1432, P.B.104
 5 - Composite of local landrace,North country Cheviot 452 United Kingdom
 6   Incrossing since 1960 from Texel Denmark, Finsk 644 Finland
 7   Numbers 1983: 6000/70000; HB: miss; stable; 79 %; Ne = 22105
 8 - Height: miss/miss cm; Weight: 110/75 kg; Herd number: miss; AI: Yes
 9   Colour: Uni white
10   Pecularity: horns 0/0, wool free medullated fibers
11 - Main use: (1) meat,(2) wool,(3) yellow fat
12   Spec. abilities: miss
13   Performance compared with STB Texel:
14      higher: litter size, wool or fiber yield
15      equal:  carcass leanness,age of sexual mat.,length of mating seas.
16      lower:  muscularity
17 - Management: stationary; housing: > 6 m.;
18 - Conservation progr.: live animals: miss;Semen: 15;Embryos: miss
19   Status: normal;              Watch: HB♀♀,%pure,%incross!
20 - Similar breeds (see group 7/11 on page 94)   EN  Country Status
21   Blackface                                    421  F       crit.end.
22   Whitefaced Woodland                          676  GB      pot. end.
23   Wicklow Cheviot                              677  IRL     normal
24   Blackface Mountain                           422  IRL     normal
```

```
 1 - Norsk Geit                                                    EN  342
 2   Norwegian Landrace
 3   Statens fagtjeneste for landbruket                            HB:1956
 4   As 1432, Moerveien 12
 5 - Autochthon local breed
 6   Incrossing since 1960 from Saanen Netherlands
 7   Numbers 1983: 3500/72100; HB: miss; stable; 100 %; Ne = 13352
 8 - Height: miss / miss cm; Weight: 80/50 kg; Herd number: miss; AI: Yes
 9   Colour: Uni grey,blue,white; sometimes combinations of these colours
10   Pecularity: horns 2/2, saddle, long hair
11 - Main use: (1) milk,(2) meat,(3) miss
12   Spec. abilities: miss
13   Performance compared with STB Saanen:
14      higher: muscularity
15      equal:  daily gain, carcass leanness, litter size, milk yield
16      lower:  % fat, % protein
17 - Management: stationary; housing: > 6 m.;
18 - Conservation progr.: live animals: miss;Semen: 125;Embryos: miss
19   Status: normal;              Watch: HB♀♀,%incross!
20 - Similar breeds (see group 10 on page 98)    EN  Country Status
21   Suomenvuohi                                  358  SF      endanger.
22   Nederlandse Landgeit                         341  NL      pot. end.
23   Svensk Lantras                               359  S       normal
24   Dansk Landrace                               322  DK      normal
```

```
 1 - Norsk Landrace                                      EN  983
 2   Norwegian Landrace; country-wide
 3   Norsk Svineavlslag                                  HB:1930
 4   Hamar 2300
 5 - Composite of Scandinavian Landrace, Large+Middle White 1023+975 GB,
 6   Landrace S, 917 DK; incrossing since 1970 from Landrace S, 917 DK
 7   Numbers 1983: 3600/70000; HB: miss; decreasing; 85 %; Ne = 13696
 8 - Height: 100/80 cm; Weight: 230/180 kg; Herd number: miss; AI: Yes
 9   Colour: Uni white
10   Pecularity: lop ears
11 - Main use: (1) meat,(2) miss,(3) miss
12   Spec. abilities: meat quality, backfat thickness 10 mm in average
13   Performance compared with STB Pietrain:
14     higher: meat quality, feed conversion rate, piglet mortality
15     equal: litter size,daily gain,age of sex. mat.,farrowing interv.
16     lower: % lean, muscularity
17 - Management: stationary; housing: 12 m.;
18 - Conservation progr.: live animals: miss;Semen: 350;Embryos: miss
19   Status: normal;          Watch: HB♀♀,trend,%pure,%incross!
20 - Similar breeds (see group 2/1 on page 101)   EN  Country Status
21   Belgische Landrasse                           907  D*      crit.end.
22   Zlotnicka biala                              1024  PL      crit.end.
23   Landrace                                      952  CS      normal
24   Belgisch Landvarken                           906  B       normal
```

```
 1 - Norsk Yorkshire                                     EN  984
 2   Large White; southeastern Norway
 3   Norsk Svineavlslag                                  HB:1930
 4   Hamar 2300
 5 - Composite of Landrace, Yorkshire 1023 United Kingdom, 1021 Finland,
 6   Sweden; incrossing since 1970 from Yorkshire Sweden
 7   Numbers 1992: 25/300; HB: miss; decreasing; miss %; Ne = 82
 8 - Height: 100/80 cm; Weight: 200/165 kg; Herd number: miss; AI: miss
 9   Colour: Uni white
10   Pecularity: erect ears
11 - Main use: (1) meat,(2) miss,(3) miss
12   Spec. abilities: meat qualitiy
13   Performance compared with STB Pietrain:
14     higher: meat quality, feed conversion rate, piglet mortality
15     equal: litter size,daily gain,age of sex. mat.,farrowing interv.
16     lower: % lean, muscularity
17 - Management: stationary; housing: 12 m.;
18 - Conservation progr.: live animals: miss;Semen: 75;Embryos: miss
19   Status: endangered;      Watch: HB♀♀,trend,%pure,%incross!
20 - Similar breeds (see group 1/1 on page 101)   EN  Country Status
21   Grand Yorkshire Belge                         937  B       normal
22   Yorkshire                                    1021  SF      normal
23   Large White Pigs                              963  IRL     normal
24   Large White                                   960  F       normal
```

```
 1 - Fjordhest                                                    EN  746
 2   Fjord; western Norway
 3   Norges Fjordhestlag                                          HB:1909
 4   Forde 6800
 5 - Autochthon Vestlandshest
 7   Numbers 1988: 62/945; HB: miss; stable; 100 %; Ne = 233
 8 - Height: 141/141 cm; Weight: 375/375 kg; Herd number: miss; AI: miss
 9   Colour: dun with dark legs
10   Pecularity: tail and erect mane central dark and outwards silver
11 - Main use: (1) sport/hobby,(2) vegetation management,(3) tourism
12   Spec. abilities: miss
13   Performance compared with STB Fjord 746:
14     higher: Breed is used
15     equal:  as standard breed,
16     lower:  no comparison possible.
17 - Management: stationary; housing: > 6 m.;
18 - Conservation progr.: live animals: miss;Semen: miss;Embryos: miss
19   Status: potential. endang.;Watch: HB♀♀!
```

20 - Similar breeds (see group 5/1 on page 110)	EN	Country	Status
21 Gotland Russ	820	SF	crit.end.
22 Nordlandshest	786	N	min. end.
23 Skogsruss	805	S	normal
24 Fjord de Norvege	745	F	normal

```
 1 - Nordlandshest, Lyngshest                                     EN  786
 2   Nordland; northern Norway
 3   Aulslagente for Nordlandshest/Lyngshest Troms               HB:1969
 4   Nordland og Sor-Norge, ODB A Solli, Lyngseidet 9060
 5 - Composite of Lyngshest, Nordlandshest and other small breeds in
 6   North-Norway; incrossing since 1950 from Finnish Pony Finland
 7   Numbers 1988: 25/124; HB: miss; increasing; 100 %; Ne = 66
 8 - Height: 130/130 cm; Weight: 275/275 kg; Herd number: miss; AI: miss
 9   Colour: all solid colours, usually dark
10   Pecularity: miss
11 - Main use: (1) sport/hobby,(2) vegetation management,(3) miss
12   Spec. abilities: miss
13   Performance compared with STB Fjord 746:
14     higher: age of sexual maturity
15     equal:  handling ease, adaptability in dressage and jumping
16     lower:  pulling power, speed in gallop and in trotters, daily gain
17 - Management: stationary; housing: > 6 m.;
18 - Conservation progr.: live animals: miss;Semen: miss;Embryos: miss
19   Status: minimally endang.; Watch: HB♀♀,%incross!
```

20 - Similar breeds (see group 5/1 on page 110)	EN	Country	Status
21 Gotland Russ	820	SF	crit.end.
22 Fjordhest	746	N	pot. end.
23 Skogsruss	805	S	normal
24 Fjord de Norvege	745	F	normal

412

```
1 - Norsk Kaldblods Traver                                    EN  789
2   Norwegian Heavy Trotter; country-wide
3   Det Norske Travelskar                                    HB:1939
4   Oslo 0515, Boks 85 Arvoll
5 - Autochthon Doele Hest 814
6   Incrossing since 1950 from Heavy Trotter stallions Sweden
7   Numbers 1988: 83/2055; HB: miss; stable; 100 %; Ne = 319
8 - Height: 150/150 cm; Weight: 400/400 kg; Herd number: miss; AI: miss
9   Colour: usually chestnut, sometimes bay
10  Pecularity: miss
11 - Main use: (1) sport/hobby,(2) miss,(3) miss
12  Spec. abilities: miss
13  Performance compared with STB Fjord 746:
14    higher: speed in trotters,pulling power,speed in gallop,daily gain
15    equal:  handling ease, adaptability in dressage and in jumping
16    lower:  miss
17 - Management: stationary; housing: > 6 m.;
18 - Conservation progr.: live animals: miss;Semen: miss;Embryos: miss
19   Status: normal;           Watch: HB♀♀,%incross!
20 - Similar breeds (see group 2 on page 108)    EN  Country Status
21   Morgan Horse                                 783  GB     endanger.
22   Lämminverinen ravuri                         773  SF     normal
23   Trotteur Francais                            813  F      normal
```

```
1 - Tyngre Doelehest                                          EN  814
2   Doele Draught Horse; southeastern Norway
3   Landslaget fur Dolehest                                  HB:1896
4   Favang 2634, Per Sylte
5 - Autochthon Doele Hest; incrossing since 1950 from Heavy Trotter 789
6   Norway, Draught Horse (1 stall.) Sweden
7   Numbers 1988: 29/306; HB: miss; stable; 100 %; Ne = 106
8 - Height: 151/151 cm; Weight: 425/425 kg; Herd number: miss; AI: miss
9   Colour: black, bay, brown
10  Pecularity: profuse mane and tail
11 - Main use: (1) sport/hobby,(2) vegetation management,(3) miss
12  Spec. abilities: miss
13  Performance compared with STB Fjord 746:
14    higher: speed in trotters+gallop,pulling power,adapt. in dressage
15    equal:  handling ease,adapt. in jumping and in military,fertility
16    lower:  miss
17 - Management: stationary; housing: > 6 m.;
18 - Conservation progr.: live animals: miss;Semen: miss;Embryos: miss
19   Status: potential. endang.;Watch: HB♀♀,%incross!
20 - Similar breeds (see group 4/4 on page 110)   EN  Country Status
21   Schleswiger Kaltblut                         799  D      endanger.
22   Den Jydske Hest                              741  DK     min. end.
23   Nordsvensk häst                              787  S      normal
24   Suomenhevonen                                809  SF     normal
```

```
 1 - Czerwona Polska                                           EN   72
 2   Polish Red; mountainous regions
 3   Cattle Breeder's  Association                             HB:1913
 4   Warszawa 01142, ul. Bodwales 23
 5 - Autochthon original slavic cattle
 6   Incrossing since 1950 from Angler 8 Germany
 7   Numbers 1983: 140/85000; HB: miss; stable; miss %; Ne = 559
 8 - Height: 135/127 cm; Weight: 775/500 kg; Herd number: miss; AI: miss
 9   Colour: Uni red
10   Pecularity: miss
11 - Main use: (1) meat,(2) milk,(3) miss
12   Spec. abilities: vitality
13   Performance compared with STB Polish Black-and-White 185:
14      higher: handling ease,% fat,% protein,calving ease,calving rate
15      equal:  milk yield, muscularity, calf mortality
16      lower:  daily gain, age of sexual maturity, milkability
17 - Management: stationary; housing: > 6 m.;
18 - Conservation progr.: live animals: miss;Semen: 21;Embryos: Yes
19   Status: normal;              Watch: HB♀♀,%pure,%incross!
```

```
20 - Similar breeds (see group 4/3 on page 78)   EN  Country Status
21   Donnersberger Rotvieh                        101  D       crit.end.
22   Harzer Rotvieh                               109  D       crit.end.
23   Rod Dansk Malkerace                          222  DK      normal
24   Rood Ras van Belgie                          224  B       normal
```

```
 1 - Nizinna Czerwono-Biala                                    EN   183
 2   Polish Red-and-White; southwestern Poland
 3   Central Animal Breeding Office                            HB:1910
 4   Warszawa 01142, str. Sokolowska no 3
 5 - Composite of local breeds, German Red Pied 74 D, MRY 161 Netherlands
 6   Incrossing since 1950 from Red-White 161 Netherlands
 7   Numbers 1986: 111/38280; HB: 23780; decreasing; miss %; Ne = 442
 8 - Height: 138/133 cm; Weight: 700/550 kg; Herd number: miss; AI: Yes
 9   Colour: Combination red, white
10   Pecularity: spotted
11 - Main use: (1) milk,(2) meat,(3) miss
12   Spec. abilities: miss
13   Performance compared with STB Polish Simmental 237:
14      higher: milk yield, milkability
15      equal:  % protein,calving ease,calving interval,age of sexual mat.
16      lower:  muscularity, daily gain, % fat
17 - Management: stationary; housing: > 6 m.;
18 - Conservation progr.: live animals: miss;Semen: 34;Embryos: 2/miss
19   Status: potential. endang.;Watch: trend,%pure,%incross!
```

```
20 - Similar breeds (see group 3/1 on page 76)   EN  Country Status
21   Blanc-Rouge de Belgique                      273  B       pot. end.
22   Ferrandais                                    85  F       pot. end.
23   Dansk Rodbroget Kvaeg                         73  DK      normal
24   Pie-Rouge                                    199  B       normal
```

```
1 - Nizinna-Czarno-Biala                                    EN  185
2   Polish Black-and-White
3   Central Animal Breeding Office                          HB:1934
4   Warszawa 01142, str. Sokolowska no 3
5 - Imported as breed from country Netherlands; incrossing since 1950
6   from Black-White 277 Netherlands, 76 Germany, Sweden, USA
7   Numbers 1986: 1298/ miss; HB: 421000; decreasing; miss %; Ne = 5176
8 - Height: 132/128 cm; Weight: 650/550 kg; Herd number: miss; AI: Yes
9   Colour: Combination black, white
10  Pecularity: spotted
11 - Main use: (1) milk,(2) meat,(3) miss
12  Spec. abilities: miss
13  Performance compared with STB Holstein-Friesian:
14     higher: muscularity, daily gain
15     equal: % fat,% protein,calving ease and interval,age of sex. mat.
16     lower: milk yield, calf mortality, milkability
17 - Management: stationary; housing: > 6 m.;
18 - Conservation progr.: live animals: miss;Semen: 354;Embryos: 42/miss
19   Status: potential. endang.;Watch: trend,%pure,%incross!
```

20 - Similar breeds (see group 1/1 on page 75)	EN	Country	Status
21 Sortbroget Dansk Malkekvaeg	245	DK	pot. end.
22 Pie-Noire-Holstein	198	B	normal
23 Deutsche Schwarzbunte	75	D	normal
24 Prim' Holstein	209	F	normal

```
1 - Simentalska                                             EN  237
2   Polish Simmental; southeastern Poland
3   Central Animal Breeding Office                          HB:1925
4   Warszawa 01142, str. Sokolowska no 3
5 - Imported as breed from country Switzerland
6   Incrossing since 1950 from Simmental 240 Switzerland, 78 Germany
7   Numbers 1986: 20/1463; HB: 622; decreasing; miss %; Ne = 57
8 - Height: 138/135 cm; Weight: 850/650 kg; Herd number: miss; AI: Yes
9   Colour: Combination red,yellow,white; white head,spotted around eyes
10  Pecularity: lyra formed horns
11 - Main use: (1) meat,(2) milk,(3) miss
12  Spec. abilities: very good legs
13  Performance compared with STB Polish Simmental 237:
14     higher: Breed is used
15     equal: as standard breed,
16     lower: no comparison possible.
17 - Management: stationary; housing: > 6 m.;
18 - Conservation progr.: live animals: miss;Semen: 10;Embryos: Yes
19   Status: minimally endang.; Watch: ♂♂,trend,%pure,%incross!
```

20 - Similar breeds (see group 3/2 on page 77)	EN	Country	Status
21 Ceske strakate	61	CZ	crit.end.
22 Pie Rouge de l'Est	89	F	pot. end.
23 Montbeliard	176	F	normal
24 Fleckvieh	88	A	normal

```
 1 - Corriedale                                                     EN  582
 2   Polish Corriedale; central Poland
 3   Warsaw Agricultural University, Division of Sheep Breeding   HB:1977
 4   Warsaw 02528, Rakowiecka 26/30
 5 - Composite of Polish Merino 583, Lincoln 532 United Kingdom
 7   Numbers 1986: 331/ miss; HB: 11566; decreasing; 95 %; Ne = 1287
 8 - Height: miss/miss cm; Weight: 93/60 kg; Herd number: miss; AI: miss
 9   Colour: Uni white
10   Pecularity: horns 0/0
11 - Main use: (1) wool,(2) meat,(3) miss
12   Spec. abilities: miss
13   Performance compared with STB Corriedale of New Zealand:
14      higher: age of sexual maturity
15      equal:  carcass leanness,litter size,milk yield,% fat,% protein
16      lower:  daily gain, muscularity, wool or fiber yield
17 - Management: stationary; housing: 12 m.;
18 - Conservation progr.: live animals: miss;Semen: miss;Embryos: miss
19   Status: normal;              Watch: trend!
```

20 - Similar breeds (see group 3 on page 88)	EN	Country	Status
21 Mouton Boulonnais	559	F	crit.end.
22 Galway	495	IRL	endanger.
23 Mouton Charollais	560	F	normal
24 Cotentin	473	F	normal

```
 1 - Kamieniecka                                                    EN  517
 2   Kamieniec; husbandry Kaminiec, palatinate Olsztyn
 3   National Association of Sheep Farmers Unions in Poland       HB: Yes
 4   Warsaw 02528, Siewierska 13
 5 - Autochthon prim. sheep population of the Pomeranin type
 6   out of Gdansk
 7   Numbers 1986: miss /160000; HB: 25000; decreasing; miss %; Ne = 4525
 8 - Height: miss/miss cm; Weight: 100/65 kg; Herd number: miss; AI: miss
 9   Colour: Uni white
10   Pecularity: horns 0/0
11 - Main use: (1) meat,(2) wool,(3) miss
12   Spec. abilities: highly resistant to diseases, esp. foot rot
13   Performance compared with STB Texel:
14      higher: miss
15      equal:  daily gain, age of sex. maturity, length of mating season
16      lower:  litter size, carcass leanness
17 - Management: stationary; housing: 2-6 m.;
18 - Conservation progr.: live animals: miss;Semen: miss;Embryos: miss
19   Status: normal;              Watch: trend!
```

20 - Similar breeds (see group 2/3 on page 88)	EN	Country	Status
21 Rauhwolliges Pommer. Landschaf	595	D*	crit.end.
22 Olkuska	571	PL	crit.end.
23 Leineschaf	529	D	pot. end.
24 Pomorska	586	PL	normal

1 - **Olkuska**   EN **571**
2   **Olkusz; Cracow region, southern Poland**
3   **Warsaw Agricultural University, Division of Sheep Breeding   HB:miss**
4   **Warsaw 02528, Rakowiecka 26/30**
5 - **Composite of local breed Pomerania 586, Friesian**
7   **Numbers 1992: 20/130; HB: miss; decreasing; 100 %; Ne = 47**
8 - **Height: miss / miss cm; Weight: 100/65 kg; Herd number: 6; AI: miss**
9   **Colour: Uni white**
10 **Pecularity: horns 0/0**
11 - **Main use: (1) meat; wool,(2) miss,(3) miss**
12 **Spec. abilities: high prolificacy (1-5 lambs)**
13 Performance compared with STB **miss:**
14   higher: **miss**
15   equal: **miss**
16   lower: **miss**
17 - Management: **miss;** housing: **miss m.;**
18 - Conservation progr.: live animals: **Yes;**Semen: **Yes;**Embryos: **Yes**
19 Status: **critically endang.;**Watch: **♂♂,HB♀♀,trend,herds!**
20 - <u>Similar breeds</u> (see group 2/3 on page 88)   <u>EN</u> <u>Country</u> <u>Status</u>
21 **Rauhwolliges Pommer. Landschaf**   **595   D*   crit.end.**
22 **Hvidhovedet Marsk**   **510   DK   min. end.**
23 **Pomorska**   **586   PL   normal**
24 **Kamieniecka**   **517   PL   normal**

1 - **Polish Merino**   EN **583**
2   **Polish Merino; northern and western Poland**
3   **Warsaw Agricultural University, Division of Sheep Breeding   HB: Yes**
4   **Warsaw 02528, Rakowiecka 26/30**
5 - **Imported as breed from countries 545 Spain, 550 Germany, 553 France**
7   **Numbers 1986: 10061/1900000; HB: 235849; decreasing; 100 %; Ne=38598**
8 - **Height: miss/miss cm; Weight: 110/65 kg; Herd number: miss; AI: miss**
9   Colour: **Uni white**
10 Pecularity: **horns 0/0**
11 - Main use: **(1) wool,(2) meat,(3) miss**
12 Spec. abilities: **long breeding season**
13 Performance compared with STB **German Merino 550:**
14   higher: **% fat**
15   equal: **daily gain, carcass leanness, age of sexual maturity**
16   lower: **milk yield,wool or fiber yield,litter size,wool thickness**
17 - Management: **stationary;** housing: **2-6 m.;**
18 - Conservation progr.: live animals: **miss;**Semen: **miss;**Embryos: **miss**
19 Status: **normal**
20 - <u>Similar breeds</u> (see group 1/5 on page 87)   <u>EN</u> <u>Country</u> <u>Status</u>
21 **Merinos de Palas**   **552   RO   normal**
22 **Merinos Transilvanean**   **556   RO   normal**
23 **Czech Merino**   **475   CZ   normal**

```
1 - Polska owca gorska                                        EN  584
2   Polish Mountain; Polish part of the Carpathian Mountains
3   Warsaw Agricultural University, Division of Sheep Breeding   HB:miss
4   Warsaw 02528, Rakowiecka 26/30
5 - Composite of Carpathian Zackiel, Transylvanian Zackiel 600 Romania,
6   East Friesian 573 Germany
7   Numbers 1986: miss /30000; HB: 5000; decreasing; 90 %; Ne = 905
8 - Height: miss/miss cm; Weight: 65/50 kg; Herd number: miss; AI: miss
9   Colour: Uni white
9   Colour: Combination black, white, sometimes spotted
10  Pecularity: horns 2/0
11 - Main use: (1) wool,(2) milk,(3) miss
12  Spec. abilities: miss
13  Performance compared with STB Valachian:
14    higher: wool or fiber yield
15    equal:  litter size, age of sex. maturity, length of mating season
16    lower:  milk yield, daily gain, % fat
17 - Management: transhumant; housing: 2-6 m.; mountain
18 - Conservation progr.: live animals: miss;Semen: miss;Embryos: miss
19  Status: potential. endang.;Watch: ♂♂,trend,%pure!
```

20 - Similar breeds (see group 7/6 on page 92)	EN	Country	Status
21 Florina	490	GR	endanger.
22 Ruda Dubrovacka Sheep	611	HR	endanger.
23 Karagouniko	518	GR	normal
24 Sazakatsaniko	429	GR	normal

```
1 - Pomorska                                                  EN  586
2   Pomeranian Coarsewool; flock of the Koszalin and of the Kaszuby type
3   National Association of Sheep Farmers Unions in Poland      HB: Yes
4   Warsaw 02528, Siewierska 13
5 - Autochthon primitive population of the Kaszuby and Koszalin region
7   Numbers 1986: miss /250000; HB: 30500; decreasing; 100 %; Ne = 5521
8 - Height: 72/67 cm; Weight: 100/70 kg; Herd number: miss; AI: miss
9   Colour: Uni white
10  Pecularity: horns 0/0,black ears,muzzle,legs;no wool on head a. legs
11 - Main use: (1) meat,(2) wool,(3) miss
12  Spec. abilities: seaside climate with low feeding require.,hardiness
13  Performance compared with STB Texel:
14    higher: litter size
15    equal:  daily gain,age of sexual maturity,length of mating season
16    lower:  muscularity, carcass leanness
17 - Management: stationary; housing: 2-6 m.;
18 - Conservation progr.: live animals: miss;Semen: miss;Embryos: miss
19  Status: normal;              Watch: trend!
```

20 - Similar breeds (see group 2/3 on page 88)	EN	Country	Status
21 Rauhwolliges Pommer. Landschaf	595	D*	crit.end.
22 Olkuska	571	PL	crit.end.
23 Leineschaf	529	D	pot. end.
24 Kamieniecka	517	PL	normal

```
 1 - Wielkopolska Sheep                                              EN  678
 2   Wielkopolska; central Poland
 3   Warsaw Agriculture University, Division of Sheep Breeding     HB:1977
 4   Warsaw 02528, Rakowiecka 26/30
 5 - Composite of local breeds, Polish Merino 583, Romney Marsh 602 GB
 7   Numbers 1986: 2203/ miss; HB: 69711; decreasing; 95 %; Ne = 8542
 8 - Height: miss/miss cm; Weight: 90/60 kg; Herd number: miss; AI: miss
 9   Colour: Uni white
10   Pecularity: horns 0/0
11 - Main use: (1) wool,(2) meat,(3) miss
12   Spec. abilities: intensive production of fat lambs
13   Performance compared with STB Corriedale of New Zealand:
14     higher: miss
15     equal: muscularity,carcass leanness,milk yield,% fat,% protein
16     lower: litter size, wool or fiber yield, daily gain
17 - Management: stationary; housing: 12 m.;
18 - Conservation progr.: live animals: miss;Semen: miss;Embryos: miss
19   Status: normal;              Watch: trend!
```

20 - Similar breeds (see group 3 on page 88)	EN	Country	Status
21 Mouton Boulonnais	559	F	crit.end.
22 Galway	495	IRL	endanger.
23 Mouton Charollais	560	F	normal
24 Cotentin	473	F	normal

```
 1 - Wrzosowka                                                      EN  680
 2   Wrzosowka; eastern Poland
 3   Sheep Breeder's  Association                                 HB:1975
 4   Warszawa 01142, ul. Swietokrzyska 12
 5 - Autochthon old primitive Polish breed
 7   Numbers 1983: 38/800; HB: miss; increasing; 4 %; Ne = 145
 8 - Height: 61/57 cm; Weight: 35/25 kg; Herd number: miss; AI: miss
 9   Colour: Combination black, grey, blue, white
10   Pecularity: horns 2/ miss, black head and legs
11 - Main use: (1) meat,(2) vegetation management (3) fur
12   Spec. abilities: miss
13   Performance compared with STB Polish Merino 583:
14     higher: litter size, lambing interval, fur, carcass leanness
15     equal: milk yield
16     lower: muscularity, wool yield, wool thickness, daily gain
17 - Management: miss; housing: miss m.;
18 - Conservation progr.: live animals: miss;Semen: miss;Embryos: miss
19   Status: potential. endang.;Watch: HB♀♀,%pure!
```

20 - Similar breeds (see group 6/3 on page 90)	EN	Country	Status
21 Dansk Landfar	477	DK	crit.end.
22 Coburger Fuchsschaf	466	D	crit.end.
23 Foroyskur Seydur	491	FR	normal
24 Gronlandsk Fär	504	DK	normal

```
1 - Duroc                                                      EN  930
2   Duroc; country-wide
3   Central Animal Breeding Office                             HB:1979
4   Warszawa 01142. str. Sokolowska no 3
5 - Imported as breed from countries 928 Germany, Denmark
7   Numbers 1992: 60/ miss; HB: 598; increasing; miss %; Ne = 218
8 - Height:miss/miss cm; Weight:miss/miss kg; Herd number:miss; AI:miss
9   Colour: Uni red
10  Pecularity: short lop ears
11 - Main use: (1) meat,(2) crossbreeding,(3) miss
12  Spec. abilities: miss
13  Performance compared with STB Large White 1019:
14    higher: miss
15    equal: % lean,feed conver.,meat qual.,daily gain,age of sex. mat.
16    lower:  litter size
17 - Management: stationary; housing: 12 m.;
18 - Conservation progr.: live animals: miss;Semen: miss;Embryos: miss
19  Status: potential. endang.;Watch: %pure!
```

20 - Similar breeds (see group 5/1 on page 103)	EN	Country	Status
21 Duroc	927	F	crit.end.
22 Duroc	932	GB	crit.end.
23 Duroc	929	I	normal
24 Duroc	926	CS	normal

```
1 - Polska biala zwisloucha                                    EN  992
2   Polish Landrace; country-wide
3   Central Animal Breeding Office                             HB:1962
4   Warszawa 01142, str. Sokolowska no 3
5 - Composite of Polish and German long-eared, Landrace Sweden
6   Incrossing since 1970 from Landrace 983 Norway, 980 NL, 920 Germany
7   Numbers 1992: 700/ miss; HB: 14469; increasing; miss %; Ne = 2671
8 - Height: miss/miss cm; Weight: 375/325 kg; Herd number: miss; AI:miss
9   Colour: Uni white
10  Pecularity: lop ears
11 - Main use: (1) meat,(2) miss,(3) miss
12  Spec. abilities: miss
13  Performance compared with STB Large White 1019:
14    higher: miss
15    equal: % lean, litter size, feed conversion rate, meat quality
16    lower:  miss
17 - Management: stationary; housing: 12 m.;
18 - Conservation progr.: live animals: miss;Semen: miss;Embryos: miss
19  Status: normal;                Watch: %incross!
```

20 - Similar breeds (see group 2/1 on page 101)	EN	Country	Status
21 Belgische Landrasse	907	D*	crit.end.
22 Zlotnicka biala	1024	PL	crit.end.
23 Landrace	952	CS	normal
24 Belgisch Landvarken	906	B	normal

```
 1 - Pulawska                                              EN  995
 2   Pulawy; central and eastern Poland
 3   Central Animal Breeding Office                       HB:1935
 4   Warszawa 01142, str. Sokolowska no 3
 5 - Autochthon local short-eared pigs,Large White 1019 Poland,Berkshire
 6   909 United Kingdom; incrossing since 1970 from Large White 1019 PL
 7   Numbers 1992: 30/294; HB: miss; stable; miss %; Ne = 109
 8 - Height: miss/miss cm; Weight: 300/240 kg; Herd number: 104; AI: miss
 9   Colour: Combination black, white; spotted
10   Pecularity: erect ears
11 - Main use: (1) meat,(2) miss,(3) miss
12   Spec. abilities: good results in bad environmental conditions
13   Performance compared with STB Large White 1019:
14      higher: litter size, handling ease
15      equal:  feed conv., meat quality, daily gain, farrowing interval
16      lower:  % lean, age of sexual maturity, muscularity
17 - Management: stationary; housing: 12 m.;
18 - Conservation progr.: live animals: miss;Semen: miss;Embryos: miss
19   Status: minimally endang.; Watch: ♂♂,HB♀♀,%incross!
```

20 - Similar breeds (see group 6/2 on page 104)	EN	Country	Status
21 Sortbroget	1005	DK	crit.end.
22 Schwarz-Weißes Bentheimer	996	D	crit.end.
23 Sibirskaya chernopestraya	1001	USSR	pot. end.
24 Gloucestershire Old Spot	936	GB	pot. end.

```
 1 - Wielka biala polska                                  EN 1019
 2   Large White; country-wide
 3   Central Animal Breeding Office                       HB:1956
 4   Warszawa 01142, str. Sokolowska no 3
 5 - Imported as breed from countries 1023 United Kingdom, 923 Germany
 6   Incrossing since 1970 from Large White 1023 United Kingdom
 7   Numbers 1992: 500/ miss; HB: 10063; decreasing; miss %; Ne = 1905
 8 - Height: miss/miss cm; Weight: 375/325 kg; Herd number: miss; AI:miss
 9   Colour: Uni white
10   Pecularity: erect ears
11 - Main use: (1) meat,(2) miss,(3) miss
12   Spec. abilities: miss
13   Performance compared with STB Large White 1019:
14      higher: Breed is used
15      equal:  as standard breed,
16      lower:  no comparison possible.
17 - Management: stationary; housing: 12 m.;
18 - Conservation progr.: live animals: miss;Semen: miss;Embryos: miss
19   Status: normal;              Watch: %incross!
```

20 - Similar breeds (see group 1/2 on page 101)	EN	Country	Status
21 Bela Zlahtna	904	SLO	crit.end.
22 Middle White	975	GB	min. end.
23 Deutsches Edelschwein	922	D*	normal
24 Vile uslechtile	1017	CS	normal

```
 1 - Zlotnicka biala                                          EN 1024
 2   Zlotniki White; Poznan region (central and western Poland)
 3   Central Animal Breeding Office                           HB:1962
 4   Warszawa 01142, str. Sokolowska no 3
 5 - Autochthon aborigin Large Polish Long-eared pigs from Lithuania
 6   Incrossing since 1970 from Landrace Sweden
 7   Numbers 1992: 8/83; HB: miss; decreasing; miss %; Ne = 14
 8 - Height: miss / miss cm; Weight: 290/240 kg; Herd number: 2; AI: miss
 9   Colour: Uni white
10   Pecularity: lop ears
11 - Main use: (1) meat,(2) miss,(3) miss
12   Spec. abilities: miss
13   Performance compared with STB Large White 1019:
14      higher: miss
15      equal: % lean, litter size, feed conv., meat quality, daily gain
16      lower: miss
17 - Management: stationary; housing: 12 m.;
18 - Conservation progr.: live animals: miss;Semen: miss;Embryos: miss
19   Status: critically endang.;Watch: ♂♂,HB♀♀,%incross,trend,herds!
```

20 -	Similar breeds (see group 2/1 on page 101)	EN	Country	Status
21	Belgische Landrasse	907	D*	crit.end.
22	Landrace Belga	956	I	endanger.
23	Landrace	952	CS	normal
24	Belgisch Landvarken	906	B	normal

```
 1 - Zlotnicka pstra                                          EN 1025
 2   Zlotniki Black and White; Mazurian region (northern Poland)
 3   Central Animal Breeding Office                           HB:1962
 4   Warszawa 01142, str. Sokolowska no 3
 5 - Autochthon aborigin Large Polish long-eared pigs from Lithuania
 7   Numbers 1992: 27/miss; HB: 269; stable; miss %; Ne = 95
 8 - Height: miss/miss cm; Weight: 260/220 kg; Herd number: miss; AI:miss
 9   Colour: Combination black, white; spotted
10   Pecularity: lop ears
11 - Main use: (1) meat,(2) miss,(3) miss
12   Spec. abilities: meat quality, halothane negative
13   Performance compared with STB Large White 1019:
14      higher: meat quality, handling ease
15      equal: age of sexual maturity,farrowing interval,piglet mortality
16      lower: % lean,muscularity,litter size,feed conv. rate,daily gain
17 - Management: stationary; housing: 12 m.;
18 - Conservation progr.: live animals: miss;Semen: miss;Embryos: miss
19   Status: minimally endang.; Watch: ♂♂,HB♀♀!
```

20 -	Similar breeds (see group 6/2 on page 104)	EN	Country	Status
21	Sortbroget	1005	DK	crit.end.
22	Schwarz-Weißes Bentheimer	996	D	crit.end.
23	Sibirskaya chernopestraya	1001	USSR	pot. end.
24	Gloucestershire Old Spot	936	GB	pot. end.

1 - Hucul   EN 763
2   Hutsul; mountainous regions
3   Horse Breeder's Association   HB:1955
4   Warszawa 01142, ul. Nowogrodzka 50
5 - Autochthon old local breed
6   Incrossing since 1950 from Hucul 762 Czechoslovakia, Romania
7   Numbers 1992: 50/170; HB: miss; increasing; miss %; Ne = 155
8 - Height: 141/135 cm; Weight: 420/380 kg; Herd number: 6; AI: miss
9   Colour: predominantly dun or bay
10 Pecularity: rarely piebald
11 - Main use:(1) tractive power,(2) veget.manag.,(3) good mountain horse
12 Spec. abilities: hardy, docile and willing
13 Performance compared with STB Halfbred:
14   higher: fertility, handling ease, age of sexual maturity
15   equal: miss
16   lower: pulling power, daily gain
17 - Management: miss; housing: miss m.;
18 - Conservation progr.: live animals: miss;Semen: miss;Embryos: miss
19 Status: potential. endang.;Watch: HB♀♀,herds,%pure,%incross!
20 - Similar breeds (see group 5/9 on page 111)

	EN	Country	Status
21 Hucul	762	CS	crit.end.
22 Koniki Polskie	771	PL	normal
23 Bosanski brdski konj	712	YU	miss

1 - Koniki Polskie   EN 771
2   Polish Konik; eastern Poland
3   Horse Breeder's Association   HB:1955
4   Warszawa 01142, ul. Nowogrodzka 50
5 - Autochthon old local breed - Tarpan Horse
7   Numbers 1983: 45/200; HB: miss; stable; 25 %; Ne = 147
8 - Height: 133/132 cm; Weight: 405/398 kg; Herd number: miss; AI: miss
9   Colour: dun, especially blue-dun, grey
10 Pecularity: sometimes zebra-striped legs
11 - Main use: (1) veget. management,(2) tractive power,(3) sport/hobby
12 Spec. abilities: miss
13 Performance compared with STB Halfbred:
14   higher: feed efficiency, handling ease, fertility
15   equal: age of sexual maturity, daily gain
16   lower: pulling power
17 - Management: miss; housing: miss m.;
18 - Conservation progr.: live animals: miss;Semen: miss;Embryos: miss
19 Status: normal;   Watch: HB♀♀,%pure!
20 - Similar breeds (see group 5/9 on page 111)

	EN	Country	Status
21 Hucul	762	CS	crit.end.
22 Hucul	763	PL	pot. end.
23 Bosanski brdski konj	712	YU	miss

```
1 - Alentejana                                                    EN     5
2   Alentejana; Alentejo (southern Portugal)
3   Associacao de Criadores da Raca Bovina Alentejana            HB:1970
4   Assumar 7450, Coutada do Assumar
5 - Autochthon old local breed
6   Incrossing since 1950 from Charolais 62, Salers 226 France
7   Numbers 1986: 450/30000; HB: 15430; stable; 40 %; Ne = 1749
8 - Height: 155/140 cm; Weight: 970/600 kg; Herd number: 65; AI: Yes
9   Colour: Uni, yellow, golden red
10  Pecularity: long horns
11 - Main use: (1) miss,(2) miss,(3) miss
12  Spec. abilities: miss
13  Performance compared with STB Charolais:
14     higher: calving ease, age of sexual maturity, calf mortality
15     equal:  daily gain, calving interval, calving rate
16     lower:  muscularity, handling ease
17 - Management: stationary; housing: no
18 - Conservation progr.: live animals: miss;Semen: 3;Embryos: miss
19  Status: potential. endang.;Watch: %pure,%incross!
```

20 - Similar breeds (see group 4/6 on page 79)	EN	Country	Status
21 Mallorquina	164	E	crit.end.
22 Menorqina	169	E	crit.end.
23 Berrenda roja andaluza	30	E	normal
24 Asturiana de Valles	12	E	normal

```
1 - Arouquesa                                                     EN    11
2   Arouquesa; mountainous regions of Viseu and Aveiro
3   Direccao-Geral de Pecuaria                                   HB:1982
4   Lisboa 1100, Largo da Biblioteca Publica 1
5 - Composite of Mirandesa 172, Barrosa 21
7   Numbers 1986: 600/15000; HB: 5500; decreasing; 95 %; Ne = 2164
8 - Height: 130/120 cm; Weight: 600/350 kg; Herd number: 15; AI: miss
9   Colour: Uni brown
10  Pecularity: miss
11 - Main use: (1) tractive power,(2) meat,(3) milk
12  Spec. abilities: miss
13  Performance compared with STB Jersey:
14     higher: pulling power, daily gain
15     equal:  muscularity,% fat,% protein,calving ease,calving interval
16     lower:  milk yield, age of sexual maturity, handling ease
17 - Management: stationary; housing: > 6 m.; mountain
18 - Conservation progr.: live animals: miss;Semen: miss;Embryos: miss
19  Status: normal;            Watch: trend!
```

20 - Similar breeds (see group 5/4 on page 80)	EN	Country	Status
21 Frieiresa	90	E	crit.end.
22 Limiana	155	E	crit.end.
23 Marinhoa	167	P	normal
24 Barrosa	21	P	normal

1 - Barrosa   EN   21
2   Barrosa; northwestern Portugal
3   Direccao-Geral de Pecuaria   HB:1985
4   Lisboa 1100, Largo da Biblioteca Publica 1
5 - miss
7   Numbers 1986: 750/35000; HB: 6000; stable; 80 %; Ne = 2667
8 - Height: 125/115 cm; Weight: 700/400 kg; Herd number: 21; AI: miss
9   Colour: Uni blond
10 Pecularity: scimitar shaped horns
11 - Main use: (1) miss,(2) miss,(3) miss
12 Spec. abilities: meat with very good paladability
13 Performance compared with STB Charolais:
14   higher: calving ease, pulling power, handling ease, calving rate
15   equal: miss
16   lower: daily gain, calf mortality, muscularity, calving interval
17 - Management: stationary; housing: 2-6 m.; mountain
18 - Conservation progr.: live animals: miss;Semen: miss;Embryos: miss
19 Status: normal;   Watch: %pure!
20 - Similar breeds (see group 5/4 on page 80)   EN Country Status
21 Frieiresa   90   E   crit.end.
22 Limiana   155   E   crit.end.
23 Marinhoa   167   P   normal
24 Arouquesa   11   P   normal

1 - Marinhoa   EN   167
2   Marinhoa; central Portugal near Aveire
3   Direccao-Geral de Pecuaria   HB:1986
4   Lisboa 1100, Largo da Biblioteca Publica 1
5 - Autochthon variety from Mirandesa 172
7   Numbers 1986: 55/4500; HB: 2750; decreasing; 50 %; Ne = 216
8 - Height: 150/140 cm; Weight: 800/550 kg; Herd number: 11; AI: miss
9   Colour: Uni yellow
10 Pecularity: miss
11 - Main use: (1) tractive power,(2) meat,(3) miss
12 Spec. abilities: miss
13 Performance compared with STB Charolais:
14   higher: calving ease, pulling power, age of sexual maturity
15   equal: calving interval, calving rate
16   lower: daily gain, muscularity, calf mortality
17 - Management: stationary; housing: > 6 m.;
18 - Conservation progr.: live animals: miss;Semen: miss;Embryos: miss
19 Status: normal;   Watch: trend,%pure,herds!
20 - Similar breeds (see group 5/4 on page 80)   EN Country Status
21 Frieiresa   90   E   crit.end.
22 Limiana   155   E   crit.end.
23 Barrosa   21   P   normal
24 Arouquesa   11   P   normal

```
 1 - Maronesa                                                      EN  168
 2   Maronesa; northern Portugal near Vila Real
 3   Estacao Zootecnica Nacional                                   HB:1989
 4   Santarem 2000, Vale de Santarem
 5 - Composite of Mirandesa 172, Barrosa 21
 7   Numbers 1986: 800/10000; HB: 4500; decreasing; 95 %; Ne = 2717
 8 - Height: 140/130 cm; Weight: 700/450 kg; Herd number: 12; AI: miss
 9   Colour: Combination black, brown
10   Pecularity: miss
11 - Main use: (1) tractive power,(2) meat,(3) miss
12   Spec. abilities: miss
13   Performance compared with STB Charolais:
14     higher: pulling power, calving ease
15     equal:  calving rate
16     lower:  daily gain, calf mortality, muscularity, calving interval
17 - Management: stationary; housing: 12 m.;
18 - Conservation progr.: live animals: Yes;Semen: miss;Embryos: miss
19   Status: normal;              Watch: trend,herds!
```

```
20 - Similar breeds (see group 5/4 on page 80)    EN  Country Status
21   Frieiresa                                     90   E    crit.end.
22   Limiana                                      155   E    crit.end.
23   Barrosa                                       21   P    normal
24   Arouquesa                                     11   P    normal
```

```
 1 - Mertolenga                                                    EN  170
 2   Mertolenga; eastern Alentejo and Ribatejo
 3   Associacao de Criadores da Raca Bovina Mertolenga             HB:1979
 4   Evora 7000
 5 - Autochthon variety of Alentejana 5
 6   Incrossing since 1950 from Charolais 62 France
 7   Numbers 1986: 300/20000; HB: 6000; stable; 60 %; Ne = 1143
 8 - Height: 130/120 cm; Weight: 550/350 kg; Herd number: 50; AI: miss
 9   Colour: Uni grey, red, some combination red, white
10   Pecularity: there is a line that is red with white spots
11 - Main use: (1) meat,(2) miss,(3) miss
12   Spec. abilities: twinning
13   Performance compared with STB Charolais:
14     higher: calving ease, calving rate
15     equal:  miss
16     lower:  handling ease, muscularity, daily gain, calving interval
17 - Management: stationary; housing: no; for harsh conditions/husb.
18 - Conservation progr.: live animals: miss;Semen: miss;Embryos: miss
19   Status: minimally endang.; Watch: %pure,%incross!
```

```
20 - Similar breeds (see group 4/6 on page 79)    EN  Country Status
21   Mallorquina                                  164   E    crit.end.
22   Menorqina                                    169   E    crit.end.
23   Berrenda roja andaluza                        30   E    normal
24   Asturiana de Valles                           12   E    normal
```

1 - **Mirandesa**   EN 172
2   **Mirandesa**; northeastern Portugal
3   Associacao dos Criadores da Raca Mirandes - Posto   HB:1959
4   Zootécnico Malhadas, Miranda do Douro 5210
5 - Composite of Berciana, Verinesa Spain
7   Numbers 1986: 3500/50000; HB: 13082; decreasing; 90 %; Ne = 11045
8 - Height: **150/140** cm; Weight: **900/600** kg; Herd number: **40**; AI: **Yes**
9   Colour: **Uni blond to black**
10 Pecularity: **miss**
11 - Main use: (1) **meat**,(2) **tractive power**,(3) **miss**
12 Spec. abilities: **miss**
13 Performance compared with STB **Charolais**:
14   higher: **calving ease,pulling power,calving interval,calving rate**
15   equal: **miss**
16   lower: **muscularity,daily gain,age of sexual maturity,handl. ease**
17 - Management: **stationary**; housing: **> 6 m.**;
18 - Conservation progr.: live animals: **miss**;Semen: **miss**;Embryos: **miss**
19 Status: **normal**
20 - Similar breeds (see group 5/4 on page 80)   EN Country Status
21 **Frieiresa**   90   E   crit.end.
22 **Limiana**   155   E   crit.end.
23 **Barrosa**   21   P   normal
24 **Arouquesa**   11   P   normal

1 - **Raca Brava**   EN 212
2   Fighting Bull; Ribatejo and Alentejo
3   Associacao dos Criadores do Touro de Lide   HB:1986
4   Samora Correia 2135
5 - Composite of Bos Taurus indigenius and Bos Taurus braquiceros
6   Incrossing since 1950 from de Lidia 257 Spain
7   Numbers 1986: 190/7000; HB: 5000; stable; 99 %; Ne = 732
8 - Height: **140/120** cm; Weight: **700/400** kg; Herd number: **15**; AI: **miss**
9   Colour: **Uni black**
10 Pecularity: **miss**
11 - Main use: (1) **sport/hobby**,(2) **meat**,(3) **miss**
12 Spec. abilities: **hardiness, adaptation to poor husbandry conditions**
13 Performance compared with STB **Charolais**:
14   higher: **calving ease, age of sexual maturity, calving rate**
15   equal: **miss**
16   lower: **handling ease, daily gain, muscularity, calving interval**
17 - Management: **stationary**; housing: **no**
18 - Conservation progr.: live animals: **miss**;Semen: **miss**;Embryos: **miss**
19 Status: **potential. endang.**;Watch: **%incross!**
20 - Similar breeds (see group 2/1 on page 76)   EN Country Status
21 **Cardena Andaluza**   60   E   crit.end.
22 **Serrana Negra**   232   E   crit.end.
23 **Race Espagnole**   41   F   pot. end.
24 **Toro de Lidia**   257   E   normal

1 - Badana   EN 406
2   Badana; northeastern Portugal
3   Direccao Regional de Agricultura   HB:1991
4   Mirandela 5370
5 - miss
7   Numbers 1986: 10000/40000; HB: 800; decreasing; 99 %; Ne = 2963
8 - Height: 85/75 cm; Weight: 60/50 kg; Herd number: 400; AI: miss
9   Colour: Uni white
10 Pecularity: horns 2/2,0; often brown face and feet
11 - Main use: (1) meat,(2) milk,(3) wool (coars wool)
12 Spec. abilities: miss
13 Performance compared with STB Portuguese Merino 547:
14   higher: milk yield, wool or fiber thickness, litter size
15   equal: age of sexual maturity,length of mat. season,lambing int.
16   lower: daily gain,muscularity,carcass leanness,% fat,% protein
17 - Management: stationary; housing: 2-6 m.;
18 - Conservation progr.: live animals: miss;Semen: miss;Embryos: miss
19 Status: normal;   Watch: trend!
20 - Similar breeds (see group 8/2 on page 94)   EN Country Status
21 Ibicenca   511   E   crit.end.
22 Palmera   578   E   crit.end.
23 Segurena   625   E   normal
24 Chamarita   449   E   normal

1 - Campanica   EN 443
2   Campanica
3   Direccao-Geral de Pecuaria   HB:1987
4   Lisboa 1100, Largo da Biblioteca Publica 1
5 - Autochthon local breed, Merino 547, Bordaleiro type
6   Incrossing since 1960 from Merino 547 Portugal
7   Numbers 1986: 900/30000; HB: 3500; decreasing; 70 %; Ne = 2864
8 - Height: 78/64 cm; Weight: 65/45 kg; Herd number: 75; AI: miss
9   Colour: Uni white
10 Pecularity: horns 2/0, small brown spots on head and legs
11 - Main use: (1) milk,(2) meat,(3) wool
12 Spec. abilities: cheese
13 Performance compared with STB Portuguese Merino 547:
14   higher: wool or fiber thickness
15   equal: litter size, % fat, % protein, age of sexual maturity
16   lower: daily gain,muscularity,carcass lean.,milk yield,wool yield
17 - Management: stationary; housing: no
18 - Conservation progr.: live animals: miss;Semen: miss;Embryos: miss
19 Status: potential. endang.;Watch: trend,%pure,%incross!
20 - Similar breeds (see group 8/5 on page 95)   EN Country Status
21 Saloia   615   P   normal
22 Serra da Estrela   626   P   normal

```
 1 - Churra Algarvia                                      EN   454
 2   Algarve Churra
 3   Direccao-Geral de Pecuaria                           HB:miss
 4   Lisboa 1100, Largo da Biblioteca Publica 1
 5 - Composite of Andalusian Churro 456, local breed
 7   Numbers 1986: 1000/22000; HB: miss; decreasing; 90 %; Ne = 3826
 8 - Height: 95/85 cm; Weight: 75/55 kg; Herd number: 120; AI: miss
 9   Colour: Uni white
10   Pecularity: horns 2/2, black spotted around eyes and feet
11 - Main use: (1) meat,(2) wool,(3) miss
12   Spec. abilities: miss
13   Performance compared with STB Portuguese Merino 547:
14     higher: wool thickness, litter size, age of sexual maturity
15     equal:  length of mating season, lambing interval, wool yield
16     lower:  muscularity, daily gain, carcass leanness
17 - Management: stationary; housing: no
18 - Conservation progr.: live animals: miss;Semen: miss;Embryos: miss
19   Status: normal;            Watch: trend!
```

20 - Similar breeds (see group 8/4 on page 95)	EN	Country	Status
21 Churra Lebrijana	456	E	endanger.
22 Rubia de El Molar	610	E	pot. end.
23 Galega Mirandesa	494	P	normal
24 Churra da Terra Quente	455	P	normal

```
 1 - Churra da Terra Quente                               EN   455
 2   Churra da Terra Quente; southern Tras-os-Montes
 3   Direccao Regional de Agricultura                     HB:1990
 4   Mirandela 5370
 5 - Autochthon Mondegueira 557
 7   Numbers 1986: 2000/70000; HB: 3000; decreasing; 90 %; Ne = 4800
 8 - Height: 92/84 cm; Weight: 90/60 kg; Herd number: 650; AI: miss
 9   Colour: Uni white
10   Pecularity: horns 2/2
11 - Main use: (1) meat,(2) milk,(3) wool
12   Spec. abilities: 60 % twinning
13   Performance compared with STB Portuguese Merino 547:
14     higher: milk yield, litter size, wool or fiber thickness
15     equal:  % fat,% protein,age of sexual mat.,length of mating season
16     lower:  muscularity,daily gain,carcass leanness,lambing interval
17 - Management: stationary; housing: 2-6 m.;
18 - Conservation progr.: live animals: miss;Semen: miss;Embryos: miss
19   Status: normal;            Watch: trend!
```

20 - Similar breeds (see group 8/4 on page 95)	EN	Country	Status
21 Churra Lebrijana	456	E	endanger.
22 Rubia de El Molar	610	E	pot. end.
23 Galega Mirandesa	494	P	normal
24 Churra Algarvia	454	P	normal

1 - Galega Bragancana e Mirandesa   EN   494
2   Braganca+Miranda Galician; northeastern Portugal
3   Direccao Regional de Agricultura de Tras-os-Montes,   HB:1989
4   Posto Zootecico, Malhadas 5210
5 - Autochthon Portuguese Churro type
7   Numbers 1986: 5600/150000; HB: 5500; decreasing; 95 %; Ne = 11099
8 - Height: 95/85 cm; Weight: 60/40 kg; Herd number: 1000; AI: miss
9   Colour: Uni white; spots around the eyes and on the legs
10 Pecularity: horns 2/2,0
11 - Main use: (1) meat,(2) wool,(3) miss
12 Spec. abilities: miss
13 Performance compared with STB Portuguese Merino 547:
14   higher: litter size, wool or fiber thickness
15   equal: milk yield, % fat, % protein, age of sexual maturity
16   lower: muscularity,daily gain,carcass lean.,length of mat. seas.
17 - Management: stationary; housing: 2-6 m.;
18 - Conservation progr.: live animals: miss;Semen: miss;Embryos: miss
19 Status: normal;   Watch: trend!
20 - Similar breeds (see group 8/4 on page 95)   EN Country Status

		EN	Country	Status
21	Churra Lebrijana	456	E	endanger.
22	Rubia de El Molar	610	E	pot. end.
23	Churra da Terra Quente	455	P	normal
24	Churra Algarvia	454	P	normal

1 - Merino Portugues   EN   547
2   Portuguese Merino; Beira Baixa and Alentejo
3   Direccao-Geral de Pecuaria   HB:1987
4   Lisboa 1100, Largo da Biblioteca Publica 1
5 - Composite of Bordaleiro, Spanish Merino, Rambouillet 553 France,
6   Precose 555 France; incrossing since 1960 from Merino 553 France
7   Numbers 1986: 30000/1000000; HB: 22000; decreasing; 80 %; Ne = 50769
8 - Height: 90/80 cm; Weight: 85/50 kg; Herd number: 390; AI: miss
9   Colour: Uni black, white
10 Pecularity: horns 2/0
11 - Main use: (1) meat,(2) milk,(3) wool
12 Spec. abilities: miss
13 Performance compared with STB Rambouillet:
14   higher: litter size, milk yield, wool or fiber thickness
15   equal: % fat,% protein,age of sex. maturity,length of mat. seas.
16   lower: muscularity,daily gain,carcass leanness,lambing interval
17 - Management: stationary; housing: no
18 - Conservation progr.: live animals: miss;Semen: miss;Embryos: miss
19 Status: normal;   Watch: trend,%pure,%incross!
20 - Similar breeds (see group 1/1 on page 87)   EN Country Status

		EN	Country	Status
21	Merina	545	E	min. end.
22	Merino de Grazalema	546	E	min. end.

```
1 - Mondegueira                                                     EN  557
2   Mondegueira; Beira
3   Direccao Geral de Pecuaria                                     HB:miss
4   Lisboa 1100, Largo da Biblioteca Publica 1
5 - Autochthon Portuguese Churro type
7   Numbers 1986: 2000/60000; HB: miss; decreasing; 90 %; Ne = 7742
8 - Height: 90/80 cm; Weight: 60/50 kg; Herd number: 1400; AI: miss
9   Colour: Uni white
10  Pecularity: horns 2/2, small brown spots on head and legs
11 - Main use: (1) milk,(2) meat,(3) wool
12  Spec. abilities: cheese
13  Performance compared with STB Portuguese Merino 547:
14    higher: milk yield, wool thickness, litter size, wool yield
15    equal:  age of sexual maturity, lambing interval
16    lower:  muscularity,daily gain,carcass leanness,% fat,% protein
17 - Management: stationary; housing: 2-6 m.;
18 - Conservation progr.: live animals: miss;Semen: miss;Embryos: miss
19  Status: normal;              Watch: HB♀♀,trend!
```

20 - Similar breeds (see group 8/4 on page 95)	EN	Country	Status
21 Churra Lebrijana	456	E	endanger.
22 Rubia de El Molar	610	E	pot. end.
23 Churra da Terra Quente	455	P	normal
24 Churra Algarvia	454	P	normal

```
1 - Saloia                                                         EN  615
2   Saloia; Estremadura, near Lisbon and Setubal
3   Direccao-Geral de Pecuaria                                     HB:1988
4   Lisboa 1100, Largo da Biblioteca Publica 1
5 - Autochthon Bordaleiro type
7   Numbers 1986: 2000/55000; HB: 3000; decreasing; 90 %; Ne = 4800
8 - Height: 75/65 cm; Weight: 60/40 kg; Herd number: 250; AI: miss
9   Colour: Uni white
10  Pecularity: horns 2/2, pale brown head and legs
11 - Main use: (1) milk,(2) meat,(3) wool
12  Spec. abilities: miss
13  Performance compared with STB Portuguese Merino 547:
14    higher: milk yield, litter size, wool or fiber thickness
15    equal:  lambing interval
16    lower:  muscularity,daily gain,carcass leanness,% fat,% protein
17 - Management: stationary; housing: no
18 - Conservation progr.: live animals: miss;Semen: miss;Embryos: miss
19  Status: normal;              Watch: trend!
```

20 - Similar breeds (see group 8/5 on page 95)	EN	Country	Status
21 Campanica	443	P	pot. end.
22 Serra da Estrela	626	P	normal

```
 1 - Serra da Estrela                                              EN   626
 2   Serra da Estrela; Guarda, Viseu and Coimbra
 3   Associacao Nacional de Criadores de Ovinos da Serra          HB:1986
 4   da Estrela (ANCOSE), Oliveira do Hospital 3400
 5 - Composite of Bordaleiro type
 7   Numbers 1986: 8000/280000; HB: 3500; stable; 90 %; Ne = 9739
 8 - Height: 90/80 cm; Weight: 70/50 kg; Herd number: 650; AI: miss
 9   Colour: Uni black, white
10   Pecularity: horns 2/2
11 - Main use: (1) milk,(2) meat,(3) wool
12   Spec. abilities: cheese
13   Performance compared with STB Portuguese Merino 547:
14     higher: milk yield, litter size, wool or fiber thickness
15     equal:  age of sexual maturity, lambing interval
16     lower:  muscularity,daily gain,carcass leanness,% fat,% protein
17 - Management: transhumant; housing: no
18 - Conservation progr.: live animals: miss;Semen: miss;Embryos: miss
19   Status: normal
```

20 - <u>Similar breeds</u> (see group 8/5 on page 95)   <u>EN</u> <u>Country</u> <u>Status</u>

		EN	Country	Status
21	Campanica	443	P	pot. end.
22	Saloia	615	P	normal

```
 1 - Charnequeira                                                  EN   318
 2   Charnequeira; Alentejo and Beira Baixa
 3   Direccao-Geral de Pecuaria                                   HB:1988
 4   Lisboa 1100, Largo da Biblioteca Publica 1
 5 - Autochthon local breed originated of Algarvia
 7   Numbers 1986: 950/35000; HB: 4000; decreasing; 95 %; Ne = 3071
 8 - Height: 75/70 cm; Weight: 50/35 kg; Herd number: 98; AI: miss
 9   Colour: Uni red, yellow
10   Pecularity: horns 2,0/2,0, wide twisted, lyra-shaped horns
11 - Main use: (1) meat,(2) milk,(3) vegetation management
12   Spec. abilities: miss
13   Performance compared with STB Saanen:
14     higher: length of mating season,% fat,% protein,age of sexual mat.
15     equal:  muscularity
16     lower:  milk yield,daily gain,carc.lean.,litter size,lamb.interv.
17 - Management: stationary; housing: no
18 - Conservation progr.: live animals: miss;Semen: miss;Embryos: miss
19   Status: normal;                Watch: trend!
```

20 - <u>Similar breeds</u> (see group 8 on page 98)   <u>EN</u> <u>Country</u> <u>Status</u>

		EN	Country	Status
21	Derivata di Siria	323	I	crit.end.
22	Cabra Mallorquina	313	E	min. end.
23	Murciana-Granadina	340	E	normal
24	Negra Serrana	316	E	normal

```
 1 - Serpentina                                              EN   354
 2   Serpentina; southern Portugal
 3   Direccao-Geral de Pecuaria                             HB:miss
 4   Lisboa 1100, Largo da Biblioteca Publica 1
 5 - Imported as breed from country Spain
 7   Numbers 1986: 3300/100000; HB: miss; decreasing; 95 %; Ne = 12778
 8 - Height: 75/70 cm; Weight: 60/45 kg; Herd number: 350; AI: miss
 9   Colour: Combination black, white
10   Pecularity: black spotted on head and hump
11 - Main use: (1) meat,(2) milk,(3) vegetation management
12   Spec. abilities: miss
13   Performance compared with STB Saanen:
14     higher: length of mating season,% fat,% protein,age of sex. mat.
15     equal:  lambing interval
16     lower:  milk yield,muscularity,daily gain,carc. lean.,litter size
17 - Management: stationary; housing: no
18 - Conservation progr.: live animals: miss;Semen: miss;Embryos: miss
19   Status: normal;              Watch: HB♀♀,trend!
20 - Similar breeds (see group 7 on page 98)     EN  Country Status
21   Vallesana                                   365  I     crit.end.
22   Walliser Schwarzhalsziege                   366  CH    normal
```

```
 1 - Serrana                                                 EN   355
 2   Serrana; north of Tagus river
 3   Direccao-Geral de Pecuaria                             HB:1985
 4   Lisboa 1100, Largo da Biblioteca Publica 1
 5 - Autochthon local mountain population
 7   Numbers 1986: 6250/241000; HB: 15000; stable; 95 %; Ne = 17647
 8 - Height: 65/60 cm; Weight: 45/35 kg; Herd number: 180; AI: miss
 9   Colour: Uni black, grey, brown
10   Pecularity: horns 2,0/2,0; long hair
11 - Main use: (1) milk,(2) meat,(3) vegetation management
12   Spec. abilities: miss
13   Performance compared with STB Saanen:
14     higher: length of mating season, age of sexual maturity
15     equal:  litter size, milk yield, % fat, % protein
16     lower:  carcass leanness,muscularity,daily gain,lambing interval
17 - Management: stationary; housing: no
18 - Conservation progr.: live animals: miss;Semen: miss;Embryos: miss
19   Status: normal
20 - Similar breeds (see group 9 on page 98)     EN  Country Status
21   Roccaverano                                 347  I     crit.end.
22   Val di Livo (extinct)                       363  I     crit.end.
23   Local breeds                                338  GR    normal
24   Corse                                       320  F     normal
```

```
1  - Alentejana                                                    EN   902
2    Alentejana; south of Tagus river (Alentejo)
3    Associacao de Criadores do Suino Alentejano                   HB:1985
4    Elvas 7350
5  - Autochthon last native breed that remains today; incrossing
6    since 1970 from Large White 1023 United Kingdom
7    Numbers 1986: 1734/8500; HB: 6861; stable; 70 %; Ne = 5537
8  - Height: miss/miss cm; Weight: 180/150 kg; Herd number: 120; AI: miss
9    Colour: Uni black, brown
10   Pecularity: miss
11 - Main use: (1) meat,(2) miss,(3) miss
12   Spec. abilities: smoked charcuterie products
13   Performance compared with STB Large White:
14     higher: meat quality, age of sexual maturity, farrowing interval
15     equal:  handling ease, piglet mortality, live weight at slaughter
16     lower:  % lean,litter size,feed conversion rate,daily gain,muscul.
17 - Management: stationary; housing: > 6 m.; extensive condit. outdoors
18 - Conservation progr.: live animals: miss;Semen: miss;Embryos: miss
19   Status: normal;              Watch: %pure,%incross!
20 - Similar breeds (see group 4/1 on page 103)   EN  Country Status
21   Gascon                                        935   F    crit.end.
22   Large Black                                   959   GB   min. end.
23   Negra Iberica                                 981   E    normal
```

```
1  - Garrano                                                       EN   749
2    Garrano; mountainous areas in northwestern Portugal
3    Direccao-Geral de Pecuaria                                    HB:miss
4    Lisboa 1100, Largo da Biblioteca Publica 1
5  - miss
7    Numbers 1986: 200/2000; HB: miss; stable; 95 %; Ne = 727
8  - Height: 130/120 cm; Weight: 380/300 kg; Herd number: 3; AI: miss
9    Colour: bay
10   Pecularity: miss
11 - Main use: (1) tractive power,(2) sport/hobby,(3) miss
12   Spec. abilities: miss
13   Performance compared with STB Arab:
14     higher: handling ease
15     equal:  fertility, age of sexual maturity
16     lower:  adaptability in jumping and in military, speed in gallop
17 - Management: stationary; housing: 2-6 m.; mountain
18 - Conservation progr.: live animals: miss;Semen: miss;Embryos: miss
19   Status: minimally endang.; Watch: HB♀♀,herds,%pure!
20 - Similar breeds (see group 5/10 on page 111)  EN  Country Status
21   Sorraia                                       807   P    crit.end.
22   Skyos Pony                                    806   GR   endanger.
23   Pottok                                        794   F    pot. end.
24   Cavallo Bardigiano                            718   I    normal
```

1 - **Lusitano**   EN   780
2   Lusitanian; Ribatejo and Alentejo
3   Associacao Portuguesa de Racas Selectas   HB:1973
4   Lisboa 1100, Rua Dom Dinis 2
5 - Autochthon local horse, Arab, Barb, nordic horses
6   Incrossing since 1950 from Andaluza 742 Spain, Arab Spain
7   Numbers 1986: 140/2000; HB: 950; stable; 75 %; Ne = **488**
8 - Height: **157/152** cm; Weight: **500/450** kg; Herd number: 30; AI: miss
9   Colour: **any solid colour**
10 Pecularity: miss
11 - Main use: (1) **sport/hobby**,(2) miss,(3) miss
12 Spec. abilities: miss
13 Performance compared with STB **Arab**:
14   higher: **handling ease, adaptability in dressage and in military**
15   equal: **pulling power, fertility, age of sexual maturity**
16   lower: **adaptability in jumping, speed in gallop**
17 - Management: **stationary**; housing: **2-6 m.**;
18 - Conservation progr.: live animals: miss;Semen: miss;Embryos: miss
19 Status: **potential. endang.**;Watch: **%pure,%incross!**
20 - Similar breeds (see group 3/1 on page 108)   EN Country Status
21 **Lipizzan**   776 F   crit.end.
22 **Senner**   801 D   crit.end.
23 **Espanol-Andaluz**   742 E   normal
24 **Lusitanien**   779 F   normal

1 - **Sorraia**   EN   807
2   Sorraia; near Elyas (Alentejo)
3   Herdade de Fontalva, Barbacena   HB:miss
4   Elvas 7350
5 - miss
7   Numbers 1986: 6/30; HB: miss; stable; 100 %; Ne = **9**
8 - Height: **145/140** cm; Weight: **450/400** kg; Herd number: 2; AI: miss
9   Colour: **dun with zebra-striped legs, "Tarpan-like"**
10 Pecularity: miss
11 - Main use: (1) **sport/hobby**,(2) miss,(3) miss
12 Spec. abilities: **well adapted to hard conditions**
13 Performance compared with STB **Arab**:
14   higher: **handling ease**
15   equal: **age of sexual maturity**
16   lower: **adapt. in jumping,pulling power,speed in gallop,fertility**
17 - Management: **stationary**; housing: **no**
18 - Conservation progr.: live animals: miss;Semen: miss;Embryos: miss
19 Status: **critically endang.**;Watch: **♂♂,HB♀♀,herds!**
20 - Similar breeds (see group 5/10 on page 111)   EN Country Status
21 **Skyos Pony**   806 GR   endanger.
22 **Garrano**   749 P   min. end.
23 **Pottok**   794 F   pot. end.
24 **Cavallo Bardigiano**   718 I   normal

```
 1 - Baltata cu negru romanesca                                    EN   19
 2   Romanian Holstein-Friesian; Moldau, Valechei
 3   Centrul National de Reproductie si Selectie a                HB:1970
 4   Animalelor Balotesti 8113
 5 - Composite of Rosie Dobrogeana, Bruna de Maramures, Sura de Stepa
 6   Incrossing since 1950 from Holstein-Friesian USA,277 NL,245 Denmark
 7   Numbers 1986: 228/650000; HB: 74021; increasing; 98 %; Ne = 909
 8 - Height: 143/132 cm; Weight: 1000/550 kg; Herd number: miss; AI: Yes
 9   Colour: Combination black, white
10   Pecularity: horns 2/2
11 - Main use: (1) milk,(2) meat,(3) tractive power
12   Spec. abilities: high fertility
13   Performance compared with STB Romanian Simmental 20:
14     higher: milk yield,calving ease and rate,calf mortal.,milkability
15     equal:  handling ease
16     lower:  muscularity, daily gain, calving interv., age of sex. mat.
17 - Management: stationary; housing: 2-6 m.;
18 - Conservation progr.: live animals: Yes;Semen: Yes;Embryos: miss
19   Status: normal;              Watch: %incross!
20 - Similar breeds (see group 1/4 on page 75)    EN  Country Status
21   Nizinne cernostrakate                        184  CS     normal
22   Schwarzbuntes Milchrind                      229  D*     normal
23   Crno-belo                                     71  YU     normal
```

```
 1 - Baltata Romanesca                                             EN   20
 2   Romanian Simmental; Siebenbürgen (Transilvania)
 3   Centrul National de Reproductie si Selectia                  HB:1914
 4   Animalelor, Balotesti 8113
 5 - Composite of Sura de Stepa, Simmental, Fleckvieh; incrossing
 6   since 1950 from Simmental 240 Switzerland, Fleckvieh 78 Germany
 7   Numbers 1986: 537/825000; HB: 112058; stable; 92 %; Ne = 2138
 8 - Height: 148/134 cm; Weight: 1100/600 kg; Herd number: miss; AI: Yes
 9   Colour: Combination yellow, white
10   Pecularity: white head, tail and feets
11 - Main use: (1) meat,(2) milk,(3) tractive power
12   Spec. abilities: good meat quality
13   Performance compared with STB German Simmental 78:
14     higher: milk yield, milkability, muscularity, daily gain, % fat
15     equal:  calving ease,calving interval,handling ease,calf mortality
16     lower:  age of sexual maturity
17 - Management: stationary; housing: 2-6 m.;
18 - Conservation progr.: live animals: Yes;Semen: Yes;Embryos: miss
19   Status: normal;              Watch: %incross!
20 - Similar breeds (see group 3/2 on page 77)    EN  Country Status
21   Ceske strakate                               61  CZ     crit.end.
22   Simentalska                                 237  PL     min. end.
23   Montbeliard                                 176  F      normal
24   Fleckvieh                                    88  A      normal
```

```
1 - Bruna de Maramures                                        EN   47
2   Romanian Brown; Maramures
3   Centrul National de Reproductie si Selectia              HB:1914
4   Animalelor, Balotesti 8113
5 - Composite of Sura de Stepa, Mocanita, Braunvieh; incrossing
6   since 1950 from Braunvieh 40 Switzerland, 190 Austria, 77 Germany
7   Numbers 1986: 287/600000; HB: 71005; decreasing; 90 %; Ne = 1143
8 - Height: 142/130 cm; Weight: 1050/550 kg; Herd number: miss; AI: Yes
9   Colour: Uni brown
10  Pecularity: miss
11 - Main use: (1) milk,(2) meat,(3) tractive power
12  Spec. abilities: miss
13  Performance compared with STB Romanian Simmental 20:
14    higher: milk yield, calving ease, calf mortality, calving rate
15    equal:  handling ease
16    lower:  muscularity, daily gain, % fat, calving interval
17 - Management: stationary; housing: > 6 m.; mountain
18 - Conservation progr.: live animals: Yes;Semen: Yes;Embryos: miss
19  Status: normal;              Watch: %incross!
```

20 - Similar breeds (see group 5/1 on page 79)	EN	Country	Status
21 Original Allgäuer Braunvieh	189	D	crit.end.
22 Agerolese	2	I	crit.end.
23 Aubrac	14	F	normal
24 Österreichisches Braunvieh	190	A	normal

ROMANIA   CATTLE

```
1 - Pinzgau de Transilvania                                   EN  201
2   Romanian Pinzgau; Siebenbürgen
3   Centrul National de Reproductie si Selectia              HB:1959
4   Animalelor, Balotesti 8113
5 - Composite of Pinzgau, Sura de Stepa
6   Incrossing since 1950 from Pinzgauer 202 Austria
7   Numbers 1986: 9/47000; HB: 2300; stable; 75 %; Ne = 18
8 - Height: 134/127 cm; Weight: 900/500 kg; Herd number: miss; AI: Yes
9   Colour: Combination red, white
10  Pecularity: red sided, broad white back
11 - Main use: (1) milk,(2) meat,(3) tractive power
12  Spec. abilities: miss
13  Performance compared with STB Romanian Simmental 20:
14    higher: calving ease, calf mortality, pulling power
15    equal:  % fat
16    lower:  daily gain,age of sex. maturity,handling ease,milkability
17 - Management: stationary; housing: 2-6 m.; mountain
18 - Conservation progr.: live animals: Yes;Semen: Yes;Embryos: miss
19  Status: critically endang.;Watch: ♂♂,%pure,%incross!
```

20 - Similar breeds (see group 3/4 on page 77)	EN	Country	Status
21 Pustertaler Schecken	210	D	crit.end.
22 Pinzgauer	200	I	crit.end.
23 Pinzgauer	202	A	pot. end.
24 Slovenske pinzgavske	243	SK	normal

```
 1 - Sura de Stepa                                          EN  248
 2   Romanian Steppe; Moldau, Donau-Delta
 3   Centrul National de Reproductie si Selectia            HB:1924
 4   Animalelor, Balotesti 8113
 5 - Autochthon Bos Taurus Primigenues
 7   Numbers 1986: 18/500; HB: 60; decreasing; 85 %; Ne = 32
 8 - Height: 130/118 cm; Weight: 600/300 kg; Herd number: miss; AI: Yes
 9   Colour: Uni grey
10   Pecularity: huge horns, black muzzle, black tail-tip
11 - Main use: (1) tractive power,(2) meat,(3) milk
12   Spec. abilities: resistant to tuberculosis, leucosis; stayability
13   Performance compared with STB Romanian Simmental 20:
14     higher: % fat, calving ease, calving interval, age of sex.maturity
15     equal:  handling ease
16     lower:  milkability,milk yield,muscularity,daily gain,calving rate
17 - Management: transhumant; housing: ≈ 2 m.;
18 - Conservation progr.: live animals: Yes;Semen: 5;Embryos: miss
19   Status: endangered;        Watch: ♂♂,HB♀♀,trend,%pure!
20 - Similar breeds (see group 6/1 on page 80)    EN  Country Status
21   Iskursko govedo                                104  BG   crit.end.
22   Katerini                                       136  GR   crit.end.
23   Piemontese                                     197  I    normal
24   Maremmana                                      166  I    normal
```

```
 1 - Karakul                                                EN  519
 2   Karakul; northern and central Moldavia
 3   Ministry of Agriculture                                HB:miss
 4   Bucharest, B-dul Carol 24
 5 - Imported as breed from country Uzbekistan
 6   Incrossing since 1960 from Karakul USSR, East Germany
 7   Numbers 1984: 12800/296000; HB: miss; increasing; miss %; Ne = 49078
 8 - Height: 64/62 cm; Weight: 63/42 kg; Herd number: miss; AI: miss
 9   Colour: Uni black, grey, brown, white
10   Pecularity: horns 2/ miss
11 - Main use: (1) wool,(2) milk,(3) meat
12   Spec. abilities: miss
13   Performance compared with STB Palas Merino 552:
14     higher: milk yield,age of sex. mat.,lambing interval,wool thickn.
15     equal:  miss
16     lower:  muscularity, daily gain, carcass leanness, litter size
17 - Management: miss; housing: miss m.;
18 - Conservation progr.: live animals: miss;Semen: miss;Embryos: miss
19   Status: normal;            Watch: HB♀♀,%incross!
20 - Similar breeds                           EN  Country Status
21   miss                                    miss  miss   miss
```

```
 1 - Merinos de Palas                                        EN   552
 2   Palas Merino; southern Moldavia
 3   Ministry of Agriculture                                 HB:1926
 4   Bucharest, B-dul Carol 24
 5 - Composite of Tsigai, Turcana, Stogosa, Rambouillet, Merino Mutton
 6   549 Germany; incrossing since 1960 from Merino Australia
 7   Numbers 1984: 54000/664000; HB: miss; increasing; miss %; Ne=199755
 8 - Height: 73/65 cm; Weight: 105/60 kg; Herd number: miss; AI: Yes
 9   Colour: Uni white
10   Pecularity: horns 2/ 0
11 - Main use: (1) wool,(2) milk,(3) meat
12   Spec. abilities: miss
13   Performance compared with STB Palas Merino 552:
14     higher: Breed is used
15     equal:  as standard breed,
16     lower:  no comparison possible.
17 - Management: miss; housing: miss m.;
18 - Conservation progr.: live animals: miss;Semen: miss;Embryos: miss
19   Status: normal;           Watch: HB♀♀,%incross!
```

20 - Similar breeds (see group 1/5 on page 87)	EN	Country	Status
21 Polish Merino	583	PL	normal
22 Merinos Transilvanean	556	RO	normal
23 Czech Merino	475	CZ	normal

```
 1 - Merinos Transilvanean                                   EN   556
 2   Transylvanian Merino; western lowland
 3   Ministry of Agriculture                                 HB:1936
 4   Bucharest, B-dul Carol 24
 5 - Composite of Hungarian Merino, Rambouillet, Negretti
 6   Incrossing since 1960 from Groznensk Merino USSR
 7   Numbers 1984: 65000/832000; HB: miss; increasing; miss %; Ne=241159
 8 - Height: 67/61 cm; Weight: 84/48 kg; Herd number: miss; AI: miss
 9   Colour: Uni white
10   Pecularity: horns 2/ miss
11 - Main use: (1) miss,(2) meat,(3) milk
12   Spec. abilities: miss
13   Performance compared with STB Palas Merino 552:
14     higher: miss
15     equal:  milk yield, wool or fiber thickness
16     lower:  muscularity, daily gain, carcass leanness, wool yield
17 - Management: miss; housing: miss m.;
18 - Conservation progr.: live animals: miss;Semen: miss;Embryos: miss
19   Status: normal;           Watch: HB♀♀,%incross!
```

20 - Similar breeds (see group 1/5 on page 87)	EN	Country	Status
21 Polish Merino	583	PL	normal
22 Merinos de Palas	552	RO	normal
23 Czech Merino	475	CZ	normal

```
 1 - Tigaie                                             EN   655
 2   Tsigai; foot hills of Transylvania
 3   Ministry of Agriculture                            HB:miss
 4   Bucharest, B-dul Carol 24
 5 - Autochthon ancient nature semi fine wool sheep
 7   Numbers 1984: 92000/2400000; HB: miss; increasing; miss %; Ne=354414
 8 - Height: 67/63 cm; Weight: 58/41 kg; Herd number: miss; AI: miss
 9   Colour: Uni white
10   Pecularity: horns 2/ 0, face and legs are brown
11 - Main use: (1) wool,(2) milk,(3) meat
12   Spec. abilities: miss
13   Performance compared with STB Palas Merino 552:
14     higher: milk yield,age of sexual mat.,lambing interval,wool yield
15     equal:  miss
16     lower:  muscularity, daily gain, carcass leanness, litter size
17 - Management: miss; housing: miss m.;
18 - Conservation progr.: live animals: miss;Semen: miss;Embryos: miss
19   Status: normal;              Watch: HB♀♀,%pure!
```

20 - Similar breeds (see group 7/7 on page 93)	EN	Country	Status
21 Cigaja	460	H	endanger.
22 Kivircik	654	GR	pot. end.
23 Cigaja	461	YU	normal
24 Cigaja	459	CS	normal

```
 1 - Turcana                                            EN   600
 2   Romanian Zackel; Carpathian Mountains
 3   Ministry of Agriculture                            HB:miss
 4   Bucharest, B-dul Carol 24
 5 - Autochthon ancient native coarse-wool breed
 7   Numbers 1984: 2500/27008; HB: miss; increasing; 50 %; Ne = 9153
 8 - Height: 67/62 cm; Weight: 65/43 kg; Herd number: miss; AI: Yes
 9   Colour: Uni black, grey, white
10   Pecularity: horns 2/2, face and legs brown
11 - Main use: (1) wool,(2) milk,(3) meat
12   Spec. abilities: miss
13   Performance compared with STB Palas Merino 552:
14     higher: milk yield,age of sex. mat.,lambing interval,wool yield
15     equal:  carcass leanness
16     lower:  muscularity, daily gain, litter size
17 - Management: miss; housing: miss m.;
18 - Conservation progr.: live animals: miss;Semen: miss;Embryos: miss
19   Status: normal;              Watch: HB♀♀,%pure!
```

20 - Similar breeds (see group 7/6 on page 92)	EN	Country	Status
21 Florina	490	GR	endanger.
22 Ruda Dubrovacka Sheep	611	HR	endanger.
23 Karagouniko	518	GR	normal
24 Sazakatsaniko	429	GR	normal

```
1 - Carpatina Cashgora                                    EN  315
2   Carpathian Goat
3   Ministry of Agriculture                               HB:miss
4   Bucharest, B-dul Carol 24
5 - Autochthon local goat of Carpathia
7   Numbers 1984: 15000/633000; HB: miss; increasing; miss %; Ne = 58611
8 - Height: 100/89 cm; Weight: 53/44 kg; Herd number: miss; AI: miss
9   Colour: Uni black, grey, brown, white
10  Pecularity: horns 2/2, long hair
11 - Main use: (1) milk,(2) meat,(3) miss
12  Spec. abilities: miss
13  Performance compared with STB Carpathian Goat 315:
14    higher: Breed is used
15    equal:  as standard breed,
16    lower:  no comparison possible.
17 - Management: miss; housing: miss m.;
18 - Conservation progr.: live animals: miss;Semen: miss;Embryos: miss
19  Status: normal;           Watch: HB♀♀!
20 - Similar breeds (see group 1 on page 97)    EN  Country Status
21  Irish Goat                                  336   IRL   min. end.
22  Blanche                                     308   B     pot. end.
23  Gessenay                                    350   F     normal
24  Bila kratkosrsta                            306   CS    normal
```

```
1 - Duroc                                                 EN  931
2   Duroc; country-wide
3   Ministry of Agriculture                               HB:1969
4   Bucharest, B-dul Carol 24
5 - Imported as breed from country USA
6   Incrossing since 1970 from Duroc USA
7   Numbers 1983: 650/6765; HB: miss; increasing; 100 %; Ne = 2372
8 - Height: miss/miss cm; Weight: 280/220 kg; Herd number: miss; AI:miss
9   Colour: Uni red
10  Pecularity: lop ears
11 - Main use: (1) meat,(2) miss,(3) miss
12  Spec. abilities: miss
13  Performance compared with STB Large White 962:
14    higher: meat quality, daily gain
15    equal:  % lean, feed conversion rate, age of sexual maturity
16    lower:  litter size
17 - Management: miss; housing: miss m.;
18 - Conservation progr.: live animals: miss;Semen: miss;Embryos: miss
19  Status: normal;           Watch: HB♀♀!
20 - Similar breeds (see group 5/1 on page 103)  EN  Country Status
21  Duroc                                       927   F     crit.end.
22  Duroc                                       932   GB    crit.end.
23  Duroc                                       929   I     normal
24  Duroc                                       926   CS    normal
```

```
1 - Hampshire                                           EN   944
2   Hampshire; country-wide
3   Ministry of Agriculture                             HB:1969
4   Bucharest, B-dul Carol 24
5 - Imported as breed from country USA
6   Incrossing since 1970 from Hampshire USA
7   Numbers 1983: 155/1740; HB: miss; decreasing; 100 %; Ne = 569
8 - Height: miss/miss cm; Weight: 270/220 kg; Herd number: miss; AI:miss
9   Colour: Combination black, white
10  Pecularity: white saddle, erect ears
11 - Main use: (1) meat,(2) miss,(3) miss
12  Spec. abilities: meat
13  Performance compared with STB Large White 962:
14     higher: % lean, muscularity
15     equal:  feed conversion rate, meat quality, age of sexual maturity
16     lower:  litter size, daily gain, handling ease
17 - Management: miss; housing: miss m.;
18 - Conservation progr.: live animals: miss;Semen: miss;Embryos: miss
19  Status: potential. endang.;Watch: HB♀♀,trend!
```

20 - Similar breeds (see group 3/2 on page 102)	EN	Country	Status
21	Limousin	967	F	crit.end.
22	Hampshire	942	D*	crit.end.
23	Porcul de Banat	993	RO	pot. end.
24	Hampshire	940	CS	normal

```
1 - Landrace                                            EN   955
2   Romanian Landrace; country-wide
3   Ministry of Agriculture                             HB:1958
4   Bucharest, B-dul Carol 24
5 - Imported as breed from countries United Kingdom, Sweden
6   Incrossing since 1970 from Landrace Sweden, 911 United Kingdom
7   Numbers 1983: 3530/39840; HB: miss; decreasing; 47 %; Ne = 12971
8 - Height: miss/miss cm; Weight: 270/220 kg; Herd number: miss; AI: Yes
9   Colour: Uni white
10  Pecularity: lop ears
11 - Main use: (1) meat,(2) miss,(3) miss
12  Spec. abilities: miss
13  Performance compared with STB Large White 962:
14     higher: % lean, age of sexual maturity, muscularity
15     equal:  litter size,feed conversion rate,meat quality,daily gain
16     lower:  piglet mortality
17 - Management: miss; housing: miss m.;
18 - Conservation progr.: live animals: miss;Semen: miss;Embryos: miss
19  Status: normal;          Watch: HB♀♀,trend,%incross,%pure!
```

20 - Similar breeds (see group 2/1 on page 101)	EN	Country	Status
21	Belgische Landrasse	907	D*	crit.end.
22	Zlotnicka biala	1024	PL	crit.end.
23	Landrace	952	CS	normal
24	Belgisch Landvarken	906	B	normal

```
 1 - Large White                                             EN  962
 2   Large White; country-wide
 3   Ministry of Agriculture                                 HB:1958
 4   Bucharest, B-dul Carol 24
 5 - Imported as breed from countries United Kingdom, USSR
 6   Incrossing since 1970 from Large White 1023 United Kingdom
 7   Numbers 1983: 7125/89815; HB: miss; increasing; 44 %; Ne = 26405
 8 - Height: miss/miss cm; Weight: 280/220 kg; Herd number: miss; AI: Yes
 9   Colour: Uni white
10   Pecularity: erect ears
11 - Main use: (1) meat,(2) miss,(3) miss
12   Spec. abilities: adapts at diets with lower protein quality
13   Performance compared with STB Romanian Landrace 955:
14     higher: piglet mortality
15     equal:  litter size,feed conversion rate,meat quality,daily gain
16     lower:  % lean, age of sexual maturity, muscularity
17 - Management: miss; housing: miss m.;
18 - Conservation progr.: live animals: miss;Semen: miss;Embryos: miss
19   Status: normal;              Watch: HB♀♀,%pure!
```

20 - Similar breeds (see group 1/2 on page 101)	EN	Country	Status
21 Bela Zlahtna	904	SLO	crit.end.
22 Middle White	975	GB	min. end.
23 Deutsches Edelschwein	922	D*	normal
24 Vile uslechtile	1017	CS	normal

```
 1 - Mangalita                                               EN  973
 2   Mangalitsa; Transilvania
 3   Ministry of Agriculture                                 HB:1958
 4   Bucharest, B-dul Carol 24
 5 - Imported as breed from countries Austria, Hungary, Serbia
 7   Numbers 1983: 70/500; HB: miss; decreasing; 50 %; Ne = 246
 8 - Height: 74/68 cm; Weight: 150/140 kg; Herd number: miss; AI: miss
 9   Colour: Uni red, white
10   Pecularity: lop ears
11 - Main use: (1) meat,(2) miss,(3) miss
12   Spec. abilities: adap. to adverse conditions of feeding and managing
13   Performance compared with STB Large White 962:
14     higher: meat quality
15     equal:  farrowing interval, handling ease, piglet mortality
16     lower:  % lean, litter size, feed conversion rate, daily gain
17 - Management: miss; housing: miss m.;
18 - Conservation progr.: live animals: miss;Semen: miss;Embryos: miss
19   Status: minimally endang.; Watch: HB♀♀,trend,%pure!
```

20 - Similar breeds (see group 2/2 on page 102)	EN	Country	Status
21 Normand	982	F	crit.end.
22 Chester White	913	GB	crit.end.
23 Mangalica	972	H	min. end.
24 Schwalbenbauch Mangalitza	1020	CH	pot. end.

```
1 - Porcul de Banat                                    EN   993
2   Bazna
3   Ministry of Agriculture                            HB:1958
4   Bucharest, B-dul Carol 24
5 - Composite of Berkshire, Mangalitza
7   Numbers 1983: 150/2200; HB: miss; stable; 50 %; Ne = 562
8 - Height: 74/72 cm; Weight: 170/150 kg; Herd number: miss; AI: miss
9   Colour: Combination black, white
10  Pecularity: white saddle
11 - Main use: (1) meat,(2) miss,(3) miss
12  Spec. abilities: adap. to adverse conditions of feeding and managing
13  Performance compared with STB Large White 962:
14    higher: meat quality, piglet mortality
15    equal:  farrowing interval, handling ease
16    lower:  % lean, litter size, feed conversion rate, daily gain
17 - Management: miss; housing: miss m.;
18 - Conservation progr.: live animals: miss;Semen: miss;Embryos: miss
19  Status: potential. endang.;Watch: HB♀♀,%pure!
```

20 - Similar breeds (see group 3/2 on page 102)	EN	Country	Status
21 Limousin	967	F	crit.end.
22 Hampshire	942	D*	crit.end.
23 Hampshire	944	RO	pot. end.
24 Hampshire	940	CS	normal

```
1 - Yorkshire                                          EN 1022
2   Yorkshire; country-wide
3   Ministry of Agriculture                            HB:1969
4   Bucharest, B-dul Carol 24
5 - Imported as breed from country USA
6   Incrossing since 1970 from Yorkshire USA
7   Numbers 1983: 70/700; HB: miss; decreasing; 100 %; Ne = 255
8 - Height: miss/miss cm; Weight: 270/220 kg; Herd number: miss; AI:miss
9   Colour: Uni white
10  Pecularity: erect ears
11 - Main use: (1) meat,(2) miss,(3) miss
12  Spec. abilities: miss
13  Performance compared with STB Large White 962:
14    higher: feed conversion rate, daily gain
15    equal:  % lean,meat quality,age of sex. maturity,farrowing interv.
16    lower:  litter size, piglet mortality
17 - Management: miss; housing: miss m.;
18 - Conservation progr.: live animals: miss;Semen: miss;Embryos: miss
19  Status: potential. endang.;Watch: HB♀♀,trend!
```

20 - Similar breeds (see group 1/2 on page 101)	EN	Country	Status
21 Bela Zlahtna	904	SLO	crit.end.
22 Middle White	975	GB	min. end.
23 Deutsches Edelschwein	922	D*	normal
24 Vile uslechtile	1017	CS	normal

1 - Slovenske pinzgavske   EN 243
2   Slovakian Pinzgau; country-wide
3   State Breeding Organization   HB:1925
4   Bratislava 85227, Starohajska cesta 29
5 - Composite of Carpathian Grey, Carpathian Red, Pinzgau 202 Austria
6   Incrossing since 1950 from Pinzgau 202 Austria
7   Numbers 1986: 70/67000; HB: 1000; stable; 100 %; Ne = 262
8 - Height: 136/128 cm; Weight: 850/550 kg; Herd number: miss; AI: Yes
9   Colour: Combination red, brown, white
10 Pecularity: broad white stripe on back and belly
11 - Main use: (1) milk,(2) meat,(3) miss
12 Spec. abilities: miss
13 Performance compared with STB Bohemian Red Pied 61:
14   higher: miss
15   equal: muscularity,daily gain,calving ease,age of sexual maturity
16   lower: milk yield,% fat,% protein,calving interval,calf mortality
17 - Management: stationary; housing: 12 m.;
18 - Conservation progr.: live animals: miss;Semen: 33;Embryos: 30/30
19 Status: normal;   Watch: %incross!
20 - Similar breeds (see group 3/4 on page 77)   EN Country Status
21 Pustertaler Schecken   210   D   crit.end.
22 Pinzgauer   200   I   crit.end.
23 Pinzgauer   203   D   pot. end.
24 Pinzgauer   202   A   pot. end.

1 - Slovenske strakate   EN 244
2   Slovakian Simmental; country-wide
3   State Breeding Organization   HB:1925
4   Bratislava 85227, Starohajska cesta 29
5 - Composite of Grey Steppe, Carpathian Grey, Carpathian Red;incrossing
6   since 1950 from Simmental 240 Switzerland, Red Pied 74 Germany
7   Numbers 1986: 150/234000; HB: 3500; stable; 100 %; Ne = 575
8 - Height: 146/135 cm; Weight: 1100/650 kg; Herd number: miss; AI: Yes
9   Colour: Combination red, yellow, white
10 Pecularity: miss
11 - Main use: (1) milk,(2) meat,(3) miss
12 Spec. abilities: miss
13 Performance compared with STB Bohemian Red Pied 61:
14   higher: calf mortality
15   equal: muscularity,daily gain,calving ease,age of sexual maturity
16   lower: milk yield, % fat, % protein,calving interval,calving rate
17 - Management: stationary; housing: 12 m.;
18 - Conservation progr.: live animals: miss;Semen: 33;Embryos: 30/30
19 Status: normal;   Watch: %incross!
20 - Similar breeds (see group 3/2 on page 77)   EN Country Status
21 Ceske strakate   61   CZ   crit.end.
22 Simentalska   237   PL   min. end.
23 Montbeliard   176   F   normal
24 Fleckvieh   88   A   normal

445

PIGS

1 - Slovenske biele mäsove   EN 1004
2   Slovakian White; country-wide
3   State Breeding Organization   HB:1980
4   Bratislava 85227, Starohajska cesta 29
5 - Composite of Czech Improved White, Landrace
7   Numbers 1986: 1185/16800; HB: 6490; stable; 19 %; Ne = 4008
8 - Height: 91/78 cm; Weight: 290/200 kg; Herd number: miss; AI: Yes
9   Colour: Uni white
10 Pecularity: miss
11 - Main use: (1) meat,(2) miss,(3) miss
12 Spec. abilities: miss
13 Performance compared with STB Large White 1017:
14   higher: daily gain, piglet mortality
15   equal: % lean, litter size, meat quality, age of sexual maturity
16   lower: feed conversion rate
17 - Management: stationary; housing: 12 m.;
18 - Conservation progr.: live animals: miss;Semen: miss;Embryos: miss
19 Status: normal;   Watch: %pure!
20 - Similar breeds (see group 2/1 on page 101)   EN Country Status
21 Belgische Landrasse   907 D*   crit.end.
22 Zlotnicka biala   1024 PL   crit.end.
23 Landrace   952 CS   normal
24 Belgisch Landvarken   906 B   normal

CATTLE

1 - Rjavo govedo   EN 221
2   Slovenian Brown; Rep. of Slovenia, Karst and mountain regions in YU
3   University of Ljubljana, Biotechnical Faculty, Zootechnical HB:1909
4   Domzale 61230, Groblje 3
5 - Imported as breed from Switzerland, Austria and USA
6   Incrossing since 1950 Braunvieh 40 Switzerland, Braunvieh 77 Germany
7   Numbers 1986: 96/150000; HB: 16000; stable; 87 %; Ne = 382
8 - Height: 152/134 cm; Weight: 1100/600 kg; Herd number: miss; AI: Yes
9   Colour: Uni brown
10 Pecularity: miss
11 - Main use: (1) milk,(2) meat,(3) miss
12 Spec. abilities: miss
13 Performance compared with STB Simmental 238:
14   higher: milk yield, milkability
15   equal: % fat,calving ease,calving interval,age of sexual maturity
16   lower: muscularity, daily gain
17 - Management: stationary; housing: 2-6 m.;
18 - Conservation progr.: live animals: miss;Semen: 30;Embryos: miss
19 Status: normal;   Watch: %pure,%incross!
20 - Similar breeds (see group 5/1 on page 79)   EN Country Status
21 Original Allgäuer Braunvieh   189 D   crit.end.
22 Agerolese   2 I   crit.end.
23 Aubrac   14 F   normal
24 Österreichisches Braunvieh   190 A   normal

1 - **Bovska Ovca**   EN **430**
2   **Bovec; country-wide**
3   **University of Ljubljana, Biotechnical Faculty, Zootechnical** HB:1983
4   **Domzale 61230, Groblje 3**
5 - **Autochthon local breed (Steinschaf)**
6   **Incrossing since 1960 from Ostfriesisches Milchschaf 573 Germany**
7   **Numbers 1986: 100/2000; HB: 100; decreasing; 50 %; Ne = 200**
8 - Height: **65/58** cm; Weight: **58/45** kg; Herd number: **miss**; AI: **miss**
9   Colour: **Uni white, some combinations black and white**
10 Pecularity: **horns 0/0**
11 - Main use: (1) **milk**,(2) **meat**,(3) **wool**
12 Spec. abilities: **miss**
13 Performance compared with STB **East Friesian 573**:
14   higher: **% fat, % protein**
15   equal: **length of mating season, lambing interval**
16   lower: **leanness, litter size, milk yield, age of sexual maturity**
17 - Management: **stationary**; housing: **2-6 m.**;
18 - Conservation progr.: live animals: **miss**;Semen: **miss**;Embryos: **miss**
19 Status: **minimally endang.**; Watch: **HB♀♀,trend,%pure,%incross!**
20 - <u>Similar breeds</u> (see group 5/2 on page 89)   <u>EN</u> <u>Country</u> <u>Status </u>
21 **Caussenard des Garrigues**   447 F   crit.end.
22 **Altamurana**   401 I   crit.end.
23 **Caussenard du Lot**   448 F   normal
24 **Basco-Bearnaise**   412 F   normal

1 - **Solcavsko-Jezerska**   EN **632**
2   **Solca; country-wide**
3   **University of Ljubljana, Biotechnical Faculty, Zootechnical** HB:1983
4   **Domzale 61230, Groblje 3**
5 - **Composite of Zaupelsheep, Bergamascasheep**
6   **Incrossing since 1960 from Romanov USSR**
7   **Numbers 1986: 100/2000; HB: 200; decreasing; 10 %; Ne = 267**
8 - Height: **75/67** cm; Weight: **90/65** kg; Herd number: **miss**; AI: **miss**
9   Colour: **Uni white, some combination black, white**
10 Pecularity: **horns 0/0**
11 - Main use: (1) **meat**,(2) **wool**,(3) **miss**
12 Spec. abilities: **breeding season 365 days**
13 Performance compared with STB **Scottish Blackface**:
14   higher: **length of mating season, lambing interval, daily gain**
15   equal: **muscularity, leanness, litter size, age of sexual maturity**
16   lower: **miss**
17 - Management: **stationary**; housing: **2-6 m.**;
18 - Conservation progr.: live animals: **miss**;Semen: **miss**;Embryos: **miss**
19 Status: **minimally endang.**; Watch: **trend,%pure,%incross!**
20 - <u>Similar breeds</u> (see group 7/2 on page 91)   <u>EN</u> <u>Country</u> <u>Status </u>
21 **Braunes Bergschaf**   431 D   crit.end.
22 **Istriana**   516 I   crit.end.
23 **Bergamasca**   415 I   normal
24 **Weißes Bergschaf**   416 D   normal

1 - **Bela Zlahtna**   EN **904**
2   Slovenian White; Slovenia, Pomurje
3   Zivinorejsko veterinarski zavod za Pomurje   HB:**miss**
4   69000 Murska Sobota
5 - Imported as breed from Edelschwein 923 Germany, Austria
6   Incrossing since 1970 from Swedish Yorkshire Sweden
7   Numbers 1991: **15/300**; HB: **miss**; **decreasing**; **70 %**; Ne = **34**
8 - Height: **80/70** cm; Weight: **220/180** kg; Herd number: **miss**; AI: **miss**
9   Colour: **Uni white**
10 Pecularity: **erect ears**
11 - Main use: (1) **meat**,(2) **miss**,(3) **miss**
12 Spec. abilities: **miss**
13 Performance compared with STB **Large White 925**:
14   higher: **meat quality, live weight at slaughter**
15   equal: **litter size, farrowing interval, handling ease**
16   lower: **% lean,feed conversion rate,daily gain,age of sexual mat.**
17 - Management: **stationary**; housing: **12 m.**;
18 - Conservation progr.: live animals: **miss**;Semen: **miss**;Embryos: **miss**
19 Status: **critically endang.**;Watch: ♂♂,HB♀♀,trend,%pure,%incross!
20 - <u>Similar breeds</u> (see group 1/2 on page 101)   <u>EN</u> <u>Country</u> <u>Status</u>
21 **Middle White**   975   GB   min. end.
22 **Yorkshire**   1022   RO   pot. end.
23 **Deutsches Edelschwein**   922   D*   normal
24 **Vile uslechtile**   1017   CS   normal

1 - **Crna Slavonska**   EN **916**
2   Black Slavonian; country-wide
3   Poljoprivredni Centar Hrvatske, Mr Blazenka Gutzmirtl   HB:**miss**
4   Zagreb Ilica 101
5 - Composite of Mangalitsa, Berkshire, Poland China, Cornwall
7   Numbers miss: **miss** / **miss**; HB: **miss**; **decreasing**; **miss %**; Ne = **miss**
8 - Height: **70/66** cm; Weight: **140/125** kg; Herd number: **miss**; AI: **miss**
9   Colour: **Uni black**
10 Pecularity: **semi-lop ears**
11 - Main use: (1) **meat**,(2) **miss**,(3) **miss**
12 Spec. abilities: **high temperature tolerance**
13 Performance compared with STB **Swedish Landrace**:
14   higher: **feed conversion rate, farrowing interval**
15   equal: **miss**
16   lower: **muscularity,% lean,daily gain,piglet mortality,litter size**
17 - Management: **transhumant**; housing: **2-6 m.**; **marsh**
18 - Conservation progr.: live animals: **Yes**;Semen: **miss**;Embryos: **miss**
19 Status: **miss**
20 - <u>Similar breeds</u> (see group 4/1 on page 103)   <u>EN</u> <u>Country</u> <u>Status</u>
21 **Gascon**   935   F   crit.end.
22 **Large Black**   959   GB   min. end.
24 **Negra Iberica**   981   E   normal
23 **Alentejana**   902   P   normal

SLOVENIA   PIGS

```
 1 - Krskopoljski crnopasasti prasic                         EN  950
 2   Krskopolje Saddleback; Slovenia, Dolenjska, Krsko Polje
 3   University of Ljubljana, Biotechnical Faculty, Zootechnical  HB:miss
 4   Domzale 61230, Groblje 3
 5 - Autochthon Krskopoljski prasic
 6   Incrossing since 1970 from Sattelschwein 903, 997 Germany
 7   Numbers 1991: 13/400; HB: miss; decreasing; 50 %; Ne = 28
 8 - Height: 70/62 cm; Weight: 185/170 kg; Herd number: miss; AI: miss
 9   Colour: Combination black, white
10   Pecularity: white saddle, lop ears
11 - Main use: (1) meat,(2) miss,(3) miss
12   Spec. abilities: miss
13   Performance compared with STB Landrace:
14     higher: meat quality, litter size, handling ease
15     equal:  farrowing interval, live weight at slaughter
16     lower:  daily gain,% lean,feed conversion rate,age of sexual mat.
17 - Management: stationary; housing: 12 m.;
18 - Conservation progr.: live animals: miss;Semen: miss;Embryos: miss
19   Status: critically endang.;Watch: ♂♂,HB♀♀,trend,%pure,%incross!
20 - Similar breeds (see group 3/1 on page 102)    EN  Country Status
21   Pie noir du Pays Basque                        987  F      crit.end.
22   Angler Sattelschwein                           903  D      crit.end.
23   British Saddleback                             912  GB     pot. end.
24   Schwäbisch-Hällisches Schwein                  997  D      pot. end.
```

SLOVENIA   HORSES

```
 1 - Ljutomerski kasac                                       EN  778
 2   Ljutomer-Trotter; country-wide
 3   University of Ljubljana, Biotechnical Faculty, Zootechnical  HB:miss
 4   Domzale 61230, Groblje 3
 5 - Composite of American Trotter x Anglo-Arab
 7   Numbers miss: miss / miss; HB: miss; miss; miss %; Ne = miss
 8 - Height:miss/miss cm; Weight:miss/miss kg; Herd number:miss; AI:miss
 9   Colour: miss
10   Pecularity: miss
11 - Main use: (1) miss,(2) miss,(3) miss
12   Spec. abilities: miss
13   Performance compared with STB miss:
14     higher: miss
15     equal:  miss
16     lower:  miss
17 - Management: miss; housing: miss m.;
18 - Conservation progr.: live animals: miss;Semen: miss;Embryos: miss
19   Status: miss
20 - Similar breeds (see group 2 on page 108)     EN  Country Status
21   Morgan Horse                                   783  GB     endanger.
22   Lämminverinen ravuri                           773  SF     normal
24   Norsk Kaldblods Traver                         789  N      normal
23   Trotteur Francais                              813  F      normal
```

1 - **Albera**   EN   **4**
2   **Alberes; Gerona**
3   **Univ. Zaragoza, Fac. de Vet., Dept. Prod. Anim. y**   HB:**miss**
4   **Ciencia de los Alim., Zaragoza 50013, Miguel Servet 177**
5 - **miss**
7   Numbers 1991: **6/900**; HB: **miss**; **miss**; **50** %; Ne = **11**
8 - Height: **miss** / **miss** cm; Weight: **350/275** kg; Herd number: **6**; AI: **miss**
9   Colour: **Uni black, brown, blond**
10 Pecularity: **short hornes (half moon), big head**
11 - Main use: (1) **miss**,(2) **miss**,(3) **miss**
12 Spec. abilities: **very rustic, longevity**
13 Performance compared with STB **miss**:
14   higher: **miss**
15   equal: **miss**
16   lower: **miss**
17 - Management: **stationary**; housing: **no**
18 - Conservation progr.: live animals: **miss**;Semen: **miss**;Embryos: **miss**
19 Status: **critically endang.**;Watch: **♂♂,HB♀♀,trend,herds,%pure!**
20 - <u>Similar breeds</u> (see group 10 on page 82)   <u>EN</u> <u>Country</u> <u>Status</u>
21 **Mostrenca**   177   E   **endanger.**
22 **Faeroesk**   84   FR   **min. end.**
23 **Inra 95**   119   F   **pot. end.**
24 **Corse**   70   F   **normal**

1 - **Asturiana de Valles, Carrenana**   EN   **12**
2   **Asturian Valley; Asturia**
3   **ASEAVA (Associacion Asturiano de Valles)**   HB:**1978**
4   **Oviedo 33011, Avdo. Fernandez Ladredo, # 14-A-1**
5 - **Incrossing since 1950 from Pardo Alpina Austria and Switzerland**
7   Numbers 1993: **1200/40190**; HB: **12459**; **increasing**; **90** %; Ne = **4378**
8 - Height: **147/136** cm; Weight: **1000/750** kg; Herd number: **miss**; AI: **Yes**
9   Colour: **Uni red, blond; black mucosa, eyelashes and tail-tip**
10 Pecularity: **lyra formed horns**
11 - Main use: (1) **meat**,(2) **miss**,(3) **miss**
12 Spec. abilities: **gene for muscle hypertrophy**
13 Performance compared with STB **Limousin**:
14   higher: **handling ease, milk yield, calving rate, pulling power**
15   equal: **daily gain, % fat, % protein, calving ease and interval**
16   lower: **muscularity, age of sexual maturity, calf mortality**
17 - Management: **transhumant**; housing: **2-6 m.; mountainous area**
18 - Conservation progr.: live animals: **miss**;Semen: **Yes**;Embryos: **Yes**
19 Status: **normal**;   Watch: **%incross!**
20 - <u>Similar breeds</u> (see group 4/6 on page 79)   <u>EN</u> <u>Country</u> <u>Status</u>
21 **Mallorquina**   164   E   **crit.end.**
22 **Menorqina**   169   E   **crit.end.**
23 **Monchina**   175   E   **normal**
24 **Berrenda roja andaluza**   30   E   **normal**

```
1 - Asturiano Montana, Casina                                    EN    13
2   Asturian Mountain; Asturia
3   ASEAMO (Associacion Espanolo Asturiano Montana)             HB:1978
4   Oviedo 33011, Avdo. Fernandez Ladredo, # 14-A-1
5 - Autochthon Asturiano de Montano
6   Incrossing since 1950 from Asturiano de Valles 12 Spain
7   Numbers 1993: 35/7500; HB: 2778; increasing; 50 %; Ne = 138
8 - Height: 134/120 cm; Weight: 750/450 kg; Herd number: > 10; AI: miss
9   Colour: Uni red, blond
10  Pecularity: miss
11 - Main use: (1) meat,(2) vegetation management,(3) miss
12  Spec. abilities: mountain climate
13  Performance compared with STB Asturian Valley 12:
14     higher: calving ease, milk yield, calving interval, milkability
15     equal: % fat, % protein, handling ease
16     lower: muscularity, daily gain, age of sex. maturity, calf mort.
17 - Management: miss; housing: miss m.; mountainous area
18 - Conservation progr.: live animals: miss;Semen: Yes;Embryos: Yes
19  Status: minimally endang.; Watch: %pure,%incross!
```

20 - <u>Similar breeds</u> (see group 4/6 on page 79)	EN	Country	Status
21 Mallorquina	164	E	crit.end.
22 Menorqina	169	E	crit.end.
23 Berrenda roja andaluza	30	E	normal
24 Asturiana de Valles	12	E	normal

```
1 - Berrenda negra andaluza                                      EN    29
2   Black Berrendo; Andalusia: Huelva and Sevilla
3   Departamento de Genetica, Facultad de Veterinaria           HB:miss
4   Cordoba 14005, Avda. Medina Azahara 9
5 - Composite of Bos Primigenius and Bos Desertorum Hispanicus
6 - Imported as breed from North of Africa
7   Numbers 1991: 34/389; HB: miss; decreasing; 90 %; Ne = 125
8 - Height: 143/138 cm; Weight: 950/600 kg; Herd number: 5; AI: miss
9   Colour: Combination black, white, black pied; like Pinzgauer
10  Pecularity: horn shape
11 - Main use: (1) meat,(2) to handle fighting cattle,(3) tractive power
12  Spec. abilities: climate with strong sunshine, lack of water supply
13  Performance compared with STB Retinta 219:
14     higher: handling ease
15     equal: milk yield, muscularity, %fat, %protein, age of sex. mat.
16     lower: daily gain, calving ease, calving interval, calf mortality
17 - Management: stationary; housing: no; arid climate, bush country
18 - Conservation progr.: live animals: miss;Semen: 1;Embryos: miss
19  Status: minimally endang.; Watch: HB♀♀,trend,herds,%pure!
```

20 - <u>Similar breeds</u> (see group 1/6 on page 76)	EN	Country	Status
21 Tuxer	259	A	crit.end.
22 Pohjoissuomenkarja	207	SF	crit.end.
23 Fjällras	86	S	endanger.
24 Gruzinskii gornyi skot	107	GO	normal

```
1 - Berrenda roja andaluza                                    EN   30
2   Red Berrendo; Andalusia: Sevilla, Cadiz and Saen
3   Departamento de Genetica, Facultad de Veterinaria          HB:miss
4   Cordoba 14005, Avda. Medina Azahara 9
5 - Composite of Bos Taurus Ibericus Red and Bos Desertorum Hispanicus
7   Numbers 1991: 90/971; HB: miss; increasing; 90 %; Ne = 330
8 - Height: 143/138 cm; Weight: 1000/600 kg; Herd number: 13; AI: miss
9   Colour: Combination red, white
10  Pecularity: big open horns
11 - Main use: (1) to handle fighting bulls,(2) meat,(3) tractive power
12  Spec. abilities: long marshes, live together with fighting bulls
13  Performance compared with STB Retinta 219:
14    higher: handling ease
15    equal:  milk yield, muscularity, % fat, % protein, calving ease
16    lower:  daily gain
17 - Management: stationary; housing: no; mediterranean conditions
18 - Conservation progr.: live animals: Yes;Semen: 2;Embryos: miss
19  Status: normal;              Watch: HB♀♀,herds,%pure!
```

20 - Similar breeds (see group 4/6 on page 79)	EN	Country	Status
21 Mallorquina	164	E	crit.end.
22 Menorqina	169	E	crit.end.
23 Monchina	175	E	normal
24 Asturiana de Valles	12	E	normal

```
1 - Blanca Cacerena                                           EN   34
2   White Caceres; Estremadura (Caceres and Badajoz)
3   Univ. Zaragoza, Fac. de Vet., Dept. Prod. Anim. y         HB:miss
4   Ciencia de los Alim., Zaragoza 50013, Miguel Servet 177
5 - Autochthon origin breed
7   Numbers 1991: 19/205; HB: 165; miss; 95 %; Ne = 45
8 - Height: miss / miss cm; Weight: 900/500 kg; Herd number: 11; AI: Yes
9   Colour: Uni white
10  Pecularity: horns like short hooks
11 - Main use: (1) meat,(2) miss,(3) miss
12  Spec. abilities: for arid climate with strong sunshine
13  Performance compared with STB miss:
14    higher: miss
15    equal: miss
16    lower: miss
17 - Management: stationary; housing: no; dry country
18 - Conservation progr.: live animals: miss;Semen: 4;Embryos: 4/miss
19  Status: minimally endang.; Watch: ♂♂,HB♀♀,herds,%pure!
```

20 - Similar breeds (see group 4/6 on page 79)	EN	Country	Status
21 Mallorquina	164	E	crit.end.
22 Menorqina	169	E	crit.end.
23 Berrenda roja andaluza	30	E	normal
24 Asturiana de Valles	12	E	normal

```
1 - Cachena                                                    EN   55
2   Cachena; southern Galicia
3   Conselleria Agricultura, Ganaderia y Montes de Xunta       HB:miss
4   de Galicia-Santiago de compostela (La Coruna)
5 - Composite of Bos Taurus Desertorum and Bos Primigenius Mauritanicus
6   of North Africa
7   Numbers 1991: 22/220; HB: 64; stable; 100 %; Ne = 42
8 - Height: 122/117 cm; Weight: 450/275 kg; Herd number: 18; AI: miss
9   Colour: Uni blond
10  Pecularity: lira formed horns
11 - Main use: (1) meat,(2) miss,(3) miss
12  Spec. abilities: meat quality, semidesert and cold and humid climate
13  Performance compared with STB Holstein-Friesian:
14    higher: calving ease,age of sex. matur.,muscularity,calf mortality
15    equal: miss
16    lower:  handling ease, daily gain, calving interval, calving rate
17 - Management: stationary; housing: no; mountain, poor soils
18 - Conservation progr.: live animals: Yes;Semen: 22;Embryos: 8/miss
19  Status: minimally endang.; Watch: ♂♂,HB♀♀!
```

20 - Similar breeds (see group 5/4 on page 80)	EN	Country	Status
21 Frieiresa	90	E	crit.end.
22 Limiana	155	E	crit.end.
23 Barrosa	21	P	normal
24 Arouquesa	11	P	normal

```
1 - Caldelana                                                  EN   56
2   Caldelana; Galicia
3   Conselleria Agricultura, Ganaderia y Montes de Xunta       HB:miss
4   de Galicia - Santiago de Compostela (La Coruna)
5 - Autochthon Bos Taurus Ibericus
6   Incrossing since 1950 from Brune 48 France
7   Numbers 1993: 18/2000; HB: 93; stable; 80 %; Ne = 37
8 - Height: 132/128 cm; Weight: 650/450 kg; Herd number: miss; AI: miss
9   Colour: Uni black
10  Pecularity: horns like hooks
11 - Main use: (1) meat,(2) tractive power,(3) miss
12  Spec. abilities: docile, hardy
13  Performance compared with STB Charolais:
14    higher: calving ease, pulling power
15    equal: miss
16    lower:  muscularity,daily gain,age of sex. matur.,calving interval
17 - Management: stationary; housing: ≈ 2 m.; cold and humid country
18 - Conservation progr.: live animals: Yes;Semen: 18;Embryos: 18/miss
19  Status: minimally endang.; Watch: ♂♂,HB♀♀,%incross!
```

20 - Similar breeds (see group 2/1 on page 76)	EN	Country	Status
21 Cardena Andaluza	60	E	crit.end.
22 Serrana Negra	232	E	crit.end.
23 Race Espagnole	41	F	pot. end.
24 Toro de Lidia	257	E	normal

1 - **Canaria**   EN   **59**
2   Canary Island; Canary Islands (Tenerife, Gran Canaria)
3   Consejaria de Agricultura y Pesca, Gobierno de Canarias   HB:**miss**
4   Apdo. 60, La Laguna, Tenerife-Canarias 38080
5 - Autochthon **Rubia Gallega**
7   Numbers 1993: 550/4050; HB: **420**; increasing; **90 %**; Ne = **953**
8 - Height: **miss/miss** cm; Weight: **1000/600** kg; Herd number: **650**; AI: **Yes**
9   Colour: **Uni brown, blond, chestnut**
10 Pecularity: **horns like hooks, good udder and developed muscles**
11 - Main use: (1) **meat**,(2) **dung production**,(3) **milk**
12 Spec. abilities: **for humid and arid climate**
13 Performance compared with STB **miss**:
14   higher: **miss**
15   equal: **miss**
16   lower: **miss**
17 - Management: **stationary**; housing: **12 m.**; **only some grazing**
18 - Conservation progr.: live animals: **miss**;Semen: **miss**;Embryos: **miss**
19 Status: **normal**;   Watch: **HB♀♀,%pure!**
20 - Similar breeds (see group 8/6 on page 82)   EN Country Status
21 **Palmera**   **192   E   endanger.**

1 - **Cardena Andaluza**   EN   **60**
2   Andalusian Grey; Andalusia: Cordoba, Huelva (dispersed)
3   Centro de la Almoraima   HB:**miss**
4   Cadiz, Castellar de la Frontera
5 - Autochthon **Iberic Branch**
7   Numbers 1991: 3/20; HB: **11**; decreasing; **100 %**; Ne = **4**
8 - Height: **165/160** cm; Weight: **900/500** kg; Herd number: **4**; AI: **Yes**
9   Colour: **Combination black, white; black mouth and white abdomen**
10 Pecularity: **strong horns, big dewlap**
11 - Main use: (1) **meat**,(2) **castrates lead fighting cattle**
12 Spec. abilities: **excelent meat, quick apprenticeship**
13 Performance compared with STB **Retinta 219**:
14   higher: **miss**
15   equal: **milk yield, muscularity, % fat, % protein, calving ease**
16   lower: **daily gain, calving interval**
17 - Management: **stationary**; housing: **no; adapted to "dehesa" land**
18 - Conservation progr.: live animals: **Yes**;Semen: **14**;Embryos: **miss**
19 Status: **critically endang.**;Watch: **♂♂,HB♀♀,trend,herds!**
20 - Similar breeds (see group 2/1 on page 76)   EN Country Status
21 **Serrana Negra**   **232   E   crit.end.**
22 **Caldelana**   **56   E   min. end.**
23 **Race Espagnole**   **41   F   pot. end.**
24 **Toro de Lidia**   **257   E   normal**

```
1 - Frieiresa                                                    EN    90
2   Frieiresa; southeast of Orense village
3   Conselleria Agricultura, Ganaderia y Montes de Xunta        HB:miss
4   de Galicia-Santiago de Compostela (La Coruna)
5 - miss
7   Numbers 1991: 14/400; HB: 62; miss; 30 %; Ne = 24
8 - Height: miss / miss cm; Weight: 950/575 kg; Herd number: 18; AI: Yes
9   Colour: Uni brown, males are sometimes darker
10  Pecularity: long horns, little head, long hair at breast
11 - Main use: (1) calf fattening,(2) tractive power,(3) miss
12  Spec. abilities: hardy
13  Performance compared with STB miss:
14    higher: miss
15    equal: miss
16    lower: miss
17 - Management: stationary; housing: 2-6 m.; cold and humid country
18 - Conservation progr.: live animals: miss;Semen: 12;Embryos: 12/miss
19  Status: critically endang.;Watch: ♂♂,HB♀♀,%pure!
20 - Similar breeds (see group 5/4 on page 80)      EN  Country Status
21  Limiana                                         155   E    crit.end.
22  Terrena                                         255   E    crit.end.
23  Barrosa                                          21   P    normal
24  Arouquesa                                        11   P    normal
```

```
1 - Limiana                                                     EN   155
2   Limiana; La Limia (Orense)
3   Conselleria Agricultura, Ganaderia y Montes de Xunta        HB:miss
4   de Galicia-Santiago de Compostela (La Coruna)
5 - Autochthon Cantabrique
7   Numbers 1991: 10/2000; HB: 56; miss; 70 %; Ne = 17
8 - Height: miss/miss cm; Weight: 1000/700 kg; Herd number: 30; AI: Yes
9   Colour: Uni brown
10  Pecularity: bulls with short hooks (horns), cows with long spiral h.
11 - Main use: (1) meat,(2) tractive power,(3) milk
12  Spec. abilities: docile, for high temperatures
13  Performance compared with STB miss:
14    higher: miss
15    equal: miss
16    lower: miss
17 - Management: stationary; housing: 2-6 m.; hilly country
18 - Conservation progr.: live animals: miss;Semen: 7;Embryos: Yes
19  Status: critically endang.;Watch: ♂♂,HB♀♀,%pure!
20 - Similar breeds (see group 5/4 on page 80)      EN  Country Status
21  Frieiresa                                        90   E    crit.end.
22  Terrena                                         255   E    crit.end.
23  Barrosa                                          21   P    normal
24  Arouquesa                                        11   P    normal
```

455

```
 1 - Mallorquina                                                    EN  164
 2   Majorcan; Mallorca
 3   PRAM (Patronato Razas Autoctonas de Mallorca)                  HB:miss
 4   INCA Mallorca 07300, Plaza Blanquer 46
 5 - Autochthon red convex Iberic
 7   Numbers 1991: 3/44; HB: 44; miss; 100 %; Ne = 5
 8 - Height: miss / miss cm; Weight: 600/325 kg; Herd number: 2; AI: miss
 9   Colour: Uni red, blond, chestnut
10   Pecularity: miss
11 - Main use: (1) meat,(2) miss,(3) miss
12   Spec. abilities: for mediterranean climate
13   Performance compared with STB miss:
14     higher: miss
15     equal:  miss
16     lower:  miss
17 - Management: stationary; housing: no; marginal vegetation
18 - Conservation progr.: live animals: miss;Semen: miss;Embryos: miss
19   Status: critically endang.;Watch: ♂♂,HB♀♀,trend,herds!
```

20 - Similar breeds (see group 4/6 on page 79)	EN	Country	Status
21 Menorqina	169	E	crit.end.
22 Murciana	179	E	crit.end.
23 Berrenda roja andaluza	30	E	normal
24 Asturiana de Valles	12	E	normal

```
 1 - Menorqina                                                      EN  169
 2   Minorcan; Menorca
 3   Gabriel Segui Mercadal e Hijo                                  HB:miss
 4   Mahon, Menorca, Isabel II, 21
 5 - Composite of Red Convex Ibric and Marinera
 7   Numbers 1991: 13/173; HB: 45; miss; 65 %; Ne = 21
 8 - Height: miss / miss cm; Weight: 800/475 kg; Herd number: 7; AI: Yes
 9   Colour: Uni red
10   Pecularity: horns 2,0/2,0; 80 % without horns
11 - Main use: (1) milk,(2) cheese "Mahon",(3) miss
12   Spec. abilities: hardy, longevity
13   Performance compared with STB miss:
14     higher: miss
15     equal:  miss
16     lower:  miss
17 - Management: stationary; housing: no; extreme mediterranean climate
18 - Conservation progr.: live animals: miss;Semen: miss;Embryos: miss
19   Status: critically endang.;Watch: ♂♂,HB♀♀,herds,%pure!
```

20 - Similar breeds (see group 4/6 on page 79)	EN	Country	Status
21 Mallorquina	164	E	crit.end.
22 Murciana	179	E	crit.end.
23 Berrenda roja andaluza	30	E	normal
24 Asturiana de Valles	12	E	normal

```
 1 - Monchina                                                    EN  175
 2   Monchina; Santander and Bay of Biscay
 3   Asociacion Espanola de Criadores de Ganado Vacuno de        HB:miss
 4   raza Monchina, Santander 39002, Juan de Herrera, 13-4 Izda
 5 - Autochthon origin breed
 6   Numbers 1987: 50/2000; HB: 1083; miss; 50 %; Ne = 191
 8 - Height: miss/miss cm; Weight: 400/250 kg; Herd number: 93; AI: miss
 9   Colour: Uni red, brown, chestnut
10   Pecularity: little udder with long hair
11 - Main use: (1) meat,(2) "corridas",(3) miss
12   Spec. abilities: hardy, aggressive
13   Performance compared with STB miss:
14      higher: miss
15      equal:  miss
16      lower:  miss
17 - Management: stationary; housing: no; live in hilly woods
18 - Conservation progr.: live animals: miss;Semen: miss;Embryos: miss
19   Status: normal;           Watch: %pure!
```

20 - Similar breeds (see group 4/6 on page 79)	EN	Country	Status
21 Mallorquina	164	E	crit.end.
22 Menorqina	169	E	crit.end.
23 Berrenda roja andaluza	30	E	normal
24 Asturiana de Valles	12	E	normal

```
 1 - Mostrenca, Palurda                                          EN  177
 2   Donana Cattle; Andalusia: Marshes of Donana
 3   Coto Nacional de Donana, Departamento de Genetica           HB:miss
 4   Facultad de Veterinaria, Cordoba 14005, Avda. Medina Azahara 9
 5 - Composite of Negra de las Campinas and Fighting bulls
 6   Incrossing since 1950 from Charolais and Limousin
 7   Numbers 1991: 20/300; HB: miss; increasing; 80 %; Ne = 54
 8 - Height: 145/135 cm; Weight: 900/550 kg; Herd number: 4; AI: miss
 9   Colour: Uni red, many combin.: black,grey,blue,red,brown,white,blond
10   Pecularity: horns 2/2, variable horn form
11 - Main use: (1) meat,(2) miss,(3) miss
12   Spec. abilities: adapted to marshes and humid lands
13   Performance compared with STB Charolais:
14      higher: miss
15      equal:  age of sexual maturity
16      lower:  muscularity, calving ease, handling ease, pulling power
17 - Management: nomadic; housing: no; long fasting periods possible
18 - Conservation progr.: live animals: Yes;Semen: miss;Embryos: miss
19   Status: endangered;       Watch: ♂♂,HB♀♀,herds,%pure,%incross!
```

20 - Similar breeds (see group 10 on page 82)	EN	Country	Status
21 Albera	4	E	crit.end.
22 Faeroesk	84	FR	min. end.
23 Inra 95	119	F	pot. end.
24 Corse	70	F	normal

1 - **Murciana**   EN **179**
2   **Murcian; Andalusia: Granada and Almeria**
3   **Conservacion de razas, Departamento de Genetica,**   HB:**miss**
4   **Facultad de Veterinaria, Cordoba 14005**
5 - Autochthon **Bos Taurus Frontosus; incrossing since 1950 continously**
6   **from Pajuna 191 Spain, Retinta 219 Spain, Limousin 156 France**
7   Numbers 1991: **5/65**; HB: **14**; **stable**; **40 %**; Ne = **6**
8 - Height: **141/131** cm; Weight: **800/550** kg; Herd number: **15**; AI: **Yes**
9   Colour: **Uni red, brown; black dorsal line**
10 Pecularity: **horns sometimes until the cheeks, dewlap**
11 - Main use: (1) **meat**,(2) **vegetation management**,(3) **miss**
12 Spec. abilities: **hardy, for dry and hot climate, rusticity**
13 Performance compared with STB **Retinta 219**:
14   higher: **milkability, milk yield, pulling power**
15   equal: **muscularity, daily gain, % fat, % protein, calving ease**
16   lower: **miss**
17 - Management: **transhumant**; housing: **> 6 m.; adapted to very poor lands**
18 - Conservation progr.: live animals: **Yes**;Semen: **3**;Embryos: **miss**
19 Status: **critically endang.**;Watch: **♂♂,HB♀♀,herds,%pure,%incross!**
20 - Similar breeds (see group 4/6 on page 79)   EN Country Status
21 **Mallorquina**   164   E   **crit.end.**
22 **Menorqina**   169   E   **crit.end.**
23 **Berrenda roja andaluza**   30   E   **normal**
24 **Asturiana de Valles**   12   E   **normal**

1 - **Negra de las Campinas andaluzas**   EN **182**
2   **Andalusian Black; Sierra Morena,Campina de Cordoba+Sevilla, Huelva**
3   **Departamento de Genetica, Facultad de Veterinaria**   HB:**miss**
4   **Cordoba 14005**
5 - Autochthon **Bostaurus Ibericus**
6   **Incrossing since 1950 from Avilena Spain**
7   Numbers 1991: **21/897**; HB: **150**; **decreasing**; **30 %**; Ne = **52**
8 - Height: **140/135** cm; Weight: **875/600** kg; Herd number: **10**; AI: **Yes**
9   Colour: **Uni black, some with white abdomen**
10 Pecularity: **big open horns with smooth hook**
11 - Main use: (1) **meat**,(2) **dam line for crossing**,(3) **miss**
12 Spec. abilities: **adapted to high temperatures and cold winter**
13 Performance compared with STB **Retinta 219**:
14   higher: **fertility, calving ease**
15   equal: **milk yield, muscularity, daily gain, % fat, % protein**
16   lower: **miss**
17 - Management: **stationary**; housing: **no; for marginal "dehesa" land**
18 - Conservation progr.: live animals: **Yes**;Semen: **1**;Embryos: **miss**
19 Status: **minimally endang.**; Watch: **♂♂,trend,herds,%pure,%incross!**
20 - Similar breeds (see group 2/1 on page 76)   EN Country Status
21 **Cardena Andaluza**   60   E   **crit.end.**
22 **Serrana Negra**   232   E   **crit.end.**
23 **Race Espagnole**   41   F   **pot. end.**
24 **Toro de Lidia**   257   E   **normal**

```
 1 - Pajuna, Serrana                                              EN  191
 2   Pajuna; Andalusia: Almeria, Granada and Saen
 3   Centro de la Almoraima, Finca del Ministerio de Agricultura  HB:miss
 4   Cadiz, Castellar de la Frontera
 5 - Composite of African Atlas branch with possible influence of
 6   Retinta, incrossing since 1950 from Murciana 179 (continously)
 7   Numbers 1991: 11/310; HB: 20; stable; 10 %; Ne = 13
 8 - Height: 165/160 cm; Weight: 600/375 kg; Herd number: 15; AI: miss
 9   Colour: Combination black, blond; white fringe around the muzzle
10   Pecularity: open hook horns, long legs, big head
11 - Main use: (1) tractive power,(2) meat,(3) miss
12   Spec. abilities: exquisite meat, adapted to cold mountain climate
13   Performance compared with STB Retinta 219:
14     higher: miss
15     equal: milk yield, %fat, %protein, calving ease, calving interval
16     lower: muscularity, daily gain, pulling power, sexual maturity
17 - Management: transhumant; housing: no; for marginal land
18 - Conservation progr.: live animals: Yes;Semen: miss;Embryos: miss
19   Status: critically endang.;Watch: ♂♂,HB♀♀,herds,%pure,%incross!
```

20 -	Similar breeds (see group 4/6 on page 79)	EN	Country	Status
21	Mallorquina	164	E	crit.end.
22	Menorqina	169	E	crit.end.
23	Berrenda roja andaluza	30	E	normal
24	Asturiana de Valles	12	E	normal

```
 1 - Palmera                                                      EN  192
 2   Palmera; La Palma Island
 3   Univ. Zaragoza, Fac. de Vet., Dept. Prod. Anim. y            HB:miss
 4   Ciencia de los Alim., Zaragoza 50013, Miguel Servet 177
 5 - Autochthon Rubia Gallega
 7   Numbers 1993: 12/140; HB: 130; stable; 90 %; Ne = 23
 8 - Height: miss / miss cm; Weight: 800/500 kg; Herd number: 55; AI: Yes
 9   Colour: Uni blond
10   Pecularity: good udder
11 - Main use: (1) meat,(2) tractive power,(3) milk
12   Spec. abilities: area with high rain fall
13   Performance compared with STB miss:
14     higher: miss
15     equal: miss
16     lower: miss
17 - Management: stationary; housing: 2-6 m.; mountainous country
18 - Conservation progr.: live animals: miss;Semen: 2;Embryos: miss
19   Status: endangered;        Watch: ♂♂,HB♀♀,%pure!
```

20 -	Similar breeds (see group 8/6 on page 82)	EN	Country	Status
21	Canaria	59	E	normal

```
 1 - Retinta                                                      EN  219
 2   Retinta; Andalusia, Estremadura
 3   Asciacion Nacional de Criadores de Ganado Vacuno             HB:1933
 4   Selecto de Raza Retinta, Cordoba 14005
 5 - Composite of Tronco Rojo Convexo, Propio del Sur Iberico
 7   Numbers 1993: 5560/137300; HB: 14251; increasing; 30 %; Ne = 15998
 8 - Height: 144/139 cm; Weight: 700/600 kg; Herd number: miss; AI: miss
 9   Colour: Uni brown
10   Pecularity: hook shaped horns
11 - Main use: (1) meat,(2) tractive power,(3) fur
12   Spec. abilities: resistance against parasites, heat
13   Performance compared with STB Andalusian Black 182:
14     higher: daily gain, pulling power
15     equal:  age of sexual maturity, handling ease, calf mortality
16     lower:  calving ease, calving interval
17 - Management: stationary; housing: ≈ 2 m.; poor nutrition
18 - Conservation progr.: live animals: miss;Semen: 20;Embryos: miss
19   Status: normal;                Watch: %pure!
```

20 - Similar breeds (see group 4/6 on page 79)	EN	Country	Status
21 Mallorquina	164	E	crit.end.
22 Menorqina	169	E	crit.end.
23 Berrenda roja andaluza	30	E	normal
24 Asturiana de Valles	12	E	normal

```
 1 - Serrana Negra                                                EN  232
 2   Serrana Black; Teruel
 3   Diputacion Provincial de Teruel                              HB:miss
 4   Finca "El Chantre", Teruel
 5 - Composite of Serrana Iberique, Avilena-Negra
 7   Numbers 1991: 4/660; HB: miss; miss; 15 %; Ne = 7
 8 - Height: miss/miss cm; Weight: 825/475 kg; Herd number: 26; AI: miss
 9   Colour: Uni black, some combinations black and brown
10   Pecularity: rustic
11 - Main use: (1) meat,(2) crossing for meat production,(3) miss
12   Spec. abilities: extrem continental climate with few rain
13   Performance compared with STB miss:
14     higher: miss
15     equal:  miss
16     lower:  miss
17 - Management: stationary; housing: no; semi desert, steep zones
18 - Conservation progr.: live animals: miss;Semen: miss;Embryos: miss
19   Status: critically endang.;Watch: ♂♂,HB♀♀,%pure!
```

20 - Similar breeds (see group 2/1 on page 76)	EN	Country	Status
21 Cardena Andaluza	60	E	crit.end.
22 Caldelana	56	E	min. end.
23 Race Espagnole	41	F	pot. end.
24 Toro de Lidia	257	E	normal

```
 1 - Terrena                                              EN  255
 2   Terrena; Alava
 3   Disputacion Foral de Alava, Servicio de Ganaderia    HB:miss
 4   Vitoria
 5 - Autochthon breed
 7   Numbers 1991: 8/200; HB: 70; miss; 5 %; Ne = 13
 8 - Height: miss/miss cm; Weight: miss/miss kg; Herd number: 50; AI: Yes
 9   Colour: Uni brown
10   Pecularity: many hairs at the udder and on ears, rustic
11 - Main use: (1) tractive power,(2) meat,(3) folklor. pulling competit.
12   Spec. abilities: longevity, females used for crossing
13   Performance compared with STB miss:
14     higher: miss
15     equal:  miss
16     lower:  miss
17 - Management: stationary; housing: no; extensive system
18 - Conservation progr.: live animals: miss;Semen: 4;Embryos: Yes
19   Status: critically endang.;Watch: ♂♂,HB♀♀,%pure!
```

20 - Similar breeds (see group 5/4 on page 80)	EN	Country	Status
21 Frieiresa	90	E	crit.end.
22 Limiana	155	E	crit.end.
23 Barrosa	21	P	normal
24 Arouquesa	11	P	normal

```
 1 - Toro de Lidia                                        EN  257
 2   Fighting bull; Andalusia, Estremadura and Salamanca
 3   Departamento de Genetica, Facultad de Veterinaria    HB:1980
 4   Cordoba 14005
 5 - Composite of Bos Taurus Indigenius and Bos Taurus Braquiceros
 7   Numbers 1986: 3177/55296; HB: 52000; increasing; 100 %; Ne = 11976
 8 - Height: 165/155 cm; Weight: 500/350 kg; Herd number: miss; AI: miss
 9   Colour: Uni black (predominantly); some combinations black,red,white
10   Pecularity: hook shaped horns
11 - Main use: (1) bullfight,(2) meat,(3) fur
12   Spec. abilities: great maternal instinct, brave, nobleness
13   Performance compared with STB Charolais:
14     higher: muscularity
15     equal:  calving ease
16     lower:  handling ease, daily gain, calving interval
17 - Management: stationary; housing: no; adapt. to hard conditions
18 - Conservation progr.: live animals: miss;Semen: Yes;Embryos: miss
19   Status: normal
```

20 - Similar breeds (see group 2/1 on page 76)	EN	Country	Status
21 Cardena Andaluza	60	E	crit.end.
22 Serrana Negra	232	E	crit.end.
23 Camargue	58	F	pot. end.
24 Race Espagnole	41	F	pot. end.

CATTLE

1 - Vianesa   EN   263
2   Vianesa; Orense
3   Conselleria Agricultura, Ganaderia y Montes de Xunta de   HB:miss
4   Galicia-Santiago de Compostela (La Coruna)
5 - Autochthon local breed
7   Numbers 1991: 14/200; HB: 84; miss; 50 %; Ne = 26
8 - Height: miss / miss cm; Weight: 850/550 kg; Herd number: 41; AI: Yes
9   Colour: Uni brown
10 Pecularity: horns of bull: hooks/half moon, cows: longer and spiral
11 - Main use: (1) meat,(2) tractive power,(3) miss
12 Spec. abilities: rustic, docile
13 Performance compared with STB miss:
14   higher: miss
15   equal: miss
16   lower: miss
17 - Management: stationary; housing: 2-6 m.; mixed system
18 - Conservation progr.: live animals: miss;Semen: 11;Embryos: Yes
19 Status: critically endang.;Watch: ♂♂,HB♀♀,%pure!
20 - Similar breeds (see group 5/4 on page 80)   EN Country Status
21 Frieiresa   90   E   crit.end.
22 Limiana   155   E   crit.end.
23 Barrosa   21   P   normal
24 Arouquesa   11   P   normal

SHEEP

1 - Cartera   EN   444
2   Cartera; Teruel and Castellon
3   Diputacion Provincial de Teruel   HB:miss
4   Arrufat, Finca "El Chantre", Teruel
5 - Composite of Merino, Aragonesa
7   Numbers 1991: 130/4650; HB: 460; miss; 80 %; Ne = 405
8 - Height: miss / miss cm; Weight: 80/60 kg; Herd number: 85; AI: miss
9   Colour: Uni white
10 Pecularity: horns 0/0, wool covers head, strong legs
11 - Main use: (1) meat,(2) wool,(3) miss
12 Spec. abilities: extreme continental climate, litter size 1.3 - 1.5
13 Performance compared with STB miss:
14   higher: miss
15   equal: miss
16   lower: miss
17 - Management: transhumant; housing: no/≈ 2 m.; 1300-1800 m high
18 - Conservation progr.: live animals: miss;Semen: miss;Embryos: miss
19 Status: normal;   Watch: HB♀♀,%pure,trend!
20 - Similar breeds (see group 8/3 on page 95)   EN Country Status
21 Rouge du Roussillon   606   F   crit.end.
22 Nostrana   570   I   endanger.
23 Barbaresca Siciliana   410   I   normal
24 Barbaresca della Campania   409   I   normal

```
1 - Chamarita                                                    EN  449
2   Chamarita; Rioja
3   AROCHA                                                       HB:miss
4   Logrono 26071, 11 de Junio 9
5 - Autochthon old iberic type
7   Numbers 1992: 68/30000; HB: 4277; miss; 80 %; Ne = 268
8 - Height: miss / miss cm; Weight: 55/35 kg; Herd number: 18; AI: miss
9   Colour: Uni black, white
10  Pecularity: horns 2,0/0, little ears
11 - Main use: (1) meat,(2) miss,(3) miss
12  Spec. abilities: lambing mostly in December/January
13  Performance compared with STB miss:
14    higher: miss
15    equal:  miss
16    lower:  miss
17 - Management: stationary; housing: no; mountainous area
18 - Conservation progr.: live animals: miss;Semen: miss;Embryos: miss
19  Status: normal;             Watch: %pure!
```

20 - Similar breeds (see group 8/2 on page 94)	EN	Country	Status
21 Ibicenca	511	E	crit.end.
22 Palmera	578	E	crit.end.
23 Segurena	625	E	normal
24 Badana	406	P	normal

```
1 - Churra Lebrijana                                             EN  456
2   Andalusian Churra; Andalusia : Huelva
3   ANCHE, Palencia 34001, Avda. Casado del Alisal 21            HB:miss
5 - Autochthon Churra branche with celtic origen
6   Incrossing since 1960 from Suffolk 642 United Kingdom
7   Numbers 1991: 35/828; HB: 72; increasing; 80 %; Ne = 86
8 - Height: 69/65 cm; Weight: 80/60 kg; Herd number: 6; AI: miss
9   Colour: Uni white, some combination, perife black eyes, ears, lips
10  Pecularity: horns 2/0, spiral, rings, charact. tuft on head
11 - Main use: (1) meat,(2) miss,(3) miss
12  Spec. abilities: resist. to foot rot and fascioliasis,adapt. to dump
13  Performance compared with STB Merino Grazalema 546:
14    higher: fiber thickness, litter size
15    equal:  age of sex. matur.,length of mating season,lambing interv.
16    lower:  wool yield, muscularity, daily gain, leanness
17 - Management: stationary; housing: no; low Guadalquivir marshes
18 - Conservation progr.: live animals: Yes;Semen: miss;Embryos: miss
19  Status: endangered;        Watch: HB♀♀,herds,%pure,%incross!
```

20 - Similar breeds (see group 8/4 on page 95)	EN	Country	Status
21 Rubia de El Molar	610	E	pot. end.
22 Churra Algarvia	454	P	normal
23 Galega Mirandesa	494	P	normal
24 Churra da Terra Quente	455	P	normal

```
 1 - Churra Tensina                                                  EN   457
 2   Tensina Churra; Huesca
 3   Comunidad Autonoma de Madrid, Consejeria de Agricultura         HB:miss
 4   Servicio de Ganaderia, Madrid 28040
 5 - Belongs to the Churra group
 7   Numbers 1991: 95/4100; HB: miss; miss; 60 %; Ne = 371
 8 - Height: miss / miss cm; Weight: 65/45 kg; Herd number: 27; AI: miss
 9   Colour: Uni white, black spots on head and legs
10   Pecularity: horns 2,0/2,0, mostly without horns; rustic
11 - Main use: (1) milk,(2) meat,(3) miss
12   Spec. abilities: cold and humid, hot and arid climate
13   Performance compared with STB miss:
14     higher: miss
15     equal: miss
16     lower: miss
17 - Management: transhumant/stationary; housing: no/2-6 m.;
18 - Conservation progr.: live animals: miss;Semen: miss;Embryos: miss
19   Status: normal;            Watch: HB♀♀,%pure,trend!
20 - Similar breeds (see group 8/4 on page 95)      EN Country Status
21   Churra Lebrijana                              456   E    endanger.
22   Rubia de El Molar                             610   E    pot. end.
23   Churra da Terra Quente                        455   P    normal
24   Churra Algarvia                               454   P    normal
```

```
 1 - Colmenarena                                                     EN   468
 2   Colmenar; Madrid
 3   Comunidad Autonoma de Madrid, Consejeria de Agricultura         HB:miss
 4   Servicio de Ganaderia, Madrid 28040
 5 - Autochthon, similar to Churra Castellana
 7   Numbers 1991: 45/6000; HB: miss; miss; 80 %; Ne = 179
 8 - Height: miss / miss cm; Weight: 50/33 kg; Herd number: 50; AI: miss
 9   Colour: Uni white, black spots at eyes, ears, mouth and legs
10   Pecularity: horns 2,0/0, has wool on the head, rustic
11 - Main use: (1) milk,(2) lamb production,(3) miss
12   Spec. abilities: litter size 1.2, cheese
13   Performance compared with STB miss:
14     higher: miss
15     equal: miss
16     lower: miss
17 - Management: stationary; housing: ≈ 2/2-6 m.; semiextensive system
18 - Conservation progr.: live animals: miss;Semen: miss;Embryos: miss
19   Status: normal;            Watch: HB♀♀,%pure,trend!
20 - Similar breeds (see group 8/4 on page 95)      EN Country Status
21   Churra Lebrijana                              456   E    endanger.
22   Rubia de El Molar                             610   E    pot. end.
23   Churra da Terra Quente                        455   P    normal
24   Churra Algarvia                               454   P    normal
```

```
 1 - Granadina, Montesina, Ojinegra, Ojalada                 EN   500
 2   Montesina; Andalusia: Granada and Jaen
 3   Departamento de Genetica, Facultad de Veterinaria         HB:miss
 4   Cordoba 14005
 5 - Autochthon, origin in the Iberic branch
 6   Incrossing since 1960 from breed Segurena 625 Spain
 7   Numbers 1986: 3594/83709; HB: miss; decreasing; 70 %; Ne = 13784
 8 - Height: 67/65 cm; Weight: 56/32 kg; Herd number: miss; AI: miss
 9   Colour: Uni white,some combin.,black spots around eyes, ears, mouth
10   Pecularity: horns 2/0,close spiral,esophagus dripping covered.w.wool
11 - Main use: (1) meat,(2) wool,(3) miss
12   Spec. abilities: three lambings in two years, meat quality
13   Performance compared with STB Merino Grazalema 546:
14     higher: fiber thickness
15     equal:  litter size,milk yield,% fat,% protein,age of sexual mat.
16     lower:  muscularity, daily gain, carcass leanness, wool yield
17 - Management: transhumant; housing: no; outdoor in winter,poor land
18 - Conservation progr.: live animals: miss;Semen: miss;Embryos: miss
19   Status: potential. endang.;Watch: HB♀♀,trend,%pure,%incross!
20 - Similar breeds (see group 7/10 on page 93)     EN  Country Status
21   Xisqueta                                       577    E    normal
```

```
 1 - Ibicenca                                                 EN   511
 2   Ibiza; Ibiza and Formentera
 3   Diputacion Provincial de Teruel                          HB:miss
 4   Arrufat, Finca "El Chantre", Teruel
 5 - miss
 7   Numbers 1991: 5/950; HB: miss; miss; 10 %; Ne = 9
 8 - Height: miss/miss cm; Weight: miss/miss kg; Herd number: 36;AI: miss
 9   Colour: Uni white, sometimes pigmentation on the head
10   Pecularity: horns 0/0, big head and ears, rustic
11 - Main use: (1) milk,(2) miss,(3) miss
12   Spec. abilities: litter size 1.5, mediterranean climate
13   Performance compared with STB miss:
14     higher: miss
15     equal:  miss
16     lower:  miss
17 - Management: stationary; housing: no
18 - Conservation progr.: live animals: miss;Semen: miss;Embryos: miss
19   Status: critically endang.;Watch: ♂♂,HB♀♀,%pure!
20 - Similar breeds (see group 8/2 on page 94)      EN  Country Status
21   Palmera                                        578    E    crit.end.
22   Maellana                                       536    E    pot. end.
23   Chamarita                                      449    E    normal
24   Badana                                         406    P    normal
```

```
 1 - Maellana                                                EN  536
 2   Maellana; Zaragoza, Teruel and Tarragona
 3   Diputacion Provincial de Teruel, Finca "El Chantre", Teruel  HB:miss
 5 - Autochthon Ovis Aries Ligeriensis (same branch as Aragonesa,
 6   Manchega)
 7   Numbers 1991: 110/3600; HB: 170; miss; 40 %; Ne = 267
 8 - Height: miss / miss cm; Weight: 80/58 kg; Herd number: 64; AI: miss
 9   Colour: Uni white
10   Pecularity: horns 0/0, long neck, lop ears, long extremities
11 - Main use: (1) meat,(2) lambs called "Ternasco",(3) miss
12   Spec. abilities: two lambings per year possible
13   Performance compared with STB miss:
14     higher: miss
15     equal: miss
16     lower: miss
17 - Management: stationary; housing: 2-6 m.; semidesert with bushes
18 - Conservation progr.: live animals: miss;Semen: miss;Embryos: miss
19   Status: potential. endang.;Watch: HB♀♀,%pure,trend!
```

20 - <u>Similar breeds</u> (see group 8/2 on page 94)   <u>EN</u> <u>Country</u> <u>Status</u>

		EN	Country	Status
21	Ibicenca	511	E	crit.end.
22	Palmera	578	E	crit.end.
23	Chamarita	449	E	normal
24	Badana	406	P	normal

```
 1 - Menorquina                                              EN  543
 2   Minorcan; Menorca
 3   Asociacion de Criadores de Ganado ovino de raza Menorquina   HB:miss
 4   Alayor, Menorca
 5 - miss
 7   Numbers 1991: 71/7000; HB: 1180; miss; 30 %; Ne = 268
 8 - Height: miss / miss cm; Weight: 60/43 kg; Herd number: 43; AI: miss
 9   Colour: Uni white
10   Pecularity: horns 2,0/0, little head, long tail
11 - Main use: (1) milk,(2) meat,(3) typical cheese
12   Spec. abilities: lambs 25-30 kg, mediterranean climate, rustic
13   Performance compared with STB miss:
14     higher: miss
15     equal: miss
16     lower: miss
17 - Management: stationary; housing: no; strong winds
18 - Conservation progr.: live animals: miss;Semen: miss;Embryos: miss
19   Status: potential. endang.;Watch: %pure,trend!
```

20 - <u>Similar breeds</u> (see group 5/2 on page 89)   <u>EN</u> <u>Country</u> <u>Status</u>

		EN	Country	Status
21	Caussenard des Garrigues	447	F	crit.end.
22	Altamurana	401	I	crit.end.
23	Caussenard du Lot	448	F	normal
24	Basco-Bearnaise	412	F	normal

```
1 - Merina                                              EN  545
2   Spanish Merino; Andalusia and Estremadura
3   Asociacion Nacional de Criadores de Ganado Merino      HB:1978
4   Madrid 28040
5 - Composite of primitive graunch,Ovis Aries Vignei;historically impor-
6   tant;incross. since 1960 from Merino Precoce 555 F, Suffolk 642 GB
7   Numbers 1991: 49/788; HB: miss; increasing; 100 %; Ne = 185
8 - Height: 82/7 cm; Weight: 83/52 kg; Herd number: miss; AI: miss
9   Colour: Uni white
10  Pecularity: horns 2/0, spiral and with triangular section, rustic
11 - Main use: (1) meat,(2) wool,(3) fur
12  Spec. abilities: Pedroches cheese, adapted to extreme temperatures
13  Performance compared with STB Precoce:
14    higher: wool yield, age of sexual maturity, lambing interval
15    equal:  litter size, length of mating season
16    lower:  daily gain, wool or fiber thickness
17 - Management: stationary; housing: no; marginal lands
18 - Conservation progr.: live animals: Yes;Semen: miss;Embryos: miss
19  Status: minimally endang.; Watch: HB♀♀,%incross!
20 - Similar breeds (see group 1/1 on page 87)    EN  Country  Status
21  Merino de Grazalema                           546  E       min. end.
22  Merino Portugues                              547  P       normal
```

```
1 - Merino de Grazalema                                 EN  546
2   Merino Grazalema; Andalusia : Cadiz and Malaga
3   Serga-Andalucia, Departamento de Genetica, Facultad de    HB:miss
4   Veterinaria, Cordoba 14005, Avda. Medina Azahara 9
5 - Composite of Churro and Merino branches
6   Incrossing since 1960 from European Merinos
7   Numbers 1991: 40/1261; HB: miss; stable; 30 %; Ne = 155
8 - Height: 70/66 cm; Weight: 60/43 kg; Herd number: 20; AI: miss
9   Colour: Uni white, combination white and brown, spots in face
10  Pecularity: horns 2/2, in males spiral with two rings
11 - Main use: (1) milk, cheese "Grazalema",(2) meat,(3) wool
12  Spec. abilities: high lands (>1000 m), with high rainfall
13  Performance compared with STB Merino Grazalema 546:
14    higher: Breed is used
15    equal:  as standard breed,
16    lower:  no comparison possible.
17 - Management: stationary; housing: no; mountainous conditions
18 - Conservation progr.: live animals: Yes;Semen: miss;Embryos: miss
19  Status: minimally endang.; Watch: HB♀♀,%pure,%incross!
20 - Similar breeds (see group 1/1 on page 87)    EN  Country  Status
21  Merina                                        545  E       min. end.
22  Merino Portugues                              547  P       normal
```

```
 1 - Pallaresa, Xisqueta                                        EN  577
 2   Pallaresa; Lerida
 3   Comunidad Autonoma de Madrid,                           HB:miss
 4   Consejeria de Agricultura, Servicio de Ganaderia, Madrid 28040
 5 - Autochthon local breed belonging to the "Ojalado"-group
 7   Numbers 1992: 100/20000; HB: miss; increasing; 45 %; Ne = 398
 8 - Height: miss / miss cm; Weight: 58/40 kg; Herd number: 175; AI: miss
 9   Colour: Uni white, black spots on head and legs
10   Pecularity: horns 2,0/0, rustic
11 - Main use: (1) meat,(2) miss,(3) miss
12   Spec. abilities: litter size 1.1-1.3, longevity
13   Performance compared with STB miss:
14      higher: miss
15      equal:  miss
16      lower:  miss
17 - Management: transhumant; housing: no; 2000-2900 m high
18 - Conservation progr.: live animals: miss;Semen: miss;Embryos: miss
19   Status: normal;              Watch: HB♀♀,%pure!
20 - Similar breeds (see group 7/10 on page 93)   EN  Country Status
21   Granadina                                     500   E    pot. end.
```

```
 1 - Palmera                                                   EN  578
 2   Palmera; Canary Islands
 3   Cabildo Insular de La Palma (Canarias), Consejeria de      HB:miss
 4   Agricultura y Pesca, Gobierno Canarias, Tenerife 38080, Apartado 60
 5 - miss
 7   Numbers 1991: 9/55; HB: 25; miss; 83 %; Ne = 12
 8 - Height: miss/miss cm; Weight: miss/miss kg; Herd number: 6; AI: miss
 9   Colour: Uni white or black, sometimes black spots
10   Pecularity: horns 2/0
11 - Main use: (1) meat,(2) wool,(3) miss
12   Spec. abilities: for humid climate, stay by banana cult. in a fence
13   Performance compared with STB miss:
14      higher: miss
15      equal:  miss
16      lower:  miss
17 - Management: stationary; housing: no; steep zones of La Palma
18 - Conservation progr.: live animals: miss;Semen: miss;Embryos: miss
19   Status: critically endang.;Watch: ♂♂,HB♀♀,herds,%pure!
20 - Similar breeds (see group 8/2 on page 94)   EN  Country Status
21   Ibicenca                                      511   E    crit.end.
22   Maellana                                      536   E    pot. end.
23   Chamarita                                     449   E    normal
24   Badana                                        406   P    normal
```

```
1 - Roja Levantina, Sudat, Guirra                              EN  598
2   Levantina Red; Valenciana region
3   Conselleria de Agricultura y Pesca de la Generalidad Valen-  HB:miss
4   ciana, Direccion Gral. de Produccion e Industrias Agrarias, Valencia
5 - Imported as breed from Beni Ahsen Marocco/Africa
7   Numbers 1991: 125/5500; HB: 1795; miss; 95 %; Ne = 467
8 - Height: miss / miss cm; Weight: 68/48 kg; Herd number: 15; AI: miss
9   Colour: Uni red
10  Pecularity: horns 0/0, long legs, rustic, good maternal character
11 - Main use: (1) meat,(2) milk,(3) miss
12  Spec. abilities: tolerates aridity and drought; litter size 1.5
13  Performance compared with STB miss:
14    higher: miss
15    equal: miss
16    lower: miss
17 - Management: stationary; housing: no; extensive system
18 - Conservation progr.: live animals: miss;Semen: miss;Embryos: miss
19  Status: normal
```

20 - Similar breeds (see group 8/3 on page 95)	EN	Country	Status
21 Rouge du Roussillon	606	F	crit.end.
22 Nostrana	570	I	endanger.
23 Barbaresca Siciliana	410	I	normal
24 Barbaresca della Campania	409	I	normal

```
1 - Roja Mallorquina, Coete                                    EN  599
2   Red Majorcan; Majorca
3   PRAM                                                        HB:miss
4   INCA 07300, Mallorca, Plaza Blanquer 46
5 - Composite of Nord African breeds, autochthon breeds of Mallorca
7   Numbers 1991: 21/1400; HB: 480; miss; 35 %; Ne = 61
8 - Height: miss / miss cm; Weight: 75/55 kg; Herd number: 23; AI: miss
9   Colour: white with red head and feet; lambs born red
10  Pecularity: horns 2,0/0, big tail, head and legs without wool
11 - Main use: (1) meat,(2) miss,(3) miss
12  Spec. abilities: rustic, long sexual activity
13  Performance compared with STB miss:
14    higher: miss
15    equal: miss
16    lower: miss
17 - Management: stationary; housing: ≈ 2 m.; desert with bushes
18 - Conservation progr.: live animals: miss;Semen: miss;Embryos: miss
19  Status: minimally endang.; Watch: HB♀♀,%pure,trend!
```

20 - Similar breeds (see group 8/3 on page 95)	EN	Country	Status
21 Rouge du Roussillon	606	F	crit.end.
22 Nostrana	570	I	endanger.
23 Barbaresca Siciliana	410	I	normal
24 Barbaresca della Campania	409	I	normal

SPAIN   SHEEP

```
1 - Rubia de El Molar                                            EN  610
2    Somosierra Blond; Madrid
3    Comunidad Autonoma de Madrid, Consejeria de Agricultura      HB:miss
4    Servicio de Ganaderia, Madrid 28040
5 - Autochthon breed, similar to "Churra robisca Burgalesa"
7    Numbers 1991: 45/6000; HB: miss; miss; 65 %; Ne = 179
8 - Height: miss / miss cm; Weight: 60/43 kg; Herd number: 35; AI: miss
9    Colour: Uni white, blond spots on head, legs and body
10   Pecularity: horns 2,0/2,0, frequency of polled animals is higher
11 - Main use: (1) milk,(2) meat,(3) miss
12   Spec. abilities: litter size 1.2, long sexual activity
13   Performance compared with STB miss:
14      higher: miss
15      equal:  miss
16      lower:  miss
17 - Management: stationary; housing: ≈ 2 m.; mountain 1000-2000 m high
18 - Conservation progr.: live animals: miss;Semen: miss;Embryos: miss
19   Status: potential. endang.;Watch: HB♀♀,%pure!
```

20 - <u>Similar breeds</u> (see group 8/4 on page 95)

		EN	Country	Status
21	Churra Lebrijana	456	E	endanger.
22	Churra Algarvia	454	P	normal
23	Galega Mirandesa	494	P	normal
24	Churra da Terra Quente	455	P	normal

SPAIN   SHEEP

```
1 - Segurena                                                     EN  625
2    Segurena; Andalusia and Levante: Almeria,Granada,Saen,Murci
3    Asociacion Nacional de Criadores de Ganado Segureno          HB:1978
4    Huescar (Granada), C/Campomanes Nr. 2
5 - Autochthon Manchega (native breed)
7    Numbers 1993: 40200/979721; HB: 20715; increasing; 75 %; Ne = 54682
8 - Height: 70/65 cm; Weight: 65/50 kg; Herd number: miss; AI: miss
9    Colour: Uni white, black and red spots around eyes, ears, legs
10   Pecularity: horns 0/0
11 - Main use: (1) meat,(2) milk,(3) wool
12   Spec. abilities: adapted to zones with irregular rain
13   Performance compared with STB Spanish Merino 545:
14      higher: litter size, fiber thickness
15      equal:  milk yield, length of mating season, lambing interval
16      lower:  wool yield, daily gain, age of sexual maturity
17 - Management: stationary; housing: no; mountainous country
18 - Conservation progr.: live animals: miss;Semen: miss;Embryos: miss
19   Status: normal
```

20 - <u>Similar breeds</u> (see group 8/2 on page 94)

		EN	Country	Status
21	Ibicenca	511	E	crit.end.
22	Palmera	578	E	crit.end.
23	Chamarita	449	E	normal
24	Badana	406	P	normal

```
1 - Blanca Serrana Andaluza                                    EN  307
2   Andalusian White; northern Andalusia
3   Cooperativa lechera QUESOL                                 HB:miss
4   Cordoba 14005, Plaza de la Magdalena
5 - Composite of primitive Prisca and Nubian goats
6   Incrossing since 1960 from Blanca Cectiberica Spain
7   Numbers 1991: 83/1737; HB: miss; decreasing; 80 %; Ne = 317
8 - Height: 82/74 cm; Weight: 93/63 kg; Herd number: 11; AI: miss
9   Colour: Uni white
10  Pecularity: horns 2/2,lyra-shaped,long open horns,triangular section
11 - Main use: (1) milk,(2) meat,(3) miss
12  Spec. abilities: adapted to marginal land and to continental climate
13  Performance compared with STB Murcia-Granada 340:
14    higher: muscularity, daily gain, carcass leanness
15    equal:  litter size, length of mating season, lambing interval
16    lower:  milk yield, age of sexual maturity
17 - Management: stationary; housing: no; live with the deers
18 - Conservation progr.: live animals: miss;Semen: miss;Embryos: miss
19  Status: potential. endang.;Watch: trend,%pure,%incross!
```

20 - Similar breeds (see group 6 on page 98)	EN	Country	Status
21 Girgentana	333	I	crit.end.
22 Istriana	337	I	crit.end.
23 Sempione	353	I	crit.end.

```
1 - Cabra Mallorquina                                          EN  313
2   Majorcan Goat; Mallorca and Levante
3   PRAM (Patronato Razas Autoctoras de Mallorca)             HB:miss
4   INCA, Mallorca 07300, Plaza Blanquer 46
5 - Autochthon breed
7   Numbers 1991: 91/1800; HB: miss; miss; 25 %; Ne = 346
8 - Height: miss/miss cm; Weight: miss/miss kg; Herd number: 45; AI:miss
9   Colour: Uni red; some combination of black, red, some black pigment.
10  Pecularity: big horns 2/2, type "Markhar", beard in 2 sexes
11 - Main use: (1) miss,(2) miss,(3) miss
12  Spec. abilities: rustic in steep zones higher than 800 m
13  Performance compared with STB miss:
14    higher: miss
15    equal:  miss
16    lower:  miss
17 - Management: transhumant; housing: no; extensive system, no control
18 - Conservation progr.: live animals: miss;Semen: miss;Embryos: miss
19  Status: minimally endang.; Watch: HB♀♀,%pure!
```

20 - Similar breeds (see group 8 on page 98)	EN	Country	Status
21 Derivata di Siria	323	I	crit.end.
22 Chevre du Rove	319	F	pot. end.
23 Negra Serrana	316	E	normal
24 Charnequeira	318	P	normal

1 - Castiza, Negra Serrana   EN 316
2   Andalusian Black; Castilla, La Mancha and northern Andalusia
3   SERGA-Andalucia, Departamento de Genetica, Facultad   HB:miss
4   de Veterinaria, Cordoba 14005, Avda. Medina Azahara 9
5 - Composite of Blanca Celtiberica, perhaps branch of Prisca type
6   Incrossing since 1960 from Malaguena 321 Spain, Murciana 340 Spain
7   Numbers 1989: 1400/25000; HB: miss; increasing; 80 %; Ne = 5303
8 - Height: 85/75 cm; Weight: 85/55 kg; Herd number: miss; AI: miss
9   Colour: Uni black; mouth and tail with white hairs
10 Pecularity: horns 2/2, Prisca and Nubian ears
11 - Main use: (1) meat,(2) milk,(3) miss
12 Spec. abilities: 160 % lambing percentage, temperament
13 Performance compared with STB Andalusian White 307:
14   higher: litter size, kid weight
15   equal: muscularity, daily gain, carcass leanness, % fat,% protein
16   lower: milk yield
17 - Management: stationary/transhumant; housing: no; marginal land
18 - Conservation progr.: live animals: miss;Semen: miss;Embryos: miss
19 Status: normal;   Watch: HB♀♀,%pure,%incross!
20 - Similar breeds (see group 8 on page 98)   EN Country Status
21 Derivata di Siria   323   I   crit.end.
22 Cabra Mallorquina   313   E   min. end.
23 Murciana-Granadina   340   E   normal
24 Charnequeira   318   P   normal

1 - Costena, Malaguena   EN 321
2   Malaga; Andalusia: Malaga and Sevilla
3   Departamento de Genetica, Facultad de Veterinaria   HB:1984
4   Cordoba 14005
5 - Composite of Ibex abisinio - Capra aegagrus
7   Numbers 1993: 22000/194517; HB: 7400; increasing; 80 %; Ne = 22150
8 - Height: 78/66 cm; Weight: 80/50 kg; Herd number: miss; AI: miss
9   Colour: Uni red, blond
10 Pecularity: horns 2,0/2,0, sabre shaped or spiral, tassels, beard
11 - Main use: (1) milk,(2) meat,(3) fur
12 Spec. abilities: rustic, fertility 85 %, precosity
13 Performance compared with STB Malta:
14   higher: miss
15   equal: daily gain,litter size,milk yield,% fat,l. of mating seas.
16   lower: % protein, age of sexual maturity
17 - Management: stationary; housing: 2-6 m.; adapted to marginal lands
18 - Conservation progr.: live animals: miss;Semen: miss;Embryos: miss
19 Status: normal;   Watch: %pure!
20 - Similar breeds (see group 5 on page 97)   EN Country Status
21 Di Benevento   305   I   crit.end.
22 Di Campobasso   324   I   crit.end.
23 Maltese   339   I   normal
24 Ionica   335   I   normal

```
 1 - Murciana-Granadina                                              EN  340
 2   Murcia-Granada; eastern Andalusia and the Levante
 3   Centro nacionale de Selección de la raza Murciana-Granadina  HB:1980
 4   Guadelope / Murcia / Spain
 5 - Autochthon Aegagrus
 7   Numbers 1993: 17550/382660; HB: 19411; increasing; 90 %; Ne = 36867
 8 - Height: 77/70 cm; Weight: 67/50 kg; Herd number: miss; AI: miss
 9   Colour: Uni brown
10   Pecularity: horns 0/0, beard in males
11 - Main use: (1) milk,(2) meat,(3) fur
12   Spec. abilities: for warm and dry climates, precocity
13   Performance compared with STB Malta:
14     higher: litter size, milk yield, % fat
15     equal:  daily gain, length of mating season, lambing interval
16     lower:  % protein, age of sexual maturity
17 - Management: stationary; housing: 2-6 m.;
18 - Conservation progr.: live animals: miss;Semen: miss;Embryos: miss
19   Status: normal
```

20 - Similar breeds (see group 8 on page 98)	EN	Country	Status
21 Derivata di Siria	323	I	crit.end.
22 Cabra Mallorquina	313	E	min. end.
23 Negra Serrana	316	E	normal
24 Charnequeira	318	P	normal

```
 1 - Payoya, Montejaquena                                            EN  343
 2   Montejaquena; Andalusia : Cadiz and Malaga
 3   Centro Experimental Agricola Gandero, Excma.             HB: Yes
 4   Diputacion de Cadiz, Jerez/Cadiz, Cta. de Arcos
 5 - Composite of Malaguena 321, Serrana Blanca 307 and Serrana negra 316
 6   Incrossing since 1960 from Granadina 340 Spain, Malaguena 321 Spain
 7   Numbers 1992: 369/6231; HB: 3500; increasing; 95 %; Ne = 1335
 8 - Height: 93/77 cm; Weight: 90/68 kg; Herd number: 40; AI: miss
 9   Colour: Combin.black,grey,red,brown,white;three colours are possible
10   Pecularity: horns 2/2, Prisca type, males with big horns, hard hair
11 - Main use: (1) milk,(2) meat,(3) cheese
12   Spec. abilities: adapted to extreme conditions (humid, change temp.)
13   Performance compared with STB Malaga 321:
14     higher: milk yield, age of sexual maturity
15     equal:  length of mating season, lambing interval
16     lower:  litter size, % fat
17 - Management: stationary; housing: > 6 m.;
18 - Conservation progr.: live animals: miss;Semen: miss;Embryos: miss
19   Status: normal;          Watch: %pure,%incross!
```

20 - Similar breeds (see group 9 on page 98)	EN	Country	Status
21 Roccaverano	347	I	crit.end.
22 Val di Livo (extinct)	363	I	crit.end.
23 Local breeds	338	GR	normal
24 Corse	320	F	normal

```
1 - Extremena retinta, Colorada, Olivenza                      EN   934
2   Extremadura Red; Andalusia, Estremadura, La Mancha
3   Departamento de Genetica, Facultad de Veterinaria              HB:miss
4   Cordoba 14005
5 - Autochthon breed
7   Numbers 1992: miss /10000; HB: miss; stable; miss %; Ne = 1810
8 - Height: 55/48 cm; Weight: 250/140 kg; Herd number: miss; AI: miss
9   Colour: Uni red
10  Pecularity: semi erect ears, very appreciated hams
11 - Main use: (1) meat,(2) miss,(3) miss
12  Spec. abilities: adapted to extensive exploitation in pasture land
13  Performance compared with STB Duroc:
14    higher: meat quality, feed conversion rate, daily gain
15    equal:  handling ease, piglet mortality
16    lower:  litter size, % lean, muscularity
17 - Management: nomadic; housing: 2-6 m.;
18 - Conservation progr.: live animals:  Yes;Semen: miss;Embryos: miss
19  Status: potential. endang.;Watch: HB♀♀,%pure!
20 - Similar breeds (see group 5/2 on page 103)    EN  Country Status
21  Mora Romagnola                                 977  I      crit.end.
22  Tamworth                                       1009 GB     min. end.
```

```
1 - Manchada de Jabugo                                          EN   971
2   Andalusian Spotted; Andalusia: Huelva
3   Departamento de Genetica, Facultad de Veterinaria              HB:miss
4   Cordoba 14005
5 - Composite of Iberico Negro 981 and Retinto 934, varieties Oropesa
6   and Puebla; incrossing since 1970 from Iberico 981 Spain
7   Numbers 1993: 1/14; HB: miss; decreasing; miss %; Ne = 4
8 - Height: 55/48 cm; Weight: 250/140 kg; Herd number: 1; AI: miss
9   Colour: Combin. black, red, blond; black spots on red and blond coat
10  Pecularity: semi-erect ears, appreciated ham
11 - Main use: (1) meat,(2) miss,(3) miss
12  Spec. abilities: adapted to grazing in "dehesa" land
13  Performance compared with STB Retinto Iberico:
14    higher: litter size
15    equal:  % lean,feed conversion rate,meat quality,age of sex. mat.
16    lower:  daily gain, live weight at slaughter
17 - Management: stationary; housing: 2-6 m.;
18 - Conservation progr.: live animals:  Yes;Semen: miss;Embryos: miss
19  Status: critically endang.;Watch: ♂♂,HB♀♀,trend,herds,%incross!
20 - Similar breeds (see group 6/2 on page 104)    EN  Country Status
21  Sortbroget                                     1005 DK     crit.end.
22  Schwarz-Weißes Bentheimer                      996  D      crit.end.
23  Sibirskaya chernopestraya                      1001 USSR   pot. end.
24  Gloucestershire Old Spot                       936  GB     pot. end.
```

<u>PIGS</u>

```
1 - Negra Iberica                                        EN  981
2   Iberian Black; Andalusia and Estremadura
3   Departamento de Genetica, Facultad de Veterinaria    HB:miss
4   Cordoba 14005
5 - Autochthon breed, incrossing since 1970 from Tamworth, Duroc
7   Numbers 1990: 6436/71994; HB: miss; stable; miss %; Ne = 23631
8 - Height: 55/48 cm; Weight: 350/140 kg; Herd number: miss; AI: miss
9   Colour: Uni black
10  Pecularity: semi-erect ears, appreciated ham
11 - Main use: (1) meat,(2) miss,(3) miss
12  Spec. abilities: adapted for grazing in "dehesa" land
13  Performance compared with STB Retinto Iberico:
14     higher: miss
15     equal: % lean, litter size, feed conversion rate, meat quality
16     lower: miss
17 - Management: stationary; housing: 2-6 m.;
18 - Conservation progr.: live animals: miss;Semen: miss;Embryos: miss
19  Status: normal;            Watch: HB♀♀,%pure,%incross!
```

```
20 - Similar breeds (see group 4/1 on page 103)   EN  Country  Status
21  Gascon                                        935   F    crit.end.
22  Large Black                                   959   GB   min. end.
23  Alentejana                                    902   P    normal
```

<u>HORSES</u>

```
1 - Espanol-Andaluz                                      EN  742
2   Andalusian; Andalusia
3   Asociación de Criadores de Caballos de Pura Raza     HB:1800
4   Espanola, Sevilla 41002, C/ Trajano 2
5 - Autochthon Old Iberic horse; incrossing since 1950 from Arabs
6   (continously) and English Thoroughbred
7   Numbers 1986: 1300/6500; HB: 2600; increasing; 60 %; Ne = 3467
8 - Height: 156/154 cm; Weight: 512/412 kg; Herd number: miss; AI: miss
9   Colour: normally grey or black, more rarely bay
10  Pecularity: hazel: with red mane and black legs; silky mane and tail
11 - Main use: (1) sport/hobby,(2) to handle fighting bulls,(3) miss
12  Spec. abilities: adapted to warm climate, rustic, nobleness
13  Performance compared with STB Quarter Horse:
14     higher: handling ease, tamer, adaptability in dressage
15     equal:  pulling power, fertility
16     lower:  adaptability in jumping,speed in gallop,speed in trotters
17 - Management: stationary; housing: ≈ 2 m.;
18 - Conservation progr.: live animals: miss;Semen: miss;Embryos: miss
19  Status: normal;            Watch: %pure!
```

```
20 - Similar breeds (see group 3/1 on page 108)   EN  Country  Status
21  Lipizzan                                      776   F    crit.end.
22  Senner                                        801   D    crit.end.
23  Lipicanac                                     775   HR   normal
24  Lusitanien                                    779   F    normal
```

1 - Fjällras   EN   86
2   Swedish Mountain; northern and central Sweden
3   Avelsföreningen för Svensk Kullig Boskap   HB:1907
4   Nyland 87052, Rossö gard
5 - Autochthon North Swedish Cattle; imported as breed from Norway,
6   Finland; incrossing since 1950 from East Friesian and Jersey Sweden
7   Numbers 1986: 40/5000; HB: miss; decreasing; 10 %; Ne = 159
8 - Height: 130/120 cm; Weight: 650/415 kg; Herd number: miss; AI: Yes
9   Colour: Uni white,combin. black,red,white;spotted,black or red ears
10 Pecularity: horns 0/0
11 - Main use: (1) milk,(2) vegetation management,(3) meat
12 Spec. abilities: miss
13 Performance compared with STB Jersey:
14   higher: calving ease, milk yield, calf mortality
15   equal: muscularity, calving interval, age of sexual maturity
16   lower: % fat, % protein
17 - Management: stationary; housing: > 6 m.; mountainous area
18 - Conservation progr.: live animals: Yes;Semen: 60;Embryos: miss
19 Status: endangered;   Watch: HB♀♀,trend,%pure,%incross!
20 - Similar breeds (see group 1/6 on page 76)   EN Country Status
21 Tuxer   259   A   crit.end.
22 Pohjoissuomenkarja   207   SF   crit.end.
23 Berrenda negra andaluza   29   E   min. end.
24 Gruzinskii gornyi skot   107   GO   normal

1 - Röd Kullig Lantras   EN 225
2   Swedish Red Polled; central and northern Sweden
3   Svenska Rödkulleföreningen   HB:1912
4   Deje 66900, Westby 3536
5 - Autochthon North Swedish Cattle; imported as breed from N, SF
6   Incrossing since 1950 from Finnish Polled, Norwegian Red Polled
7   Numbers 1993: 25/175; HB: miss; increasing; 100 %; Ne = 73
8 - Height: 130/120 cm; Weight: 650/400 kg; Herd number: 10; AI: Yes
9   Colour: Uni red, combination red, white
10 Pecularity: horns 0/0
11 - Main use: (1) milk,(2) vegetation management,(3) meat
12 Spec. abilities: miss
13 Performance compared with STB Jersey:
14   higher: calving ease, milk yield, calf mortality
15   equal: muscularity, calving interval, age of sexual maturity
16   lower: % fat, % protein
17 - Management: stationary; housing: > 6 m.; mountainous area
18 - Conservation progr.: live animals: Yes;Semen: 25;Embryos: 3/2
19 Status: minimally endang.; Watch: ♂♂,HB♀♀,herds,%incross!
20 - Similar breeds (see group 4/4 on page 78)   EN Country Status
21 Mestnaya estonskaya   171   EW   crit.end.
22 Länsisuomenkarja   153   SF   endanger.
23 Norsk rodtfe   187   N   normal
24 Icelandic Dairy Cattle   118   IS   normal

1 - Gutefar   EN 505
2   Gotland Sheep; central and southern Sweden
3   Föreningen Gutefaret   HB:miss
4   Tystberga 61060, Aspnaset
5 - Autochthon old landrace-sheep form the isle of Gotland
7   Numbers 1993: 400/4000; HB: miss; increasing; 90 %; Ne = 1455
8 - Height: 75/70 cm; Weight: 80/45 kg; Herd number: 310; AI: miss
9   Colour: Uni grey; comb. black, grey, white; pied; white head
10 Pecularity: horns 2/2, short tail without wool, dark eyerings
11 - Main use: (1) meat,(2) vegetation management,(3) wool
12 Spec. abilities: miss
13 Performance compared with STB miss:
14   higher: miss
15   equal: miss
16   lower: miss
17 - Management: stationary; housing: no/≈ 2 m.; mountain and forest
18 - Conservation progr.: live animals: miss;Semen: miss;Embryos: miss
19 Status: normal;   Watch: HB♀♀!
20 - <u>Similar breeds</u> (see group 6/3 on page 90)   <u>EN</u> <u>Country</u> <u>Status</u>
21 Dansk Landfar   477   DK   crit.end.
22 Coburger Fuchsschaf   466   D   crit.end.
23 Foroyskur Seydur   491   FR   normal
24 Gronlandsk Fär   504   DK   normal

1 - Pälsfar   EN 580
2   Swedish Fur Sheep; country-wide
3   Svenska Faravelsförbundet   HB:miss
4   Uppsala 75594, Brogarden, Jälla
5 - Autochthon old landrace from the isle of Gotland
7   Numbers 1986: 1000/39000; HB: miss; stable; 100 %; Ne = 3900
8 - Height: 75/70 cm; Weight: 80/50 kg; Herd number: miss; AI: Yes
9   Colour: Uni grey; combination grey and white
10 Pecularity: horns 0/0
11 - Main use: (1) fur,(2) meat,(3) vegetation management
12 Spec. abilities: the quality of the fur is very high
13 Performance compared with STB Finnsheep:
14   higher: fur, daily gain, carcass leanness, wool yield
15   equal: age of sexual maturity, length of mating season
16   lower: litter size, milk yield, lambing interval
17 - Management: stationary; housing: 2-6 m.;
18 - Conservation progr.: live animals: miss;Semen: 10;Embryos: miss
19 Status: normal;   Watch: HB♀♀!
20 - <u>Similar breeds</u> (see group 6/3 on page 90)   <u>EN</u> <u>Country</u> <u>Status</u>
21 Dansk Landfar   477   DK   crit.end.
22 Coburger Fuchsschaf   466   D   crit.end.
23 Foroyskur Seydur   491   FR   normal
24 Gronlandsk Fär   504   DK   normal

SHEEP

1 - Ryafar   EN 612
2   Rya Sheep; central and northern Sweden
3   Svenska Ryaklubben   HB:1936
4   Hallsberg 69400, Skogaholm
5 - Autochthon old landrace sheep of Sweden, imports from Norway
7   Numbers 1986: 200/2000; HB: miss; stable; 75 %; Ne = 727
8 - Height: 75/70 cm; Weight: 80/50 kg; Herd number: miss; AI: miss
9   Colour: Uni white; combination black, brown, white
10 Pecularity: horns 0/0
11 - Main use: (1) wool,(2) meat,(3) vegetation management
12 Spec. abilities: wool is long and curly
13 Performance compared with STB Finnsheep:
14   higher: length of fiber, wool yield, fiber thickness
15   equal: leanness, age of sexual maturity, length of mating season
16   lower: litter size, milk yield
17 - Management: stationary; housing: 2-6 m.;
18 - Conservation progr.: live animals: Yes;Semen: miss;Embryos: miss
19 Status: normal;   Watch: HB♀♀,%pure!
20 - Similar breeds (see group 6/3 on page 90)   EN   Country Status
21 Dansk Landfar   477   DK   crit.end.
22 Coburger Fuchsschaf   466   D   crit.end.
23 Foroyskur Seydur   491   FR   normal
24 Gronlandsk Fär   504   DK   normal

GOATS

1 - Svensk Lantras   EN 359
2   Swedish Landrace; central and northern Sweden
3   Svenska Getavelsförbundet   HB:miss
4   Trehörningen 89054, Djuptjärn3315
5 - Autochthon old nordic landrace, imported as breed from Norway
7   Numbers 1991: 200/4000; HB: miss; stable; miss %; Ne = 762
8 - Height: 75/65 cm; Weight: 70/40 kg; Herd number: miss; AI: miss
9   Colour: Uni white, combinations black, grey, brown, white
10 Pecularity: horns 2,0/2,0
11 - Main use: (1) milk,(2) vegetation management,(3) miss
12 Spec. abilities: miss
13 Performance compared with STB Saanen:
14   higher: miss
15   equal: muscularity, daily gain, leanness, litter size, milk yield
16   lower: wool yield, fiber thickness
17 - Management: stationary; housing: 2-6 m.;
18 - Conservation progr.: live animals: miss;Semen: miss;Embryos: miss
19 Status: normal;   Watch: HB♀♀,%pure!
20 - Similar breeds (see group 10 on page 98)   EN   Country Status
21 Suomenvuohi   358   SF   endanger.
22 Nederlandse Landgeit   341   NL   pot. end.
23 Norsk Geit   342   N   normal
24 Dansk Landrace   322   DK   normal

```
 1 - Nordsvensk häst                                          EN  787
 2   North Swedish Horse; country-wide
 3   Föreningen Nordsvenska Häst                             HB:1908
 4   Enebyberg 18246, Fenixvägen 10
 5 - Autochthon old Swedish Native Horse, imports from Norway
 6   Incrossing since 1950 from Döle breed 814 Norway
 7   Numbers 1986: 130/1500; HB: 1400; increasing; 100 %; Ne = 476
 8 - Height: 157/154 cm; Weight: 700/600 kg; Herd number: miss; AI: miss
 9   Colour: bay,brown,chestnut,black; quite often dun with black points
10   Pecularity: very few white markings
11 - Main use: (1) tractive power,(2) sport/hobby,(3) excel. timber-horse
12   Spec. abilities: miss
13   Performance compared with STB Fjord:
14     higher: pulling power, daily gain, speed in trotters
15     equal:  handling ease, adaptability in dressage and in military
16     lower:  miss
17 - Management: stationary; housing: > 6 m.;
18 - Conservation progr.: live animals: miss;Semen: miss;Embryos: miss
19   Status: normal;            Watch: %incross!
20 - Similar breeds (see group 4/4 on page 110)    EN  Country Status
21   Schleswiger Kaltblut                          799  D      endanger.
22   Den Jydske Hest                               741  DK     min. end.
23   Tyngre Doelehest                              814  N      pot. end.
24   Suomenhevonen                                 809  SF     normal
```

```
 1 - Skogsruss                                                EN  805
 2   Gotland Pony; central and southern Sweden
 3   Svenska Russavelföreningen                              HB:1942
 4   Havdhem 62011, Bols
 5 - Autochthon old Swedish pony breed from Gotland
 6   Incrossing since 1950 from Welsh Pony United Kingdom
 7   Numbers 1986: 120/800; HB: 700; increasing; 100 %; Ne = 410
 8 - Height: 124/123 cm; Weight: 250/250 kg; Herd number: miss; AI: miss
 9   Colour: commonly bay or black, all standard colours also
10   Pecularity: miss
11 - Main use: (1) sport/hobby,(2) miss,(3) miss
12   Spec. abilities: very good pony trotter
13   Performance compared with STB Exmoor Pony:
14     higher: speed in trotters
15     equal:  pulling power, handling ease, adaptability in dressage
16     lower:  miss
17 - Management: stationary; housing: 2-6 m.;
18 - Conservation progr.: live animals: miss;Semen: miss;Embryos: miss
19   Status: normal;            Watch: %incross!
20 - Similar breeds (see group 5/1 on page 110)    EN  Country Status
21   Gotland Russ                                  820  SF     crit.end.
22   Nordlandshest                                 786  N      min. end.
23   Fjordhest                                     746  N      pot. end.
24   Fjord de Norvege                              745  F      normal
```

```
 1 - Braunvieh                                                    EN    40
 2   Brown Swiss; eastern Switzerland
 3   Schweizerischer Braunviehzuchtverband                   HB:1897
 4   Zug 6300, Chamstr. 56
 5 - Composite of Schwyzer Einsiedler Appenzeller, Gurten Vieh etc.
 6   Incrossing since 1950 from Brown Swiss USA
 7   Numbers 1983: 2500/440000; HB: miss; stable; 82 %; Ne = 9944
 8 - Height: 152/135 cm; Weight: 1050/610 kg; Herd number: miss; AI: Yes
 9   Colour: Uni brown
10   Pecularity: miss
11 - Main use: (1) milk,(2) meat,(3) miss
12   Spec. abilities: miss
13   Performance compared with STB Holstein-Friesian 230:
14     higher: miss
15     equal:  daily gain, % fat, % protein, calving ease, calf mortality
16     lower:  milk yield, muscularity,age of sexual maturity,milkability
17 - Management: stationary; housing: > 6 m.;
18 - Conservation progr.: live animals: miss;Semen: 351;Embryos: 35/66
19   Status: normal;                Watch: HB♀♀,%incross!
```

20 - Similar breeds (see group 5/1 on page 79)	EN	Country	Status
21 Original Allgäuer Braunvieh	189	D	crit.end.
22 Agerolese	2	I	crit.end.
23 Aubrac	14	F	normal
24 Österreichisches Braunvieh	190	A	normal

```
 1 - Eringer Rind                                                 EN    83
 2   Herens; Cant.of Wallis SW, middle part of Rhone valley
 3   Federation d'elevage de la race d'Herens                HB:1917
 4   Chateuneuf/Sion 1950
 5 - Autochthon Castana Pezzataneza
 7   Numbers 1990: 550/6500; HB: 4700; decreasing; 95 %; Ne = 1970
 8 - Height: 128/123 cm; Weight: 700/500 kg; Herd number: miss; AI: Yes
 9   Colour: Uni black, brown
10   Pecularity: vivacious behaviour
11 - Main use: (1) milk,(2) meat,(3) cow fights
12   Spec. abilities: meat quality
13   Performance compared with STB Brown Swiss 40:
14     higher: miss
15     equal:  muscularity, % protein, calving ease, calf mortality
16     lower:  milk yield, daily gain, % fat, age of sexual maturity
17 - Management: stationary; housing: > 6 m.; adapted to mountains
18 - Conservation progr.: live animals: miss;Semen: 47;Embryos: miss
19   Status: normal;                Watch: trend!
```

20 - Similar breeds (see group 5/2 on page 80)	EN	Country	Status
21 Alpine Herens	7	F	crit.end.
22 Tarentaise	253	F	normal
23 Valdostana Castana	260	I	normal

```
 1 - Hinterwälder                                          EN  116
 2   Hinterwald; country-wide
 3   Schweizerischer Hinterwälderzuchtverein               HB:1984
 4   Saanen 3792, Chalberhöhi
 5 - Imported as breed from 115 Germany
 6   Incrossing since 1950 from Hinterwälder 115 Germany
 7   Numbers 1991: 50/317; HB: miss; increasing; 100 %; Ne = 173
 8 - Height: 125/115 cm; Weight: 700/400 kg; Herd number: 93; AI: miss
 9   Colour: Combination red, white; pied
10   Pecularity: lyra formed horns, white head and legs
11 - Main use: (1) milk,(2) meat,(3) vegetation management
12   Spec. abilities: no IBR disease, longevity, vitality
13   Performance compared with STB Simmental 240:
14      higher: calving ease, handling ease
15      equal: % fat, % protein, calving interval, age of sexual maturity
16      lower:  milk yield, daily gain, milkability
17 - Management: stationary; housing: 2-6 m.; adapted to mountains
18 - Conservation progr.: live animals: Yes;Semen: miss;Embryos: miss
19   Status: potential. endang.;Watch: HB♀♀!
20 - Similar breeds (see group 3/3 on page 77)     EN  Country Status
21   Hinterwälder                                   115  D    min. end.
22   Vorderwälder                                   266  D    min. end.
```

```
 1 - Rätisches Grauvieh                                    EN  214
 2   Raetian Grey Cattle; mountainous regions
 3   Genossenschaft der Grauviehzüchter (GdG)              HB:miss
 4   Altstätten 9050, Höhi Götziberg
 5 - Composite of Bündener Bergviehschläge; imported as breed from
 6   Austria; incrossing since 1950 from Tiroler Grauvieh 256 Austria
 7   Numbers 1986: 33/210; HB: 210; increasing; 95 %; Ne = 114
 8 - Height: 130/120 cm; Weight: 750/450 kg; Herd number: 58; AI: miss
 9   Colour: Uni grey
10   Pecularity: miss
11 - Main use: (1) milk,(2) meat,(3) vegetation management
12   Spec. abilities: meat quality
13   Performance compared with STB Simmental 240:
14      higher: handling ease, calving ease
15      equal: muscularity, % fat, calving interval, age of sexual mat.
16      lower:  milk yield, daily gain, milkability
17 - Management: stationary; housing: > 6 m.; adapted to mountains
18 - Conservation progr.: live animals: Yes;Semen: miss;Embryos: miss
19   Status: potential. endang.;Watch: %pure,%incross!
20 - Similar breeds (see group 6/2 on page 81)     EN  Country Status
21   Gascon Areole                                   99  F    crit.end.
22   Garfagnina                                      97  I    crit.end.
23   Grigia Alpina                                  105  I    normal
24   Gascon                                          98  F    normal
```

1 - Schwarzfleckvieh   EN   230
2   Holstein-Friesian; country-wide
3   Schweizerischer Schwarzfleckviehzuchtverband   HB:1898
4   Posieux 1725, Grangenve
5 - Autochthon breed; incrossing since 1950 from Schwarzbunte 76
6   Germany, Holstein-Friesian USA, Canada
7   Numbers 1983: 350/130000; HB: miss; stable; 80 %; Ne = 1396
8 - Height: 156/141 cm; Weight: 1100/640 kg; Herd number: miss; AI: Yes
9   Colour: Combination black, white
10 Pecularity: miss
11 - Main use: (1) milk,(2) meat,(3) miss
12 Spec. abilities: miss
13 Performance compared with STB Simmental 240:
14   higher: milk yield, age of sexual maturity
15   equal: daily gain, calving ease, calf mortality, calving rate
16   lower: muscularity, % fat, % protein
17 - Management: stationary; housing: 12 m.;
18 - Conservation progr.: live animals: miss;Semen: 191;Embryos: 18/35
19 Status: normal;   Watch: HB♀♀,%pure,%incross!
20 - Similar breeds (see group 1/1 on page 75)   EN Country Status
21 Sortbroget Dansk Malkekvaeg   245 DK   pot. end.
22 Nizinna-Czarno-Biala   185 PL   pot. end.
23 Prim' Holstein   209 F   normal
24 Pie-Noire-Holstein   198 B   normal

1 - Simmentaler Fleckvieh   EN   240
2   Simmental; western Switzerland
3   Schweizerischer Fleckviehzuchtverband   HB:1879
4   Zollikofen 3052, Schnitzenstr.
5 - Composite of Saanen, Frutigen, Freiburger, local breeds
6   Incrossing since 1950 from Red Holstein Canada/USA,Montbeliard 176 F
7   Numbers 1983: 3200/460000; HB: miss; stable; 87 %; Ne = 12712
8 - Height: 155/137 cm; Weight: 1050/710 kg; Herd number: miss; AI: Yes
9   Colour: Combination red, white; pied
10 Pecularity: white head
11 - Main use: (1) milk,(2) meat,(3) miss
12 Spec. abilities: miss
13 Performance compared with STB Holstein-Friesian 230:
14   higher: muscularity, % fat, % protein
15   equal: daily gain, calving ease, calf mortality, calving rate
16   lower: milk yield, age of sexual maturity
17 - Management: stationary; housing: > 6 m.;
18 - Conservation progr.: live animals: miss;Semen: 444;Embryos: 20/46
19 Status: normal;   Watch: HB♀♀,%pure,%incross!
20 - Similar breeds (see group 3/2 on page 77)   EN Country Status
21 Ceske strakate   61 CZ   crit.end.
22 Simentalska   237 PL   min. end.
23 Montbeliard   176 F   normal
24 Fleckvieh   88 A   normal

SHEEP

```
 1 - Braunköpfiges Fleischschaf                                    EN  432
 2   Oxford Down; country-wide
 3   Schweizerischer Schafzuchtverband                            HB:1900
 4   Herzogenbuchsee BE 3360, Niederönz
 5 - Imported as breed from Great Britain, Germany; incrossing since
 6   1960 from Oxford Down 575 GB, Schwarzköpfiges Fleischschaf 622 D
 7   Numbers 1991: 1204/18000; HB: 10912; increasing; 90 %; Ne = 4337
 8 - Height: 81/74 cm; Weight: 110/80 kg; Herd number: 1800; AI: miss
 9   Colour: Uni white, brown and black face
10   Pecularity: horns 0/0
11 - Main use: (1) meat,(2) wool,(3) vegetation management
12   Spec. abilities: miss
13   Performance compared with STB Swiss White Alpine 669:
14      higher: lambing interval, muscularity, daily gain, litter size
15      equal:  leanness, age of sexual maturity, length of mating season
16      lower:  miss
17 - Management: stationary; housing: 2-6 m.;
18 - Conservation progr.: live animals: miss;Semen: miss;Embryos: miss
19   Status: normal
```

20 - Similar breeds (see group 4/3 on page 89)	EN	Country	Status
21 Schwarzköpfiges Fleischschaf	623	D*	endanger.
22 Schwarzköpfiges Fleischschaf	622	D	normal
23 Oxford Down	575	GB	normal

SHEEP

```
 1 - Bündner Oberländerschaf                                       EN  441
 2   Buendner Oberland; German and Raetoromanian Switzerland
 3   Pro Specie Rara                                              HB:1985
 4   St. Gallen 9000, Schneebergstr. 17
 5 - Composite of Vrinerschaf, Medelserschaf, Tavetscherschaf
 7   Numbers 1991: 25/144; HB: miss; increasing; 100 %; Ne = 69
 8 - Height: miss / miss cm; Weight: 45/35 kg; Herd number: 39; AI: miss
 9   Colour: Combination black, grey, brown, white
10   Pecularity: horns 2/2
11 - Main use: (1) vegetation management,(2) hobby,(3) meat
12   Spec. abilities: twinning, rare foot rot
13   Performance compared with STB Swiss White Alpine 669:
14      higher: litter size, length of mating season, lambing interval
15      equal:  age of sexual maturity
16      lower:  muscularity, leanness, daily gain, wool yield
17 - Management: stationary/transhumant; housing: 2-6 m.; poor pasture
18 - Conservation progr.: live animals: Yes;Semen: miss;Embryos: miss
19   Status: minimally endang.; Watch: ♂♂,HB♀♀!
```

20 - Similar breeds (see group 7/4 on page 92)	EN	Country	Status
21 Bayernwaldschaf	665	D	crit.end.
22 Cikta	462	H	endanger.
23 Schwarzbraunes Bergschaf	621	CH	normal

```
 1 - Charollais Suisse                                              EN  451
 2   Charollais; Canton VD (Vand)
 3   Schweizerischer Schafzuchtverband                           HB:1991
 4   Herzogenbuchsee BE 3360, Niederönz
 5 - Imported as breed from 560 France, incrossing since 1960 from
 6   Charollais 560 France
 7   Numbers 1991: 29/ miss; HB: 364; increasing; miss %; Ne = 107
 8 - Height: 74/67 cm; Weight: 120/80 kg; Herd number: miss; AI: miss
 9   Colour: Uni white
10   Pecularity: horns 0/0, head without wool
11 - Main use: (1) meat,(2) miss,(3) miss
12   Spec. abilities: miss
13   Performance compared with STB Swiss White Alpine 669:
14      higher: muscularity
15      equal:  daily gain, leanness, litter size, age of sexual maturity
16      lower:  wool yield, length of mating season, lambing interval
17 - Management: stationary; housing: 2-6 m.;
18 - Conservation progr.: live animals: miss;Semen: miss;Embryos: miss
19   Status: potential. endang.;Watch: %pure,herds!
```

20 -	Similar breeds (see group 3 on page 88)	EN	Country	Status
21	Mouton Boulonnais	559	F	crit.end.
22	Galway	495	IRL	endanger.
23	Mouton Charollais	560	F	normal
24	Cotentin	473	F	normal

```
 1 - Engadiner Schaf, Besch da pader                               EN  485
 2   Engadine Red; German and Raetoromanian Switzerland
 3   Schweiz. Engadinerschafzuchtverein                          HB:1985
 4   Bern 3006, Melchenbühlweg 6
 5 - Composite of Landschläge, Steinschaf, Bergamaskerschaf
 6   Incrossing since 1960 from Braunes Bergschaf Austria
 7   Numbers 1992: 40/250; HB: miss; increasing; 95 %; Ne = 138
 8 - Height: 75/68 cm; Weight: 80/65 kg; Herd number: 58; AI: miss
 9   Colour: Uni brown; some with white markings on head, white tail-tip
10   Pecularity: horns 0/0, lop ears
11 - Main use: (1) hobby,(2) vegetation management,(3) meat
12   Spec. abilities: 3 kids per year, aseasonal, rare foot rot
13   Performance compared with STB Swiss White Alpine 669:
14      higher: litter size, length of mating season, lambing interval
15      equal:  age of sexual maturity
16      lower:  muscularity, daily gain, fiber thickness, leanness
17 - Management: stationary; housing: 2-6 m.;
18 - Conservation progr.: live animals: Yes;Semen: miss;Embryos: miss
19   Status: minimally endang.; Watch: HB♀♀,%incross!
```

20 -	Similar breeds (see group 7/3 on page 92)	EN	Country	Status
21	Brigasque	436	F	crit.end.
22	Brigasca	435	I	crit.end.
23	Frabosana	492	I	crit.end.
24	Delle Langhe	478	I	normal

1 - Roux du Valais, Walliser Landschaf　　　　　　　　　　EN　609
2 　Valais Red; Wallis and western Switzerland
3 　Pro Specie Rara
4 　St. Gallen 9000, Schneebergstr. 17　　　　HB: Yes
5 - miss
7 　Numbers 1992: 25/150; HB: 95; increasing; 95 %; Ne = 59
8 - Height: 75/70 cm; Weight: 70/50 kg; Herd number: 22; AI: miss
9 　Colour: Uni brown, some white markings on head, backside and tailtip
10 　Pecularity: horns 2/2, spiral shaped, stick out sideways
11 - Main use: (1) vegetation management,(2) hobby,(3) meat
12 　Spec. abilities: aseasonal, cold climate, poor food
13 　Performance compared with STB Swiss White Alpine 669:
14 　　higher: length of mating season, litter size, lambing interval
15 　　equal: miss
16 　　lower: muscularity, daily gain, carcass leanness, fiber thickness
17 - Management: stationary; housing: 2-6 m.; adapted to mountains
18 - Conservation progr.: live animals: Yes;Semen: miss;Embryos: miss
19 　Status: minimally endang.; Watch: ♂♂,HB♀♀!
20 - Similar breeds (see group 7/2 on page 91)　　EN　Country　Status
21 　Braunes Bergschaf　　　　　　　　　　　　　431　　D　　crit.end.
22 　Istriana　　　　　　　　　　　　　　　　　516　　I　　crit.end.
23 　Bergamasca　　　　　　　　　　　　　　　415　　I　　normal
24 　Weißes Bergschaf　　　　　　　　　　　　416　　D　　normal

1 - Schwarzbraunes Bergschaf　　　　　　　　　　　　EN　621
2 　Swiss Black-Brown Mountain; Bern, Jura
3 　Schweizerischer Schafzuchtverband　　　　　　HB:1900
4 　Herzogenbuchsee BE 3360, Niederönz
5 - Composite of Jura, Simmentaler, Saanen, Frutiger and Roux de Bagnes
7 　Numbers 1991: 828/24000; HB: 8373; increasing; 99 %; Ne = 3014
8 - Height: 78/70 cm; Weight: 100/75 kg; Herd number: 2500; AI: miss
9 　Colour: Uni black, brown
10 　Pecularity: horns 0/0
11 - Main use: (1) meat,(2) wool,(3) vegetation management
12 　Spec. abilities: litter size, long breeding season
13 　Performance compared with STB Swiss White Alpine 669:
14 　　higher: litter size, length of mating season
15 　　equal: carcass leanness, fiber thickness
16 　　lower: lamb. interval, muscularity, daily gain, age of sex. mat.
17 - Management: stationary; housing: 2-6 m.;
18 - Conservation progr.: live animals: miss;Semen: miss;Embryos: miss
19 　Status: normal
20 - Similar breeds (see group 7/4 on page 92)　　EN　Country　Status
21 　Bayernwaldschaf　　　　　　　　　　　　　665　　D　　crit.end.
22 　Cikta　　　　　　　　　　　　　　　　　　462　　H　　endanger.
23 　Bündner Oberländerschaf　　　　　　　　　441　　CH　　min. end.

1 - **Spiegelschaf**   EN **637**
2   **Spiegel; Graubuenden, central Switzerland**
3   **Pro Specie Rara**   HB: **Yes**
4   **St. Gallen 9000, Schneebergstr. 17**
5 - **Composite of Landschläge**
7   Numbers 1992: **25/110**; HB: **miss**; **increasing; 100 %; Ne = 63**
8 - Height: **70/65** cm; Weight: **75/60** kg; Herd number: **24**; AI: **miss**
9   Colour: **white,black around eyes,black ear tips,kids brown markings**
10 Pecularity: **horns 0/0, head and belly without wool**
11 - Main use: **(1) vegetation management,(2) hobby,(3) meat**
12 Spec. abilities: **modest, in hilly country**
13 Performance compared with STB **Swiss White Alpine 669**:
14   higher: **length of mating season, lambing interval**
15   equal: **litter size**
16   lower: **muscularity, daily gain, leanness, age of sexual maturity**
17 - Management: **stationary**; housing: **2-6 m.**;
18 - Conservation progr.: live animals: **Yes**;Semen: **miss**;Embryos: **miss**
19 Status: **endangered**;   Watch: **♂♂,HB♀♀!**
20 - <u>Similar breeds</u> (see group 7/2 on page 91)   <u>EN</u> <u>Country</u> <u>Status</u>
21 **Braunes Bergschaf**   431 D   crit.end.
22 **Istriana**   516 I   crit.end.
23 **Bergamasca**   415 I   normal
24 **Weißes Bergschaf**   416 D   normal

1 - **Walliser Schwarznasenschaf**   EN **666**
2   **Valais Blacknose; upper Wallis**
3   **Schweizerischer Schafzuchtverband**   HB:**1950**
4   **Herzogenbuchsee BE 3360, Niederönz**
5 - **Autochthon breed**
7   Numbers 1991: **773/16000**; HB: **11865; stable; 99 %; Ne = 2903**
8 - Height: **80/75** cm; Weight: **100/80** kg; Herd number: **1600**; AI: **miss**
9   Colour: **Uni white, black nose, ears and feet**
10 Pecularity: **horns 2/2**
11 - Main use: **(1) meat,(2) wool,(3) vegetation management**
12 Spec. abilities: **for high alpine pastures**
13 Performance compared with STB **Swiss White Alpine 669**:
14   higher: **fiber thickness, age of sexual maturity**
15   equal: **length of mating season**
16   lower: **muscularity, daily gain, carcass leanness, litter size**
17 - Management: **stationary**; housing: **2-6 m.**;
18 - Conservation progr.: live animals: **miss**;Semen: **miss**;Embryos: **miss**
19 Status: **normal**
20 - <u>Similar breeds</u> (see group 3 on page 88)   <u>EN</u> <u>Country</u> <u>Status</u>
21 **Mouton Boulonnais**   559 F   crit.end.
22 **Galway**   495 IRL   endanger.
23 **Mouton Charollais**   560 F   normal
24 **Cotentin**   473 F   normal

SHEEP

```
 1 - Weißes Alpenschaf                                        EN  669
 2   Swiss White Alpine; country-wide
 3   Schweizerischer Schafzuchtverband                        HB:1900
 4   Herzogenbuchsee BE 3360, Niederönz
 5 - Composite of Luzein.,Tavetscher,Wildhaus,Appenzell,Schwyz.Brienz.
 6   Incrossing since 1960 from Württemberger Germany
 7   Numbers 1991: 3527/120000; HB: 44666; increasing; 90 %; Ne = 13076
 8 - Height: 79/71 cm; Weight: 110/80 kg; Herd number: 12400; AI: miss
 9   Colour: Uni white
10   Pecularity: horns 0/0
11 - Main use: (1) meat,(2) wool,(3) vegetation management
12   Spec. abilities: miss
13   Performance compared with STB Oxford Down 432:
14      higher: miss
15      equal:  leanness, age of sexual maturity, length of mating season
16      lower:  lambing interval, muscularity, daily gain, litter size
17 - Management: stationary; housing: 2-6 m.;
18 - Conservation progr.: live animals: miss;Semen: miss;Embryos: miss
19   Status: normal;           Watch: %incross!
20 - Similar breeds (see group 1/6 on page 87)   EN  Country Status
21   Berrichon de l'Indre                         417   F    min. end.
22   Inra 401                                     515   F    pot. end.
23   Charmoise                                    450   F    normal
24   Berrichon du Cher                            418   F    normal
```

GOATS

```
 1 - Appenzellerziege                                         EN  303
 2   Appenzell; Canton of Appenzell
 3   Schweizer Ziegenzuchtverband                             HB:1900
 4   Bern 3018, Stöckackerstr. 106
 5 - Autochthon local breed; incrossing since 1960 from Deutsche
 6   Edelziege 367 Germany, Saanen 349 Switzerland
 7   Numbers 1988: 58/ miss; HB: 687; stable; 90 %; Ne = 214
 8 - Height: 75/70 cm; Weight: 65/45 kg; Herd number: miss; AI: miss
 9   Colour: Uni white
10   Pecularity: horns 0/0, long hair on back and hindparts
11 - Main use: (1) milk,(2) meat,(3) hobby
12   Spec. abilities: miss
13   Performance compared with STB Saanen 349:
14      higher: miss
15      equal:  muscularity, leanness, litter size, age of sexual maturity
16      lower:  daily gain, milk yield
17 - Management: stationary; housing: 2-6 m.;
18 - Conservation progr.: live animals: Yes;Semen: 4;Embryos: miss
19   Status: normal;           Watch: %pure,%incross!
20 - Similar breeds (see group 1 on page 97)     EN  Country Status
21   Irish Goat                                   336   IRL  min. end.
22   Blanche                                      308   B    pot. end.
23   Gessenay                                     350   F    normal
24   Bila kratkosrsta                             306   CS   normal
```

```
 1 - Bündner Strahlenziege                                        EN  312
 2   Grisons Striped; Graubuenden
 3   Schweizer Ziegenzuchtverband                                HB:1935
 4   Bern 3018, Stöckackerstr. 106
 5 - Composite of special type of alpine goats; incrossing since 1960
 6   from British Alpine England, Poitevine 345 France
 7   Numbers 1988: 18/ miss; HB: 504; decreasing; 100 %; Ne = 47
 8 - Height: 80/75 cm; Weight: 65/45 kg; Herd number: miss; AI: miss
 9   Colour: Uni black, white markings on head, tail and legs
10   Pecularity: horns 2,0/2,0, typical light pattern on head
11 - Main use: (1) milk,(2) meat,(3) miss
12   Spec. abilities: miss
13   Performance compared with STB Saanen 349:
14     higher: muscularity, age of sexual maturity
15     equal:  daily gain, carcass leanness, litter size
16     lower:  milk yield
17 - Management: stationary; housing: 2-6 m.;
18 - Conservation progr.: live animals: Yes;Semen: 3;Embryos: miss
19   Status: endangered;          Watch: trend,%incross!
20 - Similar breeds (see group 4 on page 97)     EN  Country Status
21   Pfauenziege                                 344  CH   crit.end.
22   Sardonaziege                                357  CH   pot. end.
23   Nera Verzasca                               352  CH   normal
```

```
 1 - Gemsfarbige Gebirgsziege                                     EN  332
 2   Chamois Coloured; Graubuenden, Berner Oberland, Freiburg
 3   Schweizer Ziegenzuchtverband                                HB:1900
 4   Bern 3018, Stöckackerstr. 106
 5 - Autochthon local Alpine goat, Oberhasli-Brienzer, Bündner Strahlen-
 6   ziege 312; incrossing since 1960 from Alpine 301 France
 7   Numbers 1988: 141/ miss; HB: 3313; increasing; 100 %; Ne = 541
 8 - Height: 80/75 cm; Weight: 65/45 kg; Herd number: miss; AI: Yes
 9   Colour: Uni brown, white, black markings on head, back and legs
10   Pecularity: horns 2,0/2,0
11 - Main use: (1) milk,(2) meat,(3) hobby
12   Spec. abilities: miss
13   Performance compared with STB Saanen 349:
14     higher: muscularity
15     equal:  daily gain, leanness, litter size, age of sexual maturity
16     lower:  milk yield
17 - Management: stationary; housing: 2-6 m.;
18 - Conservation progr.: live animals: miss;Semen: 20;Embryos: miss
19   Status: normal;          Watch: %incross!
20 - Similar breeds (see group 2 on page 97)     EN  Country Status
21   Erzgebirgsziege                             330  D    crit.end.
22   Hneda kratkosrsta                           334  CS   min. end.
23   Bunte Deutsche Edelziege                    310  D    normal
24   Alpine                                      301  F    normal
```

```
1 - Pfauenziege                                           EN   344
2   Peacock Goat; German and Italian Switzerland
3   Pro Specie Rara                                       HB:miss
4   St. Gallen 9000, Schneebergstr.17
5 - Autochthon local mountain goat, Graubuenden
7   Numbers 1992: 15/150; HB: 50; stable; 80 %; Ne = 25
8 - Height: 80/73 cm; Weight: 75/56 kg; Herd number: miss; AI: Yes
9   Colour: Combination black,white: black legs,white tail and forehead
10  Pecularity: horns 2/2, peacock marking on head and body
11 - Main use: (1) vegetation management,(2) milk,(3) meat
12  Spec. abilities: miss
13  Performance compared with STB miss:
14    higher: miss
15    equal:  miss
16    lower:  miss
17 - Management: stationary; housing: 2-6 m.;
18 - Conservation progr.: live animals: Yes;Semen: miss;Embryos: miss
19  Status: critically endang.;Watch: ♂♂,HB♀♀,%pure!
```

	20 - Similar breeds (see group 4 on page 97)	EN	Country	Status
21	Bündner Strahlenziege	312	CH	endanger.
22	Sardonaziege	357	CH	pot. end.
23	Nera Verzasca	352	CH	normal

```
1 - Saanen                                                EN   349
2   Saanen; Berner Oberland, Saanental, higher Simmental
3   Schweizer Ziegenzuchtverband                          HB:1890
4   Bern 3018, Stöckackerstr. 106
5 - Autochthon original breed
6   Incrossing since 1960 from Saanen 350 France
7   Numbers 1988: 168/ miss; HB: 4502; decreasing; 100 %; Ne = 648
8 - Height: 87/79 cm; Weight: 75/50 kg; Herd number: miss; AI: Yes
9   Colour: Uni white
10  Pecularity: horns 0/0
11 - Main use: (1) milk,(2) meat,(3) hobby
12  Spec. abilities: good fertility, healthy, prowess in marching
13  Performance compared with STB Toggenburg 362:
14    higher: milk yield
15    equal:  daily gain, leanness, litter size, age of sexual maturity
16    lower:  muscularity
17 - Management: stationary; housing: 2-6 m.;
18 - Conservation progr.: live animals: miss;Semen: 14;Embryos: miss
19  Status: normal;              Watch: trend!
```

	20 - Similar breeds (see group 1 on page 97)	EN	Country	Status
21	Irish Goat	336	IRL	min. end.
22	Blanche	308	B	pot. end.
23	Gessenay	350	F	normal
24	Bila kratkosrsta	306	CS	normal

```
 1 - Schwarzer Tessiner, Nera Verzasca                         EN   352
 2   Verzasca; Ticino
 3   Ferderation romande d'elevage du menn betail             HB:1940
 4   Forel 1606
 5 - Autochthon local breed
 7   Numbers 1988: 112/ miss; HB: 1846; decreasing; 95 %; Ne = 422
 8 - Height: 85/80 cm; Weight: 70/50 kg; Herd number: miss; AI: miss
 9   Colour: Uni black
10   Pecularity: horns 2/2
11 - Main use: (1) meat,(2) milk,(3) miss
12   Spec. abilities: good fertility
13   Performance compared with STB Saanen 349:
14     higher: age of sexual maturity, muscularity, daily gain
15     equal:  carcass leanness, litter size
16     lower:  milk yield
17 - Management: stationary; housing: 2-6 m.; adapted to mountains
18 - Conservation progr.: live animals: miss;Semen: 2;Embryos: miss
19   Status: normal;            Watch: trend!
```

20 - <u>Similar breeds</u> (see group 4 on page 97)

		EN	Country	Status
21	Pfauenziege	344	CH	crit.end.
22	Bündner Strahlenziege	312	CH	endanger.
23	Sardonaziege	357	CH	pot. end.

```
 1 - St Galler Stiefelgeiss, Sardonaziege                      EN   357
 2   St. Gallen Booted Goat; German Switzerland
 3   Pro Specie Rara                                          HB: Yes
 4   St. Gallen 9000, Schneebergstr. 17
 5 - Autochthon mountain goat
 7   Numbers 1992: 25/150; HB: 130; increasing; 95 %; Ne = 67
 8 - Height: 84/73 cm; Weight: 76/42 kg; Herd number: 35; AI: miss
 9   Colour: Combination black, brown; dorsal black stripe
10   Pecularity: horns 2/2, markings on legs, feet and head
11 - Main use: (1) vegetation management,(2) meat,(3) milk
12   Spec. abilities: CAE-carrier, none affected
13   Performance compared with STB Toggenburg 362:
14     higher: miss
15     equal:  muscularity, carcass lean., litter size, % fat, % protein
16     lower:  milk yield, daily gain, age of sexual maturity
17 - Management: stationary; housing: 2-6 m.; adapted to mountains
18 - Conservation progr.: live animals: Yes;Semen: miss;Embryos: miss
19   Status: potential. endang.;Watch: %pure!
```

20 - <u>Similar breeds</u> (see group 4 on page 97)

		EN	Country	Status
21	Pfauenziege	344	CH	crit.end.
22	Bündner Strahlenziege	312	CH	endanger.
23	Nera Verzasca	352	CH	normal

```
 1 - Toggenburger                                                    EN  362
 2   Toggenburg; Toggenburg/Zentralschweiz,Obertoggenbg.,Werdenberg
 3   Schweizer Ziegenzuchtverband                                    HB:1890
 4   Bern 3018, Stöckackerstr. 106
 5 - Autochthon local breed
 6   Incrossing since 1960 from Pure Toggenburg 346 United Kingdom
 7   Numbers 1988: 124/ miss; HB: 2115; stable; 100 %; Ne = 469
 8 - Height: 80/75 cm; Weight: 65/45 kg; Herd number: miss; AI: Yes
 9   Colour: Uni grey, brown; ears and tail are bordered in white
10   Pecularity: horns 2,0/2,0
11 - Main use: (1) milk,(2) meat,(3) hobby
12   Spec. abilities: because of pigmented skin good adapt. to climate
13   Performance compared with STB Saanen 349:
14     higher: muscularity
15     equal:  daily gain, leanness, litter size, age of sexual maturity
16     lower:  milk yield
17 - Management: stationary; housing: 2-6 m.;
18 - Conservation progr.: live animals: miss;Semen: 16;Embryos: miss
19   Status: normal
```

		EN	Country	Status
20 -	Similar breeds (see group 3 on page 97)			
21	Thüringer Waldziege	360	D	crit.end.
22	Toggenburger	361	B	endanger.
23	Poitevin	345	F	min. end.
24	Pure Toggenburg	346	GB	normal

```
 1 - Walliser Schwarzhalsziege                                       EN  366
 2   Valais Blackneck; Wallis
 3   Schweizer Ziegenzuchtverband, Bern 3018, Stöckackerstr. 106  HB:1920
 5 - Autochthon Kupferziege
 7   Numbers 1988: 132/ miss; HB: 1587; increasing; 100 %; Ne = 488
 8 - Height: 80/75 cm; Weight: 65/45 kg; Herd number: miss; AI: miss
 9   Colour: Combination black, white: black forehand, white backhand
10   Pecularity: horns 2/2
11 - Main use: (1) meat,(2) milk,(3) sport/hobby
12   Spec. abilities: CAE-cleaned
13   Performance compared with STB Saanen 349:
14     higher: muscularity, leanness, litter size, age of sexual maturity
15     equal:  daily gain
16     lower:  milk yield
17 - Management: stationary; housing: 2-6 m.;
18 - Conservation progr.: live animals: miss;Semen: 8;Embryos: miss
19   Status: normal
```

		EN	Country	Status
20 -	Similar breeds (see group 7 on page 98)			
21	Vallesana	365	I	crit.end.
22	Serpentina	354	P	normal

1 - Schwalbenbauch Mangalitza, Wollschwein   EN 1020
2   Swallow-Bellied Mangalitsa; country-wide
3   Pro Specie Rara   HB:1985
4   St. Gallen 9000, Schneebergstr. 17
5 - Imported as breed from Hungary; incrossing since 1970 from Schwal-
6   benbauch Mangalitza Germany, 972 Hungary
7   Numbers 1992: 45/200; HB: 80; increasing; 100 %; Ne = 115
8 - Height: 75/72 cm; Weight: 180/140 kg; Herd number: 67; AI: miss
9   Colour: Combination black, blond, swallow-bellied
10 Pecularity: wool,thick hair,piglets striped like wild ones,lop ears
11 - Main use: (1) hobby,(2) meat,(3) fur
12 Spec. abilities: cold resistance
13 Performance compared with STB Large White 1007:
14   higher: meat quality
15   equal: handling ease
16   lower: daily gain, live weight at slaughter, % lean, litter size
17 - Management: stationary; housing: no
18 - Conservation progr.: live animals: Yes;Semen: 3;Embryos: miss
19 Status: potential. endang.;Watch: HB♀♀,%incross!
20 - Similar breeds (see group 2/2 on page 102)   EN Country Status
21 Normand   982   F   crit.end.
22 Chester White   913   GB   crit.end.
23 Mangalita   973   RO   min. end.
24 Mangalica   972   H   min. end.

1 - Schweizerisches Edelschwein   EN 1007
2   Large White; eastern and western Switzerland
3   SSZV Schweizerischer Schweinzuchtverband   HB:1911
4   Sempach 6204, Austria, Allmand
5 - Imported as breed from United Kingdom,Germany; incrossing since 1970
6   from Edelschwein 923 D, Yorkshire 939 Netherlands, Yorkshire 1023 GB
7   Numbers 1989: 1735/ miss; HB: 17524; stable; 50 %; Ne = 6315
8 - Height: 105/95 cm; Weight: 300/210 kg; Herd number: miss; AI: Yes
9   Colour: Uni white
10 Pecularity: erect ears
11 - Main use: (1) meat,(2) miss,(3) miss
12 Spec. abilities: high fertility
13 Performance compared with STB Large White 1007:
14   higher: Breed is used
15   equal: as standard breed,
16   lower: no comparison possible.
17 - Management: stationary; housing: 12 m.;
18 - Conservation progr.: live animals: miss;Semen: 26;Embryos: miss
19 Status: normal;   Watch: %pure!
20 - Similar breeds (see group 1/2 on page 101)   EN Country Status
21 Bela Zlahtna   904   SLO   crit.end.
22 Middle White   975   GB   min. end.
23 Deutsches Edelschwein   922   D*   normal
24 Vile uslechtile   1017 CS   normal

PIGS

```
1 - Schweizerisches Veredeltes Landschwein                    EN 1008
2   Swiss Landrace; central Switzerland
3   SSZV Schweizerischer Schweinzuchtverband                  HB:1911
4   Sempach 6204, Austria, Allmand
5 - Imported as breed from Germany, Netherlands; incrossing since 1970
6   from Deutsche Landrasse 920 D,Brit. Landrace 911 GB,Landrace 970 SF
7   Numbers 1989: 354/ miss; HB: 3578; decreasing; 19 %; Ne = 1289
8 - Height: 100/90 cm; Weight: 280/200 kg; Herd number: miss; AI: Yes
9   Colour: Uni white
10  Pecularity: lop ears
11 - Main use: (1) meat,(2) miss,(3) miss
12  Spec. abilities: low frequency of PSE, Halothane gene undisseminated
13  Performance compared with STB Large White 1007:
14    higher: % lean, meat quality, age of sex. mat., farrowing interval
15    equal:  litter size, feed conversion rate, daily gain, muscularity
16    lower:  miss
17 - Management: stationary; housing: 12 m.;
18 - Conservation progr.: live animals: miss;Semen: 30;Embryos: miss
19  Status: normal;            Watch: trend,%pure,%incross!
```

	Similar breeds (see group 2/1 on page 101)	EN	Country	Status
20 -				
21	Belgische Landrasse	907	D*	crit.end.
22	Zlotnicka biala	1024	PL	crit.end.
23	Landrace	952	CS	normal
24	Belgisch Landvarken	906	B	normal

HORSES

```
1 - Demi Sang Suisse                                          EN  740
2   Halfbred; country-wide
3   Federation Suisse d'elevage chevalin                      HB: Yes
4   Bern 3011, Kramgasse 58
5 - Imported as breed from France, Germany; incrossing since 1950 from
6   Halfbred France, Halfbred Germany, Halfbred Ireland
7   Numbers 1983: 90/2500; HB: miss; stable; miss %; Ne = 348
8 - Height: 168/162 cm; Weight: 600/500 kg; Herd number: miss; AI: miss
9   Colour: all solid colours
10  Pecularity: miss
11 - Main use: (1) sport/hobby,(2) tractive power,(3) miss
12  Spec. abilities: miss
13  Performance compared with STB Thoroughbred:
14    higher: pulling power, handling ease, fertility, daily gain
15    equal: miss
16    lower: age of sexual maturity
17 - Management: stationary; housing: > 6 m.;
18 - Conservation progr.: live animals: miss;Semen: 20;Embryos: miss
19  Status: normal;            Watch: HB♀♀,%incross!
```

	Similar breeds (see group 3/2 on page 108)	EN	Country	Status
20 -				
21	Altwürttemberger	701	D	crit.end.
22	Rottaler	797	D	crit.end.
23	Holsteiner Warmblut	760	D	normal
24	Cheval de Selle Francais	727	F	normal

```
 1 - Franches-Montagnes                                          EN   747
 2   Freiberg; northwestern Switzerland
 3   Federation Suisse d'elevage chevalin                        HB:1890
 4   Bern 3011, Kramgasse 58
 5 - Autochthon Freiberger and Anglonormaner; incrossing since 1950 from
 6   Arab Poland, Shagya Arab 802 Hungary, Anglo-Norman CH, Halfbred S
 7   Numbers 1983: 95/3630; HB: miss; stable; 95 %; Ne = 370
 8 - Height: 155/147 cm; Weight: 650/550 kg; Herd number: miss; AI: miss
 9   Colour: normally bay or chestnut
10   Pecularity: miss
11 - Main use: (1) tractive power,(2) sport/hobby,(3) Swiss Army
12   Spec. abilities: miss
13   Performance compared with STB Halfbred 740:
14     higher: pulling power, handling ease, fertility
15     equal:  age of sexual maturity, daily gain
16     lower:  miss
17 - Management: stationary; housing: > 6 m.;
18 - Conservation progr.: live animals: miss;Semen: miss;Embryos: miss
19   Status: potential. endang.;Watch: HB♀♀,%incross!
```

20 - Similar breeds (see group 4/1 on page 109)	EN	Country	Status
21 Auxois	709	F	crit.end.
22 Cheval de Trait Ardennais	730	L	min. end.
23 Cheval de Trait Belge	731	B	normal
24 Cheval de Trait Ardennais	729	B	normal

```
 1 - Haflinger                                                   EN   756
 2   Haflinger; country-wide
 3   Federation Suisse d'elevage chevalin                        HB:1956
 4   Bern 3011, Kramgasse 58
 5 - Imported as breed from Austria and 754 Germany
 7   Numbers 1983: 20/750; HB: miss; stable; 99 %; Ne = 58
 8 - Height: 148/145 cm; Weight: 400/350 kg; Herd number: miss; AI: miss
 9   Colour: light to dark chestnut
10   Pecularity: full flaxen mane and tail
11 - Main use: (1) tractive power,(2) miss,(3) miss
12   Spec. abilities: miss
13   Performance compared with STB Fjord:
14     higher: pulling power, fertility
15     equal:  handling ease, age of sexual maturity, daily gain
16     lower:  miss
17 - Management: stationary; housing: > 6 m.;
18 - Conservation progr.: live animals: Yes;Semen: miss;Embryos: miss
19   Status: potential. endang.;Watch: HB♀♀!
```

20 - Similar breeds (see group 5/8 on page 111)	EN	Country	Status
21 Haflinger	757	GB	endanger.
22 Haflinger	753	F	normal
23 Avelignese	710	I	normal
24 Haflinger	754	D	normal

```
 1 - Belogolovaya ukrainskaya                            EN   27
 2   Ukrainian Whiteheaded; northwestern Ukraine
 3   Food and Agriculture Organisation of the UN         HB:1926
 4   Rome 00100, Via delle Terme di Caracalla
 5 - Composite of Groningen Whiteheaded, Ukrainian Grey, Polesian
 6   Incrossing since 1950 from Groninger 106 Netherlands
 7   Numbers 1990: 10/4100; HB: miss; decreasing; 59 %; Ne = 20
 8 - Height: 136/127 cm; Weight: 750/460 kg; Herd number: miss; AI: miss
 9   Colour: Combination black, red, white
10   Pecularity: white head, feet, belly; black spectacles around eyes
11 - Main use: (1) milk,(2) miss,(3) miss
12   Spec. abilities: nutritionally undemanding
13   Performance compared with STB Russian Black Pied 64:
14      higher: miss
15      equal:  miss
16      lower:  milk yield, % fat
17 - Management: stationary; housing: 2-6 m.;
18 - Conservation progr.: live animals: miss;Semen: miss;Embryos: miss
19   Status: critically endang.;Watch: ♂♂,HB♀♀,trend,%pure,%incross!
20 - Similar breeds (see group 1/7 on page 76)     EN  Country Status
21   Groninger Blaarkop                            106    NL    endanger.
```

```
 1 - Buraya karpatskaya                                  EN   49
 2   Carpathian Brown; Trans-Carpathian Ukraine
 3   Food and Agriculture Organisation of the UN         HB:1973
 4   Rome 00100, Via delle Terme di Caracalla
 5 - Composite of Swiss Brown, Montafon, Allgäu, local
 6   Incrossing since 1950 from Brown Swiss USA, Jersey
 7   Numbers 1990: 448/63000; HB: miss; decreasing; 84 %; Ne = 1779
 8 - Height: 137/128 cm; Weight: 820/490 kg; Herd number: miss; AI: Yes
 9   Colour: Uni brown
10   Pecularity: miss
11 - Main use: (1) milk,(2) meat,(3) miss
12   Spec. abilities: miss
13   Performance compared with STB Russian Simmental 241:
14      higher: miss
15      equal:  miss
16      lower:  milk yield, % fat
17 - Management: stationary; housing: 2-6 m.;
18 - Conservation progr.: live animals: miss;Semen: miss;Embryos: miss
19   Status: potential. endang.;Watch: HB♀♀,trend,%pure,%incross!
20 - Similar breeds (see group 5/1 on page 79)     EN  Country Status
21   Original Allgäuer Braunvieh                   189    D    crit.end.
22   Agerolese                                       2    I    crit.end.
23   Aubrac                                         14    F    normal
24   Österreichisches Braunvieh                    190    A    normal
```

```
 1 - Krasnaya polskaya                                        EN  146
 2   Polish Red
 3   Food and Agriculture Organisation of the UN             HB: Yes
 4   Rome 00100, Via delle Terme di Caracalla
 5 - Autochthon breed of Poland and Ukraine; incrossing since 1950 from
 6   Latvian Brown 50, Estonian Red 143, Byelorussian Red 149
 7   Numbers 1990: 23/52000; HB: miss; decreasing; 77 %; Ne = 82
 8 - Height: 135/124 cm; Weight: 750/470 kg; Herd number: miss; AI: miss
 9   Colour: Uni red, brown, yellow
10   Pecularity: miss
11 - Main use: (1) milk,(2) meat,(3) tractive power
12   Spec. abilities: high fertility, undemanding feed requirements
13   Performance compared with STB Russian Black Pied 64:
14     higher: miss
15     equal: % fat
16     lower: milk yield
17 - Management: stationary; housing: > 6 m.;
18 - Conservation progr.: live animals: miss;Semen: Yes;Embryos: miss
19   Status: minimally endang.; Watch: HB♀♀,trend,%pure,%incross!
```

20 - Similar breeds (see group 4/3 on page 78)	EN	Country	Status
21 Donnersberger Rotvieh	101	D	crit.end.
22 Harzer Rotvieh	109	D	crit.end.
23 Rod Dansk Malkerace	222	DK	normal
24 Rood Ras van Belgie	224	B	normal

```
 1 - Krasnaya Stepnaya                                        EN  147
 2   Red Steppe; South-European part of USSR
 3   Food and Agriculture Organisation of the UN             HB:1923
 4   Rome 00100, Via delle Terme di Caracalla
 5 - Composite of Franconian, German + Swiss Brown, Angeln,
 6   Ukrainian Grey, Friesian
 7   Numbers 1990: 17500/4763000; HB: miss; decreasing; 81 %; Ne = 69744
 8 - Height: 138/129 cm; Weight: 800/490 kg; Herd number: miss; AI: Yes
 9   Colour: Uni red
10   Pecularity: occasionally white markings
11 - Main use: (1) milk,(2) meat,(3) miss
12   Spec. abilities: adapt. to continental climate of South Ukraine
13   Performance compared with STB Russian Black Pied 64:
14     higher: miss
15     equal: % fat
16     lower: milk yield
17 - Management: stationary; housing: 2-6 m.;
18 - Conservation progr.: live animals: miss;Semen: miss;Embryos: miss
19   Status: normal;            Watch: HB♀♀,trend,%pure!
```

20 - Similar breeds (see group 4/5 on page 79)	EN	Country	Status
21 Yurinskaya	276	USSR	crit.end.
22 Krasnyi megrelskii skot	150	GO	endanger.
23 Kalmytskaya	135	USSR	normal
24 Bestuzhevskaya	31	USSR	normal

```
 1 - Lebedinskaya                                              EN  154
 2   Lebedin; Sumy, northeastern Ukraine
 3   Food and Agriculture Organisation of the UN              HB:1950
 4   Rome 00100, Via delle Terme di Caracalla
 5 - Composite of Swiss Brown, Ukrainian Grey 231
 6   Incrossing since 1950 from Brown Swiss USA
 7   Numbers 1990: 486/207000; HB: miss; decreasing; 89 %; Ne = 1939
 8 - Height: 139/131 cm; Weight: 850/550 kg; Herd number: miss; AI: Yes
 9   Colour: Uni grey, brown
10   Pecularity: similar to Swiss Brown
11 - Main use: (1) milk,(2) meat,(3) miss
12   Spec. abilities: miss
13   Performance compared with STB Russian Simmental 241:
14     higher: miss
15     equal: % fat
16     lower: milk yield
17 - Management: stationary; housing: 2-6 m.;
18 - Conservation progr.: live animals: miss;Semen: miss;Embryos: miss
19   Status: potential. endang.;Watch: HB♀♀,trend,%pure,%incross!
```

20 - Similar breeds (see group 5/1 on page 79)	EN	Country	Status
21 Original Allgäuer Braunvieh	189	D	crit.end.
22 Agerolese	2	I	crit.end.
23 Aubrac	14	F	normal
24 Österreichisches Braunvieh	190	A	normal

```
 1 - Seraya ukrainskaya                                        EN  231
 2   Ukrainian Grey; central Ukraine
 3   Food and Agriculture Organisation of the UN              HB:1935
 4   Rome 00100, Via delle Terme di Caracalla
 5 - Autochthon Grey Steppe breeds of southern Europe; incrossing since
 6   1950 from Red Steppe 147 Ukraine,Simmental 241,Swiss Brown 234 USSR
 7   Numbers 1990: 13/684; HB: miss; decreasing; 73 %; Ne = 29
 8 - Height: 137/129 cm; Weight: 780/480 kg; Herd number: miss; AI: Yes
 9   Colour: Uni grey
10   Pecularity: miss
11 - Main use: (1) meat,(2) milk,(3) miss
12   Spec. abilities: high butterfat content of milk;viability;hardiness
13   Performance compared with STB Russian Simmental 241:
14     higher: % fat, milk yield
15     equal: miss
16     lower: miss
17 - Management: stationary; housing: 2-6 m.;
18 - Conservation progr.: live animals: miss;Semen: miss;Embryos: miss
19   Status: critically endang.;Watch: ♂♂,HB♀♀,trend,%pure,%incross!
```

20 - Similar breeds (see group 6/1 on page 80)	EN	Country	Status
21 Iskursko govedo	104	BG	crit.end.
22 Katerini	136	GR	crit.end.
23 Piemontese	197	I	normal
24 Maremmana	166	I	normal

```
 1 - Mirgorodskaya                                              EN   976
 2   Mirgorod; central Ukraine
 3   Food and Agriculture Organisation of the UN                HB:1940
 4   Rome 00100, Via delle Terme di Caracalla
 5 - Composite of Large White, Middle White, Berkshire, Large Black,
 6   Tamworth, local spotted pigs
 7   Numbers 1990: 3500/15600; HB: miss; decreasing; 93 %; Ne = 11435
 8 - Height: miss/miss cm; Weight: 275/217 kg; Herd number: miss; AI:miss
 9   Colour: Combination black, white; occ. black, black-and-tan or tan
10   Pecularity: erect ears with forward pitch
11 - Main use: (1) lard,(2) miss,(3) miss
12   Spec. abilities: adapted to pasture feeding
13   Performance compared with STB Large White 951:
14     higher: miss
15     equal: % lean, feed conversion rate
16     lower: litter size, daily gain
17 - Management: stationary; housing: 12 m.;
18 - Conservation progr.: live animals: miss;Semen: miss;Embryos: miss
19   Status: normal;              Watch: HB♀♀,trend,%pure!
```

20 - Similar breeds (see group 4/2 on page 103)	EN	Country	Status
21 Berkshire	909	GB	min. end.
22 Kemerovskaya	949	USSR	pot. end.
23 Aksaiskaya cherno-pestraya	901	KAZ	normal
24 Belorusskaya cherno-pestraya	908	BEL	normal

```
 1 - Ukrainskaya stepnaya belaya                                EN  1014
 2   Ukrainian White Steppe; southern Ukraine
 3   Food and Agriculture Organisation of the UN                HB:miss
 4   Rome 00100, Via delle Terme di Caracalla
 5 - Composite of improved native, Large White
 7   Numbers 1990: 10200/87200; HB: miss; stable; 90 %; Ne = 36527
 8 - Height: miss/miss cm; Weight: 322/238 kg; Herd number: miss; AI:miss
 9   Colour: Uni white
10   Pecularity: lop ears
11 - Main use: (1) general purpose,(2) miss,(3) miss
12   Spec. abilities: better adapted to climate of S. Ukraine than L.W.
13   Performance compared with STB Large White 951:
14     higher: litter size
15     equal: feed conversion rate
16     lower: % lean, daily gain
17 - Management: stationary; housing: 12 m.;
18 - Conservation progr.: live animals: miss;Semen: miss;Embryos: miss
19   Status: normal;              Watch: HB♀♀,%pure!
```

20 - Similar breeds (see group 1/2 on page 101)	EN	Country	Status
21 Bela Zlahtna	904	SLO	crit.end.
22 Middle White	975	GB	min. end.
23 Deutsches Edelschwein	922	D*	normal
24 Vile uslechtile	1017	CS	normal

```
 1 - Ukrainskaya stepnaya ryabaya                        EN 1015
 2   Ukrainian Spotted Steppe; southern Ukraine
 3   Food and Agriculture Organisation of the UN         HB:1961
 4   Rome 00100, Via delle Terme di Caracalla
 5 - Composite of Ukrainian White Steppe, Berkshire, Mangalitsa
 7   Numbers 1990: 297/329; HB: miss; decreasing; 100 %; Ne = 624
 8 - Height: miss/miss cm; Weight: 322/238 kg; Herd number: miss; AI:miss
 9   Colour: Combination black, white
10   Pecularity: semi-lop ears
11 - Main use: (1) lard,(2) miss,(3) miss
12   Spec. abilities: well adapted to the hot climate in the S. Ukraine
13   Performance compared with STB Large White 951:
14     higher: miss
15     equal:  litter size, feed conversion rate
16     lower:  daily gain
17 - Management: stationary; housing: 12 m.; hardiness
18 - Conservation progr.: live animals: miss;Semen: miss;Embryos: miss
19   Status: potential. endang.;Watch: HB♀♀,trend!
20 - Similar breeds (see group 4/2 on page 103)    EN  Country Status
21   Berkshire                                      909  GB     min. end.
22   Kemerovskaya                                   949  USSR   pot. end.
23   Aksaiskaya cherno-pestraya                     901  KAZ    normal
24   Belorusskaya cherno-pestraya                   908  BEL    normal
```

```
 1 - Aberdeen-Angus                                      EN    1
 2   Aberdeen-Angus; country-wide
 3   The Aberdeen-Angus Cattle Society, Pedigree House   HB:1842
 4   Perth PH2 8AD, 6 King's Place
 5   Autochthon
 6   Incrossing since 1950 from: Aberdeen-Angus Canada
 7   Numbers 1990: 400/9000; HB: miss; increasing; 65 %; Ne = 1532
 8 - Height: 145/125 cm; Weight: 1000/650 kg; Herd number: miss; AI: Yes
 9   Colour: Uni black
10   Pecularity: horns 0/0, naturally polled
11 - Main use: (1) meat,(2) vegetation management,(3) miss
12   Spec. abilities: miss
13   Performance compared with STB Hereford 112:
14     higher: muscularity, calving ease
15     equal:  daily gain,calving interval,age of sex. matur.,calf mort.
16     lower:  handling ease
17 - Management: stationary; housing: ≈ 2/2-6 m.;
18 - Conservation progr.: live animals: miss;Semen: 100;Embryos: miss
19   Status: normal;              Watch: HB♀♀!
20 - Similar breeds (see group 2/2 on page 76)     EN  Country Status
21   Kerry Cattle                                   140  IRL    min. end.
22   Murray Grey                                    181  GB     pot. end.
23   Galloway                                        94  D      normal
24   Deutsche Angus                                  80  D      normal
```

1 - Ayrshire   EN   18
2   Ayrshire; dispersed country-wide
3   Ayrshire Cattle Society of Great Britain and Ireland   HB:1877
4   Ayr KA7 2DE, Racehouse Road 1
5 - Autochthon Cunninghame & Dunlop Breeds of Ayrshire Scotland
7   Numbers 1986: 1200/2000000; HB: 120000; decreasing; 60 %; Ne = 4753
8 - Height: 142/131 cm; Weight: 1000/540 kg; Herd number: miss; AI: Yes
9   Colour: Combination black, red, brown, white
10 Pecularity: lyra-shaped horns, light muzzle
11 - Main use: (1) milk,(2) meat,(3) miss
12 Spec. abilities: small fat globule good for cheese making & diets
13 Performance compared with STB Holstein-Friesian 117:
14   higher: % fat, % protein, calving ease
15   equal: milk yield, muscularity, daily gain, calving interval
16   lower: miss
17 - Management: stationary; housing: 2-6 m.;
18 - Conservation progr.: live animals: miss;Semen: 300;Embryos: Yes
19 Status: normal;   Watch: %pure!
20 - Similar breeds (see group 3/6 on page 78)   EN Country Status
21 Ayrshire   17   IRL   endanger.
22 Suomen Ayrshire   247   SF   normal

1 - Beef Shorthorn Cattle   EN   24
2   Beef Shorthorn; Scotland, England and Wales
3   The Beef Shorthorn Cattle Society   HB:1822
4   4th Street, NAC, Stoneleigh, Kenilworth, Warwickshire CV8 2LG
5 - Composite of Teeswater, Hoderness, then bred for beef
6   Incrossing since 1950 from Maine-Anjou 163 France, Poll Shorthorn
7   Numbers 1993: 300/10000; HB: 3000; increasing; 75 %; Ne = 1091
8 - Height: 146/140 cm; Weight: 1150/700 kg; Herd number: 40; AI: Yes
9   Colour: Uni red, white and combination red/white
10 Pecularity: short horns any of the three colours - red,white or roan
11 - Main use: (1) meat,(2) vegetation management,(3) miss
12 Spec. abilities: miss
13 Performance compared with STB Hereford 112:
14   higher: milkability, milk yield, % fat, calving ease, calving rate
15   equal: muscularity, daily gain, calving interv., age of sex. mat.
16   lower: miss
17 - Management: stationary; housing: no/≈ 2/2-6 m.; marginal land
18 - Conservation progr.: live animals: miss;Semen: 6;Embryos: miss
19 Status: normal;   Watch: %pure,%incross!
20 - Similar breeds (see group 4/2 on page 78)   EN Country Status
21 Armoricaine   10   F   crit.end.
22 Kurganskaya   151   USSR crit.end.
23 Lincoln Red   159   GB   normal
24 Irish Shorthorn   124   IRL   normal

```
1 - Belgian Blue                                              EN    26
2   Belgian Blue; country-wide
3   British Belgian Blue Cattle Society                       HB:1983
4   Lawns Farm, Orrel, Wigan, Lancashire WN5 8UH
5 - Imported as breed from Belgium, Denmark
6   Incrossing since 1950 from Belgian Blue 33 Belgium
7   Numbers 1986: 102/735; HB: 492; increasing; 100 %; Ne = 338
8 - Height: 150/134 cm; Weight: 1296/865 kg; Herd number: miss; AI: Yes
9   Colour: Combination black, grey, blue, white
10  Pecularity: ultra muscled, extra lean
11 - Main use: (1) meat,(2) miss,(3) miss
12  Spec. abilities: low in cholestrol
13  Performance compared with STB Hereford 112:
14     higher: calf mortality, muscularity, calving interval, milk yield
15     equal:  handling ease
16     lower:  calving ease, calving rate
17 - Management: stationary; housing: 2-6 m.;
18 - Conservation progr.: live animals: miss;Semen: 30;Embryos: miss/200
19  Status: normal
```

20 - Similar breeds (see group 7 on page 81)	EN	Country	Status
21 Belgian Blue	25	IRL	pot. end.
22 Blanc Bleu Belge	33	B	normal
23 Bleue du Nord	36	F	normal
24 Blanc-Bleu-Belge	35	F	normal

```
1 - Belted Galloway                                           EN    28
2   Belted Galloway; southern Scotland
3   Rare Breeds Survival Trust Society and                    HB: Yes
4   National Agriculture Centre, Kenilworth, Warwickshire CV8 2LG
5 - Autochthon colour variety of the Galloway
7   Numbers 1986: 239/ miss; HB: 2187; stable; 87 %; Ne = 862
8 - Height: miss/miss cm; Weight: miss/535 kg; Herd number: miss; AI:Yes
9   Colour: Combination black, white
10  Pecularity: polled, white belt
11 - Main use: (1) meat,(2) sport/hobby,(3) miss
12  Spec. abilities: miss
13  Performance compared with STB miss:
14     higher: miss
15     equal:  miss
16     lower:  miss
17 - Management: stationary; housing: no/≈ 2 m.; mountain
18 - Conservation progr.: live animals: miss;Semen: 4;Embryos: miss
19  Status: normal;              Watch: %pure!
```

20 - Similar breeds (see group 1/5 on page 75)	EN	Country	Status
21 Lakenvelder	152	NL	min. end.

```
 1 - Blonde d'Aquitaine                                    EN    38
 2   Blonde d'Aquitaine; country-wide
 3   Blonde d'Aquitaine Breeders Society                   HB:1971
 4   Faringdon Oxon SN7 7HS, 16 Market Place
 5 - Composite of Quercy, Garronais, Blonde des Pyreenees
 6 - Imported as breed from 37 France
 7   Numbers 1991: 2000/ miss; HB: 12420; increasing; 99 %; Ne = 6890
 8 - Height: 160/150 cm; Weight: 1290/917 kg; Herd number: miss; AI: Yes
 9   Colour: Uni brown, yellow, blond
10   Pecularity: miss
11 - Main use: (1) meat,(2) miss,(3) miss
12   Spec. abilities: miss
13   Performance compared with STB Hereford 112:
14      higher: muscularity, daily gain, age of sex. maturity, calf mort.
15      equal:  calving interval, calving rate
16      lower:  calving ease, handling ease
17 - Management: stationary; housing: 2-6 m.;
18 - Conservation progr.: live animals: miss;Semen: miss;Embryos: 18/64
19   Status: normal
```

20 - Similar breeds (see group 8/1 on page 81)	EN	Country	Status
21 Basco-Bearnaise	22	F	crit.end.
22 Coopelso 93 (terminated)	69	F	crit.end.
23 Villard de Lans	264	F	pot. end.
24 Blonde d'Aquitaine	37	F	normal

```
 1 - British Charolais                                     EN    43
 2   Charolais; country-wide
 3   British Charolais Cattle Society Ltd.                 HB:1962
 4   Coventry Rd 19, Cubbington, Leamington Spa, Warwickshire CV32 7JN
 5 - Imported as breed from France
 6   Incrossing since 1950 from Charolais 62 France
 7   Numbers 1986: 3000/7000; HB: 6000; increasing; 90 %; Ne = 8000
 8 - Height: 155/145 cm; Weight: 1250/880 kg; Herd number: miss; AI: Yes
 9   Colour: Uni white
10   Pecularity: miss
11 - Main use: (1) meat,(2) miss,(3) miss
12   Spec. abilities: miss
13   Performance compared with STB Hereford 112:
14      higher: calf mortality, muscularity, daily gain, calving interval
15      equal:  milk yield
16      lower:  calving ease, handling ease, calving rate
17 - Management: stationary; housing: 2-6 m.;
18 - Conservation progr.: live animals: miss;Semen: 100;Embryos: 200/miss
19   Status: normal
```

20 - Similar breeds (see group 9/2 on page 82)	EN	Country	Status
21 Charolais	62	F	normal
22 Irish Charolais	121	IRL	normal
23 Charolais	63	L	normal

```
 1 - British Limousin                                          EN   44
 2   Limousin
 3   British Limousin Cattle Society Ltd.                      HB:1971
 4   NAC, Kenilworth, Warwickshire CV( 2LG
 5 - Imported as breed 156 France
 7   Numbers 1983: 4392/ miss; HB: miss; increasing; 65 %; Ne = miss
 8 - Height: 143/130 cm; Weight: 700/470 kg; Herd number: miss; AI: miss
 9   Colour: Uni light yellow to reddish yellow
10   Pecularity: miss
11 - Main use: (1) miss,(2) miss,(3) miss
12   Spec. abilities: miss
13   Performance compared with STB miss:
14     higher: miss
15     equal:  miss
16     lower:  miss
17 - Management: miss; housing: miss m.;
18 - Conservation progr.: live animals: miss;Semen: miss;Embryos: miss
19   Status: normal;              Watch: HB♀♀,%pure!
20 - Similar breeds (see group 8/3 on page 81)      EN  Country Status
21   Alpha 16 (terminated)                           6   F      crit.end.
22   Limousin                                      156   F      normal
23   Irish Limousin                                122   IRL    normal
24   Parthenaise                                   193   F      normal
```

```
 1 - British White                                            EN   45
 2   British White; eastern Anglia
 3   British White Cattle Society                             HB:1918
 4   P. B. 35, Stoneleigh, Kenilworth, Warwickshire CV8 2XE
 5 - Autochthon Park Cattle
 7   Numbers 1990: 60/942; HB: 830; increasing; 98 %; Ne = 224
 8 - Height: 120/110 cm; Weight: 850/550 kg; Herd number: miss; AI: Yes
 9   Colour: Uni white, black and red points: muzzle, eyes, feet, teats
10   Pecularity: horns 0/0, polled
11 - Main use: (1) meat,(2) milk,(3) miss
12   Spec. abilities: resistance to tuberculosis, viral pneumonia; docile
13   Performance compared with STB Simmental 239:
14     higher: calving ease, calf mortality, handling ease
15     equal:  milk yield, % fat, % protein,calv. interval, calving rate
16     lower:  muscularity, age of sexual maturity, daily gain
17 - Management: stationary; housing: 2-6 m.; hardiness, strong hooves
18 - Conservation progr.: live animals: miss;Semen: 11;Embryos: 6/5
19   Status: normal
20 - Similar breeds (see group 9/1 on page 82)      EN  Country Status
21   White Park                                    271   GB     pot. end.
22   Whitebred Shorthorn                           272   GB     pot. end.
```

```
1 - Dexter                                                    EN    81
2   Dexter; England and Wales
3   The Dexter Cattle Society                                 HB:1900
4   Whitehouse Farm, No Mans Heath, Tamworth, Staffs. B79 0NX
5 - Imported as breed from Ireland
7   Numbers 1986: 113/700; HB: 700; increasing; 95 %; Ne = 389
8 - Height: 110/100 cm; Weight: miss/miss kg; Herd number: miss; AI: Yes
9   Colour: Uni black, red
10  Pecularity: miss
11 - Main use: (1) meat,(2) milk,(3) sport/hobby
12  Spec. abilities: miss
13  Performance compared with STB Holstein-Friesian 117:
14    higher: % protein
15    equal:  % fat
16    lower:  milk yield
17 - Management: miss; housing: no/2-6 m.;
18 - Conservation progr.: live animals: miss;Semen: 9;Embryos: miss
19  Status: normal
```

```
20 - Similar breeds (see group 2/2 on page 76)     EN   Country  Status
21  Kerry Cattle                                   140   IRL    min. end.
22  Murray Grey                                    181   GB     pot. end.
23  Galloway                                       94    D      normal
24  Deutsche Angus                                 80    D      normal
```

```
1 - English Longhorn                                          EN    82
2   Longhorn; country-wide in Britain
3   Longhorn Cattle Society                                   HB:1878
4   Bemborough Farm Office, Guiting Power, Cheltenham, Glos CL545 UG
5 - Autochthon local British cattle
7   Numbers 1987: 30/550; HB: 550; increasing; miss %; Ne = 114
8 - Height: miss/miss cm; Weight: 1000/850 kg; Herd number: miss; AI:Yes
9   Colour: Combination blue, red, brown, white
10  Pecularity: white line-back, (white flashes to flank prefered)
11 - Main use: (1) meat,(2) sport/hobby,(3) vegetation management
12  Spec. abilities: miss
13  Performance compared with STB Hereford 112:
14    higher: miss
15    equal:  milk yield,muscularity,daily gain,calv. ease,calv. interv.
16    lower:  miss
17 - Management: stationary; housing: ≈ 2 m.;
18 - Conservation progr.: live animals: Yes;Semen: 19;Embryos: miss
19  Status: potential. endang.;Watch: %pure!
```

```
20 - Similar breeds (see group 3/7 on page 78)     EN   Country  Status
21  Itäsuomenkarja                                 129   SF     crit.end.
22  Telemark                                       254   N      crit.end.
23  Irish Moiled                                   123   GB     crit.end.
24  Vosgienne                                      267   F      pot. end.
```

```
 1 - Galloway                                                      EN    96
 2   Galloway; Scotland, Borders, Devon
 3   Galloway Cattle Society                                       HB:1862
 4   Castle Douglas DG7 1HY, 15 New Market Street
 5 - Autochthon always recorded as Galloways - black polled cattle
 7   Numbers 1991: 300/ miss; HB: 8000; stable; 46 %; Ne = 1157
 8 - Height: 137/124 cm; Weight: 750/470 kg; Herd number: miss; AI: Yes
 9   Colour: Uni black, yellow
10   Pecularity: miss
11 - Main use: (1) meat,(2) vegetation management,(3) sport/hobby
12   Spec. abilities: wet conditions, poor hill grazing
13   Performance compared with STB Hereford 112:
14      higher: muscularity, calving ease
15      equal:  calving interval, age of sexual maturity, calf mortality
16      lower:  daily gain, handling ease
17 - Management: stationary; housing: no/≈ 2/2-6 m.;
18 - Conservation progr.: live animals: miss;Semen: 4;Embryos: miss
19   Status: normal;                Watch: %pure!
```

20 - Similar breeds (see group 2/2 on page 76)	EN	Country	Status
21 Kerry Cattle	140	IRL	min. end.
22 Murray Grey	181	GB	pot. end.
23 Galloway	94	D	normal
24 Deutsche Angus	80	D	normal

```
 1 - Gloucester                                                    EN   103
 2   Gloucester; England
 3   Gloucester Cattle Society                                     HB:1920
 4   Bemborough Farm Office, Gulting Power, Cheltenham, Glos GL54 5UG
 5 - Composite of Gloucester 103, Glamorgan
 6   Incrossing since 1950 from Friesian 117 GB, Jersey 133 GB
 7   Numbers 1989: 27/300; HB: 300; increasing; 100 %; Ne = 98
 8 - Height: 130/125 cm; Weight: miss /612 kg; Herd number: miss; AI: Yes
 9   Colour: Combination brown, white
10   Pecularity: white dorsal and underline, black points
11 - Main use: (1) sport/hobby,(2) milk,(3) meat
12   Spec. abilities: milk very good for cheese production, twinning
13   Performance compared with STB Holstein-Friesian 117:
14      higher: muscul.,daily gain,% fat, calv. ease,age of sex. maturity
15      equal:  calf mortality, milkability
16      lower:  milk yield, calving interval
17 - Management: stationary; housing: ≈ 2 m.;
18 - Conservation progr.: live animals: Yes;Semen: 12;Embryos: miss
19   Status: potential. endang.;Watch: HB♀♀,%incross!
```

20 - Similar breeds (see group 5/6 on page 80)	EN	Country	Status
21 Highland	114	GB	normal

```
 1 - Guernsey                                                    EN  108
 2   Guernsey; country-wide
 3   English Guernsey Cattle Society                          HB:1884
 4   The Bury Farm, Pednor Road, Chesham, Buckinghamshire HP5 2LA
 5 - Autochthon Guernsey Island breed;incrossing since 1950 from Guernsey
 6   Canada, Guernsey Guernsey Island; imports from Channel Island
 7   Numbers 1983: 100/22000; HB: miss; stable; 50 %; Ne = 398
 8 - Height: 152/137 cm; Weight: 600/500 kg; Herd number: miss; AI: Yes
 9   Colour: Combination yellow to red, white
10   Pecularity: halfmoon shaped yellow horns with dark tips
11 - Main use: (1) milk,(2) miss,(3) miss
12   Spec. abilities: high butterfat and protein production
13   Performance compared with STB Jersey 133:
14      higher: muscularity,daily gain,milk yield,calving ease,handl. ease
15      equal:  calving interval, age of sexual maturity, calf mortality
16      lower:  % fat, % protein
17 - Management: stationary; housing: 2-6 m.;
18 - Conservation progr.: live animals: miss;Semen: 50;Embryos: miss
19   Status: normal;              Watch: HB♀♀,%pure,%incross!
```

20 - Similar breeds (see group 8/4 on page 82)	EN	Country	Status
21 Froment du Leon	93	F	endanger.
22 Jersey	132	IRL	pot. end.
23 Jersiais	134	F	normal
24 Jersey	130	DK	normal

```
 1 - Hereford                                                   EN  112
 2   Hereford
 3   The Hereford Herd Book Society, Hereford House            HB:1846
 4   Hereford HR1 2LL, Offa Street 3
 5 - Autochthon breed
 7   Numbers 1986: 2500/10000; HB: 10000; stable; 100 %; Ne = 8000
 8 - Height: 152/140 cm; Weight: 1200/775 kg; Herd number: miss; AI: Yes
 9   Colour: Uni red, white, combination red, white
10   Pecularity: white head
11 - Main use: (1) meat,(2) vegetation management,(3) miss
12   Spec. abilities: miss
13   Performance compared with STB Hereford 112:
14      higher: Breed is used
15      equal:  as standard breed,
16      lower:  no comparison possible.
17 - Management: stationary; housing: no/≈ 2/2-6 m.;
18 - Conservation progr.: live animals: miss;Semen: miss;Embryos: miss
19   Status: normal
```

20 - Similar breeds (see group 3/5 on page 77)	EN	Country	Status
21 Hereford	110	F	pot. end.
22 Hereford	111	IRL	normal
23 Kazakhskaya belogolovaya	138	KAZ	normal

1 - **Highland**   EN **114**
2   **Highland; Scotland**
3   **The Highland Cattle Society**   HB:**1884**
4   **Thornhill, Dfs. DG3 4DH**
5 - **Autochthon native cattle**
7   Numbers 1986: **41/2000**; HB: **468**; increasing; 60 %; Ne = 151
8 - Height: **120/100** cm; Weight: **650/450** kg; Herd number: miss; AI: **Yes**
9   Colour: **Uni red**
10 Pecularity: miss
11 - Main use: (1) **meat**,(2) **vegetation management**,(3) **sport/hobby**
12 Spec. abilities: **wet areas, mountain**
13 Performance compared with STB **Hereford 112**:
14   higher: **age of sexual maturity**
15   equal: **calving ease, calving interval, handl. ease, calf mortal.**
16   lower: **muscularity, daily gain**
17 - Management: miss; housing: miss m.;
18 - Conservation progr.: live animals: miss;Semen: miss;Embryos: miss
19 Status: **normal**;   Watch: **%pure!**
20 - <u>Similar breeds</u> (see group 5/6 on page 80)   <u>EN</u> <u>Country</u> <u>Status</u>
21 **Gloucester**   103   GB   pot. end.

1 - **Holstein-Friesian**   EN **117**
2   **Holstein-Friesian; dispersed country-wide**
3   **The Holstein Friesian Society of GB and Ireland**   HB:**1909**
4   **Scotsbridge House, Scotshill, Rickmansworth, Herts WD3 3BB**
5 - **Imported as breed from Netherlands; incrossing since 1950 from**
6   **Friesian 277 Netherlands, Holstein Europe, Holstein USA**
7   Numbers 1991: **6189/175000**; HB: **206012**; decreasing; miss %; Ne=24034
8 - Height: **160/134** cm; Weight: **1000/650** kg; Herd number: miss; AI: **Yes**
9   Colour: **Combination black, white**
10 Pecularity: miss
11 - Main use: (1) **milk**,(2) **meat**,(3) miss
12 Spec. abilities: miss
13 Performance compared with STB **Holstein-Friesian 117**:
14   higher: **Breed is used**
15   equal: **as standard breed,**
16   lower: **no comparison possible.**
17 - Management: **stationary**; housing: **> 6 m.**;
18 - Conservation progr.: live animals: miss;Semen: 1500;Embryos: miss
19 Status: **normal**;   Watch: **%pure,%incross!**
20 - <u>Similar breeds</u> (see group 1/1 on page 75)   <u>EN</u> <u>Country</u> <u>Status</u>
21 **Sortbroget Dansk Malkekvaeg**   245   DK   pot. end.
22 **Nizinna-Czarno-Biala**   185   PL   pot. end.
23 **Prim' Holstein**   209   F   normal
24 **Pie-Noire-Holstein**   198   B   normal

```
1 - Irish Moiled                                           EN  123
2   Irish Moiled; mainly Countrys of Down and Antrim
3   Irish Moiled Cattle Society                           HB:1926
4   Springfield, Lurgan, RL-Co, Armagh BT66 7JL
5 - Autochthon breed
6   Incrossing since 1950 from Finland
7   Numbers 1989: 8/120; HB: 60; increasing; 95 %; Ne = 13
8 - Height: miss/miss cm; Weight: 600/450 kg; Herd number: miss; AI: Yes
9   Colour: Combination red, brown, white, face is often flecked
10  Pecularity: horns 0/0, polled, white line or flinching on the back
11 - Main use: (1) as a rare breed,(2) meat,(3) milk
12  Spec. abilities: miss
13  Performance compared with STB Beef Shorthorn 24:
14     higher: calving ease, handling ease, calving rate
15     equal:  muscularity, daily gain, % fat, % protein, calving interv.
16     lower:  age of sexual maturity, calf mortality, milk yield
17 - Management: stationary; housing: 2-6 m.;
18 - Conservation progr.: live animals: Yes;Semen: 4;Embryos: miss
19  Status: critically endang.;Watch: ♂♂,HB♀♀,%incross!
```

20 - Similar breeds (see group 3/7 on page 78)	EN	Country	Status
21 Itäsuomenkarja	129	SF	crit.end.
22 Telemark	254	N	crit.end.
23 English Longhorn	82	GB	pot. end.
24 Vosgienne	267	F	pot. end.

```
1 - Jersey                                                EN  133
2   Jersey
3   Jersey Cattle Society of the United Kingdom           HB:1878
4   Jersey House, 154 Castle Hill, Reading, Berkshire RG1 7RP
5 - Autochthon breed; incrossing since 1950 from Jersey Canada,
6   130 Denmark, New Zealand, USA
7   Numbers 1986: 500/8000; HB: 6000; stable; 50 %; Ne = 1846
8 - Height: 127/119 cm; Weight: 550/430 kg; Herd number: miss; AI: Yes
9   Colour: Uni blond
10  Pecularity: black muzzle
11 - Main use: (1) milk,(2) meat,(3) miss
12  Spec. abilities: % fat, kept at a higher density / hectare
13  Performance compared with STB Holstein-Friesian 117:
14     higher: % protein, calving ease, handling ease, % fat
15     equal:  calving interval, calf mortal., calving rate, milkability
16     lower:  muscul.,live weight,milk yield,daily gain,age of sex. mat.
17 - Management: stationary; housing: 2-6 m.;
18 - Conservation progr.: live animals: miss;Semen: 780;Embryos: miss
19  Status: normal;              Watch: %pure!
```

20 - Similar breeds (see group 8/4 on page 82)	EN	Country	Status
21 Froment du Leon	93	F	endanger.
22 Jersey	132	IRL	pot. end.
23 Jersiais	134	F	normal
24 Jersey	130	DK	normal

```
 1 - Lincoln Red                                              EN   159
 2   Lincoln Red; Lincolnshire
 3   Lincoln Red Cattle Society, Lincolnshire Showground,     HB:1896
 4   Grange-de-Lings, Lincoln LN2 2NA
 5 - Composite of descendent of Shorthorn
 7   Numbers 1987: 60/1854; HB: 1854; decreasing; 100 %; Ne = 233
 8 - Height: 125/107 cm; Weight: 515/347 kg; Herd number: miss; AI: Yes
 9   Colour: Uni red
10   Pecularity: horns 0/0, polled
11 - Main use: (1) meat,(2) miss,(3) miss
12   Spec. abilities: docile, able to finish on grass, rapid daily gain
13   Performance compared with STB Hereford 112:
14      higher: muscularity, daily gain
15      equal:  calving ease, calving interval, age of sexual maturity
16      lower:  miss
17 - Management: stationary; housing: 2-6 m.;
18 - Conservation progr.: live animals: miss;Semen: 4;Embryos: miss
19   Status: normal;            Watch: trend!
```

20 - Similar breeds (see group 4/2 on page 78)	EN	Country	Status
21 Armoricaine	10	F	crit.end.
22 Kurganskaya	151	USSR	crit.end.
23 Beef Shorthorn Cattle	24	GB	normal
24 Irish Shorthorn	124	IRL	normal

```
 1 - Murray Grey                                              EN   181
 2   Murray Grey; dispersed country-wide
 3   Murray Grey Beef Cattle Society Ltd.                     HB:1973
 4   P. B. 8, Stoneleigh, NAC, Kenilworth, Warwickshire CV8 2TZ
 5 - Composite of Aberdeen Angus 1, Beef Shorthorn 24
 6   Incrossing since 1950 from Murray Grey Australia, New Zealand
 7   Numbers 1991: 50/1500; HB: miss; stable; miss %; Ne = 194
 8 - Height: 116/108 cm; Weight: 460/390 kg; Herd number: miss; AI: miss
 9   Colour: Uni grey, solid color chocolate - silver grey
10   Pecularity: horns 0/0, polled
11 - Main use: (1) meat,(2) vegetation management,(3) miss
12   Spec. abilities: miss
13   Performance compared with STB Hereford 112:
14      higher: muscularity, calving ease
15      equal:  daily gain, calving interval, age of sexual maturity
16      lower:  miss
17 - Management: stationary; housing: no/≈ 2/2-6 m.;
18 - Conservation progr.: live animals: miss;Semen: 25;Embryos: miss
19   Status: potential. endang.;Watch: HB♀♀,%pure,%incross!
```

20 - Similar breeds (see group 2/2 on page 76)	EN	Country	Status
21 Kerry Cattle	140	IRL	min. end.
22 Deutsche Angus	80	D	normal
23 Angus	9	IRL	normal
24 Galloway	94	D	normal

1 - **North Devon, Red Ruby**   EN   **188**
2   Devon; western England
3   Devon Cattle Breeders Society   HB:**1851**
4   Barnlane Farm, Stoke Rivers, Barnstaple, N. Devon EX32 7LD
5 - **Autochthon Devons**
7   Numbers 1983: **250/4000**; HB: **miss**; decreasing; **90 %**; Ne = **941**
8 - Height: **136/miss** cm; Weight: **miss/miss** kg; Herd number: **miss**; AI:**Yes**
9   Colour: **Uni red**
10   Pecularity: **muzzle flesh-coloured**
11 - Main use: (1) **miss**,(2) **miss**,(3) **miss**
12   Spec. abilities: **miss**
13   Performance compared with STB **miss**:
14   higher: **miss**
15   equal: **miss**
16   lower: **miss**
17 - Management: **miss**; housing: **miss** m.;
18 - Conservation progr.: live animals: **miss**;Semen: **miss**;Embryos: **miss**
19   Status: **potential. endang.**;Watch: **HB♀♀,trend!**
20 - Similar breeds (see group 4/1 on page 78)   EN Country Status
21   **Red Poll**   **216**   **GB**   **pot. end.**
22   **Sussex**   **249**   **GB**   **normal**

1 - **Pinzgauer**   EN   **204**
2   Pinzgau
3   British Pinzgauer Cattle Society   HB:**1976**
4   Spitars, South Tawton, Okehampton, Devon
5 - **Imported as breed from Germany, Austria**
7   Numbers 1983: **miss** / **miss**; HB: **miss**; stable; **100 %**; Ne = **miss**
8 - Height: **miss/miss** cm; Weight: **520/353** kg; Herd number: **miss**; AI: **Yes**
9   Colour: **Combination red, white**
10   Pecularity: **dominant "Linch Back" meeting**
11 - Main use: (1) **miss**,(2) **miss**,(3) **miss**
12   Spec. abilities: **miss**
13   Performance compared with STB **miss**:
14   higher: **miss**
15   equal: **miss**
16   lower: **miss**
17 - Management: **miss**; housing: **miss** m.;
18 - Conservation progr.: live animals: **miss**;Semen: **miss**;Embryos: **miss**
19   Status: **miss**
20 - Similar breeds (see group 3/4 on page 77)   EN Country Status
21   **Pustertaler Schecken**   **210**   **D**   **crit.end.**
22   **Pinzgauer**   **200**   **I**   **crit.end.**
23   **Pinzgauer**   **202**   **A**   **pot. end.**
24   **Slovenske pinzgavske**   **243**   **SK**   **normal**

1 - **Red Poll**   EN **216**
2   **Red Poll; country-wide**
3   **The Red Poll Cattle Society**   HB:**1874**
4   **The Market Hill, Woodbridge, Suffolk IP12 4LU**
5 - **Composite of Suffolk Dun, Norfolk Red**
7   Numbers 1989: **39/1325**; HB: **miss**; **stable**; **99 %**; Ne = **152**
8 - Height: **150/132** cm; Weight: **374/227** kg; Herd number: **miss**; AI: **Yes**
9   Colour: **Uni red**
10 Pecularity: **horns 0/0, polled**
11 - Main use: (1) **milk**,(2) **meat**,(3) **miss**
12 Spec. abilities: **high meat quality, drought and cold climate**
13 Performance compared with STB **Holstein-Friesian 117**:
14   higher: **miss**
15   equal: **muscularity, % protein**
16   lower: **milk yield, daily gain, % fat**
17 - Management: **stationary**; housing: **2-6 m.**;
18 - Conservation progr.: live animals: **miss**;Semen: **15**;Embryos: **miss**
19 Status: **potential. endang.**;Watch: **HB♀♀!**
20 - <u>Similar breeds</u> (see group 4/1 on page 78)   <u>EN</u> <u>Country</u> <u>Status</u>
21 **Red Ruby**   **188**   **GB**   **pot. end.**
22 **Sussex**   **249**   **GB**   **normal**

1 - **Shorthorn**   EN **233**
2   **Shorthorn; country-wide**
3   **The Beef Shorthorn Cattle Society**   HB:**1822**
4   **4th Street,NAC,Stoneleigh Park,Kenilworth,Warwickshire CV8 2LG**
5 - **Composite of Teeswater, Holderness; incrossing since 1950 from**
6   **Maine-Anjou 163 France, Poll Shorthorn Australia**
7   Numbers 1986: **270/40000**; HB: **4000**; **stable**; **80 %**; Ne = **1012**
8 - Height: **143/140** cm; Weight: **1200/675** kg; Herd number: **miss**; AI: **Yes**
9   Colour: **Combination red, white**
10 Pecularity: **miss**
11 - Main use: (1) **milk**,(2) **meat**,(3) **miss**
12 Spec. abilities: **miss**
13 Performance compared with STB **Hereford 112**:
14   higher: **milkability, milk yield, % fat, calving ease, calving rate**
15   equal: **muscularity, daily gain, calv. interval, age of sex. mat.**
16   lower: **miss**
17 - Management: **stationary**; housing: **2-6 m.**;
18 - Conservation progr.: live animals: **miss**;Semen: **6**;Embryos: **miss**
19 Status: **normal**;   Watch: **%incross!**
20 - <u>Similar breeds</u> (see group 4/2 on page 78)   <u>EN</u> <u>Country</u> <u>Status</u>
21 **Armoricaine**   **10**   **F**   **crit.end.**
22 **Kurganskaya**   **151**   **USSR**   **crit.end.**
23 **Beef Shorthorn Cattle**   **24**   **GB**   **normal**
24 **Irish Shorthorn**   **124**   **IRL**   **normal**

```
 1 - Simmental                                                   EN  239
 2   Simmental; country-wide
 3   The British Simmental Cattle Society Ltd.                    HB:1970
 4   NAC, Kenilworth, Warwicks CV8 2LR
 5 - Imported as breed from Switzerland, Austria
 6   Incrossing since 1950 from Fleckvieh 78 Germany,Fleckvieh 88 Austria
 7   Numbers 1986: 650/15000; HB: miss; increasing; 95 %; Ne = 2492
 8 - Height: 147/137 cm; Weight: 1150/850 kg; Herd number: miss; AI: Yes
 9   Colour: Combination brown to red, white
10   Pecularity: white head, white hocks
11 - Main use: (1) meat,(2) milk,(3) vegetation management
12   Spec. abilities: miss
13   Performance compared with STB Hereford 112:
14      higher: muscularity, daily gain
15      equal:  calving interval, age of sexual maturity, handling ease
16      lower:  calving ease, calf mortality
17 - Management: stationary; housing: 2-6 m.;
18 - Conservation progr.: live animals: miss;Semen: 200;Embryos: 100/300
19   Status: normal
20 - Similar breeds (see group 3/2 on page 77)     EN  Country Status
21   Ceske strakate                                 61   CZ    crit.end.
22   Simentalska                                   237   PL    min. end.
23   Montbeliard                                   176   F     normal
24   Fleckvieh                                      88   A     normal
```

```
 1 - Sussex                                                      EN  249
 2   Sussex; southeastern  England
 3   Sussex Cattle Society                                       HB:1837
 4   Station Road, Robertsbridge, Sussex
 5 - Autochthon red weald cattle (1066 used as draught oxen)
 7   Numbers 1986: 300/7000; HB: 700; increasing; 50 %; Ne = 840
 8 - Height: miss/miss cm; Weight: miss/miss kg; Herd number:miss; AI:Yes
 9   Colour: Uni red
10   Pecularity: white / pale end of tail
11 - Main use: (1) meat,(2) miss,(3) miss
12   Spec. abilities: miss
13   Performance compared with STB Hereford 112:
14      higher: miss
15      equal:  musc.,daily gain,calv. ease,calv. interv.,age of sex. mat.
16      lower:  miss
17 - Management: stationary; housing: no
18 - Conservation progr.: live animals: miss;Semen: 30;Embryos: miss
19   Status: normal;              Watch: %pure!
20 - Similar breeds (see group 4/1 on page 78)     EN  Country Status
21   Red Ruby                                      188   GB    pot. end.
22   Red Poll                                      216   GB    pot. end.
```

```
 1 - Welsh Black                                              EN  269
 2   Welsh Black; Wales
 3   Welsh Black Cattle Society                               HB:1904
 4   13 Stryd Fangor, Caernarfon, Gwynedd LL55 1AP
 5 - Autochthon Welsh Black
 7   Numbers 1986: 150/ miss; HB: 2000; stable; miss %; Ne = 558
 8 - Height: 145/130 cm; Weight: 1100/750 kg; Herd number: miss; AI: Yes
 9   Colour: Uni black
10   Pecularity: miss
11 - Main use: (1) meat,(2) milk,(3) vegetation management
12   Spec. abilities: mountain, wet areas
13   Performance compared with STB Hereford 112:
14     higher: milk yield
15     equal:  daily gain, calving ease, calv. interval, age of sex. mat.
16     lower:  muscularity, handling ease
17 - Management: miss; housing: 2-6 m.;
18 - Conservation progr.: live animals: miss;Semen: 10;Embryos: miss
19   Status: normal;              Watch: HB♀♀,%pure!
```

20 - <u>Similar breeds</u> (see group 2/2 on page 76)

		EN	Country	Status
21	Kerry Cattle	140	IRL	min. end.
22	Murray Grey	181	GB	pot. end.
23	Galloway	94	D	normal
24	Deutsche Angus	80	D	normal

```
 1 - White Park                                               EN  271
 2   White Park
 3   White Park Cattle Society                                HB:1921
 4   Colonsay, Hampton Lovett, Droitwich, Worcester
 5 - Autochthon ancient breed
 7   Numbers 1992: 24/300; HB: 248; increasing; 96 %; Ne = 73
 8 - Height: miss /130 cm; Weight: 955/635 kg; Herd number: miss; AI: Yes
 9   Colour: Uni white
10   Pecularity: black points (ears, muzzle, eyelids, teats, feet)
11 - Main use:(1) meat,(2) sport/hobby,(3) amenity centres-public attract
12   Spec. abilities: growth rate: 5% superior to Limousin
13   Performance compared with STB Hereford 112:
14     higher: calving ease, age of sexual maturity
15     equal:  daily gain, calving rate
16     lower:  muscularity, handling ease, calf mortality
17 - Management: stationary; housing: 2-6 m.;
18 - Conservation progr.: live animals: Yes;Semen: 14;Embryos: miss
19   Status: potential. endang.;Watch: HB♀♀!
```

20 - <u>Similar breeds</u> (see group 9/1 on page 82)

		EN	Country	Status
21	Whitebred Shorthorn	272	GB	pot. end.
22	British White	45	GB	normal

CATTLE

```
 1 - Whitebred Shorthorn                                    EN  272
 2   Whitebred Shorthorn; Scotland, England, Wales
 3   Whitebred Shorthorn Association                        HB:1962
 4   Oak Hill, Kirkcambeck, Brampton CA8 2BL
 5 - Autochthon Cumberland Dairy Shorthorn
 7   Numbers 1992: 180/80; HB: miss; stable; 40 %; Ne = 222
 8 - Height: miss / miss cm; Weight: 800/400 kg; Herd number: 36; AI: Yes
 9   Colour: Uni white
10   Pecularity: pure white clear pink nose
11 - Main use: (1) meat,(2) crossbreeding,(3) miss
12   Spec. abilities: miss
13   Performance compared with STB Hereford 112:
14      higher: miss
15      equal: musc.,daily gain,calv. ease,calv.interval,age of sex. mat.
16      lower: miss
17 - Management: stationary; housing: no/≈ 2/2-6 m.;
18 - Conservation progr.: live animals: miss;Semen: miss;Embryos: miss
19   Status: potential. endang.;Watch: HB♀♀,%pure!
20 - Similar breeds (see group 9/1 on page 82)      EN  Country Status
21   White Park                                     271   GB   pot. end.
22   British White                                   45   GB   normal
```

SHEEP

```
 1 - Badger faced Welsh Mountain                            EN  407
 2   Badger Faced Welsh Mountain; Wales: Powys - Dyfed
 3   Badger Faced Welsh Mountain Sheep Society              HB:1976
 4   Pontsian, Llandysul, Dyfed
 5 - Autochthon native breed of Wales
 7   Numbers 1986: 150/1000; HB: 800; increasing; 100 %; Ne = 505
 8 - Height: miss/miss cm; Weight: 55/45 kg; Herd number: miss; AI: miss
 9   Colour: Combination black, brown, white; white body
10   Pecularity: horns 2/0, badger striped head, black legs and belly
11 - Main use: (1) meat,(2) miss,(3) miss
12   Spec. abilities: extremely hardy, can graze rough hill land
13   Performance compared with STB miss:
14      higher: miss
15      equal: miss
16      lower: miss
17 - Management: stationary; housing: no
18 - Conservation progr.: live animals: miss;Semen: miss;Embryos: miss
19   Status: normal
20 - Similar breeds (see group 7/11 on page 94)     EN  Country Status
21   Blackface                                      421   F    crit.end.
22   Whitefaced Woodland                            676   GB   pot. end.
23   Wicklow Cheviot                                677   IRL  normal
24   Blackface Mountain                             422   IRL  normal
```

```
 1 - Bleu du Maine                                        EN  426
 2   Bleu du Maine; Scotland and Wales
 3   Bleu du Maine Sheep Society Ltd.                     HB:1982
 4   Cod Beck Estate, Dalton, Thirsk YO7 3HR
 5 - Composite of Wensleydale, Bleu du Maine 425 France
 6   Incrossing since 1960 from Bleu du Maine 425 France
 7   Numbers 1986: 1000/6000; HB: 5000; increasing; 83 %; Ne = 3333
 8 - Height: 100/90 cm; Weight: 140/90 kg; Herd number: miss; AI: Yes
 9   Colour: white
10   Pecularity: horns 0/0, blue head
11 - Main use: (1) meat,(2) wool,(3) miss
12   Spec. abilities: large lean carcasses
13   Performance compared with STB Border Leicester 428:
14     higher: miss
15     equal: musc.,daily gain,carc. lean.,litter size,age of sex. mat.
16     lower: miss
17 - Management: stationary; housing: ≈ 2 m.;
18 - Conservation progr.: live animals: miss;Semen: Yes;Embryos: Yes
19   Status: normal;            Watch: %pure!
```

```
20 - Similar breeds (see group 2/1 on page 87)    EN   Country Status
21   Rouge de l'ouest                              605   GB   pot. end.
22   Bleu du Maine                                 425   F    normal
23   Blauköpfiges Fleischschaf                     424   D    normal
24   Rouge de l'ouest                              604   F    normal
```

```
 1 - Bluefaced Leicester                                  EN  427
 2   Bluefaced Leicester; northern United Kingdom
 3   Bluefaced Leicester Sheep Breeders Association       HB:1962
 4   Kirkbeck, Clarencefield, Dumfries, Scotland DG1 4NY
 5 - Autochthon from Bakewell's Dishley Leicester
 7   Numbers 1991: miss/34000; HB: miss; increasing; 95 %; Ne = 6154
 8 - Height: 75/70 cm; Weight: 90/70 kg; Herd number: miss; AI: Yes
 9   Colour: white; blue head covered with white haw
10   Pecularity: horns 0/0
11 - Main use: (1) meat,(2) wool,(3) miss
12   Spec. abilities: high prolificacy
13   Performance compared with STB Suffolk 642:
14     higher: litter size
15     equal: daily gain,carcass leanness,milk yield,age of sex. matur.
16     lower: muscularity, wool or fiber yield
17 - Management: stationary; housing: ≈ 2 m.;
18 - Conservation progr.: live animals: miss;Semen: 25;Embryos: miss
19   Status: normal;            Watch: HB♀♀!
```

```
20 - Similar breeds (see group 3 on page 88)      EN   Country Status
21   Mouton Boulonnais                             559   F    crit.end.
22   Galway                                        495   IRL  endanger.
23   Mouton Charollais                             560   F    normal
24   Cotentin                                      473   F    normal
```

1 - **Border Leicester**   EN **428**
2   **Border Leicester; British Isles**
3   **The Society of Border Leicester Sheep Breeders**   HB:**1898**
4   **Edinburgh EH14 1UL, Laichpark Road 7**
5 - **Autochthon Dishley Leicester**
7   Numbers 1986: **850/8800**; HB: **2450**; **increasing**; **100 %**; Ne = **2524**
8 - Height: **81/77** cm; Weight: **135/90** kg; Herd number: **miss**; AI: **Yes**
9   Colour: **Uni white**
10 Pecularity: **horns 0/0**
11 - Main use: (1) **meat**,(2) **wool**,(3) **miss**
12 Spec. abilities: **miss**
13 Performance compared with STB **Border Leicester 428**:
14   higher: **Breed is used**
15   equal: **as standard breed,**
16   lower: **no comparison possible.**
17 - Management: **stationary**; housing: **no**
18 - Conservation progr.: live animals: **Yes**;Semen: **miss**;Embryos: **miss**
19 Status: **normal**
20 - Similar breeds (see group 3 on page 88)   EN Country Status
21 **Mouton Boulonnais**   559 F   crit.end.
22 **Galway**   495 IRL   endanger.
23 **Mouton Charollais**   560 F   normal
24 **Cotentin**   473 F   normal

1 - **British Charollais**   EN **437**
2   **Charollais**
3   **British Charolais Sheep Society**   HB:**1977**
4   **Crogham Farm, Mymondham, Norfolk.**
5 - **Imported as breed from France**
6   **Incrossing since 1960 from Charolais 560 France**
7   Numbers 1988: **14800/15500**; HB: **15500**; **increasing**; **100 %**; Ne = **30284**
8 - Height: **85/75** cm; Weight: **130/85** kg; Herd number: **miss**; AI: **Yes**
9   Colour: **Uni white**
10 Pecularity: **horns 0/0, pinkish head**
11 - Main use: (1) **meat**,(2) **wool**,(3) **miss**
12 Spec. abilities: **miss**
13 Performance compared with STB **Suffolk 642**:
14   higher: **litter size**
15   equal: **musc.,daily gain,carc. lean.,milk yield,age of sex. matur.**
16   lower: **miss**
17 - Management: **stationary**; housing: **≈ 2 m.**;
18 - Conservation progr.: live animals: **miss**;Semen: **30**;Embryos: **miss**
19 Status: **normal**
20 - Similar breeds (see group 3 on page 88)   EN Country Status
21 **Mouton Boulonnais**   559 F   crit.end.
22 **Galway**   495 IRL   endanger.
23 **Mouton Charollais**   560 F   normal
24 **Cotentin**   473 F   normal

```
 1 - British Milksheep                              EN  438
 2   British Milksheep; country-wide
 3   British Milksheep Society                      HB:miss
 4   Colonsay, Hampton Lovett, Droitwich, Worcester
 5 - Composite of Bluefaced Leicester 427, Dorset Horn (Poll) 483,
 6   Prolific, Friesian Milksheep
 7   Numbers 1988: 350/5000; HB: 5000; increasing; 89 %; Ne = 1308
 8 - Height: miss/miss cm; Weight: 100/77 kg; Herd number: miss; AI: Yes
 9   Colour: Uni white
10   Pecularity: horns 0/0
11 - Main use: (1) meat,(2) milk,(3) wool
12   Spec. abilities: ∅ litter size 3.07, milk yield 400kg / 210 days
13   Performance compared with STB Border Leicester 428:
14     higher: litter size, milk yield
15     equal:  daily gain,carcass leanness,lambing interval,wool or fiber
16     lower:  muscularity,age of sexual maturity,length of mating season
17 - Management: stationary; housing: ≈ 2 m.;
18 - Conservation progr.: live animals: miss;Semen: miss;Embryos: miss
19   Status: normal
```

20 - Similar breeds (see group 5/1 on page 89)	EN	Country	Status
21 Mouton Laitier Belge	561	B	min. end.
22 Ostfriesisches Milchschaf	572	D*	normal
23 Friese Melkschaap	493	NL	normal
24 Ostfriesisches Milchschaf	573	D	normal

```
 1 - British Texel                                  EN  439
 2   Texel; country-wide
 3   The British Texel Sheep Society                HB:1972
 4   National Agriculture Center, Kenilworth, Warwickshire CV8 2LG
 5 - Imported as breed from France, Netherlands; incrossing since 1960
 6   from Lincoln,Border Leicester,Leicester,South Down,Hampshire Down
 7   Numbers 1986: 700/20000; HB: 15000; increasing; 90 %; Ne = 2675
 8 - Height: 84/79 cm; Weight: 120/90 kg; Herd number: miss; AI: miss
 9   Colour: Uni white, occasionally black spots
10   Pecularity: horns 0/0
11 - Main use: (1) meat,(2) miss,(3) miss
12   Spec. abilities: high proportion of lean tissue
13   Performance compared with STB Suffolk 642:
14     higher: miss
15     equal:  muscularity, daily gain, carcass leanness, litter size
16     lower:  age of sexual maturity
17 - Management: stationary; housing: ≈ 2 m.;
18 - Conservation progr.: live animals: miss;Semen: 50;Embryos: miss
19   Status: normal;            Watch: %pure,%incross!
```

20 - Similar breeds (see group 2/2 on page 88)	EN	Country	Status
21 Texel	648	SF	pot. end.
22 Texel	649	F	normal
23 Texel	651	IRL	normal
24 Texel	650	D	normal

```
 1 - Cambridge                                                EN  442
 2   Cambridge; England and Wales
 3   Cambridge Sheep Society Ltd.                             HB:1969
 4   Pharm House, Willaston, South Wirral L64 2TF
 5 - Composite of Clun Forest, Llyn, Llanwenog
 7   Numbers 1988: 490/1300; HB: 1300; increasing; 20 %; Ne = 1424
 8 - Height: 72/66 cm; Weight: 90/70 kg; Herd number: miss; AI: miss
 9   Colour: Uni brown, dark brown face
10   Pecularity: horns 0/0
11 - Main use: (1) meat,(2) wool,(3) miss
12   Spec. abilities: pref. for 1,2,3 year old ewes = 1.8, 2.6, 2.9
13   Performance compared with STB Suffolk 642:
14     higher: litter size
15     equal:  carcass leanness,milk yield,lamb. interval,wool thickness
16     lower:  muscularity,daily gain,age of sexual maturity,wool yield
17 - Management: stationary; housing: ≈ 2 m.;
18 - Conservation progr.: live animals: miss;Semen: 5;Embryos: miss/5
19   Status: normal;              Watch: %pure!
20 - Similar breeds (see group 3 on page 88)    EN  Country Status
21   Mouton Boulonnais                          559  F    crit.end.
22   Galway                                     495  IRL  endanger.
23   Mouton Charollais                          560  F    normal
24   Cotentin                                   473  F    normal
```

```
 1 - Castlemilk Moorit Sheep                                 EN  446
 2   Castlemilk Moorit; small flocks well distributed
 3   Castlemilk Moorit Sheep Society                         HB:1974
 4   Rare Breeds Surwival Trust,National Agric. Centre, Storeleigh, Wales
 5 - Composite of Shetland, Soay, Manx Loaghtan
 6   Incrossing since 1960 from Manx Loaghtan 539 United Kingdom
 7   Numbers 1989: 25/150; HB: 150; increasing; 100 %; Ne = 70
 8 - Height: miss/miss cm; Weight: miss/miss kg; Herd number: 20;AI: miss
 9   Colour: Combination brown, white
10   Pecularity: horns 2/2, mouflon pattern - brown legs, white belly
11 - Main use: (1) sport/hobby,(2) wool,(3) meat
12   Spec. abilities: light brown wool
13   Performance compared with STB Scottish Blackface:
14     higher: muscularity, litter size, milk yield
15     equal:  daily gain, age of sexual maturity, lambing interval
16     lower:  wool or fiber thickness,carc. leanness,wool or fiber yield
17 - Management: stationary; housing: ≈ 2 m.; easy management
18 - Conservation progr.: live animals: Yes;Semen: miss;Embryos: miss
19   Status: potential. endang.;Watch: ♂♂,HB♀♀,%incross!
20 - Similar breeds (see group 6/4 on page 91)  EN  Country Status
21   Vierhornschaf                              662  D    crit.end.
22   Manx Loaghtan                              539  GB   min. end.
23   Soay                                       631  GB   normal
24   Hebridean                                  508  GB   normal
```

```
 1 - Cheviot                                        EN  452
 2   Cheviot; southern  Scotland
 3   Cheviot Sheep Society                          HB:1892
 4   Annan DG12 6EF, Ednam Street 34
 5 - Autochthon local breed on Cheviot hills
 7   Numbers 1988: 3000/150000; HB: miss; decreasing; miss %; Ne = 11765
 8 - Height: 75/65 cm; Weight: 100/55 kg; Herd number: miss; AI: miss
 9   Colour: Uni white
10   Pecularity: horns 2/0
11 - Main use: (1) meat,(2) wool,(3) miss
12   Spec. abilities: conformation and hardiness
13   Performance compared with STB Suffolk 642:
14     higher: age of sexual maturity
15     equal:  muscularity, carcass leanness, milk yield, lamb. interval
16     lower:  daily gain, litter size, wool or fiber yield
17 - Management: stationary; housing: no
18 - Conservation progr.: live animals: miss;Semen: miss;Embryos: miss
19   Status: normal;          Watch: HB♀♀,trend,%pure!
```

20 - Similar breeds (see group 7/11 on page 94)	EN	Country	Status
21 Blackface	421	F	crit.end.
22 Whitefaced Woodland	676	GB	pot. end.
23 Wicklow Cheviot	677	IRL	normal
24 Blackface Mountain	422	IRL	normal

```
 1 - Clun Forest                                    EN  465
 2   Clun Forest; Shropshire, Hereford, Powys
 3   Rare Breed Survival Trust                      HB:1925
 4   National Agriculture Center, Kenilworth, Warwickshire CV8 2LG
 5 - Autochthon Long Mynd. (extinct)
 7   Numbers 1988: 257/4750; HB: 4750; decreasing; 35 %; Ne = 975
 8 - Height: 78/66 cm; Weight: 95/65 kg; Herd number: miss; AI: miss
 9   Colour: Uni white
10   Pecularity: horns 0/0, brown face, legs, ears
11 - Main use: (1) meat,(2) wool,(3) vegetation management
12   Spec. abilities: upland grazing
13   Performance compared with STB Suffolk 642:
14     higher: miss
15     equal:  litter size,milk yield,age of sex. matur.,lambing interval
16     lower:  muscularity, daily gain, carcass leanness
17 - Management: stationary; housing: no
18 - Conservation progr.: live animals: miss;Semen: miss;Embryos: miss
19   Status: normal;          Watch: %pure,trend!
```

20 - Similar breeds (see group 4/1 on page 89)	EN	Country	Status
21 Clun Forest	464	F	pot. end.
22 Dorset Down	481	F	pot. end.
23 Mouton Vendeen	562	F	normal
24 Hampshire	506	F	normal

1 - Colbred   EN 467
2   Colbred; England
3   Colbred Sheep Society Ltd.   HB:1956
4   Crickley Barrow, Northleach, Glos
5 - Composite of Clun Forest, Dorset Horn, East Friesian,
6   Border Leicester
7   Numbers miss: miss / miss; HB: miss; miss; miss %; Ne = miss
8 - Height: miss/miss cm; Weight: 60/80 kg; Herd number: miss; AI: miss
9   Colour: Uni white
10 Pecularity: horns 0/0
11 - Main use: (1) miss,(2) miss,(3) miss
12 Spec. abilities: miss
13 Performance compared with STB Suffolk 642:
14   higher: litter size
15   equal: muscularity,carcass leanness,milk yield,lambing interval
16   lower: daily gain, age of sexual maturity
17 - Management: miss; housing: miss m.;
18 - Conservation progr.: live animals: miss;Semen: miss;Embryos: miss
19 Status: miss
20 - Similar breeds (see group 3 on page 88)   EN Country Status
21 Mouton Boulonnais   559 F   crit.end.
22 Galway   495 IRL   endanger.
23 Mouton Charollais   560 F   normal
24 Cotentin   473 F   normal

1 - Cotswold Sheep   EN 474
2   Cotswold Sheep; southern England, Gloucesterhire
3   Cotswold Sheep Society, Holy Brook Cottage, Far   HB:1966
4   Oakridge, Stroud, Gloucestershire GL6 7PG
5 - Composite of Roman Longwool, Medieval Marsh Sheep
6   Incrossing since 1960 from Leicester 528 United Kingdom
7   Numbers 1993: 100/900; HB: miss; increasing; 90 %; Ne = 360
8 - Height: miss/miss cm; Weight: miss/miss kg; Herd number: 90;AI: miss
9   Colour: Uni white
10 Pecularity: horns 0/0
11 - Main use: (1) meat,(2) wool,(3) sport/hobby
12 Spec. abilities: longwool fleece
13 Performance compared with STB Suffolk 642:
14   higher: wool or fiber yield, carcass leanness, milk yield
15   equal: muscularity,daily gain,litter size,age of sexual maturity
16   lower: miss
17 - Management: stationary; housing: ≈ 2 m.;
18 - Conservation progr.: live animals: miss;Semen: miss;Embryos: miss
19 Status: potential. endang.;Watch: HB♀♀,%pure,%incross!
20 - Similar breeds (see group 3 on page 88)   EN Country Status
21 Mouton Boulonnais   559 F   crit.end.
22 Galway   495 IRL   endanger.
23 Mouton Charollais   560 F   normal
24 Cotentin   473 F   normal

```
1 - Derbyshire Gritstone                                    EN  479
2   Derbyshire Gritstone; N. Derbyshire,S. Lancashire,S. Yorkshire,Wales
3   Derbyshire Gritstone Sheep Breeders Society            HB:1907
4   528, Red Lees Road Cliviger, Burnley, Lancashire
5 - Autochthon Dale-o'-Goyt sheep
7   Numbers 1988: 1461/20000; HB: 3222; increasing; 80 %; Ne = 4021
8 - Height: 70/60 cm; Weight: 86/69 kg; Herd number: miss; AI: miss
9   Colour: Uni blue
10  Pecularity: horns 0/0, black spots on face and legs
11 - Main use: (1) meat,(2) wool,(3) miss
12  Spec. abilities: lamb meat, lean meat, lambing 150 %
13  Performance compared with STB Scottish Blackface:
14     higher: miss
15     equal:  musc.,daily gain,carcass leanness,litter size,milk yield
16     lower:  miss
17 - Management: stationary; housing: ≈ 2 m.;
18 - Conservation progr.: live animals: miss;Semen: miss;Embryos: miss
19  Status: normal
20 - Similar breeds (see group 7/11 on page 94)     EN  Country  Status
21  Blackface                                       421   F     crit.end.
22  Whitefaced Woodland                             676   GB    pot. end.
23  Wicklow Cheviot                                 677   IRL   normal
24  Blackface Mountain                              422   IRL   normal
```

```
1 - Dorset Down                                             EN  482
2   Dorset Down; mainly southwestern England, Wales, Scotland
3   Dorset Down Sheep Breeders' Association                HB:1906
4   Brierley House, Summer Lane, Combe Down, Bath, Avon BA2 5LE
5 - Composite of Berkshire, Hampshire, Wiltshire x Southdown ram
7   Numbers 1988: 298/3355; HB: 3355; decreasing; 90 %; Ne = 1095
8 - Height: 68/64 cm; Weight: 135/100 kg; Herd number: miss; AI: miss
9   Colour: Uni white
10  Pecularity: horns 0/0, brown face, ears, legs, feet
11 - Main use: (1) meat,(2) wool,(3) miss
12  Spec. abilities: early maturing breed
13  Performance compared with STB Suffolk 642:
14     higher: miss
15     equal:  muscularity,daily gain,milk yield,age of sexual maturity
16     lower:  carcass leanness, litter size
17 - Management: stationary; housing: ≈ 2 m.;
18 - Conservation progr.: live animals: miss;Semen: 1;Embryos: miss
19  Status: normal;          Watch: trend,%pure!
20 - Similar breeds (see group 4/1 on page 89)      EN  Country  Status
21  Clun Forest                                     464   F     pot. end.
22  Dorset Down                                     481   F     pot. end.
23  Mouton Vendeen                                  562   F     normal
24  Hampshire                                       506   F     normal
```

```
 1 - Dorset Horn, Poll Dorset                                    EN   483
 2   Dorset Horn/Poll; southern England
 3   Dorset Horn or Poll Dorset Sheep Breeders Association      HB:1892
 4   High West Street 3 Dorchester, Dorset
 5 - Imported as breed from Australia
 7   Numbers 1986: 859/31153; HB: 31153; increasing; 100 %; Ne = 3344
 8 - Height: miss/miss cm; Weight: 105/93 kg; Herd number: miss; AI: miss
 9   Colour: Uni white
10   Pecularity: horns: Dorset Horn 2/2, Poll Dorset 0/0
11 - Main use: (1) meat,(2) wool,(3) milk
12   Spec. abilities: breeding any time of year and twice in one year
13   Performance compared with STB Suffolk 642:
14      higher: miss
15      equal:  musc.,daily gain,carcass leanness,litter size,milk yield
16      lower:  lambing interval, age of sexual maturity
17 - Management: stationary; housing: ≈ 2 m.;
18 - Conservation progr.: live animals: miss;Semen: miss;Embryos: miss
19   Status: normal
```

20 - Similar breeds (see group 4/1 on page 89)	EN	Country	Status
21 Clun Forest	464	F	pot. end.
22 Dorset Down	481	F	pot. end.
23 Mouton Vendeen	562	F	normal
24 Hampshire	506	F	normal

```
 1 - Exmoor Horn                                                 EN   486
 2   Exmoor Horn; Exmoor and Dartmoor
 3   Exmoor Horn Sheep Breeders Society                        HB:1906
 4   Pickedstones, Simonsbath, Minehead SOM TA24-7LA
 5 - Autochthon local breed
 7   Numbers 1986: 400/35000; HB: miss; stable; 16 %; Ne = 1582
 8 - Height: 80/65 cm; Weight: 75/50 kg; Herd number: miss; AI: miss
 9   Colour: Uni white
10   Pecularity: horns 2/2
11 - Main use: (1) meat,(2) wool,(3) miss
12   Spec. abilities: extensive upland grazing
13   Performance compared with STB Scottish Blackface:
14      higher: daily gain
15      equal:  muscularity,carcass leanness,litter size,milk yield,% fat
16      lower:  miss
17 - Management: stationary; housing: ≈ 2 m.;
18 - Conservation progr.: live animals: miss;Semen: miss;Embryos: miss
19   Status: normal;            Watch: HB♀♀,%pure!
```

20 - Similar breeds (see group 7/11 on page 94)	EN	Country	Status
21 Blackface	421	F	crit.end.
22 Whitefaced Woodland	676	GB	pot. end.
23 Wicklow Cheviot	677	IRL	normal
24 Blackface Mountain	422	IRL	normal

```
 1 - Greyface Dartmoor                                      EN   502
 2   Greyface Dartmoor; southwestern England
 3   Rare Breed Survival Trust                            HB: Yes
 4   National Agriculture Center, Kenilworth, Warwickshire CV8 2LG
 5 - Autochthon native longwool
 7   Numbers 1986: 147/ miss; HB: 1186; increasing; 84 %; Ne = 523
 8 - Height:miss/miss cm; Weight:miss/miss kg; Herd number:miss; AI:miss
 9   Colour: miss
10   Peculiarity: horns 0/0, black or grey spots on nose
11 - Main use: (1) meat,(2) wool,(3) miss
12   Spec. abilities: miss
13   Performance compared with STB miss:
14      higher: miss
15      equal:  miss
16      lower:  miss
17 - Management: stationary; housing: 2-6 m.;
18 - Conservation progr.: live animals: miss;Semen: miss;Embryos: miss
19   Status: normal;              Watch: %pure!
```

20 -	Similar breeds (see group 3 on page 88)	EN	Country	Status
21	Mouton Boulonnais	559	F	crit.end.
22	Galway	495	IRL	endanger.
23	Mouton Charollais	560	F	normal
24	Cotentin	473	F	normal

```
 1 - Hampshire Down                                         EN   507
 2   Hampshire Down; country-wide
 3   Hampshire Down Sheep Breeders Association            HB:1890
 4   Iuy Cottage, Netheravon, Salisbury, Wiht.
 5 - Autochthon Wiltshire Horn, Berkshire knot, South Down
 7   Numbers 1993: 296/3681; HB: 3681; stable; 100 %; Ne = 1096
 8 - Height:miss/miss cm; Weight:miss/miss kg; Herd number: 163; AI:miss
 9   Colour: Uni white
10   Peculiarity: horns 0/0,dark brown face and ears,wool covered forehead
11 - Main use: (1) meat,(2) wool,(3) miss
12   Spec. abilities: miss
13   Performance compared with STB Suffolk 642:
14      higher: miss
15      equal:  musc.,daily gain,carc. lean.,milk yield,age of sex. mat.
16      lower:  litter size
17 - Management: stationary; housing: ≈ 2 m.;
18 - Conservation progr.: live animals: miss;Semen: miss;Embryos: miss
19   Status: normal
```

20 -	Similar breeds (see group 4/1 on page 89)	EN	Country	Status
21	Clun Forest	464	F	pot. end.
22	Dorset Down	481	F	pot. end.
23	Mouton Vendeen	562	F	normal
24	Hampshire	506	F	normal

```
1 - Hebridean                                                    EN   508
2   Hebridean
3   Rare Breed Survival Trust                                    HB:1973
4   National Agriculture Centre, Kenilworth, Wawickshire CV8 2LG
5 - Autochthon original breed
7   Numbers 1987: 57/556; HB: 556; increasing; 82 %; Ne = 207
8 - Height: miss/miss cm; Weight: miss/36 kg; Herd number: miss; AI:miss
9   Colour: Uni black
10  Pecularity: horns 4/4, some animals polycerate, tail half length
11 - Main use: (1) wool,(2) meat,(3) sport/hobby
12  Spec. abilities: speciality coloured wool
13  Performance compared with STB Scottish Blackface:
14    higher: muscularity, litter size
15    equal: daily gain, carcass leanness, milk yield, age of sex. mat.
16    lower: wool or fiber thickness, wool or fiber yield
17 - Management: stationary; housing: ≈ 2 m.;
18 - Conservation progr.: live animals: miss;Semen: miss;Embryos: miss
19  Status: normal;              Watch: %pure!
```

20 - Similar breeds (see group 6/4 on page 91)	EN	Country	Status
21 Vierhornschaf	662	D	crit.end.
22 Manx Loaghtan	539	GB	min. end.
23 Castlemilk Moorit Sheep	446	GB	pot. end.
24 Soay	631	GB	normal

```
1 - Herdwick                                                     EN   509
2   Herdwick; Cumbria
3   Herdwick Sheep Breeders Association                          HB:1920
4   19 Mountain View, Cockermonth, Cumbria
5 - Autochthon mountain breed
7   Numbers 1992: 1000/75000; HB: miss; stable; 75 %; Ne = 3947
8 - Height: 71/61 cm; Weight: 80/58 kg; Herd number: miss; AI: miss
9   Colour: Uni blue
10  Pecularity: horns 2,0/0
11 - Main use: (1) meat,(2) wool,(3) miss
12  Spec. abilities: able to survive on very sparse vegetation
13  Performance compared with STB Scottish Blackface:
14    higher: wool or fiber yield, wool or fiber thickness
15    equal: musc.,carc. lean.,litter size,milk yield,age of sex matur.
16    lower: daily gain
17 - Management: stationary; housing: no
18 - Conservation progr.: live animals: miss;Semen: miss;Embryos: miss
19  Status: normal;              Watch: HB♀♀,%pure!
```

20 - Similar breeds (see group 7/11 on page 94)	EN	Country	Status
21 Blackface	421	F	crit.end.
22 Whitefaced Woodland	676	GB	pot. end.
23 Wicklow Cheviot	677	IRL	normal
24 Blackface Mountain	422	IRL	normal

```
 1 - Ile-de-France                                                EN  514
 2   Ile-de-France; Northern Ireland & Wales, Scotland, England & Eire
 3   Ile de France Sheep Breed Society of GB & IRL                HB:1970
 4   Hill Road 3,Ballinaskeagh,Banbridge,Co. Down,N.  IRL  BT32 5EH
 5 - Imported as breed from France
 6   Incrossing since 1960 from Ile-de-France 513 France
 7   Numbers 1991: 300/ miss; HB: 5000; increasing; 100 %; Ne = 1132
 8 - Height: 80/67 cm; Weight: 150/94 kg; Herd number: miss; AI: Yes
 9   Colour: Uni white
10   Pecularity: horns 0/0
11 - Main use: (1) meat,(2) wool,(3) miss
12   Spec. abilities: very high muscle depth,high yielding meat carcasses
13   Performance compared with STB Suffolk 642:
14      higher: litter size
15      equal: musc.,daily gain,carc. lean.,milk yield,age of sex. matur.
16      lower: miss
17 - Management: stationary; housing: ≈ 2 m.;
18 - Conservation progr.: live animals: miss;Semen: miss;Embryos: miss
19   Status: normal
```

20 - Similar breeds (see group 1/6 on page 87)	EN	Country	Status
21 Berrichon de l'Indre	417	F	min. end.
22 Inra 401	515	F	pot. end.
23 Charmoise	450	F	normal
24 Berrichon du Cher	418	F	normal

```
 1 - Leicester Longwool                                           EN  528
 2   Leicester Longwool; eastern England
 3   Rare Breed Survival Trust                                    HB:1893
 4   National Agriculture Center, Kenilworth, Warwickshire CV8 2LG
 5 - Autochthon original breed, descendest of Dishley
 7   Numbers 1986: 105/1000; HB: 692; increasing; 87 %; Ne = 365
 8 - Height: miss/miss cm; Weight: miss/82 kg; Herd number: miss; AI:miss
 9   Colour: Uni white
10   Pecularity: horns 0/0
11 - Main use: (1) meat,(2) wool,(3) miss
12   Spec. abilities: miss
13   Performance compared with STB miss:
14      higher: miss
15      equal: miss
16      lower: miss
17 - Management: stationary; housing: 2-6 m.;
18 - Conservation progr.: live animals: miss;Semen: miss;Embryos: miss
19   Status: normal;              Watch: %pure!
```

20 - Similar breeds (see group 3 on page 88)	EN	Country	Status
21 Mouton Boulonnais	559	F	crit.end.
22 Galway	495	IRL	endanger.
23 Mouton Charollais	560	F	normal
24 Cotentin	473	F	normal

```
 1 - Lincoln Longwool                                         EN  532
 2   Lincoln Longwool; Lincolnshire, England
 3   Lincoln Longwool Sheep Breeders Association              HB:1892
 4   Lincolnshire Showground, Grange de Lings, Lincoln LN2 2NA
 5 - Autochthon Longwool sheep from Eastern England
 7   Numbers 1990: 100/1500; HB: miss; stable; 90 %; Ne = 375
 8 - Height: 90/80 cm; Weight: 113/91 kg; Herd number: miss; AI: miss
 9   Colour: Uni white
10   Pecularity: horns 0/0, blue/white face
11 - Main use: (1) meat,(2) wool,(3) sport/hobby
12   Spec. abilities: the heaviest, longest fleece; harsh climate
13   Performance compared with STB Suffolk 642:
14     higher: wool or fiber yield
15     equal: daily gain, carcass leanness, milk yield, lambing interval
16     lower: muscularity, litter size, age of sexual maturity
17 - Management: stationary; housing: no
18 - Conservation progr.: live animals: miss;Semen: miss;Embryos: miss
19   Status: potential. endang.;Watch: HB♀♀,%pure!
20 - Similar breeds (see group 3 on page 88)        EN  Country Status
21   Mouton Boulonnais                              559  F      crit.end.
22   Galway                                         495  IRL    endanger.
23   Mouton Charollais                              560  F      normal
24   Cotentin                                       473  F      normal
```

```
 1 - Manx Loaghtan                                            EN  539
 2   Manx Loaghtan
 3   Rare Breed Survival Trust                                HB:1973
 4   National Agriculture Center, Kenilworth, Warwickshire CV8 2LG
 5 - Autochthon breed
 7   Numbers 1987: 44/429; HB: 429; increasing; 76 %; Ne = 160
 8 - Height: miss/miss cm; Weight: miss/40 kg; Herd number: miss; AI:miss
 9   Colour: Uni brown
10   Pecularity: horns 4/4, some animals polycerate, tail half length
11 - Main use: (1) wool,(2) meat,(3) sport/hobby
12   Spec. abilities: coloured wool
13   Performance compared with STB Scottish Blackface:
14     higher: muscularity, daily gain, litter size, milk yield
15     equal: carcass leanness, age of sexual maturity, lambing interval
16     lower: wool or fiber thickness, wool or fiber yield
17 - Management: stationary; housing: ≈ 2 m.; easy management
18 - Conservation progr.: live animals: miss;Semen: miss;Embryos: miss
19   Status: minimally endang.; Watch: %pure!
20 - Similar breeds (see group 6/4 on page 91)     EN  Country Status
21   Vierhornschaf                                  662  D      crit.end.
22   Castlemilk Moorit Sheep                        446  GB     pot. end.
23   Soay                                           631  GB     normal
24   Hebridean                                      508  GB     normal
```

```
 1 - Norfolk Horn                                                    EN  565
 2   Norfolk Horn; eastern Anglia
 3   Rare Breed Survival Trust                                       HB:1974
 4   National Agriculture Center, Kenilworth, Warwickshire  CV8 2LG
 5 - Autochthon breed; incrossing since 1960 from Suffolk 642,
 6   Swaledale, Llanwenog all United Kingdom
 7   Numbers 1986: 39/329; HB: 329; increasing; 100 %; Ne = 140
 8 - Height: miss/miss cm; Weight: miss/72 kg; Herd number: miss; AI:miss
 9   Colour: Uni white
10   Pecularity: horns 2/2, black face and legs
11 - Main use: (1) meat,(2) wool,(3) miss
12   Spec. abilities: miss
13   Performance compared with STB miss:
14     higher: miss
15     equal: miss
16     lower: miss
17 - Management: stationary; housing: 2-6 m.;
18 - Conservation progr.: live animals: miss;Semen: miss;Embryos: miss
19   Status: minimally endang.; Watch: %incross!
```

20 - Similar breeds (see group 4/2 on page 89)	EN	Country	Status
21 Suffolk	639	F	normal
22 Suffolk	640	D	normal
23 Suffolk sheep	642	GB	normal
24 Suffolk	641	IRL	normal

```
 1 - North Country Cheviot                                           EN  567
 2   North Country Cheviot; northern Scotland and Scottish Borders
 3   North Country Cheviot Sheep Society                             HB:1945
 4   Tigh Na Machair, Davochfin, Dornoch, Sutherland IV25 3RW
 5 - Autochthon long hill sheep of Scotland
 7   Numbers 1986: 10000/500000; HB: 50000; increasing; 80 %; Ne = 33333
 8 - Height: 70/68 cm; Weight: 140/75 kg; Herd number: miss; AI: miss
 9   Colour: Uni white
10   Pecularity: horns 0/0
11 - Main use: (1) meat,(2) miss,(3) miss
12   Spec. abilities: miss
13   Performance compared with STB Scottish Blackface:
14     higher: daily gain,litter size,muscularity,age of sexual maturity
15     equal: carcass leanness,length of mating season,lambing interval
16     lower: miss
17 - Management: stationary; housing: ≈ 2 m.;
18 - Conservation progr.: live animals: miss;Semen: miss;Embryos: miss
19   Status: normal;                 Watch: %pure!
```

20 - Similar breeds (see group 7/11 on page 94)	EN	Country	Status
21 Blackface	421	F	crit.end.
22 Whitefaced Woodland	676	GB	pot. end.
23 Wicklow Cheviot	677	IRL	normal
24 Blackface Mountain	422	IRL	normal

1 - **North Ronaldsay**   EN **568**
2   **North Ronaldsay; Orkney Islands**
3   **Rare Breeds Survival Trust**   HB:**1974**
4   **National Agriculture Center, Kenilworth, Warwickshire CV8 2LG**
5 - **Autochthon breed**
7   Numbers 1986: 34/984; HB: 209; stable; 100 %; Ne = 117
8 - Height: **miss/miss** cm; Weight: **miss/25** kg; Herd number: **miss**; AI:**miss**
9   Colour: **Uni black, grey, red, white**
10 Pecularity: **horns 2/2,0; moufflon type; parti-coloured**
11 - Main use: (1) **wool**,(2) **meat**,(3) **miss**
12 Spec. abilities: **miss**
13 Performance compared with STB **miss**:
14   higher: **miss**
15   equal: **miss**
16   lower: **miss**
17 - Management: **stationary**; housing: **no**
18 - Conservation progr.: live animals: **miss**;Semen: **miss**;Embryos: **miss**
19 Status: **potential. endang.**;Watch: ♂♂,HB♀♀!
20 - <u>Similar breeds</u> (see group 6/4 on page 91)   <u>EN</u> <u>Country</u> <u>Status</u>
21 **Vierhornschaf**   662   D   crit.end.
22 **Manx Loaghtan**   539   GB   min. end.
23 **Soay**   631   GB   normal
24 **Hebridean**   508   GB   normal

1 - **Oxford Down**   EN **575**
2   **Oxford Down; country-wide**
3   **Oxford Down Sheep Breeders Association, 4 Brookfield,**   HB:**1887**
4   **Hampstwaite, Harrogate, N. Yorkshire HG3 2EF**
5 - **Composite of Hampshire Down, South Down x Cotswold rams**
6   **Incrossing since 1960 from Oxford Down Denmark**
7   Numbers 1986: 150/1500; HB: 1500; increasing; 100 %; Ne = 546
8 - Height: **75/65** cm; Weight: **120/90** kg; Herd number: **miss**; AI: **miss**
9   Colour: **Combination brown, white**
10 Pecularity: **horns 0/0, wool covered brown face and legs, white wool**
11 - Main use: (1) **meat**,(2) **wool**,(3) **terminal sire breed**
12 Spec. abilities: **heaviest British Down breed**
13 Performance compared with STB **Suffolk 642**:
14   higher:**miss**
15   equal: **daily gain, carcass leanness,litter size, milk yield**
16   lower: **muscularity**
17 - Management: **stationary**; housing: ≈ **2 m.**;
18 - Conservation progr.: live animals: **miss**;Semen: **miss**;Embryos: **miss**
19 Status: **normal**
20 - <u>Similar breeds</u> (see group 4/3 on page 89)   <u>EN</u> <u>Country</u> <u>Status</u>
21 **Schwarzköpfiges Fleischschaf**   623   D*   endanger.
22 **Schwarzköpfiges Fleischschaf**   622   D   normal
23 **Braunköpfiges Fleischschaf**   432   CH   normal

```
 1 - Portland                                              EN  587
 2   Portland; southern England
 3   Rare Breed Survival Trust                             HB:1973
 4   National Agriculture Centre, Kenilworth, Warwickshire CV8 2LG
 5 - Autochthon breed
 7   Numbers 1987: 66/431; HB: 431; increasing; 97 %; Ne = 229
 8 - Height: miss/miss cm; Weight: miss/40 kg; Herd number: miss; AI:miss
 9   Colour: Uni red
10   Pecularity: horns 2/2
11 - Main use: (1) meat,(2) sport/hobby,(3) wool
12   Spec. abilities: low fertility-max. of 1 lamb, breed all year around
13   Performance compared with STB Suffolk 642:
14      higher: length of mating season, carcass leanness
15      equal:  musc.,milk yield,age of sex. mat.,wool or fiber thickness
16      lower:  daily gain,lit. size,lambing interval,wool or fiber yield
17 - Management: stationary; housing: ≈ 2 m.;
18 - Conservation progr.: live animals: miss;Semen: miss;Embryos: miss
19   Status: normal
20 - Similar breeds (see group 4/1 on page 89)   EN  Country Status
21   Clun Forest                                  464   F     pot. end.
22   Dorset Down                                  481   F     pot. end.
23   Mouton Vendeen                               562   F     normal
24   Hampshire                                    506   F     normal
```

```
 1 - Romney Sheep                                          EN  602
 2   Romney; southeastern England
 3   Romney Sheep Breeders Society                         HB:1895
 4   School Road, St. Mary in the Marsh, Romney Marsh, Kent TN 29 ODG
 5 - Autochthon breed; incrossing since 1960 from Kent Halfbred,
 6   North Country Cheviot 567, Friesian, Llyn
 7   Numbers 1986: 2500/240000; HB: 20000; stable; 50 %; Ne = 8889
 8 - Height: 82/80 cm; Weight: 90/70 kg; Herd number: miss; AI: miss
 9   Colour: Uni white
10   Pecularity: horns 0/0, white head, nose and feet black
11 - Main use: (1) meat,(2) wool,(3) miss
12   Spec. abilities: miss
13   Performance compared with STB Suffolk 642:
14      higher: miss
15      equal:  muscul.,daily gain,carcass leanness,litter size,milk yield
16      lower:  age of sexual maturity
17 - Management: stationary; housing: no
18 - Conservation progr.: live animals: miss;Semen: Yes;Embryos: miss
19   Status: normal;                  Watch: %incross!
20 - Similar breeds (see group 3 on page 88)    EN  Country Status
21   Mouton Boulonnais                            559   F     crit.end.
22   Galway                                       495   IRL   endanger.
23   Mouton Charollais                            560   F     normal
24   Cotentin                                     473   F     normal
```

```
 1 - Rouge de l'ouest                                        EN  605
 2   Rouge de l'Ouest; northern England, Scotland
 3   British Rouge De L'ouest Sheep Society, LTD.            HB:1986
 4   Yochenthwaite, Buckden, Skipton, North Yorkshire BD23 5IH
 5 - Imported as breed from France
 7   Numbers 1986: 100/2000; HB: miss; increasing; 100 %; Ne = 381
 8 - Height:miss/miss cm; Weight:miss/miss kg; Herd number:miss; AI:miss
 9   Colour: Uni blond
10   Pecularity: horns 0/0, red head and legs
11 - Main use: (1) miss,(2) miss,(3) miss
12   Spec. abilities: miss
13   Performance compared with STB miss:
14     higher: miss
15     equal:  miss
16     lower:  miss
17 - Management: miss; housing: miss m.;
18 - Conservation progr.: live animals: miss;Semen: miss;Embryos: miss
19   Status: potential. endang.;Watch: HB♀♀!
20 - Similar breeds (see group 2/1 on page 87)    EN  Country Status
21   Bleu du Maine                                 425  F       normal
22   Rouge de l'ouest                              604  F       normal
23   Bleu du Maine                                 426  GB      normal
24   Blauköpfiges Fleischschaf                     424  D       normal
```

```
 1 - Rough Fell                                              EN  607
 2   Rough Fell; Kendal / Sedbergh, Cumbria
 3   Rough Fell Sheep Breeders Association                  HB:1926
 4   Weasdale Farm, Newbigginon on Lune, Kirkby Stephen, Cumbria
 5 - miss
 7   Numbers 1993: miss / miss; HB: miss; stable; 80 %; Ne = miss
 8 - Height: 120/95 cm; Weight: 75/45 kg; Herd number: > 10; AI: miss
 9   Colour: Uni white
10   Pecularity: horns 2/2, face and legs: black, white
11 - Main use: (1) meat,(2) wool,(3) miss
12   Spec. abilities: hardiness
13   Performance compared with STB Suffolk 642:
14     higher: age of sexual maturity, wool or fiber thickness
15     equal:  carc. lean.,milk yield,lamb. interv.,wool or fiber yield
16     lower:  litter size, muscularity, daily gain
17 - Management: stationary; housing: no
18 - Conservation progr.: live animals: miss;Semen: miss;Embryos: miss
19   Status: miss
20 - Similar breeds (see group 7/11 on page 94)   EN  Country Status
21   Blackface                                     421  F       crit.end.
22   Whitefaced Woodland                           676  GB      pot. end.
23   Wicklow Cheviot                               677  IRL     normal
24   Blackface Mountain                            422  IRL     normal
```

```
 1 - Ryeland                                                EN  613
 2   Ryeland; Great Britain
 3   Ryeland Flock Book Society Ltd.                        HB:1909
 4   Grandstand road 101, Hereford HR4 9NE
 5 - miss
 7   Numbers 1993: 400/3200; HB: miss; stable; 100 %; Ne = 1422
 8 - Height:miss/miss cm; Weight:miss/miss kg; Herd number: 211; AI:miss
 9   Colour: Uni white
10   Pecularity: horns 0/0,dull white face,dark skin round nose and eyes
11 - Main use: (1) meat,(2) wool,(3) miss
12   Spec. abilities: miss
13   Performance compared with STB Suffolk 642:
14     higher: miss
15     equal:  muscul.,daily gain,carcass leanness,litter size,milk yield
16     lower:  miss
17 - Management: miss; housing: miss m.;
18 - Conservation progr.: live animals: miss;Semen: Yes;Embryos: miss
19   Status: normal;               Watch: HB♀♀!
```

20 - Similar breeds (see group 4/1 on page 89)	EN	Country	Status
21 Clun Forest	464	F	pot. end.
22 Dorset Down	481	F	pot. end.
23 Mouton Vendeen	562	F	normal
24 Hampshire	506	F	normal

```
 1 - Shropshire                                             EN  629
 2   Shropshire; England
 3   Shropshire Sheep Breeders Ass.& Flock Book Society     HB:1883
 4   The Cottage,40 Droitwich Rd,Noah's Green,Feckenham,Worcs. B96 6RU
 5 - Composite of Cannock heath, Southdown
 6   Incrossing since 1960 from Shropshire Sweden
 7   Numbers 1986: 75/1450; HB: miss; increasing; 100 %; Ne = 285
 8 - Height: 75/70 cm; Weight: 120/80 kg; Herd number: miss; AI: miss
 9   Colour: Uni white
10   Pecularity: horns 0/0, black head and legs
11 - Main use: (1) meat,(2) wool,(3) miss
12   Spec. abilities: miss
13   Performance compared with STB Suffolk 642:
14     higher: miss
15     equal:  muscul.,daily gain,carcass leanness,litter size,milk yield
16     lower:  miss
17 - Management: stationary; housing: ≈ 2 m.;
18 - Conservation progr.: live animals: miss;Semen: miss;Embryos: miss
19   Status: potential. endang.;Watch: HB♀♀,%incross!
```

20 - Similar breeds (see group 4/1 on page 89)	EN	Country	Status
21 Clun Forest	464	F	pot. end.
22 Dorset Down	481	F	pot. end.
23 Mouton Vendeen	562	F	normal
24 Hampshire	506	F	normal

```
 1 - Soay                                                          EN   631
 2   Soay; country-wide
 3   Rare Breed Survival Trust                                     HB:1974
 4   National Agriculture Center, Kenilworth, Warwickshire CV8 2LG
 5 - Autochthon very old original breed
 7   Numbers 1986: 88/2000; HB: 436; stable; 92 %; Ne = 293
 8 - Height: miss/miss cm; Weight: 36/25 kg; Herd number: miss; AI: miss
 9   Colour: Uni brown
10   Pecularity: horns 2/2,0, short tail, moufflon pattern
11 - Main use: (1) meat,(2) wool,(3) sport/hobby
12   Spec. abilities: lean meat, foot rot resistance, low fertility
13   Performance compared with STB miss:
14     higher: miss
15     equal:  miss
16     lower:  miss
17 - Management: stationary; housing: ≈ 2 m.;
18 - Conservation progr.: live animals: miss;Semen: miss;Embryos: miss
19   Status: normal;              Watch: %pure!
```

20 - Similar breeds (see group 6/4 on page 91)	EN	Country	Status
21 Vierhornschaf	662	D	crit.end.
22 Manx Loaghtan	539	GB	min. end.
23 Castlemilk Moorit Sheep	446	GB	pot. end.
24 Hebridean	508	GB	normal

```
 1 - Southdown                                                     EN   636
 2   Southdown; South and Midlands
 3   Southdown Sheep Society                                       HB:1892
 4   Commercial Road 45, Bedford MK40 1QS
 5 - Autochthon Heath sheep
 6   Incrossing since 1960 from Southdown New Zealand
 7   Numbers 1986: 120/1000; HB: 900; increasing; 90 %; Ne = 424
 8 - Height: 67/60 cm; Weight: 75/60 kg; Herd number: miss; AI: Yes
 9   Colour: Uni white; mouse coloured face and lower legs
10   Pecularity: horns 0/0, barrel shaped, short legs
11 - Main use: (1) meat,(2) wool,(3) miss
12   Spec. abilities: finest wool fibre,early mat. meat sheep,fold toler.
13   Performance compared with STB Suffolk 642:
14     higher: miss
15     equal:  muscul.,daily gain,litter size,milk yield,% fat,% protein
16     lower:  wool or fiber thickness,carcass leanness,age of sex. mat.
17 - Management: stationary; housing: ≈ 2 m.;
18 - Conservation progr.: live animals: miss;Semen: 2;Embryos: miss
19   Status: normal;              Watch: %pure!
```

20 - Similar breeds (see group 4/1 on page 89)	EN	Country	Status
21 Clun Forest	464	F	pot. end.
22 Dorset Down	481	F	pot. end.
23 Mouton Vendeen	562	F	normal
24 Hampshire	506	F	normal

```
1 - Suffolk sheep                                           EN  642
2   Suffolk; country-wide
3   Suffolk Sheep Society - The Sheep Centre                HB:1887
4   Blackmore Park Road, Malvern, Worcs. WR13 6PH
5 - Composite of Norfolk Horned, Southdown
7   Numbers 1990: 6000/100000; HB: miss; increasing; 100 %; Ne = 22642
8 - Height: 80/76 cm; Weight: 136/91 kg; Herd number: miss; AI: Yes
9   Colour: Uni white
10  Pecularity: horns 0/0, black head and legs, white wool
11 - Main use: (1) meat,(2) wool,(3) major GB terminal sire breed
12  Spec. abilities: high proportion of meat / min. of fat cover
13  Performance compared with STB Suffolk 642:
14    higher: Breed is used
15    equal:  as standard breed,
16    lower:  no comparison possible.
17 - Management: stationary; housing: ≈ 2 m.;
18 - Conservation progr.: live animals: miss;Semen: 150;Embryos: miss
19  Status: normal
20 - Similar breeds (see group 4/2 on page 89)    EN  Country Status
21  Norfolk Horn                                  565   GB    min. end.
22  Suffolk                                       639   F     normal
23  Suffolk                                       641   IRL   normal
24  Suffolk                                       640   D     normal
```

```
1 - Teeswater                                                EN  647
2   Teeswater; mainly northern England, Wales + border region
3   Teeswater Sheep Breeders Association                    HB:1949
4   Mutton Hall, Old Hutton, Kendal, Cumbria LA8 ONW
5 - Autochthon native to Teesdale
7   Numbers 1993: 2000/ miss; HB: 1400; increasing; 95 %; Ne = 3294
8 - Height: 85/75 cm; Weight: 92/70 kg; Herd number: 160; AI: miss
9   Colour: Uni white
10  Pecularity: horns 0/0, brown or blue face and legs
11 - Main use: (1) meat,(2) wool,(3) miss
12  Spec. abilities: miss
13  Performance compared with STB Suffolk 642:
14    higher: litter size
15    equal:  daily gain,carcass leanness,milk yield,age of sex. matur.
16    lower:  muscularity
17 - Management: stationary; housing: no
18 - Conservation progr.: live animals: miss;Semen: miss;Embryos: miss
19  Status: normal
20 - Similar breeds (see group 3 on page 88)      EN  Country Status
21  Mouton Boulonnais                             559   F     crit.end.
22  Galway                                        495   IRL   endanger.
23  Mouton Charollais                             560   F     normal
24  Cotentin                                      473   F     normal
```

```
1 - Vendeen                                                    EN  661
2   Vendeen
3   Vendeen Sheep Society                                      HB:1984
4   Wyresdale, Camforth Hall Lane, Wittingham, Preston PR3 2AS
5 - Imported as breed from France
7   Numbers 1986: 500/500; HB: 500; increasing; 100 %; Ne = 1000
8 - Height: 75/70 cm; Weight: 105/65 kg; Herd number: miss; AI: miss
9   Colour: Uni white
10  Pecularity: horns 0/0, brown face and legs
11 - Main use: (1) meat,(2) wool,(3) crossbreeding sire line
12  Spec. abilities: miss
13  Performance compared with STB Texel 439:
14    higher: litter size, wool or fiber thickness
15    equal:  daily gain, carcass leanness, milk yield
16    lower:  muscularity,age of sex. matur.,lambing interval,wool yield
17 - Management: stationary; housing: ≈ 2 m.;
18 - Conservation progr.: live animals: miss;Semen: miss;Embryos: miss
19  Status: normal
```

20 - Similar breeds (see group 4/1 on page 89)	EN	Country	Status
21 Clun Forest	464	F	pot. end.
22 Dorset Down	481	F	pot. end.
23 Mouton Vendeen	562	F	normal
24 Hampshire	506	F	normal

UNITED KINGDOM   SHEEP

```
1 - Welsh Half-bred                                            EN  671
2   Welsh Half-bred; Wales, England, Scotland
3   Welsh Half Bred Sheep Breeders Association Ltd.            HB:miss
4   Great Darkgate Street, Aberystwyth, Dyfed, Wales
5 - Composite of Welsh Mountain, Border Leicester
7   Numbers 1988: miss /400000; HB: miss; increasing; miss %; Ne = 72400
8 - Height: miss/73 cm; Weight: miss/60 kg; Herd number: miss; AI: miss
9   Colour: Uni white
10  Pecularity: horns 0/0, white face with prominent ears of good body
11 - Main use: (1) production of prine lambs,(2) wool,(3) meat
12  Spec. abilities: lean. carc.,hardiness,very prolific,for marg. land
13  Performance compared with STB Border Leicester 428:
14    higher: daily gain, milk yield
15    equal:  muscularity,carcass leanness,litter size,age of sex. mat.
16    lower:  miss
17 - Management: stationary; housing: no
18 - Conservation progr.: live animals: miss;Semen: miss;Embryos: miss
19  Status: normal;              Watch: ♂♂,HB♀♀,%pure!
```

20 - Similar breeds (see group 3 on page 88)	EN	Country	Status
21 Mouton Boulonnais	559	F	crit.end.
22 Galway	495	IRL	endanger.
23 Mouton Charollais	560	F	normal
24 Cotentin	473	F	normal

1 - **Welsh Hill Speckled Face**   EN **672**
2   **Welsh Hill Speckled Face; Mid-North Wales**
3   **Welsh Hill Speckled Face Sheep Society**   HB:**1968**
4   **Broad street 10, Newtown, Powys, Wales SY16 2L2**
5 - Composite of **Kerry Hill, Welsh Mountain**
7   Numbers 1988: **700/26250**; HB: **26250**; **increasing**; miss %; Ne = **2727**
8 - Height: **miss/miss** cm; Weight: **67/50** kg; Herd number: **miss**; AI: **miss**
9   Colour: **Combination black, white**
10 Pecularity: **horns 2/0, black round eyes, nose, legs**
11 - Main use: (1) **meat**,(2) **wool**,(3) miss
12 Spec. abilities: **miss**
13 Performance compared with STB **Scottish Blackface:**
14   higher: **miss**
15   equal: **muscul.,daily gain,carcass leanness,litter size,milk yield**
16   lower: **miss**
17 - Management: **stationary**; housing: **no**
18 - Conservation progr.: live animals: **miss**;Semen: **miss**;Embryos: **miss**
19 Status: **normal**;   Watch: **%pure!**
20 - <u>Similar breeds</u> (see group 7/11 on page 94)   <u>EN</u> <u>Country</u> <u>Status</u>
21 **Blackface**   421   F   crit.end.
22 **Whitefaced Woodland**   676   GB   pot. end.
23 **Wicklow Cheviot**   677   IRL   normal
24 **Blackface Mountain**   422   IRL   normal

1 - **Welsh Mule**   EN **673**
2   **Welsh Mule; Wales, England, Scotland**
3   **Welsh Mules Sheep Breeders Association Ltd.**   HB:**miss**
4   **Great Darkgate Street, Aberystwyth, Dyfed, Wales**
5 - Composite of **Welsh Mountain, Brecknock Hill Cheviot,**
6   **Beulah Speckled Face, Welsh Hill Speckled**
7   Numbers 1988: **miss /370000**; HB: **miss**; **increasing**; miss %; Ne = **66970**
8 - Height: **miss/73** cm; Weight: **miss/65** kg; Herd number: **miss**; AI: **miss**
9   Colour: **Uni white**
10 Pecularity: **horns 0/0, face marking: speckled and white/black**
11 - Main use: (1) **production of prine lambs**,(2) **wool**,(3) **meat**
12 Spec. abilities: **lean. carc.,hardiness,very prolific,for marg. land**
13 Performance compared with STB **Border Leicester 428:**
14   higher: **daily gain, milk yield**
15   equal: **muscularity,carcass leanness,litter size,age of sex. mat.**
16   lower: **miss**
17 - Management: **stationary**; housing: **no**
18 - Conservation progr.: live animals: **miss**;Semen: **miss**;Embryos: **miss**
19 Status: **normal**;   Watch: **♂♂,HB♀♀,%pure!**
20 - <u>Similar breeds</u> (see group 3 on page 88)   <u>EN</u> <u>Country</u> <u>Status</u>
21 **Mouton Boulonnais**   559   F   crit.end.
22 **Galway**   495   IRL   endanger.
23 **Mouton Charollais**   560   F   normal
24 **Cotentin**   473   F   normal

1 - Wensleydale Longwool   EN 674
2   Wensleydale; Great Britain
3   Wensleydale Longwool Sheep Breeders Association   HB:1890
4   Kay Fold Farm, Ramsgrave, Blackburn, Lancs.
5 - Composite of Local Longwool, Leicester Longwool
7   Numbers 1986: 60/700; HB: miss; increasing; 90 %; Ne = 221
8 - Height: 88/82 cm; Weight: 130/90 kg; Herd number: miss; AI: miss
9   Colour: Uni white
10 Pecularity: horns 0/0, some sheep black - blue skin
11 - Main use: (1) meat,(2) wool,(3) miss
12 Spec. abilities: miss
13 Performance compared with STB Suffolk 642:
14   higher: litter size
15   equal: carc. leanness,milk yield,age of sex. mat.,lambing interv.
16   lower: muscularity, daily gain
17 - Management: stationary; housing: no
18 - Conservation progr.: live animals: miss;Semen: miss;Embryos: miss
19 Status: potential. endang.;Watch: HB♀♀,%pure!
20 - Similar breeds (see group 3 on page 88)   EN Country Status
21 Mouton Boulonnais   559   F   crit.end.
22 Galway   495   IRL endanger.
23 Mouton Charollais   560   F   normal
24 Cotentin   473   F   normal

1 - Whiteface Dartmoor   EN 675
2   Whiteface Dartmoor; southwestern England
3   Rare Breed Survival Trust   HB: Yes
4   National Agriculture Center, Kenilworth, Warwickshire CV8 2LG
5 - Autochthon breed
7   Numbers 1986: miss / miss; HB: 1853; stable; miss %; Ne = 335
8 - Height: miss/miss cm; Weight: 75/54 kg; Herd number: miss; AI: miss
9   Colour: Uni white
10 Pecularity: horns 2,0/0
11 - Main use: (1) meat,(2) wool,(3) miss
12 Spec. abilities: mountain
13 Performance compared with STB miss:
14   higher: miss
15   equal: miss
16   lower: miss
17 - Management: stationary; housing: no
18 - Conservation progr.: live animals: miss;Semen: miss;Embryos: miss
19 Status: minimally endang.; Watch: ♂♂,%pure!
20 - Similar breeds (see group 3 on page 88)   EN Country Status
21 Mouton Boulonnais   559   F   crit.end.
22 Galway   495   IRL endanger.
23 Mouton Charollais   560   F   normal
24 Cotentin   473   F   normal

```
 1 - Whitefaced Woodland                                    EN  676
 2   Whitefaced Woodland; Pennine Mountains
 3   Rare Breed Survival Trust                              HB:1974
 4   National Agriculture Center, Kenilworth, Warwickshire CV8 2LG
 5 - Composite of native Pennines, Cheviot, Merino
 7   Numbers 1986: 35/2500; HB: 387; decreasing; 96 %; Ne = 128
 8 - Height: miss/miss cm; Weight: miss/61 kg; Herd number: miss; AI:miss
 9   Colour: Uni white
10   Pecularity: horns 2/2
11 - Main use: (1) meat,(2) wool,(3) miss
12   Spec. abilities: mountain
13   Performance compared with STB miss:
14     higher: miss
15     equal:  miss
16     lower:  miss
17 - Management: stationary; housing: no/≈ 2 m.;
18 - Conservation progr.: live animals: miss;Semen: miss;Embryos: miss
19   Status: potential. endang.;Watch: trend!
```

20 - Similar breeds (see group 7/11 on page 94)	EN	Country	Status
21 Blackface	421	F	crit.end.
22 Blackface Mountain	422	IRL	normal
23 Dala	476	N	normal
24 Wicklow Cheviot	677	IRL	normal

```
 1 - Wiltshire Horn                                         EN  679
 2   Wiltshire Horn; England Midlands, South West and Wales
 3   Wiltshire Horn Sheep Society                           HB:1924
 4   Fairwater Farm, Hawkchurch, Axminster, Devon EX13 5XB
 5 - Autochthon breed of the West of England
 7   Numbers 1993: 300/1500; HB: 1200; increasing; 90 %; Ne = 960
 8 - Height: 83/75 cm; Weight: 126/72 kg; Herd number: 50; AI: miss
 9   Colour: Uni white
10   Pecularity: horns 2/0, large and curved
11 - Main use: (1) meat,(2) miss,(3) miss
12   Spec. abilities: little or no wool, so shearing is not required
13   Performance compared with STB Suffolk 642:
14     higher: litter size
15     equal:  muscul.,daily gain,carc. lean.,milk yield,age of sex. mat.
16     lower:  miss
17 - Management: stationary; housing: no
18 - Conservation progr.: live animals: miss;Semen: miss;Embryos: miss
19   Status: normal;           Watch: %pure!
```

20 - Similar breeds (see group 4/1 on page 89)	EN	Country	Status
21 Clun Forest	464	F	pot. end.
22 Dorset Down	481	F	pot. end.
23 Mouton Vendeen	562	F	normal
24 Hampshire	506	F	normal

```
 1 - Angora Goat                                              EN  302
 2   Angora Goat
 3   British Angora Goat Society                              HB:1984
 4   4th Strret, NAC, Kenilworth, Warwickshire CV8 2LG
 5 - Imported as breed from New Zealand, Australia
 6   Incrossing since 1960 from Angora New Zealand, Canada, South Africa
 7   Numbers 1993: 15/7000; HB: miss; decreasing; 100 %; Ne = 37
 8 - Height: 76/71 cm; Weight: 90/45 kg; Herd number: 300; AI: miss
 9   Colour: Uni white
10   Pecularity: horns 2/2
11 - Main use: (1) wool,(2) vegetation management,(3) meat
12   Spec. abilities: miss
13   Performance compared with STB Saanen:
14     higher: wool or fiber yield, muscularity, wool or fiber thickness
15     equal:  daily gain, carc. leanness, litter size, age of sex. mat.
16     lower:  milk yield
17 - Management: stationary; housing: 2-6 m.;
18 - Conservation progr.: live animals: Yes;Semen: 9;Embryos: miss
19   Status: critically endang.;Watch: HB♀♀,trend,%incross!
20 - Similar breeds                             EN  Country Status
21   miss                                       miss  miss  miss
```

```
 1 - Pure Toggenburg                                          EN  346
 2   Toggenburg
 3   Toggenburg Breeders Society, Lyngale House, Welham        HB:1911
 4   Hall, Little Gringley Lane, Retford, Notts DN22 OSF
 5 - Imported as breed from Switzerland
 6   Incrossing since 1960 from Toggenburg 362 Switzerland
 7   Numbers 1986: 60/300; HB: 300; increasing; 95 %; Ne = 200
 8 - Height: 80/70 cm; Weight: 70/60 kg; Herd number: miss; AI: Yes
 9   Colour: Combination brown, blond
10   Pecularity: horns 2/2, white facial stripes
11 - Main use: (1) milk,(2) miss,(3) miss
12   Spec. abilities: miss
13   Performance compared with STB Saanen:
14     higher: miss
15     equal:  litter size, milk yield, %fat, %protein, age of sex. mat.
16     lower:  miss
17 - Management: stationary; housing: 2-6 m.;
18 - Conservation progr.: live animals: miss;Semen: 8;Embryos: miss
19   Status: normal;              Watch: %pure!
20 - Similar breeds (see group 3 on page 97)    EN  Country Status
21   Thüringer Waldziege                        360  D    crit.end.
22   Toggenburger                               361  B    endanger.
23   Poitevin                                   345  F    min. end.
24   Toggenburger                               362  CH   normal
```

1 - Berkshire   EN **909**
2   Berkshire; England
3   British Pig Association   HB:1884
4   7 Rickmansworth Road, Watford Herts. WD1 7HE
5 - Autouchthon breed
6   Incrossing since 1970 from Berkshire Australia and New Zealand
7   Numbers 1992: 69/261; HB: miss; decreasing; 100 %; Ne = 218
8 - Height:miss/miss cm; Weight:miss/miss kg; Herd number: 131; AI: miss
9   Colour: Uni black
10 Pecularity: white on face, feet and tip of tail, erect ears
11 - Main use: (1) meat,(2) sport/hobby,(3) miss
12 Spec. abilities: miss
13 Performance compared with STB miss:
14   higher: miss
15   equal: miss
16   lower: miss
17 - Management: miss; housing: miss m.;
18 - Conservation progr.: live animals: miss;Semen: Yes;Embryos: miss
19 Status: minimally endang.; Watch: HB♀♀,trend,%incross!
20 - Similar breeds (see group 4/2 on page 103)   EN Country Status

	EN	Country	Status
21 Kemerovskaya	949	USSR	pot. end.
22 Severokavkazskaya	1000	USSR	pot. end.
23 Aksaiskaya cherno-pestraya	901	KAZ	normal
24 Belorusskaya cherno-pestraya	908	BEL	normal

1 - British Landrace   EN **911**
2   British Landrace
3   British Pig Association   HB:1953
4   7 Rickmansworth Road, Watford Herts. WD1 7HE
5 - Imported as breed from Sweden, Norway
6   Incrossing since 1970 from Landrace 970 Finland
7   Numbers 1986: 680/ miss; HB: 2638; decreasing; 22 %; Ne = 2163
8 - Height:miss/miss cm; Weight:miss/miss kg; Herd number: miss; AI: Yes
9   Colour: Uni white
10 Pecularity: lop ears
11 - Main use: (1) meat,(2) miss,(3) miss
12 Spec. abilities: miss
13 Performance compared with STB Large White 1023:
14   higher: miss
15   equal: % lean,litter size,feed conv. rate,meat quality,daily gain
16   lower: handling ease
17 - Management: miss; housing: miss m.;
18 - Conservation progr.: live animals: miss;Semen: miss;Embryos: miss
19 Status: normal;   Watch: trend,%pure!
20 - Similar breeds (see group 2/1 on page 101)   EN Country Status

	EN	Country	Status
21 Belgische Landrasse	907	D*	crit.end.
22 Zlotnicka biala	1024	PL	crit.end.
23 Landrace	952	CS	normal
24 Belgisch Landvarken	906	B	normal

```
 1 - British Saddleback                                      EN  912
 2   British Saddleback; England
 3   British Pig Association                                 HB:1920
 4   7 Rickmansworth Road, Watford Herts. WD1 7HE
 5 - Autochthon Essex and Wessex Saddleback
 7   Numbers 1992: 76/415; HB: miss; increasing; 100 %; Ne = 257
 8 - Height: miss/miss cm; Weight: miss/miss kg; Herd number: 91; AI: Yes
 9   Colour: Combination black, white
10   Pecularity: white saddle, lop ears
11 - Main use: (1) meat,(2) sport/hobby,(3) miss
12   Spec. abilities: outdoors,territorial instinct for outdoor farrowing
13   Performance compared with STB Large White 1023:
14     higher: handling ease
15     equal:  litter size,feed conv. rate,meat quality,farrowing interv.
16     lower:  % lean, daily gain, age of sex. maturity, piglet mortality
17 - Management: miss; housing: miss m.;
18 - Conservation progr.: live animals: miss;Semen: Yes;Embryos: miss
19   Status: potential. endang.;Watch: HB♀♀!
```

20 - <u>Similar breeds</u> (see group 3/1 on page 102)	EN	Country	Status
21 Pie noir du Pays Basque	987	F	crit.end.
22 Angler Sattelschwein	903	D	crit.end.
23 Presticke	994	CZ	pot. end.
24 Schwäbisch-Hällisches Schwein	997	D	pot. end.

```
 1 - Chester White                                          EN  913
 2   Chester White; England
 3   British Pig Association                                 HB:1981
 4   7 Rickmansworth Road, Watford Herts. WD1 7HE
 5 - Imported as breed from USA
 7   Numbers 1986: 12/30; HB: 30; decreasing; 100 %; Ne = 17
 8 - Height:miss/miss cm; Weight:miss/miss kg; Herd number: miss; AI:miss
 9   Colour: Uni white
10   Pecularity: lop ears
11 - Main use: (1) meat,(2) miss,(3) miss
12   Spec. abilities: miss
13   Performance compared with STB miss:
14     higher: miss
15     equal:  miss
16     lower:  miss
17 - Management: miss; housing: miss m.;
18 - Conservation progr.: live animals: miss;Semen: miss;Embryos: miss
19   Status: critically endang.;Watch: ♂♂,HB♀♀,trend,herds,%incross!
```

20 - <u>Similar breeds</u> (see group 2/2 on page 102)	EN	Country	Status
21 Normand	982	F	crit.end.
22 Mangalica	972	H	min. end.
23 Mangalita	973	RO	min. end.
24 Schwalbenbauch Mangalitza	1020	CH	pot. end.

1 - Duroc   EN 932
2   Duroc; England
3   British Pig Association   HB:1977
4   7 Rickmansworth Road, Watford Herts. WD1 7HE
5 - Imported as breed from Canada, USA
7   Numbers 1986: 29/ miss; HB: 62; decreasing; miss %; Ne = 59
8 - Height:miss/miss cm; Weight:miss/miss kg; Herd number: miss; AI: **Yes**
9   Colour: **Uni red**
10 Pecularity: **short lop ears**
11 - Main use: (1) **meat**,(2) miss,(3) miss
12 Spec. abilities: **outdoors**
13 Performance compared with STB **Large White 1023**:
14   higher: **meat quality, daily gain, piglet mortality**
15   equal: **% lean,litter size,feed conversion rate,age of sex. matur.**
16   lower: miss
17 - Management: miss; housing: miss m.;
18 - Conservation progr.: live animals: miss;Semen: miss;Embryos: miss
19 Status: **critically endang.**;Watch: **HB♀♀,trend,%pure!**
20 - <u>Similar breeds</u> (see group 5/1 on page 103)   <u>EN</u> <u>Country</u> <u>Status</u>
21 Duroc   927   F   crit.end.
22 Duroc   928   D*   pot. end.
23 Duroc   929   I   normal
24 Duroc   926   CS   normal

1 - Gloucestershire Old Spot   EN 936
2   Gloucestershire Old Spot; England
3   British Pig Association   HB:1915
4   7 Rickmansworth Road, Watford Herts. WD1 7HE
5 - miss
7   Numbers 1986: 59/ miss; HB: 345; increasing; 100 %; Ne = 202
8 - Height:miss/miss cm; Weight:miss/miss kg; Herd number:miss; AI:miss
9   Colour: **Combination black, white**
10 Pecularity: **black spots, lop ears**
11 - Main use: (1) miss,(2) miss,(3) miss
12 Spec. abilities: miss
13 Performance compared with STB miss:
14   higher: miss
15   equal: miss
16   lower: miss
17 - Management: miss; housing: miss m.;
18 - Conservation progr.: live animals: miss;Semen: miss;Embryos: miss
19 Status: **potential. endang.**;Watch: **herds!**
20 - <u>Similar breeds</u> (see group 6/2 on page 104)   <u>EN</u> <u>Country</u> <u>Status</u>
21 Sortbroget   1005   DK   crit.end.
22 Schwarz-Weißes Bentheimer   996   D   crit.end.
23 Pulawska   995   PL   min. end.
24 Sibirskaya chernopestraya   1001   USSR   pot. end.

```
 1 - Hampshire                                                      EN  945
 2   Hampshire; England
 3   British Pig Association                                        HB:1967
 4   7 Rickmansworth Road, Watford Herts. WD1 7HE
 5 - Imported as breed from Canada, USA
 7   Numbers 1986: 12/ miss; HB: 21; decreasing; miss %; Ne = 15
 8 - Height:miss/miss cm; Weight:miss/miss kg; Herd number: miss; AI: Yes
 9   Colour: Combination black, white
10   Pecularity: white saddle, erect ears
11 - Main use: (1) meat,(2) miss,(3) miss
12   Spec. abilities: heat-tolerance
13   Performance compared with STB miss:
14      higher: miss
15      equal:  miss
16      lower:  miss
17 - Management: miss; housing: miss m.;
18 - Conservation progr.: live animals: miss;Semen: miss;Embryos: miss
19   Status: critically endang.;Watch: ♂♂,HB♀♀,trend,herds,%pure!
```

20 -	Similar breeds (see group 3/2 on page 102)	EN	Country	Status
21	Limousin	967	F	crit.end.
22	Hampshire	942	D*	crit.end.
23	Hampshire	944	RO	pot. end.
24	Hampshire	940	CS	normal

UNITED KINGDOM   PIGS

```
 1 - Large Black                                                    EN  959
 2   Large Black; England
 3   British Pig Association                                        HB:1898
 4   7 Rickmansworth Road, Watford Herts. WD1 7HE
 5 - Composite of Small Suffolk, Black Dorset, Large Black (Devon/Corw)
 7   Numbers 1992: 39/247; HB: miss; decreasing; 100 %; Ne = 135
 8 - Height: miss/miss cm; Weight: miss/miss kg; Herd number: 95; AI:miss
 9   Colour: Uni black
10   Pecularity: lop ears
11 - Main use: (1) meat,(2) sport/hobby,(3) miss
12   Spec. abilities: good mothers
13   Performance compared with STB miss:
14      higher: miss
15      equal:  miss
16      lower:  miss
17 - Management: miss; housing: miss m.;
18 - Conservation progr.: live animals: miss;Semen: miss;Embryos: miss
19   Status: minimally endang.; Watch: HB♀♀,trend!
```

20 -	Similar breeds (see group 4/1 on page 103)	EN	Country	Status
21	Gascon	935	F	crit.end.
22	Alentejana	902	P	normal
23	Negra Iberica	981	E	normal

```
 1 - Middle White                                              EN  975
 2   Middle White; England
 3   British Pig Association                                   HB:1884
 4   7 Rickmansworth Road, Watford Herts. WD1 7HE
 5 - Composite of Large White and Small White
 7   Numbers 1992: 43/124; HB: miss; decreasing; 100 %; Ne = 128
 8 - Height: miss/miss cm; Weight: miss/miss kg; Herd number: 48; AI:miss
 9   Colour: Uni white
10   Pecularity: erect ears
11 - Main use: (1) meat,(2) vegetation management,(3) miss
12   Spec. abilities: miss
13   Performance compared with STB miss:
14     higher: miss
15     equal: miss
16     lower: miss
17 - Management: miss; housing: miss m.;
18 - Conservation progr.: live animals: miss;Semen: Yes;Embryos: miss
19   Status: minimally endang.; Watch: HB♀♀,trend!
```

20 -	Similar breeds (see group 1/2 on page 101)	EN	Country	Status
21	Bela Zlahtna	904	SLO	crit.end.
22	Yorkshire	1022	RO	pot. end.
23	Deutsches Edelschwein	922	D*	normal
24	Vile uslechtile	1017	CS	normal

```
 1 - Tamworth                                                  EN 1009
 2   Tamworth; England
 3   British Pig Association                                   HB:1884
 4   7 Rickmansworth Road, Watford Herts. WD1 7HE
 5 - Autochthon breed
 6   Incrossing since 1970 from Tamworth Australia
 7   Numbers 1992: 56/138; HB: miss; stable; 100 %; Ne = 159
 8 - Height: miss/miss cm; Weight: miss/miss kg; Herd number: 63; AI:miss
 9   Colour: Uni red
10   Pecularity:long snout,erect ears,Chinese breeds not incross. in past
11 - Main use: (1) meat,(2) sport/hobby,(3) miss
12   Spec. abilities: miss
13   Performance compared with STB miss:
14     higher: miss
15     equal: miss
16     lower: miss
17 - Management: miss; housing: miss m.;
18 - Conservation progr.: live animals: miss;Semen: Yes;Embryos: miss
19   Status: minimally endang.; Watch: HB♀♀,%incross!
```

20 -	Similar breeds (see group 5/2 on page 103)	EN	Country	Status
21	Mora Romagnola	977	I	crit.end.
22	Colorada	934	E	pot. end.

PIGS

```
 1 - Welsh                                                   EN 1018
 2   Welsh; England
 3   British Pig Association                                 HB:1918
 4   7 Rickmansworth Road, Watford Herts. WD1 7HE
 5 - Autochthon Welsh
 6   Incrossing since 1970 from Swedish Landrace S
 7   Numbers 1992: 97/373; HB: miss; decreasing; miss %; Ne = 308
 8 - Height: miss/miss cm; Weight: miss/miss kg; Herd number: 40; AI:miss
 9   Colour: Uni white
10   Pecularity: lop ears
11 - Main use: (1) miss,(2) miss,(3) miss
12   Spec. abilities: miss
13   Performance compared with STB miss:
14     higher: miss
15     equal:  miss
16     lower:  miss
17 - Management: miss; housing: miss m.;
18 - Conservation progr.: live animals: miss;Semen: miss;Embryos: miss
19   Status: minimally endang.; Watch: HB♀♀,trend,%pure!
```

20 - Similar breeds (see group 2/2 on page 102)	EN	Country	Status
21 **Normand**	982	F	crit.end.
22 **Chester White**	913	GB	crit.end.
23 **Mangalica**	972	H	min. end.
24 **Schwalbenbauch Mangalitza**	1020	CH	pot. end.

UNITED KINGDOM   PIGS

```
 1 - Yorkshire                                               EN 1023
 2   Large White; England
 3   British Pig Association                                 HB:1884
 4   7 Rickmansworth Road, Watford Herts. WD1 7HE
 5 - Autochthon Yorkshire/Cumberland/Leicestershire
 6   Incrossing since 1970 from Large White Sweden
 7   Numbers 1986: 1209/ miss; HB: 4858; increasing; miss %; Ne = 3872
 8 - Height:miss/miss cm; Weight:miss/miss kg; Herd number: miss; AI: Yes
 9   Colour: Uni white
10   Pecularity: erect ears
11 - Main use: (1) meat,(2) miss,(3) miss
12   Spec. abilities: miss
13   Performance compared with STB Large White 1023:
14     higher: Breed is used
15     equal:  as standard breed,
16     lower:  no comparison possible.
17 - Management: miss; housing: miss m.;
18 - Conservation progr.: live animals: miss;Semen: miss;Embryos: miss
19   Status: normal;              Watch: %pure!
```

20 - Similar breeds (see group 1/1 on page 101)	EN	Country	Status
21 **Norsk Yorkshire**	984	N	endanger.
22 **Grand Yorkshire Belge**	937	B	normal
23 **Large White**	960	F	normal
24 **Yorkshire**	1021	SF	normal

HORSES

1 - **Arab** EN 704
2 Arab; southern England
3 The Arab Horse Society HB:1788
4 Windsor House, Ramsbury, Nr Marlborough, Wiltshire SN8 2PE
5 - Imported as breed from Arabia
6 Incrossing since 1950 from Arab of other European countries
7 Numbers 1983: 1000/2000; HB: 2000; stable; 100 %; Ne = 2667
8 - Height: 150/140 cm; Weight: 550/500 kg; Herd number: miss; AI: miss
9 Colour: **50 % chestnut, 40 % grey, 10 % bay, very rarely black**
10 Pecularity: **long fine mane and tail**
11 - Main use: (1) **sport/hobby**,(2) **export of breeding stock**,(3) miss
12 Spec. abilities: miss
13 Performance compared with STB **miss**:
14 higher: **miss**
15 equal: **miss**
16 lower: **miss**
17 - Management: **stationary**; housing: **2-6 m.**;
18 - Conservation progr.: live animals: miss;Semen: miss;Embryos: miss
19 Status: **normal**
20 - <u>Similar breeds</u> (see group 1 on page 108)

		EN	Country	Status
21	**Arabialainen**	706	SF	crit.end.
22	**Täysverinen**	811	SF	crit.end.
23	**Anglo-Arab**	702	F	normal
24	**Vollblutaraber**	815	A	normal

HORSES

1 - **Cleveland Bay Horse** EN 732
2 Cleveland Bay; England
3 Cleveland Bay Horse Society HB:1884
4 York Livestock Centre, Murton, York
5 - **Composite of Cleveland Bay, Thoroughbred, Chapman Horse**
7 Numbers 1993: 42/200; HB: 200; increasing; 80 %; Ne = 139
8 - Height: 161/161 cm; Weight: 700/700 kg; Herd number: miss; AI: miss
9 Colour: **invariably bay with black points**
10 Pecularity: **the only acceptable marking is a small star**
11 - Main use: (1) miss,(2) miss,(3) miss
12 Spec. abilities: miss
13 Performance compared with STB **miss**:
14 higher: **miss**
15 equal: **miss**
16 lower: **miss**
17 - Management: **miss**; housing: **miss m.**;
18 - Conservation progr.: live animals: miss;Semen: Yes;Embryos: miss
19 Status: **normal**; Watch: **%pure!**
20 - <u>Similar breeds</u> (see group 3/4 on page 109)

		EN	Country	Status
21	**Kisberi felver**	769	H	pot. end.
22	**Mezöhegyesi felver**	782	H	pot. end.
23	**Irish Sport Horse**	765	IRL	normal
24	**Cob**	734	F	normal

```
1 - Clydesdale Horses                                            EN   733
2    Clydesdale; Scotland
3    The Clydesdale Horse Society of Great Britain and           HB:1877
4    Ireland, 24 Beresford Terrace, Ayr, Ayrshire KA7 2EG
5 - Composite of Native Scottish breed, Flemish, Shire 804
7    Numbers 1986: 95/400; HB: 400; increasing; 100 %; Ne = 307
8 - Height: 172/162 cm; Weight: 850/750 kg; Herd number: miss; AI: miss
9    Colour: bay, brown, black, rarely chestnut
10   Pecularity: large areas of white on face, legs and sometimes body
11 - Main use: (1) tractive power,(2) miss,(3) miss
12   Spec. abilities: miss
13   Performance compared with STB Percheron:
14     higher: handling ease
15     equal:  pulling power,speed in gallop,fertility,age of sex. matur.
16     lower:  miss
17 - Management: stationary; housing: ≈ 2 m.;
18 - Conservation progr.: live animals: miss;Semen: miss;Embryos: miss
19   Status: normal
20 - Similar breeds (see group 4/5 on page 110)    EN  Country Status
21   Suffolk Punch                                  808    GB   pot. end.
22   Shire Horse                                    804    GB   normal
```

```
1 - Dartmoor Pony                                                EN   739
2    Dartmoor Pony
3    Dartmoor Pony Society                                       HB:1899
4    Pizwell Farm, Postbridge, Yelverton, Devon PL20 6TN
5 - Autochthon breed
7    Numbers 1993: 85/2200; HB: 2000; stable; 100 %; Ne = 326
8 - Height: 122/122 cm; Weight: 250/212 kg; Herd number: miss; AI: miss
9    Colour: preferred bay, brown, or black
10   Pecularity: piebalds and scewbalds not accepted
11 - Main use: (1) sport/hobby,(2) miss,(3) miss
12   Spec. abilities: hardy
13   Performance compared with STB Thoroughbred:
14     higher: handling ease, pulling power
15     equal:  adaptability in dressage and in jumping, fertility
16     lower:  speed in gallop, age of sexual maturity
17 - Management: miss; housing: no
18 - Conservation progr.: live animals: miss;Semen: miss;Embryos: miss
19   Status: normal
20 - Similar breeds (see group 5/3 on page 110)    EN  Country Status
21   Welsh Pony (A, B & D)                          823    SF   crit.end.
22   New Forest Pony                                821    SF   min. end.
23   Exmoor Pony                                    743    GB   pot. end.
24   New Forest                                     784    F    pot. end.
```

```
 1 - Exmoor Pony                                              EN  743
 2   Exmoor Pony; Exmoor
 3   D. Mansell, ESQ.                                         HB:1921
 4   Glen Fern, Waddicombe, Dulverton Somerset TA22 9RY
 5 - Autochthon native breed, research has shown breed unchanged
 6   from ice age
 7   Numbers 1993: 40/250; HB: miss; increasing; 80 %; Ne = 138
 8 - Height: 130/127 cm; Weight: 227/227 kg; Herd number: 20; AI: miss
 9   Colour: bay, brown, dun; no white markings at all
10   Pecularity: mealy patches on muzzle,belly,around eyes,inside thighs
11 - Main use: (1) sport/hobby,(2) miss,(3) miss
12   Spec. abilities: miss
13   Performance compared with STB Fjord:
14      higher: handling ease, adaptability in dressage
15      equal:  fertility, age of sexual maturity, daily gain
16      lower:  pulling power, adaptability in jumping and in military
17 - Management: miss; housing: no; feral
18 - Conservation progr.: live animals: Yes;Semen: miss;Embryos: miss
19   Status: potential. endang.;Watch: HB♀♀,%pure!
```

	20 - Similar breeds (see group 5/3 on page 110)	EN	Country	Status
21	Welsh Pony (A, B & D)	823	SF	crit.end.
22	New Forest Pony	821	SF	min. end.
23	New Forest	784	F	pot. end.
24	Dartmoor Pony	739	GB	normal

```
 1 - Fell Pony                                                EN  744
 2   Fell Pony; northern England
 3   The Fell Pony Society                                    HB:1898
 4   Riccarton Mill, Newcastleton, Roxburghshire TD9 0SN
 5 - Composite of Ponies of North and South England
 7   Numbers 1993: 100/2000; HB: miss; increasing; 100 %; Ne = 381
 8 - Height: 142/142 cm; Weight: 460/460 kg; Herd number: > 10; AI: miss
 9   Colour: predominantly black, also brown, bay or grey
10   Pecularity: very few white markings
11 - Main use: (1) sport/hobby,(2) shepherding, trekking,(3) miss
12   Spec. abilities: very hardy, mountain
13   Performance compared with STB Thoroughbred:
14      higher: handling ease, speed in trotters, pulling power
15      equal:  fertility, age of sexual maturity, daily gain
16      lower:  adaptability in dressage, jumping and in military
17 - Management: stationary; housing: no; mountain, feral
18 - Conservation progr.: live animals: miss;Semen: miss;Embryos: miss
19   Status: normal;              Watch: HB♀♀!
```

	20 - Similar breeds (see group 5/4 on page 110)	EN	Country	Status
21	Highland	759	F	crit.end.

1 - Haflinger   EN   757
2   Haflinger; Midlands
3   Haflinger Society of Great Britain   HB:1970
4   Silver Hill, 482 Market Street, Whithworth Lancs OL12 8QW
5 - Imported as breed from Austria
6   Incrossing since 1950 from Haflinger Austria
7   Numbers 1986: 13/250; HB: 250; stable; 98 %; Ne = 27
8 - Height: 142/141 cm; Weight: 600/500 kg; Herd number: miss; AI: miss
9   Colour: light to dark chestnut
10 Pecularity: full flaxen mane and tail
11 - Main use: (1) sport/hobby,(2) tractive power,(3) miss
12 Spec. abilities: miss
13 Performance compared with STB Fjord:
14   higher: handling ease, daily gain, speed in trotters
15   equal: adaptability in dressage and jumping, speed in gallop
16   lower: pulling power, adaptability in military
17 - Management: miss; housing: miss m.;
18 - Conservation progr.: live animals: miss;Semen: miss;Embryos: miss
19 Status: endangered;   Watch: ♂♂!
20 - Similar breeds (see group 5/8 on page 111)   EN Country Status
21 Haflinger   756 CH   pot. end.
22 Haflinger   753 F   normal
23 Avelignese   710 I   normal
24 Haflinger   754 D   normal

1 - Morgan Horse   EN   783
2   Morgan; Hereford, Yorkshire, Lancashire
3   British Morgan Horse Society, Cleeton Turn Cottage,   HB:1975
4   Cleeton St. Mary,Cleobury Mortimer,Kidderminster, Worcester DY14 0QT
5 - Imported as breed from USA
6   Incrossing since 1950 from Morgan USA
7   Numbers 1993: 22/48; HB: miss; increasing; 100 %; Ne = 37
8 - Height: 143/142 cm; Weight: 540/450 kg; Herd number: 10; AI: miss
9   Colour: usually bay, also black, chestnut or isabelle
10 Pecularity: profuse mane and tail
11 - Main use: (1) sport/hobby,(2) miss,(3) miss
12 Spec. abilities: miss
13 Performance compared with STB Halfbred:
14   higher: age of sexual maturity
15   equal: pulling power, handling ease, fertility, daily gain
16   lower: miss
17 - Management: stationary; housing: 2-6 m.;
18 - Conservation progr.: live animals: Yes;Semen: 6;Embryos: miss
19 Status: endangered;   Watch: ♂♂,HB♀♀,herds,%incross!
20 - Similar breeds (see group 2 on page 108)   EN Country Status
21 Lämminverinen ravuri   773 SF   normal
22 Trotteur Francais   813 F   normal
23 Norsk Kaldblods Traver   789 N   normal

```
 1 - Shire Horse                                          EN  804
 2   Shire; England
 3   Shire Horse Society                                  HB:1878
 4   East of England Showground, Peterborough PE2 6XE
 5 - Autochthon Old English breed of cart horses
 7   Numbers 1986: 150/10000; HB: 5000; decreasing; 90 %; Ne = 583
 8 - Height: 183/173 cm; Weight: 1000/900 kg; Herd number: miss; AI: Yes
 9   Colour: black,bay,grey; regist. breeding-stallions must not be roan
10   Pecularity: white markings and heavy feathers on the legs
11 - Main use: (1) tractive power,(2) sport/hobby,(3) miss
12   Spec. abilities: miss
13   Performance compared with STB Percheron:
14      higher: pulling power, handling ease, adaptability in military
15      equal:  speed in gallop, age of sexual maturity, speed in trotters
16      lower:  miss
17 - Management: stationary; housing: 2-6 m.;
18 - Conservation progr.: live animals: miss;Semen: miss;Embryos: miss
19   Status: normal;              Watch: trend,%pure!
20 - Similar breeds (see group 4/5 on page 110)   EN  Country Status
21   Suffolk Punch                                  808   GB   pot. end.
22   Clydesdale Horses                              733   GB   normal
```

```
 1 - Suffolk Punch                                        EN  808
 2   Suffolk; eastern Anglia
 3   Suffolk Horse Society                                HB:1878
 4   The Market Hill, Woodbridge, Suffolk IP12 4LU
 5 - Autochthon oldest breed of draught horse of the world
 7   Numbers 1993: 25/100; HB: miss; increasing; 100 %; Ne = 61
 8 - Height: 170/160 cm; Weight: 800/680 kg; Herd number: > 10; AI: miss
 9   Colour: invariably chestnut
10   Pecularity: miss
11 - Main use: (1) tractive power,(2) miss,(3) miss
12   Spec. abilities: miss
13   Performance compared with STB Percheron:
14      higher: handling ease, fertility, pulling power
15      equal:  age of sexual maturity, daily gain
16      lower:  miss
17 - Management: stationary; housing: 2-6 m.;
18 - Conservation progr.: live animals: Yes;Semen: miss;Embryos: miss
19   Status: potential. endang.;Watch: ♂♂,HB♀♀!
20 - Similar breeds (see group 4/5 on page 110)   EN  Country Status
21   Clydesdale Horses                              733   GB   normal
22   Shire Horse                                    804   GB   normal
```

```
 1 - Bestuzhevskaya                                                    EN   31
 2   Bestuzhev; Tatar ASSR,Bashkiria,reg. of Ulyanovsk + Kuibyshev
 3   Food and Agriculture Organisation of the UN               HB:1928
 4   Rome 00100, Via delle Terme di Caracalla
 5 - Composite of Friesian, Simmental, Shorthorn, local cattle
 7   Numbers 1990: 2600/533000; HB: miss; decreasing; 71 %; Ne = 10350
 8 - Height: 140/132 cm; Weight: 850/520 kg; Herd number: miss; AI: Yes
 9   Colour: Uni red
10   Pecularity: miss
11 - Main use: (1) milk,(2) meat,(3) miss
12   Spec. abilities: resistant to tuberculosis, leucosis
13   Performance compared with STB Russian Black Pied 64:
14     higher: % fat
15     equal:  miss
16     lower:  milk yield
17 - Management: stationary; housing: > 6 m.;
18 - Conservation progr.: live animals: miss;Semen: miss;Embryos: miss
19   Status: normal;            Watch: HB♀♀,trend,%pure!
```

20 - Similar breeds (see group 4/5 on page 79)	EN	Country	Status
21 Yurinskaya	276	USSR	crit.end.
22 Krasnyi megrelskii skot	150	GO	endanger.
23 Krasnaya stepnaya	147	UR	normal
24 Kalmytskaya	135	USSR	normal

```
 1 - Cherno-pestraya                                                   EN   64
 2   Russian Black Pied; country-wide
 3   Food and Agriculture Organisation of the UN               HB:1940
 4   Rome 00100, Via delle Terme di Caracalla
 5 - Composite of local cattle, Dutch Black Pied, East Friesian
 6   Incrossing since 1950 from Holstein Friesian 277 Netherlands
 7   Numbers 1990: 60000/10128000; HB: miss; increasing; 50 %; Ne=238587
 8 - Height: 140/129 cm; Weight: 850/560 kg; Herd number: miss; AI: Yes
 9   Colour: Combination black, white
10   Pecularity: miss
11 - Main use: (1) milk,(2) miss,(3) miss
12   Spec. abilities: miss
13   Performance compared with STB Swiss Brown:
14     higher: milk yield
15     equal:  % fat
16     lower:  miss
17 - Management: stationary; housing: > 6 m.;
18 - Conservation progr.: live animals: miss;Semen: miss;Embryos: miss
19   Status: normal;            Watch: HB♀♀,%incross,%pure!
```

20 - Similar breeds (see group 1/3 on page 75)	EN	Country	Status
21 Yakutskii skot	274	USSR	min. end.
22 Istobenskaya	128	USSR	pot. end.
23 Tagilskaya	252	USSR	normal
24 Kholmogorskaya	141	USSR	normal

```
 1 - Istobenskaya                                              EN  128
 2   Istoben; Kirov
 3   Food and Agriculture Organisation of the UN            HB:1935
 4   Rome 00100, Via delle Terme di Caracalla
 5 - Composite of Kholmogory, Swiss Brown, East Friesian and
 6   Great Russian cattle
 7   Numbers 1990: 250/35000; HB: miss; decreasing; 74 %; Ne = 993
 8 - Height: 138/129 cm; Weight: 760/480 kg; Herd number: miss; AI: Yes
 9   Colour: Uni black, red; combination black, red, white
10   Pecularity: usually black or black pied, occ. red or red pied
11 - Main use: (1) milk,(2) meat,(3) miss
12   Spec. abilities: good adapt. to the local ecological conditions
13   Performance compared with STB Russian Black Pied 64:
14     higher: miss
15     equal: % fat
16     lower:  milk yield
17 - Management: stationary; housing: > 6 m.;
18 - Conservation progr.: live animals: miss;Semen: miss;Embryos: miss
19   Status: potential. endang.;Watch: HB♀♀,trend,%pure!
```

20 - Similar breeds (see group 1/3 on page 75)	EN	Country	Status
21 Yakutskii skot	274	USSR	min. end.
22 Cherno-pestraya	64	USSR	normal
23 Tagilskaya	252	USSR	normal
24 Kholmogorskaya	141	USSR	normal

```
 1 - Kalmytskaya                                              EN  135
 2   Kalmyk; north of Caspian Sea
 3   Food and Agriculture Organisation of the UN            HB: Yes
 4   Rome 00100, Via delle Terme di Caracalla
 5 - Composite of Simmental, Shorthorn, local cattle
 7   Numbers 1990: 7900/138500; HB: miss; stable; 79 %; Ne = 29895
 8 - Height: 135/126 cm; Weight: 720/430 kg; Herd number: miss; AI: miss
 9   Colour: Uni red
10   Pecularity: often white head, belly and feet
11 - Main use: (1) meat,(2) milk,(3) miss
12   Spec. abilities: harsh continental climate, high viability
13   Performance compared with STB Russian Simmental 241:
14     higher: % fat
15     equal:  miss
16     lower:  milk yield
17 - Management: stationary; housing: > 6 m.; grazing on poor vegetation
18 - Conservation progr.: live animals: miss;Semen: miss;Embryos: miss
19   Status: normal;           Watch: HB♀♀!
```

20 - Similar breeds (see group 4/5 on page 79)	EN	Country	Status
21 Yurinskaya	276	USSR	crit.end.
22 Krasnyi megrelskii skot	150	GO	endanger.
23 Krasnaya stepnaya	147	UR	normal
24 Bestuzhevskaya	31	USSR	normal

1 - Kholmogorskaya   EN 141
2   Kholmogory; Archangel
3   Food and Agriculture Organisation of the UN   HB:1927
4   Rome 00100, Via delle Terme di Caracalla
5 - Composite of local cattle, Friesian
7   Numbers 1990: 6000/1049000; HB: miss; decreasing; 70 %; Ne = 23864
8 - Height: 140/134 cm; Weight: 850/500 kg; Herd number: miss; AI: Yes
9   Colour: Combination black, red, white
10 Pecularity: miss
11 - Main use: (1) milk,(2) miss,(3) miss
12 Spec. abilities: leucosis rate less than among Black Pied breed
13 Performance compared with STB Russian Black Pied 64:
14   higher: miss
15   equal: % fat
16   lower: milk yield
17 - Management: stationary; housing: > 6 m.; adap. in diff. geog. areas
18 - Conservation progr.: live animals: miss;Semen: miss;Embryos: miss
19 Status: normal;   Watch: HB♀♀,trend,%pure!
20 - Similar breeds (see group 1/3 on page 75)   EN Country Status
21 Yakutskii skot   274   USSR min. end.
22 Istobenskaya   128   USSR pot. end.
23 Tagilskaya   252   USSR normal
24 Cherno-pestraya   64   USSR normal

1 - Kostromskaya   EN 142
2   Kostroma; central Russia, Byelorussia
3   Food and Agriculture Organisation of the UN   HB:1944
4   Rome 00100, Via delle Terme di Caracalla
5 - Composite of Swiss Brown,Babaev,Miskov,Kholmogory,Yaroslavl,Ayrshire
6   Incrossing since 1950 from Brown Swiss USA
7   Numbers 1990: 2400/209600; HB: miss; decreasing; 60 %; Ne = 9491
8 - Height: 140/132 cm; Weight: 850/520 kg; Herd number: miss; AI: Yes
9   Colour: Uni grey, brown
10 Pecularity: resembles Brown Swiss
11 - Main use: (1) milk,(2) meat,(3) miss
12 Spec. abilities: longevity, strong constitution
13 Performance compared with STB Russian Black Pied 64:
14   higher: % fat
15   equal: miss
16   lower: milk yield
17 - Management: stationary; housing: > 6 m.; hardiness
18 - Conservation progr.: live animals: miss;Semen: miss;Embryos: miss
19 Status: normal;   Watch: HB♀♀,trend,%pure,%incross!
20 - Similar breeds (see group 5/1 on page 79)   EN Country Status
21 Original Allgäuer Braunvieh   189   D   crit.end.
22 Agerolese   2   I   crit.end.
23 Aubrac   14   F   normal
24 Österreichisches Braunvieh   190   A   normal

1 - Krasnaya gorbatovskaya   EN   144
2   Gorbatov Red; Gorki
3   Food and Agriculture Organisation of the UN   HB:1921
4   Rome 00100, Via delle Terme di Caracalla
5 - Composite of Tyrolean, Prioksky
7   Numbers 1990: 44/27400; HB: miss; decreasing; 60 %; Ne = 176
8 - Height: 133/122 cm; Weight: 830/470 kg; Herd number: miss; AI: Yes
9   Colour: Uni red
10 Pecularity: pink muzzle
11 - Main use: (1) milk,(2) meat,(3) miss
12 Spec. abilities: resistant to leucosis, tuberculosis, brucellosis
13 Performance compared with STB Russian Black Pied 64:
14   higher: % fat
15   equal: miss
16   lower: milk yield
17 - Management: stationary; housing: > 6 m.;
18 - Conservation progr.: live animals: Yes;Semen: miss;Embryos: miss
19 Status: potential. endang.;Watch: HB♀♀,trend,%pure!
20 - Similar breeds (see group 4/5 on page 79)

	EN	Country	Status
21 Yurinskaya	276	USSR	crit.end.
22 Krasnyi megrelskii skot	150	GO	endanger.
23 Kalmytskaya	135	USSR	normal
24 Bestuzhevskaya	31	USSR	normal

1 - Krasnaya tambovskaya   EN   148
2   Tambov Red; Tambov, Voronesh region
3   Food and Agriculture Organisation of the UN   HB:1948
4   Rome 00100, Via delle Terme di Caracalla
5 - Composite of Tyrolean, Devon, Simmental, local breeds
6   Incrossing since 1950 from Danish Red 222 Denmark
7   Numbers 1990: 107/19900; HB: miss; decreasing; 31 %; Ne = 426
8 - Height: 136/127 cm; Weight: 700/460 kg; Herd number: miss; AI: miss
9   Colour: Uni red
10 Pecularity: miss
11 - Main use: (1) meat,(2) milk,(3) miss
12 Spec. abilities: strong constitution
13 Performance compared with STB Russian Simmental 241:
14   higher: miss
15   equal: % fat
16   lower: milk yield
17 - Management: stationary; housing: > 6 m.;
18 - Conservation progr.: live animals: miss;Semen: miss;Embryos: miss
19 Status: minimally endang.; Watch: HB♀♀,trend,%pure!
20 - Similar breeds (see group 4/5 on page 79)

	EN	Country	Status
21 Yurinskaya	276	USSR	crit.end.
22 Krasnyi megrelskii skot	150	GO	endanger.
23 Kalmytskaya	135	USSR	normal
24 Bestuzhevskaya	31	USSR	normal

1 - **Kurganskaya**   EN **151**
2   **Kurgan; southwestern Siberia**
3   **Food and Agriculture Organisation of the UN**   HB:**1949**
4   **Rome 00100, Via delle Terme di Caracalla**
5 - **Composite of Shorthorn, Simmental, Dutch, Bestuzhev, Tagil,**
6   **Red Steppe, local cattle**
7   Numbers 1990: **10/2000**; HB: **miss**; **decreasing**; **50 %**; Ne = **20**
8 - Height: **139/129** cm; Weight: **800/500** kg; Herd number: **miss**; AI: **miss**
9   Colour: **Uni red, roan; combination red, white**
10 Pecularity: **miss**
11 - Main use: (1) **milk**,(2) **meat**,(3) **miss**
12 Spec. abilities: **miss**
13 Performance compared with STB **Russian Simmental 241**:
14   higher: **miss**
15   equal: **% fat**
16   lower: **milk yield**
17 - Management: **stationary**; housing: **> 6 m.**;
18 - Conservation progr.: live animals: **miss**;Semen: **miss**;Embryos: **miss**
19   Status: **critically endang.**;Watch: **♂♂,HB♀♀,trend,%pure**!
20 - <u>Similar breeds</u> (see group 4/2 on page 78)   <u>EN</u> <u>Country</u> <u>Status</u>
21   **Armoricaine**   10   F   **crit.end.**
22   **Irish Shorthorn**   124   IRL   **normal**
23   **Lincoln Red**   159   GB   **normal**
24   **Beef Shorthorn Cattle**   24   GB   **normal**

1 - **Shvitskaya**   EN **234**
2   **Russian Brown; country-wide**
3   **Food and Agriculture Organisation of the UN**   HB: **Yes**
4   **Rome 00100, Via delle Terme di Caracalla**
5 - **Imported as breed from countries Switzerland, Germany**
7   Numbers 1990: **10100/886000**; HB: **miss**; **decreasing**; **49 %**; Ne = **39945**
8 - Height: **139/131** cm; Weight: **850/500** kg; Herd number: **miss**; AI: **Yes**
9   Colour: **Uni brown**
10 Pecularity: **miss**
11 - Main use: (1) **milk**,(2) **meat**,(3) **miss**
12 Spec. abilities: **miss**
13 Performance compared with STB **Russian Black Pied 64**:
14   higher: **miss**
15   equal: **% fat**
16   lower: **milk yield**
17 - Management: **stationary**; housing: **> 6 m.**;
18 - Conservation progr.: live animals: **miss**;Semen: **miss**;Embryos: **miss**
19   Status: **normal**;   Watch: **HB♀♀,trend,%pure**!
20 - <u>Similar breeds</u> (see group 5/1 on page 79)   <u>EN</u> <u>Country</u> <u>Status</u>
21   **Original Allgäuer Braunvieh**   189   D   **crit.end.**
22   **Agerolese**   2   I   **crit.end.**
23   **Aubrac**   14   F   **normal**
24   **Österreichisches Braunvieh**   190   A   **normal**

```
 1 - Simmentalskaya                                              EN   241
 2   Russian Simmental; country-wide
 3   Food and Agriculture Organisation of the UN                 HB:1925
 4   Rome 00100, Via delle Terme di Caracalla
 5 - Imported as breed from countries Switzerland, Germany, Austria
 6   Incrossing since 1950 from Red/White HF, Ayrshire
 7   Numbers 1990: 39400/6021200; HB: miss; decreasing; 55 %; Ne = 156575
 8 - Height: 142/133 cm; Weight: 900/600 kg; Herd number: miss; AI: Yes
 9   Colour: Combination red, yellow, white
10   Pecularity: horns 2/2
11 - Main use: (1) milk; meat,(2) miss,(3) miss
12   Spec. abilities: miss
13   Performance compared with STB Swiss Brown:
14     higher: milk yield
15     equal: % fat
16     lower: miss
17 - Management: stationary; housing: > 6 m.;
18 - Conservation progr.: live animals: miss;Semen: miss;Embryos: miss
19   Status: normal;           Watch: HB♀♀,trend,%pure,%incross!
20 - Similar breeds (see group 3/2 on page 77)    EN  Country Status
21   Ceske strakate                                61   CZ    crit.end.
22   Simentalska                                  237   PL    min. end.
23   Montbeliard                                  176   F     normal
24   Fleckvieh                                     88   A     normal
```

```
 1 - Suksunskii skot                                             EN   246
 2   Suksun; Perm
 3   Food and Agriculture Organisation of the UN                 HB:1941
 4   Rome 00100, Via delle Terme di Caracalla
 5 - Composite of Danish Red, local cattle, Angeln, Red Steppe,
 6   Estonian Red, Latvian Brown
 7   Numbers 1990: 20/8100; HB: miss; decreasing; 73 %; Ne = 60
 8 - Height: 137/129 cm; Weight: 770/480 kg; Herd number: miss; AI: miss
 9   Colour: Uni red
10   Pecularity: miss
11 - Main use: (1) milk,(2) miss,(3) miss
12   Spec. abilities: resistant to tuberculosis, leucosis
13   Performance compared with STB Russian Black Pied 64:
14     higher: miss
15     equal: % fat
16     lower: milk yield
17 - Management: stationary; housing: > 6 m.; severe clim. of cent. Ural
18 - Conservation progr.: live animals: Yes;Semen: Yes;Embryos: miss
19   Status: minimally endang.; Watch: ♂♂,HB♀♀,trend,%pure!
20 - Similar breeds (see group 4/5 on page 79)    EN  Country Status
21   Yurinskaya                                   276   USSR  crit.end.
22   Krasnyi megrelskii skot                      150   GO    endanger.
23   Kalmytskaya                                  135   USSR  normal
24   Bestuzhevskaya                                31   USSR  normal
```

```
 1 - Sychevskaya                                                    EN  250
 2   Sychevka; Smolensk
 3   Food and Agriculture Organisation of the UN                    HB: Yes
 4   Rome 00100, Via delle Terme di Caracalla
 5 - Composite of Simmental, West Russian Cattle
 7   Numbers 1990: 3569/259000; HB: miss; decreasing; 31 %; Ne = 14082
 8 - Height: 142/133 cm; Weight: 900/600 kg; Herd number: miss; AI: Yes
 9   Colour: Combination red, yellow, white
10   Pecularity: white head
11 - Main use: (1) milk; meat,(2) miss,(3) miss
12   Spec. abilities: miss
13   Performance compared with STB Russian Simmental 241:
14     higher: miss
15     equal:  milk yield, % fat
16     lower:  miss
17 - Management: stationary; housing: > 6 m.;
18 - Conservation progr.: live animals: miss;Semen: miss;Embryos: miss
19   Status: normal;              Watch: HB♀♀,trend,%pure!
20 - Similar breeds (see group 3/2 on page 77)   EN  Country Status
21   Ceske strakate                               61   CZ   crit.end.
22   Simentalska                                 237   PL   min. end.
23   Montbeliard                                 176   F    normal
24   Fleckvieh                                    88   A    normal
```

```
 1 - Tagilskaya                                                     EN  252
 2   Tagil; Sverdlovsk, southern Urals
 3   Food and Agriculture Organisation of the UN                    HB:1931
 4   Rome 00100, Via delle Terme di Caracalla
 5 - Composite of Friesian, Kholmogory, Swiss Brown, Tyrolean,
 6   local cattle
 7   Numbers 1990: 800/156000; HB: miss; decreasing; 62 %; Ne = 3184
 8 - Height: 138/130 cm; Weight: 850/480 kg; Herd number: miss; AI: miss
 9   Colour: Combination black, white
10   Pecularity: miss
11 - Main use: (1) milk,(2) meat,(3) miss
12   Spec. abilities: good beef qualities
13   Performance compared with STB Russian Simmental 241:
14     higher: % fat
15     equal:  miss
16     lower:  milk yield
17 - Management: stationary; housing: > 6 m.; mountain climate
18 - Conservation progr.: live animals: miss;Semen: miss;Embryos: miss
19   Status: normal;              Watch: HB♀♀,trend,%pure!
20 - Similar breeds (see group 1/3 on page 75)   EN  Country Status
21   Yakutskii skot                              274   USSR min. end.
22   Istobenskaya                                128   USSR pot. end.
23   Kholmogorskaya                              141   USSR normal
24   Cherno-pestraya                              64   USSR normal
```

```
 1 - Yakutskii skot                                           EN  274
 2   Yakut; Yakutia
 3   Food and Agriculture Organisation of the UN             HB:miss
 4   Rome 00100, Via delle Terme di Caracalla
 5 - Autochthon local breed
 7   Numbers 1990: 21/351; HB: miss; decreasing; 100 %; Ne = 60
 8 - Height: 122/112 cm; Weight: 525/375 kg; Herd number: miss; AI: miss
 9   Colour: Combination black, red, white
10   Pecularity: spotted with white back-line
11 - Main use: (1) meat,(2) milk,(3) miss
12   Spec. abilities: resist. to tuberc.,leuc.,brucel.;cold north climate
13   Performance compared with STB Russian Simmental 241:
14     higher: % fat
15     equal:  miss
16     lower:  milk yield
17 - Management: stationary; housing: > 6 m.; adapted to poor feeding
18 - Conservation progr.: live animals: miss;Semen: miss;Embryos: miss
19   Status: minimally endang.; Watch: ♂♂,HB♀♀,trend!
20 - Similar breeds (see group 1/3 on page 75)    EN  Country Status
21   Istobenskaya                                 128  USSR    pot. end.
22   Cherno-pestraya                               64  USSR    normal
23   Tagilskaya                                   252  USSR    normal
24   Kholmogorskaya                               141  USSR    normal
```

```
 1 - Yaroslavskaya                                            EN  275
 2   Yaroslavl; country-wide
 3   Food and Agriculture Organisation of the UN             HB:1924
 4   Rome 00100, Via delle Terme di Caracalla
 5 - Autochthon local breed
 7   Numbers 1990: 4300/391000; HB: miss; decreasing; 73 %; Ne = 17013
 8 - Height: 136/127 cm; Weight: 840/480 kg; Herd number: miss; AI: Yes
 9   Colour: Combination black, white
10   Pecularity: white head and feet frequent
11 - Main use: (1) milk,(2) meat,(3) miss
12   Spec. abilities: resistant to tuberculosis, brucellosis, leucosis
13   Performance compared with STB Russian Black Pied 64:
14     higher: % fat
15     equal:  miss
16     lower:  milk yield
17 - Management: stationary; housing: > 6 m.;
18 - Conservation progr.: live animals: miss;Semen: miss;Embryos: miss
19   Status: normal;           Watch: HB♀♀,trend,%pure!
20 - Similar breeds (see group 1/3 on page 75)    EN  Country Status
21   Yakutskii skot                               274  USSR    min. end.
22   Istobenskaya                                 128  USSR    pot. end.
23   Kholmogorskaya                               141  USSR    normal
24   Cherno-pestraya                               64  USSR    normal
```

CATTLE

1 - Yurinskaya   EN 276
2   Yurino; Mari, ASSR
3   Food and Agriculture Organisation of the UN   HB:1937
4   Rome 00100, Via delle Terme di Caracalla
5 - Composite of Gorbatov Red, Tyrolean, Swiss Brown, Chuvash Mari,
6   Simmental
7   Numbers 1990: 4/200; HB: miss; decreasing; 50 %; Ne = 7
8 - Height: 132/123 cm; Weight: 750/480 kg; Herd number: miss; AI: miss
9   Colour: Uni red, brown
10 Pecularity: occasionally white markings on lower barrel
11 - Main use: (1) milk,(2) meat,(3) miss
12 Spec. abilities: resistant to leucosis, tuberculosis, brucellosis
13 Performance compared with STB Russian Black Pied 64:
14   higher: % fat
15   equal: miss
16   lower: milk yield
17 - Management: stationary; housing: > 6 m.;
18 - Conservation progr.: live animals: miss;Semen: miss;Embryos: miss
19 Status: critically endang.;Watch: ♂♂,HB♀♀,trend,herds,%pure!
20 - Similar breeds (see group 4/5 on page 79)   EN Country Status
21 Krasnyi megrelskii skot   150 GO   endanger.
22 Krasnaya tambovskaya   148 USSR min. end.
23 Kalmytskaya   135 USSR normal
24 Bestuzhevskaya   31 USSR normal

PIGS

1 - Breitovskaya   EN 910
2   Breitov; Yaroslavl
3   Food and Agriculture Organisation of the UN   HB:1948
4   Rome 00100, Via delle Terme di Caracalla
5 - Composite of Danish Landrace, Middle White, Large White,
6   local lop eared pigs
7   Numbers 1990: 966/8300; HB: miss; stable; 80 %; Ne = 3461
8 - Height: miss/miss cm; Weight: 297/236 kg; Herd number: miss; AI:miss
9   Colour: Uni white
10 Pecularity: lop ears
11 - Main use: (1) general purpose,(2) miss,(3) miss
12 Spec. abilities: able to gain rapidly in low-concentrate feeding
13 Performance compared with STB Large White 951:
14   higher: miss
15   equal: % lean, litter size, feed conversion rate
16   lower: daily gain
17 - Management: stationary; housing: 12 m.; able to consume bulky feeds
18 - Conservation progr.: live animals: miss;Semen: miss;Embryos: miss
19 Status: normal;   Watch: HB♀♀,%pure!
20 - Similar breeds (see group 2/1 on page 101)   EN Country Status
21 Belgische Landrasse   907 D*   crit.end.
22 Zlotnicka biala   1024 PL   crit.end.
23 Landrace   952 CS   normal
24 Belgisch Landvarken   906 B   normal

```
1 - Kemerovskaya                                              EN  949
2   Kemerovo; southern Sibiria
3   Food and Agriculture Organisation of the UN            HB:1961
4   Rome 00100, Via delle Terme di Caracalla
5 - Composite of Berkshire, Large White, Siberian Black Pied,
6   Large Black
7   Numbers 1990: 1755/5500; HB: miss; stable; 60 %; Ne = 5322
8 - Height: miss/miss cm; Weight: 326/240 kg; Herd number: miss; AI:miss
9   Colour: Combination black, white; small white spots
10  Pecularity: erect ears
11 - Main use: (1) general purpose,(2) miss,(3) miss
12  Spec. abilities: severe (rough, hard) climate, vitality
13  Performance compared with STB Large White 951:
14    higher: miss
15    equal: % lean, litter size, feed conversion rate, daily gain
16    lower: miss
17 - Management: stationary; housing: 12 m.;
18 - Conservation progr.: live animals: miss;Semen: miss;Embryos: miss
19  Status: potential. endang.;Watch: HB♀♀,%pure!
20 - Similar breeds (see group 4/2 on page 103)   EN  Country Status
21  Berkshire                                     909  GB   min. end.
22  Severokavkazskaya                            1000  USSR pot. end.
23  Aksaiskaya cherno-pestraya                    901  KAZ  normal
24  Belorusskaya cherno-pestraya                  908  BEL  normal
```

```
1 - Krupnaya belaya                                           EN  951
2   Large White; country-wide
3   Food and Agriculture Organisation of the UN            HB:1932
4   Rome 00100, Via delle Terme di Caracalla
5 - Imported as breed from country United Kingdom
7   Numbers 1990: miss/3254000; HB: miss; increasing; 75 %; Ne = 5271263
8 - Height: miss/miss cm; Weight: 298/235 kg; Herd number: miss; AI:miss
9   Colour: Uni white
10  Pecularity: erect ears
11 - Main use: (1) general purpose,(2) miss,(3) miss
12  Spec. abilities: adapt. to any clim. cond., high and long fertility
13  Performance compared with STB Lithuanian White 968:
14    higher: daily gain
15    equal: % lean, litter size, feed conversion rate
16    lower: miss
17 - Management: stationary; housing: 12 m.;
18 - Conservation progr.: live animals: miss;Semen: miss;Embryos: miss
19  Status: normal;              Watch: HB♀♀,%pure!
20 - Similar breeds (see group 1/2 on page 101)   EN  Country Status
21  Bela Zlahtna                                  904  SLO  crit.end.
22  Middle White                                  975  GB   min. end.
23  Deutsches Edelschwein                         922  D*   normal
24  Vile uslechtile                              1017  CS   normal
```

1 - **Livenskaya**   EN **969**
2   **Livny; Orel, Lipetsk, Voronesh**
3   **Food and Agriculture Organisation of the UN**   HB:**1949**
4   **Rome 00100, Via delle Terme di Caracalla**
5 - **Composite of Large White, Berkshire, local lop-eared, Poland China**
7   Numbers 1990: **1000/3800**; HB: **miss**; **stable**; **84 %**; Ne = **3167**
8 - Height: **miss/miss** cm; Weight: **295/237** kg; Herd number: **miss**; AI:**miss**
9   Colour: **Uni white**
9   Colour: **Combination black, white**
10 Pecularity: **semi-lop eared**
11 - Main use: (1) **general purpose**,(2) **miss**,(3) **miss**
12 Spec. abilities: **high meat quality**
13 Performance compared with STB **Large White 951**:
14   higher: **daily gain**
15   equal: **litter size, feed conversion rate**
16   lower: **% lean**
17 - Management: **stationary**; housing: **12** m.;
18 - Conservation progr.: live animals: **miss**;Semen: **miss**;Embryos: **miss**
19 Status: **potential. endang.**;Watch: **HB♀♀,%pure!**
20 - <u>Similar breeds</u> (see group 1/2 on page 101)   <u>EN</u> <u>Country</u> <u>Status</u>
21 **Bela Zlahtna**   904   SLO   **crit.end.**
22 **Middle White**   975   GB   **min. end.**
23 **Deutsches Edelschwein**   922   D*   **normal**
24 **Vile uslechtile**   1017 CS   **normal**

1 - **Muromskaya**   EN **979**
2   **Murom; Vladimir, Moscow, Gorki**
3   **Food and Agriculture Organisation of the UN**   HB:**1957**
4   **Rome 00100, Via delle Terme di Caracalla**
5 - **Composite of Large White, Lithuanian White, local breed**
7   Numbers 1990: **225/2900**; HB: **miss**; **stable**; **83 %**; Ne = **835**
8 - Height: **miss/miss** cm; Weight: **314/257** kg; Herd number: **miss**; AI:**miss**
9   Colour: **Uni white**
10 Pecularity: **lop ears**
11 - Main use: (1) **general purpose**,(2) **miss**,(3) **miss**
12 Spec. abilities: **miss**
13 Performance compared with STB **Large White 951**:
14   higher: **miss**
15   equal: **% lean, litter size, feed conversion rate, daily gain**
16   lower: **miss**
17 - Management: **stationary**; housing: **12** m.;
18 - Conservation progr.: live animals: **miss**;Semen: **miss**;Embryos: **miss**
19 Status: **potential. endang.**;Watch: **HB♀♀,%pure!**
20 - <u>Similar breeds</u> (see group 1/2 on page 101)   <u>EN</u> <u>Country</u> <u>Status</u>
21 **Bela Zlahtna**   904   SLO   **crit.end.**
22 **Middle White**   975   GB   **min. end.**
23 **Deutsches Edelschwein**   922   D*   **normal**
24 **Vile uslechtile**   1017 CS   **normal**

```
 1 - Severokavkazskaya                                      EN 1000
 2   North Caucasus; North-Caucasus: Rostov,Volgograd,Krasnodar
 3   Food and Agriculture Organisation of the UN            HB:1955
 4   Rome 00100, Via delle Terme di Caracalla
 5 - Composite of local Kuban, Large White, Berkshire, Edelschwein
 7   Numbers 1990: 4800/9500; HB: miss; decreasing; 75 %; Ne = 12755
 8 - Height: miss/miss cm; Weight: 279/228 kg; Herd number: miss; AI:miss
 9   Colour: Combination black, white; black pied
10   Pecularity: erect or semi-erect ears
11 - Main use: (1) general purpose,(2) miss,(3) miss
12   Spec. abilities: miss
13   Performance compared with STB Large White 951:
14      higher: miss
15      equal: % lean, litter size, feed conversion rate
16      lower:  daily gain
17 - Management: stationary; housing: 12 m.;
18 - Conservation progr.: live animals: miss;Semen: miss;Embryos: miss
19   Status: potential. endang.;Watch: HB♀♀,trend,%pure!
```

20 - Similar breeds (see group 4/2 on page 103)	EN	Country	Status
21 Berkshire	909	GB	min. end.
22 Kemerovskaya	949	USSR	pot. end.
23 Aksaiskaya cherno-pestraya	901	KAZ	normal
24 Belorusskaya cherno-pestraya	908	BEL	normal

```
 1 - Sibirskaya chernopestraya                             EN 1001
 2   Siberian Black Pied; Novosibirsk Region
 3   Food and Agriculture Organisation of the UN           HB:miss
 4   Rome 00100, Via delle Terme di Caracalla
 5 - Composite of black and white variety of North Siberian White
 7   Numbers 1980: 258/349; HB: miss; decreasing; 45 %; Ne = 593
 8 - Height:miss/miss cm; Weight:miss/miss kg; Herd number:miss; AI:miss
 9   Colour: Combination black, white
10   Pecularity: miss
11 - Main use: (1) general purpose,(2) miss,(3) miss
12   Spec. abilities: miss
13   Performance compared with STB Large White 951:
14      higher: miss
15      equal: % lean, litter size, feed conversion rate, meat quality
16      lower:  muscularity
17 - Management: stationary; housing: miss m.;
18 - Conservation progr.: live animals: miss;Semen: miss;Embryos: miss
19   Status: potential. endang.;Watch: HB♀♀,trend,%pure!
```

20 - Similar breeds (see group 6/2 on page 104)	EN	Country	Status
21 Sortbroget	1005	DK	crit.end.
22 Schwarz-Weißes Bentheimer	996	D	crit.end.
23 Pulawska	995	PL	min. end.
24 Gloucestershire Old Spot	936	GB	pot. end.

1 - Sibirskaya severnaya   EN 1002
2   North Siberian; northern Omsk and Novosibirsk
3   Food and Agriculture Organisation of the UN   HB:1942
4   Rome 00100, Via delle Terme di Caracalla
5 - Composite of Large White, native short eared Siberian
7   Numbers 1990: 1500/7700; HB: miss; stable; 60 %; Ne = 5022
8 - Height: miss/miss cm; Weight: 312/238 kg; Herd number: miss; AI:miss
9   Colour: Uni white
10   Pecularity: erect ears
11 - Main use: (1) general purpose,(2) miss,(3) miss
12   Spec. abilities: hardiness,adapted to harsh climate of North-Siberia
13   Performance compared with STB Large White 951:
14   higher: miss
15   equal: litter size, feed conversion rate, daily gain
16   lower: % lean
17 - Management: stationary; housing: 12 m.;
18 - Conservation progr.: live animals: miss;Semen: miss;Embryos: miss
19   Status: normal;   Watch: HB♀♀,%pure!
20 - Similar breeds (see group 1/2 on page 101)   EN Country Status

		EN	Country	Status
21	Bela Zlahtna	904	SLO	crit.end.
22	Middle White	975	GB	min. end.
23	Deutsches Edelschwein	922	D*	normal
24	Vile uslechtile	1017	CS	normal

1 - Tarskaya (extinct)   EN 1010
2   Siberian; Novos./Krasno./Bury./Kaza
3   Food and Agriculture Organisation of the UN   HB:miss
4   Rome 00100, Via delle Terme di Caracalla
5 - Composite of local short-eared Siberian pigs, Large White
7   Numbers 1980: 1600/5900; HB: miss; decreasing; 45 %; Ne = 5035
8 - Height: miss/miss cm; Weight: 312/238 kg; Herd number: miss; AI:miss
9   Colour: Uni white
10   Pecularity: miss
11 - Main use: (1) meat,(2) miss,(3) miss
12   Spec. abilities: miss
13   Performance compared with STB Large White 951:
14   higher: miss
15   equal: % lean, litter size, feed conversion rate, meat quality
16   lower: muscularity
17 - Management: miss; housing: miss m.;
18 - Conservation progr.: live animals: miss;Semen: miss;Embryos: miss
19   Status: extinct/potential. endang.;Watch: HB♀♀,trend,%pure!
20 - Similar breeds (see group 1/2 on page 101)   EN Country Status

		EN	Country	Status
21	Bela Zlahtna	904	SLO	crit.end.
22	Middle White	975	GB	min. end.
23	Deutsches Edelschwein	922	D*	normal
24	Vile uslechtile	1017	CS	normal

```
 1 - Tsivilskaya                                          EN 1012
 2   Tsivilsk; Chuvash ASSR: between Gorki and Kasan
 3   Food and Agriculture Organisation of the UN          HB:miss
 4   Rome 00100, Via delle Terme di Caracalla
 5 - Composite of Large White, local Chuvash
 7   Numbers 1990: 558/3000; HB: miss; stable; 83 %; Ne = 1882
 8 - Height: miss/miss cm; Weight: 299/229 kg; Herd number: miss; AI:miss
 9   Colour: Uni white
10   Pecularity: ears tilted forward
11 - Main use: (1) general purpose,(2) miss,(3) miss
12   Spec. abilities: miss
13   Performance compared with STB Large White 951:
14     higher: miss
15     equal: litter size, feed conversion rate, daily gain
16     lower: % lean
17 - Management: stationary; housing: 12 m.;
18 - Conservation progr.: live animals: miss;Semen: miss;Embryos: miss
19   Status: normal;              Watch: HB♀♀,%pure!
```

20 - Similar breeds (see group 1/2 on page 101)	EN	Country	Status
21 Bela Zlahtna	904	SLO	crit.end.
22 Middle White	975	GB	min. end.
23 Deutsches Edelschwein	922	D*	normal
24 Vile uslechtile	1017	CS	normal

```
 1 - Urzhumskaya                                          EN 1016
 2   Urzhum; Kirov, Kostroma, Moscow regions
 3   Food and Agriculture Organisation of the UN          HB:1957
 4   Rome 00100, Via delle Terme di Caracalla
 5 - Composite of Large White, local lop-eared
 7   Numbers 1990: 2900/16500; HB: miss; stable; 40 %; Ne = 9866
 8 - Height: miss/miss cm; Weight: 291/245 kg; Herd number: miss; AI:miss
 9   Colour: Uni white
10   Pecularity: lop ears
11 - Main use: (1) meat,(2) used in crossbreeding systems,(3) miss
12   Spec. abilities: able to consume bulky succulent feeds
13   Performance compared with STB Large White 951:
14     higher: miss
15     equal: % lean, litter size, feed conversion rate
16     lower: daily gain
17 - Management: stationary; housing: 12 m.;
18 - Conservation progr.: live animals: miss;Semen: miss;Embryos: miss
19   Status: normal;              Watch: HB♀♀,%pure!
```

20 - Similar breeds (see group 1/2 on page 101)	EN	Country	Status
21 Bela Zlahtna	904	SLO	crit.end.
22 Middle White	975	GB	min. end.
23 Deutsches Edelschwein	922	D*	normal
24 Vile uslechtile	1017	CS	normal

```
 1 - Bushuevskaya                                              EN   53
 2   Bushuev; Uzbekistan: Syr Darya, Tashkent, Samarkand
 3   Food and Agriculture Organisation of the UN             HB: Yes
 4   Rome 00100, Via delle Terme di Caracalla
 5 - Composite of Friesian, Swiss Brown, local Zebu, Simmental
 6   Incrossing since 1950 from Holstein Friesian,Dutch Black Pied 277 NL
 7   Numbers 1990: 100/6300; HB: miss; stable; 60 %; Ne = 394
 8 - Height: 132/123 cm; Weight: 810/450 kg; Herd number: miss; AI: Yes
 9   Colour: Uni white; black ears and black spectacles around eyes
10   Pecularity: small hump in males, white with black spots
11 - Main use: (1) milk,(2) meat,(3) miss
12   Spec. abilities: resistant to blood parasites
13   Performance compared with STB Russian Black Pied 64:
14      higher: miss
15      equal: % fat
16      lower:  milk yield
17 - Management: stationary; housing: 2-6 m.; poor feeding vegetation
18 - Conservation progr.: live animals: miss;Semen: miss;Embryos: miss
19   Status: potential. endang.;Watch: HB♀♀,%pure,%incross!
20 - Similar breeds                                EN Country Status
21   miss                                          miss  miss  miss
```

```
 1 - Busha                                                     EN   52
 2   Busa; Mountains of Bosnia,Herzegovina,Serbia,Montenegro
 3   University Ljubljana, Biotechnical faculty, Zootechnical   HB:miss
 4   Domzale 61230, Groblje 3
 5 - Is indigenous
 7   Numbers 1991: miss /80000; HB: miss; decreasing; 50 %; Ne = 14480
 8 - Height: 120/115 cm; Weight: 470/300 kg; Herd number: miss; AI: miss
 9   Colour: Uni blue, brown
10   Pecularity: fine, curved upwards foreward horns
11 - Main use: (1) milk,(2) tractive power,(3) meat
12   Spec. abilities: hardy
13   Performance compared with STB Simmental 238:
14      higher: % fat, calving ease, calving interval, calving rate
15      equal: % protein, handling ease, calf mortality, milkability
16      lower:  milk yield,muscularity,daily gain,age of sexual maturity
17 - Management: stationary; housing: 2-6 m.; adapted to karst region
18 - Conservation progr.: live animals: miss;Semen: miss;Embryos: miss
19   Status: minimally endang.; Watch: ♂♂,HB♀♀,trend,%pure!
20 - Similar breeds (see group 5/5 on page 80)    EN Country Status
21   Rodopska kusoroga                            220  BG   crit.end.
22   Brachyceros                                   39  GR   pot. end.
```

1 - Crno-belo EN 71
2 Holstein-Friesian; Slovenia, Croatia, Serbia
3 University of Ljubljana, Biotechnical Faculty, Zootechnical HB:1960
4 Domzale 61230, Groblje 3
5 - Imported as breed from Denmark, Germany, USA; incrossing since 1950
6 from Danish Black Pied 245 DK, Deutsche Schwarzbunte 75/76 Germany
7 Numbers 1986: 85/150000; HB: 70000; increasing; 100 %; Ne = 340
8 - Height: 155/137 cm; Weight: 1100/650 kg; Herd number: miss; AI: Yes
9 Colour: Combination black, white, pied
10 Pecularity: miss
11 - Main use: (1) milk,(2) meat,(3) miss
12 Spec. abilities: miss
13 Performance compared with STB Simmental 238:
14 higher: milk yield, calving ease, age of sexual maturity
15 equal: % fat, % protein, calving interval, handling ease
16 lower: muscularity, daily gain
17 - Management: stationary; housing: > 6/12 m.;
18 - Conservation progr.: live animals: miss;Semen: 20;Embryos: miss
19 Status: normal; Watch: %incross!
20 - Similar breeds (see group 1/4 on page 75) EN Country Status
21 Nizinne cernostrakate 184 CS normal
22 Schwarzbuntes Milchrind 229 D* normal
23 Baltata cu negru romanesca 19 RO normal

1 - Istarsko govece EN 127
2 Istrian; Peninsula Istra
3 University of Ljubljana, Biotechnical faculty, Zootechnical HB:miss
4 Domzale 61230, Groblje 3
5 - Autochthon local Podolyan breed crossed by Romagnola bulls
6 Imported as breed from country Italy
7 Numbers 1991: 20/30000; HB: 700; decreasing; 75 %; Ne = 57
8 - Height: 150/136 cm; Weight: 900/550 kg; Herd number: miss; AI: Yes
9 Colour: Uni blue
10 Pecularity: very long horns
11 - Main use: (1) tractive power,(2) meat,(3) milk
12 Spec. abilities: miss
13 Performance compared with STB Simmental 238:
14 higher: % fat, calving ease, age of sexual maturity, pulling power
15 equal: % protein, calving interval, calf mortality
16 lower: milk yield,muscularity,daily gain,handling ease,calv. rate
17 - Management: stationary; housing: 2-6 m.; adapted to karst region
18 - Conservation progr.: live animals: Yes;Semen: miss;Embryos: miss
19 Status: potential. endang.;Watch: ♂♂,HB♀♀,trend,%pure!
20 - Similar breeds (see group 6/1 on page 80) EN Country Status
21 Iskursko govedo 104 BG crit.end.
22 Katerini 136 GR crit.end.
23 Piemontese 197 I normal
24 Maremmana 166 I normal

YUGOSLAVIA   CATTLE

```
 1 - Simentalska rasa                                           EN  238
 2   Simmental; Lowland (maize region)
 3   University of Ljubljana, Biotechnical Faculty,             HB:1906
 4   Zootechnical Dpt., Domzale 61230, Groblje 3
 5 - Imported as breed from Switzerland, Germany, Austria; incrossing
 6   since 1950 from Simmental 240, Deutsches Fleckvieh 78 Germany
 7   Numbers 1986: 280/1300000; HB: 88000; stable; 90 %; Ne = 1116
 8 - Height: 153/133 cm; Weight: 1350/650 kg; Herd number: miss; AI: Yes
 9   Colour: Combination red, yellow, white, pied
10   Pecularity: white head
11 - Main use: (1) milk,(2) meat,(3) tractive power
12   Spec. abilities: miss
13   Performance compared with STB Holstein-Friesian 71:
14     higher: muscularity, pulling power, daily gain
15     equal: % fat, calving ease, calving interval, age of sexual mat.
16     lower:  milk yield, milkability
17 - Management: stationary; housing: > 6 m.;
18 - Conservation progr.: live animals: miss;Semen: 30;Embryos: miss
19   Status: normal;            Watch: %incross!
```
```
20 - Similar breeds (see group 3/2 on page 77)    EN  Country Status
21   Ceske strakate                                61   CZ   crit.end.
22   Simentalska                                  237   PL   min. end.
23   Montbeliard                                  176   F    normal
24   Fleckvieh                                     88   A    normal
```

YUGOSLAVIA   SHEEP

```
 1 - Cigaja                                                     EN  461
 2   Tsigai; Vojvodia (Serbia)
 3   University of Ljubljana, Biotechnical Faculty,             HB:miss
 4   Zootechnical Dpt., Domzale 61230, Groblje 3
 5 - Imported as breed from Romania
 7   Numbers 1986: 500/250000; HB: 45000; decreasing; 90 %; Ne = 1978
 8 - Height: 75/67 cm; Weight: 85/60 kg; Herd number: miss; AI: miss
 9   Colour: Combination black, white, black head and legs
10   Pecularity: horns 0/0
11 - Main use: (1) milk,(2) meat,(3) miss
12   Spec. abilities: miss
13   Performance compared with STB Scottish Blackface:
14     higher: milk yield, % fat, daily gain, age of sexual maturity
15     equal:  muscularity,leanness,litter size,length of mating seasaon
16     lower:  wool yield
17 - Management: stationary; housing: 2-6 m.;
18 - Conservation progr.: live animals: miss;Semen: miss;Embryos: miss
19   Status: normal;            Watch: trend!
```
```
20 - Similar breeds (see group 7/7 on page 93)    EN  Country Status
21   Cigaja                                       460   H    endanger.
22   Kivircik                                     654   GR   pot. end.
23   Tigaie                                       655   RO   normal
24   Cigaja                                       459   CS   normal
```

YUGOSLAVIA   SHEEP

1 - Pramenka, Sjenicka, Svrljiska   EN 588
2   Yugoslavian Zackel; central and southern Yugoslavia
3   University of Ljubljana, Biotechnical Faculty,   HB:1952
4   Zootechnical Dpt., Domzale 61230, Groblje 3
5 - Autochthon native breed on Balkan
6   Incrossing since 1960 from Merino France, USSR and Spain
7   Numbers 1986: 50000/4000000; HB: 120000; stable; 50 %; Ne = 141177
8 - Height: 65/60 cm; Weight: 60/45 kg; Herd number: miss; AI: miss
9   Colour: Uni white
10 Pecularity: horns 2/0
11 - Main use: (1) meat,(2) milk,(3) wool
12 Spec. abilities: miss
13 Performance compared with STB Scottish Blackface:
14   higher: % fat, % protein, fiber thickness
15   equal: litter size, milk yield, length of mating season
16   lower: muscularity, daily gain, wool yield, carcass leanness
17 - Management: transhumant; housing: 2-6 m.;
18 - Conservation progr.: live animals: miss;Semen: miss;Embryos: miss
19 Status: normal;   Watch: %pure,%incross!
20 - Similar breeds (see group 7/6 on page 92)   EN Country Status
21 Florina   490 GR   endanger.
22 Ruda Dubrovacka Sheep   611 HR   endanger.
23 Karagouniko   518 GR   normal
24 Sazakatsaniko   429 GR   normal

YUGOSLAVIA   PIGS

1 - Dom. mesnata svinja   EN 925
2   Large White; Vojvodina, Subotica
3   University of Ljubljana, Biotechnical Faculty,   HB:1966
4   Zootechnical Dpt., Domzale 61230, Groblje 3
5 - Composite of Sub. Mangalitsa, Swedish Landrace, Dutch Landrace,
6   Large White
7   Numbers 1986: 500/30000; HB: 3000; decreasing; 90 %; Ne = 1714
8 - Height: 85/75 cm; Weight: 308/250 kg; Herd number: miss; AI: miss
9   Colour: Uni white
10 Pecularity: erect ears
11 - Main use: (1) meat,(2) miss,(3) miss
12 Spec. abilities: miss
13 Performance compared with STB Landrace:
14   higher: miss
15   equal: % lean, litter size, feed conversion rate, meat quality
16   lower: miss
17 - Management: stationary; housing: 12 m.;
18 - Conservation progr.: live animals: miss;Semen: miss;Embryos: miss
19 Status: normal;   Watch: trend,%pure!
20 - Similar breeds (see group 1/2 on page 101)   EN Country Status
21 Bela Zlahtna   904 SLO crit.end.
22 Middle White   975 GB   min. end.
23 Deutsches Edelschwein   922 D*   normal
24 Vile uslechtile   1017 CS   normal

```
 1 - Moravka                                                  EN  978
 2   Morava; Srbija
 3   University of Belgrad, Faculty of Agriculture            HB:miss
 4   Zemun
 5 - Composite of Sumandinka, Mangalitsa, Berkshire, Yorkshire
 7   Numbers 1983: miss / miss; HB: miss; decreasing; miss %; Ne = miss
 8 - Height: miss/miss cm; Weight: 135/120 kg; Herd number: miss; AI:miss
 9   Colour: Uni black
10   Pecularity: lop ears
11 - Main use: (1) meat,(2) miss,(3) miss
12   Spec. abilities: miss
13   Performance compared with STB Landrace:
14     higher: meat quality
15     equal:  handling ease
16     lower:  % lean, feed conversion rate, daily gain, muscularity
17 - Management: miss; housing: miss m.;
18 - Conservation progr.: live animals: miss;Semen: miss;Embryos: miss
19   Status: miss
20 - Similar breeds (see group 4/1 on page 103)    EN  Country Status
21   Gascon                                         935  F      crit.end.
22   Large Black                                    959  GB     min. end.
24   Negra Iberica                                  981  E      normal
23   Alentejana                                     902  P      normal
```

```
 1 - Slavenske ciernostrakate                                 EN 1003
 2   Slovakian Black Pied
 3   University of Zagreb, Faculty of Agriculture            HB:miss
 4   Zagreb 41000
 5 - Composite of Mangalitsa, Berkshire, Poland China
 7   Numbers 1983: miss / miss; HB: miss; decreasing; miss %; Ne = miss
 8 - Height: miss/65 cm; Weight: miss/miss kg; Herd number: miss; AI:miss
 9   Colour: Combination black and white
10   Pecularity: miss
11 - Main use: (1) meat,(2) miss,(3) miss
12   Spec. abilities: miss
13   Performance compared with STB Landrace:
14     higher: meat quality, piglet mortality
15     equal:  handling ease
16     lower:  % lean, feed conversion rate, daily gain, muscularity
17 - Management: miss; housing: miss m.;
18 - Conservation progr.: live animals: miss;Semen: miss;Embryos: miss
19   Status: miss
20 - Similar breeds (see group 6/2 on page 104)    EN  Country Status
21   Sortbroget                                    1005  DK     crit.end.
22   Schwarz-Weißes Bentheimer                      996  D      crit.end.
23   Sibirskaya chernopestraya                     1001  USSR   pot. end.
24   Gloucestershire Old Spot                       936  GB     pot. end.
```

```
 1 - Bosanski brdski konj                              EN  712
 2   Bosnian Pony; mountainous areas
 3   Agricultural Faculty                              HB:miss
 4   Sarajewo
 5 - Autochthon Busa Pony
 6   Incrossing since 1950 from Arab
 7   Numbers miss: miss / miss; HB: miss; miss; miss %; Ne = miss
 8 - Height:miss/miss cm; Weight:miss/miss kg; Herd number:miss; AI:miss
 9   Colour: all solid colours
10   Pecularity: miss
11 - Main use: (1) miss,(2) miss,(3) miss
12   Spec. abilities: miss
13   Performance compared with STB miss:
14      higher: miss
15      equal:  miss
16      lower:  miss
17 - Management: miss; housing: miss m.;
18 - Conservation progr.: live animals: miss;Semen: miss;Embryos: miss
19   Status: miss
```

20 - <u>Similar breeds</u> (see group 5/9 on page 111)

		EN	Country	Status
21	Hucul	762	CS	crit.end.
22	Hucul	763	PL	pot. end.
23	Koniki Polskie	771	PL	normal

6   Discussion

The objective of this publication is to present information on livestock breeds in European countries which can be used in decisions of a better use of available genetic diversity and in decisions of conservation of animal genetic resources.

In pursuit of this objective concessions to satisfactory results had to be made on several levels.

6.1 Volume and value of information in the data bank

As pointed out in chapter 2 the collection of breed information started in 1982 and covers a period of 11 years. Until 1988 this was achieved by three surveys as independent actions and later on by continous questioning by the data bank in Hannover. The surveys resulted in information on 345 breeds, the continous questioning in information on additional 524 breeds (see table 48). Obviously continous contacts with people and institutions as potential informants are necessary in order to obtain and update information which is reasonably complete, correct and relevant to the current situation.

Table 48: Number of breeds with most recent information on population size referring to the year ...

Year	Cattle	Sheep	Goats	Pigs	Horses	Total
1980	-	-	-	3	-	3
1983	12	65	4	20	5	106
1984	-	5	3	-	-	8
1986	61	81	15	30	33	220
1987	3	5	-	-	-	8
						(345)
1988	25	10	7	-	5	47
1989	3	1	2	2	-	8
1990	48	11	1	25	25	110
1991	57	62	26	11	28	184
1992	46	18	5	22	15	106
1993	22	23	4	10	10	69
						(524)
No information	-	2	1	3	2	8
Total	277	283	68	126	123	877

In spite of substantial improvements it was not possible to obtain answers to all questions of the EAAP-questionnaire. Table 49 shows which questions remained unanswered and to

570

Table 49: Percentage of breeds with missing information in given
fields of questionnaire

Field in questionnaire		Cattle (277) P	Sheep (283) P	Goats (68) P	Pigs (126) P	Horses (123) P	Total (877) P
A	1	Country	0	0	0	0	0	0
	2	Species	0	0	0	0	0	0
	3.1	Local name	0	0	0	0	0	0
	3.2	Intern.name	0	0	0	0	0	0
	4.1	Region	4	3	10	7	6	5
	5.1	Organization	0	0	0	0	0	0
	5.2	Institution	81	82	85	76	82	81
	6.1	Informant	0	2	1	6	0	1
	6.3	Date Info.	0	0	0	0	2	0
B	1.1	Local breeds	22	14	21	36	27	22
	1.2	Imports	71	79	85	61	60	72
	1.3	Known since	43	52	60	34	36	45
	1.4	Herdbook	20	35	44	27	13	27
	2	Immigration	38	75	69	52	45	55
	3	Year/numbers	0	1	1	2	2	1
	3.1	N♂+N♀*	83	91	60	85	98	86
	3.1.1	N♀ total	6	12	46	21	5	13
	3.1.2	N♀ Herdb.	32	55	35	60	41	45
	3.2	Purebreeding	9	27	37	28	20	21
	3.3	N♂	4	22	25	6	3	12
	3.4	N♂ in AI	27	84	85	62	89	64
	3.5	Trend	5	5	9	3	2	5
	3.6	Herd size	30	32	43	44	33	34
	3.6	Herd numb.*	70	73	82	79	76	74
	4 ♀	Age	33	39	38	52	31	38
	4 ♂	Age	36	40	38	52	36	40
	5.1	Cryo semen	34	88	76	72	80	67
	5.2	Cryo embryo	76	98	100	100	98	92
	5.1.1	N♂ semen	43	90	76	79	83	72
	5.2.1	N♂ embryo	84	99	100	100	99	95
	5.2.2	N♀ embryo	87	99	100	100	99	95
	5.3	Add. Info	64	90	79	78	88	79
C	1.1	Colour uni	37	9	21	33	96	34
	1.2	Colour comb.	56	89	65	67	100	75
	1.3	Colour spec.	36	43	47	66	8	40
	2	Skin col.	74	76	81	67	83	75
	3.1	Horns	1	1	1	0	0	1
	3.2	Knobs	99	98	97	0	0	70

Table 49 continued: Breeds with missing information

Field in questionnaire		Cattle (277) P	Sheep (283) P	Goats (68) P	Pigs (126) P	Horses (123) P	Total (877) P
3.3	Horn shape	70	82	75	0	0	55
4.1	Hair/wool	0	94	19	0	0	32
4.2	Wool class.	0	20	96	0	0	14
5.1 ♀	W-height	7	25	9	51	7	19
5.1 ♂	W-height	12	29	9	52	7	22
5.2 ♀	L-weight	3	4	6	20	21	8
5.2 ♂	L-weight	9	8	6	20	21	12
6	Ext.remark.	92	86	87	68	98	87
7.1	Chromos.	87	99	97	100	100	95
7.2	Gen.marker	87	94	96	84	79	88
7.3	Others	95	98	97	96	100	97
7.4	Add. Info	86	91	87	85	87	87
1/2	Main use	2	1	3	3	3	2
3.1	Human cons.	78	80	84	72	98	81
3.2	Resistance	92	95	97	89	98	94
3.3	Adaptation	67	66	47	80	86	70
3.4	Reproduction	84	78	84	87	93	84
3.5	Margin.land	61	67	78	85	86	71
3.6	Other	71	76	85	83	87	78
3.7	Reference	85	79	78	71	86	81
3.8	Add. Info	72	71	75	75	76	73
E 1	Managem. Type	5	26	25	21	10	16
2	Man. housing	5	28	25	23	33	21
3	Man. feeding	4	27	4	23	33	18
4	Spec. cond.	84	86	85	93	93	87
F 1.1	Stand.breed	12	28	29	13	23	20
1.2	Prod.level	55	68	63	66	0	54
2	Rel.combar.	14	29	32	8	0	17
3	Val.combar.	29	33	41	33	59	36
G 1	Gen.distance	88	95	94	85	95	91
2	DNA storage	99	99	100	99	99	99
3	L.anim.cons.	66	80	79	80	61	73

* New fields in the data bank, originally not in questionnaire.

which extent. For example, the information on specific questions is missing for the given percentage of breeds:

Number of females in herdbook	45 %
Number of herds per breed	74 %
Number of males represented in conserved cattle semen	43 %
Number of males represented in conserved cattle embryos	95 %
Live animal conservation programmes	73 %
Chromosome aberrations	95 %
Genetic markers	88 %
Genetic distance	91 %
DNA storage	99 %
Breed organization	0 %
Total number of females	13 %
Number of male breeding animals	12 %
Population trend	5 %
Standard breed for production comparisons	20 %
Main use of breed	2 %
Number of horns	1 %

In general the volume of information on demographic and phenotypic criteria is relatively reasonable, though not satisfactory, but the information which is closer to the genetic level is rather sparse. This shows the direction where increased efforts are needed.

Considerable efforts were made in order to check the validity of information, however, the quality of data may not be satisfactory in every case. It is our hope that this publication will stimulate comments and necessary corrections by the reader so that the usefulness of the information can be improved.

For this report information on 877 livestock breeds could be used. In table 50 additional 78 breeds are listed which were entered into the data bank, but for which the information either arrived later than August 1st., 1993, or which needs further completion.

Table 50: 78 breeds registered in data bank but not
included in this publication

Species
    Breedname   Country

Cattle: (18 breeds)

Breedname	Country
Alistana-Sanabresa	Spain
Avilena-Negra Iberica	Spain
Betizu, Betizoak, Betiso	Spain
Blonde d'Aquitaine	Belgium
Bordelaise	France
Charolaise	Belgium
Deutsches Shorthorn	Germany
Limousine	Belgium
Mantequera, Leonesa	Spain
Maraichine	France
Montbeliarde	Belgium
Morucha	Spain
Nantaise	France
Normande	Belgium
Pirenaica	Spain
Rubia Gallega	Spain
Sayaguesa	Spain
Tudanca	Spain

Goats: (19 breeds)

Breedname	Country
Blanca Celtiberica	Spain
Canaria, Majorera	Spain
Ciociara Grigia	Italy
Facciuta Bianca	Italy
Facciuta Rossa	Italy
Florida	Spain
Gallega	Spain
Grigio Alpina	Italy
Guadarrama	Spain
Ibicenca	Spain
Mantellata Posteriore	Italy
Palmera	Spain
Pirenaica	Spain
Raza de las Mesetas	Spain
Retinta	Spain
Screziata	Italy
Selvaggia	Italy
Tinerfena	Spain
Verata	Spain

574

Table 50 continued: 78 breeds registered in data bank but not
included in this publication

Species
Breedname   Country
_____

Sheep: (30 breeds)
    Alcarrena   Spain
    Ansotana   Spain
    Aranesa   Spain
    Blanca del Bierzo, Churra Berciana   Spain
    Blei du Maine   Belgium
    Canaria   Spain
    Carranzana, Vasca   Spain
    Castellana   Spain
    Churra Castellana   Spain
    Gallega   Spain
    Hampshire   Belgium
    Ile de France   Belgium
    Lacha   Spain
    Lojena   Spain
    Mallorquina   Spain
    Manchega   Spain
    Manchega Negra   Spain
    Montafoner (Stein-) Schaf   Austria
    Ojalada Soriana   Spain
    Ojinegra de Teruel   Spain
    Quadrella, Spagnola arianese   Italy
    Rasa Aragonese   Spain
    Ripollesa   Spain
    Roya Bilbilitana   Spain
    Sampeirina   Italy
    Steinschaf   Germany
    Suffolk   Belgium
    Talaverana   Spain
    Texel   Belgium
    Turchessa   Italy

Horses: (9 breeds)
    Cavallino do Monterufoli   Italy
    Cavallo del Catria   Italy
    Cavallo del Ventasso   Italy
    Cheval de Sang Belge   Belgium
    Persano   Italy
    Pony di Esperia   Italy
    Salernitano   Italy
    Samolaco   Italy
    Tolfettano   Italy

Pigs: (2 breeds)
    Hampshire   Poland
    Pietrain   Poland

6.2 International breed name

If breeds are looked at on an international level breeds are sometimes called by their local breed name, sometimes an international breed name is used. However, obviously no agreement exists on the international name of breeds. We therefore decided newly on an international name for each breed. This was done mainly on the basis of an English translation of the local breed name, tradition, origin and exterior of the breed and by use of MASON's dictionary (1969,1988). Since more than one breed may bear the same international breed name, this in combination with the country name is necessary for a clear identification. Agreement in naming of breeds is essential if one wants to search for genetic relationship among breeds.

6.3 Status of endangeredness of a breed

There is general agreement, that several conditions can affect the risk that a breed gets lost completely, that its genetic potential is being changed or that individual allels gradually decrease in frequency or get lost. It is also agreed that the main criterion for endangeredness of a breed is the population size, often expressed by the number of females. However, since male and female parents contribute equally to the allels of progeny and in real populations male breeding animals are smaller in number than females, the number of male breeding animals is the critical factor for the expectation that the genetic potential of a population remains constant over time.

In principle the estimate of the effective population size $Ne = 4N_mN_f/(N_m+N_f)$ (FALCONER, 1989) with N_m, N_f = number of male and female breeding animals, respectively, is the appropriate criterion to define the minimum number of parents necessary to restrict the increase of inbreeding to a given level. However, the assumptions for the formula, random relationship among mates and random variation in family size will hardly be met in rather small populations. We therefore used a correction for Ne < 100, which is based on the assumption that in a decreased population with only 4 males and 80 females left (Ne = 15), 50 % of the mates have one parent in common and the other 50% one grandparent. This would increase the coefficient of inbreeding to $\Delta F = 7,8\%$ compared to 3,3 % with random relationship among mates, i.e. in the order of factor 2,36. In addition it is assumed that the increased relationship among mates decreases linearly from Ne = 15 to Ne = 100.

The corrected estimate Ne_c means that more male breeding animals and a larger value of effective population size is required in order to restrict the increase of inbreeding ΔF to a given level.

One may argue that the assumed relationship among parents in a breed with 4 males and 80 females is rather high and the corresponding correction factor is too large. However, in addition to an increased relationship in the first generation of a conservation programme artificial selection among offspring will increase the variance of family size of male and of female parents (FALCONER, 1989), whose magnitude cannot be foreseen and consequently cannot be taken into account. Having this in mind our proposal appears as a realistic approach to estimate the effective population size of small populations.

576

The basis for estimating the status of endangeredness of a breed is the amount of accumulated inbreeding during 50 years of reproduction. We formed five classes of endangeredness depending on the following values of accumulated inbreeding Fx in 50 years:

	Fx
Normal	< 5 %
potentially endangered	5 - 15 %
minimally endangered	16 - 25 %
endangered	26 - 40 %
critically endangered	> 40 %

If one of the additional factors, absence of herdbook, number of females decreasing, low number of herds, incrossing, purebreeding equal or below 90 %, the breed was graded down into a lower class, unless other favourable conditions were obvious.

6.4 Similarity of breeds

Information on similar breeds is important if one has to decide whether a breed, which is endangered, should be conserved and if so, whether this should be done in cooperation with breeds which are similar to the one in question.

Our efforts to form groups of similar breeds within the five species were a first attempt at this objective. For this purpose the breeds have been grouped according to phenotypic characteristics, breed history development of the breed and the geographical origin. Of special interest were facts explaining a genetic relationship, e.g. incrossings from other breeds and imports of breeding stock from other areas.

In some cases the consistency of the groups was confirmed by several criterions. In other cases the evidence for grouping was vague, and furthermore some findings of relationships were contradictory. Some species are described in the literature in more detail than others. Due to these diverse prior conditions it was not possible to develop a homogeneous scheme for all five species and to follow this consequently.

Information on genetic polymorphisms of breeds is not available in the data bank until now. In future it would be highly desirable to collect also this type of information and to include information on genetic polymorphisms, such as blood groups, protein polymorphisms, microsatellites and RAPDs in projects for the definition of relationships or genetic distances among breeds.

The aim of this part of the publication was not to clarify all relationships completely, this would be a separate matter of an additional investigation. It should rather give some evidence for cases in which similar breeds can be used to maintain or conserve a special breed. But again the authors would be grateful for suggestions.

577

6.5 Presentation of individual breeds

In this chapter we were faced with the problem to present a maximum of information on a limited space. We decided on a total of 24 lines per breed. For example, sometimes it was difficult to present all information on origin and development of the breed in the two lines 5 and 6. A maximum of four similar breeds could be listed in lines 21 to 24. However, if more than four similar breeds exist the group and subgroup numbers as well as the page number are presented in line 20, where the respective group of similar breeds can be found.

6.6 Outlook

As it has already been mentioned, we hope that this report will be useful; but we also hope that this publication will stimulate readers and experts on breeds to give us their comments* and corrections if they discover information which is incomplete, not precise or not the most recent one. This will increase the usefulness of the EAAP Animal Genetic Data Bank and our next report.

*) Address: EAAP Animal Genetic Data Bank
                Institute of Animal Breeding and Genetics
                Hannover School of Veterinary Medicine
                Buenteweg 17 p, D-30559 Hannover, Germany

7 References

Alderson, L. 1992. The categorisation of types and breeds of cattle in Europe. Archieves de Zootecnia. Vol.41:154.

Avon, L. 1992. Survey about small breeds of cattle sheep and goats. Département Génétique et Controle des Performances, Paris.

Behrens, H., H. Doehner, R. Schelje and R. Waßmuth 1969. Lehrbuch der Schafzucht. Verlag Paul Parey, Hamburg·Berlin.

Buchenauer, D. and Simon, D. 1993. EAAP Datenbank für genetische Vielfalt bei Nutztieren. Züchtungskunde 65, (4): 241-253

Dimitriev, N.G. and L.K. Ernst (Eds) 1989. Animal genetic resources of the USSR. FAO Animal Production and Health Paper, Rome 65.

Evans, J.W., A. Borton, H.F. Hintz and L.D. van Vleck 1977. The Horse. W.H. Freeman & Company.

Falconer, D.S. 1989. Introduction to Quantitative Genetics. Third edition. Longman Scientific & Technical.

FAO 1981. Animal Genetic Resources Conservation and Management. FAO Anim. Prod. Health Paper 24: 388 pp.

FAO 1992. Animal Genetic Resources Information. FAO Anim. Prod. Paper 10:81 pp.

Frahm, K. 1990. Rinderrassen in den Ländern der Europäischen Gemeinschaft. Ferdinand Enke Verlag, Stuttgart.

Gall, Chr. 1982. Ziegenzucht. Verlag Eugen Ulmer, Stuttgart.

Goodall, D.M. 1980. Pferde der Welt. Erich Hoffmann Verlag, Heidenheim.

Hammond, J., I. Johansson and F. Haring 1961. Handbuch der Tierzüchtung, Rassenkunde. Verlag Paul Parey, Hamburg·Berlin.

Haring, F. 1976. Schafzucht. Verlag Eugen Ulmer, Stuttgart.

Hinrichsen, J.K. 1993. Personal Communication.

Kober, H. 1992. Das Schwäbisch Hällische Schwein. Bestandsaufnahme einer gefährdeten Nutztierrasse. Diss. Hannover 1992.

Künzi, I. and G. Stranzinger 1993. Allgemeine Tierzucht. KTB 1649. Verlag Eugen Ulmer Stuttgart.

Maijala, K., A.V. Cherekaev, J.M. Devillard, Z. Reklewski, G. Rognoni, D.L. Simon and D. Steane 1984. Conservation of animal genetic resources in Europe. Final report of EAAP Working Party. Livest. Prod. Sci. 11: 3-22.

Maijala, K. 1987. Surveying animal breed resources in Europe. Research in cattle Production - Danish Status and Perspectives, Copenhagen: 208-218.

Maijala, K. 1992. The EAAP endeavour to survey animal genetic diversity. In: D. Simon and D. Buchenauer (eds): Data Collection, Conservation and Use of Farm Animal Genetic Resources. Proceeding of a C.E.C. Workshop and Training Course, Dec. 7-9 1992: 9-17.

Mason, I.L., 1969. World dictionary of livestock breeds. 2nd edit. CAB Techn. Comm. 8, 272 pp.

Mason, I.L. 1988. A World Dictionary of Livestock Breeds. Types and Varieties. C.A.B. International.

Mathes, M. Sattelschweine in Deutschland - Inzucht, Verwandtschaft, Genanteile. Diss. Hannover (in preparation).

Mendel, Chr. 1993. Personal Communication.

Porter, V. 1991. Cattle - A Handbook to the Breeds of the World. Facts on File. New York· Oxford.

Reddick, K. 1976. Horses. Bantam Books Toronto·New York·London.

Sambraus, H.H. 1986. Atlas der Nutztierrassen. Verlag Eugen Ulmer, Stuttgart.

Simon, D. and H. Schulte-Coerne 1979. Verlust genetischer Alternativen in der Tierzucht - notwendige Konsequenzen. Züchtungskunde 51 (5):332-342.

Simon, D. 1989. Interim report of the Working Party on Animal Genetic Resources on the survey 1988 in EAAP-member countries. 40th Ann. Meet. EAAP, Dublin, Aug. 1989, 9 pp.

Simon, D, 1990. The global animal genetic data bank. FAO Animal Prod. Health Paper 80:153-166.

Simon, D. 1992a. Monitoring animal genetic resources and criteria for conservation. Post-Congress Proc. Sixth AAAP Animal Science Congress, Vol.V, 103-112, Bangkok.

Simon, D. 1992b. Criteria for endangered status of breeds. Data Collection, Conservation and Use of Farm Animal Genetic Resources. Proceeding of a C.E.C. workshop and Training Course, Dec. 7-9 1992:65-68.

Wright, S. 1923. Mendelian analysis of the pure breeds of livestock. The Journal of Heridity 14:339-348.

-- *Ausschuß der Deutschen Gesellschaft für Züchtungskunde zur Erhaltung genetischer Vielfalt bei Landwirtschaftlichen Nutztieren 1991.* Empfehlungen zur Erhaltung genetischer Vielfalt bei einheimischen Nutztieren. Züchtungskunde 63, (6):426-430.

-- *Ausschuß der Deutschen Gesellschaft für Züchtungskunde zur Erhaltung genetischer Vielfalt bei Landwirtschaftlichen Nutztieren 1991.* Empfehlung zur Kryokonservierung von Sperma, Embryonen und Erbsubstanz in anderer Form zur Erhaltung genetischer Vielfalt bei einheimischen landwirtschaftlichen Nutztieren. Züchtungskunde 63, (2):81-83.

Simon, D. 1992a. Monitoring animal genetic resources and criteria for conservation. Post-Congress Proc. Sixth AAAP Animal Science Congress, Vol.V, 103-112, Bangkok.

Simon, D. 1992b. Criteria for endangered status of breeds. Data Collection, Conservation and Use of Farm Animal Genetic Resources. Proceeding of a C.E.C. workshop and Training Course, Dec. 7-9 1992:65-68.

Wright, S. 1923. Mendelian analysis of the pure breeds of livestock. The Journal of Heridity 14:339-348.

-- *Ausschuß der Deutschen Gesellschaft für Züchtungskunde zur Erhaltung genetischer Vielfalt bei Landwirtschaftlichen Nutztieren 1991.* Empfehlungen zur Erhaltung genetischer Vielfalt bei einheimischen Nutztieren. Züchtungskunde 63, (6):426-430.

-- *Ausschuß der Deutschen Gesellschaft für Züchtungskunde zur Erhaltung genetischer Vielfalt bei Landwirtschaftlichen Nutztieren 1991.* Empfehlung zur Kryokonservierung von Sperma, Embryonen und Erbsubstanz in anderer Form zur Erhaltung genetischer Vielfalt bei einheimischen landwirtschaftlichen Nutztieren. Züchtungskunde 63, (2):81-83.